The
LOGOS
PAPERS

Other works by Dr. Surrendra Gangadean & The Logos Foundation:

Philosophical Foundation: A Critical Analysis of Basic Beliefs

History of Philosophy: A Critical Analysis of Unresolved Disputes

Theological Foundation: A Critical Analysis of Christian Belief

Philosophical Foundation: Trivium Study Guide

The Westminster Shorter and Larger Catechisms:
A Doxological Understanding

The Westminster Confession of Faith:
A Doxological Understanding

On Natural and Revealed Theology:
Collected Essays of Surrendra Gangadean

The Logos Curriculum:
Grammar Catechisms: Philosophical, Theological, and
Historical Foundations

Fundación Filosófica: Un Análisis Crítico de Creencias Básicas

DOXOLOGICAL REFORMED COMMENTARY SERIES:

The Book of Revelation: What Must Soon Take Place
Doxological Postmillennialism

The Book of Job: Deepening the Revelation of God's Glory for All Time
An Ironic Theodicy

The Epistle to the Romans:
The Righteousness of God Revealed from Faith to Faith
The Gospel According to St. Paul

The Biblical Worldview: Creation, Fall, Redemption
Genesis 1–3: Scripture in Organic Seed Form

The
LOGOS
PAPERS

To Make the Logos Known

SURRENDRA GANGADEAN

A DIVISION OF THE LOGOS FOUNDATION
Phoenix, Arizona

The Logos Papers: To Make the Logos Known

Copyright © 1992–2022 Surrendra Gangadean

Logos Papers Press 2022
Phoenix, Arizona
logospaperspress.com
thelogospapers.com

Printed in the United States of America

Cover design: Brian J. Phelps
Typesetting: Matthew P. Hicks & Brian J. Phelps

Library of Congress Cataloging-in-Publication Data pending

Gangadean, Surrendra, 1943–2022.
    The Logos papers: to make the Logos known
    Includes bibliographical references, footnotes, index, and glossary.
    ISBN 979-8-9880399-2-1 (hardcover)
    ISBN 979-8-9867472-3-1 (paperback)
    ISBN 978-0-578-93387-0 (e-book)

1. The Logos 2. Philosophy—Foundation 3. Theology—Foundation
4. Historic Christianity 5. Apologetics—Response to Modernity
6. Apologetics—Response to Postmodernity I. Title

To those who would seek

If you seek her as silver,
And search for her as for hidden treasures;
Then you will understand the fear of the Lord,
And find the knowledge of God.

—PROVERBS 2:4-5

But without faith it is impossible to please Him,
for he who comes to God must believe that He is,
and that He is a rewarder of those
who diligently seek Him.

—HEBREWS 11:6

CONTENTS

EDITOR'S PREFACE

Dr. Surrendra Gangadean (1943–2022), professor, pastor, husband, father, mentor, friend, and builder, was a giant in the faith, a Philosopher among philosophers, and a Theologian among theologians. He spent a lifetime refining the foundation for philosophy and theology and Historic Christianity. By recognizing the foundation, he was able to name the errors in the history of ideas due to the failure to have laid and built upon that sure foundation. He taught in the college classroom for 45 years, the seminary for over 25 years, and from the pulpit for almost 30 years. He taught Introduction to Philosophy, Logic, Ethics, Philosophy of Religion, Eastern Religions, World Religions, Introduction to Christianity, Introduction to Humanities, Philosophy of Art, The Great Books, Philosophical Theology, Biblical Worldview, Biblical History, Church History, Systematic Theology, Biblical Hermeneutics, and Existential Hermeneutics. In each of his encounters with notable thinkers and with his students, Dr. Gangadean heard, understood, and took intellectual challenges seriously. There was no known basic challenge he did not work through—first for himself, then with others in much discussion, and then in his teaching and writing. He was tenacious in going after a basic dispute or challenge, finding the assumptions underlying the challenge, and then attempting to respond and resolve the problem.

The Logos Papers is a collection of work from Dr. Gangadean, reflecting his teaching in philosophy, religion, and the humanities in the academy, in theology at Logos Theological Seminary, and pastoral teaching in the church. In unison with his other publications, it fundamentally calls for a *focus on foundation* from the Logos. The Logos is the eternal Word of God in its fullness, who makes God fully known. As expressed in the prologue to the gospel of John, the Logos, by whom all things were made, is present in all men as the light of reason, in the creation as general revelation, in history as special revelation/Scripture, and was incarnated in Jesus Christ, full of grace and truth—to restore man to the knowledge of God, which is eternal life. Christ sent the Holy Spirit to lead the Church objectively into all Truth/the Logos in its fullness (through its councils and creeds—Historic Christianity) and to bring unbelievers subjectively into the truth by regeneration and believers to a mature faith by sanctification.

In general, foundation is necessary for maturity, fruitfulness, unity, and fullness in the knowledge of God. Without foundation, there is division and apostasy in the Church, and decay and collapse in the culture. In Scripture, foundation is called for as first principles, for endurance against tempests, for lasting fruit, for unity of the faith and fullness, for a lasting culture in the City of God. Current divisions in the Church and decay in the culture show a longstanding lack of foundation and the need to get to bedrock. Failure to achieve comprehensiveness to attain to fullness of life is not new; it has been recurrent throughout history in the collapse of civilizations. A mere return to the past is insufficient for bedrock. Foundation must get to the certainty of clarity, the cornerstone, from which arises inexcusability. It must overcome skepticism and fideism by faith/understanding. In light of this, *The Logos Papers* seeks to articulate more clearly the worldview of creation–fall–redemption and its application to culture. It seeks to do so both by establishing the foundation from the Logos in general revelation, Scripture, and Historic Christianity, and by responding to ongoing challenges to the knowledge of God from within and from outside the Church.

A majority of the papers were written during the final decade of Dr. Gangadean's life; thus, they are in a sense a culmination of his life's work, being highly focused in his concern for the glory of God in light of the aforementioned challenges, displaying his masterful rhetoric, and distilling the wisdom he had attained and with which he had been blessed. Dr. Gangadean wrote increasingly succinctly; he intended to express depth of meaning with the brevity of words. He referred to this approach as "sutra style" and is the style of writing displayed in most of the papers. He always took great care to submit his work to a process of much discussion, either in the classroom or in the church. And it was a joy to see the attention he gave to revising and refining each paper.

Some papers were developed for use in the academic classroom and are noted as such. Papers that were posthumously published and were edited or developed by The Logos Foundation Editorial Board are noted as such. The Editorial Board anticipates additions to *The Logos Papers* through the months and years to come (see thelogospapers.com). We make no claim of originality with respect to the foundational teaching of Dr. Gangadean. Only his ideas have been and will be used to advance his work. We desire to convey our understanding of the quality and content Dr. Gangadean taught us over the years. Any inaccuracies or errors are our sole responsibility.

On a final note, the papers can be considered occasional—addressing a specific topic or subject. And while they are not necessarily systematic from one paper to the next, each is systematic individually. In light of the considerable breadth of material/topics addressed in the papers, a detailed and comprehensive index has been added to assist the reader, along with footnotes and a glossary of terms. Many of the papers can be referred to alongside other published work from Dr. Gangadean. The increasing number of works made available will shed light on his systematic, presuppositional, cumulative, and comprehensive approach to doctrine and life. These works, whether in philosophy, theology, or the humanities, are complementary, for they are written from the same methodology, assumptions, and the goal of taking thoughts captive for the glory of God.

—THE LOGOS FOUNDATION
EDITORIAL BOARD
Phoenix, Arizona
December 2022

THE PAPERS

Paper № 1

———

THE LOGOS PAPERS

An Introduction

CONTEXT AND PURPOSE

In the beginning was the Word, and the Word was with God, and the Word was God.[1] The Logos is the eternal Word of God who makes God known.

And the Word was made flesh and dwelt among us.[2] Jesus is the Word of God, the Logos incarnate. He is Christ, Savior and Lord, by whose rule *the earth shall be full of the knowledge of the LORD as the waters cover the sea.*[3]

Christ, by the Holy Spirit, builds the Church, which is the City of God, the Kingdom of God. The Spirit leads the Church into all truth, summed up historically in its creeds and confessions.[4] The City of God has foundations; a city without foundations cannot last.[5]

Christ is the stone the builders rejected; he was crucified by the sin of all men. Yet God raised him from the dead and has made him the

---

1. *John 1:1.*

2. *John 1:14.*

3. *Isaiah 11:9.*

4. *John 16:13; Acts 15; Paper No. 16* and *100;* Surrendra Gangadean, *The Westminster Confession of Faith: A Doxological Understanding* (Phoenix: Logos Papers Press, 2023). See Question 1.

5. *Hebrews 11:10; Revelation 21:10-20.*

cornerstone.[6] The Logos, by whom all things were made, is present in all men as reason, in the creation as general revelation, in history as special revelation/Scripture, and was incarnated in Jesus Christ, full of grace and truth.[7] This Logos is rejected by men in every way he reveals God, yet he is chosen by God to rule over all men to make God known.[8]

The Logos Papers seeks to articulate more clearly the worldview of creation–fall–redemption and its application to culture. It seeks to do so both by establishing the foundation from the Logos in general revelation, Scripture, and Historic Christianity, and by responding to ongoing challenges to the knowledge of God from within and from outside the Church.

Historic Christianity affirms: Man's chief end is to glorify God, in all that by which he makes himself known, in all his works of creation and providence.[9] Yet no one seeks God and no one understands. All have sinned and come short of the glory of God.[10] For the basic things about God and man and good and evil are clear to all who seek so that unbelief is without excuse.[11]

In the spiritual war between belief and unbelief, which is age-long and agonizing, good will overcome evil.[12] The Logos is Truth. It overthrows arguments and every pretension raised up against the knowledge of God and takes every thought captive to make it obedient to Christ.[13]

---

6. *Psalm 2:1-2; Isaiah 53:5-7; Psalm 118:22; Acts 4:11.*

7. *John 1:3-5, 10-11, 14, 18.*

8. *Matthew 28:18-20.*

9. *Westminster Shorter Catechism and Confession of Faith* (1648): *SCQ. 1, 101; WCF 4.1, 5.1; Paper No. 115.*

10. *Romans 3:11, 23; Paper No. 114.*

11. *Romans 1:20-21; 2:1, 14-15; Deuteronomy 30:11-14;* Surrendra Gangadean, *Philosophical Foundation: A Critical Analysis of Basic Beliefs,* Second Edition (Phoenix: Public Philosophy Press, 2022), 287-292.

12. *Genesis 3:15.*

13. *John 17:17; 2 Corinthians 10:4-5.*

ORDER AND PROCESS IN COMING
TO THE KNOWLEDGE OF GOD

1. **There is an *existential* order in the human condition in coming to know basic things (about God and man and good and evil).**

    i. The fear of the Lord is the beginning of knowledge.[14]

    ii. Understanding begins with seeking, and seeking begins with fear of suffering.

    iii. The curse (toil and strife, and old age, sickness, and death) is God's call to man to stop and think. The curse intensifies to war, famine, and plague in every age.[15]

    iv. Natural evil (the curse) is a universal call back from moral evil; left to oneself no one seeks God, no one understands, no one does what is right.[16]

    v. Moral evil is to neglect, avoid, resist, and deny one's reason in the face of what is clear about God. To deny one's reason brings spiritual death of meaninglessness.

    vi. Natural evil is the third and final call back from sin and the noetic effect of sin in self-deception and self-justification in not seeking God.

    vii. When the curse is imposed, the promise of redemption is also given: there will be a spiritual war (between belief and unbelief), age-long and agonizing, in which good will overcome evil.[17]

Application:

1. Begin with self-examination. Human suffering (toil and strife, and old age, sickness, and death) is a call to stop and think.

2. Acknowledge natural evil serves to restrain, recall from, and remove moral evil and spiritual death (meaninglessness, boredom, and guilt).

---

14. *Proverbs 1:7.*
15. *Genesis 3:14-19.*
16. *Romans 3:10-11; Paper No. 149.*
17. *Genesis 3:14-15.*

3. Since natural evil is imposed on man by God, as mercy, through the curse as a call back, the fear of the Lord is the beginning of wisdom. Fear acts on truth in humility.

2. There is an *ontological* order in human nature in coming to know basic things.

i. We are to love God with all our heart, our mind, our soul, and our strength.[18]

ii. Man is made in the image of God, as a triune personality. Man is a unity of diversity in all aspects of his being. The image of God in man reveals God.[19]

iii. Loving self above God shows a failure to know and acknowledge God. Man is restored to the knowledge of God by regeneration and is further transformed by knowing the truth.

iv. The order in man is: mind, soul, and strength; the intellectual, emotional, and practical; knowledge, holiness, and righteousness; prophet, priest, and king. Disregard for God's order brings divisions, apostasy, cultural decay, and collapse.

v. Man is a body/soul unity. Man does not live by bread alone but by every word of God. Male and female in the image of God reveal God as Creator and upholder of all things.

vi. Man's life is not determined by time (history and culture) or by place (geography and race) but by grace through faith. All can use reason to know what is clear.

vii. Love of the good (the knowledge of God) is the source of unity in each person and among all persons. The curse is fully removed only when the good is fully realized.[20]

---

18. *Luke 10:27.*

19. *Paper No. 144*; Gangadean, *The Westminster Confession.* See Question 25; Surrendra Gangadean, *The Westminster Shorter and Larger Catechisms: A Doxological Understanding* (Phoenix: Logos Papers Press, 2023). See Larger Catechism Question 17.

20. *Isaiah 11:6-9; 1 Corinthians 15:25-26.*

Application:

1. Begin with man's need as a rational being for understanding the meaning of things.

2. Do not place practical and psychological needs above the need for meaning and truth.

3. Observe the order within and among all aspects of human nature: within the soul and between soul and body; within gender and between nature and nurture; between the universal (common to all) and the particular (unique in each).

3. There is a *logical* order in human thought in coming to know basic things.

i. What may be known of God is objectively clear to reason so that unbelief is without excuse. Both the nature of God and the moral law are clear from general revelation.[21]

ii. Man is more or less conscious and consistent in his basic beliefs. Both skepticism and fideism fail to see what is clear, and both are rooted in uncritically held assumptions.

iii. Thinking is presuppositional—we think of the less basic in light of the more basic. Clarity begins and grows only if the most basic is in place. Reason as the laws of thought is most basic. Rational Presuppositionalism (RP) uses reason as the test for meaning in basic beliefs.[22]

iv. Foundation in worldview is built upon Common Ground (what is necessary for thought and discourse), and begins with the cornerstone (understanding good and evil).

v. In RP, meaning is more basic than truth. Experience requires interpretation in light of one's basic belief. In concept, the finite and temporal presuppose the infinite and the eternal. In argument, conclusion presupposes premises.

---

21. *Romans 1:20, 2:14-15; Paper No. 102.*

22. *Paper No. 101*; Surrendra Gangadean, *History of Philosophy: A Critical Analysis of Unresolved Disputes* (Phoenix: Public Philosophy Press, 2022), 22-23.

vi. In philosophy, ethics presupposes metaphysics, which presupposes one's epistemology. If there is agreement on what is more basic, there will be agreement on the less basic.

vii. In theology, one is to proceed from general revelation to special revelation to Historic Christianity. In Scripture, one must proceed from the foundation of creation–fall–redemption in Genesis 1–3, through each historical epoch, to the last book of Revelation. In Historic Christianity, one must proceed from the earliest council, building upon the assumptions and implications of each, to the latest council.

Application:

1. Begin with the more basic; we are to think of the less basic in light of the more basic.

2. Begin with Common Ground (what is necessary for thought and discourse).[23] Reason and Integrity will lead to Rational Presuppositionalism and the Principle of Clarity.

3. All disputes can be settled[24] (whether in philosophy or theology; whether interpersonal or international) if the more basic is in place. We are to avoid fruitless disputes by beginning with the basics.

---

23. *Paper No. 2*

24. Gangadean, *History of Philosophy*, xxi-xxvii.

Paper Nº· 2

COMMON GROUND
The Necessary Condition for Thought and Discourse

1. Common Ground

i. Common Ground (CG) is the set of epistemologically necessary conditions for thought and discourse. Without CG words are emptied of meaning; what is meaningless, due to lack of CG, is absurd. To deny CG is to deny the possibility of public discourse.

ii. CG is necessary to avoid foolish arguments (what cannot be resolved because no basis for resolution is in place). A foolish argument only causes strife.

iii. Avoiding foolish arguments is not optional; it is an imperative. Not avoiding foolish arguments would be epistemologically foolish, mistaken, a blunder, inept, and unwise. What is foolish falls into the category of moral evil (denying human nature as rational) and its inherent consequence.

iv. To avoid foolish arguments means *both* that there *is no* rational obligation to respond *and* there *is* a rational obligation *not to* respond, where a lack of CG is observed.

v. To avoid foolish arguments, all that needs to be said is: there *is* no CG in place; *or*, the other person does *not* affirm the *objective* content of the *principle* of CG. This *needs* to be said, and nothing more.

vi. CG affirms: *reason* as the laws of thought; *integrity* as a concern for consistency; *Rational Presuppositionalism* as critical thinking applied consistently; and the *Principle of Clarity* as necessary for meaning and morality. Each of the above is explained below.

vii. CG cannot consistently be denied. There is no naked public square (no public discourse devoid of CG); but one can be naked in the public square.

2. Reason

i. It is self-evident that we think: we form concepts, judgments and arguments expressed in words, sentences, and syllogisms.

ii. It is self-evident that there are laws of thought and that these laws are the laws of identity, non-contradiction, and excluded middle. These laws of thought are the laws of reason.[1]

iii. Reason as the laws of thought makes thought possible. To use reason to question reason is self-referentially absurd (SRA).

iv. Reason as the laws of thought is the test for meaning, which is necessary for truth. Reason is not neutral with respect to truth. What violates a law of thought lacks meaning and cannot be true. Common Ground is not neutral ground.

v. Reason as the laws of thought is most basic in epistemology. It is transcendental, self-attesting, and the most basic authority.

vi. Reason is ontological: it applies to being as well as thought. There are no square-circles, no uncaused events, no being from non-being. What is logically impossible does not exist in any possible world.

vii. Reason is natural, not conventional, the same in all who think. Reason is fundamental since what we think is basic to what we desire and what we choose to do.

---

1. Gangadean, *Philosophical Foundation*, 10-15; Gangadean, *History of Philosophy*, 26-35.

3. Integrity

 i. CG in reason requires a *commitment* to reason. A commitment to reason is a concern for consistency, both logical (vs. *reductio ad absurdum*) and existential (vs. *self-referential absurdity*—SRA).

 ii. The concern for consistency in thought, word, and deed is integrity.[2] Integrity is not sincerity, which confuses deep feeling with knowledge and uses words without cognitive meaning.

 iii. Integrity is opposed to hypocrisy, which lacks concern for consistency. Hypocrisy gives appearance in place of reality.

 iv. We are more or less conscious and consistent; we should be more conscious and consistent. We should use *reason* to examine our basic beliefs (*presuppositions*) for meaning.

 v. Persuasion by pseudo-arguments is opposed to proof by sound arguments. Use of informal fallacies gives the appearance of reason in the place of reason itself.

 vi. Judging by false or irrelevant standards gives the appearance of knowledge, but not knowledge itself. One may appear to have insight yet lack sight.

 vii. Examining the beliefs of others without allowing examination of one's own beliefs gives only the *appearance* of integrity, which is hypocrisy.

4. Rational Presuppositionalism

 i. Integrity requires critical thinking (CT). CT consistently applied uses reason to test basic beliefs (presuppositions) for meaning. *This* level of CT is called *Rational Presuppositionalism* (RP) in order to distinguish it from other levels and uses of reason and other epistemologies.

 ii. RP maintains that we think of the less basic in light of the more basic; that if we agree on the more basic, we will agree on the less basic; that to be concerned with the less basic before the more basic is a denial of the principle of RP and therefore of CG.

---

2. Gangadean, *Philosophical Foundation*, 199-205; Gangadean, *History of Philosophy*, 8-9.

iii. RP is first to be applied in general, the less basic in light of the more basic (/ = in light of): meaning/reason; truth/meaning; experience/basic belief; finite and temporal/infinite and eternal; conclusion/premises.

iv. RP is applied to giving proofs in philosophy: in epistemology first, then in metaphysics, and then in ethics. This will avoid interminable disputes persisting over millennia.

v. RP is applied to the order of understanding in theology: clarity of general revelation first, then Scripture, and then Historic Christianity. In Scripture: creation first, then the Fall, and then redemption; the Old Testament, then the New Testament; Genesis, then Revelation. RP applied in hermeneutics affirms contextualism vs. literalism and allegoricalism. Likewise, the cumulative insight of Historic Christianity (from councils, in creeds) is opposed to dogmatic authority (based on mere tradition or appeal to individuals as authorities).

vi. Since no experience is meaningful without interpretation, the authority of reason in RP is opposed to the authority of experience assumed in tradition, common sense, testimony, intuition, *and* science (*if* it claims that *all* knowledge is *only* from *sense* experience).

vii. RP is opposed to rationalism (reasoning without RP), as well as to skepticism (nothing is clear), and to fideism (belief without proof based on understanding).[3]

5. The Principle of Clarity

i. CG in Reason, Integrity, and RP, taken cumulatively, requires the Principle of Clarity (PC).

ii. PC states: some things are clear; the basic things are clear; the basic things (about God and man and good and evil) are clear to reason.

iii. Some things are clear. It is clear that the contradiction of "some things are clear" is "nothing is clear." If nothing is clear, then no

---

3. Gangadean, *History of Philosophy*, 19-24, 131-137.

distinction is meaningful (*reductio ad absurdum*). If no meaning is possible (*nihilism*), then thought and talk must be given up, which is *self-referentially absurd* (SRA). Therefore, it must be the case that "some things are clear."

iv. The basic things are clear. Thinking is presuppositional: we think of the less basic in light of the more basic (RP). If basic things are not clear, then nothing is clear (which is necessarily false by *reductio* and SRA). Therefore, *basic* things are clear.

v. The basic things (about God and man and good and evil) are clear to reason. The basic things are about metaphysics (God and man) and ethics (good and evil). Reason as the laws of thought is *most* basic. Therefore, the basic things are clear to reason (epistemology).

vi. PC is opposed to both skepticism and fideism. Skepticism divides mankind and then seeks to unite by relativism and political correctness (pc). PC is opposed to pc. Fideism divides mankind and then seeks to unite by authoritarian dogmatism. PC is opposed to dogmatism.

vii. To deny PC is to deny *clarity and inexcusability*, which denies the possibility of moral evil (sin and death) and mankind's need for redemption. It is to deny the Logos in all men as reason and the Logos incarnate for all men.

Paper N⁰· 3

THE PRINCIPLE OF CLARITY, RATIONAL PRESUPPOSITIONALISM, AND PROOF

The following assumes Common Ground.[1] Common Ground (CG) affirms the Principle of Clarity (PC) and Rational Presuppositionalism (RP).

1. Does PC require proof?

    i. PC affirms that the basic things about God and man and good and evil are clear to reason[2] and that failure to know what is clear to reason is inexcusable.[3]

    ii. If we know what is clear, we can show (give proof of) what is clear. To know p (for example, that God exists) in the strong sense of "know," which is necessary for inexcusability, requires having rational justification for one's belief, which constitutes proof.

    iii. Theism assumes PC (clarity and inexcusability). The apostle Paul, in his letter to the Romans, states: "For the invisible things of him from the creation of the world are clearly seen, being understood

---

1. *Paper No. 2.*

2. *Paper No. 2.* See 4.3.

3. *Paper No. 2.* See 4.4.

by the things that are made, even his eternal power and divine nature; so that men are without excuse."[4]

iv. Historic Christian Theism affirms PC. In its opening words, the Westminster Confession of Faith states, ". . . the light of nature, and the works of creation and providence do so far manifest the goodness, wisdom, and power of God, as to leave men unexcusable."[5]

2. Has theism achieved proof?

The arguments used historically and responses to them are briefly stated below.

i. The ontological argument: the greatest possible being necessarily exists.

Objection 1: The greatest possible being (an eternal being) need not be God the Creator. That there must be something eternal does not imply that only some is eternal.

Objection 2: Existence is not a predicate in the same order as other predicates (wisdom, power, and goodness).

ii. The cosmological argument: there must be a First Cause, which is God.

Objection 1: There could be an eternal cycle, and there are no unique *events* in an eternal cycle.

Objection 2: Eternal dependence of dependent dualism (Aristotle) does not establish God the Creator.

iii. The teleological argument: the natural order in the world (design) requires a designer, who is God.

Objection 1: Naturalism in science denies the existence of design and designer.

Objection 2: If there is design, the designer need not be God the Creator (Plato's demiurge).

---

4. *Romans 1:20.*

5. *WCF 1.1.*

iv. The moral argument: morality exists; moral law requires a moral lawgiver, who is God.

Objection 1: Moral law is not apart from human nature (heteronomy), nor by divine command in addition to human nature.

Objection 2: It is self-evident that human beings are by nature thinking (rational) beings, from which morality is derived.

v. The transcendental argument (TAG): God is the necessary condition for rationality.

Objection 1: Reason is common ground and is self-attesting.

Objection 2: Reason applies to all being, including God's being, and is eternal.

vi. Evidentialism: there is empirically verifiable evidence for the existence of God.

Objection 1: Probability in evidentialism is not certainty; without certainty there is no measure of probability.

Objection 2: Appeal to special revelation (miracles, divine encounter) is not general revelation (the basis of inexcusability).

vii. The *sensus divinitatis*: there is an immediate knowledge of God in everyone.

Objection 1: The account of the content of intuitive belief is varied, generally bare, and is insufficient for inexcusability.

Objection 2: If intuition is opposed by reason, intuition is not self-evident.[6]

3. Does RP offer proof?

RP is a method by which we understand, know (by proof), and settle disputes.[7]

RP revises the historic proofs and uses them cumulatively in a logical sequence.[8]

---

6. Gangadean, *Philosophical Foundation*, 24-25.

7. *Paper No. 2.* See 3.1.

8. Gangadean, *Philosophical Foundation*, 71-161.

RP seeks to show that there must be something eternal and that only some is eternal.

RP applied to general revelation argues for the following:

   i. that Common Ground is necessary to settle disputes.

  ii. that there must be something eternal.

 iii. that matter exists and matter is not eternal.

  iv. that the soul exists and the soul is not eternal.

   v. that there is natural design (on science and philosophy).

  vi. that there is moral design (on the problem of evil).[9]

 vii. that there is a moral law which is clear, comprehensive, and critical.[10]

viii. that general revelation is necessary for and requires special revelation.

4. Proof by RP

The following is a brief statement of the arguments used by RP.

   i. Since Common Ground (CG) is necessary for thought and discourse, CG is prologue to proof.

  ii. There must be something eternal (vs. none is eternal; all is becoming, impermanent, dependent co-arising, momentariness, which implies being from non-being). Therefore, a highest (eternal) being must exist. This is a revision of the ontological argument, since showing something must be eternal does not imply *only* some (God the Creator) is eternal.

 iii. a) The material world is not eternal since it is not self-maintaining (vs. material monism, ordinary dualism—Plato, and dependent dualism—Aristotle).

       b) The material world exists (vs. the idealism of Berkeley, Kant, or Shankara). The cause of what I see is not my mind or another mind but outside all minds.

---

9. Gangadean, *History of Philosophy*, 41-51.

10. Gangadean, *Philosophical Foundation*, 165-284.

iv. a) The soul exists, the mind is not the brain (vs. material monism); the soul exists, the individual self is not *maya* (vs. Absolute non-dualism/*Advaita*).

    b) The soul is not eternal—it cannot be finite and eternal (vs. dualism in Greek, Persian, and Indian thought).

v. Natural design exists (vs. claims based on dogmatic empiricism—that *all* knowledge is from sense experience).

    a. *Claim 1:* All of nature can and must be explained by natural causes only.

    b. *Claim 2:* There is no (need for) design or designer.

    c. *Response 1:* Science is not philosophy; science must have epistemological assumptions, currently empiricism, which is contrary to Common Ground.

    d. *Response 2:* How things operate (based on observed uniformity) does not explain how things originate (based on non-observed non-uniformity).

vi. Moral design exists (vs. the problem of evil—both natural and moral).

    a. The problem of evil is: if God is all good and all powerful, why is there any evil?

    b. Moral evil is an act contrary to one's nature; it is the failure to use one's reason to see what is clear.

    c. *Response 1:* Moral evil is designed to serve the good; it serves to deepen the revelation of divine justice and mercy.

    d. Natural evil (toil and strife, and old age, sickness, and death) is not original in creation nor inherent in moral evil.

    e. *Response 2:* Natural evil is imposed in mercy to restrain, recall from, and remove moral evil.

    f. To know how mercy does not set aside justice requires special revelation.

vii. The moral law: teleology (the good) vs. deontology (virtue) and consequentialism (happiness).

    a. The good for man as a rational being is the use of one's reason to the fullest.

    b. Reason is used to understand the nature of beings and the source of beings.

    c. The moral law is clearly revealed in human nature and is knowable to all.

    d. The moral law is the means to the good and is the source of unity in and for all men.

    e. The moral law is comprehensive (for all choices) and is critical (in all consequences).

    f. The moral law given in human nature is also given in summary in the Decalogue.

viii. The relation of general and special revelation.

    a. General revelation (GR) is what can be known by all men, everywhere, at all times.[11]

    b. Special revelation (SR) is redemptive revelation, given by testimony and transmitted in history.[12]

    c. GR is necessary for the possibility of SR and requires SR.[13]

    d. SR as redemptive revelation assumes and affirms the clarity of GR.[14]

    e. Appeal to SR presupposes Common Ground leading from GR to SR.

---

11. *Paper No. 102.*

12. Gangadean, *The Westminster Confession.* See Question 6.

13. See 4.6.f above on the problem of evil.

14. *Paper No. 112.*

Paper № 4

————

THE CORNERSTONE

GOOD & EVIL – LIFE & DEATH

The Beginning of the Foundation

INTRODUCTION

The following presupposes the prior papers on Common Ground[1] and PC, RP, and Proof.[2]

It assumes the clarity of general revelation[3] and the redemption of special revelation.[4]

The cornerstone is the beginning of the foundation.

The choice of good or evil is the existential first principle: it is the most basic choice for all men, everywhere, at all times.

The stone the builders rejected has become the chief cornerstone.[5]

Rejection of the Logos in creation (in general revelation) results in the rejection of the Logos incarnate (in special revelation).

---

1. *Paper No. 2.*
2. *Paper No. 3.*
3. *Paper No. 102.*
4. *Paper No. 87.*
5. *1 Peter 2:7.*

All attempts of mankind to build a lasting culture, civilization, or kingdom, while rejecting the cornerstone, have resulted in futility.[6]

1. The Good

The good is the highest value (*summum bonum*), the end in itself, chosen for its own sake and not for the sake of anything else. The good is not virtue (virtue of all kinds, duty, or moral law is the means to the good); the good is not happiness (happiness, pleasure, or joy is the effect of possessing the good). The good for a being is according to the nature of that being. The good for man is grounded in human nature, which is knowable to all. It is one and the same for all; it is the source of unity in each person and for all persons.[7]

2. Good and Evil for Man

   i. The good for man as a rational being is the use of reason to the fullest to understand the nature of beings and the source of all beings, which is God. It is the source of life: *maturity* in one's own understanding, *fruitfulness* in the increase of understanding in others, *unity* in all relations in every sphere of life, and *fullness* in all the riches of knowledge and understanding.

  ii. Evil is an act which is contrary to one's nature; it originates in the failure to seek and to understand what is clear about God. Left to oneself no one seeks God, no one understands, no one does what is right, not even one.[8] Evil is the source of spiritual death: meaninglessness (the mind is darkened), boredom (burning desire without satisfaction), and guilt (resulting in interminable self-deception and self-justification). Corporately, it results in divisions, apostasy, cultural decay, and collapse.

---

6. *Paper No. 32.* See 9-12.

7. *Paper No. 6*; Gangadean, *Philosophical Foundation*, 172-177.

8. *Romans 3:10-12.*

3. Life and Death

    i. Life is present and inherent in seeking and understanding; it is not future or extrinsic as in the common conception of reward in the afterlife in heaven.[9]

    ii. Death, which is spiritual, is present and inherent in not seeking and not understanding; it is not future and imposed as in the common conception of punishment in the afterlife in hell.

4. The Good in Biblical Revelation

The good in biblical revelation is eternal life, which is knowing God.

    i. Since creation is revelation, the whole earth is full of God's glory.[10] And since man is made in God's own image, the end of man's work of dominion is the knowledge of the glory of God.

    ii. The one desire of the psalmist is to know God: One thing have I desired of the Lord, that will I seek after; that I may dwell in the house of the Lord all the days of my life, to behold the beauty of the Lord and to enquire in his temple.[11]

    iii. The Word of God incarnate who makes God known, said in prayer: And this is eternal life: that they might know you, the only true God, and Jesus Christ whom you have sent.[12]

    iv. The apostle Paul, expressing his view of the highest good, said: I count all things a loss [compared to] the excellency of the knowledge of Jesus Christ.[13]

5. The Good in Historic Christianity

The good in Historic Christianity, as summed up in the Westminster Confession of Faith and the Shorter Catechism, is focused on the knowledge of God's glory:

---

9. *Paper No. 106* and *116.*

10. *Isaiah 6:3.*

11. *Psalm 27:4.*

12. *John 17:3.*

13. *Philippians 3:8.*

Man's chief end is to glorify God,[14] in all that whereby he makes himself known,[15] in all his works of creation[16] and providence.[17] The work of God in creation and providence is the revelation of God's glory.

6. Ten Characteristics of The Good

The good, as knowledge, is continuing, inexhaustible, comprehensive, inalienable, corporate, cumulative, communal, fulfilling, ultimate, and transformative.[18] Only the end of all knowledge in the knowledge of God satisfies all of these requirements of the good.

7. The Good and Man's Work of Dominion

The knowledge of God is through the knowledge of the creation, which is self-revelation; the knowledge of creation is through the work of dominion.[19] The work of dominion given to man at creation in the Garden is corporate, cumulative, and communal.[20] Mankind's work of dominion through history comes to completion in the City of God.[21]

8. The Good and Moral Evil

Moral evil serves to deepen the revelation of the divine justice and mercy. It deepens also the work of dominion, which extends now over sin and unbelief. In dominion, every thought raised up against the knowledge of God must be taken captive.[22] All kindreds, nations, tribes, and tongues are to be brought to the knowledge of God.

---

14. *SCQ. 1.*

15. *SCQ. 101.*

16. *WCF 4.1.*

17. *WCF 5.1.*

18. Gangadean, *Philosophical Foundation*, 208-211.

19. Gangadean, *The Westminster Catechisms*. See Appendix 4.

20. *Genesis 1–2.*

21. *Revelation 21–22.*

22. *2 Corinthians 10:4.*

9. The Good and Natural Evil

Natural evil (toil and strife, and old age, sickness, and death, increasing corporately to war, famine, and plague) serves to restrain, recall from, and remove moral evil. It is a call to stop and think about self-deception and self-justification against clarity and inexcusability regarding the existence and nature of God and the moral law.

10. The Good and Hope

i. True hope of attaining the good through the work of dominion is opposed to false hope of direct knowledge of God through a beatific vision in heaven and to no hope of skepticism and nihilism.

ii. The promise of redemption, given after man's fall, is that through a spiritual war which is age-long and agonizing, good will overcome evil; one to come, in the place of Adam, will undo what Adam did and do what Adam failed to do.

iii. The deepened work of dominion will be completed, signified in the continuation of the Sabbath, a day of rest; the earth will be filled with the knowledge of the Lord as the waters cover the sea.[23]

---

23. *Isaiah 11:9; Paper No. 104.*

Paper № 5

———

REASON

In Itself, in Its Use, and in Us[1]

1. Reason in itself

In itself, reason is the laws of thought. These are:

 i. The law of identity: *a* is *a* (a thing is what it is)

 ii. The law of non-contradiction: not both *a* and *non-a* (at the same time, in the same respect)

 iii. The law of excluded middle: either *a* or *non-a*

2. Reason in its use

 i. Formative: Reason is used to form concepts, judgments, and arguments, which are the forms of all thought. Concepts are the most basic. Judgments and arguments are built upon this.

 ii. Critical: Reason is used as a test for meaning; meaning is more basic than truth—if a law of reason is violated, there is no meaning, and wherever there is meaning, reason is being used.

 iii. Interpretive: Reason is used to interpret (give meaning to) one's experience in light of one's basic beliefs. Basic beliefs are more basic than experience.

---

1. Gangadean, *Philosophical Foundation*, 10-15; Gangadean, *History of Philosophy*, 26-35.

   iv. Constructive: Reason is used to construct a coherent world and life view.

3. Reason in us

   i. Natural: Reason is not cultural or conventional; it is universal, the same in all persons at all times. Reason is common ground among people. That is not to say that it is neutral ground.

   ii. Ontological: Reason applies to being as well as to thought—there are no square-circles and no uncaused events. Ontological applies to things in the world. Does reason apply to the being of God, if there is a God?

   iii. Transcendental: Reason is authoritative and self-attesting; it cannot be questioned but it makes questioning possible. It is the highest authority.

   iv. Fundamental: Reason is basic to other aspects of human personality; its use is the source of man's greatest good and its denial is the source of man's deepest misery.

Paper № 6

———

THE GOOD

The Source of Unity in Each and Among All

1. Ethics is rational.[1]

   i. Ethics is concerned with giving a rational justification for the answer to the question "What is the good?"

   ii. Ethics assumes choice; choice assumes values; values assume the highest value, which is the good (the *summum bonum*).

   iii. All things are not valued the same. Some things are chosen as means to an end; some are chosen for their own sake. What is chosen for its own sake is the end in itself, man's chief end, the good.

2. Ethics is teleological.[2]

   i. The good is not virtue; virtue is the means to the good.

   ii. The good is not happiness; happiness is the effect of possessing what is believed to be the good.

   iii. The good is not a being or a person. The good is achieved by choice. The good is by and for persons.

---

1. Gangadean, *Philosophical Foundation*, 165-169.

2. Gangadean, *Philosophical Foundation*, 172-177.

Without the good as the end in itself, ethics splits into focus on duty (deontology) or pleasure (hedonism) and all consequent fragmentation.[3]

3. Ethics is grounded in metaphysics (the nature of being).

i. The good for a being is according to the nature of that being. The good for a man, for a horse, or for a sheep is according to the nature of each.

ii. Man by nature thinks. Human beings are a union of mind and body. Man has sense impressions through the body, as do all animals. Yet man has more than animals. Thinking is cognitive, using concepts, judgments, and arguments. Reason in itself is the laws of thought. Therefore, man is a rational animal.

4. Ethics assumes epistemology (basic things are clear to reason).

i. It is clear to reason that God the Creator exists—that there must be something eternal and that only some is eternal: that matter exists and matter is not eternal; that the soul exists and the soul is not eternal—and that man is a rational being made in the image of God.

ii. It is clear that the good is one: it is the source of unity within each person and between all persons.

Human nature is a unity of diversity. All aspects of human nature are ordered, from the universal (common to all) to the particular (unique in each).

Human nature is formally one and the same in all human beings. To deny human nature in oneself is to deny it in all others.

iii. It is clear that the good for man as a rational being is the use of one's reason to the fullest, to understand the nature of things. The nature of things created reveals the nature of God the Creator. Therefore, the good for man as a rational being is the knowledge of God.[4]

---

3. Gangadean, *History of Philosophy*, 61-64.

4. Gangadean, *Philosophical Foundation*, 208-211.

5. Ethics in philosophy and theology are the same.

   i. The good and the moral law revealed in general revelation are the same in special revelation (Scripture) and in Historic Christianity (summed up in the Westminster Standards of 1648).[5]

Eternal life (the good, the end in itself) is knowing God.[6]

Man's chief end is to glorify God and to enjoy him forever, in all that by which he makes himself known, in all his works of creation and providence.[7]

   ii. The moral law is written on the hearts of all men;[8] it is structured into human nature.

The moral law given in Scripture (the Decalogue) is the same in content as the natural moral law given in general revelation and is derivable from it.[9]

   iii. The moral law is clear, comprehensive, and critical; it is the means to achieve the good, which is corporate, cumulative, and communal. The good is achieved when the earth is filled with the knowledge of God as the waters cover the sea.[10]

---

5. Gangadean, *The Westminster Catechisms.* See LCQ. 98, 101-148.

6. *John 17:3.*

7. *SCQ. 1, 101; WCF 4.1, 5.1.*

8. *Romans 2:14-15, Deuteronomy 30:11-14.*

9. Gangadean, *The Westminster Confession.* See Questions 83-84.

10. *Isaiah 11:9;* Gangadean, *The Westminster Catechisms.* See Appendix 4; *Paper No. 104.*

Paper № 7

THE PROBLEM OF EVIL

INTRODUCTION

1. The Problem of Evil is the deepest, most widespread objection to belief in God.

   The Problem of Evil (POE) is: If God is all good and all powerful, why is there evil (G·P·E)?

   The POE is discussed more fully in *Philosophical Foundation.*[1]

2. Responses: G·P·E is a contradiction, or an unknown, or may be easily knowable (Ironic Solution).

3. Hume: five solutions (*Dialogues Concerning Natural Religion*[2]) and response to each.

4. The Free Will Solution and a four-fold response.

5. The Ironic Solution: what is clear yet not seen; what we should expect but did not.

An application of Rational Presuppositionalism and the Principle of Clarity (PC) in answer to POE begins with agreement on definition of basic terms: the good, moral evil, and natural evil.

---

1. Gangadean, *Philosophical Foundation*, 145-161.

2. David Hume, *Dialogues and Natural History of Religion*, ed. J.C.A. Gaskin (Oxford: Oxford University Press, 1993), 95-115. See parts 10-11 for the five solutions.

PART I: BASIC TERMS

1. The Good (the highest value, the end in itself)

    i. The good for a being is according to the nature of that being.

    ii. The good for man as a rational (thinking) being (using concepts, judgments, and arguments / cognitive vs. non-cognitive) is the use of reason to the fullest.

    iii. Reason is used to understand the nature of things, which reveals the nature of God.

    iv. This assumes PC and the clarity of general revelation. Therefore, the good for man is the knowledge of God.

    v. The good for man as a rational being is cognitive, about understanding meaning (not a feeling: euphoria, ecstasy, bliss, joy, or happiness. Happiness is the effect of possessing the good, and is itself not the good).

    vi. The good is not the absence of natural evil; it is not a return to Eden or entry into Paradise, nor essentially a sensuous state of no pain or much pleasure.

    vii. The good is not a beatific vision (a mystical, direct vision of God apart from creation and history), which is without cognitive content.[3]

    viii. The good for man as a rational being is the knowledge of God, revealed in creation and providence, known through the work of dominion given to all mankind as a corporate, cumulative, and communal task, progressing from the Garden to the City of God.[4]

2. Moral Evil

    i. Moral evil is an act which is contrary to the nature of man as a rational being.

    ii. Evil is to neglect, avoid, resist, or deny reason (NARD) vs. affirming the Principle of Clarity (PC): some things are clear; the basic

---

3. *Paper No. 106* and *121*.

4. *John 17:3; Isaiah 6:3, 11:9; Genesis 1:26; Revelation 21.*

things are clear; the basic things (about God and man and good and evil) are clear to reason. PC is opposed to skepticism and fideism, both of which lead to nihilism, the loss of all meaning.

iii. If there is no clarity, then there is no meaning and no morality. If there is no clarity, then there is no inexcusability. Full evil reaches to the denial of reason.[5]

iv. Left to oneself, no one seeks God; no one understands; no one is righteous.[6]

v. Unbelief (worshiping the creation, e.g., the sun) is inexcusable.[7]

vi. If we know what is clear, we can show what is clear. If we cannot show the inexcusability of unbelief, then we lack insight and therefore the authority to speak.

vii. The consequence of moral evil (NARD) is spiritual death: meaninglessness, boredom, and guilt (which are inherent in sin; ontological, not imposed).

3. Natural Evil

i. Natural evil is suffering from circumstance, from outside of one's own moral choice.

ii. Natural evil individually consists of toil and strife, and old age, sickness, and physical death. Corporately it consists of war, famine, and plague.

iii. Physical death is not original in creation—God could–would–must–did create the world without natural evil vs. deism and theistic evolution.[8]

iv. Physical death is not inherent in moral evil.

v. Physical death is imposed by God.

---

5. *Romans 1:20.*

6. *Romans 3:10-11.*

7. *Psalm 19.*

8. See the argument presented in *Paper No. 127* and Gangadean, *Philosophical Foundation*, 190.

    vi. Physical death is not arbitrarily imposed; it is imposed by God because of moral evil.

   vii. Physical death, as imposed, is not punishment (penal/justice); spiritual death is justice.

PART II: WHY IS THERE EVIL?
MORAL, NATURAL, AND LASTING EVIL

1. Why is there moral evil?

    i. Creation is God's self-revelation: necessarily, intentionally, and exclusively.

    ii. Moral evil (unbelief) objectively deepens the revelation and subjectively obscures the revelation.

   iii. If moral evil is removed abruptly, the revelation is not deepened.

   iv. If moral evil is not removed, the revelation is not seen.

    v. Moral evil is removed gradually.

   vi. Moral evil (unbelief) comes to full expression in world history in every kind and degree of admixture with belief.

   vii. In a spiritual war, which is age-long and agonizing, good overcomes evil. The earth shall be full of the knowledge of the Lord as the waters cover the sea.[9]

2. Why is there natural evil?

    i. Natural evil is a call back from moral evil; it is a call to stop and think (vs. NARD).

    ii. Physical death is a call back from spiritual death.

   iii. Natural evil is a silent, constant, inescapable, universal, and final call to stop and think; it is the last call back from the fullest degree of moral evil. After physical death, there is no more call back; natural evil is removed when the call back ends.

---

9. *Genesis 3:15; Isaiah 11:9.*

iv. Natural evil serves to restrain, recall from, and remove moral evil.

v. Natural evil increases historically and corporately as moral evil increases.

vi. Natural evil as a call back is mercy. Natural evil as mercy requires special revelation (SR) from God to show how God can be both just and merciful at the same time to man in sin.

vii. Special revelation must be consistent with clear general revelation.

viii. Only Genesis 1–3 (creation–fall–redemption) is consistent with clear general revelation. Only what builds on Genesis 1–3 increases SR.

3. Why is there lasting evil?

The popular concept of hell exacerbates the POE. There have been many attempts to mitigate the problem of lasting evil in the POE.

i. Universalism claims that all are saved (including demons).

ii. Annihilation/soul sleep/pure consciousness/nirvana removes awareness of self and suffering.

iii. Purgatory/limbo/indulgences lessen the time and/or severity of suffering.

iv. Inclusivism includes all persons of good will, including explicit non-believers.

v. Reincarnation continues innumerable times until enlightenment occurs.

vi. It is claimed there must be a second chance for those who never heard SR (or who heard a misrepresentation of it).

vii. Some desire no time limit for repentance. The door must always be open, regardless of any final judgment. Conversion, in this view, depends on man's choice ultimately, not on God's grace.

The biblical concept of sin and death transforms the problem of a final theodicy.

   i. In the day you eat you shall surely die; the wages of sin is death.[10]

   ii. There are two kinds of death, physical and spiritual death.[11]

   iii. The wages of sin is spiritual death, not physical death, nor a literal lake of fire (maximal natural evil).

   iv. Infinite/divine justice is ontological; it is present and inherent in sin, not future and imposed.

   v. There is no essential difference between spiritual death in this life and in the next life. In rational freedom, there is never a conflict between *want* and *can*.[12]

   vi. The lake of fire is figurative for spiritual death. For man, it is the second death.[13] In general, it is destruction. Spiritual death for man is meaninglessness (darkness of mind), boredom (burning of desire), and guilt (torment of conscience—the worm that does not die), without end (the bottomless pit).[14]

   vii. Spiritual death deepens the revelation of God's justice and mercy, forever.

PART III: THE IRONIC SOLUTION

Man as a rational being in sin rejects the life of the light of reason.[15] His understanding becomes darkened (the noetic effect).[16] His thinking becomes increasingly meaningless and futile.[17] He claims to know when he does not. Because he has shut his eyes he cannot see.

The Ironic Solution is clear. The problem is not resolved; rather, it is, ironically, dissolved:

---

10. *Genesis 2:17; Romans 6:23.*

11. *Ephesians 2:1; John 11:25-26; Revelation 20:6, 14; 21:8.*

12. Gangadean, *History of Philosophy*, 153-154; Gangadean, *Philosophical Foundation*, 66, 167-168.

13. *Revelation 20:14; 21:8.*

14. Gangadean, *The Westminster Catechisms*. See LCQ. 29; Gangadean, *Philosophical Foundation*, 195-197.

15. *John 1:4-5.*

16. *Paper No. 103.*

17. *Romans 1:20-22.*

1. Because of all the evil in the world, I cannot see how God is all good and all powerful.

2. Because of all the unbelief in the world . . .

3. Because of all the unbelief in me . . .

4. Because I have neglected and avoided the use of reason . . .

5. Because I have shut my eyes, I cannot see what is clear about God.

Paper № 8

BELIEF AND UNBELIEF

THE SPIRITUAL WAR

Introductory Remarks

1. Man, created in the image of God, is fallen.[1] Left to oneself, no one seeks God, no one understands, and no one does what is right, not even one. Man's chief end is to glorify God, yet all have sinned and come short of the glory of God.[2]

2. Unbelief arises from the failure to understand and accept the Principle of Clarity and Inexcusability. General revelation concerning the divine nature and the moral law is clear so that unbelief is without excuse.[3]

3. The failure to seek and to understand what is clear is sin. This root of sin is the hidden strength of corruption and deceitfulness remaining in the human heart and must be repented of as long as sin remains.[4]

4. Not seeking and not understanding result in skepticism in the unbeliever and fideism in the believer. Skepticism claims that knowledge is not possible. Fideism is a profession of belief without understanding the meaning or the grounds for belief.

---

1. *Paper No. 103*; Gangadean, *The Westminster Confession*. See Questions 30-32.

2. *Romans 3:10-11, 23; 1:21.*

3. *Romans 1:20; 2:14-15.*

4. *Romans 1:21-32; 3:12-15.*

5. Those who fail to use reason to see what is clear cannot understand those who do. The natural man (skeptic or fideist) does not receive the things of the Spirit of God: for they are foolishness unto him: neither can he know them, because they are spiritually (that is, rationally) discerned.[5]

6. In failing to see the intellectual roots of belief and of unbelief, the skeptic-fideist becomes anti-intellectual in separating doctrine from life, the prophetic from the priestly and the kingly, the intellectual from the psychological and the practical.

7. Separating doctrine (belief about Truth) from life by not discussing doctrinal differences, divides the triune nature of man.[6] It dehumanizes man and gives rise to all forms of divisions, strife, and wars.

8. True faith is the substance (underlying support/reality/*hupostasis*) of things hoped for, the evidence (proof/*elegchos*) of things not seen. By faith we understand. Belief without understanding is fideism, not faith.[7] Those who understand what is clear can show (prove) what is clear.[8]

9. Faith, as understanding, is pleasing to God; lack of faith is not pleasing to God. Fideism and skepticism avoid the light of rational discourse about basic things. Lack of common ground in reason makes dialogue impossible.[9]

10. The life of the Logos, the eternal Word of God, is in all men as light (reason). The light shines in the darkness (of unbelief) and the darkness cannot overcome it or withstand it. The light of reason cannot be extinguished in oneself (by spiritual suicide) or in others (by spiritual murder). Fallen man is still man. The demand of human nature for meaning is inextinguishable.[10]

---

5. *1 Corinthians 2:14.*

6. Gangadean, *The Westminster Catechisms*. See LCQ. 17.

7. *Paper No. 21, 98, 128-129*; Gangadean, *Philosophical Foundation*, 121-127; Gangadean, *History of Philosophy*, 163-166. Gangadean, *The Westminster Confession*. See Questions 62-64.

8. *Hebrews 11:1-3.*

9. *Hebrews 11:6; John 3:16-21.*

10. *John 1:1, 4-5.*

Paper № 9

———

THE MORAL LAW

Derived from Human Nature

INTRODUCTION

1. The moral law is clear; it is grounded in human nature, which is easily knowable by all human beings.

2. The moral law is for all men, everywhere, at all times.

3. The moral law is teleological, aimed at the good, the end in itself, which is the knowledge of God.

4. The moral law is comprehensive; it guides all choices that express all aspects of human nature.

5. The moral law is the source of unity in each person and among all persons.

6. The moral law is spiritual; it has inherent consequences of spiritual life or death.

7. The moral law from general revelation is the same in content as the moral law given in special revelation (the Decalogue).

THE DERIVATION[1]

The following shows how each moral law (3) is derived from a fundamental feature of human nature (1), based upon analysis of that feature (2).

Moral Law 1: On the Good and God

1. By nature, we make choices concerning means and ends.

2. The end in itself is the good, which is grounded in human nature.

3. God, as creator of human nature, is the only determiner of good and evil for man.

Moral Law 2: On the Nature of Thinking and the Divine Nature

1. By nature, we think, and thinking by nature is presuppositional (we think of the less basic in light of the more basic).

2. The infinite and eternal are more basic than the finite and temporal.

3. We are not to think of the infinite, eternal, and unchangeable (God) in light of the finite, temporal, and changeable (man).

Moral Law 3: On Unity and Integrity

1. Human nature is one, a unity of diversity; to be divided against oneself is self-destructive.

2. Integrity is a concern for consistency, which preserves the unity of human nature.

3. We should have integrity in all that we think and say and do.

Moral Law 4: On Work and Rest

1. By nature, work (of dominion) is necessary to bring human life into being and to develop and to preserve that being.

2. Work is not an end in itself, but is the means to the good, which is corporate, cumulative, and communal.

---

1. Gangadean, *Philosophical Foundation*, 171-184; Gangadean, *History of Philosophy*, 61-69.

3. When the good is achieved, man will rest from the work of dominion.

Moral Law 5: On Authority and Insight

1. By nature, we are born ignorant and come to maturity through being taught.

2. Authority in teaching is based on insight into the good and the means to the good; this insight is historically cumulative.

3. Authority based on insight must be honored; authority without insight must be changed where possible.

Moral Law 6: On Human Dignity and Rationality

1. We are born human, with a dignity which distinguishes man from animal.

2. Human dignity consists in the capacity to understand by reason.

3. We are to affirm human dignity in man's ability and responsibility to understand what is clear to reason.

Moral Law 7: On Spiritual Fidelity and Infidelity

1. We are born of a sexual union between one man and one woman.

2. A sexual union is a sign and seal of love, which seeks the good for and with the other.

3. We are to avoid infidelity (failure to love the other) by pursuing spiritual fidelity (love for the good).

Moral Law 8: On Talent and Value

1. We are each born with talent, given in the uniqueness of one's being.

2. Talent is an ability to achieve some aspect of the good for the benefit of all.

3. We are to develop our talent in pursuit of the good in service to others.

Moral Law 9: On Truth and Justice

1. We are born equal; in justice equals are treated equally.

2. Truth is necessary and sufficient to prevent and to correct injustice.

3. We are to prevent and correct injustice by knowing and speaking the truth.

Moral Law 10: On Contentment and the Good

1. We are born changeable in our understanding; discontent arises from a misunderstanding of good and evil.

2. Moral evil serves the good by deepening the divine revelation; natural evil serves to restrain, recall from, and remove moral evil.

3. We are to be content in all circumstances by pursuing what truly is the good.

Paper N⁰· 10

———

THE MORAL LAW

The Origin, Nature, Law, Application, and Consequences of the Moral Laws[1]

INTRODUCTION

1. **Definition of "ethics": ethics is concerned with giving a rational justification for the answer to the question "what is the good?"**

   Ethics assumes choice, choice assumes values, and values assume the concept of the good.

   What is particularly sought in ethics is rational justification, which guarantees that we have knowledge of the good.

2. **There are necessary conditions in order to have rational justification for ethics.**

   i. There must be a metaphysical absolute.

   ii. There must be personal immortality.

   iii. There must be freedom.

   iv. There must be clarity.

   v. There must be rationality.

---

1. Gangadean, *Philosophical Foundation*, 171-184; Gangadean, *History of Philosophy*, 61-69; Gangadean, *The Westminster Catechisms*. See LCQ. 90-148.

3. There is a moral law which is clear, comprehensive, and critical.

  i. It is clear because it is grounded in human nature, and is therefore easily knowable and universal.

  ii. It is comprehensive, including all aspects of human nature and choice.

  iii. It is critical; its consequences are a matter of life and death.

MORAL LAW 1:
THE GOOD AND GOD

The first moral law is about the good and the ground of the good; it is about the good and the real or eternal; it is about the moral absolute and the metaphysical absolute.

1. On the ORIGIN of the concept of the good.

The good is grounded in human nature, in the reality of choice.

Choice assumes values and values assume the good, the highest value.

What is chosen is chosen either for its own sake, which is the good, the end in itself, or chosen as a means to the good.

2. On the NATURE of the good and the real.

  i. The good is the end in itself.

  It is chosen for its own sake, not for the sake of anything else. It is the highest value (the *summum bonum*), the source of unity, the moral absolute.

  ii. The good is not virtue.

  Virtue is a means to the good.

  There are different kinds of virtues: moral, natural, and instrumental.

  iii. The good is not happiness.

  Happiness is the effect of possessing what we believe is the good.

iv. The good is one.

As the source of unity in a person and among persons, there is one good for each person and one good for all persons.

There is one good for each person.
If there were more than one good for each person, there would be no rational basis for choice.

There is one good for all persons.
Good for a being is based on the nature of that being. The good for human beings is based on human nature. There is one human nature. Therefore, there is one good for all human beings.

v. The good is clear.

The good as based in human nature is easily knowable. It is objectively clear, knowable by all who can be held morally responsible, regardless of cultural background.

vi. The good is based on the real.

One's view of the good is based on one's view of human nature, which is based on one's view of what is real or eternal.

vii. It is clear that only some is eternal.

There must be something eternal.
Matter exists and matter is not eternal.
The soul exists and the soul is not eternal.

What is eternal brought into existence, or created, what is not eternal.
The Creator is God.

3. MORAL LAW 1: on the good and God.

God, as creator of human nature, is the determiner of good and evil for man.

4. APPLICATION: what is opposed in Moral Law 1.

i. Theism is opposed to all forms of non-theism.

Belief in God the Creator is opposed to atheism, pantheism, polytheism, and shamanism, as well as to material monism, spiritual monism, and dualism.

ii. Objective clarity is opposed to all forms of skepticism (nothing is clear) and fideism (belief without understanding or proof).

iii. Subjective clarity is opposed to emotivism and voluntarism.

It is opposed to the view that feelings and will are independent of and can be opposed to what one understands; that knowledge is not sufficient for morality; that knowledge of the truth does not set one free.

iv. Theonomy is opposed to all forms of autonomy.

God as the determiner of good and evil is opposed to all forms of man, understood apart from God, as the determiner of good and evil.

Theonomy is opposed to ethical egoism (individual happiness), utilitarianism (collective happiness), deontology (will guided by reason alone), existentialism (will apart from rational determination), naturalism (individual instinct), tradition (collective instinct), humanism (human nature as a whole understood apart from God), stoicism (denial of desires), mystical contemplation (knowledge apart from understanding).

v. The moral law is opposed to heteronomy.

The law, given in human nature and knowable by reason, is opposed to the view that the law is given by an external source, independent of reason.

It is opposed to the claim that the law is known only by special revelation.

vi. The moral law is opposed to positivism.

The moral law, given in human nature, is opposed to the divine command theory, that the law is arbitrary or positive, that whatever God commands is good, apart from human nature.

vii. Teleology is opposed to deontology and consequentialism.

Duty is not pursued for its own sake; virtue must be understood in relation to the good.

Happiness is not sought for its own sake; happiness must be understood in relation to the good.

There is not a direct relation between virtue and happiness, apart from the good.

5. CONSEQUENCES of Moral Law 1.

i. Moral evil is a denial of one's nature as a rational being.

In moral evil, one neglects, avoids, resists, and denies reason in the presence of what is clear about God.

In moral evil, man puts himself in the place of God to determine good and evil.

The consequence of the denial of reason is spiritual death. Individually, it brings meaninglessness, boredom, and guilt. Corporately, it brings the death of relationships, institutions, and cultures.

Spiritual death is present and inherent in moral evil; it is not imposed and future.

ii. To affirm what is clear about God brings a life full of meaning.

MORAL LAW 2:
THINKING AND THE NATURE OF GOD

1. On the ORIGIN of thinking and the concept of God.

By nature, we think. In thinking, reason is used to form concepts, judgments, and arguments, the forms of all thought.

By nature, we have the idea of God, that is, concepts about the nature of God.

2. On the NATURE of thinking.

Thinking is presuppositional. We think of the less basic in light of the more basic.

We think of truth in light of meaning. We think of experience in light of basic beliefs. We think of conclusion in light of premises. We think of the finite in light of the infinite, the temporal in light of the eternal.

Understanding what is more basic is necessary to understand what is less basic.

Agreement on what is more basic leads to agreement on what is less basic.

3. MORAL LAW 2: on thinking about the nature of God.

We are to think presuppositionally about God.

We are to think about the finite (man) in light of the infinite (God), not the infinite (God) in light of the finite (man) or the finite (man) in light of the finite (nature).

We are to think of man as the image of God; we are not to think of God as the image of man.

The divine nature, which is infinite, eternal, and unchangeable, is not to be likened to human nature, which is finite, temporal, and changeable.

4. APPLICATION: what is opposed in Moral Law 2.

Divisions among theists can be resolved by thinking presuppositionally.

Specifically, divisions among theists can be resolved by thinking presuppositionally about God's goodness and justice.

God's goodness and justice are not to be likened to human goodness and justice.

i. Presuppositional thinking, in general, is opposed to rationalism and to empiricism. Both fail to recognize their assumptions.

    ii. The divine nature is opposed the denial of divine providence in natural evil, and redemptive revelation in light of natural evil.

    iii. The divine nature is opposed to the denial of atonement to satisfy divine justice.

    iv. The divine nature is opposed to the denial of vicarious atonement by a representative man.

    v. The divine nature is opposed to the denial of the sufficiency of vicarious atonement, apart from human effort.

    vi. The divine nature is opposed to the denial of the nature of moral evil and its inherent consequences.

    vii. The divine nature is opposed to all forms of idolatry, both conceptual and visual.

5. CONSEQUENCES of Moral Law 2.

    i. Distortions in the concept of God, when developed, bring divisions among theists, apostasy, cultural decay, and collapse.

    ii. Affirmation of the true nature of God brings unity among theists, continuity of belief through the generations, and increase of understanding.

MORAL LAW 3:
INTEGRITY AND KNOWLEDGE

1. On the ORIGIN of the concept of integrity.

There is a natural unity in our being.

There is a natural concern not to be divided against oneself.

2. On the NATURE of integrity.

Integrity is a concern for consistency (unity) in what we say and what we do.
What we say is both implicit and explicit, to ourselves and to others.

Concern for consistency is necessary and sufficient for knowledge.

Concern for consistency is objective, not subjective. Integrity is not sincerity.

Concern for consistency is necessary for dialogue.

3. MORAL LAW 3: on integrity.

We should have integrity; we should have a concern for consistency.

4. APPLICATION: what is opposed in Moral Law 3.

i. Integrity is opposed to claiming to want to know without self-examination.

We implicitly profess to want to know, yet fail to know what is clear.

What is basic is clear.

If we examine our own basic beliefs for meaning, we can know what is clear.

ii. Integrity is opposed to dialogue without reason.

Dialogue requires reason.

Integrity requires that one does not neglect, avoid, resist, or deny reason in dialogue.

iii. Integrity is opposed to professing skepticism without accepting its implications.

iv. Integrity is opposed to professing a position without discipline to put it into practice.

v. Integrity is opposed to making a vow and not keeping it.

vi. Integrity is opposed to hypocrisy.

In hypocrisy, one avoids shame and guilt by self-deception and self-justification.

vii. Integrity is opposed to placing practical and psychological concerns above concern for truth.

5. CONSEQUENCES of Moral Law 3.

   i. As integrity decreases, stupor increases.

  ii. As integrity increases, clarity increases.

MORAL LAW 4:
WORK, THE GOOD, AND HOPE

1. On the ORIGIN of work.

To bring into being and to sustain in being requires work.

2. On the NATURE of work, the good, and hope.

   i. Work is not an end in itself. It is a means to the good.

  ii. The good is the knowledge of God.

     The good is continuing, inexhaustible, comprehensive, inalienable, corporate, cumulative, communal, fulfilling, ultimate, and transformative.

 iii. The good is achieved through work.

     Creation is revelation.
Knowledge of God is through knowledge of the creation.
The knowledge of creation is through the work of dominion.

     In dominion, man develops all the powers latent in himself and the world.

     All lives reveal human nature. Human nature reveals the nature of God.
Some lives reveal human nature through natural rule.
Some lives reveal human nature through moral rule.
Moral evil and natural evil deepen the revelation. They require a greater dominion.

 iv. Work for the good requires hope.

     Hope is based on understanding the nature of things.
From the nature of things, it is certain that the good will be attained.

The nature of man requires the good.

The nature of the good requires dominion.

The nature of God as infinitely good requires that good will overcome evil.

From considering the past—there has been progress.

From considering the present—challenges remain.

As the work of creation ended, the work of dominion will also end. As creation is revelation, the work of dominion brings knowledge of revelation.

The earth shall be full of the knowledge of God as the waters cover the sea.

3. MORAL LAW 4: on work, the good, and hope.

We should work for the good with true hope.

4. APPLICATION: what is opposed in Moral Law 4.

i. True hope is opposed to false hope.

The good cannot be achieved without work.

The hope of heaven as the good, in place of knowledge of God through the work of dominion, is false hope.

ii. True hope is opposed to no hope.

Work without hope for the good is meaningless.

Work for pleasure as the good is empty.

iii. True hope is opposed to revolutionary utopianism.

It is opposed to man's work without God's work.

Evil exists. It serves to deepen the divine revelation. It is removed gradually.

Work apart from divine grace cannot achieve the ideal community.

iv. True hope is opposed to the hope of righteousness by works.

Man's righteousness comes short and does not merit divine favor.

v. True hope is opposed to millennial supernaturalism.

It is opposed to God's work as done apart from man's work.

vi. True hope is opposed to cyclical fatalism.

There is no necessary cycle of history irrespective of human effort.

vii. True hope is opposed to the hope of mystical ecstasy.

There is no direct knowledge of ultimate reality apart from understanding the creation.

There is no beatific vision, no intuitive enlightenment.

5. CONSEQUENCES of Moral Law 4.

i. Work apart from the good is empty.

ii. Work for the good is fulfilling.

MORAL LAW 5:
AUTHORITY AND INSIGHT

1. On the ORIGIN of authority.

We are born ignorant. We need to be taught the good and the means to the good.

Authority is expressed fundamentally in teaching.

2. On the NATURE of authority and insight.

Authority is rational, not personal.

Authority is based on insight, not might.

Insight is historically cumulative, not individual.

3. MORAL LAW 5: on authority and insight.

Authority based on insight must be honored.

Authority without insight must be changed where possible.

4. APPLICATION: what is opposed in Moral Law 5.

i. It is opposed to persons without insight in positions of authority.

It is opposed to authority without insight in Family, State, School, and Church.

ii. It is opposed to principles of authority as ultimate, which are not self-attesting.

It is opposed to tradition, intuition, science, and scriptures as self-attesting.

iii. It is opposed to reversing the order of authority in each person.

There is a natural order of authority in each person: thought, feeling, and will.

iv. It is opposed to reversing the order of authority in each institution.

In an institution, the philosophical must lead the psychological and the practical.

v. It is opposed to totalitarianism among institutions.

No institution is over another; Family, Church, and State are equally under the moral law, according to their form and function.

vi. It is opposed to an autonomous State and to a theonomous Church.

The State is not over the Church; it is under the moral law.

The Church is not over the State; it is under the moral law.

vii. It is opposed to the State over the Family and the Family over the State.

It is opposed to a welfare state and to public education as religiously neutral.

It is opposed to the State over Business and to Business over the State.

5. CONSEQUENCES of Moral Law 5.

i. Authority without insight subverts and perverts the good.

ii. Authority based on insight protects and is productive of the good.

MORAL LAW 6:
HUMAN DIGNITY AND RATIONALITY

1. On the ORIGIN of human dignity.

We are born human. Human dignity distinguishes us from animals.

2. On the NATURE of human dignity.

Human dignity consists in the capacity to understand. We understand by reason.

Reason in man is natural, not conventional; it is universal—the same in all persons.

Human society is a society of rational beings. Participation in, or separation from, human society depends on the exercise of this capacity.

3. MORAL LAW 6: on human dignity and rationality.

We are to affirm human dignity.

We are to treat others as having the capacity and responsibility for understanding.

4. APPLICATION: what is opposed in Moral Law 6.

i. Affirmation of human dignity is opposed to use of force in murder and war.

Murder results from accumulated personal lack of discipline in self-control.

War results from accumulated collective failure to use reason, on both sides.

ii. Affirmation of human dignity is opposed to racism.

In racism, ethnicity is placed above our common humanity in reason.

iii. Affirmation of human dignity is opposed to gender wars.

In gender wars, we fail to understand the nature of male/female differences.

In gender wars, we fail to hold each other responsible for the use of reason.

iv. Affirmation of human dignity is opposed to abortion, euthanasia, suicide, and intervention which disregards the loss of the capacity to understand.

v. Affirmation of human dignity is opposed to psychotherapeutic programs which disregard interpretive assumptions and responsibility for our beliefs.

vi. Affirmation of human dignity is opposed to the view that temporal separation from human society by capital punishment is a denial of human dignity.

vii. Affirmation of human dignity is opposed to the view that final separation from rational human society by divine judgment is a denial of human dignity.

5. CONSEQUENCES of Moral Law 6.

i. To deny human dignity in another, one must first deny it in oneself.

ii. To affirm human dignity in oneself is to affirm it in others.

MORAL LAW 7:
SEX AND LOVE, AND MARRIAGE AND THE GOOD

1. On the ORIGIN of marriage and the good.

The origin of our being is from a sexual union of our parents.

Through the nurture of our being, by our parents, the good is achieved.

2. On the NATURE of sex and love, and marriage and the good.

   i. Sex is a sign and seal of love.

   ii. The physical union is a natural sign of a spiritual union.

  iii. A physical and a spiritual union together is a full union.

  iv. A full union is a union of persons.

   v. A full union of two persons is monogamous and lasting.

  vi. A full union is the union of marriage.

 vii. Love, in marriage, seeks the good for and with the other, and for those we bring into being.

3. MORAL LAW 7: on marriage and the good.

Marriage is to achieve the good.

There is an order for marriage which protects it.

4. APPLICATION: what is opposed in Moral Law 7.

   i. The good for marriage is opposed to regarding the other as the good.

     Friendship is reciprocal, lasting, and shares the deepest concerns. It is the effect of mutual commitment to the good.

     Marriage, as lasting, must be based on friendship.

     The good of friendship is not the good of romantic love.

  ii. The nature of persons is opposed to separating sex and love.

     A person is a union of body and soul; the physical is not to be separated from the spiritual.

     Sex without love is desecrated; the sign without the reality is contemptible.

     Respect of personhood is opposed to casual sex, prostitution, rape, and pedophilia, and whatever depersonalizes sex.

 iii. The full union of marriage is opposed to polygamy (simultaneous or serial), and to polyandry.

iv. Marriage, as lasting, is opposed to divorce, except for adultery, or willful desertion which cannot be remedied.

v. Sex, as a natural union, is opposed to what is not natural.

A natural union is mutual and simultaneous. What is otherwise is unnatural.

vi. The good for marriage is opposed to children or companionship as the good.

Children, as persons, are not the good; the good is by and for persons.

Companionship is not the good; it is the effect of mutual commitment to the good.

vii. Marriage, as lasting, is opposed to disregard of the order which protects it.

There is a natural order for marriage which protects it; what comes after requires what comes before:

1. Seek the good for oneself (love of self and God)

2. Seek the good for the other (love of neighbor)

3. Seek the good with the other (friendship)

4. Finding one's complement (courtship)

5. Endowment (preparation)

6. Vows (commitment)

7. Civil laws (sanctions)

5. CONSEQUENCES of Moral Law 7.

i. Ordinary infidelity (lack of commitment to the other) is rooted in spiritual infidelity (lack of commitment to the good).

ii. Marriage for the good increases the good in one's own life and the lives of others, through generations.

MORAL LAW 8:
VALUE AND TALENT

1. On the ORIGIN of value and talent.

We naturally value things. No one values all things alike.

2. On the NATURE of value and talent.

Value is a function of supply and demand.

Demand is a function of one's view of the good.

Supply is a function of talent.

   i. Talent is an ability to achieve some aspect of the good.

   ii. Talent is in each; it is grounded in the uniqueness of one's being.

   iii. The origin of one's talent is the origin of one's being. It is given to each, for all.

   iv. Talent is known by interest and ability, in the three categories of personality.

   v. Talent is developed through the efforts of others, as well as one's own effort.

   vi. Talent is developed fully only in the vision of the good.

   vii. Talent is irrepressible. When fully developed, it forms its function.

3. MORAL LAW 8: on value and talent.

One is to develop one's talent in pursuit of the good in service to others.

Failure to do so is to take from others what is of value that belongs to them.

4. APPLICATION: what is opposed in Moral Law 8.

   i. It is opposed to the neglect of one's talent through sloth or greed or pride.

   ii. It is opposed to misuse of talent, when it is not used for the good.

iii. The origin and social development of talent is opposed to capitalism. The origin and individual development of talent is opposed to communism.

Stewardship affirms that God as Creator owns all absolutely. Man is steward.

Capitalism affirms man individually owns absolutely.

Communism affirms man collectively owns absolutely.

Both capitalism and communism are antinomies; they share a common assumption.

iv. It is opposed to social policies which are based on finite supply (vs. talent).

v. It is opposed to economic policies which create disincentives to effort.

vi. It is opposed to wasteful spending of resources which does not advance the good.

vii. It is opposed to the unlimited accumulation of wealth by what indebts others.

5. CONSEQUENCES of Moral Law 8.

i. The neglect or abuse of talent increases the poverty of life for all.

ii. The use of talent for the good increases the richness of life for all.

MORAL LAW 9:
TRUTH AND JUSTICE

1. On the ORIGIN of justice.

We are born equal. In justice, equals are to be treated equally.

2. On the NATURE of truth and justice.

i. Ultimate justice is ontological. Consequences are inherent by creation.

In mercy, justice is satisfied by grace.

ii. Social justice is first distributive, then contractual, and finally retributive.

iii. Full social justice is both preventative and corrective.

iv. Truth is necessary and sufficient for justice.

v. To have justice, one must know the truth and speak the truth.

Justice, in a court of law, requires us to speak the truth, the whole truth, and nothing but the truth.

vi. Full justice requires knowing and speaking the whole truth.

vii. Knowing the whole truth is a function of the whole of one's life.

3. MORAL LAW 9: on truth and justice.

We are to seek justice by knowing and speaking the truth.

4. APPLICATION: what is opposed in Moral Law 9.

i. It is opposed to ignorance as excusable.

If we seek, we can know what is clear. We can remove oppression justified by false worldviews.

ii. It is opposed to fideism.

Fideism is not knowledge. It declares what is believed to be true without answering objections. It nullifies its testimony.

iii. It is opposed to privacy in decisions affecting public affairs.

It is opposed to privacy for bribery to influence public decisions.

iv. It is opposed to restrictions on freedom of speech.

It is opposed to closed societies, restricted public forum, and prohibited books.

v. It is opposed to abuse of freedom of speech as the right of rational discourse.

It is opposed to slander, contempt, harassment, and incitement to violence.

vi. It is opposed to false advertising.

It is opposed to profit-making by withholding information regarding possible harm from the product sold.

vii. It is opposed to public exposure of what is private.

What is private is situational.

There is both a right to privacy and an obligation to privacy for spiritual and physical nakedness.

5. CONSEQUENCES of Moral Law 9.

i. An unfaithful witness shares in injustice and its consequences.

ii. A faithful witness brings about justice.

MORAL LAW 10:
SUFFERING AND THE GOOD

1. On the ORIGIN of suffering

We are born changeable. We can change in what we think about good and evil.

Suffering arises when we think we cannot possess what we believe to be the good.

2. On the NATURE of suffering and the good.

i. The good is not virtue—natural, moral or instrumental. Virtue is a means to the good.

ii. The good is not happiness. Happiness is the effect of possessing what we believe is the good.

iii. Suffering results from evil—moral and natural.

iv. Moral evil, at root, is an act contrary to our nature as rational beings.

It is to neglect, avoid, resist, or deny reason in the face of what is clear about God.

It is to put oneself in the place of God to determine good and evil.

v. The inherent consequence of moral evil is spiritual death: meaninglessness, boredom, and guilt. Socially, it is the death of relationships, institutions, and cultures.

vi. Natural evil consists in toil and strife, and old age, sickness, and death.

It is not original in creation, nor inherent in moral evil, but imposed because of moral evil.

Natural evil, at times, is intensified to famine, war, and plague.

vii. Natural evil is imposed by God upon man, not as punishment, but as a call back, to stop and think.

Natural evil is the last, and continuing, call back from moral evil, self-deception, and self-justification.

Natural evil serves to restrain, to recall from, and to remove moral evil.

3. MORAL LAW 10: on suffering and the good.

We are not to be discontent in pursuing our own view of the good, but to be content in pursuing what truly is the good.

4. APPLICATION: what is opposed in Moral Law 10.

i. It is opposed to envy of others in their circumstances, abilities, and honors.

ii. It is opposed to stoicism, as a hardening of oneself, to avoid suffering, seen as useless.

iii. It is opposed to resentment, complaint, and bitterness, under circumstances seen as a hindrance to the good.

iv. It is opposed to discouragement in hardships in contrast to patience and perseverance in hope.

v. It is opposed to the self-indulgence of hedonism to escape emptiness or to compensate for pain.

vi. It is opposed to cynicism, which sees the reality of evil without seeing the reality of grace.

vii. It is opposed to fatalism, a resignation to evil, seen as merely natural, not imposed as a call back.

5. CONSEQUENCES of Moral Law 10.

i. To those who do not seek the good, suffering from natural evil is avoided as meaningless.

ii. To those who seek the good, all things are seen as working together for the good.

Paper № 11

FROM GENERAL REVELATION
TO SPECIAL REVELATION
Prologue to Scripture

Abbreviations:

general revelation (GR)	justice (J)
special revelation (SR)	mercy (M)
natural evil (NE)	if . . . then . . . (⊃); and (·); therefore (∴)
moral evil (ME)	restrains, recalls from, and removes (RRR)
physical death (PD)	neglect, avoid, resist, and deny reason (NARD)
spiritual death (SD)	less basic/more basic (LB/MB)

1. The NECESSITY for Special Revelation:[1]

  i. Natural evil (NE) exists: PD is not natural/original (could–would–must–did argument[2]).

  ii. NE ⊃ ME: NE assumes ME; NE RRR ME; PD calls back from SD.

  iii. If NE and ME exist, then justice and mercy exist. (NE · ME ⊃ J · M)

---

1. For an expanded version of this point, see *Paper No. 12*.

2. *Paper No. 127*; Gangadean, *Philosophical Foundation*, 190; Gangadean, *The Westminster Confession*. See Question 5.

    iv. J · M ⊃ M must satisfy J (vs. M can set aside J).

    v. If NE is by one representing all, then SR is necessary to show righteousness by one representing all.

2. The CONTENT of SR:[3]

    i. SR must be consistent with clear GR:

        a. only some (God the Creator) is eternal

        b. original creation is without natural evil

        c. all are affected by one

    ii. SR must show how M satisfies vs. sets aside divine J.

3. The ORIGIN of SR: Given by God and only from God.[4]

    i. From the nature and existence of ME in man, it cannot be from man (no one seeks and no one understands—NARD).

    ii. From the necessity of SR (SR as such is from God).

    iii. One's seeking and understanding is by divine grace.

4. The EXISTENCE of SR: Genesis 1–3 is the first, basic unit of biblical revelation.[5]

    i. Only Genesis 1–3 affirms God the Creator, man's purpose and destiny, and the original goodness of creation.

    ii. Only Genesis 1–3 affirms covenant representation and the fall of man.

    iii. Only Genesis 1–3 affirms man's redemption through curse and promise—M satisfies J through vicarious atonement.

    iv. Therefore, only Genesis 1–3, and what builds on this, is SR.

---

3. Gangadean, *The Westminster Confession*. See Question 6.

4. Gangadean, *The Westminster Confession*. See Question 7.

5. *Paper No. 13* and *14*; Gangadean, *History of Philosophy*, 50-58.

5. The TRANSMISSION of SR: Is SR preserved pure and entire?

G ⊃ P   If SR is given by God (G), then it is preserved by God (P)

G   SR is given by God

∴ P   Therefore, SR is preserved (pure and entire) by God

   i. Since it must be given in light of ME in man, and it is given to restore man from evil, it is therefore preserved from evil (NARD).

  ii. vs. Gnostic and neo-Gnostic—neither given nor preserved by God.

 iii. vs. Islam and Mormonism—both claim that SR was given, but not preserved in the past, yet given and preserved now.

6. The COMPLETION of SR:

Scripture is redemptive revelation—it is based on promise and fulfillment.

The promise is for another to come in the place of Adam to undo what Adam did and to do what Adam failed to do. When the promise is fulfilled, then SR is completed.

F ⊃ C   If the promise is fulfilled (F), then SR is completed (C)

F   The promise is fulfilled

∴ C   Therefore, SR is completed

   i. If Christ has come, then the promise is fulfilled.

  ii. Christ has come if the Spirit has been sent. It is the work of the Messiah (anointed by the Spirit) to send the Spirit after his death and resurrection.

 iii. The Spirit has come if the kingdom of God is expanding to all nations.

 iv. Since the kingdom is expanding into all nations, the promise is fulfilled.

7. The TRANSLATION of SR:[6]

i. Words express concepts and judgments, which are cognitive (true or false).

ii. Concepts are universal (the same in all); words are conventional (differ from language to language).

iii. Therefore, translations are possible.

iv. Since Scripture is meant for all, then translations are necessary and desirable.

v. Translations as desirable are opposed to the use of original languages only, or to the use of one language only, or to paraphrases in the place of translations.

8. The CLARITY of SR:[7]

If GR is clear by thinking of the less basic in light of the more basic (LB/MB), then SR also is clear by thinking of the LB/MB.

i. Clarity is opposed to hindering all from searching the Scriptures.

ii. Clarity is opposed to Gnostic mysteries and to hidden esoteric meanings.

iii. The meaning of any passage is one, not many; applications may be many.

iv. Clarity of SR is opposed to contradictions or to apparent contradictions.

v. Clarity is opposed to resignation to doctrinal divisions in the Church.

vi. Clarity is not opposed to the work of the Holy Spirit leading the Church through its pastor-teachers into all truth.

---

6. Gangadean, *The Westminster Confession*. See Question 10.

7. Gangadean, *The Westminster Confession*. See Question 9.

9. The SUFFICIENCY of SR:[8]

i. *Sola Scriptura* is opposed to all other forms of SR: traditions, opinions of ancient writers, new revelations of the Spirit vs. applications of Scripture.

ii. *Sola Scriptura* is not opposed to the use of reason or to appeal to clear GR; Scripture assumes both reason and clear GR.

iii. *Sola Scriptura* requires the use of good and necessary consequences in noting assumptions and implications; it is not only explicit statements.

10. The INTERPRETATION of SR:[9]

i. Thinking is presuppositional—we must think of the less basic in light of the more basic (LB/MB): meaning/reason, truth/meaning, experience/basic belief, conclusion/premises, finite and temporal/infinite and eternal, SR/GR, Revelation/Genesis.

ii. Contextualism is opposed to literalism (denial of the presence of interpretation) and allegoricalism (use of foreign or arbitrary assumptions in interpretation).

iii. Context consists of:

a. what is clear from GR

b. the biblical worldview of Genesis 1–3 (creation–fall–redemption)

c. historically cumulative insight (the work of the pastor-teachers in Church councils, summed up in the Westminster Confession of Faith)

---

8. Gangadean, *The Westminster Confession*. See Question 8.

9. *Paper No. 15.*

THE NECESSITY FOR SCRIPTURE

General Revelation Requires
Special Revelation

Understanding the necessity for Scripture is the first step in the process of rationally going from General Revelation to Special Revelation. After Necessity, there is understanding Content, Origin, Existence, Transmission, Completion, Translation, Clarity, Sufficiency, and Interpretation.[1]

The existence of moral evil in man and the existence of natural evil as a call back (mercy) require special revelation/Scripture (SR) to show how God can be both just and merciful to man.

1. Moral evil is an act contrary to human nature as a rational being. It is the failure to use reason to see what is clear. It is to not seek, not understand, and not do what is right.[2] It is to neglect, avoid, resist, and deny reason (NARD) in the face of what is clear about God. If there is no clear general revelation, there is no inexcusability (sin).[3]

2. The inherent consequence of moral evil (NARD) is meaninglessness, boredom, and guilt. This is spiritual death (the wages of sin

---

1. *Paper No. 11.*

2. *Romans 3:10.*

3. *Romans 1:20.*

is death;[4] in the day that you eat you will surely die;[5] you that were dead in your trespasses and sins[6]). The just punishment for sin is inherent in sin and therefore present, now and always, not merely future and imposed (popular view of hell).

3. Natural evil (NE) is suffering from circumstance. It is suffering from toil and strife, and old age, sickness, and (physical) death. It can be intensified corporately to war, famine, and plague.

 i. NE is not original in creation. If God is all good and all power-ful, then he could, would, must have, and therefore did make a world that was good, that is, without NE/physical death.

 ii. NE is not inherent in moral evil; spiritual death is inherent in moral evil, not physical death.

 iii. NE is therefore imposed by an act of God.

 iv. NE as imposed is not inherent and therefore is not punishment.

 v. NE is not imposed arbitrarily; it is imposed because of the moral evil of one person.

 vi. NE is not imposed unnecessarily but because of the depth of moral evil (NARD).

 vii. NE is imposed as a call back from moral evil; suffering is a call to stop and think.

 viii. NE serves to restrain, recall from, and remove moral evil. Phys-ical death is a call back from sin and spiritual death.

 ix. NE as a call back is therefore mercy, not justice (punishment).

 x. NE as mercy requires SR (Scripture) to show how God can be both just and merciful at the same time: mercy cannot set aside God's justice; mercy must satisfy justice since God is infinite, eternal, and unchangeable in his justice.

---

4. *Romans 6:23.*

5. *Genesis 2:17.*

6. *Ephesians 2:1.*

4. Since by one man, as representative head, physical death entered the world and passed to all, by one man, as representative head, it must be removed.

5. One can never know apart from SR how another man can be found who will take away the sin of the world. Only SR makes known the mystery of the Incarnation of the one who takes away the sin of the world.

Paper № 13

———

THE BIBLICAL WORLDVIEW
CREATION–FALL–REDEMPTION
Concise Version

CREATION

1. Creation is revelation: necessarily, intentionally, and exclusively.

2. This revelation is full and clear.

3. Eternal life is knowing God.

4. The knowledge of God is through the work of dominion.

5. The earth shall be full of the knowledge of the Lord as the waters cover the sea.

FALL

1. The covenant of creation: representation, probation, and manifestation; the covenant of marriage.

2. Temptation: the purpose, the agent, and the argument.

3. Sin: not seeking, not understanding, and not doing what is right.

4. Death: two kinds of death: physical and spiritual; the wages of sin is spiritual death.

5. Theodicy: why is there evil? Evil deepens the divine revelation.

REDEMPTION

1. The first call back: shame (inward/conscience).

   The first response: self-deception (cover up).

2. The second call back: self-examination (outward/the question).

   The second response: self-justification (blaming others).

3. The third call back: the promise and the curse.

   The promise: spiritual war, age-long and agonizing; good will overcome evil.

   The curse: toil, strife, and old age, sickness, and death; war, famine, and plague.

   The third response: repentance and faith (names his wife Eve).

4. Justification: forgiveness of sin through the death of another (the coats of skin).

5. Sanctification: cleansing from sin through suffering (the expulsion).

Paper N⚊. 14

THE BIBLICAL WORLDVIEW
CREATION–FALL–REDEMPTION
Expanded Version

INTRODUCTION

The biblical worldview of creation–fall–redemption in Genesis 1–3 is foundational for all of life.

Foundation is necessary to go on to maturity, fruitfulness, unity of the faith, and fullness of the knowledge of God.[1]

Foundation is laid in one's life at every level of learning: grammar, dialectic, and rhetoric; at the levels of knowledge, understanding, and wisdom. It must be factually remembered, in order; it must be rationally justified, at every step; and it must be applied, with social virtuosity.

ON CREATION

1. Creation is revelation: necessarily, intentionally, and exclusively.

   i. Necessarily: A being is revealed in its acts; the acts of God in creation and providence reveal the nature of God.

   ii. Intentionally: Creation is good; it was what God intended; God created to reveal himself and rules to reveal himself.

---

1. *Ephesians 4; Hebrews 6.*

iii. Exclusively: There is no knowledge of God without revelation; there is no revelation apart from the works of creation and providence.

2. This revelation is full and clear.

This revelation is full.

i. The whole earth is full of his glory.[2] The length, breadth, depth, and height of God's glory is seen in his filling everything in every way.

ii. The vast array of the creation, each after its kind, and the multitudes of human beings in history are a full revelation of God's glory.

iii. Providence of the Fall and of redemption are a full revelation of God's justice and mercy; nothing more is added to what is full.

This revelation is clear.

iv. The eternal power and divine nature are clearly revealed in the things which are made; the law of God is written on the hearts of all men.[3]

v. The clarity of general revelation makes the unbelief of mankind without excuse.

vi. Clarity is opposed to all forms of skepticism (no knowledge is possible) and to fideism (belief without proof/understanding).

3. Eternal life is knowing God.

i. From general revelation: the good for man as a rational being is understanding creation and providence, which reveal God; the good is the knowledge of God.

ii. From special revelation: eternal life is knowing God;[4] it begins in this life and grows unendingly in the next life.

---

2. *Isaiah 6:3.*

3. *Romans 1:20; 2:14-15.*

4. *John 17:3.*

iii. From Historic Christianity: man's chief end is to glorify God and to enjoy him forever; [5] to glorify God is to know his glory and to make his glory known.

4. The knowledge of God is through the work of dominion.

i. The knowledge of God is through knowledge of God's self-revelation in the creation unfolding in providence/history.

ii. The knowledge of the creation is through the work of dominion. In dominion, man is to be fruitful and multiply and fill the earth and rule over it.[6] The work of dominion is corporate, cumulative, and communal. It requires all of mankind, working together through all of history, to be achieved. Dominion requires naming (grasping the nature of) all beings in all their parts and relations, and developing this nature/essence, the excellence/glory in all beings, so as to make known the glory of God. The outcome of the work of dominion is the City of God.[7]

iii. The work of dominion under the Fall and redemption requires making disciples of all nations and taking every thought captive which is raised up against the knowledge of God.[8]

5. The earth shall be full of the knowledge of the Lord as the waters cover the sea.

i. Man is the image of God; as God's work of creation and providence is revelation, so man's work of dominion brings knowledge of God as Creator and Ruler.

ii. As God completed the work of creation, man will complete the work of dominion.

The Sabbath day of rest is instituted by God to remind man of his origin and his destiny in eschatological hope.

---

5. *SCQ. 1.*

6. *Genesis 1.*

7. *Revelation 21.*

8. *Matthew 28:20; 2 Corinthians 10:4.*

iii. The work of dominion will be completed when the earth is filled with the knowledge of God as the waters cover the sea.[9]

ON THE FALL

1. The Covenant of Creation

i. Purpose of the covenant: to establish mankind in a permanent (positive) relationship with God.

ii. Representation: all of life and history is centered in the Garden of Eden; the act of one man, Adam, will affect all.

iii. Probation: Adam is to be tested concerning his pursuit of God's purpose for mankind: the knowledge of God through the work of dominion.

iv. Manifestation: the inward, invisible choice of good and evil is manifested in the outward act of obedience regarding eating from the two trees.

v. The visible covenant of marriage between man and woman reveals the invisible covenant of creation between God and man.

2. Temptation

i. The temptation is a test of one's faith/understanding of good and evil (both objectively and subjectively).

ii. Neither the tempter nor the test is the cause of sin, but rather the outward occasion that reveals sin.

iii. The test comes in the form of an argument addressed to the understanding: a reason (premise): "for you shall be as God knowing good and evil" is given to support the conclusion: "you shall not surely die."

iv. Eve was deceived: she justified her act on the basis of seeking wisdom apart from any reference to God.

---

9. *Isaiah 11:9.*

v. Adam had turned back: he had ceased to seek the knowledge of God as the good for himself and for his wife. He failed to keep in mind the clear difference between God the Creator and man the creature with respect to knowing good and evil. He determined good autonomously by what pleased him.

3. Sin

i. From general revelation: sin is an act contrary to one's nature as a rational being, made in the image of God; it is to neglect, avoid, resist, and deny reason in the face of what is clear about God.

ii. From special revelation: sin is not seeking, not understanding, and not doing what is right;[10] the root sin of not seeking and understanding leads to the fruit sin of not doing.

iii. Sin is unbelief as lacking understanding, which leads to the outward act of disobedience; because of the clarity of general revelation unbelief is inexcusable.

iv. Sin is disobedience; the outward act of eating of the tree of the knowledge of good and evil reveals the inward reality of determining good and evil for oneself.

v. Sin, in its essence, is autonomy:

a. It is putting one's self in the place of God to determine good and evil.

b. It is doing what is right in one's own eyes.

c. It is doing whatever pleases oneself.

d. It is being a law unto oneself.

e. It is lawlessness—not being subject to the law of God in any area of life, beginning with the first form of the Word of God to man as the laws of reason.

---

10. *Romans 3:10-11.*

4. Death

    i. There are two kinds of death—physical death and spiritual death.[11]

    The wages of sin is spiritual death, not physical death. "In the day you eat you shall surely die."[12] "The wages of sin is death."[13]

    ii. Spiritual death is present and inherent in sin, not future and imposed; it is not hell conceived of as a literal, physical lake of fire.

    iii. The inherent consequence of moral evil is self-destruction of the soul; it is meaninglessness, boredom, and guilt, increasing without end; it is spiritual death.

    iv. Spiritual death is spoken of as darkness (of mind), burning (of desire without satisfaction), torment (of conscience), as a bottomless pit, and as the second death. The lake of fire is (symbolically) the second death.[14]

    v. Physical death is imposed by God as a call back from spiritual death.

5. Theodicy

    i. Moral evil as unbelief serves subjectively to obscure and objectively to deepen the revelation of God (particularly the divine justice and mercy).

    ii. If moral evil is removed abruptly, then the revelation will not be deepened; if moral evil is not removed, then the revelation will not be seen.

    Therefore, moral evil is removed gradually.

    iii. Moral evil as unbelief is allowed to work itself out in world history in every form and degree of admixture with belief.

    In the spiritual war between belief and unbelief, which is agelong and agonizing, good will overcome evil.

---

11. *John 5:25, 28; 11:25; Ephesians 2:1.*
12. *Genesis 2:17.*
13. *Romans 6:23.*
14. *Revelation 20:6, 14; 21:8.*

iv. Natural evil (as toil and strife, and old age, sickness, and death, and war, famine, and plague) is imposed by God to restrain, recall from, and remove moral evil; it is a call to stop and think; physical death is a call back from spiritual death.

v. Physical death as a call back is mercy; it requires special revelation as redemptive revelation to show how God is both just and merciful at the same time.

ON REDEMPTION

1. First call back: shame. Response: self-deception.

i. The outward effect of sin: their eyes were opened and they realized their nakedness.

ii. The inward effect of sin: in one's thoughts, feeling shame from one's own conscience is the first call back to repentance from sin.

iii. In the body/soul unity, the visible reveals the invisible; under sin, physical nakedness is a reminder of spiritual nakedness.

iv. Outward response to the shame of nakedness: shame is avoided by making a covering of leaves, yet the covering is still seen and still reminds.

v. Inward response: by self-deception a person avoids acknowledging the sin of not seeking and not understanding what is clear about God.

2. Second call back: call to self-examination. Response: self-justification.

i. The second call back by word goes beyond the first: it is outer and from another vs. inward and from within oneself.

ii. The second call back comes by word, from God, as a question: "Where are you?"

iii. The question, coming from God who is all-knowing, is a call for Adam's self-examination, not a call for his self-disclosure.

iv. From hiding in guilt and fear, man is called to confession of sin: "Have you eaten from the tree of which I commanded you . . . ?"

v. Man's response: man justifies himself by blaming both the woman and God: "The woman whom you gave to be with me . . ."

3. Third call back: the promise and the curse.

i. The promise consists in establishing a spiritual war between belief and unbelief, which will be age-long and agonizing, in which good will overcome evil; the seed of the woman, in the place of Adam, will do what Adam failed to do.

ii. The curse in the third call back is in deed, beyond word: it is imposed by God on all mankind throughout history through Adam's representation.

iii. The curse consists of toil and strife, and old age, sickness, and death; at times the curse is intensified corporately to war, famine, and plague.

iv. The curse is not punishment, but mercy; it is the final, continuing call back from sin and self-deception and self-justification.

v. The suffering of natural evil, imposed through the curse, serves to restrain, to recall from, and to remove moral evil; it is a call to stop and think.

4. Justification: God's response to man's response: repentance and faith.

i. Adam accepts life for mankind under the curse, with hope in the promise of redemption.

ii. Adam calls his wife's name Eve, the mother of all the living; he chooses to obey in repentance, with faith in the promise.

iii. God clothes Adam and Eve with garments of skin: vicarious atonement, through the sacrifice of another in the place of Adam, will undo what Adam did.

iv. Under the covenant, there is triple imputation: Adam's guilt is imputed to all whom he represents; the guilt of all who accept the promise is imputed to the one promised in the place of Adam; the righteousness of the one sacrificed is imputed to all who believe.

v. Wearing the garments of skin vs. the covering of leaves is a continual reminder of God's justification (the forgiveness of sin and provision of righteousness) through the one who is to come in the place of Adam.

5. Sanctification through the truth.

i. Sanctification is the cleansing from sin; it assumes one has received God's forgiveness of sin and his justification.

ii. Sanctification is by knowledge of the truth;[15] this knowledge comes through suffering under the curse; natural evil serves variously to restrain, to recall from, and to remove moral evil in every form.

iii. Man is driven from the Garden of Eden, to live under the curse, to be cleansed from sin and self-deception and self-justification.

iv. The call back through the curse cannot be avoided; the way to the tree of life is guarded; all born of Adam must die physically.

v. Sanctification for those who are justified continues until death; it is incomplete until death and ends with death.

---

15. *John 17:17.*

Paper № 15

HERMENEUTICS:
PRINCIPLES OF INTERPRETATION
Applied to General Revelation and to Scripture

PART I:
INTERPRETATION IN GENERAL

Thinking is Presuppositional: we think of the less basic in light of the more basic; if there is agreement on the more basic, there can be agreement on the less basic.

1. Presupposition is the set of basic beliefs we use to interpret (give meaning to) our experience.

    i. Basic belief in general revelation (GR) is Philosophical Foundation (PF).[1]

    ii. Basic belief in special revelation (SR) is Theological Foundation (TF).[2]

---

1. Surrendra Gangadean, *Philosophical Foundation: A Critical Analysis of Basic Beliefs*, Second Edition (Phoenix: Public Philosophy Press, 2022); Surrendra Gangadean, *History of Philosophy: A Critical Analysis of Unresolved Disputes* (Phoenix: Public Philosophy Press, 2022).

2. Surrendra Gangadean, *Theological Foundation: A Critical Analysis of Christian Belief* (Phoenix: Logos Papers Press, 2023).

iii. Basic belief in Historic Christianity (HC), summed up in Church creeds and confessions, is Historical Foundation (HF).[3]

2. There are two sets of basic beliefs in GR:

   i. In epistemology: basic things (about God and man and good and evil) are clear to reason (the Principle of Clarity—PC) vs. basic things are not clear (skepticism and fideism).

   ii. In metaphysics: only some is eternal (theism) vs. all or none is eternal (non-theism).

   iii. In ethics: the good is the end in itself (teleology), not virtue (which is the means to the good) or happiness (which is the effect of possessing what is the good) vs. virtue is the good (deontology) or happiness is the good (hedonism).

   The two sets of beliefs are contradictories; they cannot both be true and they cannot both be false. One must be true and the other must therefore be false.

3. We are more or less conscious and consistent in holding our basic beliefs (unbelief remains in the believer and belief remains in the unbeliever). We should be more conscious and consistent. The degree of one's consciousness and consistency in basic belief depends on one's personality focus (intellectual, emotional, or practical), one's intellectual background (developmental factors), and one's spiritual mood (existential consistency).

4. History is an outworking of the conflict in basic beliefs in each and among all. In theodicy, every degree of admixture of belief and unbelief comes to expression in world history and in Church history. Internal and external challenges to belief are trials of faith to become more conscious and consistent in one's faith.

5. Unbelief leads to (intellectual) meaninglessness, boredom (with all excess of lawlessness), and guilt (covered over by self-deception and self-justification). Belief leads to meaningfulness (ever increasing meaning), fruitfulness, unity, and fullness. Only cultures that

---

3. Surrendra Gangadean, *The Westminster Confession of Faith: A Doxological Understanding* (Phoenix: Logos Papers Press, 2023); Surrendra Gangadean, *The Westminster Shorter and Larger Catechisms: A Doxological Understanding* (Phoenix: Logos Papers Press, 2023).

retain meaning can last. Since (in redemption) some culture will last, then belief will overcome unbelief.

Application:

1. Because unbelief remains in the believer, divisions in the Church are to be expected; in the autonomy of unbelief each goes his own way.

2. Discipleship (teaching *to* observe *all* of God's will) is the means to overcome divisions; the Church is to make disciples (not merely make converts).

3. Laying foundation from GR, SR, and HC is necessary and sufficient for discipleship to attain maturity, fruitfulness, unity, and fullness.[4]

PART II:
INTERPRETATION FROM
PHILOSOPHICAL FOUNDATION

1. **Epistemology: PF must show the clarity of GR beginning with epistemology.**

   Epistemology begins with Common Ground (CG), which concludes with PC: the basic things about God and man (metaphysics) and good and evil (ethics) are clear to reason (epistemology).[5]

   i. Clarity (PC) is opposed to all recurring forms of skepticism and fideism.

   ii. Clarity of GR (cGR) is necessary and sufficient for inexcusability of unbelief.

   iii. Clarity begins with the self-evident:

   a. It is self-evident that we are thinking beings and that the three acts of thought are concept, judgment, and argument. (To doubt the existence of the self and of the external world is initially self-referentially absurd and ultimately logically absurd.)

---

4. *Hebrews 6; Ephesians 4; 1 Corinthians 1–3.*

5. *Paper No. 53*; Gangadean, *Philosophical Foundation*, 287-292.

b. It is self-evident that there are laws of thought—reason in it-self (vs. reason in its various uses) is the laws of thought: the laws of identity, non-contradiction, and excluded middle.

c. It is self-evident that man has sense impressions (through the five senses); that the senses are not (the source of the three acts of) reason; that man is a rational animal; that (since man is created by God) man is the image of God.

d. It is self-evident that reason as the laws of thought is most basic and is the test for meaning; that reason alone is self-at-testing; that reason therefore is authoritative (if there is no meaning, there can be no truth).

e. It is self-evident that man should act according to his nature as a rational being; that he should be committed to reason; that he should have integrity—a concern for consistency in thought and action.

iv. Clarity (as reason and integrity) leads to Rational Presupposition-alism (RP),[6] which is the use of reason as the test for meaning of basic beliefs. RP thinks of the less basic in light of the more basic; if there is agreement on the more basic, there can (will) be agreement on the less basic.

a. RP is an application of critical thinking to basic beliefs in GR, beginning first with (1) epistemology, then (2) metaphysics, and then (3) ethics.

b. RP, as applied to SR, is contextualism. There are several layers of context: from cGR, to Biblical Foundation (creation–fall–redemption in Genesis 1–3), through redemptive history in the biblical narrative, to the book, chapter, verse, and word.

c. RP differs from empiricism (all knowledge is from experience: common sense, intuition, testimony, science). RP maintains that no experience is meaningful without interpretation in light of one's basic beliefs.

---

6. *Paper No. 101.*

d. RP differs from rationalism. A set of beliefs is not a system of beliefs ordered from more to less basic; the formative, interpretive, or constructive use of reason is not the critical use of reason.

e. RP differs from fideistic presuppositionalism, which affirms circularity in the relation of God and reason. Reason alone is self-attesting and is the most basic form of the Word of God to man.[7]

f. RP differs from Reformed Epistemology (RE).[8] The logically basic (for all) is not the properly basic (for me). The logically basic is clear to reason; the properly basic may lack or lose warrant, leaving it defeasible.

g. RP in hermeneutics is not literalism that fails to notice multiple layers of context in understanding the meaning of Scripture grasped by good and necessary consequences.[9]

h. RP is not allegoricalism that uses foreign or unwarranted (gnostic) assumptions rather than cGR to interpret Scripture.

i. RP is not postmodern (or ancient) skepticism/relativism/ multiculturalism, which ends with asserting a pluralism of meta-narratives (that is, assuming that *all* is interpretation). Basic beliefs can and should be tested for meaning by RP in order to see cGR.

j. RP leads to the Principle of Clarity (PC), which asserts cGR.

v. PC argues to cGR in three steps: (1) that some things are clear (vs. nothing is clear), (2) that the basic things are clear (based on RP), (3) that the basic things (which are about God and man and good and evil) are (in principle) clear to reason.

a. Reason, Integrity, RP, and PC (together, and in that order) constitute Common Ground (CG), the necessary condition for all thought and discourse.[10]

---

7. *John 1:4.*

8. Gangadean, *History of Philosophy*, 175-177.

9. *Paper No. 60.*

10. *Paper No. 2.*

b. PC, which *asserts* cGR, requires a *demonstration* (proof) of cGR.

c. Understanding cGR (the Philosophical Foundation) is necessary to understand cSR (the Theological Foundation).

2. Metaphysics and Ethics: PF must show cGR in metaphysics and ethics.

i. PF must show that only some is eternal (God the Creator) vs. all forms of non-theism (all is eternal: material monism, spiritual monism, dualism; and none is eternal: process philosophy—Western and Eastern).[11]

ii. PF must show the moral law is clear, comprehensive, and critical.[12]

iii. PF must answer the Problem of Evil; it must show the reality of moral evil and natural evil, and the relation between the two—how natural evil (on all) is due to moral evil (from one)—how the act of one affects all—the Fall.[13]

iv. PF must show the requirement for SR as redemptive revelation to show the divine justice and mercy (theism vs. deism).[14]

v. PF shows creation, the Fall, and the necessity for SR (CFR). PF does not show the specific content, but only the formal content required of SR.

a. Only what is consistent with CFR in PF can qualify as SR.

b. Only Genesis 1–3 is consistent with CFR, therefore only Genesis 1–3 qualifies as SR.[15]

c. Only what is consistent with the Theological Foundation of SR (CFR in Genesis 1–3) can be added to SR.

d. PF (through Philosophical Theology) must show the full extent of SR.[16]

---

11. *Paper No. 3*; Gangadean, *Philosophical Foundation*, 71-161.

12. *Paper No. 9* and *10*; Gangadean, *Philosophical Foundation*, 165-264.

13. *Paper No. 7*.

14. *Paper No. 12*.

15. *Paper No. 11*.

16. See Ten Steps from GR to SR, *Paper No. 11*.

PART III:
INTERPRETATION FROM
THEOLOGICAL FOUNDATION

1. The Logos as reason and GR show the need for the Logos in SR, and SR shows the reality of the Logos incarnate.

2. The Logos incarnate in Jesus Christ shows Christian theism vs. all non-Christian interpretations of theism.

3. Understanding PF in cGR is necessary to understand TF in cSR.

4. Divisions in understanding cSR show failure to agree on cGR.

5. Divisions within Christian theism show lack in having the foundation from cGR, from cSR, and from HC.[17]

Application:

1. Divisions in the doctrine of Creation in SR (creation vs. evolution) are rooted in not understanding PF in cGR.

2. Divisions in the doctrine of the Fall (the origin of evil) are rooted in not understanding the doctrine of Creation.

3. Divisions in the doctrine of Redemption (the curse and the promise, and justification and sanctification) are rooted in not understanding the more basic doctrines of the Fall and Creation.

4. Divisions in understanding what comes after TF in Genesis 1–3, from the rest of the Book of Genesis to the Book of Revelation, are rooted in not understanding CFR in Genesis 1–3 and the unfolding of the curse and the promise in redemptive history.

5. In summary: theological differences in the history of Christianity can be resolved by thinking of the less basic in light of the more basic, that is, by critically examining assumptions, which is Rational Presuppositionalism.[18]

---

17. *Hebrews 6; Ephesians 4; 1 Corinthians 1–3.*

18. *Paper No. 101.*

PART IV:
INTERPRETATION FROM
HISTORICAL FOUNDATION

1. Historic Christianity (HC) is the work of the Holy Spirit sent by Christ to lead the Church into all truth.[19]

2. Disputes that persist are due either to insufficient attention to HC, or show the need for a deeper understanding of uncritically held assumptions (that is, for Philosophical Theology), or reveal challenges made more acute in the current context of the age-long spiritual war between belief and unbelief.

3. Divisions within Christianity arise from holding to Church creeds and confessions more or less consciously and consistently. The latest and most conscious and consistent development of these creeds came to expression in The Westminster Confession of Faith of 1648.[20]

4. Significant departure from the creeds (beginning with the earliest) is a departure from HC, the holy, catholic, and apostolic faith. The Holy Spirit continues to lead the Church into all truth through deeper challenges of the modern era (since 1648). This requires deepening the foundation from GR, SR, and HC.

Application:

Among continuing disputes, previously addressed in Church councils, are:

1. The necessity of sacraments for salvation (vs. Hebrew literalism, addressed in the Council of Jerusalem, A.D. 51).

2. The reality and significance of the Incarnation (vs. Greek gnostic dualism, addressed in the Apostles' Creed, *ca.* A.D. 180).

3. The nature of unity and diversity in the Triune God (addressed in the Council of Nicea, A.D. 325).

4. Confirmation of the canon of Scripture (addressed in the Council of Carthage, A.D. 397).

---

19. *Paper No. 16.*
20. *Paper No. 16* and *17.*

5. Christ is fully God and fully man (addressed in the Council of Chalcedon, A.D. 451).

6. Pelagian and semi-Pelagian free will vs. predestination and grace (addressed in the Council of Orange, A.D. 529).

PART V:
INTERPRETATION AND DEEPENING
THE FOUNDATION FOR UNITY OF THE FAITH

1. Current Challenges

Some external challenges to Christianity have become acute and the need for a more definitive response, consistent with GR, SR, and HC, has become pressing. Among them are:

i. Faith vs. Reason and Science vs. Scripture. An adequate response must be based on the clarity of general revelation, which is clear to reason.

ii. Secularism (focus on this life) vs. Heaven (focus on the afterlife, either as Edenic hedonism or beatific mysticism).[21] An adequate response must be focused on the good as the knowledge of God through the work of dominion, given to mankind from the beginning.[22]

iii. Religion as private vs. religiously neutral public life (the naked public square). An adequate response must distinguish revealed religion found in SR from natural religion found in GR and inescapably held by all in some form or other. What is clear to reason from GR should be common to all in public life.[23]

iv. Postmodern pluralism/inclusivism vs. Christian exclusivism. An adequate response must reckon with man's basic and therefore critical need for meaning, found only in the worldview and culture of creation–fall–redemption. To include all in the inevitable

---

21. *Paper No. 106* and *116*.

22. Gangadean, *The Westminster Catechisms*. See Appendix 4.

23. *Paper No. 20*.

nihilism of postmodern skepticism is not the blessing sought by all mankind. Man does not live by bread alone.

2. Current Focus Needed

i. Christianity has not yet had much discussion about the good, which is the chief end of man, the central question of man's purpose in life. Its default position has been the goal of heaven, from remnants of the dualism of Plato and Aristotle, brought into Christianity through Augustine and Aquinas.[24] A little leaven has leavened the whole lump. Is there hope this will change? The need for change in the Church in light of the state of the world has become urgent.[25]

ii. The RP hermeneutic establishes and builds on the foundation from cGR, cSR, and HC. cGR affirms that the good for man as a rational being is the use of his reason to the fullest, which is to know the Logos revealed in the creation. cSR in the first book of Genesis (1–3) affirms that man is made in the image of God, to know God, through the work of dominion, which will be completed as signified in the Sabbath. In the last book of Revelation, the consummation of history is revealed in a sevenfold vision of the spiritual war, which is age-long and agonizing, and in which good overcomes evil. HC, in The Westminster Standards, affirms the doxological focus: man's chief end is to glorify God,[26] in all that by which he makes himself known,[27] in all his works of creation and providence.[28] [29]

CONCLUSION

The foundation from GR, SR, and HC affirms the same outcome: the earth will be full of the knowledge of God as the waters cover the

---

24. Gangadean, *History of Philosophy*, 87-105, 111-114, 121-130.

25. *Matthew 5:13; Paper No. 58.*

26. *SCQ. 1; Paper No. 115.*

27. *SCQ. 101.*

28. *WCF 4.1; 5.1.*

29. *Paper No. 16.*

sea.[30] The Logos is the fullness of the Word of God who makes God known. Understanding the Logos is the source of hermeneutical and functional unity in each person and among all persons. RP seeks to deepen the philosophical, theological, and historical foundation for the knowledge of God.

---

30. *Isaiah 11:9; Paper No. 104.*

Paper №· 16

———

THE HISTORIC CHRISTIAN FAITH
The Holy Spirit Guides the Church into All Truth

PART I:
INTRODUCTION:
AUTHORITY AND INSIGHT

1. Authority in teaching is based on insight into the Word of God, the Logos, which is Truth.[1]

2. Authority is rational, not personal; it begins with Foundation, with basic things about God and man and good and evil that are clear to reason.

3. Authority based on insight has power to understand the good (man's chief end—eternal life) and the means to the good through the moral law; it is not based on mere might.

4. The insight of authority is historically cumulative, not individual; it is not set aside or decreased, but transmitted and increased through every generation. This insight in the Church is the Historic Christian Faith.

5. Historical Foundation of Christianity presupposes Theological Foundation from Scripture and Philosophical Foundation from general

---

1. *John 17:17.*

revelation (GR). If there is agreement on what is more basic, there can be agreement on what comes after.

PART II:
THE SPIRIT AND THE TRUTH

1. Jesus sent the Holy Spirit to guide the Church into all Truth in order to accomplish its mission.[2]

    i. The Church is the pillar and ground of the Truth.[3]

    ii. The Church is to be salt and light in the world.[4]

    iii. The Church is to witness unto Christ by the power of the Holy Spirit which came at Pentecost.[5]

    iv. The Church is to make disciples of all peoples.[6]

    v. The Church is to sanctify its members and bring them to maturity and to the unity of the faith through the Truth.[7]

    vi. The Church is to take thoughts captive raised up against the knowledge of God.[8]

    vii. The Church is to complete its mission to fill the earth with the knowledge of God as the waters cover the sea.[9]

2. The Holy Spirit works to bring the Truth into focus[10] and to bring the Truth into the hearts of persons by regeneration[11] and by sanctification.[12]

---

2. *John 16:13*; Gangadean, *The Westminster Confession*. See Question 1.

3. *1 Timothy 3:15.*

4. *Matthew 5:13-16.*

5. *Acts 1:8.*

6. *Matthew 28:19-20.*

7. *John 17:17; Ephesians 4:11-16.*

8. *2 Corinthians 10:4; Paper No. 47.*

9. *Isaiah 11:9; Paper No. 104.*

10. *Acts 15:28.*

11. *John 3:3.*

12. *John 17:17.*

3. The Holy Spirit brings the Truth into focus:[13]

   i. through the pastor-teachers (the ordinary, regular, continuing, post-apostolic authority in the Church),

   ii. in response to challenges (from the faulty worldviews of converts),

   iii. after much discussion,

   iv. coming to agreement summed up in creeds (understood by good and necessary consequences),

   v. which agreement is delivered unto the churches for the unity of the faith.

4. There is a process in coming to the Truth:

   i. The Truth is by a deliberative process, not from one, but from many, not accretion by tradition without challenge and much discussion, not without agreement made known to the Church.

   ii. What enters apart from these conditions is not part of Historic Christianity. What departs from the unity of the faith is not part of Historic Christianity.

   iii. The process is continuing until the Church's mission is completed.

   iv. The progress of the unity of the faith in the history of the Church is the Holy Catholic and Apostolic Faith.

5. Insight based on deliberation is cumulative:

   i. Historic Christianity makes explicit the teaching of Scripture and its practice in liturgy and cannot be used to set aside Truth from either general revelation or from Scripture, which is more basic.

   ii. There have been several councils in the history of the Church. Not everything in councils has been subject to much discussion, but some things may have been assumed.

   iii. Historic Christianity (HC) continues to respond to challenges raised up against the knowledge of God.

---

13. *Acts 15.*

iv. Later confessions cannot set aside what has been agreed upon in HC without addressing prior deliberation. HC includes more than the seven early ecumenical councils.

PART III:
THE FIRST COUNCIL AT JERUSALEM:
SACRAMENT AND SALVATION

1. The First Church Council at Jerusalem (A.D. 51) dealt with the question of sacrament and salvation: Is circumcision necessary for salvation? Against the teaching that you must be circumcised and obey the law to be saved, the Council answered: "We gave no such command."[14]

2. A sacrament is a sign of reality:

   i. Circumcision is an outward sign of an inward reality, of a new heart, of regeneration. The reality of circumcision is of the heart, not the flesh.[15]

   ii. Baptism in the New Testament, like circumcision in the Old Testament, signifies regeneration. It is possible to have the sign without the reality and to have the reality without the sign.

   iii. Jesus called for the reality: unless you are born again you cannot be saved, that is, enter the kingdom of God.[16]

   iv. Mistaking sign for reality blinds one to the need for the reality of regeneration.

3. Gentiles who believed and who were without circumcision and without baptism had been given the gift of the Holy Spirit and so were saved. So, neither the sign of circumcision nor baptism were necessary for salvation.[17]

4. Sacraments are ordinary parts of instruction in the faith and of covenant renewal. Yet the sign is not necessary for the reality signified.

---

14. *Acts 15:24.*

15. *Deuteronomy 10:16, 30:6; Jeremiah 4:4; Romans 2:29.*

16. *John 3:3-5.*

17. *Acts 10:43-48; 15:6-11.*

So, neither is the sign of the Passover or the Lord's Supper necessary for entering the kingdom of God.

5. The error of literalism:

   i. Hebraic literalism, not distinguishing sign and reality, led to ceremonial legalism and has been a major stumbling block to faith past and present.

   ii. Unbelief concerning sign and reality can range from ignorance in Nicodemus,[18] to the error of Saul of Tarsus,[19] to those who would pervert the Gospel,[20] to Peter's dissimulation.[21]

   iii. The First Council of Jerusalem rejected the insistence that sacraments are necessary for salvation.

   iv. The Historic Christian Faith affirms this teaching.

PART IV:
THE APOSTLES' CREED

1. The Apostles' Creed (*ca.* A.D. 180) summarizes the Church's response to the challenge to the truth from the Greek worldview of epistemological gnosticism (vs. cGR), metaphysical dualism (both matter and spirit are eternal), and ethical dualism (separating the soul from the hindrances of the body).

2. Against metaphysical dualism, the Church affirms God as Creator of heaven and earth. God in the flesh (the Incarnation) is real, not apparent, and bodily existence continues forever (in the resurrection).

3. Far from being (the source of) evil or a distraction or a matter of indifference, the world as created is good and reveals God.

4. Lifelong withdrawal from the affairs of this life through celibacy and monasticism (except for a limited time and for a specified purpose) is uncalled for, not a higher calling.

---

18. *John 3:10.*

19. *Philippians 3:1-9.*

20. *Galatians 1:7.*

21. *Galatians 2:11-13.*

5. The life of mystical contemplation consummated in a disembodied beatific vision is a dualist conceit, not part of man's calling to fill the earth with the knowledge of God through the work of dominion, consummated in the resurrection of the body.

PART V:
THE NICENE CREED:
THE TRINITY

1. At Nicea (A.D. 325), the Church summarized its understanding that God is one over and against misunderstanding which has survived in several forms through history (Arianism, Socinianism, Deism, Unitarianism, Judaism, and Islam).

2. What is one is a unity, and unity is a unity of diversity. God, the Most High, is a unity of the highest reality, that of Persons.

3. "In the unity of the Godhead there be three persons, of one substance, power, and eternity: God the Father, God the Son, and God the Holy Ghost: the Father is of none, neither begotten, nor proceeding; the Son is eternally begotten of the Father; the Holy Ghost eternally proceeding from the Father and the Son."[22]

4. Prior to the doctrine of the Trinity is the doctrine of God and the unity and diversity (the simplicity) in the divine nature: God is a Spirit, infinite, eternal, and unchangeable, in his being, wisdom, power, holiness, justice, goodness, and truth.[23] The doctrine of God assumes the doctrine of being and the doctrine of the eternal. It is clear to reason from GR that there must be something eternal and only some (God the Creator) is eternal.

5. The doctrine of the Trinity begins with the doctrine of the Father and the Son, co-eternal with the Father, the brightness of his glory, the express image of his person.[24] The Son reveals God and is the

---

22. *WCF 2.3.*

23. *SCQ. 4.*

24. *Hebrews 1:3.*

Word of God: *In the beginning was the Word, and the Word was with God, and the Word was God.*[25]

6. God reveals himself in his works of creation and providence. Man cannot know God as God knows himself. To man, as creature, the Triune God in himself is incomprehensible, and as revealed is inexhaustible. The mystery of God, Father, Son, and Holy Spirit is revealed in the great acts of creation and redemption as revealed in Scripture.

7. The depth of personhood in the Trinity is revealed in man the image of God, created in knowledge, holiness, and righteousness, and in Christ the new head of mankind as Prophet, Priest, and King. Man is called to the unity of the Trinity in Christ's prayer: that they all may be one, as we are one, that the world may believe you sent me.[26]

PART VI:
THE COUNCIL OF CARTHAGE:
THE CANON OF THE NEW TESTAMENT SCRIPTURE

1. At the Council of Carthage (A.D. 397), the Church identified all the books and only the books that constitute the Scripture of the New Testament, the Word of God written, the rule of faith and life for all Christians.

2. The canon of the Old Testament was received by testimony of the Church under the Old Testament.

3. The canon of the New Testament was received by testimony of the Church under the New Testament.

4. Scripture in every age must be spoken in the name of God (consistent with cGR and with any prior SR). Scripture must be accompanied by a sign (what is spoken comes to pass[27]). Scripture has been received by the testimony of the Church.

---

25. *John 1:1.*

26. *John 17:21.*

27. *Deuteronomy 18:22.*

5. Scripture, as redemptive revelation, is given only by God, and being given by God is kept pure and entire by God in every age, so that nothing is to be added to it or taken away from it, contrary to all contradictory claims.

6. Scripture in the OT testifies to the person and work of Christ, the Redeemer to come. The NT records the accomplishment of redemption in the coming of Christ and its application in the Church by apostolic witness. Scripture, as redemptive revelation, is therefore complete.

PART VII:
THE COUNCIL OF CHALCEDON:
CHRIST IS GOD AND MAN

1. At the Council of Chalcedon (A.D. 451), the Church affirmed the doctrine of Christ as fully God and fully man. In the Incarnation, "two whole, perfect, and distinct natures, the Godhead and the manhood, were inseparably joined together in one person, without conversion, composition, or confusion."[28]

2. The doctrine of Christ as God and man affects every aspect of understanding the person and work of Christ as creator of all things, upholder of all things, redeemer of all things, and heir of all things.[29]

3. He is the eternal Son of God, the Logos who was in the beginning, who was with God and is God, and who makes God known.[30]

4. He is the new head of humanity, the second Adam in the place of Adam, who came to undo what Adam did (as the Lamb of God who takes away the sin of the world) and to do what Adam failed to do (to rule over all—to exercise dominion—to make God known).[31]

5. He is God the Son incarnate (born of the Virgin Mary); He was sinless (though tempted in all points as man); He was crucified for our sins (vicarious atonement); He was raised from the dead (in his

---

28. *WCF 8.2.*

29. *Hebrews 1:1-3.*

30. *John 1:1.*

31. *Isaiah 11:1-9.*

righteousness and for our justification); He ascended into heaven and rules with all authority, sending the Holy Spirit to apply redemption accomplished; He will come again (to raise the dead and to judge all mankind by his Word).

6. He is the only mediator between God and man; He is the head of the Church, his body; He is Prophet, Priest, and King over the Church; He will rule until all things are subdued unto him;[32] He is the seed of the woman who will destroy the kingdom of darkness; He will demolish every pretension raised up against the knowledge of God.[33]

7. He is the Word of God who makes God known in every way; He will complete the work of dominion by making disciples of all nations; He will bring mankind from the Garden of Eden to the City of God; He will glorify God (fill the earth with the knowledge of God as the waters cover the sea); His kingdom will last forever; He is the Alpha and the Omega (the Beginning and the End), the fullness of God who fills everything in every way.[34]

PART VIII:
THE COUNCIL OF ORANGE:
SIN AND SALVATION

1. At the Council of Orange (A.D. 529), the Church affirmed the doctrine of sin (man is fallen in Adam) and salvation (man is saved by grace) in response to Pelagian and semi-Pelagian error.

2. The Church affirmed the distinction of liberty and ability in the fourfold state of man: (1) before the Fall, it was possible to sin; (2) after the Fall, it is not possible not to sin; (3) after regeneration, it is possible not to sin; (4) in man's glorified state, it is not possible to sin. While ability changes, liberty (doing what I want) does not change.

3. Grace is given by God, sovereignly, as he wills. Grace is not dependent on man's willing, but by grace man is made willing.

---

32. *1 Corinthians 15:25.*

33. *2 Corinthians 10:4-5; Revelation 19:11-21.*

34. *Revelation 1:8, 22:18; Ephesians 1:23.*

4. Grace does not operate against human nature or apart from human nature, but by grace human nature is changed by regeneration (signified) in baptism.

5. All acts by which we are saved—whether we "believe, will, desire, strive, labor, pray, watch, study, seek, ask or knock"[35]—are by grace, the gift of God, not of ourselves, so that no man can boast.

PART IX:
THE WESTMINSTER ASSEMBLY:
THE DOXOLOGICAL FOCUS ON THE GLORY OF GOD

1. The Reformation (1517–1648) attempted to restore the Church to the Historic Christian Faith based upon the historically cumulative insight of earlier Church councils. It specifically responded to the challenges of sacramentalism and synergism addressed in the Councils of Jerusalem and Orange.

2. The Westminster Confession of Faith (WCF) built upon earlier creeds of the Reformation: Augsburg (Lutheran); Thirty-Nine Articles (Anglican); Belgic (French); Helvetic (Swiss); Heidelberg (German); Dort (Dutch). It is the last and most conscious and consistent creed of the Reformation and of Church History.

3. The Westminster Standards (WCF and its Catechisms) affirm the clarity of GR and the inexcusability of unbelief,[36] the use of reason (the light of nature and good and necessary consequences) to understand GR and SR,[37] the doxological focus on the knowledge of the glory of God,[38] divine sovereignty in creation–fall–redemption, and the law of God for all of life.

4. Reformation soteriology has been summed up in the *ordo salutis*— the order of the application of redemption: effectual calling (regeneration), conversion (repentance and faith), justification (based on Christ's righteousness received by faith alone), adoption (having all

---

35. *Council of Orange, Canon 6.*

36. *WCF 1.1.*

37. *WCF 1.1, 1.6.*

38. *SCQ. 1, 101; WCF 4.1, 5.1.*

the privileges of children of God), sanctification (being made holy through knowing the truth), glorification (the removal of all sin at death and the removal of death by the resurrection of the body).

5. In response to the challenge of Arminian semi-Pelagianism at Dort, WCF affirmed (from Dort) the doctrines of Total Depravity, Unconditional Election, Limited Atonement, Irresistible Grace, and Perseverance of the Saints.

6. The spirit of the theology of the Reformation has been summed up in the affirmation of the Five Solas: *Sola Scriptura* (by Scripture alone), *Sola Fide* (by faith alone), *Sola Gratia* (by grace alone), *Solus Christus* (by Christ alone), *Soli Deo Gloria* (for the glory of God alone).[39]

7. Uncritically held assumptions remain in the Church and have been the source of divisions in the Church which have scandalized the world. The Church must acknowledge the nature of the spiritual warfare between belief and unbelief present at every level, enter into the process of much discussion by which the Holy Spirit leads the Church into all truth, and take every thought captive raised up against the knowledge of God from unbelief, both in the Church and in the world.

PART X:
RESPONSE TO ONGOING CHALLENGES

1. The modern era (1650–1950) has been a challenge to the Church in several areas. The postmodern period (1950–present) has intensified that challenge.

2. The Church's fideism has been challenged by the world's skepticism, seen in the discourse of faith vs. reason and science vs. religion. The Church must affirm the clarity of GR and show the nature of faith vs. fideism and skepticism.

3. The Church's other-worldliness has been challenged by secular this-worldliness. The Church must affirm the doctrine of eternal life (in the knowledge of God through the work of dominion) and

---

39. *Paper No. 17.*

spiritual death (meaninglessness, boredom, and guilt present and inherent in sin) vs. a merely future view of heaven and hell.

4. The Church has been challenged in the area of imposing religion in public life. The Church must affirm that human beings as rational beings require reason for human life and that what is clear to reason from GR, which is equally accessible to all, is the basis of public life.

5. The Church has been challenged in its claim to exclusivism and universalism (*only* through Christ are *all* to be saved) by rising global consciousness. There are other exclusivist and triumphalist faiths as well as simultaneous calls to universal tolerance and inclusivism. The Church must affirm the universality of sin and spiritual death, the universality of the curse (as God's call back from sin) and the promise (Christ in the place of Adam) for all mankind, from the beginning of history.

Paper № 17

———

THE FIVE SOLAS
Summary of the Reformation Principles

1. *Sola Scriptura:* The Authority for Faith Is Scripture Alone[1]

   i. The authority of Scripture as special revelation (SR) is opposed to the authority of all other forms of special revelation (including the opinions of men or of private spirits).

  ii. *Sola Scriptura* (SS) is not opposed to the use of reason in making good and necessary consequences, but assumes it.

 iii. SS is not opposed to the clarity of general revelation (GR), but assumes it (see the five-point relation between GR and SR below).

 iv. SS is not opposed to historically cumulative insight, the work of the Holy Spirit leading the Church into all truth, summed up in its creeds and confessions, but anticipates it.

  v. SS requires all of the Scriptures and only the Scriptures, understood with good and necessary consequences, to be used in interpreting the Scriptures.

Interpretation, therefore, is contextual, not literal or allegorical—in light of foreign assumptions.

———

1. Gangadean, *The Westminster Confession*. See Questions 4-12.

2. *Sola Fide:* Justification Is by Faith Alone[2]

    i. Justification is based on a person having righteousness.

    ii. This righteousness is from Christ, whose righteousness is perfect and complete, and not from oneself.

    iii. Christ's righteousness is imputed to the believer. This act of imputation assumes that Adam's sin is imputed to all men and that man's sin is imputed to Christ.

    iv. The righteousness of Christ is received by faith alone.

    v. Justification is not sanctification; imputation of righteousness is not infusion of righteousness; forgiveness of sin is not cleansing from sin, but cleansing flows from forgiveness.

3. *Sola Gratia:* Salvation Is by Grace Alone

    i. Salvation is by grace alone, from beginning to end, without any admixture of human works. Both faith and works that glorify God are by grace.

    ii. The grace of salvation is sovereignly bestowed, by God's predestination, apart from any condition in the person.

    iii. The context of the bestowal of grace is summed up in the acronym TULIP.[3]

    iv. In the order of application of redemption (*ordo salutis*), God's act of effectual calling (regeneration) precedes man's conversion (repentance and faith).

    v. Predestination is not opposed to but upholds freedom—properly understood as liberty to do what one desires, rather than ability to do otherwise.

---

2. Gangadean, *The Westminster Confession.* See Questions 53-57.

3. *Paper No. 18.*

4. *Solus Christus:* **Salvation Is by Christ Alone**[4]

   i. Salvation is through Christ alone, and not through Christ and the Church as mediator of grace.

   ii. Salvation is through Christ alone, and not through Christ and the merits or intercession or mediation of any other.

   iii. Salvation is through Christ alone, and not through Christ and any practice of penance in this life or in the next, or through any supposed good deeds.

   iv. Salvation is through Christ alone and not apart from Christ; there is no salvation without atonement, or without the vicarious atonement of Christ.

   v. Salvation is through Christ alone and in this life alone, after which is the final judgment, which vindicates the divine justice in judging man in unbelief.

5. *Soli Deo Gloria:* **All of Life Is for the Glory of God Alone**[5]

   i. God's glory, which is intrinsic in his being, cannot be added to but is only manifest in, by, unto and upon all his creatures.[6]

   ii. God manifests his glory in all his works of creation and providence, which purpose is extended to the fall of man.[7]

   iii. Man's chief end is to glorify and enjoy God in all that by which he makes himself known, in all his works of creation and providence.[8]

   iv. The purpose of the work of dominion in the creation mandate and of the work of Christ in making disciples of all nations is the knowledge of God, which is eternal life.[9]

---

4. Gangadean, *The Westminster Confession.* See Questions 39-46; Gangadean, *The Westminster Catechisms.* See LCQ. 36-56.

5. Gangadean, *The Westminster Confession.* See Question 3.

6. *WCF 2.2.*

7. *WCF 4.1, 5.1, 6.1.*

8. *SCQ. 1, 101; WCF 4.1, 5.1.*

9. *Genesis 1:28; Matthew 28:20; John 17:3.*

    v. The outcome of Christ's work through the Church is that the earth will be filled with the knowledge of the Lord as the waters cover the sea.[10]

The Relationship Between General and Special Revelation[11]

1. If there is no clear general revelation (cGR), then there is no consistent possibility of any meaningful belief regarding GR or SR (nihilism).

2. If there is no cGR, then there is no possibility of inexcusability or moral evil, and therefore, no necessity of SR as redemptive revelation.

3. GR, in understanding the problem of moral and natural evil, shows the necessity for SR.[12]

4. SR and Historic Christianity presuppose and teach cGR.

5. SR must be consistent with cGR and must show how God is both just and merciful to man in sin.

    The steps from GR to SR must show first the necessity of SR, then its content, origin, existence, transmission, completion, translation, clarity, sufficiency, and interpretation.[13]

---

10. *Isaiah 11:9.*

11. *Paper No. 112.*

12. *Paper No. 12.*

13. *Paper No. 11.*

Paper N𝐨. 18

_____

SALVATION BY GRACE

The Sovereignty of God in the Salvation of Man

INTRODUCTION

1. Sovereignty of grace is one aspect of the sovereignty of God expressed in all of creation and providence.

2. Sovereignty expressed in predestination is one aspect of soteriology (the doctrine of salvation). It requires the context of creation–fall–redemption in order to be understood.

3. Disputes about predestination can be traced back to uncritically held assumptions in disputes about freedom and determinism in the history of philosophy.

4. Resolving disputes requires clarifying the compatibility of freedom and causality, the relation between *ought*, *can*, and *want* in relation to freedom, and freedom with respect to the use of reason to see what is clear. It also requires special care to distinguish the revealed and the decreed will of God.

5. The Church has upheld the teaching of predestination in contrast to Pelagianism (in its varying degrees) through Augustine, the Council of Orange, Luther, Calvin, The Thirty-Nine Articles of the Church of England, the Canons of Dort, and the Westminster Confession of Faith (WCF).

TULIP

TULIP is an acronym for the five points (addressed in the Canons of Dort) listed below and which are briefly explained.

1. Total Depravity

i. Sin affects the whole (total) heart of man so that no one seeks God, no one understands, and no one is righteous.[1]

ii. Sin (moral evil) has become rooted in self-deception and self-justification so that the curse of toil and strife, and old age, sickness, and death was imposed by God to restrain, recall from, and remove moral evil in man.[2]

iii. While sin is total in extent, sin varies in degrees (men are more or less conscious and consistent in their unbelief) and it may increase to ever-deeper depravity.

iv. The sin of not seeking results in culpable ignorance of what is clear about God and the moral law. Inconsistencies within one's understanding result in inconsistencies within one's feelings and within one's actions.[3]

v. The understanding of fallen man (learned or unlearned) is deficient so that it is knowing the truth that makes one holy and sets one free.[4]

2. Unconditional Election

i. Election unto salvation is not based on any condition (past, present, or future) in man, but wholly on God's purpose, which is, in wisdom, to make his glory known.

ii. Election unto salvation is not apart from or against secondary causes, such as seeking and understanding or repentance and

---

1. *Romans 3:10-11.*
2. *Genesis 3.*
3. *Paper No. 120.*
4. *John 17:17, 8:32.*

faith; predestination is not of ends without means, but of both ends and means.

iii. Election of men presupposes the Fall (infralapsarianism), either to leave one in sin and death or to restore one to life and righteousness.

iv. Unconditional election is not arbitrary regarding justice; spiritual death is always due to sin, and mercy never sets aside justice but satisfies justice through vicarious atonement by Jesus Christ.

v. God has mercy on whom he chooses. Showing mercy to some is not unfair to others; what is unfair is to deny justice to any.

3. Limited Atonement

i. The intent and effect of Christ's atonement makes salvation actual for the elect, not merely possible for all but actual for none.

ii. It is the revealed will of God that no one *should* sin and that all who sin *should* repent of sin and come to salvation. It is the decreed will of God to *permit* sin and the persistence of some in sin against calls to repentance.

iii. It is the decreed will of God (by promise) that good *will* overcome evil, that all nations *will* be blessed, that all nations *will* be discipled, that the earth *will* be filled with the knowledge of the Lord as the waters cover the sea.[5]

iv. It is by the decree of God that the limit of atonement *does* include the salvation of the whole world as the kingdom of God grows to its fullness.

v. The decree of God to save the world reveals the length, breadth, depth, and height of the love of God for mankind.[6]

4. Irresistible Grace

i. The grace of salvation is prevenient to the time of one's salvation; it operates to preserve and prepare a person for salvation.

---

5. *Isaiah 11:9.*

6. *John 3:16; Ephesians 2:14-21.*

ii. Salvation begins with effectual calling in which a person is raised from spiritual death to life, which is to be regenerated by spiritual rebirth, or to be recreated as a new creature in Christ.

iii. Regeneration is wholly of God and not from man, either positively (by man's will cooperating with God's will) or negatively (by man's will not resisting God's will).

iv. By regeneration a person is made both willing and able to seek and to understand and to do the will of God so that regeneration precedes and *naturally* results in repentance and faith.

v. The grace of salvation continues after regeneration throughout one's life to make a person willing and able to know and do the will of God.

5. Perseverance of the Saints

i. Those who are effectually called (regenerated) are kept by the power of God unto salvation.

ii. A person who is outwardly called (but not effectually called) may fall away from their profession of faith.

iii. A person who is effectually called may fall away for a time or be left to walk in darkness, but is never utterly destitute of the seed of God.[7]

iv. Assurance of salvation is not of the essence of faith; a true believer may lack assurance, but may through the right use of ordinary means attain assurance.[8] Assurance based on false teaching or practice is presumptuous.

v. Perseverance of believers is not *regardless* of sin, but a *perseverance* and growth in faith and righteousness.

---

7. *WCF 18.4.*
8. *WCF 18.3.*

Paper № 19

FOUNDATION FOR
PHILOSOPHY OF HISTORY

1. Meaning and Worldview

    i. Human beings as thinking beings seek to make sense of their world through forming a worldview.

    ii. Presuppositions are the basic beliefs we use to interpret our experience.

    iii. No experience is meaningful without interpretation.

    iv. Experiences are interpreted differently in varying worldviews.

    v. A worldview must be internally coherent in order to retain meaning.

2. Basic Beliefs

    i. There are two alternative basic beliefs in each foundational feature of a worldview: in epistemology, in metaphysics, and in ethics.

    ii. These basic beliefs are contradictories, not contraries; both cannot be true and both cannot be false; one must be true and the other false.

    iii. In epistemology: either knowledge is possible or knowledge is not possible.

If knowledge is possible, then in principle: some things are clear; the basic things are clear; the basic things (about God and man and good and evil) are clear to reason.

If knowledge of basic things is not possible, then either skepticism or fideism results, both of which lead to nihilism (the loss of all meaning).

   iv. In metaphysics: either all is eternal in some form or other, or only some is eternal.

If all is eternal, then either matter or spirit or both or neither (i.e., nothing) is eternal.

If only some is eternal, then what is eternal brought into existence (created) what is not eternal.

   v. In ethics: either there is rational justification for the good (the moral absolute) or there is no such justification.

The good is grounded in human nature, which is determined by what is eternal.

If what is eternal cannot be known, then human nature cannot be known and there can be no rational justification for the good.

3. Consciousness and Consistency

   i. Human beings are more or less conscious and consistent in holding their basic beliefs.

   ii. There is an admixture of contradictory beliefs in each person.

   iii. One of the contradictory beliefs is existentially more basic and therefore more prevailing in each person.

   iv. One's consciousness and consistency depend on one's presupposition, personality, background, and mood.

   v. We should seek to be more conscious and consistent.

4. History and Conflict

   i. History is the outworking of these conflicting beliefs in each person, in each culture, and in world history.

   ii. Suffering of toil and strife, and old age, sickness, and death (and collectively, of war, famine, and plague) challenges each person to make greater sense of the world.

  iii. The conflict is between understanding and misunderstanding, between belief and unbelief.

  iv. The conflict is between the use of reason (to act according to one's nature) and lack of the use of reason (to neglect, avoid, resist, or deny reason regarding what is clear).

   v. The conflict is between meaningfulness and meaninglessness, between life and death, between good and evil.

5. Reason and Hope

   i. In the conflict between contradictory beliefs, only what is meaningful will last.

  ii. Every form and degree of admixture between belief and unbelief will come to expression in culture in world history.

  iii. The darkness of misunderstanding cannot overcome or withstand the demands of the light of reason in human nature.

  iv. Evil serves only to deepen the revelation of the nature of things.

   v. In the spiritual war, which is age-long and agonizing, good will overcome evil.

Paper № 20

———

CHRISTIANITY, PHILOSOPHY, AND PUBLIC EDUCATION
Reflections Upon Retirement

For all those who would sit in the chair of Philosophy

APRIL 2014

THE IDEA OF A CHRISTIAN PHILOSOPHER in a secular university raises a set of related concerns. First, there are Church and State First Amendment issues (more generally, religion and public life). Second, the definitions of philosophy and religion and their relation to each other. Third, what special obligations are there for a Christian who is a philosopher in public education. (I assume there is no such thing as Christian philosophy or Christian math.) And fourth, is there any resolution to the dilemma inherent in the very notion of public education today.

There is an ever-increasing presumption of a wall of separation between religion and public life. In private life, one is free to be religious; in public life, one is to be free from religion. It is either not good form or unconstitutional (or both) to expose one's religion in public life. The public realm is either common ground or neutral ground and religion appears to be neither. But common ground and/or neutral ground appear equally elusive. Can philosophy offer help? Can the philosopher who is a Christian offer wisdom?

What are some minimum characteristics of philosophy that lead us to expect help from philosophy?[1] There is public philosophy and philosophy addressed primarily to fellow philosophers (that is, academic philosophy). Public philosophy deals with questions that are of interest to the public at large. These are the questions that moved us at first to love philosophy, the big questions, the basic, enduring questions, what may be called the classic tradition in philosophy. These are the questions of epistemology (how is knowledge possible?), metaphysics (what is real/eternal?), and ethics (what ought I to do?). And is it still philosophy if we have left our first love, if we do not seek answers to the big questions?

We had wanted (needed) knowledge if at all possible, and if it was not possible, then we faced despair.[2] (Could we, with integrity, be heroes of the Absurd?) We critiqued every answer for a sufficient reason, having outgrown mere authoritarianism. If nothing is clear, if knowledge is not possible, if we don't (can't) even know what knowledge is, have we become mere sophists (if we get paid for teaching) or nihilists (if we don't sell out)? And if knowledge *is* possible, must we be the gadfly (or midwife) to our fellow citizens who are complacent in mere opinion (fideism)? And what is our knowledge about if not about basic things, about what is eternal (God, *or not*) and about human nature (man) and about what we ought to do as *human* beings (about good and evil)? If philosophy is not about what is clear to reason about God and man and good and evil, what is it about?

Philosophy engages in critical thinking about basic things, therefore philosophy is not neutral about basic things. Some views will not withstand scrutiny.[3] If philosophy concludes one way or another about what is eternal, is that a *religious* conclusion? If so, is critical thinking in public education therefore unconstitutional? Are we then to avoid critical thinking and merely list opinions? Would that still be philosophy? When Socrates exposed false claims to knowledge, those

---

1. Gangadean, *Philosophical Foundation*, 6-10; Gangadean, *History of Philosophy*, 73-78.

2. Gangadean, *History of Philosophy*, 169-170.

3. Gangadean, *Philosophical Foundation*, xxiii-xxvi; Gangadean, *History of Philosophy*, xxi-xxvii.

so exposed struck back. Questioning authority (by reason) was said to "corrupt the youth." Instead of countering Socrates' reasoning or else acknowledging the conclusions of reason, he was condemned by popular vote, based on widespread prejudice, and executed, not being willing to retract.

If we think out loud (do public philosophy and question illegitimate authority *du jour*) there will be push back. What shall we do? We can deny God (give up his call to think, that is, to be human) or do the expedient thing (leave Athens/the Academy/public life), or, we can seek to dispel popular prejudice (on what is religion and on the wall of separation) while there is still time.[4]

One such popular prejudice concerns the definition of religion. Religious Studies departments are still "working on it." Clergy are still "working on it." Philosophy can/should offer help. So, I make a modest proposal, without irony, because it is truly modest, not a clever innovation, but merely a reminder. Religion is the belief or set of beliefs we use to give meaning to our experience. Both theists and non-theists give meaning to their experience. All who hold any belief about what is eternal, implicitly or explicitly, hold a belief about the existence (or the non-existence) of God. All who hold beliefs about God, affirmative or negative, using these to interpret experience, are therefore equally religious. Consequently, we can readily admit that all are religious. And since basic beliefs affect all other beliefs, then all of life (public and private) is religious.

This does not mean there is no distinction between public and private life. A further distinction about religion is to be made. Some religions are revealed, based on special revelation (on a sacred text or tradition handed down by testimony), and some religions are natural, based on general revelation (what can be known about God and man and good and evil by all men, everywhere, at all times). All human beings have equal access to general revelation. Equal access to knowledge is a natural requirement for public life. Natural religion belongs in public life; revealed religion belongs in private life. The credibility of this application depends on understanding the boundaries of what is public and private, and the (objective) clarity and comprehensiveness of general revelation.

---

4. Gangadean, *History of Philosophy*, 3-9.

Public life in America began with the Declaration of Independence, which affirms basic beliefs in epistemology, metaphysics, and ethics. "We hold these truths to be self-evident *(epistemology)*, that all men are created equal *(metaphysics—about God and man)*, that they are endowed by their Creator with certain unalienable Rights *(ethics)* . . ." There is no revealed religion here, only general revelation. The *principle* of beginning with basic beliefs which are clear to all is right; the *claim* that these are the self-evident truths on which all can agree is dubious. The assumptions of Reid's Common Sense philosophy used in the Declaration encounter defeaters by which they lose their *prima facie* warrant. More work is needed, without which the Declaration sinks into a mere assertion of *fideism* and is therefore inadequate for public life, even though it is natural and not revealed religion. Social doctrine based on naturalism or spiritual monism is currently equally fideistic and equally inadequate for public life. We need, in place of fideism and skepticism, what is clear to reason, with proofs to show clarity.[5] This is a job for public philosophy. But given the long history of disputes, is there hope to show what is clear about basic things?[6]

It is not enough therefore to avoid revealed religion in public life by appeal to natural religion. It is necessary to avoid fideism in natural religion as well, beginning with any dogmatism in epistemology. Currently (in postmodern Academic life) a dogmatic skepticism prevails, as much as dogmatism has prevailed in the past in revealed religion. We face dogmatism in the antinomy of skepticism and fideism. We are at an impasse unless public philosophy can show what is clear to reason as a basis for public life as well as for private life. Public philosophy must use critical thinking to attain knowledge for the benefit of both the individual and society. Discourse in public philosophy must not be hindered by the prejudice that it is establishing a (revealed) religion if it reaches a conclusion in natural religion, or that it is prohibiting anyone in the free private exercise of religion if it critiques any form of fideistic religion (revealed or natural).

Christian philosophers (as persons of wisdom) are committed in principle to special (redemptive) revelation found in the Scriptures of

---

5. Surrendra Gangadean, *Philosophical Foundation: A Critical Analysis of Basic Beliefs*, Second Edition (Phoenix: Public Philosophy Press, 2022).

6. Surrendra Gangadean, *History of Philosophy: A Critical Analysis of Unresolved Disputes* (Phoenix: Public Philosophy Press, 2022).

the Old and New Testaments, the written word of God. They understand good and evil in basic ways. They understand the difference and relation between general and special revelation (GR and SR): that if there is no clear GR, there can be no (need for) SR;[7] that understanding the claims of GR leads to understanding the necessity for and the existence of SR; that SR presupposes clear GR. They understand that the good for a being is according to the nature of that being, and that the good for man, the image of God, a thinking, sentient being, is the knowledge of God gained through self-knowledge, attained by the full exercise of one's powers.

Understanding good and evil motivates by fear and love the Christian philosophers' search for the *Logos*, the Word of God in its fullness, revealed in every aspect of life.[8] They are willing to prepare themselves through much discussion and historically cumulative insight to glorify God in all that by which he makes himself known, in all his works of creation and providence. They speak prophetically the law of God, deeply structured into human nature[9] to all of life, in Church and State and Family; in economics and law and psychology. Wherever we go, behold, he is there!

He is there in public education. Wisdom stands in the high places and cries out at the city gates to all, both wise and simple. The university is the life of the mind, enabled through dialogue. It is not the silence of the mind in mysticism or skepticism or fideism. Without the life of reason, the university loses its *raison d'être* and fragments into voices muttering from the dust. Without reason as common ground, public education splits into antinomies: if it is public, it must be religiously neutral; but if it is education, interpreting life through basic beliefs, it cannot be religiously neutral. The dilemma can be resolved by recognizing that common ground is not neutral ground. The critical use of reason is not and cannot be neutral with respect to meaning and truth.

Since reason as the laws of thought and the test for meaning is common to all (and to which all have equal access), and since the public square (including public education) must be accessible to all, we must

---

7. *Romans 1:20.*

8. *John 1:1-18.*

9. *Romans 2:15.*

abandon the chimera of religious neutrality for the universality of natural religion, accessible to all through reason as common ground. In place of the dilemma, we can say: If it is public, it must be rational; if it is not rational, it must be (kept) private. Through reason, legitimate authority is upheld. No one is killed/enslaved/oppressed/loses freedom as a rational being. Only those who use brute force rather than reason are restrained. Philosophy has a role to play in public life. The Christian who is a philosopher has a double obligation to lead the way.

All human beings are more or less conscious and consistent in holding their basic beliefs. Philosophy, through critical thinking, must lead the way in becoming more conscious and consistent. All the more so must Christian philosophers lead the way as persons of the Logos, the Word of God in its fullness. Nebuchadnezzar found Daniel ten times wiser than others because he was not taken captive by the worldview of the court astrologers.

All discourse requires common ground, all the more explicitly if it addresses longstanding disputes. If we cannot agree on anything (even that *a* is *a*), how can we begin to think or talk? Common ground is not arbitrary. Philosophy merely points out the necessary conditions which make discourse possible. Reason as the laws of thought makes thought (and therefore discourse) possible. As such, reason is the test for meaning which is necessary for truth (a meaningless utterance is neither true nor false). The laws of thought (identity, non-contradiction, and excluded middle) are most basic and authoritative (they cannot be questioned, but make questioning possible). Reason, objectively, and commitment to reason, subjectively (as a concern for consistency both logical and existential), are the beginnings of common ground.

Thinking by nature is presuppositional; we think of the less basic in light of the more basic: truth in light of meaning; conclusion in light of premises, etc. If we can agree on the more basic, we can agree (settle disputes) on what is less basic. Applied in principle, if any discourse is possible at all, we will hold to the Principle of Clarity as self-evident: that some things are clear; that the basic things are clear; that the basic things (about God and man and good and evil) are clear to reason. Reason, Integrity (concern for consistency), Rational Presuppositionalism (the less basic in light of the more basic), and the Principle of Clarity are elements of common ground, the basis of discourse and public life.

The task of the Christian philosopher then is to make dialogue possible by establishing common ground through which we can find meaning and settle disputes. And, failing that, we can point out that the lack of common ground in the most basic matters is the cause of the death of dialogue. Since dialogue is the source of public life, we must live or die together. Let us live together!

Paper № 21

FAITH AND REASON
IN CHRISTIANITY

1. The Logos is the eternal Word of God who makes God known.[1]

   The life of the Logos is in all men as light, that is, reason.[2]

   Jesus is the Logos incarnate.[3]

   Where this is understood in Christianity, there is no conflict between faith and reason.

2. Faith and reason are inseparable. Faith is to reason as truth is to meaning.

   As truth cannot be separated from meaning, so faith cannot be separated from reason. By faith we believe a statement to be true; by reason we understand its meaning.

   Faith grows as understanding grows; faith is tested as understanding is tested.

3. Faith is not contrasted with reason, but with sight.

---

1. *John 1:1.*
2. *John 1:4.*
3. *John 1:14.*

Faith is the substance (*hupostasis*/underlying support) of things hoped for, the evidence (proof) of things not seen.[4]

The proof of things not seen is based on understanding: By faith we understand that the worlds were framed by the Word of God.[5]

4. Scripture presupposes that the basic things about God and man and good and evil are clear to reason.[6]

   The clarity of general revelation is the basis of the inexcusability of unbelief.

   The clarity of GR in the problem of evil shows the necessity for Scripture, to show how God can be both just and merciful to man in the state of sin.[7]

5. Scripture requires the use of reason (good and necessary consequences—inference) to understand the meaning of Scripture in context.

   Reason, through inference, recognizes rational assumptions and implications.

   Hermeneutics is contextual, from more basic to less basic, not presumed to be literal, and not allegorical (using foreign or unwarranted assumptions).

6. What is clear in GR can be known by critical thinking about basic belief (presupposition).

   Reason, as the laws of thought, is most basic and is the test for meaning.

   Therefore, critical thinking, as the test of meaning, when applied to basic belief, is called Rational Presuppositionalism (RP).

   Understanding what is clear in GR by RP is necessary to understand what is clear in SR.

---

4. *Hebrews 11:1.*

5. *Hebrews 11:3.*

6. *Romans 1:20; 2:14-15.*

7. *Paper No. 12.*

7. Faith and reason are exemplified in Abraham, the father of the faithful, when he was called to sacrifice his only son Isaac as a burnt offering.[8]

   Abraham reasoned, from all the particulars of his life, that God would raise Isaac from the dead to fulfill the promise through Isaac.[9]

   In doing so, Abraham came to see what God would himself do to fulfill the promise of redemption to mankind.[10]

8. Christ commends those who hear with understanding: Who has ears to hear, let him hear.[11]

   The faithful are those who hear and understand the Word of God and so produce fruit.[12]

   Christ reproved the lack of faith in his disciples, then enabled them to hear the Scriptures by opening their understanding.[13]

9. Paul reasoned in his speaking and in his writing to both believers and non-believers.

   Paul presented the faith rationally by starting with what is foundational.[14]

   Paul described spiritual warfare as rational activity: demolishing arguments and every pretension raised up against the knowledge of God.[15]

10. The Historic Christian Faith is the work of the Holy Spirit leading the Church into all truth,[16] through the pastor-teachers[17] who,

---

8. *Genesis 22.*

9. *Hebrews 11:17-19.*

10. *John 8:56.*

11. *Matthew 13:9, 13.*

12. *Matthew 13:23.*

13. *Luke 24:25, 45.*

14. *1 Corinthians 3:10; Hebrews 6:1.*

15. *2 Corinthians 10:4.*

16. *John 16:13.*

17. *Ephesians 4:11-14.*

after much discussion in response to challenges, come to agreement summed up in its creeds and confessions.[18]

Discussion is the process of mutual questioning and reasoning to come to a common understanding.

Insight has accumulated from the Council of Jerusalem (*ca.* A.D. 51), to the Apostles' Creed (*ca.* 180), to the Council of Nicea (325), to Chalcedon (451), and has reached its current level in the Westminster Confession of Faith (1648).

---

18. *Acts 15.*

Paper N<u>o.</u> 22

———

THE UNITY OF THE FAITH
That the World May Believe

PART I:
WHAT IS THE UNITY OF THE FAITH?

1. **The unity of the faith is about the *basic* beliefs of the Christian Faith; about what is foundational; about God and man and good and evil.**[1]

    i. It is not about what is fundamental for initial conversion; it is about what is foundational for maturity in Christ.[2] Foundation is for fullness and what is maximal includes what is minimal.

    ii. It is not about the unity of the Spirit (in professing one Lord, one faith, one baptism), *which already exists* and is to be preserved in the bond of peace, but about the fullness of Christ *to be attained.*[3]

    iii. It is not about ecclesiastical unity (church government), which comes naturally if there is unity of the faith.

    iv. It is not about what is less basic (the outward before the inward—in piety, law, or sacrament); if we agree on what is more basic, we can (will) agree on what is less basic.

---

1. *Ephesians 4:13.*

2. *Hebrews 6:1.*

3. *Ephesians 4:3, 13.*

v. It is about *basic* beliefs that are clear from general revelation (Philosophical Foundation),[4] from Scripture (Theological Foundation),[5] and from Church history (Historical Foundation).[6]

2. The unity called for is:

i. The unity in the Trinity: that they may be one as we are one; that they may be one *in us* that the world may believe.[7] (All diversity originates in God who is one.)

ii. The unity in Christ himself: is Christ divided (in his function as prophet, priest, and king)? (vs. I am of Paul or Apollos or Cephas).[8]

iii. The unity in the Truth, attained by the work of the Holy Spirit through the pastor-teachers in Church history.[9]

iv. The unity in the good, in the meaning and purpose of life, in man's chief end, which is to glorify God.[10]

PART II:
IS UNITY OF THE FAITH
NECESSARY AND URGENT?

1. The necessity for unity depends on one's view of the good.

i. In the popular view of knowledge by direct experience, the fullness of blessing is received only in heaven after death. Or, only Christ

---

4. Surrendra Gangadean, *Philosophical Foundation: A Critical Analysis of Basic Beliefs*, Second Edition (Phoenix: Public Philosophy Press, 2022); Surrendra Gangadean, *History of Philosophy: A Critical Analysis of Unresolved Disputes* (Phoenix: Public Philosophy Press, 2022).

5. Surrendra Gangadean, *Theological Foundation: A Critical Analysis of Christian Belief* (Phoenix: Logos Papers Press, 2023).

6. Surrendra Gangadean, *The Westminster Confession of Faith: A Doxological Understanding* (Phoenix: Logos Papers Press, 2023); Surrendra Gangadean, *The Westminster Shorter and Larger Catechisms: A Doxological Understanding* (Phoenix: Logos Papers Press, 2023).

7. *John 17:21, 15:7.*

8. *1 Corinthians 1:12-13.*

9. *John 16:13; Acts 15; Ephesians 4:11-13.*

10. *John 17:1-4.*

by his return and direct rule can remove evil on earth. In this view, unity of the faith is not necessary for attaining the good.[11]

ii. In the view that knowledge of God is by understanding God's self-revelation in creation and history, the fullness of blessing is received only by Christ ruling through the Church to complete the work of dominion given to man in the Garden of Eden. In this view, unity of the faith is necessary for the good.

2. Is the unity of the faith urgent?

i. Without foundation (understanding basic things, beginning with the meaning and purpose of life) we do not thrive. We do not go on to maturity, fruitfulness, unity, and fullness. We remain infants rather than become teachers.[12]

ii. Without foundation we have meaninglessness (increasing loss of meaning), and consequently boredom (with transgression), and guilt.

iii. Without foundation the family breaks down. By divisions and apostasy, the Church ceases to be pillar and ground of the Truth (it is taken captive, not taking thoughts captive). It is not salt and light (it is the tail, not the head). The culture without God, in education, in economics, and in politics decays and collapses.

iv. The cup appears to be nearly full. Not being salt and light, we will be cast out and trampled underfoot. If this is so, then unity is urgent.

PART III:
WHAT PROPOSALS ARE THERE
FOR PROGRESS TOWARD UNITY?

Proposals begin with five areas of basic agreement and seek to become more conscious and consistent. By taking a step-by-step approach to

---

11. *Paper No. 12.*

12. *Hebrews 5:12; John 15:8, 16.*

unity of the faith, the origin of differences can thereby be identified and addressed.

1. Man's chief end: the good—eternal life—the knowledge of God[13]

    i. Man's chief end is to glorify God and to enjoy him forever.[14]

    ii. We are to glorify God in all that by which he makes himself known, in all his works of creation and providence.[15]

    iii. Eternal life is knowing God.[16]

    iv. The good is grounded in human nature and never changes. The knowledge of God is the goal of the work of dominion, given to man in the beginning.[17]

    v. The work of dominion now extends over sin; it moves from the Garden of Eden to the City of God.[18]

    vi. The work of dominion will be completed as signified by the Sabbath.[19]

    vii. Christ, through the Church, will rule to complete the work of dominion so that the earth shall be full of the knowledge of the Lord as the waters cover the sea.[20]

2. Common Ground: the necessary condition for thought and discourse[21]

    i. It begins with the self-evident: we are thinking beings and reason in itself is the laws of thought.

---

13. *Paper No. 4* and *117*; Gangadean, *The Westminster Catechisms*. See Appendix 4.
14. *SCQ. 1.*
15. *SCQ. 101, WCF 4.1, 5.1.*
16. *John 17:3.*
17. *Genesis 1:26-28.*
18. *Revelation 21–22.*
19. *Genesis 2:1-3.*
20. *Isaiah 11:9; Paper No. 104* and *118-119.*
21. *Paper No. 2.*

ii. *Reason* as the laws of thought is most basic; it is the test for meaning and it is self-attesting.

iii. We should be committed to reason. *Integrity* is a concern for consistency (logically and existentially).

iv. *Rational Presuppositionalism* (RP): thinking is presuppositional—we think of the less basic in light of the more basic; if we agree on the more basic, we can agree on the less basic. RP tests basic beliefs for meaning.[22]

v. *The Principle of Clarity* (PC): some things are clear; the basic things are clear; the basic things about God and man and good and evil are clear to reason. PC is opposed to both skepticism and fideism, which end in nihilism.[23]

vi. Clarity makes unbelief inexcusable. One has to neglect, avoid, resist, or deny one's reason to avoid what is clear.

vii. Understanding PC is necessary in order to understand sin and spiritual death. If there is no sin and death, there is no need for Christ and him crucified.

3. The Moral Law is clear, comprehensive, and critical[24]

i. The moral law is clear: it is grounded in human nature and also given in Scripture as the Decalogue.[25] The moral law is universal (for all men) and perpetual (for all time).

ii. The moral law is comprehensive: it is total (for all choices) and spiritual (for all levels) and is summed up in the commandment to love. Love is not higher than the moral law, but is expressed in obeying God's law.

iii. The moral law is critical: its consequence leads to life (the knowledge of God in the kingdom of God) or spiritual death (personal

---

22. *Paper No. 101.*

23. *Paper No. 53*; Gangadean, *Philosophical Foundation*, 287-292.

24. *Papers No. 9* and *10*; Gangadean, *Philosophical Foundation*, 165-284; Gangadean, *History of Philosophy*, 61-69.

25. *Romans 2:14-15; Deuteronomy 30:11-14*; Gangadean, *The Westminster Catechisms*. See LCQ. 91-148.

and cultural). It reveals the meaning of autonomy, idolatry, hypocrisy, and hope.

iv. The moral law given in human nature is neither arbitrary (merely posited by divine command) nor foreign to human nature (heteronomy).

v. The moral law is teleological, aimed at the good; it is not deontological, aimed at virtue (the means to the good), or consequential, aimed at happiness (the effect of possessing what is the good).

vi. The moral law aimed at the good is corporate, cumulative, and communal, for oneself as well as for others; it is personal as well as cultural. It achieves the good through the Kingdom of God, the City of God.

vii. The moral law is over all institutions; no institution is total (over any other). Sanctions differ according to the form and function of each institution. Civil sanctions apply only to crime, which is but one distinct aspect of moral evil.

4. Foundation in Scripture: Creation–Fall–Redemption[26]

i. Foundation consists of the elementary truths of the faith; it is milk, not meat. Foundation is necessary for a lasting culture (the City of God).[27]

ii. Foundation is necessary for maturity, fruitfulness, unity, and fullness. It is possible not to have the foundation in place or not to build on the foundation.[28]

iii. Theological Foundation from Scripture is found in Genesis 1–3: creation–fall–redemption.

iv. The account of creation reveals: God's purpose for creating man in the image of God; the good and the means to the good through the work of dominion; the Sabbath hope that the good will be attained.

---

26. *Papers No. 13, 14,* and *15.*

27. *Hebrews 5:12-14; 11:10; Revelation 21:14, 19-20.*

28. *Hebrews 6:1; Matthew 7:24-27; 1 Corinthians 3:10-15.*

v. The account of the Fall reveals: the covenant of creation; clarity and inexcusability in temptation and sin; spiritual death in meaninglessness, self-deception, and self-justification.

vi. The account of Redemption reveals: God's call to repentance in the curse and the promise; vicarious atonement; justification and sanctification.

vii. Christ in the place of Adam will undo, as the Lamb of God, what Adam did. And he will do, as King, what Adam failed to do—exercise dominion through his people.

5. Historic Christianity[29]

i. Historic Christianity is the work of the Holy Spirit leading the Church into all Truth.[30]

ii. This work is through the pastor–teachers, in response to challenges, after much discussion, coming to agreement.[31]

iii. Agreements are summed up in creeds and delivered to the churches for the unity of the faith.[32]

iv. What began in Jerusalem, continued in the Apostles' Creed, Nicea, Carthage, Chalcedon, and Orange.

v. The Reformation built on the previous councils.

vi. The Westminster Confession built on the earlier creeds of the Reformation.

vii. The work of the Holy Spirit leading the Church into all Truth is continuing until the end of history.

---

29. *Paper No. 16.*

30. *John 16:13.*

31. *Acts 15.*

32. *Acts 15–16.*

A Response to
Critics of Clarity

*Common Ground Applied to
Avoid Meaningless Disputes*

PART I

THE NECESSITY FOR COMMON GROUND

Common Ground (CG) is the set of conditions necessary for thought and discourse. To engage in discourse without CG is to engage in meaningless disputes.

CG consists of the following:

1. *Reason* as the laws of thought (identity, non-contradiction, and excluded middle) is the test for meaning and is self-attesting.

2. *Integrity* is a commitment to reason as a concern for consistency.

3. *Rational Presuppositionalism* (RP) affirms the necessity to address the more basic before the less basic.

4. *The Principle of Clarity* (PC) affirms: some things are clear; the basic things are clear; the basic things concerning metaphysics (about God and man) and ethics (about good and evil) are clear to reason—epistemology.

For skeptics, to deny CG is to deny any possibility of knowledge, which is self-referentially absurd. For theists, to deny clarity is to deny inexcusability (of unbelief) and the need for redemptive revelation.

OBJECTIONS TO COMMON GROUND
AND RESPONSES

The following objections deny Common Ground. A response is made to each objection.

1. *Objection:* Being can come from non-being. Since laws do not apply to non-being, no law *ontologically* prevents being coming from non-being.

   Response: If being can come from non-being, then there is *logically* no way to distinguish being from non-being. It is a meaningless distinction. Since being and non-being is the most basic distinction, then all other distinctions resting on this are meaningless. If all words are meaningless, then all thought and discourse end.

2. *Objection:* We cannot know *a is a*; we may have an incorrigible memory lapse (fallibilism). Yet the claim *a is a* is probably true.

   Response: If there is no rational basis for certainty (re: *a is a*), there is no rational basis for certainty about anything, including probability.

3. *Objection: a is a* is pragmatically true, not logically true.

   Response:

   i. Can the logical contradiction (*a is not a*) be possibly true in any sense? If it makes no sense, then it is necessarily false and its contradiction (*a is a*) is necessarily true, not just pragmatically true.

   ii. What is pragmatically true is about "what works for me," or "what I like." Expressions of feelings are non-cognitive (neither true nor false) and not subject to discussion.

4. *Objection:* Nothing (including reason) is self-attesting, therefore nothing is certain.

Response: Pure skepticism is self-referentially absurd (SRA): is it certain that nothing is certain? Or, can any degree of certainty (probability) be distinguished with certainty?

5. *Objection:* Fideism: reason is not self-attesting; only Scripture is self-attesting.

   Response:

   i. Which, of many, is the self-attesting true Scripture?

   ii. Why is there need for any Scripture?

   iii. Which interpretation of Scripture is self-attesting?

   iv. SR *requires* cGR and reason; and cGR *requires* SR.

   v. Any thought requires reason as the laws of thought.

   vi. Scripture is the Word of God *written*. (From SR) the Word of God is in all men *first* as light, that is, reason.

   vii. Since reason is self-attesting, (from SR) it would be the Word of God as reason that is self-attesting.

6. *Objection:* Reason is not self-attesting; only God is. ("When God speaks, you know"—affirmed in existential theology and in simple piety).

   Response:

   i. No experience is meaningful without interpretation; and every interpretation must be tested for meaning (by reason).

   ii. The experience of regeneration is not self-attesting; it may not be known by oneself if one has had the experience.

   iii. Many make the claim that "God spoke to me," which claims contradict each other.

   iv. Since reason applies to the being of God (God is not both eternal and not eternal, at the same time and in the same respect), God cannot contradict himself. Miracles do not contradict reason, which is uncreated, but transcend the laws of nature, which are created.

7. *Objection:* The simple pious cannot be expected to know these things.

   Response:

   i. All can know what is clear; all can know foundational (grammar level) truths; all can grow to maturity.

   ii. It is not a matter of learning, but of seeking. Left to oneself, no one (learned or unlearned) seeks God.

   iii. All suffer under the curse (of toil and strife, and old age, sickness, and death), therefore all are being called to seek.

8. *Objection:* Higher Consciousness ("HC") goes beyond reason.

   Response:

   i. God's being is rational (not both eternal and not eternal, at the same time and in the same respect); God's "HC" is not beyond his rational being.

   ii. If "HC" goes beyond the laws of thought, it makes no assertion (it isn't is; it isn't isn't; it isn't both; it isn't neither). "HC" moves to silence.

   iii. "HC" without reason cannot distinguish itself from lower consciousness or no consciousness.

   iv. Only reason by RP can achieve the higher consciousness of unity of diversity.

9. *Objection:* If you can get *a* from *non-a*, you can get being from non-being.

   Response:

   i. A particular form of being is not identical with all of being (being as such).

   ii. It is not chicken (*a*) from the egg (*non-a*), but being (both chicken and egg—both *a* and *non-a*) from non-being.

10. *Objection:* You can get being from non-being, in quantum physics or in creation *ex nihilo*.

Response:

> i. Quantum foam is not particle physics, but (like energy) it is not non-being.
>
> ii. God the Creator is Spirit, not matter, but Spirit is not non-being.

11. *Objection:* To every argument an equal argument can be opposed. Therefore, judgment is suspended and mental tranquility is achieved (Sextus Empiricus).

    Response:

    > i. *Some is eternal* is not equal in rationality to *none is eternal* (that is, all came into being from non-being).
    >
    > ii. Because *being from non-being* is meaningless (necessarily false, false in every possible world), *some is eternal* is necessarily true, and maximally clear, and certain.

12. *Objection:* There are uncaused events (Epicurus—the atomic swerve/*clinamen* theory).

    Response:

    > i. If an uncaused event could happen once, it could happen more than once, perhaps often or always.
    >
    > ii. There is no way empirically to distinguish a caused from an uncaused event.
    >
    > iii. If thoughts can be uncaused events, then uncaused thoughts making distinctions about cause become rationally meaningless.
    >
    > iv. Talk about uncaused events is therefore SRA.
    >
    > v. SRA's are non-starters—they end thought and discourse before they begin.

13. *Objection:* Reason cannot get you very far beyond *a is a*.

    Response:

    > i. Reason is *first* the test for meaning. What violates a law of thought lacks meaning; a meaningless statement cannot be true, but is necessarily false (by *reductio ad absurdum*).

ii. The contradiction of what is necessarily false *must* be true.

iii. We can know by reason that there *must* be something eternal and that *only* some is eternal; we can know by reason that the good for a being is according to the nature of that being.

iv. Therefore, the basic things about God and man and good and evil are clear to reason (PC).

v. The Principle of Clarity has substantial content that can be extended by the Principle of Rational Presuppositionalism, both of which are affirmed in Common Ground.

(See Paper No. 107 for response to further objections)

SUMMARY

1. Neither skepticism nor fideism can set aside reason.

2. Critics of clarity try to set aside reason to avoid discussion, which shows the inexcusability of unbelief.

3. The light of reason is irresistible: it cannot be overcome and it cannot be withstood.

4. Reason in man (made in the image of God) cannot be eradicated from human nature.

5. The light shines in the darkness and the darkness comprehended it not.[1] Reason is self-attesting.

---

1. *John 1:5.*

Paper № 24

THE MORAL LAW

Universal, Perpetual, Total, and Teleological

1. **Autonomy:** disregarding what is clear about God and man and good and evil; determining the good as other than the knowledge of God through the work of dominion; original sin.

2. **Idolatry:** any false view of God; likening the infinite, eternal, unchangeable Creator to the finite, temporal, changeable creature.

3. **Hypocrisy:** self-deception and self-justification arising from not seeking and not understanding what is clear about God.

4. **Eschatology:** hope that through the work of dominion the earth shall be full of the knowledge of the Lord as the waters cover the sea.

5. **Authority:** authority is based on insight into the good and the means to the good. Authority is rational, not personal. Insight is historically cumulative.

6. **Human Dignity:** man is the image of God, with the ability and responsibility to know what is clear to reason.

7. **Fidelity:** spiritual fidelity to the good prevents ordinary infidelity, and the consequence of cultural decay.

8. **Property**: the wealth of nations is from the use of talent in pursuit of the good.

9. **Equity**: justice for all is from knowing and speaking all of the truth that is relevant.

10. **Serenity**: contentment in the good prevents discontent with divine providence.

Paper № 25

Moral Law and Culture
The City With Foundations

PART I:
FOUNDATION AND CULTURE

1. The City of God has foundations.[1] The City of God embodies the corporate life of the people of God in its fullness—the Christian worldview expressing itself in culture.

2. The wise man builds his house on the rock, and so it endures.[2]

3. A wise masterbuilder lays the foundation; anyone who builds on this foundation has lasting fruit.[3]

4. Foundation is necessary for maturity, fruitfulness, unity, and fullness.[4] Without foundation, there is division and apostasy in the Church and decay and collapse in the culture.

5. The foundational, elementary, first principles of faith (in the City of God) must displace the first principles (*stoicheia*) of unbelief in the world (in the City of Man).[5]

---

1. *Hebrews 11:10; Revelation 21:19-20.*
2. *Matthew 7:24-25.*
3. *1 Corinthians 3:10-15.*
4. *Hebrews 6:1-2; Ephesians 4:11-13.*
5. *Colossians 2:8, 20; 2 Peter 3:10, 12; Galatians 4:3, 9; Hebrews 5:12; 6:1.*

PART II:
SEVERAL LEVELS OF FOUNDATION

1. Philosophical Foundation is grounded in the clarity of general revelation. It affirms that the basic things about God and man and good and evil are clear to reason. It proceeds from epistemology to metaphysics to ethics.[6]

2. Theological Foundation is grounded in the basic teachings of special revelation (Scripture). It affirms the doctrines of creation– fall– redemption (Genesis 1–3) and interprets Scripture in light of this worldview.[7]

3. Historical Foundation is based upon the work of the Holy Spirit leading the Church into all truth, summed up in its creeds and confessions. By challenge and response, the Church becomes more conscious and consistent in its faith.[8]

PART III:
BIBLICAL FOUNDATION FOR CULTURE:
The knowledge of God is through the work of dominion

1. Man is created in the image of God for dominion: "Let us make man in our image . . . and let them have dominion."[9]

2. Dominion is the call to name the creation, the natural and the human world, and to rule over both.

3. Naming is the work of the sciences and the humanities; ruling is the work of technology and all the human arts. Technology develops

---

6. Surrendra Gangadean, *Philosophical Foundation: A Critical Analysis of Basic Beliefs*, Second Edition (Phoenix: Public Philosophy Press, 2022); Surrendra Gangadean, *History of Philosophy: A Critical Analysis of Unresolved Disputes* (Phoenix: Public Philosophy Press, 2022).

7. Surrendra Gangadean, *Theological Foundation: A Critical Analysis of Christian Belief* (Phoenix: Logos Papers Press, 2023).

8. *John 16:13; Acts 15; Ephesians 4:10-16;* Surrendra Gangadean, *The Westminster Confession of Faith: A Doxological Understanding* (Phoenix: Logos Papers Press, 2023); Surrendra Gangadean, *The Westminster Shorter and Larger Catechisms: A Doxological Understanding* (Phoenix: Logos Papers Press, 2023).

9. *Genesis 1:26.*

the powers latent in nature. The arts communicate the truth concerning the human condition and develop the powers latent in man.

4. Dominion requires the work of all of mankind throughout all of history: "Be fruitful and multiply, fill the earth and subdue it and rule over it."[10]

5. By dominion, mankind develops culture, from the Garden of Eden[11] to the City of God.[12]

6. The goal of dominion is the earth being filled with the knowledge of God as the waters cover the sea.[13]

7. The hope that man will complete the work of dominion is given and reaffirmed continually in the Sabbath.[14]

8. Creation is revelation.[15] The Fall was permitted to deepen the revelation of God. Unbelief in every form and degree of admixture with belief is permitted to come to expression in world history.

9. Through a spiritual war, which is age-long and agonizing, good will overcome evil. Every thought raised up against the knowledge of God will be made subject to Christ. Dominion now extends over sin.[16]

10. The work of dominion will be completed by Christ, the seed of the woman in the place of Adam, through the Church, the body of Christ. He must rule until all his enemies are subdued to him.[17]

---

10. *Genesis 1:28.*

11. *Genesis 1.*

12. *Revelation 21.*

13. *Isaiah 11:9.*

14. *Genesis 2:2-3.*

15. Gangadean, *The Westminster Catechisms.* See Appendix 4.

16. *Genesis 3:15; 2 Corinthians 10:4; Paper No. 8, 58,* and *60.*

17. *1 Corinthians 15:25.*

PART IV:
NECESSARY AND SUFFICIENT CONDITIONS:
Completing the work of dominion which
comes to expression in the City of God

1. The unity of the Historic Christian Faith: that they may be one that the world may believe.[18]

2. Common Ground is the set of conditions necessary for thinking and discourse by which we find meaning and settle disputes. Common Ground affirms reason, integrity, Rational Presuppositionalism, and the Principle of Clarity. The Principle of Clarity is opposed to fideism in the Church and skepticism in the world.

3. The good is one, not many; it is the source of unity in each person and among all persons.

     i. The good for man as a rational being (made in the image of God) is meaning, which is grounded in the knowledge of God.

     ii. Eternal life is the highest good (the *summum bonum*), not merely the common good. Eternal life is knowing God.[19]

     iii. Man's chief end is to glorify God, and to enjoy him forever. Man is to glorify God in all that by which he makes himself known, in all his works of creation and providence.[20]

4. The Prologue prepares man to hear the gospel: it requires understanding clarity and inexcusability, sin and death, and the curse as a call back (given *with* the promise). The Foundation of the gospel requires understanding the promise (Christ in the place of Adam), repentance and faith, and justification and sanctification. Without Prologue and Foundation, the gospel is not preached.[21]

5. There is a moral law which is clear, comprehensive, and critical. It is the basis of all culture.

---

18. *John 17:21.*

19. *John 17:3*; Gangadean, *Philosophical Foundation*, 208-211; Gangadean, *The Westminster Catechisms*. See LCQ. 1.

20. *SCQ. 1, 101; WCF 4.1, 5.1.*

21. *Genesis 1–3; John 1; Romans 1–3.*

PART V:
THE MORAL LAW IS THE BASIS OF CULTURE

1. The Moral Law (ML) is given to every human being in human nature. It is also given by special revelation in the Ten Commandments (the Decalogue), which summarily comprehends the revealed
will of God for all men.[22]

2. The ML is universal, for all mankind, whatever their present culture; it is not heteronomous (imposed by another from outside)
since it is given in the nature of each, which is the same in all. It is
the source of unity for all mankind.

3. The ML is not positive (merely posited arbitrarily) either by the will
of man (autonomous human law) or by the will of God (theonomous divine command). It is clear to all, already present in man's
heart (structured into his being/nature) and in his mouth (present
in his thoughts and words).

4. The ML is perpetual, the same for all time, from the time of man's
creation in the image of God to time everlasting. It does not change
from age to age, through varying dispensations of God's covenant.
The civil application of the moral law varies from age to age, but
the general equity remains the same.

5. The ML is total, comprehensive, for all moral actions in every area
of life. Its application is knowable by good and necessary consequences, through meditating on the law day and night.

6. The ML is spiritual, not merely legal; it reaches to the thoughts and
intents of the heart. It is not comprehended by legalism, but it is
summarily comprehended by the command to love God with the
whole heart and love one's neighbor as oneself.

7. The ML is teleological, aimed at the good; it is not deontological,
aimed at virtue, which is the means to the good; it is not consequential or hedonic, aimed at happiness, which is the effect of possessing the good. Virtues without the good become vices; happiness
without the good becomes empty, leading to excess.

---

22. *Deuteronomy 30:11-14; Romans 2:14-15; SCQ. 39-42.*

8. There is one ML over all institutions: Family, Church, and State (vs. one institution over all other institutions, i.e., totalitarianism). The moral law is applied differently in each institution according to the form and function of each institution. The civil law of the State applies to crime only, not to all sin. It is only one part of the moral law. The moral law is a unity; no civil law can set aside the moral law.

9. The ML cannot be understood apart from the good, which is the knowledge of God. Both the good and the moral law are objectively clear so that ignorance from not seeking is without excuse. Each law assumes and aims at the good. The good cannot be achieved apart from the moral law.

10. There is no knowledge of God apart from God's self-revelation, and no self-revelation by God apart from his works of creation and providence (including redemptive history and redemptive revelation). There is therefore no direct (beatific) vision of God in heaven. The good can be achieved only through the cultural work of dominion based on the moral law. The good is achieved when the earth is filled with the knowledge of God as the waters cover the sea.[23]

---

23. *Isaiah 11:9.*

Paper № 26

―――――

THE GOSPEL AND THE
CALL TO REPENTANCE

1. The Good[1]

Man's chief end is to glorify God in all that by which he makes himself known, in all his works of creation and providence. Man is created in the image of God and given dominion over the creation. Man is called to fill the earth with the knowledge of God through the work of dominion. The good is eternal life, the knowledge of God.

2. Sin[2]

Man's sin is rooted in disregard of what is clear about God and man and good and evil. Left to oneself no one seeks, no one understands, and no one does what is right. All have sinned and come short of the glory of God; not glorifying God as God is man's original sin.

3. Death[3]

The inherent consequence of sin is spiritual death. In disregarding what is clear about God, man's thinking is emptied of meaning; he

---

1. Gangadean, *Philosophical Foundation*, 171-177, 208-211; Gangadean, *The Westminster Catechisms*. See LCQ. 1.

2. *Paper No. 103.*

3. Gangadean, *The Westminster Confession*. See Questions 31-32.

seeks to avoid and resist the light of reason. Man in sin falls into a state of meaninglessness and boredom and guilt, without end.

4. Curse and Promise[4]

God calls man to repentance through the curse and the promise.

The curse of toil and strife, and old age, sickness, and death serves to restrain, recall from, and remove sin, covered up by self-deception and self-justification.

The promise is that through a spiritual war, which is age-long and agonizing, good will overcome evil: the seed of the woman will crush the head of the serpent.

5. The Gospel[5]

Christ, the seed of the woman in the place of Adam, came to undo what Adam did and to do what Adam failed to do.

Christ is the Lamb of God who takes away the sin of the world.

Christ is Lord, who rules through his people to fill the earth with the knowledge of God as the waters cover the sea.

6. The Church's Calling[6]

The Church is the pillar and ground of the Truth. It is to be salt and light in the world. It is to make disciples of all nations, teaching them to observe all things Christ has commanded.

The Church in sin is divided, not one. It is the tail of the culture, not the head. It has been taken captive; it has not taken captive thoughts raised up against the knowledge of God.

---

4. *Paper No. 149-150.*

5. *Paper No. 114.*

6. *Paper No. 33, 40, 58,* and *60.*

7. The Church's Repentance[7]

Unless the Church repents of root sin in misconceiving the cornerstone of good and evil, it will be cast out and trampled underfoot.

Unless the Church repents of its divisions and apostasy, the culture will decay until its collapse.

Unless the Church builds on its foundation, it cannot go on to maturity, fruitfulness, unity, and fullness.

8. The Church's Foundation

The Church's foundation is built upon the clarity of general revelation, the biblical worldview of creation–fall–redemption, and the cumulative insight of the Historic Christian Faith.

General revelation concerning God and man and good and evil is clear to all so that unbelief is without excuse.[8]

Biblical revelation concerning creation–fall–redemption is clear to all affirming Scripture, so that divisions within theism are without excuse.[9]

The cumulative insight of Historic Christianity, summed up in its creeds and confessions, is clear to all professing Christ as Savior and Lord, so that divisions within Christianity are without excuse.[10]

---

7. *Paper No. 58* and *60-62.*

8. *Paper No. 102.*

9. *Paper No. 13-14* and *141-150.*

10. *Paper No. 16.*

Paper №· 27

THE LIMITS OF THE STATE

The Purpose and Function of Human Government Applied to Current Debates

1. The State (Human Government) with laws and courts (for law enforcement) assumes that:

    i. Human beings are rational beings who may act contrary to their rational nature.

    ii. Human society is a society of rational beings.

    iii. Participation in human society depends on the exercise of that rationality.

   Laws and courts are meant for human beings who are rational; they are not meant for animals that are non-rational. Law enforcement is meant for lawbreakers who have engaged in a form of moral evil, which in essence is an act contrary to human nature that is the same in all human beings. Law enforcement involves the use of force to remove someone from human society (by jail or fine or death) because they resorted to non-rational means (force or falsehood) to get their way. The very existence of the State therefore assumes both human rationality and violation of that rationality in oneself and in others.

2. The State is an institution which, by use of force, is to protect human life from harm by force.

   The State is authorized to use force ("the sword"); no other institution may use force to enforce its laws. The State uses force against lawbreakers who harm others through the wrongful use of force, as in murder or theft or other violations of one's person. Speech is not the use of force, even when it is deemed offensive. Man is first a rational being, capable of self-governance by thought, and whose feelings arise in the context of one's set of beliefs.

3. The State may not make and enforce laws that are contrary to man's life as a rational being.

   Since the State necessarily assumes man is rational, and is to be protected because he is rational, in contrast to animals which may be used for food and brute labor or kept as pets, the State may not violate the very reason for its existence, which is to protect human dignity from harm by force, but must support what promotes man's dignity as a rational being.

4. The State is one institution among others, including the Family and the Church. No institution is total (over other institutions); each institution is, according to its form and function, under the Moral Law given in human nature as rational.

   Each institution may exclude members from participation in its function to varying degrees, but does so in different ways. On an individual level, degrees of self-disclosure in friendships are regulated naturally by the perceived reasonableness of the other, that is, by their "commitment to the good."

5. The Family as an institution is to protect and promote the origin and nurture of human life.

   The Church as an institution is, by teaching (not by force as used by the State), to restore man from moral evil—what is contrary to human nature as rational.

6. Human beings may neglect, avoid, resist, and deny their nature as rational beings, and seek to express that denial individually and institutionally.

   The sanctions in each institution are to protect and promote human dignity rooted in rationality.

   The denial of human nature as rational tends to diminish rational discourse and public life.

   (Points 5 and 6 are evident enough. Further comment can be given if need arises.)

7. The institution of the Family protects and promotes the origin and nurture of human life:

   i. Human life originates from the physical union of one man and one woman.

   ii. Parents have a natural right *and* obligation to nurture their child.

   iii. The State must recognize that right and uphold that obligation.

   iv. Human beings, in denying their nature, have denied rights and obligations that are institutionally protected.

   v. The State may not allow institutional sanctions of rights and obligations to be denied.

   The moral and legal aspects of the institution of the Family originate in the ontology of our being, in how we originate (that is, come into existence), which is by the union of one man and one woman, *and* from the needs of our existence as dependent infants. There are natural rights and obligations accompanying the manner of our coming into existence. The Family as an institution, with recognized rights and obligations, originates in the manner of our coming into being. Persons are not produced as artifacts or traded as such. Marriage is a moral and legal bond that protects and promotes *both* the origin *and* the nurture of our being.

8. No human law (at any level) may set aside the sanctions of human institutions by denying human nature.

Where human nature is disputed, the State must protect and promote public discourse, not deny or decide the dispute.

Neither federal nor state law, nor decree of a ruler, nor the will of a majority can set aside our rationality as human beings, nor the manner in which we come into existence—from the union of one man and one woman. Therefore, no human law can set aside the institution of marriage with its sanctions that protect and promote natural rights and obligations.

Since human beings are finite, temporal, *and* changeable, they may act against their nature as rational *and* dispute their nature as rational. However, disputes themselves reflect our rationality, even when thinking proceeds from uncritically examined assumptions which may be erroneous. So, disputes at a deeper level are an affirmation of human rationality that makes disputes possible. Furthermore, the very existence of the State with laws and courts assumes human rationality, so the State cannot decide against or abandon rationality. But it can protect and promote public discourse by which disputes may be rationally resolved or mediated.

9. There has been a long history of human beings denying human nature and infringing on human rights and obligations in principle and in practice, personally and institutionally through the State.

   In the past two centuries the courts in the United States have:

   i. Decided who is (or is not) a person and thus permitted slavery.

   ii. Not recognized the obligations of the Family in the welfare state.

   iii. Supported taxation for education as belonging in the public realm rather than in the private realm.

   iv. Disregarded obligations in marriage in no-fault divorce.

   v. Decided the right to privacy outweighed the right to life and thus permitted abortion.

   The humanity of others cannot be denied without first denying our own human essence as rational beings, since the essence is one and the same in all. The degradation of slavery for both slaveholder and slave consists of this denial of human dignity common to both. The law may not allow the dignity of a person to be denied by forced servitude.

Welfare that fails to hold *both* parents responsible for their obligation to nurture their child undermines the institution of the Family.

Education, as an integral part of nurture in families, belongs in the private realm, not in the public realm.

Obligations within marriage bonds, which were upheld by sanctions, were denied by no-fault divorce.

When human life begins (and by implication when it ends) *and* a person's right to life were disregarded by the Court in favor of another person's right to privacy.

10. Currently, the State is being asked to decide what constitutes the institution of the Family.

    The State may not, through its courts, go beyond its jurisdiction to decide on what constitutes the Family or to deny natural rights and obligations protected and promoted by the institution of the Family.

    The State may not, contrary to assumptions inherent in its own existence—that human society is a society of rational beings—deny the assumptions underlying the existence of other institutions such as Family and Church.

    The State may not, by its laws, ask its citizens to go against their reason and their conscience.

Summary:

No institution is total.

Each institution, according to its form and function, is under the Moral Law given in human nature.

May 16, 2015

Paper № 28

PREPARE THE WAY OF THE LORD

By Faith We Understand

PART I: FAITH
By faith we understand that:

1. Philosophical Foundation is based on the clarity of general revelation and the inexcusability of unbelief.

2. Theological Foundation is based on the biblical worldview of creation–fall–redemption (Genesis 1–3) in light of which all of Scripture is to be understood.

3. Historical Foundation is based on the work of the Holy Spirit leading the Church into all truth, summed up cumulatively in its creeds and confessions.

4. Man's chief end is to glorify God and to enjoy him forever, by filling the earth with the knowledge of God through the work of dominion.

5. God calls man back from sin and death through the curse and the promise. (The curse consists of toil and strife, and old age, sickness, and death, increasing to war, famine, and plague; the promise is that Christ, in the place of Adam, will undo what Adam did and do what Adam failed to do.)

PART II: THE CHURCH
The Church is to be salt and light.

1. The Church is divided; it is not one, as the Father and Son are one, that the world may believe that God sent his Son, Jesus Christ.

2. The Church has not attained the unity of the faith; it has neglected the historically cumulated insight of its creeds and confessions by emptying them of their meaning.

3. The Church has lost ground in the spiritual war; it has not taken thoughts captive that are raised up against the knowledge of God, but is instead taken captive by these thoughts.

4. The Church is the pillar and ground of the truth; repentance must therefore begin with the house of God.

5. If the Church will not be salt and light to the world, it will be cast out and trampled underfoot.

PART III: THE WORLD
The world and its desires pass away.

1. Moral decay has penetrated deeply every aspect of human life and every sphere of human culture; the cup is now full.

2. The world has become global *and* unstable; it is both highly interdependent economically, and yet highly divided culturally.

3. Civil governments have become totalitarian in disregarding the boundaries of each sphere of life: Family, Church, State, Business, and Education.

4. The economy, driven by greed of the many and the few, has become exposed to collapse under the weight of accumulating debt.

5. Ideologies of civilizations, each seeking world dominance through power, deny human dignity and rights.

PART IV: WISDOM
The fear of the Lord is the beginning of wisdom.

1. We must prepare the way of the Lord by calling the Church to repentance; we must prepare for the day of the Lord if the Church does not repent.

2. To prepare the way of the Lord requires spiritual discipline in order to gain understanding and to engage in works of service. We live by our faith; the rule for life is faith: to each and from each according to the measure of one's faith.

3. God's judgment comes on man's lack of repentance by the increase of the curse; preparation is needed for restoration after his judgment.

4. Abraham sought for a city with foundations. This city is *of* God and *is* the promised kingdom of God, sought by the faithful in every age. Those who have gone before cannot receive the completion of the promise without us.

5. The work of dominion, moving from the Garden of Eden to the City of God, will be completed when the earth is filled with the knowledge of the Lord as the waters cover the sea.

August 3, 2015

Paper № 29

———

REPENTANCE AND HOPE
Thy Kingdom Come

All Have Sinned

Human beings are all under the charge of sin: all have sinned and come short of the glory of God. All fail to seek the knowledge of God through the work of dominion, to fill the earth with the knowledge of God.

What may be known of God, his eternal power and divine nature and the moral law, is clear so that unbelief is without excuse.

No one seeks God; no one understands; no one does what is right.

The inherent consequence of sin is spiritual death: meaninglessness, boredom, and guilt, without end.

Unbelief in Believers

The curse of toil and strife, and old age, sickness, and death, increasing to war, famine, and plague, is imposed on all men to restrain, recall from, and remove sin, beginning with self-deception and self-justification regarding sin.

Sin as failure to seek and understand remains in the believer even if unbelief does not reign over all his beliefs. God's call to repentance is over all, in the believer first and also in the non-believer.

The name of God is blasphemed by the non-believer due to sin that remains in believers.

Sin remaining in believers disregards and distorts the meaning of sin, which must be grounded in clarity and inexcusability. The consequence of not seeking and not understanding basic things that are clear to reason empties Christian faith of meaning over time.

Heaven vs. the Knowledge of God

Preparing the way of the Lord requires demolishing arguments and every pretension raised up against the knowledge of God, first in believers, and then in non-believers.

In the Church, the commonly held goal of heaven comes short of the glory of God and has been the chief hindrance to the goal of the knowledge of God through the work of dominion.

In the Church, several uncritically held epistemological assumptions prevail: literalism, fideism, intuitionism, and voluntarism together hinder the knowledge of God and have been used to support salvation focused on heaven rather than eternal life in knowing God.

Four False Epistemological Assumptions

Some in the Christian community have placed immediate knowledge by intuition (the *sensus divinitatis*)[1] above knowledge by reason and inference (understanding the nature of God from the things made).

Some have taught voluntarism[2] (where the will is free to act against the intellect in knowingly doing evil) in place of culpable ignorance (arising from not seeking and not understanding and where knowing the truth sets a person free).

Some have taught that faith is above and at times against reason, in place of identifying faith with understanding, which grows as understanding grows.[3]

---

1. Gangadean, *History of Philosophy*, 127-130; *Paper No. 120*. See Part V.

2. *Paper No. 120*.

3. Gangadean, *History of Philosophy*, 111-112, 122-123, 163-166; *Paper No. 70*.

Some have taught the Principle of Literalism[4] in which one word is said to have one meaning, in place of the Principle of Clarity that understands the less basic (word) in the context of more basic principles.

Hope in Repentance

We are to take thoughts captive that are raised up against the knowledge of God. These faulty assumptions, and other arguments that are raised up against the knowledge of God, will soon be addressed more fully in subsequent papers.

While all have sinned in not seeking and understanding, repentance must begin with the believer. When we avoid and resist repentance, the curse deepens. In repentance, there is hope that the kingdom of God will come: *Repent, the kingdom of heaven is at hand.*

---

4. *Paper No. 15* and *60.*

Paper № 30

THE WORD OF GOD
The Logos Is Truth

1. *In the beginning was the Word:* The Logos is the Word of God in its fullness. The Word of God is eternal. The Word of God is God the Son who makes God known. The Son of God is the Creator by whom all things were made.

2. *The life of the Logos was the light of men:* The Word of God is in all men made in the image of God. The life of the Word is the light of men. That light, by which we see and understand, is reason. The darkness of unbelief cannot withstand the light of reason.

3. *The Logos was in the world:* The Word of God is revealed in all his works of creation and providence. The whole earth is full of his glory. Yet no one seeks and no one understands what is clear about God.

4. *He came unto his own:* The Word of God came to the covenant people of God in history through the prophets. The prophets were not received, but their word became Scripture, the Word of God written.

5. *And the Word was made flesh:* The Word of God became incarnate in Jesus Christ, full of grace and truth. He is the Lamb of God who takes away the sin of the world. He is the risen Lord who rules to make God known.

6. *He will guide you into all Truth:* Christ the Lord sends the Spirit to lead the Church into all Truth.[1] The historically cumulative insight summed up in the Church's creeds and confessions is the holy, catholic, and apostolic faith, the basis of the unity of the faith for all who believe.

7. *Sanctify them by thy Truth:* The Word of God is in each believer by the work of the Holy Spirit. Each believer is born again by the living Word of God.[2] Each believer is sanctified by the Truth. The Word of God (the Logos) is Truth.[3]

---

1. *John 16:13.*
2. *1 Peter 1:23.*
3. *John 17:17.*

Paper № 31

_____

DIVISIONS AMONG THEISTS
Sources and Response

1. Clarity and Inexcusability: "The invisible things of God from the creation of the world are clearly seen, being understood by the things that are made, even his eternal power and divine nature; so that they are without excuse."[1]

   What is clear to reason from general revelation is assumed and affirmed in special revelation (Scripture)[2] and made still more explicit in Historic Christianity (in its creeds and confessions).[3]

2. What is clear from general revelation, Scripture, and Historic Christianity concerning the nature of God: God is a Spirit, infinite, eternal, and unchangeable, in his being, wisdom, power, holiness, justice, goodness, and truth. Man is the image of God, finite, temporal, and changeable in his being, wisdom, power, holiness, justice, goodness, and truth. This is the universal aspect of man, the image of God. There are several other aspects of the image of God in man not addressed here.

3. Divisions and sin: There are divisions among theists regarding the nature of God. In light of the clarity of general revelation, these

_____

1. *Romans 1:20.*

2. *Paper No. 112.*

3. Gangadean, *The Westminster Confession.* See Question 4.

divisions are without excuse. Misconceiving the nature of God is idolatry, which produces spiritual death (meaninglessness and boredom and guilt). All divisions among theists are rooted in idolatry, which must be repented of as sin. Repentance requires confession of sin in order to receive forgiveness and cleansing from God.

These general divisions among theists will be more explicitly applied to the various forms of theism in subsequent papers.[4]

4. The first division among theists concerns the infinite power and goodness of God: "If God is all good and all powerful, why is there evil?" Original creation is very good; it reveals the glory of God. Natural evil (toil and strife, and old age, sickness, and death) is not in the original creation. In the Fall, the moral evil of one man (Adam) affects all men by the covenant of creation. Moral evil serves to deepen the revelation of the glory of God. Man is redeemed from sin and death by the curse (natural evil) and the promise (of one to come in the place of Adam). Natural evil is imposed by God to restrain, recall from, and remove moral evil.

5. The second division concerns God's justice and mercy. If God is infinite, eternal, and unchangeable in *both* justice and mercy, then mercy cannot set aside God's justice, but must satisfy justice. If God is neither just nor merciful by nature, then he is without a nature and the word *God* becomes meaningless. In Christ alone, in place of Adam, by vicarious atonement, the justice and mercy of God are fully revealed and reconciled. Christ alone is necessary *and* sufficient for salvation.

6. The third division concerns Scripture and the Word of God. The Word of God is first eternal. Scripture is the Word of God written. The Word of God comes to man in several ways, which are ordered: reason, general revelation, Scripture, incarnate, through councils in creeds, and existentially (by regeneration and sanctification). There is no contradiction in the Word of God; what comes after must be

---

4. *Paper No. 34, 47, 58, 60-62, 64-65, 91, 94, 97, 106, 109, 111, 113, 120-122, 127*, and *140*.

consistent with what is prior. The Word of God is the Logos and is Truth in its fullness.

7. The fourth division concerns the Trinity. Jesus is the eternal Word of God, the Son of God, incarnate. The Son of God is eternal, *before* taking to himself human nature by incarnation. He is not a mere man claiming to be God, but fully God *and* fully man. The infinite includes the finite; it is not opposed to or does not exclude the finite. The finite cannot include the infinite.

8. The fifth division concerns divine sovereignty, predestination, and freedom.[5] God is sovereign by virtue of creating (as first cause) the nature of all things (second causes). God as first cause in creation *and* by re-creation predestinates all things through the nature of second causes. Human beings as rational beings are always free at the most basic level of their being to use their reason if they want to. This is so because the first cause does not deny, or allow to be externally overridden, but upholds the nature of second causes.

9. The sixth division concerns the worship of God.[6] Man is to worship God in spirit and in truth. Due to sin remaining in man, corporate worship is regulated: we are to worship God only as he has commanded in Scripture or we sink into idolatry. Only the book of Psalms is given by God for singing in worship. Only the book of Psalms for singing embodies the Truth of God in its fullness.

10. The seventh division concerns eschatology.[7] Man's chief end is to glorify God and to enjoy him forever. Mankind is to glorify God in all that by which he makes himself known, in all his works of creation and providence. Through the work of dominion, given to man at creation, man is to fill the earth with the knowledge of the Lord as the waters cover the sea. The Sabbath signifies to man, both before and after the Fall, that the work of dominion will be completed.

---

5. *Paper No. 18* and *97.*

6. *Paper No. 105* and *134-135.*

7. *Paper No. 104, 118,* and *119.*

Paper №. 32

_____

RELIGION AND CIVILIZATION
Prologue: Philosophical Foundation

1. Df. religion: the set of basic beliefs (BB) used to give meaning to experience; the set consists of basic beliefs in epistemology, metaphysics, and ethics.

   Meaning is necessary for man as a thinking (rational) being.

   Meaning is more basic than truth. The need for meaning is most basic.

   No experience is meaningful without interpretation in light of basic beliefs (vs. empiricism of all forms).

2. There are two sets of BB which are ordered (epistemology, metaphysics, ethics) and which are contradictory (both cannot be true and both cannot be false).

   Epistemology (clarity): the basic things about God and man and good and evil are clear to reason vs. the basic things are *not* clear to reason.

   Metaphysics (reality): all is eternal is some form or other (material monism, spiritual monism, dualism) vs. *only some* is eternal (God the Creator).

   Ethics (morality): there is rational justification for the moral law vs. there is no rational justification for any moral law.

3. BB are held more or less consciously and consistently depending on presupposition, personality, background, and mood.

   There is an admixture of both contradictory sets in each person.

   In each person, one set is existentially more basic than the other.

4. History is an outworking of the conflict of BB in each and between each person and each group (family, Church, nation, and all—in belief vs. unbelief).

5. BB serve to give meaning.

   Only BB that retain meaning will last.

   Moral evil (ME) is an act contrary to human nature as rational. It is to neglect, avoid, resist, and deny reason vs. clarity.

   ME is self-destructive and cannot last. The inherent consequences are: meaninglessness, boredom, and guilt.

6. History is redemptive; it assumes Creation and Fall. Redemption restores man from ME.

   ME exists and man is being called back from ME.

   Natural evil (NE) is a non-intrinsic source of suffering (toil and strife, and old age, sickness, and death / war, famine, and plague).

   God imposes NE on man, in providence, to call man back from ME.

7. Creation is not Providence; Theism is not Deism; First cause is not Second cause.

   Creation is any bringing into being of what previously did not exist (by God or man). Subsequent creation is sequential (and cumulative). What is new can be a thing or a person or an idea.

   In Providence, God upholds, directs, disposes, and governs all creatures, actions, and things, from the least to the greatest . . . for *his* purpose.[1]

---

1. *WCF,* Chapter 5.

Creation and Providence assume each other; they are not antinomies.

Providence is not hidden; what is hidden is the divine plan, until it is revealed.

8. What is new, after creation, is the covenant of creation (and the Fall), and redemption (the curse and the promise).

9. God rules in history; he is the judge of all the earth; God comes in several ways; the rule of God is redemptive.

10. Cultures come into being and pass out of being.

    There is a distinct process of formation and decay.

    Due to ME, men and cultures left to themselves tend to decay. Many cultures have decayed. ME results intrinsically in meaninglessness and boredom (with excess) and guilt (with attendant self-deception and self-justification).

    Without foundation, there is division, apostasy, decay, and collapse. With foundation, there is maturity, fruitfulness, unity, and fullness.

    Foundation consists of BB from general revelation, special revelation, and Historic Christianity.

11. Most civilizations have perished; only five major civilizations remain: Christian, Islam, Indian, Chinese, and Naturalism (Secular Humanism).

    These are all deeply divided within themselves and among themselves.

    The conflict of BB within each and among each is still being worked out.

12. Only what retains meaning will last.

    What is divided within itself cannot stand as it becomes more conscious and consistent.

    Only one culture will last. Only what retains meaning can be true. Only Truth can last. Good by its nature will overcome evil.

Paper № 33

———

THE CHURCH

**The Church Is the Body of Christ, the Bride of Christ,
the Kingdom of God, the City of God.**[1]

1. The Church is the pillar and ground of the truth. The Holy Spirit leads the Church into all truth (the Historic Christian Faith). The Logos, the Word of God in its fullness, is Truth.

2. The Church is for worship and discipleship. Worship of God determines service to God.

3. We are to worship God in Spirit and in truth, according to the regulative principle of worship.

4. The Church is to make disciples of all nations, baptizing them and teaching them to observe all that Christ has commanded.

5. Truth begins with foundation, the first principles, the elementary teachings: clarity and inexcusability, sin and death, curse and promise, repentance and faith, justification and sanctification, baptism and calling, resurrection and reward.[2]

6. Redemption through the curse and promise requires the discipleship of the Church.

---

1. Gangadean, *The Westminster Confession*. See Questions 111-113.

2. *Paper No. 36* and *37*.

7. Discipleship is based on membership vows. Vows require preparation before and practice afterward.[3]

8. The Church is salt and light in the world. If it loses its effectiveness, it will be cast out and trampled underfoot.

9. The Church today is divided. It has been taken captive by unbelief. There is widespread apostasy. The culture is in decay and near collapse.

10. The sources of unity are Common Ground, the good, the moral law, the Church's foundation, and the Historic Christian Faith.

---

3. Gangadean, *The Westminster Catechisms*. See Appendices 10-11.

Paper No. 34

———

GLOBALISM AND NATIONALISM
A Biblical Perspective

The biblical perspective of creation–fall–redemption must be used to understand the historical tension between globalism and nationalism.

Creation

Man is created in the image of God to have dominion.

Let us make man in our image and let him have dominion.

The work of dominion is corporate, cumulative, and communal; it will take all of mankind all of history to complete the work of dominion.

Man's chief end is to glorify God and to enjoy him forever.

Through dominion man is to *fill the earth with the knowledge of the Lord as the waters cover the sea.*

The Sabbath is a sign that the work of dominion will be completed.

Fall

When they knew God, they glorified him not as God.

All have sinned and come short of the glory of God.

No one seeks God, no one understands, no one does what is right.

Without understanding, man sinks into the spiritual death of meaninglessness, and boredom, and guilt, without end.

God permits sin to deepen the revelation of his justice and mercy.

Unbelief in every form is allowed to work itself out in world history.

Redemption

Man is redeemed from sin and death by the curse and promise.

The curse of toil and strife, and old age, sickness, and death is imposed by God on man to restrain, recall from, and remove moral evil (sin and self-deception and self-justification).

The promise is that one in the place of Adam will come to undo what Adam did and to do what Adam failed to do (rule to make God known).

There will be a spiritual war, which is age-long and agonizing, in which good will overcome evil (belief will overcome unbelief).

From the Fall to the Flood

In the first epoch of world history, believers fell into apostasy and the world sank into moral decay.

Every inclination of the thought of his heart is only evil all the time.

The judgment of the Flood removed moral evil outwardly, and the curse was intensified greatly to further restrain moral evil. Universal evil, which brought universal judgment, was *never* to occur again.

From the Flood to Babel

In the second epoch of world history, apostasy, manifest in a central government, soon reappeared.

Let us build a city so that we make a name for ourselves and not be scattered.

The Lord said, if as one people speaking the same language they have begun to do this, then nothing they plan to do will be impossible for them.

To prevent a return to universal decay and judgment, mankind was scattered by a division of language.

From Babel to Pentecost

From this scattering over two millennia arose the nations, kindreds, tribes, and tongues in the world today.

Mankind was restrained from unity in unbelief by wars and famines and plagues.

Generations came and passed, as a tale that is told. Nations rose and fell as they forgot God. The chosen nation Israel languished through cycles of unbelief, until Christ came to fulfill the promise given to mankind after the Fall.

From Pentecost to Postmodernism[1]

At Pentecost, Christ sent the Spirit to the Church to make disciples of all nations, to bring back the scattering from Babel. After two millennia, even through recurrent cycles of apostasy in the Church, the world has come into a physical community, but without a unity of faith. The postmodern world is putting aside the assumptions of Modernity for a post-Christian, secular source of unity.

From a Postmodern Present to an Unknown Future

For those who affirm creation–fall–redemption, history is determined by God's rule in Providence. There can never be a return to the unity in unbelief at Babel. Unity can come about only if nations are under the moral law, which is grounded in human nature and given also by special revelation in the Decalogue (Ten Commandments).

The Church is to be salt and light in the earth, to teach the law of God to the nations of the world.

Thy will be done on earth as it is in heaven.

If the Church ceases to be salt, it will be cast out and trampled underfoot.

Attempts to put out the light of Christian culture remaining in the nations of the West in order to hasten a globalist agenda will only hasten divine judgment. Both the Church and Globalism will be scattered once again in unbelief.

A remnant must then rebuild the Church on a deeper and more sure foundation.

---

1. Gangadean, *History of Philosophy*, 171-174, 181-191.

Paper № 35

THE CLARITY OF
GENERAL REVELATION

The doctrine of clarity is from three sources: general revelation, special revelation, and Historic Christianity.

1. General Revelation[1]

General revelation consists of what may be known about God and man and good and evil by all men, everywhere, at all times.

The clarity of general revelation (cGR) is opposed to all that is raised up against the knowledge of God; it is opposed to skepticism (knowledge is not possible) and to fideism (knowledge, as proof based on understanding, is not necessary).

cGR is the *first* elementary teaching in philosophical and theological foundation.

  i. It is self-evident that we think: we have concepts, judgments, and arguments. Acts of thinking by reason are distinct from sense impressions.

  ii. It is self-evident that there are laws of thought—**reason in itself** (the laws of identity, non-contradiction, and excluded middle) is the laws of thought.

---

1. *Paper No. 102.*

iii. **Reason in its use** is *formative* (used to form concepts, judgments, and arguments which are the forms of all thought). It is *critical* (used as the test for meaning). It is *interpretive* (used to interpret experience in light of basic beliefs). It is *constructive* (used to construct a coherent worldview).

iv. **Reason in us** is *natural* (not conventional; the same in all who think). It is *ontological* (it applies to being as well as to thought). It is *transcendental* (authoritative, self-attesting; it cannot be questioned since it makes questioning possible). It is *fundamental* in human nature, the basis for understanding good and evil, which directs human desires and actions.

v. **Common Ground** is the necessary condition for thought and discourse (public life). Human society is a society of rational beings. Participation in human society depends on the exercise of one's capacity to use reason.

vi. The **Content of Common Ground** consists of *reason* (as the laws of thought), *integrity* (as a concern for consistency vs. the logical and existential absurd), *Rational Presuppositionalism* (we must think of the less basic in light of the more basic) and *The Principle of Clarity* (that the basic things are clear to reason).

vii. **The Principle of Clarity** affirms that the basic things about God and man and good and evil are clear to reason. One must *neglect, avoid, resist, and deny* reason in order not to see what is objectively clear. Not seeing what is clear to reason is without excuse. All acts that are contrary to one's nature as a rational being are morally evil. The inherent consequence of moral evil is meaninglessness and boredom and guilt.

viii. **Clarity and God's Existence**—It is clear to reason that there must be something eternal and that *only* some (God the Creator) is eternal: matter exists and matter is not eternal; the soul exists and the soul is not eternal.

ix. **Clarity and the Moral Law**—It is clear to reason that there is a moral law grounded in human nature and that this law is objectively clear, comprehensive (for all of life), and critical (a matter of life and death in *every* sense).

x. **Clarity and Special Revelation**—In response to the Problem of Evil (if God is all good and all powerful, why is there evil?), cGR *requires* special revelation to show how God can be both just *and* merciful to man in sin and death.[2]

2. Special Revelation

Special revelation, given by God and committed to writing, *is* Scripture, and is set over and against all other claims of special revelation. This is the doctrine of *Sola Scriptura*.

Scripture is not set over and against reason and cGR. Scripture presupposes the existence of reason *and* cGR and must be consistent with both reason and cGR.

Only Genesis 1–3, which teaches creation–fall–redemption, and what builds on this, qualifies as Scripture.

The Word of God (the *Logos*) which is eternal, is in all men as reason, is in creation as general revelation, is in history as Scripture, is incarnate in Jesus Christ, and by the Holy Spirit is in the Church as the Historic Christian Faith and in the believer by regeneration and sanctification. The *Logos* is Truth.[3]

i. Man is the image of God, a person, who can know God. There are several aspects of the image of God, each of which reveals God.

ii. Man, as the image of God, is to exercise dominion in the earth: he is to name and rule in the creation by natural law (science and technology) and by moral law (humanities and the arts).

iii. The goal of dominion is the knowledge of God, which is eternal life, man's chief end, the good.

iv. The work of dominion, which is corporate, cumulative, and communal, *will* be completed, as signified by the Sabbath: the earth shall be full of the knowledge of the Lord as the waters cover the sea.[4]

---

2. Gangadean, *The Westminster Confession*. See Questions 8-9.

3. *John 1:1-18, 3:3, 16:13, 17:17.*

4. *Isaiah 11:9.*

v. The invisible things of God from the creation of the world are clearly seen, being *understood* by the things that are made, even his eternal power and divine nature, so that they are without excuse.[5]

The law of God is written in the hearts of all men.[6]

Through faith we *understand* that the worlds were framed by the word of God.[7] Faith *is* understanding.

vi. Man is fallen:[8] no one seeks God; no one *understands*; no one is righteous. All have sinned and come short of the glory of God. The wages of sin is *spiritual* death, inherent in not understanding—meaninglessness and boredom and guilt, without end.

vii. The Fall serves to deepen the revelation of divine justice and mercy. Moral evil is not removed abruptly. Unbelief in every form and degree of admixture with belief is allowed to work itself out in world history.

viii. Natural evil (the curse of toil and strife, and old age, sickness, and physical death, increasing at times to war, famine, and plague), is imposed by God on mankind to restrain, recall from, and remove moral evil, covered over by self-deception and self-justification. The curse is given *with* the promise.[9]

ix. The promise is that through a spiritual war, which is age-long and agonizing, good will overcome evil; one to come in the place of Adam will undo what Adam did and do what Adam failed to do—rule to make God known.[10]

x. In this spiritual war, believers are to demolish arguments and every pretension that is raised up against the knowledge of God and take every thought captive to make it obedient to Christ.[11]

---

5. *Romans 1:20.*

6. *Romans 2:15, Deuteronomy 30:12-14.*

7. *Hebrews 11:3.*

8. *Paper No. 103.*

9. *Genesis 3:7-19.*

10. *Genesis 3:15.*

11. *2 Corinthians 10:4-5.*

3. Historic Christianity

Christ sent the Holy Spirit to lead the Church into all Truth.

The Historic Christian Faith (HCF) is the work of the Holy Spirit leading the Church into all Truth through the pastor-teachers, in response to challenges, coming to agreement after much discussion, expressed in its creeds, for the unity of the faith.[12]

This unity of the faith is the holy, catholic, and apostolic faith, which grows until the Church comes to the full measure of the stature of Christ, who fills everything in every way.[13]

i. HCF is corporate (it is the work of many, in councils, not simply notable individuals), cumulative (it must build on what comes before), and communal (it is increased by sharing). Councils may err on some matters that were not sufficiently discussed, and those that have erred were corrected after more discussion.

ii. The present high-water mark of HCF is the Westminster Confession of Faith (WCF, 1648). It includes six creeds from before the Reformation and six creeds from the beginning of the Reformation. Challenges of the past four centuries remain to be answered.

iii. The WCF is doxological in focus. The doxological focus goes beyond what is traditional, soteriological, and cultural (law and kingdom) to the praise of the glory of God.

iv. Man's chief end is to glorify God and to enjoy him forever, in all that by which he makes himself known, in all his works of creation and providence.[14] If we *do not* glorify God, we *cannot* enjoy God.

v. The light of nature (reason) and the works of creation and providence (general revelation) do so far manifest the goodness, wisdom and power of God as to leave men inexcusable.[15]

---

12. Gangadean, *The Westminster Confession*. See Questions 1-2.

13. *John 16:13; Ephesians 4:10-16; Acts 15.*

14. *SCQ. 1, 101; WCF 4.1, 5.1.*

15. *WCF 1.1.*

vi. If there is no cGR, then there can be no inexcusability and therefore no sin, no need for Christ, and no need for Scripture as revelation concerning the coming of Christ's redemption.

vii. If there is no cGR and no inexcusability, then the Church cannot call men to repentance and faith. All such faith will prove to be in vain when subject to scrutiny under trials of faith.

viii. If there is no cGR, then the Church cannot make disciples of all nations. Nations will inevitably sink into moral decay and collapse. No secular utopia can supply meaning.

ix. If there is no cGR, then the Church cannot glorify and enjoy God forever. No mystical state or heaven without the knowledge of God is an escape from meaninglessness.

x. The Church is the pillar and ground of the Truth; it is the salt and light of the world. The Church must now therefore *show* cGR in order to *establish* its foundation, that it may overcome its divisions and reach unity of the faith, that the world may believe the Truth. The *Logos* is Truth.

Paper № 36

THE PILLAR AND GROUND

OF THE TRUTH

Rebuilding the Church's Foundation

INTRODUCTION

The Church is the pillar and ground of the Truth. It is the body of Christ who is the incarnate Word of God (the *Logos*, Truth in its fullness). The Church is called to be the salt of the earth and the light of the world. Yet it is now deeply divided. It has lost its headship where it once flourished. It languishes in captivity to the world. The Church is to worship God in spirit and in truth and to make disciples of all nations. To do so it must rebuild on a deeper foundation. What is that foundation?

Foundation comes from three sources: *philosophical*, from the clarity of general revelation; *theological*, from the biblical worldview of creation–fall–redemption; and *historical*, from the cumulative insight of the Church's creeds and confessions. Foundation is given in narrative form from the beginning of Scripture in Genesis 1–3.[1] It is also given theologically in summary form as seven pillars of the faith: clarity and inexcusability, sin and death, curse and promise, repentance and faith, justification and sanctification, baptism and calling, resurrection and

---

1. *Paper No. 14* and *141-150.*

reward.[2] Sin empties these terms of their meaning. Rebuilding on rock must deepen their meaning. To introduce the task at hand, the following is a brief comment on these seven pillars.

1. Clarity and Inexcusability[3]

Foundation must begin with the clarity of general revelation. If there is no clarity, there can be no meaning, no morality, and therefore no Christian faith. The basic things about God and man and good and evil are clear to reason. The invisible things of God, his eternal power and divine nature, are clearly seen, being understood by the things that are made so that unbelief concerning what is clear about God is without excuse. It is clear that there must be something eternal and that only some (God) is eternal: matter exists and matter is not eternal; the soul exists and the soul is not eternal. Man is created in the image of God, a body/soul unity, a rational animal. The moral law is clearly revealed in human nature. It is clear that God is good and that he created the world very good (without any form of natural evil) and that natural evil as a call back from moral evil requires special revelation to show God's justice and mercy.

Clarity has been largely ignored. Without clarity and inexcusability, the Church lapses into fideism (belief without understanding) and the world lapses into skepticism (doubt without understanding). We have become deeply mired in this antinomy without the doctrine of clarity.

2. Sin and Death[4]

Sin or moral evil is an act contrary to man's nature as a rational being. It is to neglect, avoid, resist, and deny reason concerning what is clear about God. Left to oneself, no one seeks God, no one understands, no one does what is right. Man's chief end is to glorify God and to enjoy him forever. Through the work of dominion man was to fill the earth with the knowledge of God. But all

---

2. *Paper No. 37.*

3. *Paper No. 35, 39,* and *102.*

4. *Paper No. 103*; Gangadean, *The Westminster Confession.* See Questions 30-34.

have sinned and come short of the glory of God. Without glorifying God, no one can enjoy God.

The wages of sin is death. This death is spiritual, present and inherent in the sin of not seeking and not understanding. It is meaninglessness (words are more and more empty of meaning); it is boredom (desires are without satisfaction); and it is guilt (self-accusation without relief). Denial of spiritual death by the doctrine of hell, taken literally as future and imposed, is a denial of God's justice, a perpetuation of self-deception and a removal of the fear of the Lord that is the beginning of wisdom.

3. Curse and Promise

Man is called back from sin and death by the curse and promise. Original creation was very good. Natural evil (the curse) was due to moral evil. The curse of toil and strife, and old age, sickness, and death (increasing at times to war, famine, and plague) is God's third and final call back from sin and self-deception and self-justification. Natural evil is not punishment for sin. It is God's call back from moral evil. Natural evil serves to restrain, recall from, and remove moral evil. It is God's call to stop and think.[5]

The promise is that through a spiritual war, which is age-long and agonizing, good will overcome evil. God permitted evil to deepen the revelation of his glory. Evil is made to serve the good. Christ in the place of Adam will undo what Adam did and will do what Adam failed to do. Christ is the Lamb of God who takes away the sin of the world. He rules at the right hand of God through the Church until all thoughts raised up against the knowledge of God are taken captive to the obedience of Christ. Redemption does not bypass man's original calling in creation nor sets aside man's chief end, but fulfills them in a deeper way.[6]

---

5. *Paper No. 147-150.*

6. Gangadean, *The Westminster Confession*. See Questions 30 and 36.

4. Repentance and Faith

Repentance[7] begins with a change of mind from unbelief to belief regarding the manifold Word of God. It begins with the root sin of not seeking and understanding what is clear about God from general revelation. It arises from a personal conviction of sin and death. This conviction arises from regeneration that restores man to the life of reason. A change in thinking brings about a change in action. If a person seeks, they will understand. If they understand what is clear, they will be able to show what is clear. They will use reason to understand the meaning of Scripture. They will accept the work of the Holy Spirit leading the Church into all truth through its councils and creeds.

Biblical faith is belief based on understanding.[8] Understanding gives evidence for (or reasons to believe) what is not seen. The general object of faith is the worldview of creation–fall–redemption. The particular object of faith is a saving understanding of the person and work of Jesus Christ. Faith without understanding is fideism, a blind dogmatism, not biblical faith. Faith is inseparable from reason as truth is inseparable from meaning. Faith grows as understanding grows; faith is tested as understanding is tested.

5. Justification and Sanctification[9]

Justification assumes vicarious atonement, which assumes the fall of man in Adam. Adam's sin is imputed to all in him. Our sin is imputed to Christ. Christ's righteousness is imputed to all in him. Believers are accounted righteous (justified) on the basis of Christ's righteousness received by faith alone. In the order of redemption (*ordo salutis*) justification comes after regeneration (effectual calling) and conversion (conviction of sin and death and repentance and faith). It is followed by sanctification. If we confess our sins,

---

7. Gangadean, *The Westminster Confession.* See Questions 65-69.

8. *Paper No. 21, 28, 98, 128,* and *129*; Gangadean, *History of Philosophy,* 163-166; Gangadean, *Philosophical Foundation,* 121-127; Gangadean, *The Westminster Confession.* See Questions 62-64.

9. Gangadean, *The Westminster Confession.* See Questions 33-34.

he is faithful and just to forgive us our sins and to cleanse us from all unrighteousness.

Sanctification is the process of being cleansed from all unrighteousness to become more like Christ. It is distinct but inseparable from and presupposes justification. We are sanctified by knowing the Truth. (The *Logos* is Truth.) Knowing the Truth is through a life-long process of trials of faith. Sanctification ends with physical death, the end of natural evil and suffering in trials of faith. All of salvation is by grace alone, through Christ alone. Works are a fruit of grace, not a source of merit.

6. Baptism and Calling

Baptism[10] signifies regeneration (being born again) even as circumcision signified a new heart. Regeneration is also spoken of as a new creation and as a resurrection from the dead spiritually. The (sacramental) sign of baptism is not the reality of regeneration. Sign and reality may each exist apart from the other; baptismal regeneration collapses the distinction between sign and reality. Regeneration is solely a sovereign act of God who works when and where he wills. Baptism is in the name of the Father, the Son and the Holy Spirit. It acknowledges our union with each person of the Triune God, each in his distinct work: God the Father decrees; God the Son accomplishes redemption; God the Holy Spirit applies redemption.

Our distinct work (calling) is based on the work of Christ as prophet, priest, and king who carries out the will of the Father through the Church, the body of Christ, by the Holy Spirit. Christ came to undo the sin of Adam and to do what Adam failed to do: to glorify God through the work of dominion, given to all mankind in the beginning. Dominion requires us to name the creation (the natural and the human world) in all its parts and aspects, and to rule over all through the natural law and the moral law. Each person is to love God with the whole heart (mind, soul and strength); yet each is to serve all in their varying offices as prophet, priest, and king under Christ.

---

10. Gangadean, *The Westminster Catechisms*. See LCQ. 165-167; Gangadean, *The Westminster Confession*. See Questions 119-122.

7. Resurrection[11] and Reward

Man is created a body/soul unity in the image of God. Physical death is not original at creation; it is part of the curse imposed by God as a call back from sin and spiritual death. By man came death. Under the curse: Dust you are and to dust you shall return. But as in Adam all die, even so in Christ shall all be made alive. All in the grave (both the just and the unjust) will be raised from the dead when all has been subdued to Christ. The last enemy to be destroyed is death. After the resurrection comes the rapture. We shall not all sleep (die), but we shall all be changed, to have bodies no longer subject to death. After the general resurrection of all the dead, those who are alive and remain shall be changed and caught up together with all resurrected believers to meet the Lord in the air. Therefore, a premillennial rapture is a false hope.

After the resurrection of all comes the Last Judgment[12] in which all must give an account of their thoughts and words and deeds. Man's chief end that is corporate, cumulative, and communal is to glorify God and to enjoy him forever. Since God is glorified through the work of dominion, one's reward is according to work that has lasting fruit. In the work of dominion, history unfolds from the Garden of Eden to the City of God, the Kingdom of God, which is the inheritance of all who believe. Hope for the good, eternal life, the knowledge of God in its fullness, apart from the completion of the work of dominion is therefore a false hope.

CONCLUSION

The Church's foundation enables believers to go on to maturity, fruitfulness, unity of the faith, and the fullness of Christ. Without the foundation, the Church has division and apostasy and the culture has decay and collapse.

---

11. Gangadean, *The Westminster Catechisms.* See LCQ. 87; Gangadean, *The Westminster Confession.* See Questions 133-134.

12. Gangadean, *The Westminster Confession.* See Questions 135-137.

Paper № 37

THE SEVEN PILLARS
OF THE FAITH
A Brief Summary

1. Clarity and Inexcusability

   i. It is the clarity of general revelation that makes unbelief without excuse.

   ii. The invisible things of God from the creation of the world are clearly seen, being understood by the things that are made, even his eternal power and divine nature, so that they are without excuse.[1]

   iii. The light of nature and the works of creation and providence do so far manifest the goodness, wisdom, and power of God as to leave men unexcusable.[2]

The Principle of Clarity states:

   iv. Some things are clear (vs. nihilism).

   v. The basic things are clear (vs. skepticism).

   vi. The basic things about God and man and good and evil are clear to reason (vs. fideism—belief without understanding).

---

1. *Romans 1:20; 2:14-15.*

2. *WCF 1.1*, the opening lines.

2. Sin and Death

    i. Man's chief end is to glorify God and to enjoy him forever. But all have sinned and come short of the glory of God.[3]

    ii. No one seeks and no one understands what is clear about God.[4]

    iii. No one who takes the name of God in vain is held guiltless.[5]

    iv. The wages of sin is (*spiritual*) death.[6]

    v. Spiritual death is *inherent* in the sin of not seeking and not understanding.

    vi. Spiritual death is meaninglessness, and boredom, and guilt, without end.

3. Curse and Promise

    i. The curse is God's third and final call back from sin and self-deception and self-justification.[7]

    ii. The curse consists of toil and strife, and old age, sickness, and death.

    iii. The curse serves to restrain, recall from, and remove moral evil.

    iv. The promise is that through a spiritual war, which is age-long, and agonizing, good will overcome evil.

    v. Christ, in the place of Adam, will undo what Adam did and do what Adam failed to do.

    vi. Christ, through the Church, will make disciples of all nations.

4. Repentance and Faith

    i. Repentance begins with the root sin of not seeking and understanding what is clear about God.

---

3. *SCQ. 1; Romans 3:23.*

4. *Romans 3:11.*

5. *Exodus 20:7; 34:6-7.*

6. *Genesis 2:17; Romans 6:23; Ephesians 2:1.*

7. *Genesis 2:25; 3:7, 9, 14-19.*

ii. True repentance produces fruit in keeping with repentance.

iii. If we know what is clear, then we can show what is clear.

iv. Faith is belief based on understanding; faith without understanding is blind (empty) faith.[8]

v. Faith grows as understanding grows; faith is tested as understanding is tested.

vi. Faith begins with the first principles (foundation) of the faith.[9]

5. Justification and Sanctification

i. Adam's sin is imputed to all in him by natural generation.

ii. The sin of believers is imputed to Christ, the Lamb of God.

iii. The righteousness of Christ is imputed to all in him by faith.[10]

iv. Sanctification is through knowing the Truth.[11]

v. The Logos (the Word of God in its fullness) is Truth.

vi. Knowledge of the Truth is through suffering (trials of faith).

6. Baptism and Calling

i. Baptism is in the name of the Father, Son, and Holy Spirit.

ii. Believers are to be one as the Father, Son, and Holy Spirit are one, that the world may believe.[12]

iii. Christ as prophet, priest, and king is not divided; our work in Christ is not to be divided.[13]

iv. The Holy Spirit leads the Church into all truth, for works of service, for the unity of the faith.[14]

---

8. *Hebrews 11:1-3.*

9. *Hebrews 6:1-3.*

10. *Genesis 3:21.*

11. *John 17:17.*

12. *John 17:21.*

13. *1 Corinthians 1:13.*

14. *John 16:13; Acts 15; Ephesians 4:12-13.*

   v. We are to love God with the whole heart: mind and soul and strength.

  vi. Each, together, is to seek first the kingdom of God and his righteousness in all the relationships of life.[15]

7. Resurrection and Reward

    i. There is only one physical resurrection of the dead.[16]

   ii. The resurrection comes after Christ has subdued all his enemies.[17]

  iii. The rapture comes after the resurrection.[18]

   iv. The reward for believers is the new heavens and the new earth.[19]

    v. This earth will be made new by removing all evil *from* it.[20]

  vi. The earth shall be full of the knowledge of the Lord as the waters cover the sea.[21]

---

15. *Matthew 6:33.*

16. *John 5:28-29; 11:25-26.*

17. *1 Corinthians 15:25-26.*

18. *1 Corinthians 15:51-52; 1 Thessalonians 4:15-17.*

19. *Revelation 21:1-2.*

20. *Revelation 21:5, 4, 8.*

21. *Isaiah 11:9.*

Paper № 38

_____

THE HOLY CATHOLIC AND APOSTOLIC FAITH

Given for the Unity of the Faith

1. Challenges remaining after five hundred years

On the five-hundredth anniversary of the beginning of the Reformation there are unresolved challenges remaining that hinder the
unity of the faith in Christendom: the principle of authority expressed in the *magisterium* and that authority expressed in the theology of the sacraments.

2. The magisterium

The magisterium is the authority and power of the Church to teach
religious truth. This authority has been located variously: in Church
councils, in the head of the church of Rome, in particular persons
from time to time.

3. The Holy Spirit leads the Church into all truth[1]

This authority is grounded in the truth; and knowing this truth is
the work of the Holy Spirit, sent by Christ, to lead the Church into
all truth.[2] Being led into *all* truth applies not to individuals or to

_____

1. Gangadean, *The Westminster Confession.* See Questions 1-2.

2. *John 16:13.*

the Church in the first century, but to ever deepening understanding of the Word of God through history. The Holy Spirit makes the truth known to individuals through regeneration and sanctification.

4. The First Church Council at Jerusalem

Leading the Church into all truth is an ongoing work: it was first expressed in the First Church Council at Jerusalem in A.D. 51.[3] In response to challenges, the pastor-teachers/elders and apostles, after much discussion, came to agreement, expressed in a statement of faith and delivered to all churches for the unity of the faith. There have been several creeds and confessions through Church history (Jerusalem, the Apostles Creed, Nicea, Carthage, Chalcedon, Orange, and Westminster—summing up the Reformation); and there is still more work needed to respond to remaining challenges. A creed is valid if it builds upon (or explicitly corrects) what has gone before.

5. The response to sacramentalism[4]

The Jerusalem Council responded to the theology of sacramentalism: "unless you are circumcised you cannot be saved."[5] Circumcision was an outward sign pointing to the inward reality for the need for a new heart (to the need to be recreated, regenerated, resurrected from spiritual death).[6] Circumcision was the same in substance as baptism.[7] One may have the outward sign without the inward reality, and, vice versa, one may have the spiritual reality without the outward sign. This is true of all sacraments as outward signs, including Passover in the Old Testament, continued as the Lord's Supper/Communion (the Eucharist/Mass) in the New Testament. The physical sign never becomes the spiritual reality in any meaningful sense of the term.

---

3. *Acts 15.*

4. *Paper No. 16* and *60.*

5. *Acts 15:1.*

6. *Romans 2:28-29.*

7. *Colossians 2:11-13.*

6. The authority of the Council

The Jerusalem Council was authoritative: against the subversive teachers of sacramentalism, it declared: "to whom we gave no such command."[8] Its declaration was sent to all the churches.[9] Its declaration was the work of many, led by the Holy Spirit, not of one.[10] It declared against a recurrent false principle of literalism (vs. contextualism), which takes the sign for the reality, or takes a metaphor literally.[11] It affirmed that salvation was by grace,[12] through faith,[13] not by works.[14]

7. The locus of the magisterium

The magisterium resides in the Church councils, led by the Holy Spirit,[15] through much discussion[16] based on scriptural revelation,[17] and new revelations in the acts of the Holy Spirit in redemptive history as were here reported by Paul and Peter.[18] The cumulative insight of the Church's declarations, thus assembled and led through the centuries, constitutes the true (holy, catholic and apostolic) faith, the basis of the unity of the faith for all who believe. This faith is one form of the Word of God (the Logos—truth in its fullness), subordinate to prior forms of the Logos.

8. The Church and the keys of the kingdom

The Church, now visible on earth, is the pillar and ground of the truth,[19] and is constituted of all those who profess the true faith and

---

8. *Acts 15:24.*
9. *Acts 15:23.*
10. *Acts 15:22, 23, 25, 28.*
11. *John 2:18-22; 3:3-4, 9-10, 14-15; 4:15,* etc.
12. *Acts 15:11.*
13. *Acts 15:9.*
14. *Acts 15:10.*
15. *Acts 15:28.*
16. *Acts 15:7.*
17. *Acts 15:15, 21.*
18. *Acts 15:7, 12.*
19. *1 Timothy 3:15.*

their children. Those who continue in Christ's word are his disciples.[20] Authority to include the repentant and to exclude the unrepentant—the keys of the kingdom—is given to the Church,[21] through the apostles[22] based upon the apostolic teaching that Jesus is the Christ.[23]

9. Justification in the covenant by imputation[24]

The Church affirms the covenant of creation[25] in which Adam's sin is imputed to all in him by natural generation. It affirms that Christ, the seed of the woman, is the Lamb of God, in the place of Adam, who takes away the sin of the world. The sin of those who are united to Christ by faith is imputed to Christ, and the righteousness of Christ is imputed to those who believe in him (as Adam, who upon repentance, was covered with the coat of skin[26] signifying Christ to come).

10. Sanctification[27] vs. penance, purgatory, and indulgences

The Church affirms both the forgiveness of sins and cleansing from sins as distinct but inseparable.[28] We are sanctified by knowing the truth: God's Logos is truth.[29] We come to know the truth through suffering trials of faith. Natural evil (the curse of toil and strife, and old age, sickness, and death) is imposed by God as a call back from moral evil (sin). Adam, being justified, was expelled from the Garden to be cleansed from sin; he must learn the truth through suffering under the curse.[30] Cleansing is mercy, not punishment

---

20. *John 8:31.*
21. *Matthew 18:15-21.*
22. *John 20:21-23.*
23. *Matthew 16:15-20.*
24. Gangadean, *The Westminster Confession.* See Question 53.
25. *Genesis 2.*
26. *Genesis 3:21.*
27. Gangadean, *The Westminster Confession.* See Questions 59-61.
28. *1 John 1:9.*
29. *John 17:17.*
30. *Genesis 3:21-24.*

to be paid for by penance or indulgences, in this life or in the next (in an imagined purgatory). For to be absent from the body, for the justified believer, is to be present with the Lord.[31]

11. Scripture and the Word of God[32]

Scripture is the Word of God written; the Logos is the Word of God (Truth) in its fullness; Christ is the Logos incarnate who makes God known through the working of the Holy Spirit.[33] We know Scripture (special revelation/SR) is the Word of God written, not by testimony of the Church, but from the clarity of the Word of God in general revelation (GR).[34] GR shows the necessity for SR: natural evil as a call back is mercy and mercy requires SR to show how God can be *both* just and merciful to man in sin and death. SR must be consistent with what is clear about God and man and good and evil from GR, that is, it must be spoken in the name of the Lord.[35] Of all religious teachings, only Genesis 1–3 affirms creation–fall–redemption, so only Genesis 1–3 (and what builds on it) is Scripture. We know that Scripture, being given by God to redeem man from sin, is kept pure and entire by God from being corrupted by sin.

12. Clarity and contextualism vs. literalism and allegoricalism[36]

We understand Scripture, not by any church's teaching, but by interpreting what is less basic in light of what is more basic; what logically comes after by what is logically prior. We understand Scripture in light of reason, the Word of God in all men,[37] and the clarity of GR, through good and necessary consequences. We understand redemption in light of the Fall, and the Fall in light of creation. We understand man's purpose as a rational creature in light

---

31. *2 Corinthians 5:8.*

32. Gangadean, *The Westminster Confession.* See Questions 4-10.

33. *John 1:1-18; 16:13; 17:17.*

34. *John 1:4,10; Romans 1:20.*

35. *Deuteronomy 18:21-22.*

36. Gangadean, *The Westminster Confession.* See Questions 11-12; *Paper No. 15* and *141.*

37. *John 1:4.*

of God's purpose: that creation is revelation, necessarily, intention-ally, and exclusively and that all things are directed to the good—the knowledge of the glory of God. Contextual interpretation is opposed both to literalism (which treats context as non-existent or irrelevant) and to allegoricalism (which rejects that interpretation is bound by the clarity of GR, or maintains that there is no clear GR, or that we cannot know what is clear from GR).

Paper № 39

———

CLARITY

And Its Application

1. Scripture on Clarity[1]

i. What may be known of God from the creation—his eternal power and divine nature—is clearly revealed so that unbelief (the failure to know and acknowledge God) is without excuse.[2]

ii. Left to oneself, no one seeks God; no one understands; no one does what is right, no, not one.[3] Not seeking and not understanding what is clear about God is the root of not doing what is right.

iii. Man's chief end (the good, eternal life) is to glorify God (to know his glory and to make his glory known) and to enjoy him forever. But all have sinned and come short of the glory of God.[4]

iv. The wages of sin—of not seeking and not understanding what is clear about God—is spiritual death.[5] The inherent consequence of not seeking and not understanding is meaninglessness and boredom and guilt.

---

1. Gangadean, *The Westminster Confession*. See Questions 8-9.

2. *Romans 1:20; SCQ. 46.*

3. *Romans 3:11-12.*

4. *SCQ. 1; Romans 3:23.*

5. *Romans 6:23.*

v. The gospel calls all men, everywhere to repent (beginning with root sin), and to seek first the kingdom of God by which God is glorified. Because we all come short in seeking God, and resist acknowledging this, natural evil—the curse of toil and strife, and old age, sickness, and death—is God's constant call back to all from moral evil.

vi. Christ is the eternal Word of God, the *Logos* incarnate, who makes God fully known.[6] The Logos is in all men as the light of reason,[7] in creation as general revelation,[8] in history as Scripture.[9] He sends the Spirit to lead the Church into all truth,[10] to regenerate unbelievers[11] and to sanctify believers by his Word.[12]

vii. The gift of God is eternal life through Jesus who is Christ, the Lord.[13] He comes in the place of Adam to undo what Adam did (he is the Lamb of God, which takes away the sin of the world[14]), and to do what Adam failed to do (he is the Lord who rules to make God known).

2. The Principle of Clarity[15]

i. The gospel assumes the Principle of Clarity and with it, the inexcusability of unbelief. If there is no clarity, then there can be no inexcusability, no moral evil/sin, and no need for Christ in redemption.

ii. Clarity and inexcusability is the beginning of the foundation of Christianity. Foundation is bedrock, and clarity is cornerstone.

---

6. *John 1:1-18.*

7. *John 1:4.*

8. *John 1:10.*

9. *John 1:11.*

10. *John 16:13; Acts 15.*

11. *John 3:3.*

12. *John 17:17.*

13. *Romans 6:23.*

14. *John 1:29.*

15. *Paper No. 3* and *53*; Gangadean, *Philosophical Foundation*, 287-292.

iii. The Principle of Clarity says: some things are clear; the basic things are clear; the basic things about God and man and good and evil are clear to reason.

iv. Some things are clear: there are no square-circles; no being from non-being; no uncaused events. If nothing is clear, then no distinction (between being and non-being, true and false, good and evil) would be meaningful. Skepticism and fideism (belief without proof based on understanding) assume that nothing is clear and end in nihilism—the loss of all meaning.

v. The basic things are clear: we think of the less basic in light of the more basic: meaning in light of reason (meaning/reason), truth/meaning, the meaning of experience/basic beliefs, finite and temporal/infinite and eternal, conclusions/premises. If we agree on the more basic, we will agree on the less basic. Reason as the laws of thought is most basic and is the test for meaning.

vi. The basic things about God and man (metaphysics) and good and evil (ethics) are clear to reason (epistemology).

One has to deny one's nature as a human (rational) being—neglect, avoid, resist, and deny reason—to fail to see what is clear to reason. To deny one's nature is spiritual suicide (moral evil/sin), the inherent consequence of which is spiritual death: the darkness of meaninglessness, the burning of boredom in all forms of excess, and the torment of guilt, all without end.

vii. To fail to see what is clear about God is to take God's name in vain.[16] God does not hold him guiltless who takes his name in vain.

3. Application of Clarity[17]

i. If one knows what is clear, one can show what is clear. If a person repents of root sin, they will seek and understand what is clear about God.

---

16. *SCQ.* 55.
17. *Paper No. 23, 107,* and *110.*

If one cannot show what is clear, one has not yet repented of root sin. Without repentance of root sin, one cannot go on to spiritual maturity. That person is not in a position to teach others the first principles of the faith.[18]

ii. If one knows what is clear, one can go on to understand the other first principles (pillars of the faith) in the foundation.

Understanding the foundation brings maturity, fruitfulness, unity, and fullness in Christ.

Without foundation, there is division and apostasy in the Church, and decay and collapse in the culture.

Since the Church is the salt of the earth and the light of the world, the present state of the culture reveals the state of the Church—that clarity and foundation are lacking in the Church.

iii. If one knows what is clear, one can engage in spiritual war; one can demolish arguments and every pretension that is raised up against the knowledge of God and take every thought captive to the obedience of Christ.[19]

iv. If one knows what is clear, longstanding disputes can be settled by consistently applying presuppositional thinking: if we agree on the logically more basic, we can, should, and will agree on the logically less basic. The logical is more basic than the psychological and the practical.

---

18. *Hebrews 5:12–6:3.*

19. *2 Corinthians 10:4-5.*

Paper № 40

THE CHURCH
The Pillar and Ground of the Truth

1. The Church[1]

The Church is the people of God, the body of Christ, the Kingdom of God, expressing itself in all of culture.

The Church consists of all those who make a credible profession of the Historic Christian Faith, and their children.

2. The Pillar and Ground of the Truth

Christ is the eternal Word of God (the *Logos*) incarnate who makes God fully known. The Logos is Truth in its fullness.

The Church, as the body of Christ, is therefore the pillar and ground of the Truth to all mankind.

3. Man's Chief End[2]

God created and rules over all things for his own glory.

Man is created in the image of God. Man's chief end is to glorify God and to enjoy him forever.

---

1. *Paper No. 33, 36, 64,* and *100*; Gangadean, *The Westminster Confession*. See Questions 111-112.

2. *Paper No. 6, 104,* and *106*; Gangadean, *Philosophical Foundation*, 171-177, 208-211; Gangadean, *The Westminster Catechisms*. See SCQ. 1 and Appendix 4.

Through the work of dominion given to mankind at creation, man is to fill the earth with the knowledge of God as the waters cover the sea.

4. Fall and Redemption

Mankind is fallen in Adam. Although they knew God, they glorified him not as God.[3]

Christ comes in the place of Adam to undo what Adam did (he is the Lamb of God which takes away the sin of the world), and to do what Adam failed to do (he is the Lord who rules to make God known).

5. Worship[4] and Discipleship[5]

To worship God is to know and acknowledge him as he has revealed himself, and not in the imagination of one's own heart.

The Church is gathered out of the world to worship God in spirit and in truth and to make disciples of all nations.

6. Salt and Light

The Church is the salt of the earth and the light of the world.

As Christ makes known the Truth of God to the Church, the Church makes that Truth known to the world.

Without the Truth, there is division and apostasy in the Church and decay and collapse in the culture.

7. Marks of a True Church

The marks of a true church are doctrine (Truth), sacraments (signs and seals of the Truth), and discipline through its oversight (upholding the practice of Truth in the Church).

---

3. *Romans 1:21.*

4. *Paper No. 134-135.*

5. Gangadean, *The Westminster Confession.* See Question 112 and Appendix 10.

Churches are more or less pure according to the presence in each of the marks of a true church.

8. Truth in the Church

Christ, the Word of God (the Logos) incarnate, sends the Holy Spirit to lead the Church into all Truth: by reason, by the clarity of revelation in creation, and by Scripture; by its councils and creeds, by regeneration of unbelievers, and by the sanctification of believers.

9. From the Garden to the City of God[6]

The Church is to grow from the Garden of Eden to the City of God, the Kingdom of God in its fullness.

The Church must be taught to obey all that Christ has commanded.

The Church is to take captive every thought raised up against the knowledge of God to the obedience of Christ.

10. The Discipline of Instruction

The Church is to be instructed in all knowledge, understanding, and wisdom, at every stage in the lives of its members in order to do its work.

The Church is to be established on its philosophical, theological, and historical foundation by the discipline of instruction as called for by all vows made by its members.

The Church must express the worldview built upon its foundation in all of culture, until man's work of dominion is completed.

---

6. *Paper No. 54.*

Paper № 41

WHAT IS CLEAR ABOUT GOD

The Clarity of General Revelation

1. Common Ground[1]

Common Ground is the set of conditions necessary for thought and discourse. Clarity begins with Common Ground. Common Ground requires Reason, Integrity, Critical Thinking, and the Principle of Clarity.

i. Reason

    a. Reason is natural: it is self-evident that we think (we form concepts, judgments, and arguments); it is self-evident that there are laws of thought (the law of identity, non-contradiction, and excluded middle—reason in itself *is* the laws of thought); reason is natural, *not* conventional, the same in all who think.

    b. Reason is ontological; it applies to being as well as thought: there are no square-circles, no being from non-being, no uncaused events. It applies to all being, the highest being, God's being. The laws of reason are eternal, not created.

    c. Reason is transcendental: as the laws of thought, it cannot be questioned but makes questioning possible; it is self-attesting—only reason is self-attesting; as the test of meaning, which is more basic than truth, reason is authoritative.

---

1. *Paper No. 2, 50-53,* and *107.*

d. Reason is fundamental: it is basic to feeling and will; its use or abuse is the source of good and evil, life and death; reason is neither finite nor fallen, but man is both (reason is the life of the *Logos*—the eternal Word of God—in all men); one's failure to use reason critically is a denial of one's own essential nature.

ii. Integrity

We are more or less conscious and consistent; we should be more conscious and consistent.

Integrity is a concern for consistency, both logical and existential; we should be neither logically absurd nor self-referentially absurd—the absurd ends all conversation.

Without integrity, we are in self-deception and self-justification about our failure to use reason (the noetic effect of the Fall): we neglect, avoid, resist, and deny reason regarding what is clear.

iii. Critical Thinking

Thinking is presuppositional—we think of the less basic in light of the more basic. If we agree on the more basic, we will agree on the less basic.

We think of meaning in light of reason (meaning/reason), truth/meaning, the meaning of experience/basic beliefs, finite and temporal/infinite and eternal, conclusion/premises. Reason is most basic.

We should think critically about the meaning of our basic beliefs (presuppositions). The conscious and consistent application of the critical use of reason to our basic beliefs is called *Rational Presuppositionalism.*

iv. The Principle of Clarity

The Principle of Clarity states: some things are clear; the basic things are clear; the basic things about God and man and good and evil are clear to reason.

a. Some things must be clear: if nothing were clear, no distinction would be clear (meaningful) and no thought or discourse would be possible.

b. The basic things are clear: thinking is presuppositional; if basic things were not clear, then nothing would be clear.

c. The basic things, which are about God and man (metaphysics) and good and evil (ethics), are clear to reason (epistemology).

2. The Concept of God[2]

i. Minimally, God is a higher being.

ii. God is the highest being, and higher than all.

iii. God is eternal, dependent on no other for his being.

iv. Only God is eternal: he is both higher than all, and the highest.

v. If God is eternal and all else is temporal, then God is Creator *ex nihilo* of all else.

vi. God, as Creator *ex nihilo* of heaven and earth, is a Spirit, infinite, eternal, and unchangeable in being, wisdom, and power.

vii. As Creator of man, in his own image, God is infinite, eternal, and unchangeable in being, wisdom, power, holiness, justice, goodness, and truth.

3. There Must Be Something Eternal[3]

It is clear to reason that there must be something eternal. This first step is a paradigm of proofs to follow.

i. If nothing were eternal, then all would be temporal, all would have had a beginning, all would have come into being, all would have come into being from non-being.

ii. Being from non-being is not possible.

---

2. Gangadean, *The Westminster Catechisms*. See LCQ. 7.

3. Gangadean, *Philosophical Foundation*, 61-65; Gangadean, *History of Philosophy*, 40-44.

(Non-being is not energy, or quantum foam, or a transformation of being, or a fluctuation in a field, or an uncaused event, which denies any distinction between being and non-being.)

iii. Therefore, there must be something eternal.

4. Only Some Is Eternal[4]

Matter exists and matter is not eternal; the soul exists and the soul is not eternal.

Matter exists: the cause of what I perceive is not in my mind or in any other mind, but outside of all minds (vs. all forms of idealism).

Matter is not eternal: it is not self-maintaining, in general, in its parts, or as a whole.

The soul exists: the mind/self is not an illusion; and the mind is not the brain: neither in perception (a mental image is not a neural impulse and the self/perceiver is not a mental image), nor in conception (a judgment is not reducible to motion of atoms in the brain).

The soul is not eternal: if the soul were eternal, it would have sufficient knowledge to have achieved any goal.

Therefore, only some (God, the Creator) is eternal.

5. The Moral Law[5]

There is a moral law which is clear, comprehensive, and critical.

The moral law is clear because it is grounded in human nature, which is easily knowable to all.

The moral law is comprehensive, expressed in every choice we make. It is the same in content as the Decalogue.

The moral law is critical, aimed at the good, man's chief end, eternal life vs. spiritual death, which is emptiness in all of one's life.

---

4. Gangadean, *Philosophical Foundation*, 71-161; Gangadean, *History of Philosophy*, 47-58; *Paper No. 3* and *93*.

5. Gangadean, *Philosophical Foundation*, 171-284; Gangadean, *History of Philosophy*, 61-69; Gangadean, *The Westminster Catechisms*. See LCQ. 91-148.

6. Natural Evil Is Due to Moral Evil

Moral evil is an act contrary to one's nature; it begins with failure to know and acknowledge what is clear about God in creation. Natural evil is suffering imposed by God through circumstance: toil and strife, and old age, sickness, and death.

Since God is all good and all powerful, original creation was very good; God could, would, must, and did create a world without natural evil.

Natural evil is not justice; it is mercy: it is not justice which is inherent, proportional, and lasting; it is mercy, imposed by God on all mankind as a call back from the moral evil through one man, representing all (by covenant, from the beginning—that is, the Fall).

7. Scripture Is Necessary and Scripture Exists[6]

A call back as mercy requires special (redemptive) revelation (given in Scripture) to show how God can be both just and merciful to man in sin and death.

Special revelation must be consistent with creation–fall–redemption seen in general revelation.

Only biblical revelation (from Genesis to Revelation) is consistent with creation–fall–redemption, and is given by God.

---

6. Gangadean, *The Westminster Confession*. See Questions 5-10; Gangadean, *The Westminster Catechisms*. See LCQ. 4-7; *Paper No. 11* and *12*.

Paper N⁰· 42

THE MORAL LAW:
THE FIRST COMMANDMENT
You Shall Have No Other Gods Before Me

1. The good for a being is determined by the nature of the being.

  i. The moral absolute; central to all moral concerns; assumes choices, highest value; "good" in relation to the good.

  ii. Grounded, objectively, in the nature of things (metaphysics).

  iii. Easily knowable: in the human heart.[1]

  iv. In human nature: not arbitrary (Divine Command Theory), not subjective, not culturally relative.

  v. In human nature: the good is one; human nature (in one being) is a unity of diversity.

  vi. In human nature: the same in all; the source of unity: one and the same for all.

  vii. What determines human nature determines the good for man (2 possibilities) (not 3).

---

1. *Romans 2:14-15; Deuteronomy 30:11-13.*

2. Man is made in the image of God, to know God.

> i. Man has the capacity to use reason to understand the nature of things in forming concepts, judgments, and arguments.

> ii. Man is a rational animal (distinct from all other animals by reason) and is therefore not made in the image of animals.

> iii. Man is a unity of body and soul, not a duality of a soul only for a time present in a body.

> iv. Human nature is complex and ordered in a unity of diversity.

> v. What is most basic is universal, the same in all persons, everywhere, at all times.

> vi. We are first human in our common formal features, then distinguished by conflicting basic beliefs, then by diversity of personality, by body/soul relation, by one's gender identity, by cultural identity, and by the uniqueness of personal identity.

> vii. Only by loving God with the whole heart, in the unity of our being, can the good be achieved.

3. As the image of God, man, through dominion, is to fill the earth with the knowledge of God.[2]

> i. Creation is revelation: necessarily, intentionally, and exclusively.

> ii. This revelation is full and clear: the whole earth is full of his glory.

> iii. God is a Spirit, immortal, invisible, whom no man has seen or can see.[3]

> iv. There is no direct knowledge of God, in this life or the next, apart from God's works.

> v. Through dominion mankind is to name and rule over the world of nature (under natural law) and the human world (under moral law).

---

2. Gangadean, *The Westminster Catechisms*. See Appendix 4.

3. *1 Timothy 6:16.*

vi. Through dominion man is to develop culture so as to fill the earth with the knowledge of God as the waters cover the sea.[4]

vii. To bypass the knowledge of God through dominion, for a beatific vision of God in the afterlife, is to deny the nature of God and man and the good and the significance of human history.

4. Man's chief end is to glorify God and to enjoy him forever.

i. Man's chief end is the end in itself (the end of all ends), the highest good or, the good, simpliciter.

ii. The (highest) good is eternal life, which is the knowledge of God.[5]

iii. To glorify God is to know his glory and to make his glory known.

iv. The first commandment requires us to know and acknowledge God to be the only true God and to be our God, and to worship and glorify him accordingly.[6]

v. In the first petition of the Lord's Prayer, we pray that God would enable us and others to glorify him in all that by which he makes himself known.[7]

vi. God makes himself known through all his works of creation and providence.[8]

vii. To enjoy God is inseparable from and intrinsic to glorifying God. What we enjoy is God himself in contemplating his glory revealed in every relationship with him.

5. The Law is teleological, aimed at the good, eternal life.

i. Man's chief end (the good) is not virtue, the means to the good.

ii. Man's chief end (the good) is not happiness, the effect of possessing the good.

---

4. *Isaiah 11:9.*
5. *John 17:3.*
6. *SCQ. 46.*
7. *SCQ. 101.*
8. *WCF 4.1, 5.1.*

   iii. Both virtue ethics and happiness ethics come short of the glory of God.

   iv. Virtue, doing what is right, as an end in itself, apart from the good, is deontology, which tends to legalism.

   v. Pursuit of happiness as an end in itself, apart from the good, is hedonism, which tends to antinomianism.

   vi. Virtue and happiness without the good misunderstand God's law, which is aimed at the good: they are ever-recurrent antinomies which go to the right and left of the law of God.

   vii. Love seeks the good for oneself and for others. Love is the chief virtue: it binds all other virtues in perfect unity in pursuit of the good.

6. All have sinned and come short of the glory of God.[9]

   i. The sin of all is not glorifying God as God.

   ii. Left to oneself no one seeks God, no one understands, no one is righteous, not even one.

   iii. God's eternal power and divine nature are clearly revealed so that unbelief is without excuse.[10]

   iv. The first sin of the first man broke the first commandment. It is original and paradigm.

   v. Root sin is not seeking and not understanding; radical evil is to put oneself in the place of God to determine good and evil.

   vi. The wages of sin is spiritual death; meaninglessness, boredom, and guilt without end are present and inherent in root sin. Death arises from denying one's nature.

   vii. The gospel calls all men, everywhere, at all times to repent of root sin and to glorify God in seeking first the kingdom of God in all of life.

---

9. *Paper No. 103.*

10. *Romans 1:20; Psalm 19.*

7. There are ten characteristics of the good.[11]

   i. Continuing: it must continue from this life to the next.

   ii. Inexhaustible: one can grow in the good forever.

   iii. Comprehensive: it must include all deliberate human activity.

   iv. Inalienable: it cannot be lost by force or inadvertence.

   v. Corporate: it is and must be achieved by many (through dominion).

   vi. Cumulative: it is and must be achieved through many generations.

   vii. Communal: it must increase by sharing.

   viii. Fulfilling: it must be most satisfying; only what and what only satisfies.

   ix. Ultimate: it must be rooted in what is infinite and eternal.

   x. Transformative: it must have power to bring change, against evil and for good.

Only the knowledge of God can have these ten characteristics.

The good for man is the knowledge of God.

---

11. Gangadean, *Philosophical Foundation*, 208-211.

Paper N⁰· 43

―――

MY LAST LECTURE
Focus on Foundation

APRIL 2018

My Last Lecture reflects my years of teaching in philosophy, religion, and the humanities in the academy, in theology at Logos Theological Seminary, and pastoral teaching in the church. It calls for a focus on foundation.

1. The Necessity for Foundation

   i. In general, foundation is necessary for maturity, fruitfulness, unity, and fullness. Without foundation, there is division and apostasy in the Church, and decay and collapse in the culture.

   ii. In Scripture, foundation is called for as first principles,[1] for endurance against tempests,[2] for lasting fruit,[3] for unity of the faith and fullness,[4] for a lasting culture in the City of God.[5]

   iii. Current divisions in the Church and decay in the culture show a longstanding lack of foundation and the need to get to bedrock.

―――――――

1. *Hebrews 6.*
2. *Matthew 7.*
3. *1 Corinthians 2.*
4. *Ephesians 4.*
5. *Hebrews 11:10; Revelation 21.*

iv. Foundation must get to the certainty of clarity, the cornerstone, from which arises inexcusability. It must overcome skepticism and fideism by faith.[6]

v. Failure to achieve comprehensiveness to attain to fullness of life is not new; it has been recurrent throughout history in the collapse of civilizations. A mere return to the past is insufficient for bedrock.

2. The Cornerstone: understanding good and evil (and life and death, and heaven and hell); without the cornerstone, the foundation cannot be laid and the worldview cannot be built.

i. The good is the highest value, the end in itself, chosen for its own sake and not for the sake of something else; it is neither virtue (means to the good) nor happiness (the effect of the good).

ii. The good is clear: the good for a being is according to the nature of that being; the good for man as a rational being is the use of reason to the fullest to understand the nature of things. The nature of things created reveal the nature of God. It is *not* a non-cognitive state of a beatific vision.

iii. The good is one: it is the source of unity in each person and the source of unity among all persons.

iv. The good must have several characteristics: continuing, inexhaustible, comprehensive, inalienable, corporate, cumulative, communal, fulfilling, ultimate, and transformative.

v. The good is the first *moral* concept, depending on one's epistemology and metaphysics. It is the most basic *existential* concept that moves a person to or from critical self-examination.

vi. Moral evil is an act contrary to one's nature as a rational being; all have sinned, all come short of the glory of God.

vii. It is to neglect, avoid, resist, and deny reason regarding basic things that are clear to reason. Clarity makes unbelief inexcusable.

---

6. *Romans 1:20; Hebrews 11:1.*

viii. Moral evil of not seeking and not understanding is *root* sin and is the source of all *fruit* sin.

ix. Natural evil (toil and strife, and old age, sickness, and death) is due to autonomy in moral evil; it is a lasting and final call back to stop and think, to restrain, recall from, and to remove moral evil.

x. The inherent consequence of moral evil is meaninglessness, boredom, and guilt; it is *not* a state that is merely future or imposed.

3. Common Ground and the Word of God

i. Common Ground (CG) is the set of conditions necessary for thought and discourse. It consists of reason (as the laws of thought), integrity (as a concern for consistency), critical thinking (applying reason critically as the test of meaning to basic beliefs/presuppositions) and the Principle of Clarity, that the basic things (about God and man and good and evil) are clear to reason (vs. skepticism and fideism).

ii. The *Logos* is the eternal Word of God, Truth in its fullness, who makes God known.[7] The Logos, by which all things were made, is in all men as light/reason,[8] in creation as general revelation,[9] in history, through the prophets,[10] in person, incarnate in Jesus Christ, full of grace and truth.[11] He sends the Spirit of truth to lead the Church into all truth,[12] to bring unbelievers into the truth by regeneration,[13] and to sanctify the believer through knowing the truth.[14]

iii. It is self-evident that we think and it is self-evident that there are laws of thought. Reason as the laws of thought (identity, non-contradiction, and excluded middle) is the most basic form

---

7. *John 1:1-18.*

8. *John 1:4.*

9. *John 1:10.*

10. *John 1:11.*

11. *John 1:14.*

12. *John 16:13.*

13. *John 3:3.*

14. *John 17:17.*

of the Word of God to all men. Only the Word of God as reason is and can be self-attesting, and therefore authoritative. What is self-attesting does not need justification *and cannot be* questioned because, as the laws of thought, it makes questioning possible. By reason we understand the clarity of general and special revelation. Reason as the beginning of Common Ground and of the Logos in man is not neutral ground. Any act of thought (including unbelief) assumes reason and the darkness of unbelief cannot withstand the light of reason.[15] One must stop thinking and talking to avoid the use of reason, and no one can stop the spontaneity of thought. The use of reason leads to belief in God, and consequently, in Scripture. And, belief in God assumes reason is ontological, for neither God's being *nor any being* can be contradictory (both eternal and not eternal, at the same time and in the same respect).

4. The Clarity of General Revelation: It is clear to reason that God the Creator and Ruler exists.[16]

i. The concept of God: God is not only a higher being (one among many) but the highest being (above all else). He is not only eternal (uncreated) but *the only eternal* (the Creator of all).

ii. It is clear to reason that there must be something eternal (being cannot come from non-being), and that only God is eternal. Matter exists (vs. idealism) and matter is not eternal (self-maintaining). The soul exists (the mind is not the brain), and the soul is not eternal (having all knowledge in infinite time).

iii. It is clear that creation is revelation, necessarily, intentionally, and exclusively. Man is created a body/soul unity, a rational animal, created in the image of God, not in the image of (or from) non-rational animals, to rule over the creation, to know and make known the glory of God. Original creation was very good, without natural evil (toil and strife, and old age, sickness,

---

15. *John 1:5.*

16. Gangadean, *Philosophical Foundation*, 71-161; Gangadean, *History of Philosophy*, 47-58; Gangadean, *The Westminster Catechisms*. See LCQ. 2; *Paper No. 3* and *93.*

and death). The good for man, grounded in human nature, is the knowledge of God.

iv. It is clear to reason that man is fallen, that God rules over man by an act of *special* providence, that *by covenant* the act of one affects all. Since God's eternal power and divine nature are clear, unbelief is without excuse. No one knows and acknowledges what is clear about God; no one seeks and understands—all have sinned and come short of the glory of God and all are in self-deception and self-justification about seeking and understanding. It is clear that natural evil, which is not original, is now *imposed on all* (by God, through covenant) to restrain, recall from, and remove moral evil, that a call back is not punishment but mercy, that mercy requires special (redemptive) revelation to show how God can be both just and merciful to man in sin and death. Since moral evil is permitted in order to deepen the revelation, it must be removed gradually if the revelation is both to be deepened and be seen. In the conflict between good and evil, belief will gradually overcome unbelief, through another in place of the first covenant head.

The clarity of general revelation regarding God and man and good and evil is necessary metaphysical foundation for the unity of mankind scattered in every form of unbelief.

5. Moral Law: It is clear from general revelation that there is a moral law which is clear, comprehensive, and critical.[17]

i. Good and evil are grounded in human nature. God, as Creator of human nature therefore determines good and evil for man. Man is not, and cannot be, the author of his being (vs. all forms of *autonomy*).

ii. Misconceptions of God arise from likening the infinite (Creator) to the finite (creature), rather than thinking of the finite/less basic in light of the infinite/more basic (vs. all forms of *idolatry*).

---

17. Gangadean, *Philosophical Foundation*, 171-284; Gangadean, *History of Philosophy*, 61-69; Gangadean, *The Westminster Catechisms*. See LCQ. 91-148.

  iii. Lack of integrity (concern for consistency, both logical and existential) empties words of meaning. *Hypocrisy* is without excuse and leads to mental stupor.

  iv. Man's work of dominion is based on God's work of creation. As creation is revelation, dominion brings knowledge of revelation. As creation is completed, dominion will be completed (vs. false and no hope).

   v. Authority is rational and is based on insight, which is historically cumulative. Authority based on insight must be honored; authority without insight must be changed where possible.

  vi. Human dignity is based on man's capacity to understand. Human society is a society of rational beings. Participation in human society is based on the exercise of one's capacity to understand.

 vii. Lack of love in marriage is due to lack of love of the good. Ordinary adultery is rooted in spiritual adultery.

viii. Value arises from the exercise of talent in pursuit of the good. Talent, given in one's being, is from God, the author of our being. Only God therefore owns value absolutely; man is steward of the talent given to him.

  ix. Truth is necessary and sufficient for justice. One must know and speak the full truth to attain full justice.

   x. The good is inalienable. Natural evil is a call back from moral evil. All things work together for good to those who seek the good.

The moral law, given in human nature, is universal, perpetual, total, and spiritual; it is teleological (aimed at the good), and defines what love is. It is therefore foundational and the source of unity in all and for all.

6. Biblical Foundation (Narrative Form): Creation–Fall–Redemption (CFR) (Genesis 1–3)[18]

   i. Scripture

      a. Clear general revelation through the problem of evil requires special revelation/scripture.

      b. Only what is consistent with clear general revelation (4–5 above) can be special revelation.

      c. Only biblical revelation (Genesis 1–3 and what builds on it) affirms CFR, as it is understandable from clear general revelation.

      d. Therefore, only biblical revelation, and no other text, can qualify as special revelation from God.

   ii. Creation

      a. God's purpose in creation is revelation: necessarily, intentionally, and exclusively.

      b. This revelation is full and clear.

      c. Man's purpose, as created in the image of God, is for dominion.

      d. The good for man, man's chief end, eternal life, is the knowledge of God through dominion.

      e. The Sabbath signifies the hope that man's work of dominion will be completed, that the earth will be filled with the knowledge of God as the waters cover the sea.

   iii. Fall

      a. God relates to man by covenant; by representation, the act of one affects all; the visible covenant of marriage established in the Garden of Eden reveals the invisible covenant of creation.

      b. In probation, man's understanding of good and evil is tested—knowing what is the good and the ground of the good is tested by the claim: "you shall be as gods knowing good and evil."

---

18. *Paper No. 14*, and *141-150*.

c. Had Adam been seeking God he would have understood that only God as Creator can determine good and evil.

d. Adam's sin revealed that left to oneself no one seeks God and no one understands what is clear about God. All have sinned and come short of the glory of God.

e. God permits the fall of man to deepen the revelation of his glory, especially his justice and mercy.

iv. Redemption

a. Man is called back from sin and death, first through conscience (shame regarding nakedness), which is avoided by self-deception (the covering of leaves).

b. Man is then called to self-examination by the question "where are you?" which is resisted by self-justification, blaming the woman and God.

c. Man's final and enduring call back is through the curse (toil and strife, and old age, sickness, and death) and the promise—"I will put enmity between you and the woman" (through a spiritual war, which is age-long and agonizing, good will overcome evil). Through the seed of the woman, Christ to come in the place of Adam, will undo what Adam did (as the Lamb of God signified by the coats of skin) and do what Adam failed to do (make God known by crushing the lies of the devil (the head of the serpent)).

d. Adam believes the promise, repents, and obeys (he wears the coats of skin—he is *justified* in being covered through the death of another), and he calls his wife's name Eve, the mother of all living—he will be fruitful for the work of dominion.

e. Adam is to be *sanctified* by knowing the truth through suffering; he is driven from the Garden to live under the curse.

v. CFR is a complete summary of the biblical worldview.

CFR is affirmed in Genesis 1–3, the foundation of all of redemptive revelation.

All of Scripture must be understood in light of CFR. If we do not understand CFR, we cannot understand Scripture.

CFR gives unity to all of Scripture and to all who affirm Scripture.

7. Biblical Foundation (Theological Form): the Seven Pillars[19]

Foundation has many layers; the City of God[20] has twelve.

Theological Foundation is summed up in Hebrews[21] in its assumptions and implications, and in the proclamation of the gospel—repent, for the kingdom of heaven is at hand.

Repentance assumes *sin and death*, which assumes *clarity and inexcusability*.

Faith towards God assumes the *promise* of redemption, given with the *curse* as God's continuing call to repentance.

Repentance and faith is accompanied by *justification and sanctification*.

A repentant sinner is received by the Church through *baptism* (signifying regeneration and identification with the work of each person of the Triune God). The Church prepares its members for their particular work (*calling*) in the kingdom of God, based on God's work. Commitment to work in the kingdom is renewed in corporate worship each Lord's Day and in the sacrament of the Lord's Supper *until he comes*.

Christ returns when all things are subdued to him, consummated by the *resurrection* of the dead, followed by the Last Judgment and *reward*, each according to one's work.

i. Clarity and inexcusability

Basic things about God and man and good and evil are clear to reason so that unbelief is without excuse.

---

19. *Paper No. 37.*
20. *Revelation 21.*
21. *Hebrews 6:1-2.*

If there is no clear general revelation, there is no possibility of meaning or morality, no sin and death, and no need for Christ as redeemer.

All who fail to acknowledge clarity and inexcusability, in some degree, fail to repent of (root) sin and (spiritual) death, and persist in self-deception and self-justification. The Church disciples its members to deepen their faith in understanding the first principles of the faith, and not to remain spiritual infants, unable to teach others.

ii. Sin and Death

Sin is an act contrary to one's nature as a rational being. In sin, man neglects, avoids, resists, and denies reason regarding what is clear about God.

Root sin is universal: no one seeks God and no one understands; all have sinned and come short of the glory of God.

The wages of sin (spiritual suicide) is spiritual death: meaninglessness, boredom, and guilt, ever increasing in this life and the next.

Root sin is *not* fruit sin, and spiritual death is *not* a literal lake of fire.

iii. Curse and Promise

The curse consists of toil and strife, and old age, sickness, and death, and is imposed by God on all as his continuing and final call back to stop and think, to restrain, recall from, and remove moral evil.

As sin increases culturally, the curse increases corporately to war, famine, and plague.

The promise, given with the curse, is that through a spiritual war (between belief and unbelief), which is age-long and agonizing, good will overcome evil.[22]

Christ, the seed of the woman, in place of Adam, will undo what Adam did (as the Lamb of God he will take away the sin of the

---

22. *Genesis 3:15.*

world), and will do what Adam failed to do (rule through the work of dominion to make God known).

iv. Repentance and Faith

Man is called by the gospel to repent of (root) sin and to seek first the kingdom of God by which God is glorified and through which man enjoys eternal life—the knowledge of God now and ever increasing forever.

Repentance in principle must grow in practice: faith grows as man through discipleship becomes more conscious and consistent in understanding and in obedience, putting away all sin, root and fruit.

v. Justification and Sanctification

Upon repentance and faith in Christ's atoning sacrifice on the cross, a person receives forgiveness of sin and is justified solely on the basis of Christ's righteousness imputed to him and is received by faith.

This imputation of Christ's righteousness to those in him is real, even as Adam's sin is imputed to all in him, and as our sin is imputed to Christ.

Imputation of Christ's righteousness for justification is once for all and is not by any works or to be confused with sanctification, by which a believer continues to be cleansed from sin throughout his life.

Sanctification comes through knowing the Truth, the fullness of the Word of God.[23] Knowing the Truth comes through trials of faith by which we are disciplined through suffering under the curse in this life. Sanctification is completed at and through death and does not continue in the next life through any kind of purgatory.

---

23. *John 8:32, 17:17.*

vi. Baptism and Calling

Upon a credible repentance and faith, the Church receives a repentant sinner by baptism in the name of the Father, Son, and Holy Spirit.

Baptism signifies regeneration, and union with God, even as circumcision under the Old Testament, and is similarly applied, in principle.

In light of the work of the Triune God, each man is called to a particular work in the kingdom of God, recognized, at times, by the laying on of hands.

Commitment to discipleship in following Christ is renewed in corporate worship on the Lord's Day and in the Lord's Supper, done in remembrance of him *until he comes.*

vii. Resurrection and Reward

Christ returns when all has been subdued to him. The last enemy, physical death, is removed by the resurrection of all, followed by the rapture of believers who remain alive at the time.[24]

In the Last Judgment, believers, separated from unbelievers, inherit, in Christ, the kingdom of God, the City of God with foundations, built throughout history, according to plan, from the beginning.[25]

Christ is ruling now through the Church in a spiritual war through history to make God known; there is no future millennium in which he will come to rule from any place.

The reward of believers is the kingdom of God now being advanced on earth, not a beatific vision of God apart from the earth being filled with the knowledge of God.

---

24. *1 Corinthians 15:51; John 5:28-29; 1 Thessalonians 4:15-17.*

25. *Matthew 25:31-34.*

8. The Historic Christian Faith[26]

Christ sends the Holy Spirit to lead the Church into all Truth.[27]

In response to challenges, the pastor-teachers, building on the work of the apostles and prophets, after much discussion come to agreement, expressed in creeds and confessions delivered to the Church for the unity of the faith.[28]

This is the holy, catholic and apostolic faith, the basis of the magisterium—the teaching authority of the Church, departure from which divides the body of Christ.

i. The Council of Jerusalem (*ca.* A.D. 51)

The Council of Jerusalem addressed the question of sacrament and salvation: must I be circumcised (or be baptized) to be saved?

Since any sacrament is a sign and not the reality of grace, the Church's answer is no.

The First Council rejected the underlying principle of literalism which confuses sign and reality and both polarizing antinomies of this error: the sign is *not* the reality, nor is it always accompanied by the reality.

ii. The Apostles' Creed (*ca.* A.D. 180)

The Apostles' Creed rejected Greek dualism which denigrated the reality and value of bodily existence in the incarnation, crucifixion, and resurrection of Christ.

Creation is very good and is revelation and the knowledge of God through dominion is man's original and lasting calling.

It therefore implicitly rejects celibacy as a regular calling for the priesthood, monasticism as a higher service, and direct, mystical contemplation as the good.

---

26. *Paper No. 16*; Gangadean, *The Westminster Confession*. See Questions 1-3.

27. *John 16:12-13.*

28. *Ephesians 4; Acts 15.*

iii. The Council of Nicea (*ca.* A.D. 325)

The Council of Nicea affirmed the unity of diversity in the Trinity: One God in three Persons, Father, Son and Holy Spirit; the ultimate reality of personhood; diversity and relationships of persons who are equal in power and glory, and ordered without subordination.

The Word of God (the *Logos*) is the co-eternal Son of God, who makes God known.

iv. The Council of Carthage (*ca.* A.D. 397)

The Council confirmed the canon of the New Testament to be all and only the writings commonly received. The Old Testament canon, affirmed by the Hebrew priesthood to whom it was entrusted, consists of all and only the writings commonly received, and excludes all inter-testamental writings.

The canon of Scripture is the Word of God *written* and is authoritative over all other special revelations of spirits and traditions of men. Scripture itself affirms the authority of the Word of God in its manifold forms in John's prologue, and throughout Scripture, understood by good and necessary consequences.

v. The Council of Chalcedon (*ca.* A.D. 451)

The Council of Chalcedon affirmed the unity of two natures (the Godhead and manhood) united in one person, Jesus Christ, without conversion, composition or confusion.

The infinite (God) includes the finite (man) without contradiction or paradox. The finite cannot include the infinite.

The mysteries of the faith are neither from reason, nor against reason, but in accord with reason, and requires care not to be misrepresented.

vi. The Council of Orange (*ca.* A.D. 529)

The Council of Orange affirmed the fall of man against all degrees of Pelagianism.

Only sovereign grace can restore man from sin and death.

Man is always free (to seek and to understand), but left to himself, no one seeks and no one understands.

vii. The Westminster Confession of Faith (*ca.* A.D. 1648)

The Westminster Confession (and its Catechisms) builds upon earlier confessions of the Reformation in response to the Church of Rome.

Salvation is by faith alone, by grace alone, through Christ alone, based on Scripture alone, for the glory of God alone.

Westminster affirms the earlier creeds prior to the Reformation and represents the current high-water mark of the Historic Christian Faith.

9. From the Reformation to the Present: Challenges from the past continue

i. Divisions in Christendom

Divisions among Christians persist since the Reformation, and have increased.

A false magisterium in Rome has been opposed by no magisterium in current Protestantism.

The true magisterium in the Historic Christian Faith, the work of the Holy Spirit leading the Church into all Truth and which is the holy catholic and apostolic faith, is the source of unity for all who believe.

ii. The Enlightenment

The Enlightenment whose motto was "Dare to Reason" failed to see what was clear to reason, that there must be something eternal, and only some (God) is eternal.

The Enlightenment split into the antinomy of rationalism (Descartes, Spinoza, Leibniz) and empiricism (Locke, Berkeley, Hume).

The synthesis proposed by Kant failed and resulted in varying degrees of idealism (Hegel, Schopenhauer, Bradley).

iii. Secularism

   Secularism affirmed the reality perceived through the senses alone.

   In the name of naturalistic science, it pronounced against the invisible realities grasped by reason alone: essences, the soul/mind, personal immortality, and God (Marx, Darwin, Nietzsche, Freud).

iv. Postmodernism

   Post-Kantian modernism in existentialism (Kierkegaard/Barth, Heidegger, Sartre) and Positivism's verification theory (Russell, Ayer) or Ordinary Language (Wittgenstein, Moore) gave way to postmodern pragmatic skepticism (Dewey, Rorty) and its eventual nihilism (Derrida, Foucault, and cultural Marxism).

The spiritual war (between belief and unbelief) that is age-long and agonizing is currently being expressed in the many dimensions of the culture war today. Response still requires the fullness of redemption through Christ.

10. Response of the Word of God (the *Logos*): Redemption from the sin of unbelief and the death of meaninglessness is by Christ through the Church.

   i. The Church is the body of Christ, the Word of God incarnate, who rules to make God known.

   ii. The Church is the pillar and ground of the Truth. It is the salt of the earth and the light of the world, without which the culture decays and collapses. The first principles of the foundation must be in place for the Church to be the pillar and ground of the Truth.

   iii. The Church is for worship and discipleship.

   We are to worship God in spirit and in Truth.

   Only the Psalms for singing in corporate worship preserve pure and entire the biblical worldview of creation–fall–redemption.

   iv. The Church is to make disciples of all nations, teaching them to observe all things that Christ has commanded.

Only the Church which holds to the Historic Christian Faith has the authority of cumulative insight to make disciples.

v. The Church is to be sanctified by the Truth that it may be one that the world might believe.

The Holy Spirit is sent to lead the Church into all Truth in the Historic Christian Faith, the basis of the unity of the faith.

vi. The Church is to preach the gospel in the fullness of Truth: repent of (root) sin of not seeking and not understanding what is clear, and seek first the kingdom of God in all relations of life by which God is glorified.

vii. The Church has and must affirm the promise that through a spiritual war (between belief and unbelief) which is age-long and agonizing, good will overcome evil.

viii. The Church, by the Word of God (the *Logos*, Truth in its Fullness) is to demolish arguments and every pretension raised up against the knowledge of God and take every thought captive to Jesus Christ.

ix. The Church, under Christ, through the work of dominion, is to fill the earth with the knowledge of God as the waters cover the sea.

x. The Church, under Christ, builds the City of God with foundations, and inherits that kingdom, into which all nations flow, and which lasts forever.

Paper № 44

REASON IN ITSELF[1]

Order in Discourse on Reason

1. It is *self-evident* that we think; we form concepts, judgments, and arguments. Denial of the self-evident is self-referentially absurd.

2. It is self-evident that there are laws of thought: identity (*a* is *a*), non-contradiction (not both *a* and *non-a*, at the same time and in the same respect), excluded middle (either *a* or *non-a*). These laws are the laws of *reason in itself*.

3. Reason as the laws of thought is *natural*, not conventional, the same in all who think.

4. Reason as the laws of thought is the test for meaning; what violates a law of thought cannot be thought—it has no meaning. Meaning is more basic than truth: if there is no meaning there can be no truth. Reason is *authoritative*.

5. Reason is *ontological*; it applies to being as well as thought: there are no square-circles; no being from non-being; no uncaused events. It applies to all being, to the highest being, to God's being—God cannot be both eternal and not eternal, at the same time and in the same respect. Reason (unlike the laws of nature) is an uncreated aspect of eternal being.

---

1. Gangadean, *Philosophical Foundation*, 10-11; Gangadean, *History of Philosophy*, 26-28.

6. Reason as the laws of thought is *transcendental*: it cannot be questioned since it makes questioning possible.

7. *Only* reason as the laws of thought is *self-attesting*; it requires no justification. Attempts to justify reason results from failure to understand reason as the laws of thought. All else requires justification.

8. Reason is used to understand *all* revelation—general (creation and providence) and special (Scripture).

9. Reason is used to understand the *clarity* of general revelation;[2] what is against clarity is against reason and cannot be true.

10. The life of the Logos, the eternal Word of God, is first in all men as light. Reason is the light by which we see/understand what is not visible. Reason is the self-attesting Word of God in all men.

11. Reason is the *ground* of the Principle of Clarity: the basic things (about God and man and good and evil) are clear to reason.

12. Failure to acknowledge what is clear to reason is *inexcusable*; it results in spiritual death—the increasing loss of meaning and morality.

---

2. *Romans 1:20.*

Paper Nº· 45

———

THE LOGOS THESES

In the beginning was the Logos

The Logos is the eternal Word of God who makes God known.

And the Word was made flesh and dwelt among us

1. That the life of the Logos is in all men as light and that light is reason, the light of nature, by which we understand creation and providence.

2. That the basic things about God and man and good and evil are clear to reason; that one has to neglect, avoid, resist, and deny reason to not see what is clear.

3. That the good for a being is according to the nature of that being; that the good for man as a rational being is the knowledge of God through the work of dominion; that through the work of dominion the earth shall be full of the knowledge of God as the waters cover the sea.

4. That the clarity of general revelation is necessary for the inexcusability of unbelief of all of mankind; that there is no inexcusability without clarity.

5. That all fruit sin is due to the root sin of all; that the root sin of all consists in not seeking and not understanding what is clear about God; that meaninglessness, boredom, and guilt/spiritual death is

inherent in not seeking and not understanding; that the gospel calls men everywhere to repent of root sin.

6. That foundation, the first principles of the faith, are necessary for spiritual maturity, fruitfulness, unity, and fullness in Christ; that only in the full work of Christ is there fullness of redemption.

7. That Christ sent the Holy Spirit to lead the Church into all truth, through the pastor-teachers, which truth is cumulatively stated in the Church's confessions and creeds, and is the Historic Christian Faith.

8. That the Historic Christian Faith is the basis of the unity of the faith for all believers; that to depart from this faith is to divide the body of Christ.

9. That the Church is the pillar and ground of the Truth; that the unity of the faith is necessary for making disciples of all nations; that the Church must be one that the world might believe that God has sent Jesus Christ.

10. That the Logos is Truth in its fullness, and alone makes God fully known; that the Logos is in all men as reason, is in the creation as general revelation, is in redemptive history as Scripture, is incarnate only in Jesus Christ, is in the Church, by the Holy Spirit, as the Historic Christian Faith, is restored in all believers by regeneration, and grows in all believers by sanctification.

11. That only the biblical worldview of creation–fall–redemption is consistent with and required by the clarity of general revelation; that only the Bible is the Word of God written.

12. That the Church is for worship and discipleship; that believers everywhere must worship God in spirit and in truth; that only the book of Psalms for singing preserves pure and entire the biblical worldview of creation–fall–redemption; that believers everywhere must seek out a church where they can both worship God in spirit and truth and be discipled to know the Truth.

13. That believers are to demolish arguments and every pretension that is raised up against the knowledge of God and to take every thought captive to the obedience of Jesus Christ.

14. That Christ is now reigning, being seated at the right hand of God; that his reign must continue until all his enemies are subdued to him; that at the coming of Christ there will be a resurrection of all who have died, and a transformation of all who are still alive.

15. That after the resurrection of the dead, there will be the Last Judgment in which all men will be rewarded according to their work; that believers will inherit the kingdom of God that grows through history to its fullness and is the City of God.

Paper № 46

THE LOGOS CURRICULUM
Foundational Principles

1. Man's chief end is to glorify God, in all that by which he makes himself known, in all his works of creation and providence. The lasting joy of eternal life comes from knowing God.[1]

2. Man is made in the image of God, to know God through the work of dominion, to fill the earth with the knowledge of God as the waters cover the sea. In dominion, man is to name the creation, which reveals God's glory, and to rule over it: in the realm of nature—under natural law, through science and technology; in the human realm—under the moral law, through the humanities and culture.[2]

3. The skills required for learning and for the work of dominion include the language arts and mathematics. *The Logos Curriculum* (TLC) recommends specific curricula already available in those areas, along with assistance in implementation.

4. TLC incorporates the classical Trivium: grammar (K-4), dialectic (5-8), and rhetoric (9-12). The Trivium is based on the student's intellectual readiness to progress from fact-based knowledge, to reasoned understanding, to wisdom in applying what has been learned to oneself and to the world.

---

1. *SCQ. 1, 101; WCF 4.1, 5.1; John 17:3.*
2. *Genesis 1; Isaiah 11:9.*

5. TLC is first *preparatory*, for further academic study and for lifelong learning. TLC emphasizes *critical thinking*, applying reason to critically examine assumptions and presuppositions for meaning. TLC understands particular beliefs, values and actions as integral parts of a person's *worldview* built more or less coherently upon a set of basic philosophical assumptions. And last, TLC seeks to appreciate the highest achievements of all of human culture, manifest, in part, in the *Great Books Tradition*.

6. TLC builds upon a scope and sequence of core knowledge needed at each grade level. Layers of enrichment are added to the core. TLC offers layers of assistance for parents and students in implementing the curriculum.

7. The Humanities answers the question "What is Man?" by examining man's view of himself in the varying worldviews and cultures. The Humanities consists of Philosophy and Theology and History and Literature and the Arts and Music. History focuses attention on the age-long and agonizing conflict between good and evil, between truth and falsehood, in every aspect of human existence, in the hope that only what retains meaning will last.

8. The *Logos* Curriculum seeks to recover, to advance, and to secure the highest achievements of civilization built upon the *Logos*, the eternal Word of God, who makes God fully known.[3]

The Logos is in all men as the light of reason. The basic things about God and man and good and evil are clear to reason. Only what builds on the *Logos* can last.[4]

---

3. *John 1:1, 4-5, 10, 11, 14; 16:12-13; 3:3; 8:31-32; 17:17.*

4. *John 1:4; Romans 1:20.*

Paper No. 47

THE UNITY OF THE CHURCH

That They May Be One
That the World May Believe

1. The Church is God's ordained institution for redemption. Redemption assumes the order of creation and man's fall away into sin and death. Sin assumes the objective clarity of general revelation, affirmed in all sources of revelation.[1] Clarity increases subjectively with integrity. The Church consists of those called out by God from their fallen condition of sin and death.

2. The Church is the pillar and ground of the truth: it is the body of Christ, who is the Word of God, the *Logos* incarnate, who makes the truth of God fully known.[2] The Church is the salt of the earth and the light of the world.[3] If the Church fails, the world fails.

3. There is division in the Church due to its manifold apostasy, resulting in decay and collapse in the culture. The Church once was the head of the culture; now it is the tail, in captivity to the world. In this spiritual war, between belief and unbelief, unbelief once again has the upper hand, worldwide.

---

1. *Romans 1:20.*

2. *1 Timothy 3:15; 1 Corinthians 12:27; John 1:14.*

3. *Matthew 5:13-14.*

4. The Church is to *preserve* the unity of the Spirit; *attain* to the unity of the faith; and *operate* in the functional unity of the body of Christ as each part does its work.[4]

5. The good/the goal, is the source of unity, in all and for all:

   i. from general revelation: the good for a being is according to the nature of that being; the good for man as a rational being is the use of reason to the fullest; reason is used to grasp the nature of things; the nature of things created reveal the nature of God; therefore, the good for man is the knowledge of God.

   ii. from special revelation: man is made in the image of God, to know God, through the work of dominion; eternal life *is* knowing God.[5]

   iii. from Historic Christianity: man's chief end is to glorify God, in all that by which he makes himself known, in all his works of creation and providence.[6]

6. The moral law, summed up in the Ten Commandments, is the means to the good. It is objectively clear to all, being written on the hearts of all men.[7] This moral law is both central and basic.

7. Common Ground is the most basic source of unity as the prerequisite for all thought and discourse. If we can agree on the more basic, we will agree on the less basic. Common Ground consists of *reason* as the laws of thought in all; *integrity* as a concern for consistency (logical *and* existential); *Rational Presuppositionalism* as the most consistent application of critical thinking, and consequently, the *Principle of Clarity*: the basic things about God and man and good and evil are clear to reason.

8. Scripture is clear in affirming the biblical worldview in the narrative of creation–fall–redemption in Genesis 1–3 as foundational to all

---

4. *Ephesians 4:3, 13, 16.*

5. *Genesis 1:26; John 17:3.*

6. *SCQ. 1, 101; WCF 4.1, 5.1.*

7. *Romans 2:14-15; Deuteronomy 30:11-14.*

of Scripture. This foundation is also affirmed theologically in Scripture, summed up in the Seven Pillars of the faith.[8]

9. The Holy Spirit leads the Church into all truth for the unity of the faith.[9] The Historic Christian Faith is progressively summed up in the Church's creeds from its councils. To depart from Historic Christianity is to depart from the holy catholic and apostolic faith, and is to divide the body of Christ. There are seven major, cumulative councils and creeds from Jerusalem (A.D. 51) to Westminster (1648).

10. Church discipline is necessary for discipleship by which we come to understand and to obey the Truth. The Word of God/the *Logos* is Truth in its fullness.[10] The *Logos* is the eternal word of God who makes God known. The *Logos* is in all men as the light of reason; is in the creation as general revelation; is in redemptive history as Scripture; is incarnate in Jesus Christ; is in Church history as the Historic Christian Faith summed up in its creeds. It gives life to each believer by regeneration; and this life grows in each believer by sanctification through deepening understanding of the truth.[11]

11. The fear of the Lord (which is to see the connection between *root* sin and *spiritual* death, and between the curse—consummated in physical death—and the promise) is the beginning of wisdom. The completion of wisdom is through the love of God (which is to seek the good—the knowledge of God through the work of dominion, in order to fill the earth with the knowledge of God as the waters cover the sea[12]).

12. The unity of the Church is necessary to disciple all nations, to complete the work of dominion, to subdue all things to Christ, to take all thoughts captive to Christ, for Christ to return, for us to inherit the kingdom of God, and to enjoy the fullness of God.

13. Recovery begins with preaching the gospel *in its fullness*: repent; the kingdom of heaven is at hand.

---

8. *Romans 1:20; Hebrews 6:1-2; Paper No. 36 and 37.*

9. *John 16:13; Acts 15; Ephesians 4:11-13.*

10. *John 8:31-32; 17:17.*

11. *John 1:1, 4, 10, 11, 14, 16:13, 3:3, 17:17.*

12. *Isaiah 11:9.*

———

REASON AND
THE WORD OF GOD
An Apologetic for Reason

1. It is self-evident that we think: we form concepts, judgments, and arguments: a word or term expresses a concept; judgments only are either true or false; arguments for a judgment are either sound or unsound.

2. It is self-evident that there are laws of thought: the law of identity (*a* is *a*); the law of non-contradiction (not both *a* and *non-a*, at the same time and in the same respect); the law of excluded middle (either *a* or *non-a*).

   Reason in itself is the laws of thought.

   Reason in its use is formative, critical, interpretative, and constructive.

   Reason *in us* is natural, ontological, transcendental, and fundamental.

3. Reason as the laws of thought is the test for meaning. If a law of thought is violated, there is no *logical* meaning.

   Meaning is more basic than truth; if there is no meaning, there can be no truth.

   If there is no *logical* meaning, there can be no *existential* meaning.

4. Reason is ontological; it applies to being as well as thought: there are no square-circles; no being from non-being; no uncaused events.

Reason applies to all being, the highest being, God's being (God is not both eternal and not eternal, at the same time and in the same respect).

Reason is an aspect of being and is as eternal as the highest being.

5. Reason as the laws of thought is self-attesting; it cannot be questioned but makes questioning possible.

Reason is transcendental and it is therefore authoritative.

6. Only reason in itself as the laws of thought is self-attesting.

Nothing else (neither testimony, nor any person, nor common sense, nor intuition, nor empiricism—all knowledge is from sense experience, nor tradition) is self-attesting.

No experience is meaningful without interpretation; and every interpretation must be tested for meaning by reason.

Coherence, by good and necessary consequences, is the test for meaning and is more basic than correspondence (by naïve realism) as the test for truth.

7. The *Logos* is the eternal Word of God who makes God fully known.[1]

The Word of God comes *to* man and *into* man in several ways (explained throughout the gospel of John). Jesus Christ is the *Logos* incarnate.

The Holy Spirit is sent by Christ to lead the Church into all truth, through the work of the pastor-teachers, in response to challenges, coming to agreement after much discussion, summed up in its creeds, which is the Historic Christian Faith.[2]

8. The life of the *Logos* is in all men as light. Man is created by God, in his own image, to know God.

---

1. *John 1:1-18.*
2. *John 16:13; Acts 15, Ephesians 4:10-16.*

The light by which we see/understand the invisible things about God is the light of reason.

The light of reason is in all men as the light of nature.[3]

9. Reason is the beginning of Common Ground (the necessary conditions for thought and discourse).

Common Ground consists of reason, integrity (as a concern for consistency in thought and life), critical thinking (examining assumptions for meaning), all of which lead to the *Principle of Clarity*: some things are clear; the basic things are clear; the basic things (about God and man and good and evil) are clear to reason.

If we know what is clear, we can show what is clear.

Common Ground is not neutral ground. One has to neglect, avoid, resist, and deny reason to avoid what is clear about God. The darkness of unbelief cannot withstand the light of reason.[4]

Failure to seek and understand what is clear about God is sin. Sin brings spiritual death—meaninglessness, boredom, and guilt without end.

One must repent of sin in coming to Christ, the Word of God incarnate.

10. Reason is the self-attesting form of the Word of God in all men.

Man, in himself, is now fallen; he fails to use reason self-critically or fully. This failure is in man, not in reason. Reason in itself is not and cannot be fallen.

Man is restored to the life of reason by regeneration, and sanctified through trials of faith leading to deeper understanding.

By reason, man is to demolish arguments and every pretension which exalts itself against the knowledge of God and take every thought captive to the obedience of Christ and silence what opposes the Word of God.[5]

---

3. *Psalm 8:5; John 1:4; Romans 1:20; WCF 1.1.*

4. *John 1:5.*

5. *2 Corinthians 10:4-5.*

Paper № 49

_____

ESCHATOLOGY
Summary and Response to FAQ

1. The SABBATH: the first, most basic and lasting eschatological declaration: as God completed his work of creation and rested, man,
   the image of God, *will* complete his work of dominion *and* rest. As
   creation is revelation, so dominion brings knowledge of this revelation: the *earth* shall be full of the knowledge of the LORD as the
   waters cover the sea.[1]

2. The PROMISE of redemption: the curse as call back, given *with* the
   promise, assumes creation and fall, and restoration to and through
   a deepened revelation. Through a spiritual war which is age-long
   and agonizing, good will overcome evil: Christ (the seed of the
   woman in the place of Adam) will undo, as the Lamb of God, what
   Adam did, and do what Adam failed to do—through his body, the
   Church, Christ will crush the head of the serpent in subduing all
   things to himself.[2]

3. NOAH: he gives *rest* as he preserves the pre-flood work of dominion, through universal apostasy and universal judgment, with God's
   promise after the flood of "never again."

_____

1. *Isaiah 11:9.*

2. *Genesis 3:15.*

4. ABRAHAM: the promise is renewed and deepened: through Abraham's seed all the families of the earth shall be blessed; seen in the offering up of Isaac.[3]

5. MOSES: the theology of the Law—moral, civil and ceremonial; through the Law the kingdom grows; through the priesthood the people are sanctified: daily—by Word, worship and witness; by learning to distinguish clean and unclean, we learn the blessings and curses of our response to the precepts of holiness; through the holy days we learn God's plan of redemption.

6. The PSALMS: in the theology of the Psalms, at every level of the spiritual war which is age-long and agonizing, good overcomes evil: in the believer, in the Church and in the world—in every nation, kindred, tribe, and tongue.

7. The PROPHETS: in each prophet, there is a call to repentance of sin, both root sin of not seeking and understanding what is clear about God and all fruit sin; and with each judgment of the curse, the promise of redemption through Christ is reaffirmed and further clarified.

8. CHRIST: the king comes, in fulfillment of the promises given in Scripture, to inaugurate the kingdom, teaching through miracles, parables, prayer, sacraments, and the Great Commission that he will rule by his Spirit, through his people, until he returns to consummate the kingdom.

9. PAUL: in the theology of the hope of the resurrection: there is only *one* general resurrection of the dead; this resurrection comes only *after* Christ completes his rule of subduing all things; only *after* this resurrection comes the rapture.[4]

10. JOHN: the eschatology of the *Book of Revelation* is given in seven visions of Christ now ruling, from heaven, through the spiritual war, by the curse *and* the promise (given by proclamation of the gospel), to subdue all things unto himself, after which he returns to consummate the kingdom.

---

3. *Genesis 12:3; Genesis 22:1-14; John 8:56.*
4. *John 5:28-29; 1 Corinthians 15:25; 1 Thessalonians 4:15-18.*

RESPONSE TO FAQ

FAQs arise from the deficiencies of a literalist hermeneutic; response is based on a contextual hermeneutic: the less basic understood in light of the more basic.

1. **Antichrist:** there are many, not one, antichrist; anyone who denies that Jesus is the Christ (the Son of God incarnate) is antichrist.[5] Antichrist is *not* the man of sin who exalts himself as god in the Temple of God in Jerusalem, still standing in A.D. 70.[6]

2. **The Mark of the Beast—666:** used in imitation of God's law, which was to be placed as a reminder on the forehead and on the hand of believers; man's law, apart from and against God's law, is put where God's law is meant to be.[7]

3. **The Harlot:** represents the values of the economic system based on the corrupt desires of this world/kingdom of darkness, put in place of what is of lasting value in the kingdom of God.

4. **The False Prophet:** all non-Christian teaching in education and in its outworking in every form of propaganda, through all of media, journalism and the arts; based on a worldview without God and denial of reason as the Word of God, the light of nature in all men.

5. **Armageddon:** a *spiritual* war, fought throughout this age with the Word of God (the sword coming out of the mouth) by Christ and the Church (his army) against the world of unbelievers, small and great, ending in victory of belief/truth over unbelief.[8]

6. **The Millennium:** the period of the rule of Christ from his first to his second coming; all who take part in the first (spiritual) resurrection by being born again, the second (spiritual) death has no power over them; this is true of all believers throughout this age. After this millennial age, the devil is cast out, to be tormented forever.[9]

---

5. *1 John 4:4; 2 John 7.*

6. *2 Thessalonians 2:3-4.*

7. *Deuteronomy 6:1-9.*

8. *Revelation 19:11-21.*

9. *Revelation 20.*

7. **The Tribulation and the Coming of Christ:** tribulation arises as the curse increases with sin. The greatest tribulation came on the generation that rejected Christ, in the destruction of the Temple in A.D. 70 and the second diaspora.[10] Christ warned of that judgment, coming in season, yet suddenly. No one knew the day or the hour, as travail comes on a woman in childbirth. Those who took heed escaped; those left behind suffered much.

8. **The Rapture:** refers only to the change in believers remaining alive on earth at the time of Christ's return. Immediately after the resurrection of all the dead,[11] the bodies of believers will be changed in a moment, from mortal to immortal, and they will be caught up to meet Christ in the air.[12]

9. **The Second Coming:** As the old self is renewed by rebirth, and as our present bodies are renewed by resurrection, so the present heaven and earth is renewed by the removal of all evil.[13] After the resurrection at the return of Christ, all are judged in the Last Judgment. Believers then inherit the kingdom of God, in which unbelievers have no part, but continue in spiritual death: meaninglessness, boredom, and guilt, without end.

10. **The Historic Christian Faith:** Man's chief end is to glorify God and to enjoy him forever.[14] We are to glorify God in all that by which he makes himself known.[15] God makes himself known in all his works of creation and providence.[16] Implicitly, the outcome is the earth filled with the knowledge of the LORD as the waters cover the sea.[17]

---

10. *Matthew 24:21, 34.*

11. *John 5:28-29.*

12. *1 Thessalonians 4:15-18.*

13. *2 Peter 3:10-13; Revelation 21:1-5.*

14. *Shorter Catechism Question 1.*

15. *SCQ. 101.*

16. *Westminster Confession of Faith 4.1 and 5.1.*

17. *Isaiah 11:9.*

Paper № 50

———

COMMON GROUND

PART I

Reason

Common Ground in its most basic sense is the set of conditions necessary for thought and discourse.

Common Ground consists of Reason (objectively), Integrity (subjectively), and Rational Presuppositionalism (methodologically), all of which lead to the Principle of Clarity, necessary for inexcusability: some things are clear; the basic things are clear; the basic things, about God and man and good and evil, are clear to reason.

Reason

1. It is self-evident that we think: we form concepts, judgments, and arguments, the forms of all thought; a concept is expressed by a word or term, which assumes rationality; the rational use is not the non-cognitive use of words; the cognitive is most basic.

2. It is self-evident that there are laws of thought: identity (*a* is *a*), non-contradiction (not both *a* and *non-a*, at the same time and in the same respect), and excluded middle (either *a* or *non-a*); the laws of thought are properly called the laws of reason or reason-in-itself.

3. Reason as the laws of thought is the test of meaning: if a law of reason is violated, then there is no cognitive meaning (no distinction

between *a and non-a*); if there is no cognitive meaning, then truth, in any form, is not possible.

4. Reason is ontological—it applies to being as well as to thought: there are no square-circles, no being from non-being, no uncaused events; it applies to all being, to the highest being, to God's being; since God's being is eternal, reason-in-itself is eternal.

5. Reason in man is natural: it is the same in all men as the light of nature; this light is that by which we see, with the mind, that is, understand; both the book of Nature/general revelation and the book of Scripture/special revelation are clear to reason and can be understood by all who seek.

6. Reason is man's essence as rational animal: reason distinguishes man from animals; his essence is fundamental to all other aspects of his being; reason in man cannot be denied without sinking into meaninglessness. The good for man must therefore be rational, not mystical.

7. Reason in man is transcendental—authoritative: it cannot be questioned but makes questioning possible; reason as the laws of thought is self-attesting; only reason is self-attesting.

8. Reason is the first form of the Word of God that comes to man: the life of the *Logos*, the eternal Word of God, is in all men, made in the image of God, as the self-attesting light of reason. The Word of God in its fullness is Truth in its fullness and makes God fully known.[1]

---

1. *John 1:1-18; 17:17.*

Paper № 51

COMMON GROUND

PART II

Integrity

Integrity is a concern for consistency, both logical and existential.

Man is a natural unity; we should act according to our nature and not be divided.

We are more or less conscious and consistent in our basic beliefs. We should be more conscious and consistent. We should have integrity, through self-examination.

1. All persons implicitly profess to seek to know. If we had integrity, we would seek and understand what is clear. If we cannot show what is clear, then we do not know what is clear. Therefore, we lack integrity.

   We make our most explicit commitments through vows. If we had integrity, we would keep our vows. We often come short in keeping our vows. Therefore, we often lack integrity.

2. If our thoughts are not logically consistent at the basic level, then they are incoherent and absurd; we cannot think what is absurd.

If our lives are not existentially consistent with basic things we profess, then our lives are self-referentially absurd; we cannot live what is absurd.

3. Integrity is necessary and sufficient for knowledge of basic things. One has to neglect, avoid, resist, and deny reason to avoid what is clear about God.

To place the psychological and the practical above, apart from or against the rational concern for truth is to first dehumanize oneself and, in turn, others. The unexamined life is less than human life. It is a disintegration downward toward the anti-human.

Examples: Man that is in honor without understanding is like the beasts that perish.[1] Man does not live by bread alone.[2] The birds of the air have nests, but not the Son of man.[3] My mother and my brothers are those who hear the word of God and do it.[4] Denial of reason can descend to the Luciferian level.

Truth is not reducible to beauty (Keats), or to power (Pilate), or to comfort (traditionalism), or to anything else.

4. Lack of integrity is hypocrisy, which requires self-deception and self-justification (the third degree of moral evil).

Suffering under natural evil (the curse of toil and strife, and old age, sickness, and death) is necessary to restrain, recall from, and remove moral evil, in every degree.

5. Clarity increases with integrity. Stupor increases with hypocrisy.

The Church's doors are open to repentant sinners, but not to hypocrites.

Repentance must begin with the root sin of not seeking and understanding what is clear about God and man and good and evil.

Lack of Church discipline to prevent hypocrisy destroys the Church.

---

1. *Psalm 49.*
2. *Matthew 4:4.*
3. *Matthew 8:20.*
4. *Luke 8:21.*

6. Lack of integrity (hypocrisy) is inexcusable; it is to take God's name (his self-revelation) in vain.[5]

Disregard of what is clear is not held guiltless; the foolish heart becomes further darkened. From the one who has not will be taken what he has.

7. Discipline is necessary for integrity, to seek *first* the kingdom of God.

The Church is for worship and discipleship; it is the pillar and ground of the Truth. It is the salt of the earth and the light of the world.[6]

The Church is to make disciples of all nations, to worship God in spirit and in truth.

The *Logos*, the eternal word of God *is* Truth in its fullness. We are sanctified through knowing the Truth. God's Word is Truth.[7]

8. Discipleship brings us to know and to practice the truth.

"If you continue in my word then you are my disciples indeed, and you shall know the truth and the truth shall make you free."[8]

Discipleship requires us to deny ourselves, take up our cross daily and follow Christ.[9]

Discipline requires us to take time out to stop and think: first by self-restraint; then, when necessary, by restraint through church oversight; and always, by the restraint through suffering under the curse of natural evil.

---

5. *Matthew 23; Exodus 20:7.*

6. *Matthew 5:13-14.*

7. *John 1:1-18; 17:17.*

8. *John 8:31-32.*

9. *Luke 9:23.*

Paper № 52

COMMON GROUND

PART III

Rational Presuppositionalism

1. Rational Presuppositionalism (RP) uses reason as the laws of thought to test our basic beliefs (presuppositions) for meaning, hence the name RP.

   RP is a more conscious and consistent form of critical thinking, the method used in philosophy that can settle longstanding disputes.

2. Thinking by nature is presuppositional: we must think of the less basic in light of the more basic (the finite—man in light of the infinite—God).

   If we agree on the more basic, we can and will agree on the less basic.

3. Reason as the laws of thought is used to understand the meaning of both general revelation (creation and providence) and special revelation (Scripture). Reason as the laws of thought is *most* basic; as the test for meaning, reason is more basic than meaning, and meaning is more basic than truth. *Only* reason, as the laws of thought, is self-attesting.

4. In the order of thought, concept comes before judgment, which comes before argument. On the level of concept, we must think of the finite and temporal in light of the infinite and the eternal (not the infinite in light of the finite, or the finite in light of the finite).

On the level of judgment (which is true *or* false), we must think of truth in light of meaning. On the level of argument, we must think of conclusion in light of premises.

5. Philosophical foundation (PF) from general revelation (GR) comes before theological foundation (TF) from Scripture (special revelation—SR). If there is no clear general revelation, there can be no inexcusability and no need for redemption or for Scripture as redemptive revelation (RR). If basic things are clear to reason (epistemology), then we can know the nature of God and man (metaphysics), from which we can know good and evil (ethics).

6. PF *requires* RR; RR *assumes* clarity and inexcusability from PF. RR must be consistent with PF. RR in *Genesis* must affirm creation, in light of which the Fall must be understood, and, in light of creation and the Fall, redemption must be understood. In RR, the later (*Revelation*) must be understood in light of the earlier (worldview of *Genesis*). The understanding of RR in relation to GR progresses in history and this historically cumulative insight is summed up in the creeds and confessions of Historic Christianity (HC).

7. In hermeneutics, RP requires contextualism vs. literalism and allegoricalism. Contextualism requires several ordered layers for interpretation: first, clear GR; second, the biblical worldview of creation–fall–redemption; third, the historical context of RR; fourth, the book in historical context; then chapter; then verse; then word. Literalism begins with *word*. Allegoricalism begins with a *denial of clear GR*. RP is opposed to *all* forms of empiricism, rationalism, fideism, and skepticism about what is basic.

8. Man is the image of God, a triune personality; he is to love God with his whole heart: mind, soul, and strength. Reason in man is fundamental, that is, essential: it is basic to other aspects of his being, and, as light, is irresistible.[1] Thoughts precede feeling and will; the rational precedes the psychological and the practical. The prophetic precedes the priestly and the kingly; knowledge precedes holiness and righteousness. Unity comes from giving heed to the triune order in man; divisions come from neglect or denial of this triune order.

---

1. *John 1:4-5.*

Paper № 53

COMMON GROUND

PART IV

The Principle of Clarity

Common Ground (CG) in Reason, Integrity, and Rational Presuppositionalism leads to the Principle of Clarity (PC).

PC states that some things are clear; the basic things are clear; the basic things (about God and man and good and evil) are clear to reason.

1. Some things are clear.

  i. If nothing were clear, then no distinction (*a* and *non-a*, being and non-being, true and false, good and evil, more and less) would be clear.

  ii. Without clarity, all distinctions of reason lose their meaning, logically and existentially. Words express concepts and concepts grasp essence. Words without concepts are empty; concepts without essence are blind. From the ancient to the postmodern, sophistry is recurrent.

  iii. One has to deny reason as the laws of thought to fail to see what is clear to reason. Denial of reason is the last step which culminates a long process that neglects, avoids, resists, and then finally denies reason, contrary to human nature as rational.

iv. The denial of reason itself is radical doubt and results necessarily in meaninglessness or nihilism, that is, spiritual death, the increasing loss of *all* meaning.

v. Radical doubt is a universal solvent that denies even the *possibility* of thought. The increasing loss of all meaning, in every word and thought, is a bottomless pit.

vi. Radical doubt is self-referentially-absurd, a disregard for integrity, which ends the possibility of all discourse. It reduces itself to silence.

vii. Radical doubt, the denial of reason itself—in whatever form it takes—is toxic, sinking to the level of demonic doubt; its harmfulness must be recognized as such and avoided by all.

viii. The light of reason shines in the darkness of unbelief and the darkness cannot overcome it or resist it.[1] Some things *are* clear.

2. The basic things are clear.

i. Thinking is presuppositional: we think of the less basic in light of the more basic (see earlier explanation of Rational Presuppositionalism).

ii. If there is agreement on the more basic, there will be agreement on the less basic, in a step-by-step process.

iii. To resolve a dispute logically, it is *necessary* to get to the more basic.

iv. To resolve *all* disputes, it is necessary to get to the *most* basic level: to the philosophical, theological and historical foundations; to the logically most basic—reason, as the self-attesting Word of God; and to the existentially most basic—one's view of good and evil.

v. If the more basic were not clear, then nothing would be clear. But some things *are* clear (from 1 above). Therefore, *basic* things are clear.

---

1. *John 1:5.*

vi. No experience is meaningful without interpretation (vs. all forms of empiricism).

vii. All experience is interpreted in light of one's set of basic beliefs. There are just *two* (contradictory) sets of basic beliefs.

viii. Basic beliefs must be tested for meaning by the critical use of reason. It is clear to reason that only one set of basic beliefs can be and *is* coherent.

3. The basic things (about God and man and good and evil) are clear to reason.

i. The basic things are about the most basic questions we can ask: how do I know? (epistemology); what is real? (metaphysics); and, what ought I to do, or, what is good and evil? (ethics).

ii. The basic things are about the basic/foundational beliefs, which begin with the cornerstone of epistemology, and develop into one's overall worldview that expresses itself in culture.

iii. The basic things about God and man (metaphysics) and good and evil (ethics) are clear to reason (epistemology). While epistemology is logically most basic, ethics is existentially most basic. Ethics is derived from the nature of things: good for a being is according to the nature of that being, which nature is metaphysically most basic.

iv. If there is no clear general revelation (cGR), then there is no possibility of inexcusability (for man as a rational being), no actuality of sin and death, no necessity for redemption (the focus of the Christian faith), or for a redeemer (Christ), or for redemptive revelation (Scripture)—since all words lose their meaning.

v. Redemptive revelation (RR) assumes cGR[2] and cGR requires RR through the answer to the problem of evil (POE).

a. The POE is the most common obstacle logically and existentially to belief in God.

---

2. *Romans 1:20.*

b. Due to the noetic effect of sin/evil, evil is most commonly misunderstood.

c. Evil (moral and natural), when understood is, ironically, the strongest reason *for* theism (belief in creation *and* redemption) vs. deism (belief in creation *without* redemption).

vi. Both general and special revelation become clear subjectively if and only if all the elements of Common Ground are in place existentially.

vii. Foundation begins existentially if and only if the cornerstone of good and evil are seen as clear to reason. Reason as the laws of thought is the light of the *Logos* in all men,[3] and is understood as distinct from *all* forms of empiricism (tradition/testimony, common sense, intuition, science). Understanding is an act of reason which arises *only* by diligently seeking, *not* spontaneously by intuition. *All* are called to seek diligently.[4]

viii. If the cornerstone is in place from general revelation, Scripture, and the historically cumulative insights of Christianity, then we can go on, through all the steps, from foundation to fullness.[5]

---

3. *John 1:4.*

4. *Hebrews 11:6; Romans 3:10-11.*

5. *Isaiah 11:9.*

Paper №· 54

_____

FROM FOUNDATION
TO FULLNESS

*A Biblical Worldview for Maturity,
Fruitfulness, Unity, and Fullness*

1. **Common Ground:** the set of conditions necessary for thought and discourse.

    i. Reason in itself is the laws of thought; in its use it is formative, critical, interpretive, and constructive; in us it is natural, ontological, transcendental and fundamental.

    ii. Integrity is a concern for consistency—logical and existential; it is necessary and sufficient for knowing clear general revelation.

    iii. Rational Presuppositionalism tests basic beliefs (presuppositions) by reason for meaning; if we *can* agree on what is more basic, we *will* agree on what is less basic.

    iv. The Principle of Clarity affirms: some things are clear; the basic things are clear; the basic things (about God and man and good and evil) are clear to reason.

2. There Must Be Something Eternal: the ontological argument argues from logos (reason) to ontos (being).[1]

    i. "Eternal" is our most basic concept. What is eternal is minimally without beginning and without end in time, or, is outside of time.

    ii. There are four propositions on the eternal: A: all is eternal; E: none is eternal; I: some is eternal; and O: some is not eternal. I and E, and A and O, are contradictories.[2]

    iii. None is eternal implies all came into being, from non-being, which is impossible; therefore, its contradictory *some* is eternal *must* be true.

    iv. No being from non-being is clear to reason, by which we distinguish being and non-being. This is not yet proof that *only some* is eternal.

3. Only Some Is Eternal: what is eternal brought into existence (created *ex nihilo*) what is not eternal.[3]

    i. Matter exists vs. ordinary idealism.

    ii. Matter is not eternal (the material world is not self-maintaining).

    iii. The soul exists (the mind is *not* the brain; and, there is *not* one mind only).

    iv. The soul is not eternal (it grows in time).

4. Special Creation

    i. Man is created a body/soul unity, a rational animal, made in the image of God, with the capacity to know God by understanding oneself and the creation.

    ii. The moral law is written on the heart of man (structured into human nature).

---

1. Gangadean, *Philosophical Foundation*, 61-65; Gangadean, *History of Philosophy*, 40-44.

2. See *Paper No. 75* for the relation of these propositions on the square of opposition.

3. Gangadean, *Philosophical Foundation*, 71-161; Gangadean, *History of Philosophy*, 47-58; Gangadean, *The Westminster Catechisms*. See LCQ. 2; *Paper No. 3* and *93*.

iii. Good for a being is according to its nature; evil is what is contrary to its nature.

iv. Good for man as a rational being is the knowledge of God through the work of dominion, which is corporate, cumulative, and communal.

5. The Problem of Evil[4]

i. If God is all good and all powerful why is there evil?

Moral evil is to neglect, avoid, resist, and deny reason regarding what is clear about God.

Natural evil is suffering from circumstance: toil and strife, and old age, sickness, and physical death, intensifying through history from time to time.

If God is all powerful, he *could* create a world without natural evil; if God is all good, he *would* create a world without natural evil; if he could and would, then he *must* have; and if he must have, then he *did*.

ii. Moral evil is *not* original; it is permitted in order to deepen the revelation of God's nature unfolding in providence.

iii. Natural evil is *not* original; it is imposed, to restrain, recall from, and remove moral evil.

iv. Natural evil is not punishment, which is inherent, but a *call back* from moral evil.

6. The Necessity for Redemptive Revelation[5]

i. Natural evil, understood from general revelation as a call back (mercy), requires special (redemptive) revelation to show how God can be both just and merciful to man in moral evil.

---

4. Gangadean, *Philosophical Foundation*, 145-161.

5. Gangadean, *The Westminster Confession*. See Questions 5-10; Gangadean, *The Westminster Catechisms*. See LCQ. 4-7; *Paper No. 11* and *12*.

ii. Redemptive revelation must be consistent with what is clear from general revelation (creation–fall–redemption); if it is not consistent, then it is not special revelation.

iii. Redemptive revelation must show how mercy does not set aside but satisfies divine justice.

iv. Only God, who is *both* just and merciful, can show how *his* mercy satisfies *his* justice.

7. Only Genesis Is Special Revelation[6]

i. Only Genesis affirms creation–fall–redemption; no other source does.

ii. Only Genesis shows how God is just and merciful in the curse and promise.

iii. The seed of the woman (Christ) in the place of Adam, is to undo what Adam did—through vicarious atonement, signified in the coats of skin, and do what Adam failed to do—rule to make God known, signified by crushing the head of the serpent.

iv. Only Genesis, and what builds on creation–fall–redemption, qualifies as the Word of God in scripture or special/redemptive revelation.

8. Christ Has Come

i. The curse and promise is unfolded in all of Scripture, awaiting fulfillment in Christ.

ii. Christ came in fulfillment of and to fulfill all of Scripture.

iii. By his incarnation, obedience, crucifixion, and resurrection, Christ accomplished redemption, according to Scripture.

iv. Christ, given all authority, sent the Spirit, at Pentecost, to apply redemption, by making disciples of all nations, currently in progress.

---

6. Gangadean, *The Westminster Confession*. See Question 6.

9. The Historic Christian Faith

   i. The Spirit guides the Church into all truth.[7] In response to challenges, the Church leaders (pastor-teachers), after much discussion in its councils, come to agreement, summed up in its creeds, for the unity of the faith.[8]

  ii. There have been seven major councils and creeds so far in Church history:

    a. The Council of Jerusalem (*ca.* A.D. 51) answered a Hebraic literalist view of the sacraments.

    b. The Apostles' Creed (*ca.* 180) answered the worldview of Greek dualism.

    c. Nicea (325) answered misunderstandings of the Trinity and of unity of diversity.

    d. Carthage (*ca.* 397) affirmed the canon of the New Testament. The Old Testament canon, before Christ, was affirmed by the Jews.

    e. Chalcedon (451) answered misunderstanding of Christ as fully God and fully man, having two whole natures, in unity, without conversion, composition or confusion.

    f. Orange (529) affirmed the fall of man and the sovereignty of God's grace in redemption, against all degrees of Pelagianism.

    g. Westminster (1648) summed up more consciously and consistently the earlier creeds of the Reformation, building upon the Historic Christian Faith of the earlier creeds through Orange.

 iii. What disregards and fails to build on the Historic Christian Faith have divided the Church and have brought widespread apostasy.

 iv. Modern skepticism and secularism vs. the Church's fideism and otherworldliness, resulted in postmodern multicultural pluralism and culture wars, leading to cultural decay, nearing collapse.

---

7. *John 16:12-13.*

8. *Acts 15, Ephesians 4.*

The Church must respond. The foundation must be laid more deeply, on solid rock.

10. Complete the Work![9]

i. From Genesis to Revelation, the promise of redemption stands firm. There will be a spiritual war, age-long and agonizing, in which good *will* overcome evil.[10] Revelation, in its set of seven visions, each of the *entire* Church age, affirms that good *will* overcome evil.[11]

ii. Based on the cornerstone of clarity and inexcusability,[12] the Church is to demolish arguments and *every* pretension raised up against the knowledge of God.[13] Christ, out of whose mouth goes a sharp sword, leads the Church, united in faith, in this *spiritual* war.[14]

iii. The work of dominion, given in the Garden of Eden, *will* be *completed*, signified in the Sabbath.[15] All believers who have died await the *completion* of the City of God by believers yet to come.[16]

iv. Man's chief end is to glorify God and to enjoy him forever, in all that by which he makes himself known, in all his works of creation and providence.[17] The outcome of glorifying God is the *earth* shall be *full* of the knowledge of the Lord as the waters cover the sea.[18]

---

9. Gangadean, *The Westminster Catechisms*. See Appendix 4; *Paper No. 104.*

10. *Genesis 3:15.*

11. *Revelation, Chapters 6-20.*

12. *Romans 1:20.*

13. *2 Corinthians 10:4-5.*

14. *Revelation 19:11-21.*

15. *Genesis 1:24–2:3.*

16. *Hebrews 11:39-40.*

17. *SCQ. 1, 101; WCF 4.1, 5.1.*

18. *Isaiah 11:9.*

Paper No· 55

Z ARGUMENTS

Against Beliefs that Divide and Lead to Apostasy and Cultural Decay

1. Heaven[1]

    i. Man's chief end is to glorify God and to enjoy him forever, in all that by which he makes himself known, in all his works of creation and providence.[2]

    ii. The outcome of glorifying God is the *earth* filled with the knowledge of the Lord as the waters cover the sea.[3]

    iii. Man's chief end (the good, eternal life) therefore is *not* a beatific vision of God in heaven. There is no direct knowledge of God apart from creation, and no knowledge of creation apart from the work of dominion.[4]

2. Hell[5]

    i. Man is created a body/soul unity. There are, therefore, two kinds of death and two kinds of resurrection, physical and spiritual.[6]

---

1. *Paper No. 106* and *116*.

2. *SCQ. 1, 101; WCF 4.1, 5.1.*

3. *Isaiah 11:9.*

4. *Genesis 1:26-28.*

5. Gangadean, *Philosophical Foundation*, 195-197.

6. *Genesis 2:7; John 11:25-26; 5:25, 28-29.*

The first death is physical; the second, and lasting, is spiritual. The first resurrection is spiritual; the second is physical.[7]

ii. The wages of sin is *spiritual* death, present and inherent in sin, not future and imposed.[8] In a person, it is meaninglessness, boredom, and guilt; in a relation, it is alienation; in a culture, it is decay and collapse; in general, it is destruction (according to its kind).

iii. The lake of fire *is* the second death, present and inherent in sin. There is, therefore, no literal lake of fire which is future and imposed. What *is* future is full manifestation of God's glory in the Last Judgment and final separation of good and evil.[9]

3. Faith

i. Faith is the substance of things hoped for, the evidence of things not seen.[10]

ii. By faith we understand (we *see* the invisible, through the use of reason); faith grows as understanding grows; faith is tested as understanding is tested.

iii. Faith therefore is *not* fideism—belief without proof based on understanding.

4. Reason

i. In itself, reason is the laws of thought: identity, non-contradiction, and excluded middle. Reason in itself is not reason in its use, *or* lack of use, *or* misuse.

ii. As the laws of thought, reason is transcendental (makes thought possible), authoritative (the test for meaning), and self-attesting (irrepressible and irresistible).[11]

---

7. *Revelation 20:6.*

8. *Genesis 2:17; Ephesians 2:1.*

9. *Revelation 19:20; 20:6, 10, 14-15; 21:8.*

10. *Hebrews 11:1-3.*

11. *John 1:4-5.*

iii. Reason is most basic in knowing any and all revelation; it is the life of the *Logos*, by which God makes himself fully known.[12]

5. The Rapture: on a distinctive of popular-level, current evangelicalism

i. There is only one general resurrection of all those who have died physically.[13]

ii. The physical resurrection occurs only after all has been subdued to Christ through the Church.[14]

iii. The rapture of believers occurs only after the general resurrection of the dead, at the end of history.[15]

6. Rejecting paedobaptism: on a distinctive of Baptists[16]

i. There is only one covenant of grace, administered differently in the covenants of the Old and New Testaments.

ii. The sacraments of the one covenant of grace signify the same reality in the Old and New Testaments—circumcision and baptism both signify regeneration.[17]

iii. The sacrament of baptism is therefore to be administered similarly in the New Testament, as in the Old Testament, applied to infants in circumcision.

7. Charismatic Worship

i. Christ sent the Spirit to enable the Church to make disciples of all nations.

ii. In the transition from the Old to the New Testament, the Spirit came with signs and wonders.

---

12. *John 1:1-18.*

13. *John 5:28-29.*

14. *1 Corinthians 15:25.*

15. *1 Thessalonians 4:15-17.*

16. *Paper No. 140.*

17. *Romans 2:28-29; Colossians 2:11-13; John 3:3.*

    iii. With the completion of the New Testament, the time of transition (with charismatic gifts in signs and wonders) came to an end. Ecstatic utterances, without understanding, are *not* biblical tongues.[18]

8. Sacramentalism: on a distinctive of Roman Catholicism

    i. Roman Catholicism affirms sacramentalism, that the sacramental sign becomes the reality it signifies.

    ii. Historic Christianity does not affirm, but denies sacramentalism—circumcision is *not* necessary for salvation.[19]

    iii. Roman Catholicism therefore, on the sacraments, does not build on the Historic Christian Faith.

9. Atonement

    i. By the covenant of creation, Adam represented all in him.[20] In the Fall, Adam's original sin is imputed to all—by one man's sin, death entered the world.[21]

    ii. Christ came in the place of Adam to undo (as the Lamb of God) what Adam did, and to do what Adam failed to do (rule to make God known). Our sin is imputed to Christ and Christ's righteousness is imputed to all in him.

    iii. All who deny the covenant of creation deny also the Fall and redemption in Christ; and all who deny redemption by vicarious atonement have denied (the covenant of) creation and the Fall. Creation–fall–redemption are inseparable.

10. On Islam

    i. Creation–fall–redemption is clear from general revelation.[22]

---

18. *1 Corinthians 13, 14:4.*
19. *The Council of Jerusalem, Acts 15.*
20. *Genesis 2.*
21. *Romans 5:8-12; 1 Corinthians 15:21-22.*
22. *Paper No. 54.* See points 1-5.

ii. Islam is not based on creation–fall–redemption.

iii. Islam therefore is not the Word of God.

11. Worship

i. We are to worship God in spirit and in truth, not in zeal without knowledge, or in ritual without understanding.[23]

ii. Only the Psalms preserve pure and entire the biblical worldview of creation–fall–redemption.

iii. Only the Psalms, given for singing, are to be sung in the worship of God. All else leads to idolatry.

12. Conscience

i. We are to live according to the measure of our faith: we are not to violate *our* conscience, but one's conscience is not Lord of others.

ii. What we eat or drink must be to the glory of God, not merely in word but with understanding. Whatever is not of faith is sin.

iii. Conscience must be informed: necessary but insufficient conditions are *not* in themselves causes of sin, *nor* means, occasions, and appearances thereof, and provocations thereunto.[24]

13. Politically-Correct Pluralism and Multi-Cultural Skepticism

i. All worldviews are not equally rational.

ii. What is rational (based on insight) must rule.

iii. What is not rational lacks meaning and will perish.

14. Eco-Green

i. Only God, as Creator, determines the nature of things, not the environment.

---

23. *John 4:23.*

24. *LCQ. 99.6.*

ii. Only God, as Creator, is to be worshipped and served, not the environment.

iii. Only the worship and service of God can lift the curse and restore the environment to its pristine state.[25]

15. On Gender

i. There are two genders in God, which are spiritual, and two in man, made in the image of God, male and female, which are physical.[26]

ii. Male and female in humans are for the good, the knowledge of God through the work of dominion, requiring all of mankind through all of history.

iii. The two genders in humans are in unity—without conversion, composition or confusion. Any confusion, due to the Fall, is to be *redeemed*, not marginalized *or* normalized.

16. Feminism or Patriarchy vs. the Good—the rule for households

i. Male and female in creation–fall–redemption are equal and different.

ii. Male and female are a unity of diversity, to achieve the good.

iii. Without the good, there is no hope for unity between male and female.[27]

17. Marriage

i. Marriage is instituted by God, in creation, to serve *his* holy purposes, and continues, even *through* the Fall, *to* redemption.[28]

ii. Marriage originally is instituted for the origin and the nurture of our being, and is by mutual consent.

---

25. *Isaiah 11:1-9; Romans 8:19-23.*

26. *Genesis 1:26-27.*

27. *1 Timothy 2:8-15; 3:4, 12.*

28. *Genesis 2:18-25.*

iii. Marriage therefore, by God's institution, is between one man and one woman. Anything else is due to the Fall and is other than marriage.

18. Nationalism vs. Globalism

i. God created all men of one blood to dwell on the face of all the earth.[29]

ii. In unbelief, mankind was scattered by God on the face of all the earth.[30]

iii. The times and boundaries of nations are determined by God, according to their seeking and knowing God, *not* by mere human will.

19. Totalitarianism

i. Only God's law is total (*Lex Rex*). Totalitarianism puts man's law in the place of God's law. The Mark of the Beast (666) is put on man's hand and forehead where only God's law is to be placed.

ii. Neither the Left (Socialism) nor the Right (Fascism) can have total rule over man.

iii. No institution—Family, State, Church, or Corporation—by its very form and function, can be total, over any other. All are equally under the moral law, written on the hearts of *all* men.

20. Racism

i. Nations, kindreds, tribes, and tongues originated due to unbelief at Babel.[31]

ii. Faith is by grace alone, according to God's sovereign will.[32]

iii. Heritage from faith is by grace, and is therefore *not* by race (racism).

---

29. *Acts 17:24-28.*

30. *Genesis 11:1-9.*

31. *Genesis 11:1-9.*

32. *Ephesians 2:8-9.*

21. Human Dignity

   i. Murder is rooted in disregard for the dignity of man, made in the image of God, with ability and responsibility to know what is clear about God and man and good and evil.

   ii. Murder begins with spiritual suicide, the foolishness of pride in claiming to know what one does not know, and anger if corrected.

   iii. Human society is a society of rational beings; participation in society depends on the exercise of one's reason, *not* on the use of non-rational means against others.

22. Abortion

   i. A person is a body/soul unity, from conception, made in the image of God.[33]

   ii. A person is forever, not merely until death. *All* will be resurrected, in the body, including those who die before birth.

   iii. In the resurrection, we shall all stand before the judgment seat of Christ, to give an account before all, for all the deeds done in our body.[34]

23. The Origin of Wealth and the Commonwealth

   i. The origin of lasting value is from the use of talent in pursuit of the good.

   ii. Talent is from God, given to each, for the benefit of all.

   iii. God therefore is Lord of the wealth of nations. Man is steward of the manifold grace of God, given to each, for all.

---

33. *Genesis 2:7; Psalm 51.*
34. *Romans 14:10-12.*

24. Social Justice[35]

    i. In justice, equals are treated equally; justice is both ontological, in the nature of things, *and* social: first distributive, then retributive, and lastly corrective.

    ii. Truth is necessary and sufficient for justice; the whole truth is necessary for full justice.

    iii. Whatever does not aim at the whole truth is less than the justice of God, and tends to mere self-righteousness (virtue signaling).

25. The Pathologies of Discontent

    i. Discontent arises from a misconception of the good, leading to a belief that one cannot possess the good, to despair, and to all its attendant pathologies.

    ii. The good is the knowledge of God in all that by which he makes himself known. The good itself is *in*alienable.

    iii. No condition in all of creation can separate us from the love of God. Love, joy, and peace are the fruit of faith, hope, and love.[36]

---

35. Gangadean, *History of Philosophy*, 181-191.

36. *Romans 8:38-39; Galatians 5:22; 1 Corinthians 13:13.*

Paper № 56

THE GOSPEL:

A SUMMARY WITH EXPLANATION

Repent: For the Kingdom of Heaven Is at Hand

INTRODUCTION

1. Jesus Christ is the Lamb of God who takes away the sin of the world.

2. He comes in the place of Adam to undo what Adam did and to do what Adam failed to do.

3. He is the Word of God (the Logos) incarnate, Truth in its fullness who makes God known.

4. Man's chief end is to glorify God and to enjoy him forever, in all that by which he makes himself known, in all his works of creation and providence.

   Man is to fill the earth with the knowledge of God as the waters cover the sea.

5. Yet all have sinned and come short of the glory of God. No one seeks God; no one understands; no one is righteous, not even one.

6. Root sin leads to fruit sin: not seeking and not understanding what is clear about God is without excuse and leads to all acts of unrighteousness.

7. The Word of God calls all men to repent of root sin and to seek first the kingdom of God and his righteousness in all relationships of life.

EXPLANATION

1. The Lamb of God is a central theme through all of Scripture.

    i. Slain from before the foundation of the world.

    ii. Revealed in the coats of skin by which God covered the spiritual nakedness and shame of our first parents in the Garden.

    iii. In the sacrifice offered by Abel, Noah, and by Abraham offering up his son, his only son Isaac.

    iv. In the Passover lamb.

    v. In the sacrifice on the Day of Atonement.

    vi. In the prophets: *Isaiah 53*—But he was wounded for our transgressions, he was pierced for our iniquities.

    vii. By John pointing to Christ: Behold, the Lamb of God who takes away the sin of the world.

    viii. By Christ in the Eucharist, in fulfillment of the Passover: this is my body . . . this is my blood.

    ix. In the Church's worship of the One who reigns in history: Worthy is the Lamb that was slain to receive power, and riches, and wisdom, and strength, and honor, and glory, and blessing.

    x. In the consummation of history in the marriage supper of the Lamb, in the full union of Christ and his people forever.

2. He comes in the place of Adam.

    i. God made a covenant with Adam to establish all of mankind in righteousness.

    ii. In that covenant, Adam represented all men; he was tested regarding his pursuit of good over evil; his obedience was to be made manifested in not eating of the tree of the knowledge of good and evil.

    iii. In the temptation, Adam disobeyed and all mankind fell with him. By covenant representation his guilt is imputed to all in him.

iv. Christ in the place of Adam obeyed, even unto his death on the cross.

v. Our sin is imputed to Christ on the cross and the righteousness of his obedience is imputed to all united to him by faith.

Thus, Christ undid what Adam did: he took away our sin by his death on the cross and his righteousness is imputed to us by the covenant.

vi. Made in the image of God, Adam was given the task of dominion; he was told to be fruitful and multiply and fill the earth and subdue it.

vii. By dominion, requiring all of mankind through all of history, he was to name the creation and rule over it. Naming the natural world is the task of science; ruling over it is the task of technology. Naming the realities of the human world is the task of the humanities; ruling over it is the task of all forms of the arts of human culture.

viii. The full expression of the work of dominion was to result in the highest expression of human civilization embodied in the City of God.

ix. Christ, in the place of Adam, calls his people to make disciples of all nations. Discipleship begins with baptism, on the basis of which all nations are taught to obey the law of God in all of life.

x. Christ subdues all things to himself through his people. All thoughts raised up against the knowledge of God are taken captive. He fills the earth with the knowledge of God as the waters cover the sea.

3. The Word of God.

i. God makes himself known through his Word. There is no direct knowledge of God apart from his Word.

ii. The Word of God is eternal; it is eternally of God and with God. And the Word is God, the eternal Son who makes God known.[1]

---

1. *John 1:1.*

iii. The Word of God makes God known through his works of creation and providence. All things were made by him[2] and by him all things consist.[3] In him are hid all the treasures of wisdom and knowledge.[4] He ascended far above all heavens that he might fill everything in every way.[5]

iv. In him (the Logos, the Word of God) was life, and the life was the light of men who are made in the image of God.[6] The life of the Logos is in all men as light, by which they see/understand what is clear about God. That light by which we understand is reason. Fallen man turns from the light, but the darkness cannot overcome or withstand the light.[7]

v. The Logos is revealed in the creation and is the object of study in biology, psychology, epistemology, and all academic disciplines. Yet man fails to see what is clear.[8]

vi. The Logos comes to God's people in history through the prophets, yet that Word was not heeded.[9]

vii. The eternal Word of God, rejected as reason in clear general revelation and in special revelation, became incarnate in Jesus the Christ, full of Grace and truth, to take away the sin of the world and to make God known.[10]

viii. Christ sends the Holy Spirit to lead the Church into all Truth. In response to challenges to the faith, after much discussion, the pastor-teachers come to agreement summed up in the Church's creeds and confessions. This historically cumulative insight is the holy catholic and apostolic faith, the basis of the unity of the faith for all who believe.

---

2. *John 1:3.*

3. *Colossians 1:17.*

4. *Colossians 2:3.*

5. *Ephesians 4:10.*

6. *John 1:4.*

7. *John 1:5.*

8. *John 1:10.*

9. *John 1:11.*

10. *John 1:14.*

ix. The Holy Spirit brings each believer to faith through regeneration, which restores a person to the life of the Logos, working conviction of sin and death, repentance and faith by which that person is justified before God.

x. The Holy Spirit sanctifies each believer through knowing the truth. The Word of God (the Logos) is Truth in its fullness. Through suffering in trials of faith believers are led to seek and understand what is clear about God.

4. Man's chief end.

i. Man's chief end is to glorify God and to enjoy him forever.[11] If one does not glorify God, one cannot enjoy God. And the emptiness of enjoying the world in place of God leads to all excess of unrighteousness.

ii. God is to be glorified in all that by which he makes himself known,[12] in all his works of creation and providence.[13] To glorify God is to know the glory of God and to make his glory known.

iii. The good is clear to reason: the good for man as a rational being is the knowledge of God. It is the same as man's chief end. Virtue is the means to the good. Happiness is the effect of possessing the good. Eternal life, the highest good, the end in itself, is knowing God.

iv. Man is to glorify God through the work of dominion. It requires all of mankind through all of history to complete the work of dominion.

v. The good, manifest in the Kingdom of God, which is the City of God, is corporate, cumulative, and communal: it requires the unity of mankind in all aspects of man's diversity to complete the work of dominion.

vi. The Sabbath, the day of rest, is the sign of hope that man will complete the work of dominion and rest from that work.

---

11. *SCQ. 1.*

12. *SCQ. 101.*

13. *WCF 4.1, 5.1.*

vii. The work of man without the good is empty. The City of Man has no foundation. The good without work is false hope. There is no beatific vision of God in heaven; God is known only through his Word.

viii. God has a zeal for his own glory: Holy, holy, holy is the Lord of hosts: the whole earth is full of the glory of God.[14]

ix. In exercising dominion through a spiritual war, the Church is to demolish arguments and every pretension raised up against the knowledge of God and take every thought captive to Jesus Christ.

x. Christ now rules to make God known. He must rule until all has been subdued to him. He will rule through his people until the earth is filled with the knowledge of the Lord as the waters cover the sea.

5. All have sinned.

i. All have sinned by coming short of the glory of God.[15] It is a denial of man's chief end, the good, eternal life as knowing God. This is the most concise, focused summary of what sin is.

ii. Sin is an act contrary to one's nature as a rational being. By nature we think, and reason in itself is the laws of thought. What may be known about God is clear to reason, being understood by what is made so that unbelief is without excuse.[16] It is to neglect, avoid, resist, and deny reason in the face of what is clear about God.

iii. Sin begins in not seeking God. He that comes to God must believe that he is and that he rewards those who diligently seek him.[17] Yet no one seeks God, no one understands, no one is righteous, not even one.[18]

iv. Sin is unbelief, not just an outward act. The fool says in his heart there surely is no God. Or, God does not act in history.

---

14. *Isaiah 6:3.*

15. *Romans 3:23.*

16. *Romans 1:20.*

17. *Hebrews 11:6.*

18. *Romans 3:10-11.*

Or, God is not infinite, eternal, and unchangeable in both justice and mercy. Or, there is no historically cumulative insight in the creeds of the Church, always progressing subjectively from neglect to denial.

v. Sin is autonomy: putting oneself in the place of God to determine good and evil; being a law unto oneself; doing what is right in one's own eyes. It is contrary in spirit to Christ who said: "not my will but your will be done"; "deny yourself, take up your cross daily and follow me."

vi. Sin is any want of conformity or transgression of the law of God. The law, summed up in the Decalogue, is written on the hearts of all (clear); it is broad and deep (comprehensive). The consequence of obedience is a matter of life or death, individually and culturally (critical). It is opposed to the antinomy of legalism (virtue as/or without the good) and antinomianism (pleasure/happiness is the good). It is not general and abstract, but comes to concrete expression in precepts, statutes, and ordinances, all aimed at the kingdom of God and the knowledge of God.

vii. Sin is in human nature being fallen in Adam. We are conceived in sin and go astray from the womb.[19] From the guilt of original sin imputed to all proceeds all actual transgression. (But where sin abounded—in Adam, grace did much more abound—in Christ).

viii. The wages of sin is death. There are two kinds of death: physical and spiritual.[20] The wages of sin is spiritual (not physical) death, which is present and inherent in sin,[21] not future and imposed. The lake of fire is figuratively the second (or spiritual) death.[22]

ix. The spiritual death inherent in the sin of not seeking and not understanding is meaninglessness (the darkened mind, pictured as outer darkness), boredom (burning desire without satisfaction, pictured as the fire that is not quenched), and guilt (the torment of conscience, pictured as the gnawing worm that does not die); all of which is unending, pictured as the bottomless pit.

---

19. *Psalm 51.*

20. *John 11:25-26*

21. *Ephesians 2:1.*

22. *Revelation 20:6, 14.*

x. All have sinned in that all die physically. All are under the curse of toil and strife, and old age, sickness, and (physical) death. The curse is imposed by God to restrain, recall from, and remove moral evil (the sin of not seeking and not understanding). It is God's third and final call back from, not only sin, but self-deception and self-justification. This call back is mercy and is always (to be) given with the promise of redemption.

6. Root sin and fruit sin.

i. Sin is both root sin and fruit sin. Root sin leads to fruit sin. Root sin is seldom recognized. Fruit sin, manifest in doing what is not right, is what is noticed. (By their fruits you shall know them). Yet without removing root sin, fruit sin will remain or recur.

ii. Root sin is universal; it is one and the same in all: no one seeks God; no one understands; no one does what is right, not even one.[23]

iii. Not seeking and not understanding leads to any and all fruit sin of unrighteousness. The root sin of not understanding is culpable ignorance; it cannot be excused but requires forgiveness: "Father, forgive them; for they know not what they do."

iv. General revelation concerning God and man and good and evil is objectively clear. It is clear to reason by which we understand. In every age, understanding is by seeking, not requiring one or many "great teachers" in history. Understanding is by seeking, not by spontaneous intuitive knowledge (*sensus divinitatis*). If we understand God and man, we can understand (have rational justification for) good and evil. To lose rational justification based in metaphysics is to (eventually) lose ethics (as in the Enlightenment).

v. It is the objective clarity of general revelation that makes unbelief inexcusable. If there is no clarity and inexcusability, then there can be no sin and no Christianity in which Christ is the Lamb of God who takes away the sin of the world.

---

23. *Romans 3:10-11.*

vi. The one who comes to God must believe (with understanding) that he exists and that he rewards (with understanding) those who diligently seek him. Failure to see what is clear about God (his eternal power and divine nature) shows that one is not seeking. If we see (know/understand) what is clear, we can show what is clear.

vii. The root sin of not seeking and not understanding what is clear remains because the shame and guilt of its inexcusability is avoided by self-deception and resisted by self-justification. In pride, we think we know. Professing oneself to be wise one becomes a fool.

viii. The Word of God (the Logos) makes God known in every way. It begins with reason and general revelation before redemption in special revelation. Clarity and inexcusability is the cornerstone of the foundation. By it, all else comes into place. The stone which the builders rejected is become the head stone of the corner. This is the Lord's doing; it is marvelous in our eyes.[24]

ix. There are degrees of sin in both root and fruit sin. The degree depends on the amount of light one has (or claims) and the nature of the sin (omission or commission). All have sinned but not all are blameless. Teachers are blameless only if they hold fast to the first principles (the foundation from clear general revelation, from the worldview of Scripture and from the Historic Christian Faith).

x. The best of men have root sin remaining: Job: now my eyes see you, wherefore I abhor myself and repent in dust and ashes;[25] David: you desire truth in the inward parts . . . wash me and I shall be whiter than snow;[26] Christ reproving the unbelief of the Apostles: O fools, and slow of heart to believe all the prophets have spoken: Ought not Christ to have suffered these things, and (then) to enter into his glory?[27]

---

24. *Psalm 118:22-23.*

25. *Job 42:5-6.*

26. *Psalm 51:6-7.*

27. *Luke 24:25-26.*

7. Repent: for the kingdom of heaven is at hand.

i. The Word of God calls all men everywhere to repent that they may enter the kingdom of God. To repent is to change one's mind of the sin of unbelief regarding the truth of God. All men are to repent of the root sin of not seeking and understanding what is clear about God and to pursue the good in the kingdom of God.

ii. Repentance is based on the conviction of one's own sin and death, which originates in the grace of regeneration (spiritual rebirth). Repentance acknowledges the justice of God, which would leave a person to perish in the unending miseries of sin and spiritual death. It apprehends also the mercy of God in the promise of eternal life in the kingdom of God.

iii. Repentance begins when one confesses one's guilt and helplessness as a sinner against God and seeks mercy offered by God in the gospel concerning the person and work of Jesus Christ, the eternal Son of God incarnate. The prayer attitude of the repentant is summed up in the words: Lord have mercy upon me, a sinner.

iv. Sin must be confessed particularly: if we confess our sins, he is faithful and just to forgive us our sins and to cleanse us from all unrighteousness.[28] The Commandments guide confession of sin both root and fruit, both omission and commission, both inward thought and outward act. Confession of sin is only to those whom we sin against (God and man).

v. We sin in not seeking and understanding what is clear about God: we take God's name in vain in that we lightly and thoughtlessly disregard God's self-revelation in creation, in history, in Scripture. We are in self-deception (hypocrisy—Moral Law 3): we think and say we seek, but we do not know and acknowledge what is clear (Moral Law 1); instead, we misconceive of God's nature in every form of idolatry through world history (Moral Law 2). Root sin results in every form of fruit sin/unrighteousness.

vi. In the forgiveness of sin, Christ represents us in the place of Adam. Adam's sin is imputed to all in him. Our sin is imputed to Christ who bears the penalty of our sins in his death on the

---

28. *1 John 1:9.*

cross, on which basis our debt is forgiven. And Christ's righteousness is imputed to those in him by faith.

vii. Forgiveness and cleansing are distinct but inseparable. (Justification is not sanctification and vice versa). Sanctify them through thy Truth. Thy Word (logos) is Truth.[29] Knowing truth in its fullness (from foundation to worldview) sanctifies. Knowing the truth requires discipline (through the Church and through trials of faith).

viii. The kingdom of God is Christ's rule over his people in all the relationships of life. All who have repented and believed in Christ are the people of God, the body of Christ, the Church, which is the pillar and ground of the truth and is the kingdom of God on earth. The Church is the salt of the earth and the light of the world as it obeys Christ. In repenting, believers are called to seek first (before all else) the kingdom of God and his righteousness, the goal of which is to glorify God in all that by which he makes himself known.

ix. The Church today is badly divided. It has not built on its first principle but is compromised by worldly first principles. Its teachers, without its philosophical, theological, and historical foundations is unable to disciple its members, who in turn are to make disciples of all nations. Seeking first the kingdom of God requires first that the Church become established on its foundations.

x. God has appointed Christ to rule. The Scriptures, when read contextually and not literally or allegorically, and while acknowledging the full extent of human sin, bursts throughout with the hope that Christ, in his present rule through his people, will subdue all things to himself until the kingdoms of this world become the kingdom of the Lord and of his Christ. And he shall reign forever and ever (so let it be!).

The message of the gospel is therefore:
Repent, for the kingdom of heaven is at hand.

---

29. *John 17:17.*

Paper № 57

REASON

1. It is self-evident that we think: we form concepts and make judgments and inferences, the forms of all thought, expressed in words, statements, and arguments. Thought is an act of the mind, not an event of the senses.

2. It is self-evident that there are laws of thought: the law of identity—*a* is *a;* the law of non-contradiction—not both *a* and *non-a,* at the same time and in the same respect; the law of excluded middle—either *a* or *non-a.* These laws of thought are reason-in-itself.

3. Reason-in-itself as the laws of thought is transcendental; they make thought possible. Reason is the test of meaning, which is more basic than truth—if a law of thought is violated, there can be no meaning. Reason is authoritative: if there is no meaning, there can be no truth.

4. Reason is ontological: it applies to being as well as thought. There are no square-circles, no uncaused events, no being from non-being. Reason applies to all being, to the highest being, to God's being: God cannot be both eternal and not eternal, at the same time and in the same respect. Reason (as the *Logos*) is eternal; miracles transcend created laws of nature, not the laws of reason. Paradox, complexity and incomprehensibility cannot set aside the laws of reason.

5. Reason is self-attesting; only reason is self-attesting. It is irrepressible: it arises spontaneously so that we cannot cease from thinking by withdrawal to any mystical state. Any attempt to neglect, avoid,

resist, or deny reason is futile: the light shines in the darkness of un-belief and the darkness cannot withstand it. The light illuminates itself, and all else, and is not illuminated by anything else.

6. Reason in man is fundamental: it is not one among many aspects, but basic to the unity of all aspects of man's being. Reason distinguishes man from animals: non-rational and anti-intellectual attitudes are self-destructive. The good for man is based on man's rational nature needing cognitive meaning. Truth is not reducible to beauty or power.

7. Reason in man is natural; it is not conventional, but the same in all who think. Man, by nature, is a rational animal, created in the image of God to know God in all of creation and providence. The *Logos* is the eternal Word of God who makes God fully known. The life of the *Logos* is in all men as the light of reason by which all of God's self-revelation is understood.

Paper № 58

———

THE SPIRITUAL WAR

PART I

On the State of the Church and the World

1. Man is created in the image of God to know God through the work of dominion. Man's chief end is to glorify God and to enjoy him forever.

   Man is fallen in Adam, by his failure to seek and to understand what is clear about God and man and good and evil.

   Man is redeemed from evil by a spiritual war between belief and unbelief, which is age-long and agonizing, in which good eventually overcomes evil.

2. The conflict between belief and unbelief is within each person, in each household, in each church, and in each nation, kindred, tribe, and tongue.

   This conflict is *comprehensive*, between the kingdom of God and the fallen world as the kingdom of Darkness, between Christ as Prophet, Priest, and King, ruling in the Church through knowledge, holiness, and righteousness, and Satan ruling through the institutions of the False Prophet, the Harlot, and the Beast in the world's fallen culture. Spiritual war is *total* war. The outcome is life full of meaning or meaningless existence.

3. The curse of toil and strife, and old age, sickness, and death, increasing with sin, to war, famine, and plague, is imposed by God as a call back from sin, and self-deception and self-justification. The curse is a call back—not punishment, which is intrinsic and ultimate—given with the promise of redemption through Christ.[1] As the Lamb of God, Christ will undo what Adam did (take away the sin of the world). As the Word of God incarnate, he will do what Adam failed to do (rule to make God known).

4. Evil (unbelief) serves to deepen the revelation of God's justice and mercy. Unbelief in every kind and degree of admixture with belief is allowed to work itself out in world history. In this conflict, belief will eventually win out. Unbelief leads to spiritual death—meaninglessness, boredom (with excess), and guilt. Only what is meaningful can bring everlasting life and a lasting culture.

5. In world history, there have been many cycles of apostasy—departure from faith/belief—with resulting cultural decay, and collapse under divine judgment. The first was the Flood, in Noah's day. The second was at Babel, against the attempt to set up a world government in unbelief. The scattering of mankind by language restrained man from descending again into a universal apostasy and the resulting universal judgment of the Flood. Since Babel, many civilizations have risen in unbelief, flourished for a time, then decayed and perished.

6. Now, in world history, we enter our deepest crisis as the ending of four cycles converge. These cycles began 4000, 2000, 500, and 75 years ago.

    i. Post-Babel—the end of human scattering to prevent a return to universal apostasy and the emergence of an anti-national globalism.

---

1. *Genesis 3:15.*

ii. Post-Western—the end of Christian cultural influence in the West and the re-emergence of anti-rational neo-paganism.

iii. Post-Protestant—the decline of the distinctives of the Reformation focused on *the glory of God alone* and the rise of cultural despair.

iv. Post-Colonial—the completion of Fourth Generation apostasy (post-WWII) and the rise of postmodern cultural nihilism.

7. In the redemptive history of the Church in the Old Testament, there have been many cycles of apostasy, beginning after the exodus from Egypt, in the wilderness, and again after the conquest of Canaan, in the cycle of Judges. After Solomon, apostasy grew in Israel until its destruction by the Assyrians, and also in Judah, until it was removed by exile to Babylon. During the time of the kings, the prophets declared the curse (war, famine, and plague) as God's call back, and reaffirmed the promise of Christ to come.

8. Christ, the Word of God incarnate, came full of grace and truth. The evil of unbelief in the religious establishment crucified Christ. (He prayed, "Father, forgive them; for they know not what they do.") But the death of Christ on the cross atoned for the sin of mankind. He was raised from the dead, ascended into heaven, and sent the Holy Spirit to lead the Church into all Truth. The Spirit came at Pentecost, to begin the ingathering of all nations into the kingdom of God.

9. There have been many Church councils addressing the challenges of unbelief in the Church: Jerusalem (*ca.* A.D. 51), The Apostles' Creed (*ca.* 180), Nicea (325), Carthage (397), Chalcedon (451), Orange (529), several creeds of the Reformation culminating in Westminster (1648). The challenges of the modern era (1650–1950) from naturalism and secularism, and the challenges from the postmodern period (1950 to the present) from skepticism and anti-rationalism, remain to be answered, in due time, by yet another Church council.

10. The Church is much divided in understanding good and evil. The cornerstone of clarity and inexcusability is rejected in place of fideism (belief without proof based on understanding). Clarity and

inexcusability are avoided by self-deception and resisted (sometimes fiercely) by self-justification. A future heaven and hell are proclaimed in place of a present *spiritual* life and death. Without common ground among believers, there is no hope for agreement on the state of the Church and the world, or for understanding the signs of the times, or whether prudence requires preparation to persevere. To see *anything* clearly, redemption requires repentance of *root* sin—not seeking and not understanding what is clear about God—the *original* sin, universal—in all human beings, in their inmost being.

11. There is one kingdom of Darkness, under one ruler, called Satan, the Devil, Lucifer, The Ancient Serpent (from the Garden of Eden), and the Dragon.

    This one kingdom of Darkness is divided under many principalities and powers—fallen angels, ruling the earth through the ages over regions as their gods (Egypt, Assyria, Babylon, Persia, Greece, Rome). They are the rulers of the darkness of this world, the spiritual wickedness in high places.[2] There was war in heaven, between the good and the evil angels. The good prevailed.[3] Nevertheless, *all* evil beings and *all* forces of nature are *always* subject to God's *sovereign* power.

12. This one kingdom of Darkness rules on earth through the highest level (mostly invisible) of human power (sometimes called the Deep State). The Dragon's power is manifest through the False Prophet (education without God), the Harlot (economics without God), and the Beast (politics without God).[4] There are various levels of human hierarchy (the Swamp) below the Deep State which carry out its rule, often in culpable ignorance.[5]

13. The kingdom of Darkness rules in opposition to the foundation of the kingdom of God. It opposes general revelation that is clear

---

2. *Ephesians 6:12.*

3. *Revelation 12:7-9.*

4. *Revelation 12–20.*

5. *2 Timothy 2:23-26.*

to reason by the antinomies of skepticism and fideism/mysticism. It opposes the good (man's chief end/teleology) by the antinomies of hedonism (happiness as the good rather than the *effect* of the good) or deontology (virtue as the good rather than the *means* to the good—virtues *in place of the good* become our vices). It opposes the moral law—given in human nature, by the antinomies of anarchy (freedom from all law) or totalitarian law (man's law/666/the mark of the Beast) in the place of God's law—on the hand and forehead.

14. The City of God (the kingdom of God) has foundations, walls, and gates. It is the body of Christ, the Logos/Truth incarnate and is therefore the pillar and ground of the Truth. It is called to be the salt of the earth and the light of the world. It is called to make disciples of all nations. It is called to be one that the world might believe. The Church is in captivity in many places where once it led the culture. It built on sand, not on the rock. It must rebuild on the cornerstone of clarity. It must lay again, *more consciously and consistently*, the foundation from clear general revelation, from Scripture, and from the Historic Christian Faith, many layers, *all set in order*. Only by the foundation in its fullness can the Church avoid divisions, apostasy, decay, and collapse and attain to maturity, fruitfulness, unity, and fullness.

15. The *Logos* is the eternal Word of God, the Son of God, the fullness of Truth who makes God fully known. It is in all men as the light of reason. It is in creation as general revelation. It is in redemptive history as Scripture. It is incarnate in Jesus Christ. It is in the Historic Christian Faith by the Holy Spirit leading the Church into all Truth. It is restored in each believer by regeneration. It grows to maturity by sanctification.[6]

Only the Word of God can sanctify in one's inmost being.[7]

Only the Word of God can discern the thoughts and intents of the heart.[8]

---

6. *John 1:1-18; 3; 16; 17.*

7. *John 17:17; Psalm 51.*

8. *Hebrews 4:12.*

Only the Word of God can demolish arguments raised up against the knowledge of God, take every thought captive to Christ, bind Satan, and destroy his kingdom.[9]

This Word of God endures forever.[10]

---

9. *2 Corinthians 10:4-5; Revelation 19:11-21; 20:1-3.*

10. *Isaiah 40:8.*

Paper N⁰· 59

THE LOGOS FOUNDATION
An Outline for The Logos Paideia

1. The Gospel of the Kingdom

    i. Repent (of root/original sin), for the kingdom is at hand.

    ii. The Kingdom of God is the City of God, the Church—the People of God, obeying God's law in all of life/culture.

    iii. The City of God has foundations (twelve) and walls and gates, to attain to the fullness of God in redemption vs. the City of Man/ the World without God/Satan's kingdom of Darkness.

    iv. The promise of the kingdom is from the beginning: man, the image of God, is to have dominion—rule to make God known, to fill the earth with the knowledge of God as the waters cover the sea.[1]

    v. The hope of the promise, now through Christ in the place of Adam, is *still* assured in the Sabbath. There will be rest when the work of dominion is completed.

2. Summary I: The Foundation is from three sources.

    i. General revelation is objectively clear to all by reason.

    ii. Special revelation (Scripture) is clear, in light of general revelation.

---

1. *Isaiah 11:9.*

iii. Historic Christianity is the work of the Holy Spirit leading the Church into all Truth.[2]

iv. The Church is to make disciples of all nations, teaching them to observe *all* that Christ has commanded.[3] Foundation is *first* principles.

v. The old foundation learned by tradition[4] must be *replaced*. The new cannot be added to the old without harm of loss.[5]

3. Summary II: The Moral Law is given to all in human nature,[6] then in Scripture by the Ten Commandments. The Law is applied in precepts, statutes, and ordinances and understood by meditation on the Law, day and night.

i. God, as Creator, is the determiner of good and evil (theonomy vs. autonomy).

ii. True worship of God who is infinite, eternal, and unchangeable in all his attributes is opposed to all idolatry (gods created in one's own image as finite, temporal, and changeable).

iii. Integrity vs. hypocrisy—self-deception and self-justification in not seeking God.

iv. Sabbath: only by completing the work of dominion (moral and then natural) can mankind achieve rest.

v. Authority, in all institutions, is rational not personal, based on insight, not might.

vi. Man is the image of God: to affirm man's rationality is to affirm human dignity.

vii. True love in marriage (fidelity) is opposed to spiritual and physical infidelity.

---

2. *John 16:13.*
3. *Matthew 28:19-20.*
4. *Colossians 2:8.*
5. *Luke 5:37-38.*
6. *Deuteronomy 30:11-14; Romans 2:14-15.*

    viii. Lasting value is by the use of talent in pursuit of the good vs. all forms of stealing.

    ix. Truth (the whole truth and nothing but the truth) is necessary and sufficient for justice.

    x. Contentment (vs. all forms of discontent) is found only in pursuit of the good.

4. Summary III: From foundation to maturity, fruitfulness, unity, and fullness.

    i. Common Ground requires reason, integrity, critical thinking, and clarity.

    ii. There must be something eternal since there can be no being from non-being.

    iii. It is clear that only some is eternal and that therefore God the Creator exists.

    iv. By special creation, all of life is created each after its own kind, not by evolution.

    v. In the solution to the problem of evil, natural evil (the curse) is due to moral evil.

    vi. Scripture is necessary since natural evil is a redemptive call back from moral evil.

    vii. Only Genesis, and what builds on clear general revelation, qualify as Scripture.

    viii. Christ has come, in the place of Adam, according to the promise in Scripture.

    ix. The creeds of Historic Christianity are by the work of the Holy Spirit.[7]

    x. Complete the work: take captive all unbelief in Modernity and in Postmodernity.

---

7. *John 16:13.*

5. Common Ground (CG) is the set of epistemological conditions necessary for thought and discourse.

    i. *Reason*, as the laws of thought, is the test for meaning. There are no square-circles, no *a* that is *non-a*. If a law of thought is violated, there can be no meaning. Reason is the self-attesting light of nature in all men made in the image of God. It is the light of the *Logos*, the Word of God in all men. The darkness of unbelief cannot overcome it or withstand it.[8]

    ii. *Integrity* is the concern for consistency (both logical and existential) vs. lack of consistency in incoherence/absurdity/nihilism. The self-deception and self-justification of hypocrisy require increasing natural evil to confront one's own moral evil in not seeing what is clear.

    iii. Critical Thinking, consistently applied as a test for meaning to unexamined assumptions, is *Rational Presuppositionalism* (RP). If there is agreement on what is more basic, there can/will be agreement on what is less basic. RP stands in contrast to empiricism/literalism and to non-cognitive mystical allegoricalism.

    iv. The *Principle of Clarity* (PC) affirms that some things are clear; the basic things are clear; the basic things about God and man and good and evil are clear to reason, so that unbelief is without excuse.[9] Clarity is the cornerstone of the foundation.

6. The foundation is given in Scripture, first in narrative form, in Genesis 1–3, then in theological form derived from all of Scripture, particularly Hebrews 6:1-2.

    i. The biblical worldview of creation–fall–redemption[10] is understood only by diligently seeking, using good and necessary consequences, in a step-by-step process, beginning with the context of clear general revelation, as opposed to literalism *and* allegoricalism.

---

8. *John 1:1-5.*

9. *Romans 1:20.*

10. *Genesis 1–3.*

ii. The foundation in theological form is summarized in the Seven Pillars of the faith, by using good and necessary consequences to grasp assumptions and implications: clarity and inexcusability, sin and death, curse and promise, repentance and faith, justification and sanctification, baptism and calling, and resurrection and reward.[11]

iii. Contextualism is Rational Presuppositionalism applied to hermeneutics. It begins with the full clarity of general revelation, then with the biblical worldview of creation–fall–redemption, then with the unfolding history of redemption, then with the form of the book in that history, then with context of the chapter, then grammar of the sentence, and word.

iv. The Word of God in its fullness (the *Logos*) comes to man in several ways: in all men as reason, as general revelation in creation, as Scripture in redemptive history, in person in the Incarnation, in creeds in Church history, by regeneration in each believer, and by sanctification as each grows in faith (John's gospel—all).

7. The Historic Christian Faith is by the work of the Holy Spirit leading the Church into all truth.[12] In response to challenges to the faith, the pastor-teachers, meeting in councils, after much discussion, come to agreement, summed up in creeds, delivered to all the churches for the unity of the faith. This is the holy, catholic, and apostolic faith by which doctrine and life must be examined. Councils may err and are subject to Scripture.

i. The Council of Jerusalem (*ca.* A.D. 51) addressed (Judaic) literalism (recurrent in the Church) regarding the sacraments (here, circumcision).

ii. The Apostles' Creed (*ca.* 180) addressed the worldview of Greek dualism (evil is from the body) and by implication its gnosticism and mystical otherworldliness (vs. the *earth* filled with the knowledge of God).

---

11. *Paper No. 36* and *37.*

12. *John 16:13.*

iii. Nicea (325) addressed the unity of diversity in the Triune Godhead, and by implication in human nature.

iv. Carthage (*ca.* 397) settled the canon of Scripture for the New Testament. The Jews preserved the Old Testament pure and entire.

v. Chalcedon (*ca.* 451) declared that two whole natures, divine and human, were united in Christ without conversion, composition, or confusion.

vi. Orange (*ca.* 529) affirmed the sovereignty of grace in the salvation of man against all degrees of Pelagianism, correcting false views of free will.

vii. The Westminster Confession of Faith (1648) summed up six prior creeds of the Reformation as well as six in prior Church history in the context of the doxological focus of God's work of creation and providence.

viii. The challenges of Modernity (1650–1950) of naturalism and secularism (against Greek dualism in the Church's theology), and Postmodernity (1950 to the present) of skepticism and pluralism (against fideism and pietism in the Church's doctrine and life) require answers from yet another Church council. The Church must rebuild from the cornerstone of clarity.

Paper № 60

THE SPIRITUAL WAR

PART II

Church Councils and Settling Current Divisions in the Church

Common Ground (CG) is the set of conditions necessary for thought and discourse.

CG consists of understanding *reason* as the laws of thought, a commitment to reason—*integrity*, the use of reason as the test for meaning, starting with basic beliefs—*Rational Presuppositionalism* (RP), and the *Principle of Clarity* (PC): some things are clear; the basic things are clear; the basic things about God and man and good and evil are clear to reason.

Where there is no CG, conversation with those in any dispute will end.

Conversation can continue in so far as there is CG, with pastors willing to seek unity of the faith.

Pastors themselves, to begin with, will have different positions on basic things.

The first major Church dispute (Acts 15) was settled in council, after much discussion.

Today, all must learn to apply the whole Word of God, including CG, to settle disputes.

There are preliminary considerations in the appeal to Acts 15.

1. The Jerusalem Council of Acts 15 was decisive in the dispute. It was not a reconciliation. The response was then sent to all the churches for instruction for the unity of the faith.

2. This First Church Council (*ca.* A.D. 51) was against sacramentalism, which was based on literalism. The sign of regeneration (circumcision) is not the reality of regeneration.

3. Literalism is grounded in empiricism (appeal to experience) and subjective persuasion in contrast to objective proof. Persuasion is not proof nor are they necessarily connected.

4. Literalism splits into antinomies in Church history: many believe regeneration itself is by baptism; many others believe regeneration is by the believer's decision, and/or appeal to *discontinuity* between the old and new testaments—where new means another, not a new administration of the one covenant of grace.

5. Literalism neglects, avoids, resists, and denies the logical distinction of less and more basic. Empiricism opposes the use of reason to understand meaning by good and necessary consequences, by appeal to context, by Rational Presuppositionalism (RP).

6. Without RP, the meaning of every word is disputed, endlessly. Without CG, a person does not have ears to hear.

7. We are to avoid foolish disputes, which lack CG. They gender strife from those who sit in the seat of the scornful.[1]

8. Correction from literalism is called for according to membership vows that are based on the Historic Christian Faith, beginning with Acts 15.

9. In any church that holds to the Historic Christian Faith, no man can be released from his vow to God to heed correction in doctrine and life by duly appointed church oversight.

---

1. *Psalm 1:1; 2 Timothy 2:23; Jude 9, 11.*

Paper №· 61

_____

THE PRESENT AND FUTURE STATE OF THE CHURCH

To and For the Church

Logos Papers No. 61 & 62 (along with others) are written to and for the Church. They concern the present and future state of the Church. They presuppose the clarity of general revelation, addressed throughout *The Logos Papers*.

The Church is divided in its current inability and resistance to dealing with its doctrinal differences. As a result, it is in apostasy, in varying degrees, by its departing from the Historic Christian Faith found in its creeds and confessions.

These papers call the Church to repentance and to the reformation of the Church. A process of much discussion is needed to deal with its divisions.

To those who affirm the clarity of general revelation and Historic Christianity, these papers are a call to lay the Church's foundation on solid rock, and to rebuild the walls and gates of the City of God.

The call to repent and to rebuild comes with the call to be thoughtful: "He that has an ear to hear, let him hear . . ."

1. The Church is the body of Christ, the Word of God (The *Logos*) incarnate. The Logos is the Word of God in its fullness, who makes God fully known.

2. As the body of Christ, the Church is the pillar and ground of the Truth. Only the foundation of general revelation knowable always to all men, and special revelation given in Scripture, makes knowing the fullness of Truth possible.

3. The Church, therefore, is called to be the salt of the earth and the light of the world. Without salt and light, the culture is now in moral decay, nearing collapse.

4. The Church is for the worship of God and discipleship of its members. The Church is to worship God in spirit and in truth—not in zeal without knowledge, or in ritual without understanding. Only in true worship can the Church disciple its members.

5. The doors of the Church are always open to repentant sinners, who repent of root sin (of not seeking and understanding what is clear about God), as well as fruit sins. The Church's doors are closed to unrepentant sinners. Unless you are born again, and repent, you cannot enter the kingdom of God.

6. The Church is to make disciples of all nations, teaching them to observe all that Christ has commanded. The Church prays, continually: "Thy will be done in earth, as it is in heaven."

7. The Church must be one, as the Father and Son are one, that the world might believe. The Church is now badly divided, and is therefore mostly disregarded, if not scorned.

8. The Church must have its foundation laid on the solid rock of clarity and inexcusability, to withstand the current storms of unbelief in the form of skepticism and secularism. The Church is now in captivity to fideism (belief without understanding), and to an otherworldly focus on heaven and hell.

9. The Church was once the head in Western civilization. It is now the tail of the culture, due to its unbelief. The Church has not taken unbelief captive; it has not demolished pretensions raised up against the knowledge of God.

10. From its beginning, the Church (as those called out of the world) was to engage in a spiritual war with unbelief. Evil, like the good, has been corporate, cumulative, and communal. Four cycles of world history now converge for a perfect storm: post-Babel, post-Pentecost, post-Reformation, and post-Modern. War with unbelief has been age-long and agonizing, but the promise stands: good *will* overcome evil, even if we must go through judgment, again. The Church must repent, or all but a remnant will perish.

Paper N⁰· 62

———

THE NEXT REFORMATION
Prepare the Way of the Lord

WE NEED A SECOND REFORMATION; the first Reformation is spent. The Church's message is no longer being heard after 500 years: it is disregarded, if not scorned, by the immediate heirs of the first Reformation. The Church is divided, as much as it could be, and is treated with indifference. It is the tail of the culture; it has lost its headship and is in captivity to the unbelief of the world. In response to centuries of empiricism and skepticism, it has sunk into fideism (belief without understanding). In response to naturalism and secularism, it has sunk into superstitious super-naturalism and otherworldly mysticism. In response to the relativism of political correctness and the decay of nihilism, it has sunk into legalism and pietism. The life and culture-transforming power of the gospel is not being preached. We need a second Reformation. In short, the first Reformation is dead; long live the second Reformation!

It is clear what is needed for a second Reformation. The Church's foundation must be laid again, this time more deeply; it must be built upon the rock, not sand. That rock is clarity, not fideism. Only by the clarity of general revelation can the inexcusability of unbelief be understood. The basic things about God and man and good and evil are clear to reason. The Church must repent of its root sin of not seeking and understanding what is clear to reason.

The Church must be one, that the world might believe. It must come into the unity of the faith. It must affirm, with understanding, the Historic Christian Faith summed up in its creeds and confessions. Christ sent the Holy Spirit to lead the Church into all Truth. In response to challenges of unbelief, internal and external, the pastor-teachers, after much discussion, come to agreement expressed in its creeds and confessions, for the unity of the faith. The creeds must be understood by reason, which recognizes relevant assumptions and implications.

Laying foundation more deeply requires responding to the most explicit challenges of unbelief since the first Reformation. Both Modernity and Postmodernity require a philosophical response based on the clarity of general revelation. General revelation requires Scripture (redemptive revelation), and Scripture assumes clear general revelation. Therefore, foundation from clear general revelation must come first, *before* foundation from Scripture, and enable the understanding of Scripture.

Foundation from Scripture begins with the biblical worldview of creation–fall–redemption. In light of challenges of Modernism and Postmodernism, biblical revelation must be understood more deeply, coherently, and relevantly. Only by diligently seeking can understanding (faith) be deepened. General and specific challenges to the knowledge of God from within and outside the Church must be responded to by the illumining work of the Holy Spirit. The theological pillars of the Christian faith must be carefully laid, again, in the lives of all penitent believers: clarity and inexcusability, sin and death, curse and promise, repentance and faith, justification and sanctification, baptism and calling, and resurrection and reward.

Philosophical and Theological Foundations (PF and TF) are completed by Historical Foundation (HF). The historically cumulative insight of HF is corporate, cumulative, and communal. HF begins with the Council of Jerusalem (*ca.* A.D. 51) against Judaic literalism, and applies against all continuing literalist hermeneutics. The Apostles' Creed applies against the worldview of Greek dualism, from Plato and Aristotle, coming down through Augustine and Aquinas. Nicea affirmed (the principle of) unity and diversity in the Trinity. Carthage established the canon of the New Testament once and for all. Chalcedon affirmed Christ as fully God and fully man, *two* whole natures everlastingly joined in *one* person, without conversion, composition, or confusion. Orange affirmed the effects of the fall of man and the sovereignty of divine grace against all degrees of Pelagianism. Westminster

(1648) brought the work of the first Reformation into full focus and left its effect in all the earth.

Challenges from before and after the past Reformation remain. The Church, in its spiritual war against unbelief, must demolish every pretension raised up against the knowledge of God, beginning from within, with Church leaders. The Church, as the body of Christ, the Word of God (the *Logos*) incarnate, is the pillar and ground of the Truth, the salt and light of the world. The Church is to worship God in spirit and in truth (not in zeal without knowledge, or by ritual without understanding), if it is to disciple its members and all peoples.

Who will lead? All who understand the need for foundation. Only with Foundation (PF, TF, and HF) can the Church go on unto maturity, fruitfulness, unity, and fullness. Those who understand good and evil most consciously and consistently will naturally lead in the spiritual war of good against evil. All who share that faith will naturally join the age-long and agonizing war. The ultimate outcome is certain; reading near Providence is less than certain. Four cycles, from four thousand years of history, now converge. A perfect storm is upon mankind. We know the times and the seasons; the day and the hour are unknown. Both justice and mercy are unfolding; either way, the time is short. All in and out of the Church must repent of root sin, of not seeking and not understanding what is clear about God and man and good and evil. All must bring forth fruit in keeping with repentance. All must seek the kingdom of God, through the law God, for the knowledge of God.

The way of life and death are in the nature of our being. The ancient lie denied this: "You shall not surely die." All of history has, and will, prove otherwise.

Paper №· 63

———

Theological Foundation
Prologue

THE CITY OF GOD HAS FOUNDATIONS. It has walls and gates. Once she was sought after—Abraham sought for the city with foundation; and Augustine. One enters through her gates by understanding. By faith we understand, good and evil. Now she lies desolate—walls broken down by divisions within. Her children depart from her. Unless the Lord had left us a remnant, we would have been like Sodom, and like Gomorrah, a graveyard, full of dead men's bones.

Son of man, can these bones live? Prophesy unto her the Word of the Lord. The stone the builders rejected has become the head of the corner. This is the Lord's doing, and it is marvelous in our eyes.

Hear the Word of the Lord:
In the beginning was the Word, and the Word was with God,
and the Word was God.
The same was in the beginning with God.
All things were made by him; and without him
was not any thing made that was made.
In him was life; and the life was the light of men.
And the light shines in the darkness;
and the darkness comprehended it not.

Man, made in the image of God, is crowned with light and honor, and given rule over the creation, by which he comes to know God, in all that by which he makes himself known. But man turned aside. All have sinned and come short of the glory of God. No one seeks God. No one understands. No one is righteous, no, not one. All lie in the slumber of sin and death, in the darkness of meaninglessness.

And God said, Let there be light. Grace and Truth—in its fullness, came by the Word of God, incarnate, in Jesus, the anointed—*Christos*, the *Messiah*. By the Spirit, he sends out his Word, like a river, that brings life once again to the City of God. He *is* the resurrection and the life, who raises the dead, spiritually, by rebirth, by re-creation. And, he cleanses us from all sin, by the Truth. The *Logos* is Truth.

She, who sat in the dust, will be without spot or stain or wrinkle, glorious, with *his* glory. Arise, shine, for thy light has come! All kings of the earth shall bring their glory into her. She, who once was forsaken, will be the Everlasting City. In the strength and joy of beauty, she will be the City with foundations.

Paper No. 64

AARON'S ROD:

GOD'S TEACHING AUTHORITY

IN THE CHURCH

A Call to Repentance

I N UNDERSTANDING GOD'S TEACHING AUTHORITY in the Church (summed up in the budding of Aaron's rod[1]), there are three tight-ly-connected parts that need to be considered. *First*, we are not to strain at gnats and swallow camels. If we cannot make this distinction, then there are problems. *Second*, we are not to put new wine into old wine-skins. Again, if we cannot make this distinction, we will have trouble. Without these, we cannot get to the *third* part—we are to heed God's order in the Church to bring teaching and correction in doctrine and in life. The grounds for this are shown in a particularly powerful way that is summed up in Aaron's rod that budded, and blossomed, and brought forth fruit. This was placed in the Ark of the Testimony as a permanent testimony to this authority in the Church—authority that we have inherited and are to apply today.

---

1. *Numbers 17.*

PART I

We are not to strain at gnats and swallow camels. Over the months and years, there have been divisions/disputes that have arisen and not been settled in the church (locally and globally). Some have made attempts (as all should) to settle these by proceeding from the more basic to the less basic, from Common Ground,[2] using the method of Rational Presuppositionalism (*if we agree on the more basic, we will agree on the less basic*)[3] and laying out a foundation over the months and years. This has not been fruitful for the reason given in the second point: *we are not to put new wine into old wineskins.* Although these disputes have become more manifest over time, they go back months and years beyond this. It has affected various ministries, teaching (and the prerequisites for that), use of school curriculum, existential hermeneutics, the laying out of foundation given by oversight (God's teaching authority) in the church, as well as the laying out of Common Ground, and the ten steps from foundation to fullness.[4]

In the course of these disputes, personal background factors have emerged—most prominently, a certain kind of literalism from an evangelical background from which many have come. This literalism does not distinguish fact from interpretation and does not speak about a system in which there is more basic and less basic. In this way of thinking, all things are equally basic and therefore the gnat/camel distinction is blurred and perhaps rendered meaningless—it does not make sense in the frame of reference of literalism. As a matter of fact, because of this background factor, which has emerged more and more as a default position, we find ourselves going in opposite directions in trying to settle disputes. When speaking about straining at gnats, there *is* a straining— there have been contentions and contentiousness, and there has been no way out, as long as we cannot get this more basic piece in place.

2 Timothy 2:23 says that *we are to avoid foolish arguments, they gender strife.* And Titus 3:9 says again, *we are to avoid foolish arguments,* and that if contentions continue after the second admonition, *we are to avoid it by cutting it off*—do not pursue that, have nothing to do with

---

2. *Paper No. 2.*

3. *Paper No. 52.*

4. *Paper No. 54.*

that. There is this reality in the Church, and while it may and has manifested in the present in particular ways, it has been there longer. As a matter of fact, this problem is very old in history—in the history of the Church. It goes back to the dispute concerning circumcision. This dispute came out in Acts 15—*unless you are circumcised, you cannot be saved.* The outward reality of circumcision was observed, but the inward reality spoken of by Moses from the beginning, the circumcision of the heart, was not observed. This is an example of literalism—looking at the outward/the visible and not the spiritual reality signified (circumcision is circumcision is circumcision). Historically, this has also occurred particularly with respect to baptism. There are major divisions in the Church concerning this. Between the Reformed view and Baptist view—Baptists make a distinction between the Old and the New Testament in which the New Testament is said to be new in the sense of another, not a renewal and continuity of the Old Testament. They think that unless you have it *explicitly* stated that you must baptize children, then it is not to be practiced. There have also been disputes with Catholics concerning baptismal regeneration. They think that if you are baptized, you are saved—somewhat like, *if you are circumcised, you are saved.* Again, there is a kind of literalism on either side, in an antinomy that has not been settled. So, this is not new—there are longstanding disputes that have not been settled.

Another example of this is Christ's statement, "this is my body," and the idea of the Eucharist and transubstantiation. People feel very strongly about this because the words are right there. It is literal. It means what it says and it says what it means. Another example: "Thou art Peter, and upon this rock I will build my church." This is another form that has been highly disputed—contentious—and much blood has been shed over this. Or, another: *The doctrine of heaven and hell*—mansions and glory and the literal fire into which people are cast, versus the idea of spiritual life and death to which these things point. And for good measure, consider how one should understand *Armageddon from Revelation 19*—speaking about *a sword coming out of the mouth.* This cannot and should not be taken literally. Or, *the mark of the beast,* that is *666, put on the hand and the forehead,* taken literally. There are many examples of literalism and some have come out of that background, especially in evangelicalism—in the baptistic form of evangelicalism. Many people have been raised in this and are not even aware when this is occurring in their thinking. To say "don't strain at gnats and swallow camels" does not make sense because this distinction is undermined by literalism.

Some in the church have claimed that they believe in the teaching about clarity,[5] just not with the way it is applied by the leaders in church oversight. There are some implications that follow from this claim. First, oversight does not know clarity well enough to apply it correctly. Secondly, some say "we understand clarity better than oversight, so we can apply it better—in the academy, in seminary, and in the church." In connection with this, it may manifest itself in such views and attitudes as: "We have outgrown our need for a CEO," or "This is the Lord's church, not oversight's," or "Many are ready to go on without oversight, or in spite of oversight." This should raise a lot of red flags—especially when this is inquired of by oversight, but never engaged with.

These things are the camels. When oversight tries to address these, it becomes difficult when they are shunted into procedural moves. And while this is brought to the attention of others in the church, many do not deal with or disavow it. God will and has made known the heart in due time. So, there is this camel in the room about challenging the understanding of oversight—about the doctrine of clarity and how it is to be applied. No one is talking about it. This is a camel and it is what we should be talking about, not the gnats. We should not strain at gnats while swallowing camels. There is a distinction and it is scriptural. The Lord says we should deal with the camels first—the bigger things first, the more basic things first. We should take the beam out of our own eye first, and then we will see clearly to correct others— particularly to correct oversight. That is the first point: *we are not to strain at gnats and swallow camels.*

PART II

We are not to put new wine into old wineskins. Specifically, we are not to put the new wine of the doxological focus into the old wineskins

---

5. See the teaching on clarity throughout *The Logos Papers* and Gangadean, *Philosophical Foundation.*

of our tradition,[6] which did not speak of clarity or the need to repent for failing to see clarity. Put another way, many have brought their backgrounds with them and sought to add clarity to them. That is to put new wine into old wineskins. Again, just as it can be said the very distinction between camels and gnats is undermined, the distinction about clarity itself may be undermined.

When referring to clarity, this is speaking about something that is objectively clear to reason. This is the laws of thought, the test for meaning, versus something subjectively clear to experience. The following are some examples: 1) Some have said that the existence of God is clear to intuition—it is sometimes referred to as the *sensus divinitatis*. This says that we have this intuitive, immediate, innate sense. We don't have it by seeking diligently; everyone just has this knowledge. That is an example of subjective clarity—clear to experience/intuition, but not objectively clear to reason. 2) *We hold these truths to be self-evident, that all men are created equal...* This has been challenged for the last 250 years and it has been found wanting. In the Judeo-Christian tradition, we may think of this as a self-evident truth, and maybe we will fall back on the intuitional knowledge to make it such, but it has not held up upon challenge. It has been set aside more and more. Maybe that is something that we are comfortable with as part of our tradition—we take that to be self-evident or clear. 3) Some say, "*some things are clear to my conscience.*" That is a subjective inward testimony that is going on in terms of our conduct, consistent with what we believe to be true, but that is a subjective standard again, not objective. Conscience is not Lord; the Word of God is Lord over conscience, and our conscience may not be well-informed. We may try to impose that on others. 4) *Common sense*—it has been taken for granted that it is clear that the sun rises in the east, or that the earth is flat, or the sky is blue—this may happen (maybe for a long time) until we are able to understand we are taking the position of the observer for granted and we should not. These are examples of common-sense experience on which many rely. This was used much in the schools in New England coming over from the Scottish Enlightenment, but that has proven to be inadequate. We have these histories of what is *subjectively* clear to experience rather than *objectively* clear to reason.

---

6. *Paper No. 35.* See 3.3 and 3.4; *Paper No. 16.* See Part IX.

We should not hold to clarity *simpliciter*. We are to hold to clarity *and* inexcusability. This is not speaking about 'I believe in clarity, I just don't agree with how you apply it'; this is speaking about clarity *and* inexcusability, and this is to be applied to oneself *first*, which often generates an *existential crisis*. This is the application of *existential hermeneutics*. This inexcusability is revealed in the conviction of sin and death—not understanding the meaning of things and with that meaninglessness, boredom, and guilt. This is death, and this is due to sin— root sin of not diligently seeking. We must repent of the past that we have had without any teaching of clarity, rather than build on it and add to it. This is one of the reasons that clarity and inexcusability has not taken hold. It is not that it hasn't been taught, but we are trying to build on this past/tradition, we are trying to put new wine into old wineskins, and this does not work.

Many have said, "I always believed in God, but not Christ. I didn't see my need for Christ." What are we to make of this statement? What "God" did we believe in if we did not see the need for Christ? Is it the God whose eternal power and divine nature are clearly revealed in general revelation? We fool ourselves into thinking that we believe in God and say we do not believe in Christ. This religion is a very old religion. It goes all the way back to Cain—it is the religion of Cain. He believed in God, spoke/responded to God, but did not see the need for the atonement and how this points to Christ—even though his parents wore coats of skin and he was supposed to understand what this signified. This is the religion of the deists. It is the religion of Judaism— they do not see the need for Christ, but believe in God. And it is the religion of Islam. So, we must not allow ourselves to add this teaching of clarity to our old/past tradition, without the foundation in place. After many years we will find the teaching has not taken hold, according to Hebrews 5:12, and the effort has been wasted. This is to add new wine into the old wineskin. This will cause the wineskin to burst, the wine to spill out, and there will be a waste. Again, this is what has occurred in the cases where we try to put the new wine of the doxological focus into the old wineskin of a background from evangelicalism, or other traditions, as mentioned above.

PART III

We are to heed God's order in the Church to bring teaching and correction in doctrine and in life. Historically, many churches have had membership standards which affirm this. This is summed up well in the biblical account of Aaron's rod that budded, blossomed, and bore fruit. This is not an incidental thing. This has been made a permanent witness to the Church through all the ages. God prepares those who are to teach the Law. In the Old Testament, a group was set aside—the priests and the Levites helping them. The account in the book of Numbers from chapters 1–17 brings this into focus. As we get the context in place and see how much the focus is placed on the preparation for the work of the Levites, we will be able to see more clearly Korah's opposition—his rebellion. We should remember that the book of Numbers is given after the book of Leviticus and presumes this, just as Leviticus is given after Exodus, and the understanding of how to build the tabernacle. These build one on the other.

1) The book of Numbers begins with the census of all the tribes, and then in that context, 2) the Levites are selected out in connection with all the tribes. They are selected out in a particular way, which is in place of the firstborn (this is mentioned several times in Numbers chapters 3 and 8). After this, 3) the camp is arranged and it is laid out so things are done decently and in order. And duties among the Levites are specified as part of the preparation of God setting up the order. 4) Next, there is an application of their work—the unclean are removed from the camp and the Law is being applied. It is necessary that discipline is maintained and the Levites are to exercise that duty. The unclean are removed from the camp because they could not continue among others as if there was not a problem of uncleanness. Interestingly, it speaks about the Nazarite vow, which is taking a vow to separate yourself and live under greater restrictions that will cause you to be more devoted for holiness. Whether it is the Levites or those outside like the Nazarite, they can draw near, but there is need for preparation. The Levites have this preparation regularly and in an ongoing way.

5) There is a priestly benediction on the people, the altar is dedicated, the candelabra is lit, and the Levites are cleansed in order to be in the Holy Place, where God reveals himself. The Passover is observed and, again, in a special way the Passover spared the firstborn in Israel,

and the Levites now stand in place of the firstborn as being particularly dedicated to God. The tabernacle is set up, and the cloud signifying the presence of God comes upon the tabernacle. All of this is by way of preparation for the order for teaching in the Church by the Levites. 6) A special function was given to the priests (not just the Levites) to call to the assembly of the people. The trumpets are to be blown by Aaron and his sons. Calling a holy assembly is the work of those who are most dedicated to the service of God in holiness.

7) At this point, the Israelites depart from Sinai and they lust for food—for meat (remember the previous preparation of food and water given to the people during this time). And God sends them quail and sends judgment upon them. In light of the burden of the people's murmuring and complaining on Moses, a new layer is added at this time—a new layer of leadership—the 70 of the elders of Israel. We should keep this in mind as there will be murmuring and complaining that Moses did not lead them into the Promised Land. But we should notice what is happening and why they do not go in.

8) Next, we have a very particular objection to the teaching of Moses through Miriam and Aaron. We should consider what Miriam and Aaron should have known by way of Moses' life from the very earliest way in which God set him aside and prepared him. But they overlook that—something about Moses being married to an Ethiopian woman is brought up by Miriam which shows her lack of knowledge. She challenges Moses—Is teaching the Word of God only through Moses? Her pride is revealed and she is struck with leprosy as an outward sign of her pride. She is unclean for a period of time and set outside the camp until she can come back in. All of this would have been known by everyone in the camp and they should have been learning from this. The question is, did they learn?

9) Next, we have the account of the twelve spies and of those twelve, only two are faithful. Though they had seen God's glory revealed in many ways, they did not pay attention.[7] The Third Commandment is violated. They took God's name in vain and God did not hold them guiltless. He said that they will not go into the land for their unbelief. 10) The unbelief is the reason for their wandering in the wilderness and in their presumption to overcome that, they were struck down by

---

7. *Numbers 14:20-25.*

Amalek. All of this teaching is going into, and leading up to, the event with Korah. 11) Then there was a Sabbath-breaker and the Law was applied. We should notice the objective revelation—there is objective clarity and the lawbreaker was executed. 12) The Israelites were told to wear fringes on their garments to remember to do all of the Law.

13) Now, we come to Korah and his denial of God's authority.[8] He does this in a particular way. From the King James Version:

> "Now Korah, the son of Izhar, the son of Kohath, the son of Levi, and Dathan and Abiram, the sons of Eliab, and On, the son of Peleth, sons of Reuben, took men: [they stirred up others to join them]
> And they rose up before Moses, with certain of the children of Israel, two hundred and fifty princes of the assembly, famous in the congregation, men of renown: [they have stirred up a rebellion among a significant number of leaders]
> And they gathered themselves together against Moses and against Aaron, and said unto them, Ye take too much upon you, seeing all the congregation are holy, every one of them, and the Lord is among them: wherefore then lift ye up yourselves above the congregation of the Lord?"

Scripture singles this out in the book of Jude, along with the religion of Cain and the error of Balaam, as ways in which we go astray. *The gainsaying of Korah.* His claim is self-refuting. If *all are holy and equally holy*, why then is there a need for anyone above any other and therefore, why should anyone teach? He is undermining the whole office. That is the deeper claim of Korah. It is antiauthoritarian—not just against Moses' authority, but, if we follow that reasoning, all views are equally valid. If our approach is at the level of gnats and subjective clarity, all views are equal. Unless we can get to the more basic, we cannot resolve this. One gnat is as good as another; one subjective certitude is as good as another. Korah came at it in this way and it was confronted and exposed.[9] The three families who were leaders were cut off in a particular way—the earth opened and swallowed Korah, Dathan, and

---

8. *Numbers 16.*

9. *Numbers 16–17.*

Abiram. They had challenged the teaching authority that God set up in the Church.

After this, the 250 princes who had put fire in a censer and drew near to God were consumed by fire. And on the next day, 14,700 of the congregation were struck down in their continued murmuring and complaining. Finally, to settle all of this, God calls them to bring out the rod of every tribe and to lay them before him. The rods are laid before God, and he says the one that blossoms is the one chosen by him. When they are brought out the next day, Aaron's rod had sprouted, and brought forth buds, and bloomed blossoms, and yielded almonds. This was shown to the people and "the Lord said unto Moses, Bring Aaron's rod again before the testimony, to be kept for a token against the rebels; and thou shalt quite take away their murmurings from me, that they die not."[10]

Aaron's rod is the perpetual sign to believers in all ages that God has set up authority in his Church. They teach and they bring correction. Those who teach are to have preparation, and this does not come by way of genetics, in terms of sonship. The preparation to teach is by their way of life and part of this is that they hold to the Historic Christian Faith. Many who step into that office without holding to the Historic Christian Faith are arrogating to themselves a position they have no right to step into—they have not been prepared by the work that has gone before. This is something very specific that can be seen objectively. Merely being around in history and having a tradition is not the same as the Historic Christian Faith—this is what we should look to. And we should not only hold to the Historic Christian Faith, we should seek to hold to it as consciously and consistently as we can. Korah had complained saying, *we didn't get the promised land, and we had it better off in Egypt, and you want privileges.* He fully denied and overlooked God's miracles through which Moses showed that he was sent by God. He had a disregard of what was objectively clear. It was on this basis that he was able to take the steps that he did. Heeding God's order in the Church to bring teaching and correction in doctrine and in life is epitomized in this account of Aaron's rod that budded over and against Korah's rebellion.

---

10. *Numbers 17:10.*

CONCLUSION

As was mentioned at the beginning, the three main parts above are tightly connected. The following further draws out these connections and some implications with respect to our becoming more conscious and consistent in our commitment to heeding God's teaching authority in the Church.

First, if we cannot distinguish between the *more basic* and *less basic* (camels and gnats), and if we cannot distinguish between *objectively clear to reason* and *subjectively clear to experience*, then there is no objective clarity, no need for teachers in the Church, and no need for Christ. We can come to the knowledge of the existence of God by going from the more basic to less basic. If that does not hold, then there is no way to get to the clarity of general revelation (objectively clear to reason). And if we cannot distinguish between what is objectively clear to reason versus subjectively clear to experience/intuition, then we cannot get to objective clarity. Without objective clarity, there is no need for teachers (to bring teaching and correction) because there is nothing to be taught. Without objective clarity, there is no way to speak about inexcusability. Without inexcusability, there is no sin and therefore no need for Christ.

Second, if there is clarity by going from the more basic to less basic, and objective versus subjective clarity, then objectors must submit from their hearts to oversight and learn what they need to learn. They should not continue to object—especially when teaching and correction is brought down to the level of what is clear. We are not to reject what is clear to reason.

Third, if we cannot submit to teaching based on what is clear, and to oversight that brings this, that is unprofitable for us and harmful to the church.[11]

Fourth, by way of application, we should continually renew/reaffirm our commitment to the standard of heeding God's teaching authority in the Church. There are many reasons for speaking about renewal. Deuteronomy 31:10-12 speaks about the Law being read every seven years to everyone. There is a sabbatical pattern in our lives where there is to be renewal every seven years. Teachers renew their commitment

---

11. *Hebrews 13:17.*

yearly. There is a renewal of all the vows we take whenever we hear these taken by others. There is a renewal when we observe the sacrament. We are called to make a renewal when we engage in the process of cumulative self-examination with respect to our growth in understanding the Word of God, and in our godliness, service, and witness. We are called to examine ourselves considering the reality of the curse as a call back from sin and death—this is continual/lifelong. And particularly, when disputes arise concerning understanding the doctrine of clarity and how this is applied in practice, we are called to reaffirm our understanding and commitment to the standard of heeding God's order in the Church to bring teaching and correction in doctrine *and* in life.

This paper is posthumously published
based upon the original work of Dr. Surrendra Gangadean
and has been edited by The Logos Foundation Editorial Board.

Paper Nº· 65

_____

AARON'S ROD:

A PERMANENT WITNESS AGAINST THOSE WHO CHALLENGE GOD'S AUTHORITY IN THE CHURCH

Existential Hermeneutics Applied

INTRODUCTION

This paper is a summary of three previously mentioned applications for the Church.[1] Each precept is tightly connected and if properly applied will help to resolve longstanding disputes. These are:

1. We are not to strain at gnats (the less basic) and swallow camels (the logically more basic).

2. We are not to put new wine (the doxological focus) into old wineskins (tradition/fideism).

3. We are to heed God's order in the Church to bring teaching and correction in doctrine and in life (Existential Hermeneutics).

Existential Hermeneutics is the application of the doctrine of clarity and inexcusability (the whole Word of God) to the whole of one's own life.

The teaching authority in the Church is to bring the Word of God to bear on divisions/disputes that arise.

_____

1. *Paper No. 64.*

When Korah, Dathan, and Abiram challenged the authority that God had given to Moses and Aaron, the Lord dealt most harshly with all those who brought division. As a permanent witness, Aaron's rod that budded, blossomed, and brought forth fruit was placed in the Ark of the Testimony.

All are called to repent and submit to the Word of God lest we go the way of Korah.[2]

1. We are not to strain at gnats and swallow camels.

   i. The Word of God distinguishes between camels and gnats (the logically *more basic* and *less basic*). The Lord says we should deal with the camels *first*—these are the bigger things, the weightier things, the more basic things.

   ii. The method of Rational Presuppositionalism (RP) affirms: *if we agree on the more basic, we will agree on the less basic*. We are to proceed from Common Ground[3] to the foundation to fullness.[4]

  iii. Disputes which remain unresolved show there is a lack of Common Ground (not agreeing on the more basic).

  iv. Without addressing the more basic (the camel in the room), there will be a straining (at the less basic gnats) which can and has produced strife.[5] Without the more basic in place, there is no way to proceed in resolving the divisions/disputes—the meaning of every word is disputed, endlessly.

   v. Divisions make manifest those that are proven. Personal background factors emerge, revealing opposing epistemic frameworks—among these, most prominently, is a literalism from an evangelical background (subjective Christianity).

  vi. Contextualism (RP) is opposed to literalism. Literalism neglects, avoids, resists, and denies the logical distinction of less and more basic. It cannot understand the distinction because it

---

2. *Jude 1:11.*

3. *Paper No. 2.*

4. *Paper No. 54.*

5. *2 Timothy 2:23.*

undermines it. It renders the distinction meaningless by making all things equally basic.

vii. Literalism is a very old problem in the history of the Church.[6]

viii. Many *profess* the teaching of clarity. Few *understand* it enough to apply it.[7]

ix. When one professes to know clarity (or how to apply it) better than God's teaching authority, this presumption should raise red flags—it is the camel in the room with which all should engage.

x. We should take the beam of literalism out of our own eye *first*, then we can see clearly to correct others (particularly God's teaching authority).

2. We are not to put new wine into old wineskins.

i. We are not to put the new wine of the doxological focus into the old wineskins of our tradition/background.[8]

ii. We are not to add the teaching of clarity to our tradition, but we are to repent for failing to see clarity rooted in our tradition. Our old tradition cannot see clarity because it undermines it.

iii. By clarity is meant what is *objectively* clear to reason (using RP) vs. what is *subjectively* clear to experience. Some common examples of subjective clarity include:

a. *Sensus divinitatis*—intuitive, immediate, innate sense vs. objectively clear to reason by seeking diligently.

b. *"I always believed in God, but I didn't see my need for Christ"*— what "God" did we believe in if we did not see our need for Christ? Is it the God whose eternal power and divine nature are clearly revealed to all (objectively) in general revelation, so that all are without excuse?

---

6. *Paper No. 16.* See Part III; *Paper No. 38.* See point 5; *Paper No. 49.* See Response to FAQ; Also, see the problem of literalism addressed throughout *The Logos Papers.*

7. See *The Logos Papers* and Gangadean, *Philosophical Foundation.*

8. *Paper No. 35.* See 3.3 and 3.4; *Paper No. 16.* See Part IX.

c. *"We hold these truths to be self-evident..."*—we may take *truths* to be self-evident or clear intuitively in the comfort of our Judeo-Christian tradition vs. showing truth to be objectively clear to reason.

d. *"Some things are clear to my conscience"*—subjective standard of inward testimony. Conscience is not Lord; the Word of God is Lord over conscience, and our conscience may not be well-informed.

e. *Common sense*—assumes it is clear that appearance is reality (the sun rises in the east, the earth is flat, the sky is blue). Common sense takes the position of the observer for granted.

iv. By clarity is meant clarity *and* inexcusability (not clarity *simpliciter*). Clarity requires the application of *existential hermeneutics*—clarity *and* inexcusability applied to oneself *first*.

v. Inexcusability is revealed in the conviction of death (meaninglessness, boredom, and guilt) due to our root sin of not seeking diligently.

vi. Adding the teaching of clarity to past traditions will not hold, causing the wineskin to burst, the wine to spill out, and the effort to be wasted.[9]

vii. Objections arise against clarity from the old wineskin of subjective Christianity: faith without proof based on understanding (fideism), zeal without knowledge (pietism), and the outward letter of God's law (legalism).

3. We are to heed God's order in the Church to bring teaching and correction in doctrine and in life.

i. The biblical account of Aaron's rod is a perpetual sign to believers in all ages that God has set up an order of authority in his Church.[10]

---

9. *Hebrews 5:12.*

10. *Numbers 17.*

ii. The context of Numbers 1–17 gives a cumulative focus on the preparation for the work of the priests and Levites.[11]

The teaching authority is shown through preparation by a way of life, speaking in the name of God—showing what is objectively clear, and building on the Historic Christian Faith.

iii. In light of the objective clarity of the cumulative revelation of God's glory, the people murmur and complain, object to God's order, and take the name of God in vain, bringing God's judgment.

iv. The denial of God's order of authority culminates in the gainsaying of Korah.[12]

Korah's claim, *all are holy and equally holy* (all views are equally valid), is self-refuting and antiauthoritarian—it undermines the whole order of teaching authority established by God.

Those who side-step, disregard, or rebel against God's order arrogate to themselves God's teaching authority in pride, presumption, arrogance, and contumacious behavior.

A particular disregard of what is objectively clear brings God's judgment in a particular way.

v. The choosing of Aaron's rod—God is the final judge among us. Resurrection life comes through the Word of God.

IMPLICATIONS

1. If we cannot distinguish between the *more basic* and *less basic*, and *objectively clear to reason* and *subjectively clear to experience*, then there is no objective clarity, and therefore no inexcusability, no need for teachers in the Church, and no need for Christ.

2. If there is objective clarity, we should submit from our hearts to the Word of God and his authority in the Church which brings teaching and correction based on clarity.

---

11. *Paper No. 64.* See Part III.

12. *Numbers 16.*

3. If we cannot submit to teaching and correction, it is unprofitable to us and harmful to the peace and purity of the Church.[13]

4. We should continually renew/reaffirm our understanding and commitment to the standard of heeding God's order in the Church to bring teaching and correction in doctrine (understanding) *and* in life (application)—especially when disputes arise.

This paper is posthumously published
based upon the original work of Dr. Surrendra Gangadean
and has been developed by The Logos Foundation Editorial Board.

---

13. *Hebrews 13:17.*

Paper № 66

———

WHAT IS PHILOSOPHY?[1]
On the Nature and Necessity of Philosophy

Philosophy can be defined in terms of its several features.
It is an area, an attitude, a method, an application, and a system.

1. AREA—foundation and goal

Philosophy is concerned with the most basic issues we can logically think about. It deals with questions that are foundational to all our thoughts, in each of its three branches.

Epistemology: How do I know?

i. Is knowledge of basic things (concerning the existence and nature of God and man and good and evil) possible? Is knowledge of basic things necessary, or is belief based on testimony (human or divine) sufficient?

ii. How is knowledge of basic things possible? Is it by sense experience (in science) or by intuition (in art, morality, or religion) or by reason (in philosophy)?

Metaphysics: What is real (eternal)?

i. Ontology: What is the nature of being? Is everything made of matter or does spirit also exist, or is all spirit?

---

1. Gangadean, *Philosophical Foundation*, 6-10; Gangadean, *History of Philosophy*, 73-75; *Paper No. 20*.

ii. Cosmology: How did things come to be as they are? Is everything eternal in some form or other, or is only some (God) eternal, or is nothing eternal? Is there an eternal process or did God create the heavens and the earth?

Ethics: What ought I to do?

Philosophy is also concerned with ultimate questions about the meaning of life. What is the goal or purpose of human existence? What is the highest good, the end in itself, sought for its own sake, and the source of happiness? Is this good the same for all? Is morality possible if basic things are not objectively clear (knowable by all who seek to know)?

Q1. Are these questions of philosophy the most basic of all questions?

Q2. Must these questions be asked and answered or can they be assumed?

Q3. Can other disciplines (physics, psychology, etc.) answer these questions? Do they attempt to?

Q4. Is philosophy foundational for all other areas of thought (the sciences, the arts, and religion based on special revelation)?

2. ATTITUDE—love of wisdom

"Philosophy" literally means "love of wisdom." One has wisdom if one knows the good and how to achieve it.

Beliefs about what is real and what is the good direct our lives and so are crucially important. The alternative is to think one knows when one does not know or to not be concerned to know. Failure to know and seek the good is the source of all the miseries of life. Fear of not having the good is the beginning of wisdom. Love of the good brings one to the fullness of wisdom.

Q1. Is wisdom necessary for all or for only some? Is it possible for all?

Q2. Can one seek wisdom if one is mistaken about being wise?

Q3. How is wisdom or lack of wisdom experienced?

Q4. Is it possible to study philosophy without this attitude?

3. METHOD—critical use of reason

By reason is meant the laws of thought:

i. identity: *a* is *a*

ii. non-contradiction: not both *a* and *non-a* (at the same time, in the same respect)

iii. excluded middle: either *a* or *non-a*

Reason is the test for meaning, which is more basic than truth: one has to know what a statement means before knowing if it is true or not. A statement is meaningless (cannot be thought) if it violates a law of thought. A statement which is meaningless cannot be true. Reason is used critically when basic assumptions are recognized and analyzed for meaning.

Q1. Can reason itself (the laws of thought) be doubted?

Q2. Is man fundamentally rational?

Q3. Do the laws of thought apply to the world?

Q4. Is it necessary to test basic beliefs for meaning?

Q5. Is reason the test for meaning?

Q6. Can there be truth without meaning?

4. APPLICATION—self-examination

The first application of philosophy is to examine one's own basic beliefs for meaning. The Socratic dictum, "the unexamined life is not worth living [is less than human existence]," is basic in philosophy. To live an unconscious and uncritical life is less than the life of reason and is therefore less than human existence. Unthinking life for humans is wasted life. Self-examination is necessary for integrity, and integrity is necessary and sufficient for knowledge.

Q1. Can you identify your most basic belief and test it for meaning? Can we fail to do so?

Q2. Can reason be used critically without self-examination?

Q3. If there is a lack of knowledge of basic things, is there a lack of integrity?

5. SYSTEM—world and life view

Philosophy uses reason constructively to develop the implications of one's assumptions (basic beliefs) for every area of life. A worldview supplies meaning to all of life. A civilization or a culture is a system of shared beliefs, attitudes, and values which are developed theoretically and come to expression institutionally in every area of human life.

Worldviews are held more or less consciously and more or less consistently in every culture and civilization. History shows that there are various philosophical views that have come to cultural expression through the process of internal and external challenges of reason. Many cultures and civilizations have ceased to exist when their worldview ceased to be credible.

Q1. Is philosophy fundamentally relevant to all of life?

Q2. Is thinking by nature presuppositional? If there is agreement on what is more basic, will there be agreement on what is less basic?

Q3. What are some of the philosophical views expressed in history?

Q4. How do differences in culture reflect different basic beliefs?

Q5. Are all worldviews equally coherent?

Q6. Can a culture or civilization survive if its worldview fails to achieve coherence when challenged?

*This paper was originally developed for an
Introduction to Philosophy course.*

———

CONCEPTUAL MAP
To Find Meaning and Settle Disputes

A conceptual map helps us to locate where we are intellectually. It enables us to locate differences appropriately and thus help to avoid secondary disputes and to address the more basic disputes. A conceptual map therefore helps to find meaning and to settle disputes.

1. Epistemology

    i. Definition of "know": cognitivism; justified true belief vs. objections.

    ii. Skepticism: knowledge is not possible; Fideism: belief without proof/understanding.

    iii. Empiricism: common sense, science, intuition, mystical experience.

    iv. Rationalism: reason as a source of truth (vs. test for meaning).

    v. Testimony: human (tradition), divine (scripture).

    vi. Rational Presuppositionalism: thinking of the less basic in light of the more basic.

2. Metaphysics

i. Definition of "being": being and non-being; aspects of being; existence and essence; substance: matter and spirit; temporal and eternal; finite and infinite.

ii. Becoming without being: none is eternal—all is process.

iii. Material monism: all is eternal—matter.

iv. Spiritual monism: all is eternal—spirit.

v. Dualism: all is eternal—matter and spirit.

vi. Theism: only some is eternal—God the Creator.

3. Ethics

i. Definition of "the good": the end in itself, the highest value, the source of unity, the moral absolute—not the effect or a means, based on human nature, one, clear.

ii. Ethical relativism: there is no rational justification for a universal moral standard.

iii. Hedonism: pleasure/happiness is the good; individual vs. collective.

iv. Deontology: some things are right or good in themselves.

v. Humanism: instinctual, theoretical, existential forms of human autonomy.

vi. Moral Law: there is a moral law which is clear—based on human nature, comprehensive—applies to all choice, and critical—consequence of life or death.

This paper was originally developed for an
Introduction to Logic course.

Paper № 68

———

RESPONSES TO
POPULAR SKEPTICISM[1]

1. *There are so many views.*

   R1: There are not many basic views, only two (all or only some is eternal).

   R2: There are many degrees of rational consistency with which a basic view is held.

2. *It doesn't matter anyway which view you hold. They are all the same.*

   R1: This may be true on a practical or psychological level, but even here only in the short run.

   R2: If large-scale, long-term, differences in human lives are not important, then nothing is important—including anything you say.

3. *Who is to say which view is right?*

   R1: It is not who is to say, but what is to say.

   R2: Reason (the laws of thought in all of us) must be observed if we are to avoid talking nonsense.

---

1. Gangadean, *Philosophical Foundation*, 18-21.

4. *It is all a matter of interpretation.*

R1: That is true, but philosophy does not end here—it begins here.

R2: Every interpretation must be tested for rational consistency.

5. *It is all relative.*

R1: Yes, it is—to one's own basic belief.

R2: Basic beliefs can be tested for meaning.

6. *I don't know what I believe.*

R1: We do have basic beliefs held more or less consciously.

R2: We can know our basic beliefs by looking at our actions.

7. *I'll go with the flow (the simple, easy, what comes natural approach).*

R: Ok. Go ahead. Perhaps we will meet again.

This paper was originally developed for an
Introduction to Philosophy course.

Paper N⁰· 69

———

SOURCES OF SKEPTICISM[1]

Skepticism (intellectual despair) is rooted
in our uncritically held assumptions.

1. Informal Fallacies

It involves the use of irrelevant appeals as a substitute for the use of reason and logical argument. For example: ad hominem; straw man; question begging; arguing in a circle; appeal to pity, fear, popularity, etc.[2] It assumes that if a pseudo-argument does not succeed, no argument will succeed.

2. Tradition and Custom

It assumes what we are most comfortable with is true. For example: since it has been around a long time it is true; it is right because that is the way I have been taught; most people I know think and act this way, etc. This certainty melts in our exposure to other cultures or hardens into prejudice.

3. Common Sense

It assumes that appearance is reality (naïve realism). For example: the earth is flat; the sun rises in the east; the color of the ocean is blue, green, gray, clear. Common sense takes the condition of the perceiver for granted.

---

1. Gangadean, *Philosophical Foundation*, 17-31.

2. *Paper No. 71.*

4. Intuition

It assumes that the natural sign is always accompanied by the reality, or the sign is the reality. For example: truth is beauty, beauty truth; pleasure and goodness; sex and love; smile (good vibrations) and friendliness. It assumes this is a morally ideal world.

5. Science

It is being misused and becomes a source of skepticism when its methods are over-extended to a philosophical principle. For example:

i. When empiricism is assumed (all knowledge is ultimately from sense experience—there are no innate ideas of reason apart from experience).

ii. When it goes beyond its empirical boundary (in assuming only natural or material forces must be used to explain phenomena).

iii. When it fails to distinguish data (pure experience) from fact—data interpreted in light of philosophical assumptions.

iv. When it fails to notice that science does and must have philosophical foundations, which have to be critically analyzed for coherence of meaning.

v. When skeptical disclaimers (tentativeness and pragmatism) are used to forgo philosophical criticism of its assumption.

6. Reason

It is a source of skepticism when it is misused or not fully used.

i. It is misused when used as a source of truth rather than as a test for meaning.

ii. It is not fully used when it is used constructively only and not first and fundamentally used critically to examine basic assumptions for coherence of meaning.

*This paper was originally developed for an
Introduction to Philosophy course.*

Paper № 70

―――――

SOURCES OF FIDEISM[1]
Popular, Theological, Personal

Fideism is holding a belief without proof. Proof is seen either as not relevant or not possible or may not actually be present. Fideism may occur on both sides of an assertion. It may be both theistic and anti-theistic. It may be naturalistic or supernaturalistic. It may be sophistic or simplistic. Fideism assumes basic things are not clear. Belief without proof based on understanding loses all meaning.

1. *Sensus Divinitatis:* Is knowledge of God immediate or inferred?

"Deep down everyone knows that God exists."

Response:

i. What is the content of this knowledge? Is it the same as Romans 1:20—God's eternal power and divine nature? The account from upholders of the SD view is varied and generally bare.

ii. If one has this knowledge, one should be able to prove it.

iii. SD assumes a common sense realism or intuition.[2]

When arguments arise against this immediately held belief, it is not self-evident that intuition must override reason. How can one rationally choose between two *prima facie* justifiable

―――――――――

1. Gangadean, *Philosophical Foundation*, 32-45.

2. *Paper No. 69.*

beliefs? Reason and argument (strong justification) is necessary for knowledge.[3]

2. Knowledge and Accountability: What is the basis of inexcusability?

"Because they really know deep down (and suppress it), they are without excuse."

Response:

i. This view assumes that if one does not have knowledge, one cannot be held responsible (vs. culpable ignorance—responsible for the failure to seek and understand/know what is maximally clear about God).

ii. Failure to seek and understand describes a universal, basic, moral failure. "Father, forgive them; for they know not what they do," assumes ignorance is culpable.

iii. This view assumes that knowing the truth does not set a person free from moral bondage.

3. The Magisterial vs. Ministerial Use of Reason: Is reason to be understood as only servant, and not judge of the truth of revelation?

"Reason cannot and should not be the judge of the truth of revelation."

Response:

i. Some are willing to use reason in its formative, interpretive, and constructive use, but not critically with respect to their *own* revelation (truth). To apply the critical use of reason to other revelation and not to one's own is arbitrary in the extreme.

ii. Since reason is necessary to receive *and to understand* revelation, revelation must necessarily pass the minimal test of intelligibility. What is actually contradictory (vs. apparently) is unintelligible and cannot be thought, and therefore cannot be believed.

---

3. *Paper No. 72* and *75*.

Reason used critically, as the test for meaning (which is more basic than truth), is necessary to understand revelation.

4. Ontology and Epistemology: Can reason grasp ultimate reality?

"Reason cannot grasp ultimate reality."

Response:

i. Reason is ontological—it applies to all being, to the highest being, to God's being (God, in his being, is not both eternal and not eternal, at the same time and in the same respect). If God's being is eternal, then reason is eternal, and therefore uncreated, and unlike the laws of nature which began at creation.

ii. Human knowledge is and will forever be finite (even though it may grow). But, by reason and argument, we know in part. And since thinking is presuppositional, we begin with what is most basic, without having exhaustive knowledge.

iii. The basic things (about God and man and good and evil) are known by revelation through the acts of creation and providence (necessarily, intentionally, and exclusively).

iv. Reason is transcendental (authoritative and self-attesting)—it cannot be questioned but makes questioning (intelligibility) possible. Since reason applies to the being of God, it need not be, nor can it be, established by appeal to God's being or will, which already presupposes reason.

5. Faith and Reason: Are faith and reason compatible?

"Faith is other than reason; it goes beyond and sometimes is opposed to reason."

Response:

i. Does not truth presuppose meaning? Can a belief be held more strongly than the understanding of the meaning of its content? If not, then faith *is* understanding, and "I believe *in so far as* I understand" (vs. "I believe in order that I may understand").

ii. As truth cannot be separated from meaning, so faith cannot be separated from reason. It is by reason that meaning is grasped. Faith grows as understanding grows. Faith is tested as understanding is tested.

6. **Reason and the *Testimonium Spiritu Sancti:* What is the role of reason and the work (witness) of the Holy Spirit with respect to faith (salvation)?**

"Reason is finite and fallen. Reason cannot persuade; the Holy Spirit does. Salvation is by grace, not works."

Response:

i. Is reason the most basic form of the Word of God that comes to man (the life of the *Logos* in man, as light, by which man sees/understands all of the revelation of God)?

ii. If so, does the Holy Spirit (HS) work by and with reason (the Word) or apart from reason? Does the HS work to convince, persuade, enlighten, and illuminate the mind with sound argument or apart from sound argument?

iii. Does the HS make an argument sound by a supernatural act? Or is the argument sound by its own characteristics?

iv. Is the purpose of a sound argument only to persuade, or can it also compel a person to shut their eyes (turn off their mind) to avoid the force of a sound argument?

v. Is it reason that is finite and fallen, or is it man that is finite and fallen? Is it reason that fails to understand, or man who fails to seek and understand through reason?

vi. Is the use of reason opposed to or independent of grace, or itself a work of grace? Is the use of and proper response to sound argument a purely natural occurrence, or is it itself something of a miracle?

7. **Reason and the Particular: Can reason grasp the particular/individual/unique or only the universal and abstract?**

"Reason grasps the universal and abstract, not the particular concrete (known only in existential encounter). Faith must suspend and leap beyond reason, the universal, and the ethical, to grow in faith and obey God (as seen in Abraham, the man of faith)."

Response:

   i. The individuality/uniqueness of Abraham is comprehensible only in understanding all the particulars of his life story in its entirety. Abraham's particular act of offering up Isaac (obedience in faith) should be seen in the continuity of his faith (understanding), developed and expressed throughout his life.

   ii. The elements of his faith (understanding man's origin and destiny, God's purpose in world history, sin and death, the curse and promise, the necessity for the resurrection) were in place before leaving the City of Man for the City of God.

   iii. These elements (universals) were deepened through all the particulars of his life (the meaning of world history, sacrifice, circumcision, the name "Isaac," and the promise/blessing being through Isaac—himself, a sinner).

   iv. From this faith, Abraham *reasoned* that God could and would raise Isaac from the dead to fulfill the promise God made. This was a deepened understanding (faith) of what he already believed when he first received the call and promise in Ur.

8. **Reason and Rationalism: Can we escape the bi-polar mindset between faith and reason, between fideism and skepticism, between the right and left?**

"Religion leads to wars, abuses, and superstitions. Therefore, it's reason without God."

"Reason removes God from creation and providence (seen as unnecessary), leading to extreme immorality, dehumanization, and nihilism. Therefore, it's God without reason."

Response:

    i. No one is obligated to choose between reason without God or God without reason (antinomies).

    ii. There is a common failure to use reason to understand the clarity of general revelation on both sides (in the name of reason and in the name of God). Both rationalists and fideists fail to address the problem of evil (the latter, from both general *and* special revelation—which gives them more light).

    iii. A deeper sense of reason as the *Logos* in man, and a deeper use of reason in light of clarity, would shatter pretentions on both sides and get us past the dangers of competing idolatries.

9. Reason and Hermeneutics: Is reason/how is reason to be used in interpreting the Scripture?

"God's Word means what is says and says what it means; the words are right there; God says it and I believe it. We shouldn't add our own interpretations/imaginations to the Word of God. The Bible should be read literally."

"The Scripture is much deeper in meaning with its very symbolic and metaphorical language. Reading the Bible literally leaves it bare and boring and it often becomes absurd. The Bible should be read allegorically."

Response:

    i. Interpretation of Scripture should be by contextualism (applying all layers of context with a presuppositional hermeneutic—understanding the logically less basic in light of the more basic). This is opposed to the antinomies of literalism (one word, one meaning) and allegoricalism (brings in arbitrary/unwarranted assumptions to the text).

    ii. Taken strictly, the Reformation principle of *Sola Scriptura* becomes literalist, excluding the use of external and internal context of interpretation.

    iii. *Sola Scriptura* should be understood as a principle of authority set against all other claims based on special revelation. It is not set against, but presupposes, reason (in making good and necessary consequences) and the clarity of general revelation as its most basic context. Therefore, it should be consistent with this context.

10. Piety and Intellect: Can we allow for an anti-intellectual split in human personality or piety (head/heart split)?

"The Scripture warns against vain philosophy and being puffed up by knowledge. God hides truths from the wise but reveals them to babes, and uses the weak and foolish things to confound the strong and wise. He desires us to not lean on our own understanding, but to be like little children in simple piety, for which he will reward us in heaven face-to-face in a beatific vision."

Response:

i. One is called to love God with the whole heart, including the mind, beginning with the understanding.

ii. One is called to go on to maturity from infancy in understanding, in order to attain to the fullness of God.

iii. One is warned against zeal without knowledge and called to piety (holiness), which comes from knowing the truth.

iv. One is reminded that all suffer under natural evil as a call to stop and *think*, to earnestly seek God.

v. One is called to take every thought (raised against the knowledge of God) captive to the obedience of Christ.

vi. The wisdom literature exalts understanding and warns against the folly of fools and the complacency of the simple.

vii. The outcome (the goal) of life is not an individual beatific vision in heaven, but the earth being filled with *the knowledge of God* through a corporate, cumulative work of mankind in history.

11. Reason and the Mysteries of the Faith: Are mysteries of the faith beyond or against reason?

"Mysteries are beyond and against reason; they are supremely objects of faith."

Response:

i. How can it be known what is to be believed within a religion or between religions, if reason is to be suspended in matters of faith?

ii. Mysteries are things formerly hidden and now revealed (in special, not general, revelation). They arise first from the reading of Scripture. Then, as differences in understanding arise, a consensus is reached through a process of much discussion (by leaders and teachers in councils). Through the use of reason (good and necessary consequences), faulty and contradictory misunderstandings of doctrine are removed for a more precise confession of faith. Future generations who neglect this often repeat old questions and old errors.

iii. The differences are often misunderstandings rooted in uncritically held assumptions from general revelation used to interpret special revelation.

iv. In the course of progressing in understanding, what appeared to be against reason (paradox) is seen to be not against reason, but in accord with reason, and eventually it may be seen to be what reason should expect.

12. Reason and Personality: With the diversity in human nature, is there hope for unity?

"Some people are inclined to the life of thought, some to feeling, and some to action. We are just different."

Response:

i. There is a real diversity among persons, but properly understood it is the basis of unity, not disunity.

ii. There is a *natural unity* and a *natural order* for unity in each person—3 functions: intellect, emotion, will (in that order). Unity among persons begins with unity in a person.

iii. Our personality inclination (to the life of thought, or feeling, or action) has an epistemological lifestyle implication (to rely on reason, or intuition, or sense experience as a primary source of knowledge).

iv. Through proper education, self-examination/discipline, and wise guidance, knowledge of oneself and of the good is cultivated. Knowledge of the good is the source of unity (within a person and between persons), through which the good is fully realized. Reason as the source of the knowledge of the good is the primary source of unity.

*This paper is posthumously published
based upon the original work of Dr. Surrendra Gangadean
and has been developed by The Logos Foundation Editorial Board.*

Paper № 71

INFORMAL FALLACIES[1]

1. APPEAL TO FEAR: Use of threat to persuade to action. It succeeds where one fears losing a secondary good over a primary good. Used against Socrates, unsuccessfully.

2. APPEAL TO PITY: Abuse of the listener's disposition to compassion. It succeeds where the good of the recipient is not kept clearly in mind. It is often used to avoid responsibility where hardship is necessary.

3. STRAW MAN: Arguing against a misrepresentation of a position rather than the real thing. Honesty and care are necessary to avoid the use of straw man.

4. APPEAL TO AUTHORITY: Appealing to someone as an authority where he or she is not an authority. This is often used where there is insufficient respect for the authority of reason.

5. AD HOMINEM: Speaking against the person rather than against what the person said. Personal attack often used when we don't have a counter-argument.

6. AD POPULUM: Relying on the tendency of people to believe or go along with what is commonly accepted or done. It succeeds against those who find safety in numbers, or custom, or the establishment.

---

1. Gangadean, *Philosophical Foundation*, 45-48.

7. BEGGING THE QUESTION: Assuming to be true what one claims to be proving to be true. Used often where a person is not aware of his or her assumptions.

8. RED HERRING: Sidetracking the argument by bringing in what is irrelevant. Often based on associative thinking and taking things out of the original context.

9. APPEAL TO IGNORANCE: Assuming a belief to be true if it has not been disproven. It sometimes involves an appeal to the unknown through the use of indefinable terms.

10. POST HOC: After this, therefore because of this. Faulty causal reasoning based on insufficient observation or analysis.

11. HASTY GENERALIZATION: Making a general statement based on insufficient observation. Often involved in stereotyping.

12. COMPLEX QUESTION: A question that assumes more than the listener is ready to assent to. Also known as the loaded question.

*This paper was originally developed for an
Introduction to Philosophy course.*

————

WHAT IS KNOWLEDGE?
Concise Version

Epistemology (the logos of *episteme*) is concerned with an account of knowledge regarding the certainty of basic beliefs. The term "knowledge" is ambiguous; there are several senses in which knowledge can be understood. It is the last sense below—*justified true belief*—that is of primary importance in addressing contemporary challenges in epistemology.

1. *Knowledge by acquaintance* is direct, or non-inferential, sense perception of a thing, or the properties of a thing. For example: the taste of a lemon, the smell of a rose, or the color of blue.

2. *Factual knowledge* is the comprehension of some "fact." For example: "I know that today is Tuesday." *Know-how* is the comprehension of how to execute a task. For example: "I know how to ride a bicycle."

3. *A priori* knowledge is propositional knowledge independent of sense perception. For example: "All bachelors are unmarried men." *A posteriori* knowledge is propositional knowledge that is dependent upon the senses. For example: "The sun is shining today."

4. *Propositional knowledge* is understanding the meaning of a judgment (S is P), affirming the content of that judgment, and having logical inferential support for the truth claim of that judgment. For example: "I know that something is eternal."

5. In attempting to define propositional knowledge, Plato says that knowledge is true opinion with an account. Contemporary philosophers, claiming to follow Plato, define knowledge as: *justified true belief.* This definition of knowledge may be stated more formally by saying:

> A person S knows a proposition *p* if and only if:
>
> i. *p* is true
>
> ii. S believes *p*
>
> iii. S is justified in believing that *p*

6. To have a *belief* is to have a mental affirmation of a proposition. Consider the existential state of holding a belief.

   Truth is what corresponds with reality. Consider the difference between a subjective and objective definition of truth.

   Justification is what guarantees true belief.

7. The three conditions (of justified, true, belief) are said to be necessary and sufficient for knowledge. These conditions have been challenged as being neither necessary nor sufficient for knowledge.

   i. Edmund Gettier, through his counterexamples, challenges the sufficiency of justification for knowledge.

   ii. Alvin Plantinga, in response to challenges to the sufficiency of justification, restates the definition of knowledge as *warranted true belief*, and denies the necessity of justification for knowledge.

8. The challenge is plausible only until an ambiguity in understanding the third condition of justification is clarified, and by addressing primary (logically basic), rather than secondary (properly basic), beliefs.

9. We may retain the *justified true belief* formulation of knowledge by removing the ambiguity between Plato's rationalist account and Gettier and Plantinga's empiricist accounts. Knowledge is *justified true belief* where:

i. *Weak justification* is sensory data that provides a high probability of truth (sufficient for most of our everyday judgments). This does not guarantee knowledge.

ii. *Strong justification* is by reason and argument such that the opposite is impossible (necessary for foundational philosophical claims). Strong justification requires an understanding of reason.[1] This guarantees knowledge.

10. To believe the conclusion of a sound argument because the argument is seen as sound is to possess knowledge.

*This paper is posthumously published
based upon the original work of Dr. Surrendra Gangadean
and has been developed by The Logos Foundation Editorial Board.*

---

1. *Paper No. 5* and *75.*

Paper №· 73

———

WHAT IS KNOWLEDGE?
Expanded Version

Epistemology is the logos of *episteme* or the account of knowledge. Contemporary philosophers have had interminable disagreements about the nature of knowledge and the means of attaining knowledge, which has resulted in skepticism. We can and should overcome skepticism and, through contemporary challenges, see more clearly what knowledge is and that these challenges do not undermine the classical definition of knowledge.

Epistemology is concerned with an account of knowledge regarding the certainty of basic beliefs. There are several senses in which knowledge can be understood; it is the last sense that is of primary importance in addressing contemporary challenges in epistemology. The term "knowledge" is ambiguous; ambiguity can be removed by defining its uses.

1. *Knowledge by acquaintance* is direct, or non-inferential, sense perception of a thing or the properties of a thing. For example, the taste of a lemon, the smell of a rose, or the color of blue.

2. *Factual knowledge* is the comprehension of some "fact." For example: "I know that today is Tuesday." *Know-how* is the comprehension of how to execute a task. For example: "I know how to ride a bicycle."

3. *A priori* knowledge is propositional knowledge independent of sense perception. For example: "All bachelors are unmarried men." *A*

posteriori knowledge is propositional knowledge that is dependent upon the senses. For example: "The sun is shining today."

4. *Propositional knowledge* is understanding the meaning of a judgment (S is P), affirming the content of that judgment, and having logical inferential support for the truth claim of that judgment. For example: "I know that something is eternal."

5. In attempting to define propositional knowledge, Plato says that knowledge is true opinion with an account. Contemporary philosophers, claiming to follow the tradition of Plato, define knowledge as: *justified true belief.* This definition of knowledge may be stated more formally by saying:

   A person S knows a proposition *p* if and only if:

   i. *p* is true

   ii. S believes *p*

   iii. S is justified in believing that *p*

6. The distinction between Plato's original formulation of the definition of knowledge and Gettier's contemporary definition is the difference between a rationalist account of knowledge and an empiricist account.

7. The three conditions (of justified, true, belief) are said to be necessary and sufficient for knowledge. These conditions have been challenged as being neither necessary nor sufficient for knowledge.

   i. Edmund Gettier, through his counterexamples, challenges the sufficiency of justification for knowledge.

   ii. Alvin Plantinga, in response to challenges to the sufficiency of justification, restates the definition of knowledge as *warranted true belief,* and denies the necessity of justification for knowledge.

8. The challenge to the necessity and sufficiency of justification is plausible only until an ambiguity in understanding the third condition of justification is clarified, and by addressing primary (logically basic), rather than secondary (properly basic), beliefs.

9. Clarifying the ambiguity in the condition of justification requires examination of the context of the original definition of knowledge and the contemporary definition of knowledge, and testing each for meaning.

   i. Plato defines knowledge in the dialogue *Theaetetus*.

      a. The context of the dialogue: assumptions of materialism (flux doctrine), empiricism (all knowledge is through the senses), skepticism (knowledge is not possible), and sophism (persuasion).

      b. Plato clarifies the meaning of knowledge by negation—what knowledge is not: Knowledge is not perception (vs. empiricism). Perception is of what is changing and impermanent. Knowledge is of what is unchanging and permanent (vs. materialism).

      c. Knowledge is not relative (to the individual or to society). Perception is subjective, not shared, and is relative. Knowledge is objective and shared (vs. skepticism).

      d. Knowledge is not opinion. Opinion may or may not be true. What distinguishes opinion from knowledge is rational justification.

      e. Knowledge is not true opinion (TO).

         1. TO may be obtained by chance.

         2. TO may be changed when opposed because it is not "tied down."

         3. TO is sufficient for right action.

      f. Knowledge is true opinion with an account—a logos.

         1. Opinion is a judgment: X is Y.

         2. True is what accords with reality and is objective.

         3. A logos is a reason that "ties down," guarantees, or certifies true belief.

            i. A logos is an account or reasons (not sense data).

ii. A logos is necessary truth that couldn't be otherwise.

iii. A logos is proof, often derived by elimination of the logical contradiction.

iv. A logos is what is needed for philosophical claims (not for scientific claims or poetic claims).

v. In the allegory of the line, Plato shows that there are levels of cognitive commitment (imagination, opinion, true opinion, and knowledge).

vi. An example of knowledge is that "something must be eternal." Proof: the impossibility of the opposite "nothing is eternal."[1]

4. Knowledge is of fundamental philosophical claims about God (Is matter all there is?), man (Does the soul exist? Is the soul eternal?), and good and evil for man.

5. Knowledge is the source of the good for human beings.

6. Knowledge is gained by conversation (the dialectic) in community as a source of unity.

ii. Objections to Plato's definition of knowledge.

a. Gettier and justified true belief (JTB); Plantinga and warranted true belief (WTB).

1. Gettier's justification is not a rational account; it assumes empiricism. Gettier examples all rely on empirical data or testimony, which can never provide certainty. Plato would disagree with Gettier's empirical approach and definition of knowledge.

2. Gettier's account of knowledge is closer to Plato's true opinion.

3. Plantinga's reformulation of justification assumes Gettier's definition (JTB) and his empiricism. Plantinga's WTB (cognitive faculties functioning properly in an appropriate environment, according to a good design plan) does

---

1. Gangadean, *Philosophical Foundation*, 49-62.

not escape the problem of skepticism and leads to religious fideism.

    4. Neither Gettier nor Plantinga get to a rational account that guarantees true belief based on a logos. Neither Gettier nor Plantinga get to what is clear to reason.

  b. What about certainty?

    1. An account "certifies" or proves objectively. Objective "certification" is not the same as subjective "certainty." Proof is not the same as persuasion.

    2. If something is knowledge, then an account can be provided.

    3. If someone claims to know, then an account should be provided.

  c. What about fallibility?

Human beings are fallible in knowing. Knowledge itself is something objectively true, and so fallibility is not applicable (to say knowledge is fallible is a category mistake). Certainty without knowledge can be shaken; certainty from knowledge cannot be shaken.

  d. What about moral culpability?

    1. If something is easily knowable (clarity), and human beings ought to know it, there is moral culpability for failing to know (inexcusability).

    2. How is moral culpability for failing to know experienced?

      i. Failure to know the basic things leads to ignorance of what is true and what is good for humans. It leads to meaninglessness, boredom, and guilt.

      ii. Ignorance is harmful to the individual (darkness of mind) and to society. It leads to the death of relationships, cultures, and civilizations.

iii. A fillip to mollify Gettier: We may retain the justified true belief formulation of knowledge by removing the ambiguity between

Plato's rationalist account and Gettier and Plantinga's empiricist accounts. Knowledge is justified true belief where:

a. *Weak justification* is sensory data that provides a high probability of truth (sufficient for most of our everyday judgments). This does not guarantee knowledge.

b. *Strong justification* is by reason and argument such that the opposite is impossible (necessary for foundational philosophical claims). Strong justification requires an understanding of reason.[2] This guarantees knowledge.

10. To believe a sound argument because the argument is seen as sound is to possess knowledge. We can know the basic things that are clear to reason through sound arguments.

This paper is posthumously published
based upon the original work of Dr. Surrendra Gangadean
and has been developed by The Logos Foundation Editorial Board.

---

2. *Paper No. 5 and 75.*

Paper № 74

———

CONCEPTS AND APPLICATIONS

CONCEPTS[1]

1. In a concept, the mind grasps the essence of a being or class of beings (or states, relations, activities, or properties of beings).

2. The essence of a being or class of beings is the quality or set of qualities that all members have, that they always have, and that distinguishes them from all non-members.

3. A concept is the first act of reason. All thinking beings as rational would have concepts.

4. A concept is not an image or perception, which is an act of the senses.

5. A concept is universal—it applies to all members of a class. An image is always particular, applying to one being only.

6. A concept is universal—it is the same in all thinkers since it grasps the essence of a class of beings. An image differs in each perceiver.

7. A concept is expressed by a word (or other conventional sign) (e.g., man, red, happy, run, near). Words are taught; concepts cannot be taught, but are grasped. Words can be ambiguous; concepts are not ambiguous.

---

1. Gangadean, *Philosophical Foundation*, 51-54.

8. A concept is not a feeling. It is not an association of an image and a sensation (e.g., of pain).

9. A concept is not orderly behavior. It is not the same as instinct.

10. There are many causes of orderly activities or events apart from concept or perception. Consider order in the amoeba, bee, bird, heart, and computer in relation to perception.

APPLICATIONS

1. "Do animals think?" is the same as "do animals have concepts?" It is not the same as "do animals perceive?" or "do animals behave orderly?" or "do they have sensations or make associations?"

   Argument:

   If animals could think, we could communicate with them as with other human beings.

   We cannot communicate with animals as with other human beings.

   Therefore, animals do not think.

   If animals could think, they would have the same concepts as any thinking being. The only difference would be one of language, such as the difference between French and Chinese.

2. Is there an essential difference between humans and animals?

3. What are the implications of essential difference or non-difference for theories of origin? Can humans evolve from animals if there is an essential difference between humans and animals?

4. What are the implications of essential difference or non-difference for rights and dignity?

*This paper was originally developed for an
Introduction to Philosophy course.*

Paper № 75

REASON AND ARGUMENT[1]

1. By *reason* is meant the laws of thought, or logic: identity: *a* is *a*; non-contradiction: not both *a* and *non-a* (at the same time and in the same respect); excluded middle: either *a* or *non-a*. These laws are natural laws.

2. Reason is used as a test for meaning primarily and as a test for truth only secondarily. If a law of thought is violated, then there is no meaning. Wherever there is meaning, reason is being used.

3. Reason is used to form concepts, judgments (propositions), and arguments (inferences).

4. In a *concept*, the mind grasps the essential nature of a thing. A concept is expressed by a *word* or *term*. A *definition* expresses the meaning of a word or the concept expressed in the word. The *essence* of a class of things is the set of qualities that all members and only members always have. Word, definition, meaning, concept, and essence are closely related. In all of the above, *a* is distinguished from *non-a* by reason (law of identity). Concepts are logically ordered from the most basic to less basic.

5. In a *simple judgment*, two concepts are joined by affirmation or separated by negation. In a *compound judgment*, two propositions are joined by "or," "if/then," or "and." Simple judgments are either true or false and are expressed by propositions.

---

1. Gangadean, *Philosophical Foundation*, 55-56.

The four forms of propositions differ by *quantity* (all/some) and *quality* (is/is not):

All S is P   universal affirmative   (A)
No S is P   universal negative   (E)
Some S is P   particular affirmative (I)
Some S is not P   particular negative   (O)

These are related in the square of opposition.

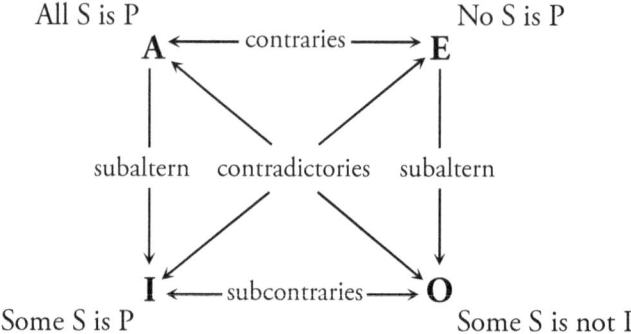

Contradictions (A/O; E/I): differ in quantity and quality; both cannot be true; both cannot be false.

Contraries (A/E): may both be false; both cannot be true.

Subcontraries (I/O): may both be true; both cannot be false.

Subalterns (A/I; E/O): if the universal is true the particular is true, but not reversed.

The meaning of a proposition is made clear by analyzing its concepts and its form. To oppose a position, the contradictory of the position must be established.

6. The following apply to deductive arguments only:

An *argument* uses premises (reasons) to support a conclusion (the point being proven).

An argument is *valid* if the premises logically support the conclusion.

An argument is *sound* if it is valid and the premises are true (needed for rational belief).

The following argument or syllogism forms are commonly used:

i. *Categorical syllogism:* two concepts related to a third are related to each other.

> All S is M
> All M is P
> ∴ All S is P

(S and P being related to M can be related to each other)

ii. *Hypothetical syllogism:* If a cause is present, so is the effect; if no effect, then no cause.

> If $P \supset Q$ If $P \supset Q$
> P   and $\sim Q$
> ∴ Q   ∴ $\sim P$

(These are the only valid forms of this argument)

iii. *Disjunctive syllogism:*

> Either A ∨ non-A
> $\sim A$
> ∴ it must be non-A

iv. *Reductio ad absurdum:* proof by showing that the contradiction leads to an absurdity.

All these argument forms rely on the laws of thought (reason) in order to infer valid conclusions.

7. For any rationally held belief, reasons can be given in support of the belief (conclusion). The alternative to the use of reason ultimately is meaninglessness (spiritual death).

This paper was originally developed for an
Introduction to Logic course.

———

PRESUPPOSITION[1]
Our Most Basic Belief

Most Basic Concept

1. Our most basic belief is about our most basic concept.

2. Logically, the most basic concept is that of existence.

3. Existence is of two kinds: temporal (with beginning) and eternal (without beginning).

4. Eternal existence is prior (logically and ontologically) to temporal existence.

5. We have a precise concept (not image) of what eternal means.

Eternality

1. Eternal is not the same as everlasting or aeveternal (in time).

2. What is eternal is independent, self-existing, self-maintaining, and self-explaining.

3. There are no unique events in an eternal being or process.

   i. If there was an infinite amount of time, it could not be explained why a unique event did not happen before it did.

---

1. Gangadean, *Philosophical Foundation*, 56-59.

   ii. How can a unique event happen at all in an eternal (infinite) series?

      a. An infinite series cannot be crossed in finite time.

      b. There cannot be an infinite series since what is infinite is indivisible.

      c. Since time is divisible, time must not be an infinite series.

There Must Be Something Eternal

1. There must be at least something eternal (assuming anything exists at all).

2. *Reductio* Argument:

   i. The contradiction of "some is eternal" is "none is eternal."

   ii. If "none is eternal," then all is temporal, all had a beginning, all came into being.

   iii. If all came into being, then being came into existence from non-being.

   iv. Being from non-being is not possible.

   v. Therefore, "none is eternal" is not possible and its contradiction "some is eternal" must be true.

Two Basic Presuppositions

1. Presupposition is the most basic belief that is used to interpret experience.

2. There are two presuppositions: *all is eternal* (in some form or other) or *only some is eternal.*

3. No one is fully conscious or consistent in their presupposition; there is an admixture of both in varying degrees in each person, with one being more basic than the other.

4. History is reason (logos) unfolding the meaning of one's presupposition in time.

5. Rationally, one or the other must be true (both can't be true by the law of non-contradiction and both can't be false by the law of excluded middle).

Historic Belief Systems

1. Logically, all historic belief systems can be classified as *all* or *only some* is eternal.

2. All is eternal: material monism, spiritual monism, dualism, pluralism, etc.

3. Only some is eternal: theism (Judaism, Christianity, Islam) and deism.

This paper was originally developed for an
Introduction to Philosophy course.

Paper № 77

___

CONCEPT OF BEING[1]

1. Being and Non-Being

    i. creation *ex nihilo* (no pre-existing material)

    ii. unmanifest being (energy)

    iii. invisible being (spirit)

    iv. imaginary being (fictional)

    v. *a* from *non-a* (child/parents)

    vi. void (medium of waves)

Philosophical examples: naked singularity; Thales and change; Buddhism; Hegel.

2. Being and Aspect of Being

Aspects are states (happy); relations (near); properties (red); activities (thinking).

3. Being and Thought

Thoughts are not beings but the product of thinking; and beings are not thoughts. Philosophical idealism corrects naïve realism, but over-extends itself.

___

1. For further development of this material, see: Surrendra Gangadean, *History of Philosophy*, 35-40.

4. Being and Substance

Substance is defined as:

i. that which exists in itself and not in another (in contrast to aspects of being)

ii. being without the form of a particular being

iii. that out of which a being is formed

iv. not made up of anything else

v. that in which qualities inhere

vi. not a mode or dimension; there are two kinds of substances: matter and spirit—matter is extended and non-conscious; spirit is non-extended and conscious

5. Being and A Being

A being is substance of a particular form (or essence) that has been individuated. A being has functional unity.

6. Being and Essence

An individual being has an essence that is general for a class, and particular for one only. Existence cannot be separated from essence.

Philosophical application: Existentialism; God in Islam; Brahman in Indian thought; Anaximander's *Apeiron* (transcends all qualities); voluntarism in freewill.

7. Being and Existence

All being has existence; being is existence.

8. Being and Unity

i. numerical unity: one and the same

ii. same essence; same nature as

iii. non-dual—all is one, without any difference

iv. unity of diversity (consider several forms of unity of diversity)

v. ethical (same purpose as)

vi. part of (natural vs. collective unity)

9. Being and Eternal Existence

i. eternal is without beginning and without end, minimally

ii. eternal is independent, self-existing, self-maintaining, self-explaining

iii. eternal is not aeveternal—eternal in time; eternal is timeless

iv. eternal is not temporal (with a beginning) or everlasting (merely without end)

v. whatever is eternal is also infinite

vi. there are no unique events for an eternal being (the sun or the soul)

vii. eternal is our most basic quality of being, logically and ontologically

viii. there must be something eternal

*This paper was originally developed for an
Introduction to Philosophy course.*

Paper № 78

———

MATERIAL MONISM[1]

1. Material monism is the ontological position that there is only one
    kind of substance or being (monism), that this substance is ma-
    terial, and that this substance is eternal. According to materialist
    cosmology, all phenomena can (and must) be explained in phys-
    ical or material terms. Contrast this with spiritual monism, dual-
    ism, and theism.

2. Materialist lifestyles differ according to social-economic background,
    degree of rational consistency, and personality disposition. Socio-eco-
    nomic: dropouts, blue collar, bourgeois, professional, epicurean
    (refined version of materialism—fine things in life). Personality:
    instinctual primitivism, secular humanism, mystical materialism.

3. Materialism arose out of a desire for explanation in reaction to ex-
    cess and failure in supernatural explanations. In ancient Greece, the
    Milesians (Pre-Socratics) replaced the superstitions of finite gods
    depicted in popular religion (myths and epics) with natural expla-
    nations. In the modern world, religious strife and otherworldliness
    lead to the rejection of popular and Historic Christianity in favor
    of deism at first, and later naturalism. As overextended natural ex-
    planations fail, the culture swings back without reflection to the an-
    tinomy of overextended supernaturalism.

---

1. Gangadean, *Philosophical Foundation*, 71-100; Gangadean, *History of Philosophy*, 81-85;
   Paper No. 90 and *130*.

4. Given the assumption that all is matter, certain implications follow necessarily. Consider the following: the origin of the cosmos, the origin of life, the destiny of man, human equality, the origin of thought, the good, freedom, rationality, and political authority. These are important parts of a materialist worldview and answers are derived by reason seeking consistency and are not and cannot be a matter of experience.

5. The first argument against materialism is based on the relation of the most fundamental feature of the physical universe (change) and our most basic concept (eternal).

    Major premise: If the material world were eternal, it would be self-maintaining.

    Minor premise: The material world is not self-maintaining.

    Conclusion: The material world is not eternal.

    Is this argument sound: Is it valid and are the premises true? This argument is *modus tollens*, and is valid.

6. The major premise assumes:

    i. There must be something eternal and what is eternal is not dependent on anything for its continuing existence. If all is matter, then matter must be eternal.

    ii. If something is self-maintaining, it will continue without any change, or if it changes it is a matter of recycling.

7. There are no unique events in an eternal being.[2]

8. The reason for the minor premise:

    i. In general:

        1. The physical universe is highly differentiated in terms of hot and cold.

        2. These differences interact.

---

2. *Paper No. 76*

3. The interaction continues until sameness is reached.

4. Sameness remains sameness—it cannot return to differentiation.

  ii. In its parts: the sun (and all stars) will burn out:

1. The sun is finite in size.

2. The sun is giving off heat.

3. Being finite, this process cannot go on forever. Therefore, the sun and stars will burn out.

  iii. As a whole:

A materialist response has been an appeal to the Big Bang oscillating universe theory.

The non-materialist reply is:

1. On empirical grounds, there is not enough matter in the physical universe for gravity to pull everything back together (need about 10x as much).

2. On logical grounds, the model of the Big Bang does not overcome the problem of entropy (sameness). At some point, the force pulling in will have to equal the force pushing out.

3. In the true vacuum to false vacuum theory of the beginning of the universe, when the true vacuum is described as empty of matter and energy in contrast to the false vacuum as empty of matter but not energy, the change so described involves being coming into existence from non-being. How can you go from a position where you have no energy to having energy?

The reason for the minor premise is not overcome by appeal to black holes, antimatter, antiuniverses, etc.

9. To explain change and diversity from an original unity and oneness in materialists' terms has often involved appeal to uncaused events:

  i. Epicurus (300 B.C.)—the atomic swerve theory (atoms ran into other atoms and developed material)

  ii. Dirac (1930)—evenly heated vacuum theory

    iii. Hoyle (1950)—the Steady-State theory (atoms kind of giving birth to other atoms)

    iv. B. Russell (1960)—cold ash heap view (the universe will end in a cold heap and run down)

    v. Currently widespread—the Big Bang oscillating universe theory

    vi. S. Hawking and others (1980)—true vacuum/false vacuum theory

    vii. Historically, appeals have been made to something non-material to account for change in light of the difficulties in materialists' explanations (e.g., Aristotle's dualistic view of a Prime Mover)

10. *Non-Materialist:* appeal to an uncaused event violates the laws of reason.

    Materialist: why should reason be an absolute; reason itself evolves as man evolves.

    Non-Materialist: if reason is not absolute, then "all is matter" is not rationally true; its logical opposite is not false if it is true; both may be true at the same time.

    Materialist: "all is matter" is pragmatically true; it works for me.

    Non-Materialist: what works (satisfies) is a statement about one's feelings, not about what is real.

    Materialist: about what is real I make no statement (c.f. Sextus Empiricus' move to silence (gave up reason)).

    Non-Materialist: as rational beings, we cannot give up reason; we can only give up integrity.

11. The second argument against materialism is based on the reality of thought that must be explained in terms of materialism. (How can chemistry explain thinking?)

    Major premise: If all is matter, then thinking must be motion of atoms in the brain.

    Minor premise: Thinking is not motion of atoms in the brain.

    Conclusion: It is not the case that all is matter.

The argument must be tested for soundness: Is it valid? Are the premises true?

12. The reason for the minor premise:

    Motion of atoms can be described in terms of fast or slow, straight or curved, up or down, etc. None of these qualities or combinations can be identified as true or false which is an essential quality of thought. Therefore, thinking is not motion of any kind. In thinking, we have concepts which are meaningful or not; judgments which are true or false; and arguments which are valid/sound or not. The argument above is saying that thinking is motion. Do they share the same qualities?

13. Reducing thought to motion is one form of reductionism. Historically, attempts were made to reduce space to number, force to space, chemistry to physics, biology to chemistry, etc. The distinctiveness of the diverse aspects of reality has asserted itself in each case. Other attempts to reduce thought to non-rational categories are:

    Marx: a person's belief is determined by class-consciousness based on economic factors.

    Freud: a person's belief is based on psychological factors originating in early childhood.

    Skinner: a person's belief is based on conditioning by pleasure/pain stimuli.

    Whenever a reductionist theory is applied to itself in order to see if it can be justified, the result is a dissolving of the very possibility of any rational justification whatsoever. In effect, epistemologically, reductionist theories are moves that abandon reason. The three examples cited are explicit in their materialist assumption.

14. The third argument against materialism is based on the problem of perception. The materialist maintains that belief in the reality of the physical world is a matter of immediate perception, whereas belief in spirit has no such support in experience. The many common claims to experience of a non-physical reality can be more convincingly explained in materialistic terms.

The non-materialist reply is that in looking for spirit, one has to know what one is looking for in order to know where and how to look. If spirit exists at all, I would have a spirit or be a spirit. I could not have a spirit without knowing it. In looking for spirit, one is looking for something so constantly obvious that one is likely to overlook it.

The third argument against materialism:

Major premise: The most immediately known is the most certainly known.

Minor premise: The self is most immediately known.

Conclusion: The self is most certainly known.

Is this argument sound?

15. The reason for the minor premise is based on the analysis of "immediately" perceived. Perception of the table is analyzed in terms of light waves, neural impulses, mental image, and self as perceiver of the mental image.

   i. Light waves are said to be more immediate than the (cause of the) table that I see. But light waves are not seen, nor are they conceived to be in the shape of the table that I see.

   ii. Neural impulses are formed from light waves interacting with the optic nerves. They are more immediate than light waves, yet they too are not seen nor conceived to be in the shape of the table I see. Since neural impulses are the last brain activity, one has to go beyond neural impulses and the brain to get to the table that is seen.

   iii. Where is the table that is seen? It cannot conceivably be in the brain, but must be a mental image in the mind. Finally, the mental image does not perceive itself or another mental image and it changes continually (many), but I am immediately aware that I am the perceiver (one) of all the mental images. I am other than the mental images and know myself as consciousness itself, having no physical characteristic. This consciousness is also known as mind, self, soul, or spirit. This consciousness is so constantly present, that it is not noticed without deliberate attention.

16. The objections to the minor premise retrace the steps in the reason for the minor premise by attempting to reduce the self to mental images, and then either show mental state terms are dispensable or can be identified indirectly with a physical reality.

  i. Hume: when I look inside, I see no self but only various mental images; if there is a self, it must be a bundle of mental images.

  Response: what is doing the looking?

  ii. Analytical behaviorism: mental state terms can be analyzed completely into statements containing only behavior terms. Consider pain and pain behavior. On this principle, any distinction between animal, artificial, and human intelligence is denied.

  Response: contradictory beliefs are compatible with the same behavior, so the meaning of the belief cannot be analyzed in terms of behavior; e.g., "x believes there is a fire nearby" and "x does not believe there is a fire nearby" as in meditative self-immolation.

  iii. Neutral identity thesis: while pain cannot be directly identified with a physical fiber, both can be identified with a neutral third—fibain. The very thing (fibain) that is aching unbearably (pain) is conducting nerve impulses (fiber).

  Response: this works for non-essential properties but not for essential properties. For example, the very thing that has no size (pain) has size (fiber). No neutral thing can have these properties at once.

If what is known immediately is mental, the problem is to avoid idealism which says there is no material world. This can be done by analyzing the cause of what is seen.[3]

*This paper was originally developed for an
Introduction to Philosophy course.*

---

3. *Paper No. 88*; Gangadean, *Philosophical Foundation*, 107-109.

Paper № 79

THE CREATION VS. EVOLUTION CONTROVERSY[1]

INTRODUCTION

There has been lengthy and heated discussion from both sides without resolution. This is an indication that the assumptions in the dispute are not being adequately addressed.

Three issues are involved in the controversy:

1. By what method is the dispute to be settled—by appeal to science, or to scripture, or to the critical use of reason in philosophy? This also requires analysis of fact, data, presupposition, and interpretation.

2. If differing assumptions are being used to interpret what is observed, which assumption, given the existing common ground, best interprets the data?

3. Are the two views mutually exclusive, or is there a compromise position (theistic evolution) which would be acceptable to both sides, without compromising fundamental features of either?

---

1. Gangadean, *Philosophical Foundation*, 86-100.

ISSUE #1:
By what method can origins be known:
science or scripture or philosophy?

1. Science assumes material monism and that only natural forces operate; it has not attempted to prove this.

2. Christian theism assumes the existence of God the Creator; it does not attempt to prove this.

3. The question of proof of first principles belongs to the realm of philosophy (critical use of reason).

Consider the example of the carbon dating method to see the penetrating presence of assumption in science:

1. Does C-14 dating of bones require the principle of uniformity—that the present is like the past, that the forces now operating in nature have always operated and in essentially the same magnitude as today? For example, is the rate of C-14 formation today the same as two million years ago?

2. If uniformity is required, is it verifiable by observation or is it an assumption of science?

3. If it is an assumption, on what basis is the alternative assumption of non-uniformity (catastrophism) excluded?

4. If non-uniformity is allowed in some places, must it be allowed elsewhere, and if it is disallowed, must it be disallowed everywhere?

5. Does consistent uniformity allow only natural forces to be used in explanation (methodological naturalism), and if so, does uniformity rest on the assumption of material monism, to the exclusion of theism?

The "fact" of the age of the fossil is an interpretation of data in light of a basic belief (material monism) and is warranted only as much as the assumption is warranted. Philosophy is the discipline which deals with basic beliefs.[2]

---

2. *Paper No. 78.*

ISSUE #2:
By what assumption is the data to be explained:
uniformity or non-uniformity?

In all three areas of geology, biology, and astronomy, uniformity based on naturalism is not required to explain what is observed, nor does it best explain the data. The following will raise some brief points.[3]

1. Geological Data: fossil beds, coal beds, sedimentary strata, mountain uplifts, volcanic plateaus, ocean levels/depths (underwater canyons), and meteorological changes.

    Were these formed gradually by forces operating at the present rates, or were there catastrophic forces at work at some time in the earth's history?

2. Biological Data—four stages: 1) From non-life to life (the origin of life); 2) From life to more complex life (the increase of complexity); 3) From more complex life to hominid (the origin of the species); 4) From hominid to human (the origin of man).

    The dispute is not about microevolution (changes within a species, for example, the beaks of finches), but about macroevolution (changes between kinds, for example, from amoeba to man).

    i. Can macro-mutation be explained as the gradual accumulation of micro-mutations?

    ii. Could natural forces, through some sort of gradual process (uniformity), have produced all the forms of life (four stages)? Can chance account for each step through gradual/greater complexity up to human beings?

    iii. Does the fossil record bear this out? (Current saltational theories deny the likelihood of finding any missing links in light of the completeness of the fossil record.)

    iv. If there are gaps between the various kinds of living things, are these gaps original (by creation), or were there sudden fortuitous changes from one kind to another?

---

3. For a more detailed explanation of each, see *The Fourth Argument Against Materialism* in Gangadean, *Philosophical Foundation*, 86-97.

    v. Can anomalies (what is contrary to expectation) count as evidence against a theory?

3. Astronomical Data: fine-tuning and the age of the universe.

Fine-tuning of the cosmos

    i. Recent discoveries in astronomy have revealed how finely tuned the forces of the cosmos must be in order for there to be a universe at all, and furthermore to have one that can make life possible. Scores of instances of fine-tuning have been identified and summarized.

    ii. Appeal to necessity and chance to explain the origin of the universe itself in natural terms alone, apart from intelligent design, is to shift from calculating probabilities within the actual world to calculating probabilities between logically possible worlds.

Age of the cosmos

    i. Uniformitarian assumptions in thinking about the age of the universe are not warranted in light of commonly held views about 1) the expanding universe (Big Bang/white hole cosmology) and 2) gravity's effect on time.

    ii. From 1 and 2, as the universe expanded, with less matter at the center, the event horizon (EH) (determined by the field of gravity surrounding the white hole) grew smaller. The greater part of the universe exists outside the EH, compared to what is at or near the center. Gravity affects clocks outside differently than within the EH. So, the age of the universe is not uniform.

ISSUE #3:
Is a compromise position (theistic evolution) possible?

There are four points which are at issue: 1) the concept of man as a body/soul unity, 2) the concept of human equality, 3) the concept of divine goodness, and 4) the concept of science and divine intervention.

	Naturalism	Historic Theism	Theistic Evolution
Man as a Body/Soul Unity	No soul	Body/soul unity; soul survives death; soul = life	Soul survives death; soul infused by God (hominid to human); soul ≠ life
Human Equality	Evolution continuing; some more fit than others	Created equal in the image of God; creation has ended	Evolution continuing; some more fit than others
Divine Goodness	Struggle to Survive and death as natural	Original creation very good (no natural evil); natural evil imposed in connection with moral evil	Struggle to survive and death as natural; compatible with divine goodness
Science and Divine Intervention	No divine intervention (unnecessary and too arbitrary)	God creates, sustains, and rules the creation; this is the basis for scientific investigation	Divine intervention in soul infusion and every micro-mutation

A compromise position (theistic evolution) is not acceptable to consistent naturalism and to consistent theism. The issue must be resolved at the level of assumption through the critical use of reason.

This paper was originally developed for an Introduction to Philosophy course, and has been edited by The Logos Foundation Editorial Board.

Paper № 80

SPIRITUAL MONISM[1]

1. Spiritual monism is the ontological position that there is only one kind of being and that this being is spirit and that all spirit is eternal. Material objects only appear to exist. It is distinct from dualism and from theism.

2. Points of contact with spiritual monism are in reincarnation, karma, yoga, the Hare Krishna Movement, Transcendental Meditation, New Age, and several other instances of Eastern thought. Note that some forms of Indian thought are not monist.

3. The appeal of spiritual monism is that it is believed to offer:

   i. an alternative to the emptiness of materialism.

   ii. a hopeful view of the afterlife in which a person reincarnates until enlightenment is achieved.

   iii. an explanation of why events in this life occur in terms of influence from one's previous lives.

4. Some objections to reincarnation are:

   i. Explanation using reincarnation is ad hoc—it explains too much.

   ii. Since innumerable lifetimes are involved, the assumption is that knowledge is difficult to attain, yet we suffer until we know.

---

1. Gangadean, *Philosophical Foundation*, 101-118; Gangadean, *History of Philosophy*, 107-110, 115-119, 142-144.

    iii. If the soul is eternal, how long has reincarnation been going on—is there real hope that the goal can be attained?

    iv. How can a unique event (enlightenment) occur for an eternal being?

5. Some responses of spiritual monism to these objections:

    i. Against the view of a unique beginning or end, the process of reincarnation is cyclical, without beginning and without end.

    ii. If an endless cycle makes striving for release meaningless, the response is that ultimately the cycle itself is an illusion.

    iii. If the illusion is inexplicable, then the problem is with reason; ultimately, there is no difference between ordinary existence (*samsara*) and enlightened existence (nirvana).

6. There are two forms of spiritual monism:

    i. Absolute non-dualism, one without parts, called historically *Advaita* Vedanta and espoused by Shankara (A.D. 800) and in Transcendental Meditation (where you meditate to transcend the confines of space and time and the self is realized as the ultimate reality).

    ii. Qualified non-dualism, one with parts, called historically *Dvaita* Vedanta and espoused by Ramanuja (A.D. 1200) and in the Hare Krishna movement. Ramanuja is looking back at Shankara's position and critiquing it.

7. The central teaching of *Advaita* Vedanta is that *atman* is *Brahman*; the self is the ultimate reality. The nature of *atman/Brahman* is pure existence, consciousness, bliss (*sat chit ananda* (Sanskrit words)). That is what the real self is (*tat tvam asi*—that thou art). There is one mind only and its ideas. The world is *maya* (illusion) or *avidya* (due to ignorance).

8. The reasons for spiritual monism are based on the analogy of a dream (*maya* or *avidya*):

    i. A shared illusion, as in a dream, is not a guarantee of objective reality.

    ii. In a dream, just because we think we are real does not mean that we are real.

    iii. As in a dream, there is one self behind the many apparently real selves.

    iv. As in a dream, the only way in which the illusory nature of the individual self and the world can be realized is through mystical experience of self-realization, *samadhi*, enlightenment, awakening. You know it's a dream by waking up.

9. The general objection to appeal to experience is fourfold:

    i. No experience (of awakening—becoming one with the one) is meaningful without interpretation.

    ii. This experience (pure consciousness) has been interpreted in many ways (monist, dualist, Buddhist, theist, etc.).

    iii. A valid interpretation is internally consistent.

    iv. This interpretation (absolute non-dualism) is incoherent in many ways.

10. Consider the criticisms raised by the qualified non-dualists (Ramanuja):

    i. Where does the illusion reside? It cannot be in either Brahman or in the individual self.

    ii. How can Brahman be concealed given its nature as (infinite) pure consciousness?

    iii. How can the world—*maya*—be neither positive nor negative nor both nor neither?

    iv. How can the world be neither real nor unreal (nor both nor neither)?

11. Since Shankara believes all is One and therefore all is eternal, things must be either real/eternal or unreal/nonexistent; they cannot be

temporal given his assumption. He says that reason cannot grasp the nature of the world as neither real nor unreal. He is faced with giving up his presupposition or reason. He chooses to give up reason. (Those caught in the meshes of intellect are like an elephant stuck in deep mud. The highest philosophy is silence. It isn't is, it isn't isn't, it isn't both, it isn't neither. Silence. – Quote from Shankara)

12. In the second form of non-dualism (one with parts), we are all part of the One (God).

     The three possible interpretations are:

     i. all parts are the same—finite

     ii. all parts are the same—infinite

     iii. all parts are not the same; some part(s) are infinite and some finite

13. Objections to qualified non-dualism:

     i. If all parts are finite, then the whole (God) cannot be infinite. Further, beings cannot be finite (growing—going through unique events) and be eternal.

     ii. If all parts are infinite, each would be complete in itself and therefore not have or need parts to make it whole.

     iii. If some parts are infinite (and eternal) and some finite (and temporal), this would be Creator/creation rather than non-dualism/spiritual monism.

*This paper was originally developed for an
Introduction to Philosophy course.*

Paper № 81

———

ON REINCARNATION[1]

1. Belief in reincarnation is the belief that the soul which departs from the body at death re-enters at birth another body (human or animal). This belief assumes the preexistence of the soul and that the soul is eternal, without beginning. Belief in reincarnation also assumes that the process of reincarnation will come to an end when the soul has achieved an enlightened state. Belief in reincarnation is held in all forms of Hinduism and Buddhism and in many forms of dualism. Sometimes this belief is held by maintaining different levels of truth. Belief in reincarnation, like all other beliefs about the afterlife, is a basic belief, affecting all aspects of thinking about individual human destiny and human culture.

2. Empirical reasons for belief in reincarnation and responses to these reasons.

   i. Déjà vu is the sense that *I have seen this before*, although it could not have been in this life. Therefore, it must have been in a previous life.

   Response: the sense that one is remembering rather than perceiving for the first time can be explained as an unusual phenomena of brain chemistry or double neural firings.

   ii. Hypnotic regressions are said to bring to light memories of previous lives.

---

1. Gangadean, *Philosophical Foundation*, 102-105.

Response: that what comes to mind is memory from previous lives rather than knowledge imparted some other way cannot be verified; and, since reports from hypnotic regressions conflict (several persons report being Napoleon etc.) they are not to be accepted on the face of it.

   iii. Special psychic powers displayed by some persons are said to have been acquired in a previous life.

   Response: these powers can be explained in other ways, either naturally (as clever tricks) or supernaturally (as operations of spirits).

3. Philosophical reasons for belief in reincarnation and responses to these reasons.

   i. Reincarnation is said to be an alternative to no afterlife.

   Response: there are other alternatives: one can learn as well by living one longer life; the soul may go on without the body; there could have been no death originally; one may change from mortality to immortality without death.

   ii. Reincarnation is said to explain circumstances of this life in terms of previous lives.

   Response: explanations from previous lives do not justify particular conduct in this life—the actor's tale of adultery; explanations from previous lives do not necessitate explanations in this life—the doctor's tale of hard cases; explanations from previous lives are not conclusive—the lottery winner's tale of changing fortunes.

   iii. Reincarnation is said to be just, since we suffer for our own karma (deeds) from previous lives.

   Response: it is not just to suffer through many births and deaths to know what is objectively not clear.

   iv. Reincarnation is said to be hopeful since we have many lives to get it right rather than one life only.

   Response: it is not hopeful if we have been through innumerable lives before this one.

   v. Reincarnation is said to be necessary if the soul is eternal.

Response: it is not possible for reincarnation to reach its goal of enlightenment since there cannot be a unique event in an eternal being.

4. Higher levels of truth claims regarding reincarnation and responses to these claims.

   i. If there is no unique event in an eternal being, then it is said that reincarnation is a beginningless and endless cycle, contrary to the popular view.

   Response: if there is no beginning nor end, then striving for release is meaningless.

   ii. If an endless cycle makes life meaningless, then reincarnation (*samsara*) is said to be an illusion (*maya*), or ignorance (*avidya*), contrary to popular view.

   Response: if our existence is an illusion, then it cannot be explained in whose mind the illusion resides. It cannot be in our minds, since our minds are the product of the illusion; and it cannot be in God's mind, since God cannot have an illusion.

   iii. If the nature of the world as illusion (*maya*) cannot be explained, then this problem must be due to the limitation of reason. One must give up reason at this point.

   Response: reason cannot be given up and any belief kept. This would be a lack of integrity. The meaningless belief should be given up in the name of reason.

5. Is theistic reincarnation possible?

   In this view, the soul is created by God and therefore the soul had a beginning. It is not beginningless. It reincarnates until enlightenment is reached. Reincarnation assumes that the knowledge to be achieved is objectively unclear.

   Response:

   i. If we suffer through many births and deaths to know what is objectively unclear, then God is not just. But if it is objectively clear, then we do not need many lives in order to know it. One life is sufficient.

ii. If the human soul may pass through many life forms without preserving any distinct human quality in these other life forms, then the soul would be an essenceless reality, contrary to logical possibility.

6. Is it possible that the soul in this life already knows everything?

i. It is self-evident that the soul does not know everything.

ii. If the soul knows everything, then it must always have known everything, to avoid the problem of a unique event in an eternal being.

iii. If the soul knows everything, then its present reincarnation is not necessary.

iv. If the soul knows everything, then no form of enlightenment is needed or possible.

v. To avoid saying "I know" and "do not know," at the same time and in the same respect, the unity of the self as knower must be denied, contrary to our most basic intuition.

*This paper was originally developed for an
Introduction to Philosophy course.*

Paper No. 82

DUALISM[1]

1. Dualism is the ontological position that there are two kinds of beings (substances)—matter and spirit—both of which are eternal. It is distinct from monism and from theism. Historical examples of dualism include:

    i. Greek—Plato and Aristotle

    ii. Persian—Zoroastrianism

    iii. Indian—Samkhya Yoga

    iv. Mormonism—heterodox Christianity

2. The appeal of dualism lies in it being the nearest logical alternative to material and spiritual monism, which avoids the same criticisms raised against both. It also offers a solution to the problem of evil, generally by locating the problem in matter vs. spirit.

3. Objections to its appeal:

    i. If the soul is eternal, how can it go through a unique event, for example, growth in knowledge, liberation, or attainment of heaven?

    ii. If the soul is inherently good and eternal and independent of the body, why is it in an evil body?

---

1. Gangadean, *Philosophical Foundation*, 129-137; Gangadean, *History of Philosophy*, 87-105, 111-114.

    iii. One can conceive of an evil spirit (the devil) or of evil not based in bodily needs (Eden).

4. Dualistic attitudes are reflected in popular theism in several ways:

    i. The world is evil; one should flee it or avoid it—monastic withdrawal, ascetic distrust of the sensuous, celibacy as a higher spiritual state.

    ii. The world is corruptible especially in the sins of the flesh and must be guarded against (vs. evil as disregard of reason).

    iii. The world is morally neutral in its basic institutional structures; personal piety is all that is needed.

    iv. The world is good as the creation of God, but not as good as the world to come—heaven.

5. A philosophical alternative to dualistic otherworldliness of popular theism is to regard creation and history as revelation of the divine nature, the source of the knowledge of God, which is the greatest good, and the goal of reading this revelation is that "the earth shall be full of the knowledge of God as the waters cover the sea."[2] No other revelation exists.

6. Two forms of dualism:

    i. Ordinary dualism in which matter is eternal and independent of spirit—Plato. The first argument against materialism holds against ordinary dualism.[3]

    ii. Dependent dualism in which matter is eternal and dependent on spirit—Aristotle.

7. In accounting for change and permanence, Aristotle analyzes the world in terms of form and matter, potentiality and actuality. Matter without form is pure potentiality (an acorn is potentially a big oak tree). The source of all change is the Unmoved Mover, pure actuality, spirit without matter. The dilemma is: if matter has some

---

2. *Isaiah 11:9.*

3. *Paper No. 78.*

actuality without spirit (then matter is independent), then it so far is ordinary dualism (matter not being self-maintaining refutes this), but if matter has no actuality without spirit, then matter would be created and temporal. The dilemma has to figure out the relationship between matter and the Unmoved Mover.

This paper was originally developed for an
Introduction to Philosophy course.

THEISM[1]

It is clear that matter exists and that matter is not eternal, that the soul exists and that the soul is not eternal.

Only some is eternal, in contrast to material monism, spiritual monism, and dualism.[2]

INTRODUCTION

1. If only some is eternal, then God the Creator exists. What is eternal brought into existence, or created, *ex nihilo* (from nothing) what is not eternal. The Creator is God.

2. Creation *ex nihilo* is not being from non-being. In creation, God is eternal. In creation, God acts to bring creation into being. The universe did not appear from nowhere as an uncaused event.

3. Creation is not a change of God's being. Theism is not pantheism. The analogy for creation of matter is in the experience of a mental event causing a physical event, as in the intention to move one's arm and the movement of one's arm. The analogy for the creation of spirit is in the experience of procreation—life flows from parents and becomes other than parents, without the parents being decreased.

---

1. Gangadean, *Philosophical Foundation*, 139-161, 185-198; Gangadean, *History of Philosophy*, 51-58; *Paper No. 127.*
2. *Paper No. 78, 80,* and *82.*

4. Creation is not a unique event in time, but that by which time comes to be. Time is not a thing in itself, but a relation between things created—of physical things in motion or in thought as a succession of ideas in finite minds. Time began with creation. There was no time before creation. God is eternal in the sense of being timeless (outside time).

5. Creation is not a completion of God's being. In creating, there is no need in God that is being fulfilled. God creates because He is. To be is to express one's being. In creating, the nature of God is being expressed. Creation is revelation necessarily, intentionally, and exclusively. There is no knowledge of God apart from creation and its history (providence).

6. God the Creator is a Spirit, infinite, eternal, and unchangeable, in his being, wisdom, power, holiness, justice, goodness, and truth. Man as the image of God has these attributes in a finite, temporal, and changeable way. What distinguishes the divine and the human nature are the three incommunicable attributes. Historic theism is more or less conscious and consistent in understanding the nature of God.

7. General revelation is what can be known of God by all persons, everywhere, at all times. Special revelation, written as scripture, is what can be known of God through transmission alone. Scripture, as redemptive revelation, assumes the existence of moral evil in the denial of clear general revelation.

8. Theism is not fideism. Theism is grounded in the clarity of general revelation. Fideism is belief without proof or understanding what is clear. As truth is inseparable from meaning, so faith is inseparable from reason.

HUME AND THE PROBLEM OF EVIL

1. In his *Dialogues Concerning Natural Religion*, David Hume presents the problem of evil as seen from three points of view:

i. Demea, the orthodox believer, who speaks of God analogously (God is like man in having wisdom, but unlike man in that God's wisdom is infinite).

ii. Cleanthes, the rational empiricist, who speaks of God univocally (God's wisdom is essentially like man's—greater, but still finite.)

iii. Philo, the skeptic-mystic, who speaks of God equivocally (God's wisdom is totally unlike man's—perfect, but incomprehensible).

2. Demea and Philo agree that religion arises from a sense of misery. This view is common (Marx, Freud, popular theism).

   To critique this view, consider:

   i. Is this true of all religion or some?

   ii. What is religion?

   iii. Are all or only some persons religious?

   iv. Does religion arise or only change?

   v. If religion is the set of beliefs by which we give meaning to experience (including misery), can religion arise?

3. Demea and Philo also agree that the world is full of misery (natural evil) and wickedness (moral evil). Consider the many attempts to avoid facing the full extent of this (see *The Extent of Natural and Moral Evil* section below).

4. From 2 and 3 above, evil should bring man to God. But to what God? Philo springs on Demea the problem of evil: if God is all good and all powerful, why is there evil? The problem is either a contradiction (these three (G × P × E) are contradictory) or remains unsolvable. (He does allow, for all we know, the possibility of an easy solution.)

5. First solution (Philo): God's goodness is perfect, but incomprehensible.

   Response: This is an appeal to an unknown. If God's goodness is unknowable, then all religion (prayer and praise) ends.

6. Second solution (Demea): We know in part now. We will have full knowledge in the future (afterlife) when we see the whole picture (in which all difficulties are answered).

   Response: Appealing to the future begs the question. This assumes that to know anything one must know everything, which is impossible for finite beings.

7. Third solution (Cleanthes): There is more good than evil in the world.

   Response: Knowledge of the amounts of suffering in comparison is impossible (e.g., the intensity of pain is incomparable); and why should there be any suffering at all?

8. Fourth solution (Cleanthes): God's power is great, but finite.

   Response: Even with a finite deity, one would expect a better world. Furthermore, God cannot be Creator and finite.

9. Fifth solution (Philo): No natural evil is necessary; God is indifferent to good and evil (he is amoral).

   Consider:

   i. Animal pain is not necessary—not for death, accident, learning, or appreciation.

   ii. Evil could be greatly reduced by secret divine intervention (small miracles).

   iii. Greater natural endowment or diligence would vastly improve life.

   iv. The excesses of nature are not necessary.

   Response: God created the moral sense of man with infinite, deliberate, wisdom. God cannot be Creator and be morally indifferent.

THE EXTENT OF
NATURAL AND MORAL EVIL[3]

1. Nature vs. nature

2. Nature vs. man

3. Man vs. man

4. Man vs. woman

5. Man vs. self

6. Bad attitude

7. Ignorance is bliss

8. Island of bliss in a sea of misery

9. Suicide

10. Hope

11. Family and friends

12. Culture

13. Nature

14. Knowledge

Beyond Hume:

15. Full extent and cause of natural evil—physical death

16. Full extent of the denial of reason/logos—deicide

17. Full consequence of the denial of reason—spiritual death

THE FREE WILL SOLUTION
TO THE PROBLEM OF EVIL

1. The Free Will Solution to the problem of evil is frequently used. It affirms that:

    i. Natural evil is due to moral evil.

---

3. For explication of these points, see Gangadean, *Philosophical Foundation*, 147-151.

    ii. Moral evil is due to free will.

    iii. Free will is necessary for human dignity.

2. Response:

    i. Free will makes moral evil possible, not actual.

    ii. If moral evil becomes actual, that does not make it necessary.

    iii. Free will does not have to make moral evil possible (God is free without the possibility of evil; in the final state, man is free without the possibility of evil).

    iv. One can pass from innocence to virtue without moral evil (temptation is not sin).

THE IRONIC SOLUTION
TO THE PROBLEM OF EVIL

1. Introduction

    i. The problem of evil is an intellectual problem. It is a problem for man as a rational being. The concern is to know why there is evil (how can it make sense if God exists?), not merely how to remove it practically. As such, if it is to be solved, it will require a clearer, deeper, and more consistent understanding of good and evil.

    ii. Definition of "good":

        a. Good for man as a rational being is the use of reason to the fullest.

        b. Reason is used to understand the nature (meaning) of the world.

        c. The nature of the world as created reveals the nature of God.

        d. Therefore, good for man is the knowledge of God.

    iii. Definition of "evil":

        a. Evil for man as a rational being is the failure to use reason to the fullest.

b. It is the failure to understand the nature of things.

c. Therefore, evil for man is the failure to know God.

d. It is to neglect, avoid, resist, or deny reason in the face of what is clear about God.

2. Why is there moral evil?

Consider the parable of the prodigal son.[4]

Moral evil (unbelief) serves two purposes:

i. Evil as unbelief serves to obscure the revelation of the divine nature. (The younger son, living daily with his father, had a clear revelation of his father's love, yet failed to see it because of his unbelief about what is good.)

ii. Evil as unbelief serves to deepen the revelation of the divine nature. (The sequence of events brought about by unbelief deepens the revelation of divine justice and mercy.)

There are two parts to this solution:

i. If evil (unbelief) is removed abruptly, then the revelation will not be deepened; if evil (unbelief) is not removed, then the revelation will not be seen.

ii. The solution is to remove evil gradually. Evil (unbelief) in every possible form and degree of admixture and conflict with the good (belief) is allowed to work itself out in world history. In this conflict, good eventually overcomes evil. Consider worldview conflicts in world history.

The assumptions of this solution:

i. There is a clear general revelation.

ii. There is no other way to deepen the revelation.

iii. The good, as the knowledge of God, justifies evil.

---

4. *Luke 15:11-32.*

3. Why is there natural evil?

    i. Natural evil consists in toil and strife, and old age, sickness, and death.

    ii. Natural evil is not original; natural evil is due to moral evil; natural evil is imposed as a call back from moral evil.

    iii. Natural evil is imposed to restrain, recall from, and remove moral evil. It calls man to stop and think deeply about basic things.

    iv. Natural evil assumes the existence of self-deception and self-justification when we neglect, avoid, resist, and deny reason in the face of what is clear.

4. The Ironic Solution

It is the nature of evil to reverse the order of things, to call good evil and evil good, to blind a person to the nature of good and evil. With this understanding of good and evil, the problem becomes transformed. The problem is not resolved; rather, it is, ironically, dissolved:

    i. Because of all evil in the world, I cannot see how it can be said that God is all good and all powerful.

    ii. Because of all the unbelief in the world, I cannot see how it can be said that God is all good and all powerful.

    iii. Because of all the unbelief in me, I cannot see how it can be said that God is all good and all powerful.

    iv. Because I have neglected and avoided the use of reason, I cannot see what is clear about God.

    v. Because I have shut my eyes, I cannot see what is clear about God.

The solution to the problem of evil thus understood is objectively easy, but subjectively difficult.

*This paper was originally developed for an
Introduction to Philosophy course.*

Paper № 84

———

ETHICS[1]

1. Ethics is concerned with giving a rational justification for the answer to the question "what is the good?"

Ethics assumes choice, choice assumes values, and values assume the concept of the good. What is particularly sought in ethics is rational justification.

2. The main concepts of ethics are the good, virtue, and happiness.

   i. The good is what is sought as an end in itself, for its own sake, and not for the sake of something else. It is clear what cannot be sought for its own sake and what can be.

   ii. Virtue is what is sought as the means to the good. Consider examples of virtues, classification, and interrelations.

   iii. Happiness is the effect of possessing what we believe is the good. It cannot be sought directly. Consider the difference between happiness and lasting happiness.

   iv. Ethics is teleological (goal oriented), not deontological (virtue oriented), or utilitarian (happiness or pleasure oriented).

---

1. Gangadean, *Philosophical Foundation*, 165-169.

3. The following are formal features of the good.

i. The good is the moral absolute. It is not relative to other moral judgments, but other moral judgments (about virtue and happiness) are relative to the good.

ii. The good is the source of unity within a person, between two persons, and between groups of persons.

iii. The good is based on human nature, which is based on what is real (or eternal). So, the moral absolute (the good) is based on the metaphysical absolute (the real).

iv. The good must be easily knowable if there is to be moral responsibility.

4. There are necessary conditions for morality.

i. If there is no *metaphysical absolute* (if all is eternal and nothing is absolute or transcendent), there can be no justified distinction between good and evil and therefore no morality. Consider the implications of pantheism, polytheism, naturalism, and secular humanism. Is God therefore necessary for morality?

ii. If there is no *personal immortality*, there can be no morality. If there is no personal continuity, there can be no future and no purpose, and if there is no purpose, there can be no goal or good.

iii. If there is no *freedom*, there can be no morality. The good as the end in itself is achieved through choice. If there is no freedom, there can be no choice and therefore the good is not achievable.

iv. If there is no *clarity*, there can be no morality. If it is not clear what is good, then one cannot be held accountable for pursuing the good. If there is no clarity, then there is skepticism, and if there is skepticism, then there is relativism.

v. If there is no *rationality*, then there can be no clarity and therefore no morality. What is clear could not possibly be otherwise. Its contradiction is logically impossible. One has to stop thinking to avoid seeing what is clear.

This paper was originally developed for an Introduction to Philosophy course.

Paper № 85

AN INTRODUCTION
TO CHRISTIANITY

INTRODUCTION

1. Historic Christianity is based on the Bible (special revelation or Scripture).[1]

2. The basic themes of biblical revelation are creation, fall, and redemption.

3. Scripture is redemptive revelation. It assumes the reality of sin in the rejection of the Word of God in man as reason and in the creation as clear general revelation.

4. Scripture is the Word of God written. It reveals how God is both just and merciful to man in sin.

5. Scripture focuses on the person and work of Christ, the Word of God incarnate, who restores mankind to life in the knowledge of God.

6. Biblical revelation is organic, a unity that grows. In Genesis 1–3 is given the foundation of Scripture in organic seed form. Scripture builds on, is to be understood by, and is the development of what is revealed here. Understanding the beginning is necessary for understanding all that follows.

---

1. Gangadean, *The Westminster Confession*. See Questions 4-12; Gangadean, *The Westminster Catechisms*. See LCQ. 4-6; *Paper No. 14, 26, 56, 112, 114*, and *141-150.*

7. Understanding the Bible assumes the use of reason and knowledge of general revelation to understand its terms and the implications of its statements.

GENESIS 1:
CREATION[2]

1. Original creation is *ex nihilo*; there was no pre-existent material. This is opposed to pantheism (everything is a part of God) and to dualism (both matter and spirit are eternal). Only God is eternal. God is a Spirit, infinite, eternal, and unchangeable in being, wisdom, and power.

   Subsequent creation are acts of *forming* (by separation) of the original substance of creation and *filling*.

2. Creation is revelation. The whole earth is full of the glory of God.

   The acts of God necessarily reveal his nature.

   The revelation was intentional. Everything created was good, as intended.

   The revelation of creation is exclusive. There is no other revelation apart from creation.

3. Each kind of being is created directly by God. This is opposed to theistic evolution.

4. Man is created in the image of God. Man is finite, temporal, and changeable in being, wisdom, power, holiness, justice, goodness, and truth. These are formal characteristics which man never ceases to have regardless of how their content may change. Man will always be devoted (be holy) whether he is devoted to God or to self. Man will always have beliefs about truth, whether he believes God exists or believes there is no God.

   Male and female are both aspects of the image of God. These characteristics are in God, spiritually, and originate from God.

---

2. Gangadean, *The Westminster Catechisms*. See Appendix 4; *Paper No. 141-144.*

5. Knowledge of God is through the work of dominion. Man's calling is to rule in the creation. By this rule, he is to develop the powers latent in himself and in the creation. As God's work of creation is revelation of the glory of God, so man's work of dominion is to fill the earth with the knowledge of the glory of God.

6. Original creation was very good. There was no moral or natural evil. Animals were given the green vegetation for food. Human beings did not die.

7. The Sabbath signifies that the work of creation is completed. A new work, the work of providence, upholding and directing the creation, begins and continues.

   The Sabbath is to be observed by man who is the image of God. As God completed his work of creation, so man will complete his work of dominion.

   The Sabbath is a perpetual reminder to man of his origin—God created all things; of his destiny—through dominion man is to fill the earth with the knowledge of God; and of hope—man's work will be completed.

GENESIS 2:
THE COVENANT OF CREATION[3]

The purpose of the covenant made with man in the Garden is to accomplish God's gracious purpose to bring man from a state in which he could sin, to a state in which he cannot fall away from God.

1. Man is created a body/soul unity.

   Man is not created as an angel, nor is he a soul that happens to be in a body.

   Man is not an already living body to which a soul is added.

   The separation of soul and body by physical death is unnatural.

   The state of the soul in heaven without the body is an unnatural condition due to sin. Redemption requires the resurrection of the body.

---

3. *Paper No. 145.*

2. Man is created to dwell on the earth. All natural needs are provided for in Eden.

   Eden is the biological, geographical, and historical center of life on earth: all human life flows from Eden; all plant and animal life flow from Eden.

3. Man has a choice between good and evil, between life and death. These two ways are visibly represented by the tree of life and the tree of the knowledge of good and evil.

   By understanding the nature of things, Adam had understanding of good and evil and life and death. Good for man is based on his nature, made in the image of God, and capable of understanding. Evil is to act contrary to that nature. Good was to acknowledge his nature and purpose as determined by God, to know God. Evil was to deny one's creatureliness and seek to determine good and evil independently of God who, as creator of the nature of things, determines good and evil.

4. God's covenant with man involves representation and probation. As covenant head of the human race, Adam represents the entire race. His act will affect all men and all of nature. The probation is a time of testing regarding his choice of good or evil. The outward act of eating or not eating from the tree of the knowledge of good and evil will reveal whether he has pursued the knowledge of God as the good or whether he has denied God as Creator and is determining good and evil from himself. In the day he denies God, he will die, spiritually.

5. The covenant of marriage reflects man's relationship with God and is fulfilled in man's relationship with God.

   Adam begins his work of dominion; in naming the creation, he shows his understanding of the revelation of God in the creation. In doing this work, he sees his need for help and his difference from the rest of creation. God's creation of a suitable helper establishes the context of marriage. Marriage is to serve God's purpose for man, not man's purpose for himself. Marriage is for dominion and the knowledge of God. Companionship is an effect of serving this purpose, and children, in the generations to come, are to serve this purpose. All mankind together are to glorify and enjoy God forever. Marriage and childbearing ends when the work of dominion is completed.

In the creation of a suitable helper, what was one in man became two persons, and the two persons are to become one in marriage, establishing a new unity. She is called "woman" for she was taken "out of man." There is an equality of persons in that she is flesh of his flesh and bone of his bone. There is a diversity of persons in distinct functions—the man leaves his father and mother; the woman is given in marriage.

GENESIS 3:
THE FALL OF MAN[4]

1. Man is created in a state of moral innocence and purity. They felt no shame in either their inward or outward condition.

   The fall of man is a change in the condition of man from righteousness and life to sin and death.

   The account of the fall of man depicts the original sin and accounts for how sin at its root originates.

2. The temptation of man is not the cause of sin, but is a test which serves to reveal the inward condition of man, whether he has been pursuing the knowledge of God as the good.

3. Temptation begins with questioning the meaning of God's command. It goes on to deny the consequence of spiritual death for disobedience (you shall not surely die), and offers instead the impossible promise of attaining divinity (you shall be like God, knowing good and evil.)

4. Before the outward act of sin, the inward act of believing what is false about sin and death and about the difference between God and man, had already occurred. This lack of understanding the difference between the finite creature and the infinite God reveals that

---

4. Gangadean, *The Westminster Confession*. See Questions 30-34; Gangadean, *The Westminster Catechisms*. See LCQ. 21-29; *Paper No. 145-147.*

man had ceased seeking to know God and had not retained elementary truth about God. Inwardly, he had already put himself in the place of God to determine good and evil. The outward act of eating from the tree of the knowledge of good and evil naturally followed this inward reality.

5. In the account of the fall of man, there is a clear revelation of the nature of sin.

   Sin is not seeking God, not understanding, and not doing what is right.

   Sin is unbelief, unholiness, and unrighteousness.

   Sin is the failure to see what is clear (the difference between the infinite Creator God and finite man.)

   Sin is the failure to use reason to see what is clear.

   Sin is the denial of one's nature as a rational being to avoid what is clear.

   Sin is autonomy, the denial of one's creaturely dependence on God.

   Sin is putting oneself in the place of God.

6. The inherent consequence of sin is spiritual death. It is the necessary consequence of the denial of one's nature. Inwardly, it is meaninglessness, boredom, and guilt. Outwardly, it is the breakdown and reversal of the order established by creation.

GENESIS 3:
REDEMPTION[5]

1. Redemption is the act of God by which man is brought out of sin and death to righteousness and life. It begins with the call to repentance, the forgiveness of sin, and the removal of the power of sin. It culminates in the completion of dominion and the earth being filled with the knowledge of God.

---

5. Gangadean, *The Westminster Confession*. See Questions 39-61; Gangadean, *The Westminster Catechisms*. See LCQ. 30-90; *Paper No. 148-150.*

2. The first call to repentance is inward, through one's conscience, and is felt as shame. Man's response is to avoid it by covering up sin in self-deception.

3. The second call to repentance is outward, through a question, "Where are you?"—calling for self-examination. Man's response to this call is to avoid it by self-justification. He blames the woman and God for his act of disobedience.

4. The third call to repentance is through the curse and the promise. It is the final and continuing call to all men, made necessary by man's continuing self-deception and self-justification. The curse is not punishment which is inherent to sin; it is the imposition of natural evil on man and the creation in increasing intensity, to call man to stop and think. It serves to restrain, recall, and restore man from moral evil. It is first manifested in toil and strife, and old age, sickness, and death. It is more fully manifested in war, famine, and plague. Natural evil will be removed when moral evil is removed and there is no more call to repentance.

5. In the promise, the order of creation is to be restored through spiritual warfare, age-long and agonizing, until good overcomes evil. The promised seed of the woman will bring this about.

6. Man's response to the third call is repentance and faith. He accepts the curse and believes the promise and will obey and be fruitful. His faith and obedience is seen in naming his wife Eve.

7. God's first response to man's faith is to justify man by covering his guilt through an atoning sacrifice. Man is given the garment of skin to cover his nakedness.

8. God's second response is to sanctify man by expulsion from the Garden to suffer the effects of the curse. He is prevented from re-entering the Garden to avoid the curse of death. There is no life apart from the knowledge of God, and now, under sin, there is no knowledge of God apart from suffering in the work of dominion.

REDEMPTIVE HISTORY

1. Biblical history is the unfolding of man's response to God's revelation in creation and Scripture. Original creation was very good. It revealed the glory of God. Evil was permitted to serve God's purpose. It deepened the revelation of God's glory. Evil is allowed to work itself out in history in every form of unbelief and every cultural expression of unbelief.

2. Biblical history unfolds through several epochs of apostasy, curse, deepened revelation, and renewal, leading up to the coming of Christ. Biblical revelation ends in a vision of continued spiritual warfare between belief and unbelief until the work of dominion is completed, in which good overcomes evil and the earth is filled with the knowledge of God.

This paper was originally developed for an
Introduction to Christianity course.

Paper № 86

———

CHRISTIANITY

An Overview

1. The Old Testament tells of the person and work of the Messiah that is to come. The New Testament shows how Jesus of Nazareth fulfilled, and is fulfilling, what was written of the Messiah. The substance of the Old Testament continues in effect while the outward form is done away with (ceremonial law), or changed (civil law).

2. The main events of the life of Jesus are his birth (incarnation); his baptism and temptation; his calling of his disciples; his ministry of teaching and healing; his conflict with the religious leaders (concerning the meaning of the Law and his authority); his arrest and trial; his crucifixion, death, and burial; his resurrection from the dead; and his ascension to exercise authority for the extension of his kingdom.

3. The reasons for the rejection of Jesus as the Messiah centered on the question of his identity as not only the son of David but as the Son of God, his interpretation of the Law in contrast to the traditions of the elders, and the nature of the kingdom he came to establish.

4. The main point of his teaching concerned the kingdom of God. The opening words of his ministry called for repentance because the kingdom was at hand. His parables were about the nature of the kingdom and its king. The Sermon on the Mount was about the character of the members of this kingdom. He taught the true

meaning of the law of the kingdom. He taught entry to this kingdom was by spiritual birth. He revealed himself to be the king of this kingdom. Lastly, he commissioned his disciples to bring all nations into this kingdom.

5. The prologue of John's gospel speaks of the Word of God as the one by whom all things were made. This Word that has been rejected as reason, general revelation, and Scripture becomes incarnate to restore man to the knowledge of God. In John, Jesus progressively reveals himself, through his miraculous signs and by his teaching, to be the Messiah, the Son of God, the Word incarnate, through whom alone man has eternal life (knowledge of God).

6. The book of Acts records the growth of the kingdom of God. It begins with Pentecost (the coming of the Holy Spirit), preaching and large numbers of conversions in Jerusalem (1–6); persecution and the spread of the gospel to Judea and Samaria (7–8); the conversion of Paul and the gospel going to the gentiles throughout the world (to Asia Minor, Greece, and Rome through the missionary journeys of Paul).

7. The book of Romans is a systematic statement of the Christian faith. All men have clear general revelation of the nature and existence of God and the law of God and so are without excuse for unbelief and sin (1–2). Since no one is righteous, a person is accepted by God on the basis of the righteousness of God which comes through faith in Jesus Christ. Abraham too was accepted by faith (3–4). This reconciliation by grace through Christ's atoning death has benefits far greater than the effects of Adam's sin. It not only forgives sin, but frees from the power of sin. It extends to the whole of creation and triumphs over every opposition (5–8). This grace comes into a person by God's sovereign choice and though Israel does not now believe, God will bring both the gentiles and Israel to believe (9–11). In view of God's mercy, men are to devote themselves to God and to do his will in all things. The will of God in many applications of the law is urged upon those who believe (12–16).

8. In the letters to the Corinthians, Paul deals with divisions in the Church particularly with respect to the diversity of gifts. True ministry is a spiritual warfare involving much suffering, ending in triumph. In the letter to the Galatians, Paul affirms that no human effort can be added to or mixed with the free gift of salvation by God's grace. In the letter to the Ephesians, Paul speaks of the full extent of salvation in Christ who through his Church is to fill everything in every way. The Church's maturity consists in attaining to the whole measure of the fullness of Christ. In the letter to the Philippians, Paul sets forth Christ's life as the example of service. In the letter to the Colossians, Paul affirms the believer's completeness in Christ who is fully God against Gnostic teaching of Christ as a higher being in a spiritual hierarchy. In the letters to the Thessalonians, Paul corrects faulty teaching about the return of Christ and irresponsible behavior connected with this. The letter to the Hebrews shows how Christ is the reality of the types and shadows through which they had been taught about Christ and exhorts them to persevere in faith.

9. The pastoral letters to Timothy and Titus are teachings and exhortations about the responsibility and conduct of pastors. The general epistles (James, Peter, John, Jude) give instruction and exhortation on living the Christian life.

10. The Book of Revelation speaks of the then current state of spiritual warfare and the eventual triumph of the kingdom of God. The certainty of the triumph is deepened by the repetition of the vision from seven perspectives (the seals, the trumpets, the woman and the dragon, the plagues, the harlot, the great war, the thousand-year rule).

11. Church councils expressed the Church's response to challenges to the foundation of Christianity. The Council of Jerusalem about A.D. 51 addressed the distinction of the Old and New testaments. The Council of Nicea in 325 affirmed the doctrine of the Trinity, that God is Father, Son, and Holy Spirit. The Council of Chalcedon

in 451 affirmed that Christ is the Son of God incarnate, both God and man. These councils are ecumenical.[1]

12. Augustine (d. 430)[2] shaped the Church's thinking for centuries in his development of the doctrine of original sin (the fall of Adam and its effects on mankind), in his teaching about predestination and man's need for divine grace, in his teaching about the Church in history in its conflict with unbelief.

13. During the period of the rise of the papacy (500-1200) the major developments were the rise of monasticism (ascetic withdrawal and otherworldliness), expansion during the Dark Ages and admixture of superstition, feudal society, and the Church over the State.

14. Aquinas (d. 1274)[3] dealt with both the defense of the faith and the exposition of the faith. He worked out a synthesis of faith and reason in relating the supernatural and natural realms. He developed the doctrine of the sacraments as administered by the Church as the sole source of divine grace to man.

15. The main concerns in the first phase of the Reformation (under Luther) concerned the ultimate authority of Scripture vs. the teaching authority of the Church; justification is by faith alone apart from works and sacrament; the priesthood of every believer vs. the need for priests as intermediaries with God.

16. The focus of the Reformation under Calvin was on the divine sovereignty over all aspects of life; the purity of worship apart from human traditions; Church order is synodical (the joint rule of all pastor-teachers) vs. hierarchical or local independence.

17. The Enlightenment was the reliance on reason and experience as sufficient guides for human affairs. Some accepted the Enlightenment first by synthesis with Scripture, then in conflict with Scripture (deism), then displacing Scripture (secularism/naturalism),

---

1. *Paper No. 16.*
2. Gangadean, *History of Philosophy*, 111-114.
3. Gangadean, *History of Philosophy*, 121-126.

then against the original principle (existentialism/Postmodernism). Others reacted. Some reaffirmed historical creeds. Others accommodated experience as valid (evangelicalism), then literalism vs. liberal rationalism, and fundamentalism vs. apostasy.

18. The liberals claimed hold to reason and the findings of science and attempted to accommodate the Scripture to this. The conservatives claimed hold to Scripture and those fundamentals necessary for salvation. Some fundamentalists claimed to hold to a strict literal understanding of all of Scripture. This antinomy assumes the possibility of conflict between faith and reason. It can be resolved by critically examining assumptions.

19. The main dividing lines within Christianity are: the sole authority of Scripture (Catholic/Protestant, liberal/conservative); divine sovereignty (historical/popular); the principle of worship and Church government.

20. Some of the principal challenges facing Christianity today are: the doctrine of clear general revelation vs. every form of non-theistic thought; the Church's otherworldliness vs. the this-worldliness of secular thought; faith vs. reason and the very nature of religion.

This paper was originally developed for a
World Religions course.

Paper No. 87

———

SCRIPTURE

INTRODUCTION[1]

1. Scripture is redemptive revelation. It assumes the rejection of the Word of God in man as reason and in the creation as clear general revelation.

2. Scripture is the Word of God written. It reveals how God is both just and merciful to man in sin.

3. Scripture focuses on the person and work of Christ, the Word of God incarnate, who restores mankind to life in the knowledge of God.

4. Genesis is the book of beginnings, of creation, of sin, and of redemption; and of continuity and increase of covenant blessing in the midst of apostasy and judgment.

5. In Genesis 1–3 is given the foundation of Scripture in organic seed form. Scripture builds on, is to be understood by, and is the development of what is revealed here.

---

1. Gangadean, *The Westminster Confession*. See Questions 4-12; Gangadean, *The Westminster Catechisms*. See LCQ. 4-6; *Paper No. 14, 26, 56, 112, 114,* and *141-150.*

GENESIS 1:
CREATION[2]

1. Original creation is *ex nihilo*; it is the origin of the clarity of general revelation.

2. Subsequent creation is by forming and filling what is without form and empty.

3. God's purpose in creation is revelation. This is so necessarily and intentionally.

4. Creation of life is each after its own kind rather than of no kinds or all from one kind.

5. Creation of man is in the image of God. He is ruled by God and is to rule the creation.

6. Original creation was very good; there was no natural evil.

7. The completion of the work of creation is sealed in the Sabbath.

GENESIS 2:
CREATION OF MAN, THE IMAGE OF GOD[3]

1. Man is created of one kind. Man is finite, temporal, and changeable in all his attributes.

2. Man is created in triune personhood, in knowledge, in holiness, and in righteousness.

3. Man is created a body/soul unity.

4. Man is created a male/female unity.

5. Man is created a temporal being whose nurture is historically conditioned.

6. Man is created each with a unique personal identity.

7. Man is created in a corporate unity centered in Eden.

---

2. Gangadean, *The Westminster Catechisms*. See Appendix 4; *Paper No. 141-144*.

3. Gangadean, *The Westminster Confession*. See Question 23; Gangadean, *The Westminster Catechisms*. See LCQ. 17; *Paper No. 144*.

8. Man is created with unity in purpose, for dominion and the knowledge of God.

9. Man is created with the moral law written on his heart, with the choice of good and evil.

10. Man is created in covenant unity, to be established in righteousness by representation.

11. Man is created changeable: in innocence, in sin, in regeneration, and in sanctification.

12. Man in the Sabbath-hope is to complete dominion as God completed the work of creation.

GENESIS 3:1-7:
THE FALL[4]

1. The temptation of man reveals the state of man in the pursuit of good or evil.

2. Sin as unbelief and not understanding is revealed in man's rejection of God's Word.

3. Sin as unholiness is revealed in man not seeking the knowledge of God.

4. Sin as unrighteousness is revealed in man's eating of the tree of the knowledge of good and evil.

5. Sin as autonomy is revealed in man's choosing to determine good and evil for himself.

6. Sin at root is revealed as the denial of God as infinite, eternal, and unchanging Creator.

7. Sin at root is revealed as man's denial of being finite, temporal, and changeable creature.

8. Sin is revealed as the denial of the clear difference between the finite and the infinite.

---

4. Gangadean, *The Westminster Confession.* See Questions 30-34; Gangadean, *The Westminster Catechisms.* See LCQ. 21-29; *Paper No. 103* and *145-147.*

9. Sin is revealed as the denial of human nature in denying reason to avoid what is clear.

10. The consequence inherent in sin is spiritual death: meaningless-ness, boredom, and guilt.

GENESIS 3:7-24:
REDEMPTION[5]

1. The first call to repentance is through shame. Man covers it up through self-deception.

2. The second call is by a question for self-examination. Man avoids it by self-justification.

3. The third call of promise and curse reveals God's goodness to man in hardness of heart.

4. The promise brings spiritual warfare, age-long and agonizing, until good overcomes evil.

5. The curse brings toil with nature, strife with man, and old age, sick-ness, and death.

6. Man's response to the third call is repentance and faith shown in obedience to be fruitful.

7. God's first response is to justify man by covering his guilt through an atoning sacrifice.

8. God's second response is to sanctify man by expulsion, to be cleansed through suffering.

This paper was originally developed for a
Philosophy of Religion course.

---

5. Gangadean, *The Westminster Confession.* See Questions 39-61; Gangadean, *The Westminster Catechisms.* See LCQ. 30-90; *Paper No. 148-150.*

Paper No. 88

———

Philosophy of Religion

1. **Definition of religion: the beliefs or set of beliefs we use to give meaning to our experience.**

   Religion cannot be defined as belief in a higher power, or as belief in a Scripture, or as a set of practices. Many religions do not have these features.

   Implications of this definition of religion:

   i. *All persons are religious since all persons give meaning to their experience.*

   Both theism and atheism are formally paired beliefs which are used in the same way to interpret experience.

   ii. *Religion is fundamentally cognitive.*

   It has to do with beliefs which are either true or false.

   Religion is not fundamentally mystical/experiential or a set of social rules.

   iii. *No experience is meaningful without interpretation.*

   One's basic belief cannot arise from experience.

   Experience has meaning when interpreted in light of one's basic belief using reason.

   iv. *As truth cannot be separated from meaning, so faith cannot be separated from reason.*

It is by reason that meaning is grasped. Reason is the test for meaning.

Faith grows as understanding grows. Faith is tested as understanding is tested.

Faith is contrasted with sight; it is not contrasted with reason, proof, or understanding.

v. *No one is fully conscious of or consistent in their basic beliefs.*

All have a mixture of the two basic beliefs (all or only some is eternal), with one being more at one's core.

History is an outworking of the conflict of these two beliefs in each person, each culture, and in world history.

2. Levels of religion

i. *Popular (95+%):*

Concerned mostly for practical and psychological needs.

Generally unaware of historical creeds.

ii. *Historical (4-5%):*

What the best minds have agreed upon after much discussion.

This understanding is summed up in the great creeds of the faith.

iii. *Philosophical (1% or less):*

Addresses questions that have not yet been discussed historically.

Addresses questions that remain from internal and external challenges.

3. Minimal definition of "God"

i. God is a higher power.

ii. God is the highest power (none higher).

iii. God is eternal (not dependent on another for his being).

iv. Only God is eternal (God is higher than all others).

v. Only some is eternal (there are other beings besides God than which he is higher).

vi. Some is eternal and some is not eternal (direct implication of the above).

vii. What is eternal brought into existence what is not eternal (being from non-being is impossible).

viii. The eternal (God) is Creator (to bring into being is to create).

4. There must be something eternal.

i. Contradictory statements cannot both be true and cannot both be false (at the same time and in the same respect).

ii. A self-contradictory statement cannot be true (there are no square-circles).

iii. The contradiction of "some is eternal" is "none is eternal."

iv. "None is eternal" implies a contradiction since it implies:

    a. all is temporal, which implies,

    b. all had a beginning, which implies,

    c. all came into being, which implies,

    d. all came into being from non-being.

v. Being from non-being cannot be true.

So, (d), (c), (b), (a), and the original (iv) "none is eternal" cannot be true, since they all mean the same thing.

vi. So, the contradictory of (iv), "some is eternal," must be true.

5. The material world is not eternal.

(What is eternal is independent, self-existing, self-maintaining, and self-explaining)

The argument to show the material world is not eternal is:

Major premise: If the material world were eternal, it would be self-maintaining.

Minor premise: The material world is not self-maintaining.

Conclusion: The material world is not eternal.

The reasons for the minor premise are:

i. In general (the universe is entropic—tends to randomness and sameness).

    a. The physical universe is highly differentiated (some parts are hot and some cold).

    b. These differences interact.

    c. The interaction continues until sameness is reached.

    d. When sameness is reached in everything, it remains in sameness.

ii. In its parts (the suns and the stars will burn out).

    a. The sun is finite (limited in size).

    b. The sun is giving off heat.

    c. The sun (and all stars) will burn out.

iii. As a whole (the Big Bang cannot occur again).

    a. There is not enough mass (it needs 10 times as much mass for gravity to pull everything back again).

    b. The force in will equal the force out (at some point in the process of oscillation).

    c. The theory of a change from a true vacuum (no matter and no energy) to a false vacuum (no matter and energy) involves an appeal to being coming into existence from non-being, which is impossible.

6. The soul exists.

Proof for the existence of the soul is proof for what is obvious, not for what is hidden.

The soul is the same as the self or the mind, and the mind is not the brain.

That the mind is not the brain can be seen from an analysis of perception of any object.

The argument to show the mind is not the brain is:

Major premise: The most immediately known is the most certainly known.

Minor premise: The self is most immediately known.

Conclusion: Therefore, the self is most certainly known.

The reason for the minor premise "the self is most immediately known" is based on the analysis of perception in terms of light waves, neural impulses, mental image, and the self.

i. The light waves (coming from the table to the eyes) are more immediate (to the perceiver than the cause of the table that is seen); the light waves are not seen; they are not conceived to be shaped like a table.

ii. The neural impulses (formed from the light wave interacting with the optic nerve) are more immediate (in the process of perception than the light waves); they are not seen; they are not shaped like a table; they are the last brain activity. One has to go beyond the brain to get to the table that is seen.

iii. The mental image of the table is more immediate than the neural impulse; the mental image is seen; the mental image is shaped like a table; the mental image is therefore not a neural impulse; the mental image does not perceive itself.

iv. The self is more immediately known than the mental image; it is known as the perceiver of the mental image; the self is known as having no size but as having consciousness. The self is known as the spirit, mind, soul, and consciousness.

The objections to the reasons for the minor premise attempt to reduce the self to a bundle of mental images (Hume), to do away with talk about mental state terms (analytical behaviorism), or to identify the physical with the non-physical, indirectly (the neutral identity thesis). There are responses refuting each of these objections.

i. Hume: When I look inside, I see nothing but mental images. If there is a self, it must be the bundle of mental images.

Response: What is doing the looking when "I" look inside is the self.

ii. Analytical behaviorism: Mental state terms can be explained fully by behavior terms. Pain means the same as pain behavior.

Response: It is easy to conceive of pain without pain behavior and vice versa.

iii. The neutral identity thesis: The very same thing (fibain, having the properties of nerve fibers and pain) that is conducting nerve impulses is aching unbearably.

Response: The same thing (fibain) that has no size (pain) has size (nerve fiber).

7. The soul is not eternal.

The argument to show the soul is not eternal is:

Major premise: If the soul were eternal, I would have infinite knowledge.

Minor premise: I do not have infinite knowledge.

Conclusion: Therefore, the soul is not eternal.

The reason for the major premise:

i. The soul has one thought after another and is therefore in time.

ii. If it is eternal in time, it would have been in existence for an infinite amount of time.

iii. Since the soul grows in knowledge in time, however slowly, in infinite time it would have infinite knowledge.

iv. It is self-evident that I do not have infinite knowledge.

The argument holds for any view of an eternal soul going through a unique event, such as liberation from reincarnation, or going to heaven.

8. The material world exists.

The argument to show the material world exists is:

Major premise: The cause of what I see is either my mind or another mind or outside all minds.

Minor premise: The cause is not my mind or another mind.

Conclusion: Therefore, the cause of what I see is outside all minds.

The reasons for the minor premise:

i. If my mind were the cause of what I see, then I would have total control of what I see.

 I do not have total control of what I see.

 Therefore, the cause is not my mind.

ii. If another mind were the cause of what I see, then I would have no control of what I see.

 I do have some control of what I see.

 Therefore, another mind is not the cause of what I see.

9. The objections to *Advaita* Vedanta (one mind only and its ideas; the world is illusion).

i. Where does the illusion reside? (it cannot be in my mind or in pure consciousness)

ii. How can pure consciousness be concealed from itself?

iii. How can the world be neither a thing nor a thought?

iv. How can the world be neither real (eternal) nor unreal (non-existent)?

To say reason cannot grasp it and we must give up reason is not possible. We cannot give up reason. The assumption "the world is an illusion" is what should be given up.

10. The objections to *Dvaita* Vedanta or qualified non-dualism (we are all part of God).

    i. If all the parts are the same, finite, then the whole (God) would not be infinite. And parts cannot be finite and eternal, going through unique events.

    ii. If all the parts are the same, infinite, then they would be both complete and incomplete at the same time.

    iii. So, the parts are not all the same: some are finite-temporal and some infinite-eternal.

This paper was originally developed for a
Philosophy of Religion course.

Paper № 89

———

HISTORY OF RELIGION

1. **Definition of religion: the beliefs or set of beliefs we use to give meaning to our experience.**

   Religion cannot be defined as belief in a higher power, or as belief in a Scripture, or as a set of practices. Many religions do not have these features.

   Implications of this definition of religion:

   i. *All persons are religious since all persons give meaning to their experience.*

      Both theism and atheism are formally paired beliefs which are used in the same way to interpret experience.

   ii. *Religion is fundamentally cognitive.*

      It has to do with beliefs which are either true or false.

      Religion is not fundamentally mystical/experiential or a set of social rules.

   iii. *No experience is meaningful without interpretation.*

      One's basic belief cannot arise from experience.

      Experience has meaning when interpreted in light of one's basic belief using reason.

   iv. *As truth cannot be separated from meaning, so faith cannot be separated from reason.*

It is by reason that meaning is grasped. Reason is the test for meaning.

Faith grows as understanding grows. Faith is tested as understanding is tested.

Faith is contrasted with sight; it is not contrasted with reason, proof, or understanding.

v. *No one is fully conscious of or consistent in their basic beliefs.*

All have a mixture of the two basic beliefs (all or only some is eternal), with one being more at one's core.

History is an outworking of the conflict of these two beliefs in each person, each culture, and in world history.

2. Definition of basic belief

i. Our most basic belief has to do with our most basic concept—that of eternal existence.

ii. There are two basic beliefs: all is eternal and only some is eternal.

iii. None is eternal cannot be held since it implies being came from non-being.

iv. Under "all is eternal" are the following religions:

Secular Humanism (all is matter, matter is eternal, there is no spirit or soul)

Hinduism (all is one, *atman* is Brahman, *Advaita*: the world is *maya*/illusion)

Buddhism (all is *dukkha*, all is an eternal process)

Dualism (matter and spirit are both eternal: Greek, Persian, Indian, Mormon)

Taoism, Confucianism, and Shintoism

Shamanism (belief in spirits in nature, and magical powers)

v. Under "only some is eternal" (or God the Creator) are the following religions:

Judaism (Orthodox, Reformed, Conservative, Reconstruction, Hasidic)

Christianity (Eastern Orthodox, Roman Catholic, Protestant)

Islam (Sunni, Shi'a, Sufi)

Deism (God created the world, but does not actively rule in the world)

3. Definition of "God"

i. In theism, God is a spirit, infinite, eternal, and unchanging in being, wisdom, power, holiness, justice, goodness, and truth.

ii. In atheism, there is no God as spirit. "God" has sociological or psychological meaning only, if at all.

iii. In deism, God is Creator but not ruler.

iv. In pantheism, God is all and all is God.

v. In polytheism, there are many gods, each having rule over a particular function of nature. Or, the god is connected to the local people.

vi. In dualism, God is maker but not Creator.

vii. In Shamanism, the gods are local spirits or impersonal forces.

4. Levels of religion

i. *Popular (95+%):*

Concerned mostly for practical and psychological needs.

Generally unaware of historical creeds.

ii. *Historical (4-5%):*

What the best minds have agreed upon after much discussion.

This understanding is summed up in the great creeds of the faith.

iii. *Philosophical (1% or less):*

Addresses questions that have not yet been discussed historically.

Addresses questions that remain from internal and external challenges.

5. **Recent developments in religion: the move from theism to shamanism**

    i. The ongoing conflict between impersonal/natural explanations and personal/supernatural explanations beginning with the Greeks.

    ii. The shift from the Dark Ages and Medieval Christianity to the Renaissance and the Reformation.

    iii. The development of science from theism and from the Reformation view of work.

    iv. The shift to deism and the extension of natural explanations; the collapse of the Old Order in the revolutionary period.

    v. The naturalism of Darwin, Marx, Nietzsche, and Freud.

    vi. The miracles of technology and the trust in science.

    vii. World War I, World War II, The Cold War, and the collapse of Modernism: post-colonialism and Postmodernism.

6. **Meaning, faith, and reason in popular religion**

    i. Liberals and conservatives

    ii. Fundamentalism and literalism

    iii. The concept of hell—4 contrasts

    iv. The concept of heaven—4 contrasts

    v. The concept of the second coming of Christ—4 contrasts

7. **Meaning, faith, and reason in science, religion, and philosophy**

    i. Does the soul exist?

    ii. Creation and Evolution—geology

    iii. Creation and Evolution—biology

iv. Creation and Evolution—astronomy

v. Creation and Evolution—theistic evolution

This paper was originally developed for a World Religions course.

CHRISTIANITY AND SECULAR HUMANISM

The Difference

There is a worldview difference between Secular Humanism (SH) and Christianity manifest in every aspect of life.

SECULAR HUMANISM

1. SH denies that God exists or that it is clear that God exists. SH affirms that all is matter, that matter is eternal, and that all of reality can and must be explained in material terms only. Theism is thus seen as a mere by-product of past human ignorance.

2. SH denies that man is the image of God, that man is a *rational* animal, that man is a body/soul unity, that man has or *is* an immortal soul. SH affirms that man is an evolved animal, entirely a product of the environment, that the mind is identical with the brain and that we cease to exist entirely when we die.

3. SH affirms empiricism, that *all* knowledge is from sense experience, that knowledge is pragmatically based, that science is the only means to knowledge, that science (not reason or philosophy) has authority and is therefore the basis of public discourse and policy.

There are corollaries to naturalism (material monism) grounded in empiricism, which lead to reductionism:

   i. Thought is identical with motion of atoms in the brain.

   ii. A mental image is identical with a neural impulse.

   iii. Analytical behaviorism analyzes pain as pain-behavior.

   iv. The self is a bundle of mental images (the perceiver *is* the perceived).

4. SH affirms that the good for man individually is pleasure (vs. pain), consistent with ethical egoism, the will to power, the superman (*ubermensch*). The good for man collectively is utilitarian—the greatest good/pleasure/happiness for the greatest number, the collective, an earthly utopia (heaven on earth). There is no way to mediate the dispute between individualism and collectivism except through power. To change man's thinking one must change his environment, by force/pain if necessary. Change in thinking is not by the use of reason but by non-rational (anti-intellectual) means, since thinking is merely rationalization of one's perceived self-interest.

5. SH denies that there are any moral absolutes (besides pleasure individually or power collectively). Skepticism about clarity leads to moral relativism (and the socio-political doctrine of moral equivalence), which requires tolerance and political correctness. All speech that causes distress must be removed by sensitivity training or by exclusion from the realm of public discourse (loss of freedom of speech).

6. SH believes that all power differences are produced by one group exercising power over another group at the other's expense and rationalizing the difference by ideology. Differences are not produced by basic beliefs based on the use of reason prior to and apart from social contact among groups. In SH, the worldview of science and its material benefits (and hence power differences in societies) cannot be said to be "better than" the worldview of sorcery. In SH, differences arise from taking advantage of another. Therefore, all differences must be leveled by "social justice." Mere participation in power differences makes one a capitalist, or a racist, or a sexist.

7. SH believes that atheism is *not* a religion based on fideism (belief without proof), that *all* religions are a hindrance to human happiness (the secular utopia), that (all) religion is the opiate of the masses, that (all) religion is infantile dependence, that (all) religion is opposed to (all) science, that science is *not* based on philosophical assumptions subject to critical analysis, that only science is free from dogmatic assumptions and that empiricism and uniformitarianism (the forces now operating have *always* operated and in essentially the *same* degree) are held not as dogmas, but as *pure* facts.

CHRISTIANITY

1. Historic Christianity and the Scriptures affirm the clarity of general revelation (cGR) regarding the existence and nature of God and the moral law grounded in human nature, so that unbelief is without excuse. The difference with SH lies in the critical use of reason to understand cGR—basic things that can be known by all men, everywhere, at all times, prior to any appeal to special revelation (SR). The difference between Christianity and SH is therefore first philosophical *before* it is theological.

2. SR presupposes cGR and cGR leads to and requires SR. All thought and discourse requires Common Ground (CG), which leads to the Principle of Clarity (PC)—that the basic things are clear to *reason*. The difference therefore between SH and Christianity is first epistemological: are basic things clear to reason or to sense experience? Reason as the laws of thought is most basic and is authoritative as the test for meaning. By reason, we know there are no square-circles, no being from non-being, no uncaused events. By reason, we know that there must be something eternal. Senses give sensations, which are appearances, not reality. We cannot know *anything* about reality by the senses alone. Empiricism, which holds that *all* knowledge is from sense experience, is therefore unwarranted and is merely a naïve dogma, based on neither sense experience nor reason.

3. By reason, I can know that the material world exists (the *cause* of what I perceive is outside all minds) and that the material world is not eternal (self-maintaining) due to entropy at every level of the

material world. The material world is brought into existence (created *ex nihilo*) by Spirit. By reason, I can know the soul exists (the mind is not the brain: thinking cannot be reduced to motion of atoms in the brain; in perception, a mental image (of a table) in my mind cannot be reduced to a neural impulse in the brain). By reason, I can know the soul is not eternal (an eternal soul would have all knowledge). Therefore, *only some* (God) is eternal.

4. By reason, I know there are logical (not merely empirical) gaps in every stage of the naturalistic evolutionary explanation of the origin of man: from non-life to life, from life to more complex life, from more complex life to hominid, from hominid to human. By reason, I know that man is the image of God, not the image of the animal, that since God is all good and all powerful, original creation was very good (without natural evil), and that theistic evolution must deny original creation was very good, that natural evil entered *after* moral evil. By reason, I know that a concept is not an image (a universal is not a particular), that reason distinguishes man from animal, that man is of a different *kind*, not evolved from animal. By reason and experience, I know that major geological data is best explained by non-uniformity rather than uniformity, and that the finely tuned universe is neither by chance nor by necessity, but ordered by the wisdom of God.

5. By reason, I know that the good for a being is according to the nature of that being, that evil for man is an act contrary to human nature as rational. Moral evil is to neglect, avoid, resist, and deny reason in the face of what is clear to reason, that evil therefore is an act of *self*-destruction, *not* an act caused from outside. By reason, I know that the good for man as a rational being is the use of reason to understand the nature of things, which, as created, reveal the nature of God, that the good for man therefore is the knowledge of God. By reason, I know that virtue is not the good but the *means* to the good, and that happiness is not the good but the *effect* of possessing the good; that the inherent effect of not seeking and not understanding is meaninglessness and boredom and guilt and that no amount of pleasure apart from meaning can overcome boredom and its excess.

6. Given that God is all good and all powerful, by reason, I know that the physical death of man is not original in creation, that death, which is universal, entered by one man (the Fall), that the just consequence of moral evil is spiritual death, not physical death. By reason, I know that physical death, imposed by God on all men, is not punishment, but the last, final, and merciful call back from sin and self-deception and self-justification (regarding not seeking), that sin as unbelief remains in all men (both believers and non-believers), that natural evil (the curse of toil and strife, and old-age, sickness, and physical death) *as mercy* requires SR (Scripture) to show how God can be *both* just *and* merciful to man in sin and spiritual death.

7. By reason, I know that SR must be consistent with cGR, that redemption in SR must meet the (covenant) requirements of the Fall, that another *man* in place of the first must undo what the first did and do what he failed to do. By reason, I know that Genesis 1–3 which teaches creation–fall–redemption (and any further SR which builds on the worldview of Genesis) satisfies the demand of cGR. By reason, I know what evil is and *why* God permits evil (theodicy), that it is *only* because God is all good and all powerful that good *will* overcome evil and that SH can never bring about a lasting culture.

What is known from cGR is assumed throughout SR, and both cGR and SR are made still more explicit in the Historic Christian Faith, which is cumulatively summed up by Church councils in their creeds.

Paper N⁰· 91

CHRISTIANITY AND ISLAM
The Difference

The difference between Christianity and Islam is not merely a few isolated doctrines, but a worldview (systematic) difference rooted in their different view of the Logos, the Word of God, which first comes to man as reason. This root difference becomes more apparent as each position becomes more conscious and consistent.

There are several interrelated levels in a worldview, beginning with what presents itself more immediately and reaches to what is most basic.

The *first* level concerns Christ and him crucified, the Scriptures, the Trinity, predestination, divine law, view of the good, civil liberties, and human dignity.

The *second* level of differences can be summed up in understanding the biblical worldview of creation–fall–redemption.

The *third* level of differences arises at the philosophical level of general revelation in the assumptions of epistemology, metaphysics, and ethics.

At the *fourth* and deepest level the question of common ground (for all thinking and discourse) arises. What is the highest authority? What is the self-attesting Word of God?

In the 10 points that follow, all these levels will be addressed; points 1–7 address issues on the first level.

1. Islam denies that Christ died on the cross. Islam professes to build on the Old Testament (OT) and the New Testament (NT), yet denies what is central to both: in the OT, vicarious atonement on *Yom Kippur* (the Day of Atonement) and in the NT, which fulfills the OT, the death of Christ on the cross to atone for the sin of the world. If there is no redemption in Islam, then God is not great in justice and mercy and *"Allahu Akbar!"* is empty of meaning.

2. Islam professes to build on the OT and the NT. While the OT and the NT are commonly believed to be *given* by God, according to Islam the OT and the NT are not *preserved* by God, whereas the Quran is *both* given *and* preserved by God. Why the latter is preserved and the former is not, has not (and cannot be) explained on the shared assumption of being given by God: either God has changed, which is impossible, or no scripture is given by God, which is also impossible for Islam, or the Quran contains error where it disagrees with what is given by God *earlier*. If the Quran *were* given by God, it would not contain error, therefore the Quran must not be given by God.

3. Islam denies the Trinity as error. It denies that Jesus is the Son of God the Father by Mary his mother. But it is an error to say the NT teaches this. The gospel of John says: "In the beginning was the Word (Logos), and the Word was with God, and the Word was God." The Word of God, who is eternally *with* God, and *is* God, is the eternal Son of God. It is the Word of God, the eternal Son of God, who became flesh: "And the Word was made flesh . . . ." The Son of God took upon himself human nature by being born of the Virgin Mary. If the Son of God is co-eternal with the Father (no Son without the Father and no Father without the Son—Father and Son are relational terms), then the Quran is in error to argue against a straw man. What contains error cannot be the Word of God.

4. Islam and Historic Christianity both teach the doctrine of predestination, but in very different ways and with very different outcomes. In Islam, the end is decreed apart from the means (second causes *in* the nature of things). In Christianity, *both* the end (salvation) *and* the means (through human desire and beliefs grounded in the use

of reason) are predestined. The Islamic view of ends without means is *partial* predestination and results in paradoxes of freedom and responsibility. Rather than question uncritically held assumptions about freedom and divine omnipotence, Islam moves to give up reason. However, the failure is not *in* reason but in the *failure* to use reason critically. The injunction to submit to scripture and not to reason is uncalled for, and ends in the use of force rather than reason.

5. Islam believes in divine law embodied in *sharia* and obligatory upon all to whom it comes. Islamic law is entirely from *direct* divine command apart from any supposed nature of God or man. It is known from testimony alone and cannot be and must not be questioned. Biblical law is summed up in the Ten Commandments, but is first written in the hearts of all men (i.e., in human nature). It is therefore objectively clearly revealed to all men and is easily knowable by all who seek. In Islamic law there is no distinction between Church and State or between crime and sin. *Sharia* law is totalitarian; it is to be enforced upon all persons and in all aspects of life.

6. In Islam, God is pure will, unconstrained by any divine nature, so creation cannot be revelation. The good in Islam is virtue or piety as an end in itself, expressed in behavior of obedience or submission. The reward for virtue is happiness or pleasure, conceived of as a sensual paradise, in which women are for the pleasure of men. In Christianity, man's chief end is to glorify and to enjoy God in all that by which he makes himself known, in all his works of creation and providence. Through the cumulative work of dominion, by all human beings through all of history, the earth shall be full of the knowledge of the Lord as the waters cover the sea. Eternal life for Christianity is knowing God.

7. Islam means submission. Man's will everywhere must be made to submit to God's will, and through submission comes peace. Force (*jihad*) may be used to bring about submission (Islam). The force may be either the force of law (civilizational *jihad*) or the force of violence (terrorism). No one is free to make converts out of Islam, and the penalty for any person who converts out of Islam is death. In Christianity, man is made in the image of God, with the ability

and the responsibility to know God. The inherent consequence of not using reason to know what is clear about God is meaningless-ness and boredom and guilt. Because of its theology, Islam has re-lied on force rather than reason. The use of force in the place of reason in forming basic beliefs is a violation of man's dignity as the image of God. What violates human dignity can never be a lasting foundation for civilization.

8. Islam and Christianity differ in their understanding of creation–fall–redemption. Because creation is understood differently, Islam denies the reality of the Fall and the necessity for redemption.

Creation in Islam:

i. Creation is not revelation; there is no nature of God to be re-vealed in the acts of creation.

ii. Man is not the image of God understood as a rational being. Therefore, the good for man cannot be the knowledge of God through the work of dominion.

iii. Original creation of all things cannot be said to be very good be-cause there is nothing in God that requires it to be good. Phys-ical death was present in the original creation of man.

The Fall in Islam:

i. There is no Fall of man in Islam.

ii. There is no covenant of creation with Adam in the beginning. Adam's act does not affect all men.

iii. Death does *not* come by *one* man; it was there from the begin-ning of the creation of man.

Redemption in Islam:

i. There is no redemption in Islam through curse and promise.

ii. Natural evil (the curse of toil and strife, and old age, sickness, and death) is not imposed as a call back from moral evil. It was there at the creation of man.

iii. Moral evil does not serve to deepen the revelation of God's jus-tice and mercy.

iv. There is no promise of Christ to come in the place of Adam to undo what Adam did (Christ is not the Lamb of God who takes away the sin of the world), and to do what Adam failed to do (rule to make God known).

9. There are fundamental differences in philosophical first principles based in general revelation, between belief and unbelief, wherever they occur, especially between the theistic faiths of Islam and Christianity.

   i. In Epistemology: Islam does not affirm the Principle of Clarity, that the basic things about God and man and good and evil are clear to reason.

   ii. In Metaphysics: In Islam, there is no infinite, eternal, and unchangeable *nature* of God. Man is not therefore the finite, temporal, and changeable image of God, who is rational in essence.

   iii. In Ethics: In Islam, there is no rational justification for the good as the knowledge of God. The good in Islam is not teleological, distinguished from virtue (as means to the good), and happiness (as effect of possessing the good). Ethics is either deontological (virtue is the end in itself) or consequential (happiness/pleasure is the good and virtue is the means to happiness, *extrinsically* given by God).

10. At the deepest level of difference between Christian theism and Islamic theism lies the doctrine of the Logos as the Word of God in its fullness. The Logos is Truth.

   i. The eternal Word of God, the Logos, comes to man first as reason, the laws of thought. Reason as the laws of thought is the test of meaning. It is therefore authoritative and self-attesting. Reason applies to being as well as thought, to all being, to the highest being, to God's being. God is not both eternal and not eternal, at the same time and in the same respect. What violates reason cannot be the Word of God.

   ii. Commitment to reason as a concern for consistency is integrity, which is necessary and sufficient to know the truth. Lack of integrity disregards what is existentially absurd or logically absurd.

iii. Thinking by nature is presuppositional: we think of the less basic in light of the more basic. Reason as most basic must be applied as a test of meaning to basic beliefs. This epistemological process is called *Rational Presuppositionalism*. If we agree on the more basic, we can and will agree on what is less basic. Where critical thinking has been disallowed disputes have festered for centuries.

iv. The Logos is present in creation as clear general revelation: the basic things about God and man and good and evil are clear to reason. What is clear objectively is not seen subjectively because of sin: left to oneself no one seeks God and no one understands.

v. Consistent with the disregard of reason and clear general revelation, the Logos comes to the people of God as Scripture in the Old Testament, which also is disregarded.

vi. The Logos comes once more to man, incarnate in Jesus Christ, full of grace (to forgive sin) and truth (to make God known).

vii. Christ sends the Holy Spirit to lead the Church objectively into all truth (through its councils and creeds) and to bring believers subjectively into the truth by regeneration and sanctification.

The Logos is Truth in its fullness, coming to man through general revelation, Scripture, and Historic Christianity, both objectively and subjectively. The Logos distinguishes Christianity from Islam.

Paper Nº· 92

THE RELEVANCE OF REASON
An Apologetic for Logic

1. Introduction: Logic and Reason

The term "logic" comes from the Greek term "*logos*" which means reason, account, word, explanation.

The Logos is the focus of the Prologue to the Gospel of John: In the beginning was the Word (*Logos*). The Logos is the Word of God that reveals God in every way. The Logos is Truth in its fullness.

The Logos is the object of study in all academic disciplines: biology, psychology, epistemology, etc.

The purpose of the study of logic is to develop confidence and competence in the use of reason, to find meaning and to settle disputes.

The following is an apologetic for logic, which explains the relevance of reason.

2. Reason and Thought

i. It is self-evident that we think: we form concepts, judgments, and arguments, the forms of all thought.

ii. It is self-evident that there are laws of thought: the law of identity: *a* is *a*; non-contradiction: not both *a* and *non-a* (at the same time and in the same respect); excluded middle: either *a* or *non-a*. The laws of thought are reason in itself.

iii. When a law of thought is violated, thinking ceases. One cannot think *a is non-a*; *a is non-a* as a whole is meaningless.

3. Reason and Meaning

i. Reason in itself as the laws of thought *is* the test for meaning.

ii. If a law of thought is violated, then thinking ceases and meaning therefore ceases.

iii. Reason is not neutral with respect to truth. Meaning is more basic than truth. Where there is no meaning there can be no truth.

4. Reason and Authority

i. Reason as the test for meaning is authoritative for all thought. There can be no objection to thought by what is non-thought (by the non-cognitive, by what is neither true nor false).

ii. Reason as the laws of thought cannot be questioned since it makes questioning possible. It is unquestionable, needing no proof.

iii. Reason as the laws of thought is self-attesting. Only reason is self-attesting. The highest authority must be self-attesting.

5. Reason and Human Nature

i. Human nature is man's essence—the set of qualities that all men have, that they always have, and that distinguishes them from all other beings.

ii. Man is a thinking being having a real body. He is a mind *and* a body, a rational animal. He is both body and soul in the unity of one being.

iii. Man is the image of God, crowned with the light of reason (to know God) and honor (to rule over the creation).

6. Reason and the Word of God

i. God makes himself known through his Word. The Logos is the eternal Word of God who makes God known. All things were made by him (the Logos).[1]

ii. The life of the Logos is in all men as light. That light, by which we see (that is, understand), is reason. Reason in man is ineradicable and irresistible.[2]

iii. By reason, all other forms of revelation are understood: in creation (general revelation);[3] in history (special revelation in Scripture);[4] in person (incarnate in Jesus Christ);[5] in the Church (in its councils and creeds);[6] in believers (through regeneration and sanctification).[7]

iv. Reason is the most basic form of the Word of God for human knowledge; it is the self-attesting Word of God present in all men.

7. Reason and Common Ground

i. Common Ground is that set of conditions necessary for thought and discourse. Common Ground begins with reason. Discourse without Common Ground is futile.

ii. Human society is a society of rational beings. Full participation depends on the exercise of one's full capacity to reason.

iii. Human dignity is affirmed when we are treated as rational beings responsible for the use of reason.

iv. Common Ground also includes: integrity as a concern for consistency; addressing what is more basic *before* the less basic; and a commitment to the Principle of Clarity—that some things are clear to reason.

---

1. *John 1:1-3.*
2. *John 1:4-5.*
3. *John 1:10.*
4. *John 1:11.*
5. *John 1:14.*
6. *John 16:13.*
7. *John 3:3; 17:17.*

8. Reason and Clarity

i. The Principle of Clarity states: some things are clear; the basic things are clear; the basic things about God and man (metaphysics) and good and evil (ethics) are clear to reason (epistemology).

ii. If nothing is clear to reason, then meaning and morality (inexcusability) are not possible. Then Christianity, which assumes the clarity of general revelation and the inexcusability of unbelief,[8] is not possible.

iii. If what can be known of God through general revelation *is* clear to reason, then there is a meaningful answer to the problem of evil and the necessity for redemptive revelation can be understood.

9. Faith and Reason[9]

i. Biblical faith is belief based on understanding. Faith is not dogmatism or fideism, which is belief without understanding. Without faith it is impossible to please God.[10]

ii. Understanding is by the use of reason. Understanding connects disparate pieces of knowledge so that one can see the Truth.

iii. Faith is inseparable from reason as truth is inseparable from meaning.

iv. Faith grows as understanding grows; faith is tested as understanding is tested.

10. Reason and Being[11]

i. Reason is ontological; it applies to being as well as thought.

---

8. *Romans 1:20.*

9. Gangadean, *Philosophical Foundation*, 32-45, 121-127; Gangadean, *History of Philosophy*, 3-12, 163-167; *Paper No. 21, 28, 98,* and *128-129.*

10. *Hebrews 11:6.*

11. Gangadean, *History of Philosophy*, 35-44, 107-110, 151-162, 167-170; Gangadean, *Philosophical Foundation*, 14-15, 27-31, 73-80, 109-110.

ii. Reason applies to all being; to the highest being; to God's being. For instance, God is not both eternal and not eternal, at the same time and in the same respect.

iii. What violates a law of reason cannot be thought *and* cannot exist: there are no square-circles; there are no uncaused events; there is no being from non-being.

iv. Miracles do not violate the uncreated laws of reason, but supervene by an act of God on the created laws of nature.

11. Reason and Good and Evil

i. The good for a being is according to the nature of that being; evil is what is contrary to the nature of that being.

ii. The good for man as a rational being is the use of reason to the fullest, to understand the nature of things, which reveal the nature of God. The good for man therefore is the knowledge of God.

iii. Moral evil is to neglect, avoid, resist, or deny reason regarding what is clear about God. The inherent consequence of not seeking God is not understanding the meaning of things. It is meaninglessness, boredom, and guilt—without end.

12. Reason and Integrity[12]

i. Integrity is a concern for consistency in thought and action.

ii. Integrity is necessary to avoid the logically absurd and the existentially (self-referentially) absurd.

iii. Integrity is a *commitment* to reason as a rational being. It is necessary and sufficient to see what is clear.

iv. Lack of integrity produces an intellectual stupor resulting from self-deception and self-justification regarding one's commitment to reason.

---

12. Gangadean, *Philosophical Foundation*, 199-205; Gangadean, *History of Philosophy*, 8-9, 169-170; *Paper No. 51, 64-65,* and *110.*

13. Reason and History

i. Presuppositions are basic beliefs used to give meaning to one's experience.

ii. There are two sets of basic beliefs: in epistemology: some things are clear vs. nothing is clear; in metaphysics: all is eternal vs. only some is eternal; in ethics: the good is the end in itself vs. the good is virtue (means to the end) or happiness (the effect of the end).

iii. These sets of beliefs are contradictory: they cannot both be true and they cannot both be false. We are more or less conscious and consistent in our basic beliefs. We should be more conscious and consistent.

iv. History is an outworking of the conflict of basic beliefs in each person and each culture.

v. Only what retains meaning will last; what is inherently contradictory cannot last.

14. Reason and Regeneration[13]

i. Left to oneself, no one seeks God; no one understands; no one does what is right.[14] In himself, man is spiritually dead.

ii. Man is restored from spiritual death to life by regeneration.[15] In regeneration, man is restored to the life of the Logos in him as light (reason).

iii. Restoration to the self-critical use of reason produces conviction of sin and death and the need for repentance and faith (conversion).

---

13. Gangadean, *Philosophical Foundation*, 36-37; Gangadean, *The Westminster Confession*. See Questions 49-52; Gangadean, *The Westminster Catechisms*. See LCQ. 67.

14. *Romans 3:10-11.*

15. *John 3:3.*

15. Reason and Unity

   i. Man is sanctified (made more Christ-like) through knowing the Truth. The Logos is Truth.[16]

   ii. Understanding the Truth comes through suffering (trials of faith).

   iii. The Holy Spirit leads the Church into all Truth.[17] In response to challenges, after much discussion, the Church comes to agreement summed up in creeds, delivered to all believers for the unity of the faith.[18]

   iv. The first principles are the foundation of the faith.[19] Without foundation, there are divisions and apostasy in the Church, and decay and collapse in the culture. With foundation, there is maturity, fruitfulness, unity, and fullness.[20]

16. Conclusion: Reason and Hope

In the spiritual war (between belief and unbelief), which is age-long and agonizing, good will overcome evil.[21]

In the clarity of the Logos, the light shines in the darkness: unbelief cannot overcome or withstand belief.[22]

In the rule of Christ, through his body, the Church, the earth shall be full of the knowledge of the LORD as the waters cover the sea.[23]

---

16. *John 17:17.*
17. *John 16:13.*
18. *Acts 15.*
19. *Hebrews 6:1.*
20. *Ephesians 4:10-16.*
21. *Genesis 3:15.*
22. *Romans 1:20; John 1:5.*
23. *Isaiah 11:9; Revelation 19:11-21.*

Paper Nº· 93

THE LOGIC OF
APOLOGETICS

The Goal, the Method, the Content

1. The Goal

i. The goal of Christian Apologetics is determined by the goal of the Christian life: the knowledge of God is the good, man's chief end, which is eternal life.

ii. Christian Apologetics seeks to remove all obstacles to the knowledge of God. "We demolish arguments and every pretension that raises itself up against the knowledge of God."[1] Every objection includes internal and external objections, as well as objective proofs and subjective persuasion.

iii. Christian Apologetics assumes and seeks to defend the Christian Worldview of creation–fall–redemption:

a. Creation: creation is revelation: the basic things about God and man and good and evil are clear to reason so that unbelief is without excuse.[2] Apologetics requires us to show the clarity of general revelation.

---

1. *2 Corinthians 10:4-5.*

2. *Romans 1:20.*

b. Fall: man is fallen; he is in a state of sin and death: no one seeks God, no one understands, no one is righteous.[3] The noetic effect of sin is such that man neglects, avoids, resists, and denies reason in the face of what is clear in order to retain his autonomy.

c. Redemption: man is called back from sin and death by the curse and promise. God imposes the curse of toil and strife, and old age, sickness, and death on man to restrain, recall from, and remove moral evil. The promise is that through a spiritual war (between belief and unbelief) that is age-long and agonizing, good will overcome evil.

iv. Christian Apologetics seeks to take *all* thoughts captive to the obedience of Christ[4] resulting in the earth being filled with the knowledge of God as the waters cover the sea.[5]

v. Thinking by nature is presuppositional: we think of the (logically) less basic in light of the more basic. If we agree on the more basic, we can and will agree on the less basic. Apologetics seeks to apply this principle to resolve philosophical and theological disputes.

2. The Method: Rational Presuppositionalism

i. Thinking by nature is presuppositional: we think of the less basic in light of the more basic: meaning in light of reason; truth in light of meaning; experience in light of basic belief; finite and temporal in light of the infinite and eternal; conclusion in light of premises.

ii. Reason as the laws of thought is most basic; it is self-attesting; it cannot be questioned because it makes questioning possible. Reason is authoritative for all thought.

iii. The application of reason as the test of meaning to basic beliefs (presupposition) is Rational Presuppositionalism (RP). Critical

---

3. *Romans 3:10-11.*

4. *2 Corinthians 10:5.*

5. *Isaiah 11:9.*

thinking examines uncritically held assumptions. RP is critical thinking applied more consciously and consistently.

iv. Presuppositions are basic beliefs used to give meaning to experience. No experience is meaningful without interpretation. We interpret experience in light of basic beliefs. Basic beliefs can and should be tested for meaning.

v. RP is distinct from mere presuppositionalism: the latter is belief without proof (fideism); the former is belief based on understanding.

RP is distinct from mere rationalism; the latter uses reason constructively without first using it critically, and also uses reason as a source of truth rather than as a test for meaning.

RP is distinct from all forms of empiricism: common sense (naïve realism which takes appearance for reality); intuition (inner experience, mysticism, or spontaneously arising beliefs—*sensus divinitatis*); science based on empiricism (the claim that all knowledge is from sense experience alone).

3. Rational Presuppositionalism Applied

i. Common Ground (CG) consists of the set of conditions necessary for thought and discourse: reason, integrity, RP, and the Principle of Clarity (PC). To begin with what is most basic, one must begin with CG. There is no naked public square. Common Ground is not neutral ground.

ii. General revelation (GR) consists of what can be known of basic things by all men, everywhere, at all times. Philosophy asks the most basic questions based on GR. RP in GR must first deal with epistemology (clarity and inexcusability), then metaphysics (the nature of God and man), and then ethics (the moral law grounded in human nature).

iii. Special revelation in Scripture (Genesis 1–3) affirms creation–fall–redemption. Creation must be understood before one can understand the Fall. Redemption is to be understood in light of creation and the Fall. The life of Abraham must be understood in light of what comes before (Genesis 1–11). The book of Revelation must be understood in light of all else that comes before, beginning with Genesis and clear GR.

iv. Hermeneutics (interpretation, understanding the meaning of) is contextual (the less basic in light of the more basic). It is neither literal (without context) nor allegorical (using foreign context). There are several layers of context: first clear GR, then the biblical worldview of creation–fall–redemption, then what came before in history, then the book, chapter, sentence, and word. The less basic is connected to the more basic by reason (using good and necessary consequences). Understanding also comes by connecting related and relevant parts of knowledge to see the picture in full dimension.

v. In theology, doctrines which divide the Church can be resolved by having foundational doctrines in place: clarity and inexcusability, sin and death, curse and promise, repentance and faith, justification and sanctification, baptism and calling, resurrection and reward.

4. The Content: Understanding Clear General Revelation

If one understands the clarity of GR, then one can:

i. Show the necessity for clear general revelation.

ii. Show there must be something eternal, and, only some (God) is eternal (vs. material monism, spiritual monism, and dualism).

iii. Show the nature of God (infinite, eternal, and unchangeable in being, wisdom, power, holiness, justice, goodness, and truth) and show man is the image of God (in the sevenfold aspect of human nature).

iv. Show how the moral law is clear, comprehensive, and critical by showing how the moral law is grounded in human nature and how the moral law from GR is the same in content as the Decalogue from SR.

v. Show the necessity for and existence of SR from clear GR.

5. The Content: Addressing Divisions Within Theism

    i. Show God is Creator and ruler (vs. deism).

    ii. Show vicarious atonement in biblical revelation vs. post-biblical Judaism.

    iii. Show Christianity and the clarity of general revelation vs. Islam.

    iv. Show the Historic Christian Faith in the Church's councils and creeds vs. divisions within Christianity.

    v. Show the Theological Foundation (the Seven Pillars) vs. divisions within Christianity.

CONCLUSION

RP Apologetics differs from other forms of Apologetics by its **goal** (it is opposed to *all* that is raised up against the knowledge of God), by its **method** (it secures agreement by understanding the (logically) less basic in light of the more basic), and by its **content** (it addresses *all* objections *to* theism and *all* divisions *within* theism).

Paper N<u>o.</u> 94

———

CURRENT APOLOGETIC METHODS AND GENERAL CRITIQUE

DEFINITIONS

1. Definition of Apologetics: defense based on proof vs. persuasion to believe.

2. Definition of the Christian Faith: Christ is Savior and Lord.

3. Definition of Christian Apologetics: showing that Christ is Savior and Lord.

   i. Savior: requires showing the clarity of general revelation and inexcusability of unbelief.[1]

   ii. Lord: requires taking thoughts captive which divide the Church and mankind.[2]

4. Definitions of Current Christian Apologetic Methods:

   i. Evidentialism: reliance on experience (internal or external) as self-evident.

   ii. Presuppositionalism: reliance on intuition (*sensus divinitatis*) or testimony (Scripture) as self-evident.

———

1. *Romans 1:20.*
2. *2 Corinthians 10:4-5.*

iii. Classical: reliance on pluralistic cumulative arguments (vs. logically cumulative arguments—from more basic to less basic).

iv. Cultural: reliance on human flourishing as self-evident.

GENERAL CRITIQUE OF
CURRENT APOLOGETIC METHODS

1. A reason for one's belief (warrant/reasonableness) does not show inexcusability for unbelief (sin and need for Christ as Savior).

2. Appeal to experience as common sense/naïve realism/pragmatism does not address the distinction between appearance and reality.

3. Appeal to experience (inner or outer) does not address the assumptions used to interpret the experience/event, which assumptions can/should be tested for meaning.

4. Appeal to experience (historical fact of the resurrection) does not address the inexcusability of all, based on the clarity of general revelation.

5. Appeal to experience (observation in science) does not critique the naturalistic assumptions used to interpret the data.

6. Appeal to testimony, handed down as scripture, must address scriptural pluralism as well as the need for any scripture.

7. Reason as the laws of thought is neither finite nor fallen, but is the test for meaning and is self-attesting.

8. Reliance on pluralistic cumulative arguments leaves logical gaps in proving Christian Theism.

9. Use of standard theistic arguments must answer historical objections or offer revised arguments, which are logically cumulative.

10. Standard theistic arguments do not address inexcusability of unbelief of all.

11. Cultural apologetics must show the inherent connection between sin and death; fideism is not a rational response to skepticism.

12. Appeal to human flourishing does not sufficiently distinguish and relate the good, virtue, and happiness in order to achieve rational justification in ethics. The natural moral law is the foundation for lasting culture.

RATIONAL PRESUPPOSITIONALISM[3]

1. Thinking by nature is presuppositional—we think of the less basic in light of the more basic. If we agree on the more basic, we can agree on the less basic.

2. Rational Presuppositionalism responds to all the above critiques of current apologetic methods.

---

3. *Paper No. 101.*

Paper № 95

———

RATIONAL PRESUPPOSITIONAL APOLOGETICS

Prolegomenon

DEFINITION AND METHOD

1. Definition of Apologetics

    i. A rational defense of one's basic beliefs in response to challenges; required of all who engage in public discourse.

    ii. Christian apologetics is a rational defense of Christian basic beliefs. A rational defense offers proof; proof is not persuasion (evangelism, witnessing etc.).

2. Definition of the Christian Faith: Christ is Savior and Lord

    i. Christ is Savior from sin and death.

    ii. Christ is Lord who rules to make God known.

3. Due to sin remaining, the Christian is more or less conscious and consistent in understanding the meaning of confessing Christ as Savior and Lord.

    Apologetic methods differ according to the measure of one's faith, that is, understanding.

4. Current apologetic methods can be classified as follows, with many degrees of admixture:

    i. Evidentialism: reliance upon human experience (empiricism) for knowledge.

    ii. Presuppositionalism: reliance upon non-inferred sources (intuition and testimony) for the knowledge of God.

    iii. Classical: infers the knowledge of God from what can be known by all.

    iv. Cultural: infers the need for God from life without God.

5. Rational Presuppositionalism (RP): reliance on reason to understand meaning and settle disputes.

    RP seeks to consistently argue from the more basic to the less basic at every stage of discourse.

    RP begins with Common Ground, lays foundation from general revelation (GR), scripture/special revelation (SR), and Historic Christianity (HC), and seeks fullness through a worldview expressed in culture.

CHRISTIAN APOLOGETICS MUST SHOW THAT CHRIST IS SAVIOR

1. Sin

    i. Christ is the Lamb of God who takes away the sin of the world[1] from the beginning[2] to the end.[3]

    ii. All have sinned and come short of the glory of God.[4]

    Sin is rooted in autonomy, putting self in the place of God to determine good and evil.

    Unbelief is without excuse in light of the clarity of general revelation.[5]

---

1. *John 1:29.*
2. *Genesis 3:21.*
3. *Revelation 22:3.*
4. *Romans 3:23.*
5. *Romans 1:20.*

   iii. Left to oneself, no one seeks God, no one understands, no one does what is right.[6]

   iv. From general revelation: moral evil (sin) is an act contrary to one's nature as a rational being.

      It is to neglect, avoid, resist, or deny reason in what is clear about God.

2. Death

   i. The wages of sin is death.[7] This death is spiritual, not physical. It is present and inherent in sin, not future and imposed. Sin and death reveal God's justice (J).

   ii. Physical death and every form of the curse/natural evil is imposed because of moral evil.

3. Natural Evil

   i. Natural evil (toil and strife, and old age, sickness, and death / war, famine, and plague) is a call back from moral evil, not punishment.

   ii. Natural evil serves to restrain, recall from, and remove moral evil. It is a call to stop and think.

4. Mercy

   i. Natural evil as a call back is mercy (M).

   ii. Natural evil requires special revelation to show J and M.

5. Scripture

   i. Christian Apologetics must show the need for special revelation.

   ii. SR must show J and M in Christ and him crucified for sin and death, grounded in the clarity of general revelation and the inexcusability of unbelief.

---

6. *Romans 3:10.*

7. *Romans 6:23.*

CHRISTIAN APOLOGETICS MUST SHOW
THAT CHRIST IS LORD

1. Jesus Christ is the eternal Word of God incarnate who rules to make God known.[8]

2. Christ exercises Lordship through a spiritual war (between belief and unbelief), which is age-long and agonizing, and in which good overcomes evil.[9]

3. The truth of God begins with foundational doctrine from GR/SR/HC.

   Foundation leads to worldview, to culture (a way of life), to the City of God, to the earth filled with the knowledge of God.[10]

4. Christ sends the Holy Spirit to lead the Church into all truth through the pastor-teachers who, in response to challenges and after much discussion, come to agreement summed up in creeds and confessions, the basis for unity of the faith of all believers.

   The Holy Spirit brings persons into the truth through the work of regeneration and sanctification.

5. In the spiritual war, every thought raised up against the knowledge of God which divides the Church and divides mankind must be made obedient to Christ.[11]

---

8. *John 1:1-18.*

9. *Genesis 3:15; Revelation 19:17-21.*

10. *Isaiah 11:9.*

11. *2 Corinthians 10:4-5; Matthew 28:18-20.*

Paper N<u>o.</u> 96

———

THE PROJECT OF RATIONAL PRESUPPOSITIONAL APOLOGETICS

**Rational Presuppositionalism shows
Christ is Savior and Lord by showing:**

1. The clarity of general revelation (God the Creator)

Only some (God the Creator) is eternal.

   i. There must be something eternal.

   ii. Matter exists and matter is not eternal.

   iii. The soul exists and the soul is not eternal.

   iv. Natural order is by special creation.

   v. Moral order is by theodicy for the good (the problem of evil).

2. The clarity of general revelation (the natural moral law)

There is a natural moral law which is clear, comprehensive, and critical.

   i. The natural moral law is for the good (teleology); the good is not virtue (deontology) or happiness (consequentialism).

    ii. The natural moral law is grounded in human nature.

    iii. The moral law given in human nature is also given in the Decalogue.

3. The clarity of general revelation (inexcusability: sin and death)

    i. The nature and existence of moral evil (sin).

    ii. The nature and existence of spiritual death.

    iii. The nature and existence of natural evil (physical death).

4. Christ is Savior (redemption accomplished)

Christ is the Lamb of God who takes away the sin of the world.

    i. The relation of general revelation (GR) and special (redemptive) revelation (SR).

    ii. Christian Theism: the promise and fulfillment of redemption in SR.

    iii. The steps from GR to SR: necessity, content, origin, existence, transmission, completion, translation, clarity, sufficiency, and interpretation of SR.

5. Christ is Lord (redemption applied)

Christ, the eternal Word of God incarnate, rules to make God known through the Holy Spirit.

    i. The Holy Spirit enables the Church to make disciples of all nations.

    ii. The Holy Spirit leads the Church into all truth through historically cumulated insight.

    iii. The Holy Spirit leads the believer into the truth through regeneration and sanctification.

Paper №. 97

─────

FREEDOM AND PREDESTINATION
A Concise Critical Analysis

1. Locus of the problem

  i. Is there freedom with respect to the use of reason to see what is clear about God?

  If I want to use my reason, can I use my reason?

  ii. Does "want" imply "can" here?

  The problem is not to be relocated at a secondary level where "want" does not imply "can."

  iii. The problem becomes: because I have shut my eyes, I cannot see.

  Because I do not want to see, I cannot see.

  iv. At the basic level, "want" implies "can," always.

  v. The problem is not in the power of reason itself, or in the power to use reason, but in the power to see without the use of reason.

2. Definition of freedom: liberty and ability[1]

Liberty, at the basic level, is not the ability to do otherwise.

Liberty is doing what I want.

    i. "Which do you want?" is the same as "which do you choose?"

   ii. God is free: God does what he pleases; God cannot do evil.

  iii. Freedom as the ability to do otherwise requires that what I do is uncaused.

       If the cause is present, the effect necessarily follows. I could not have done otherwise (cf. history of libertarian freedom).

       If "my act" is uncaused by me (my beliefs and desires), then it is not *my* act and therefore not my *free* act. Freedom is impossible.

       Reason as a cause is not possible.

       If one event can be uncaused, all events can be uncaused, and there is no way to know if any event is in fact caused.

3. Objections and responses

    i. Even if I can't want otherwise, still I get what I want, always. If I always get what I want, there is no basis for complaint.

   ii. If I can't want to use reason, then I can't use reason, and therefore I am not using reason. But I am now using reason.

  iii. "Why have you made me so?" If this is a call for help, then there is help. If this is an attempt at self-justification, then it is not intelligible: "I want a reason why I don't want to use reason."

This paper was originally developed for a
Philosophy of Religion course.

---

1. Gangadean, *Philosophical Foundation*, 66, 167-168; Gangadean, *History of Philosophy*, 113-114, 153-154.

Paper №· 98

FAITH AND

THE WORD OF GOD

The Object of Faith

1. The Word of God is that by which God makes himself known. The Logos is the Word of God in its fullness. The sum of all God's Word is truth. The object of faith is always and only the Word of God.[1]

2. Faith is the substance of things hoped for, the evidence of things not seen. Without faith it is impossible to please God. He that comes to God must believe that he is, and that he rewards those who diligently seek him. Left to oneself, no one seeks God, no one understands. All have sinned and come short of the glory of God.

3. Faith is inseparable from proof (evidence) based on understanding. Faith without understanding is like words without meaning. Faith grows as understanding grows; faith is tested as understanding is tested. Faith without understanding is dead; fideism (belief without proof based on understanding) is not faith.

4. By faith we understand that the worlds were framed by the Word of God, so that things which are seen were not made of things

---

1. Gangadean, *Philosophical Foundation*, 32-45, 121-127; Gangadean, *History of Philosophy*, 3-12, 163-167; *Paper No. 21, 28,* and *128-129.*

which do appear.[2] The invisible things of him from the creation of the world are clearly seen, being understood by the things that are made, even his eternal power and Godhead; so that they are without excuse (*anapologia*).[3]

5. Due to sin (remaining in all, and ruling in some) there is resistance to request for proof, manifest in many/every degree(s), both inside and outside the Church. The gospel calls men everywhere to repent of failure to seek and understand what is clear about God and man and good and evil, and to seek first the kingdom of God in all relations of life.

6. Faith is to reason as truth is to meaning. By reason we see (understand) the invisible things of God. Without understanding the meaning of experience, man is like the beast that perishes. Faith is based on reason; it is not based on uncritically examined tradition; it is not based on mere persuasion (by informal fallacies vs. sound argument); it is not based on mere appearance (common sense); it is not based on intuition (the sign is not the reality); it is not based on science in so far as it assumes empiricism (all knowledge is from sense experience); it is not based on the constructive use of reason building on dogmatic assumptions.

7. Faith begins with the light of reason (the life of the Logos in all men made in the image of God).[4] By reason, as the laws of thought, we understand the Logos in general revelation.[5] By reason, we understand Scripture—the Word of God written.[6] The Logos, rejected as reason, general revelation, and special revelation, became incarnate in Jesus Christ, full of grace and truth.[7] The Holy Spirit is sent by Christ to lead the Church into all truth[8] summed up in the creeds

---

2. *Hebrews 11:3.*

3. *Romans 1:20.*

4. *John 1:4.*

5. *John 1:10.*

6. *John 1:11.*

7. *John 1:14-18.*

8. *John 16:13.*

through Church councils.[9] The Spirit restores persons to the life of faith sovereignly by regeneration[10] and brings them to a mature faith by sanctification.[11]

8. Faith (Word of God, Truth, doctrine, belief) is fundamental to all other aspects of life—to the psychological (feeling) and the practical (outward/actional). Yet we live (existentially are aware of and operate) on the less basic level. So, divisions are seldom addressed as disputes about faith and they persist through one lifetime and are passed on to the third and fourth generations. What becomes long-standing and deep-seated requires both repentance and forgiveness up to seventy times seven.

9. What is more basic is not the ethical or the metaphysical, but the epistemological (how we know—by the Word of God, the object of faith). Meaning is more basic than truth; and reason—the life of the Logos in all men as light[12]—that by which we understand meaning, is the most basic form of the Word of God in man. In our fallen state, we neglect, avoid, resist, and deny reason as the laws of thought to avoid what is clear about God. We avoid the inexcusability of the light of reason—in ourselves and in others.

10. Unbelief regarding clarity has been avoided by excusing or accusing: doctrine divides; theological hairsplitting; dry-as-dust theology; faith is above or against reason; faith of the simple (most); only (very) few can do metaphysics; proof is by evidence for special revelation (miracles, prophesy, the Resurrection) vs. from clear general revelation; all men already know—deep down (without seeking and understanding); all must know (and suppress) to be culpable (vs. culpable ignorance); belief in God is properly basic—*prima facie* warrant only (like the external world and other minds); one must presuppose God to reason (vs. reason is the self-attesting Word of God[13]). None of these apologetics aim at clarity and inexcusabili-

---

9. *Acts 15.*

10. *Ephesians 2:8-9; 1 Peter 1:23.*

11. *John 17:17.*

12. *John 1:4.*

13. *John 1:4-5.*

ty. All, therefore, miss the mark (*hamartia*). All sin comes short of the glory of God. All sin brings death. The emperor has no clothes. Without rational justification for belief in God we are all naked. Rational justification is avoided by self-deception (fig leaves—comes in many styles and every size and color) and self-justification. The unexamined life is not worth living (Socrates). Man that is in honor, without understanding, is like the beasts that perish.[14]

11. Professing believers, drawn to the doctrine of clarity, without repentance of root sin (the lack of faith—belief in God without proof/fideism) in themselves first and in their tradition, merely add the proofs of clarity to their apologetic arsenal. Addition without repentance puts new wine (the worldview arising from the cornerstone of clarity) into old wineskins (built on a faulty foundation). To preach clarity without repentance of one's inexcusability is to preach a fatal distortion of clarity (clarity-lite). The old wineskins burst sooner or later, and all labor is lost.[15]

12. The stone the builders rejected has become the cornerstone.[16] Clarity (and inexcusability) is cornerstone, the bedrock of the foundation. All else is sand. The Church has not withstood the challenges of Modernity and Postmodernity. There has been division and apostasy in the Church. Without the Church as salt and light, the culture is in decay, nearing collapse. But the promise stands: with the foundation, the Church can grow to maturity, fruitfulness, unity, and fullness. All flesh is grass. Only the Word of God, grasped by faith, stands forever.[17]

---

14. *Psalm 49:20.*

15. *Hebrews 5:12.*

16. *Psalm 118:22.*

17. *Isaiah 40:8.*

Paper № 99

THE ORIGIN AND GROWTH
OF EVIL IN THE WORLD

From Original Sin to the Kingdom of Darkness

1. Human evil begins in the hearts of fallen human beings.[1]

2. Man, in self-centered existence, does not seek God: all have sinned and come short of the glory of God.

3. Without glorifying God, man cannot enjoy God. He turns to the creation without God for enjoyment.

4. The world cannot satisfy man's need for meaning found only in the knowledge of God. Man goes to excess in greed and lust, and transgresses the law of God.

5. Sin is done in secret, and in the darkness of self-deception and self-justification. Sin is done in collusion with others.

6. Sin grows over one's lifetime, and over generations, in families and groups that benefit from sin. Sin grows like leaven and leavens the whole lump.

7. Those at the top seek to preserve and advance their unjust gain, and structure the world around them to this end.

---

1. *Paper No. 103.*

8. Without the good as the knowledge of God, and the moral law as means to the good, unbelievers justify a worldly view of the good and worldly means to it. This ideology cannot be opposed by any who share in such a false view of the good.

9. Those at the top secretly seek to eliminate all that opposes their view. Secret societies, of many kinds, accumulating power over centuries, infiltrate, like a cancer, every organ in the body politic. Education without God (the false prophet), economics without God (the harlot), and politics without God (the beast), unite to achieve full control through a one world government.

10. At this point in history, the kingdom of darkness comes into full display against the kingdom of God. The conflict is now all out. The cup is full. The end (resolution one way or the other) is near. If the Church does not repent and take the world's unbelief captive, evil will prevail and this will bring judgment, as at Babel, to prevent a one world government under unbelief.

Paper № 100

———

HISTORICAL FOUNDATION

The Work of the Holy Spirit
Leading the Church Into All Truth

HISTORIC CHRISTIANITY IS THE WORK OF the Holy Spirit lead-ing the Church into all truth,[1] through the centuries, through the work of pastor-teachers. Pastor-teachers are given to the Church by Christ to bring believers to the unity of the faith, to the full mea-sure of the stature of Christ.[2]

Challenges occur in every age, to which the Church must respond in order to attain to the fullness of Christ, and to accomplish its task to disciple all nations. Without the teachings of Historic Christiani-ty firmly established in the lives of believers, there is no ordinary basis for hope for attaining maturity in the fullness of Christ.

In every age, as the Church expands, new believers bring into the Church ideas and practices from their culture which challenge the truth of the Gospel. After much discussion, the pastor-teachers come to agreement on the teaching of Scripture in response to these challenges.

The First Church Council was held in Jerusalem in response to the challenge of Judaic legalism.[3] The early gentile converts were influenced by Greek dualism, and raised the challenge of Gnosticism, which was answered by the Apostles' Creed (*ca.* A.D. 180), recited in churches

---

1. *John 16:13.*

2. *Ephesians 4.*

3. *Acts 15.*

through the centuries. The Council of Nicea (A.D. 325) addressed challenges to the doctrine of the Trinity. The Council of Carthage (A.D. 397) identified all the books and only the books that constitute the Scripture of the New Testament. The Council of Chalcedon (A.D. 451) clarified the doctrine of the Incarnation (that Christ is fully God and fully man), and the Council of Orange (A.D. 529) affirmed the doctrine of sin (man is fallen in Adam) and salvation (man is saved by grace) in response to Pelagian and semi-Pelagian error.

The Westminster Confession of Faith (A.D. 1648) is the high-water mark of Historic Christianity at the beginning of the modern era. Building on the work of the pastor-teachers in the early Church councils, it responded to the challenges of systemic distortions in the Church at the time of the Reformation.[4]

It affirmed the authority of Scripture over against all other sources of special revelation. It affirmed the sovereignty of God over all, and its application in salvation through one covenant of grace over against all admixtures of grace with human effort.

It affirmed the work of the pastor-teachers meeting in synods/councils over against hierarchical and independent ecclesiastical authority. And it affirmed the regulative principle of worship, that the worship of God, which God has commanded in Scripture, must be kept pure and entire.

In the modern age, the Church has been challenged in terms of its claim to knowledge (reason and science vs. faith and scripture), and in its view of human purpose (life on earth vs. eternal life in heaven, the secular vs. the sacred).

The Church has not yet come to the unity of faith in meeting these challenges and has steadily been losing ground where it once led the culture in Western civilization. Current globalization has intensified contact with non-Western cultures and worldviews in Asia, Africa, and South America.

The more supernatural forms of Christianity growing in these areas are yet to face the acid tests of skepticism and secularism. By building on Historic Christianity, as summed up in the Westminster Confession of Faith, these challenges can be met.

---

4. *Paper No. 16.*

The challenge of reason and science vs. faith and scripture can be met by the biblical teaching on the clarity of general revelation and the inexcusability of unbelief.[5]

The Westminster Confession opens with the affirmation of this teaching: "The light of nature [reason], and the works of creation and providence do so far manifest the goodness, wisdom, and power of God, as to leave men unexcusable." Believers today are being challenged by skepticism to show the clarity of general revelation and to take thoughts captive which are raised up against the knowledge of God.[6]

Believers today are being challenged by secularism—life in this world vs. eternal life in heaven. This can be met by the biblical teaching that eternal life is the knowledge of God,[7] and that man's purpose on earth is to fill the earth with the knowledge of God as the waters cover the sea.[8]

The Westminster Confession of Faith affirms that God's purpose in creation and providence is the revelation of his glory;[9] that the first commandment requires us to know and acknowledge God;[10] that the first petition in the Lord's Prayer is that God would enable us and others to glorify him in all that by which he makes himself known;[11] that man's chief end is to glorify God and enjoy him forever.[12]

---

5. *Romans 1:18-20; 2:14.*

6. *2 Corinthians 10:4-5.*

7. *John 17:3.*

8. *Isaiah 11:9.*

9. *WCF 4.1, 5.1.*

10. *SCQ. 46.*

11. *SCQ. 101.*

12. *SCQ. 1.*

_____

RATIONAL
PRESUPPOSITIONALISM
Critically Examining Assumptions for Meaning

RATIONAL PRESUPPOSITIONALISM IS AN epistemological method used to settle philosophical disputes by critically analyzing assumptions for meaning. It applies reason as a test for meaning to what is presupposed in a dispute.

Rational Presuppositionalism (RP) affirms that some things are clear. The basic things are clear. The basic things about God and man and good and evil are clear to reason.[1] RP is an answer to skepticism and fideism. It is an alternative to rationalism and to empiricism, both of which make uncritically held assumptions.[2]

Thinking is presuppositional. We think of the less basic in light of the more basic. We think of truth in light of meaning, experience in light of basic belief, conclusions in light of premises, and the finite and temporal in light of the infinite and eternal. If we understand what is more basic, we can understand what is less basic; if we agree on what is more basic, we can agree on what is less basic.

RP seeks to avoid needless disputes by examining if there is agreement on what is more basic. It seeks to avoid straining at gnats while swallowing camels. It looks at both the objective and the subjective

---

1. Gangadean, *Philosophical Foundation*, 287-292.

2. Gangadean, *History of Philosophy*, 131-149.

aspects of knowledge and dialogue. Dialogue presupposes a commitment to reason along with an understanding of the nature of reason.

Having knowledge presupposes a concern to know, which presupposes integrity as a concern for consistency, both theoretically and personally. If there is commitment to reason, with integrity, disputes can be settled.[3]

Skepticism claims that knowledge is not possible. It is rooted in uncritically held assumptions, that if rationalism (for example, Descartes) and empiricism (for example, Hume) cannot give knowledge, then no knowledge is possible.[4] Consistently held, skepticism leads to nihilism, in which no distinction is clear, including the distinction of *a* and *non-a*, being and non-being, true and false, and good and evil.

Skepticism denies reason, makes dialogue impossible, and leads to silence as well as a cessation of all thought. It dissolves the meaning of its terms—*knowledge* and *possible*. Pragmatism cannot overcome the meaninglessness of skepticism.[5] And fideism (appeal to faith apart from proof based on understanding) becomes an arbitrary affirmation of one view from among many.

RP affirms that sense experience gives knowledge of appearance but not of reality, and that the data of experience (common sense, scientific or mystical) must be interpreted in order to be meaningful. RP does not allow the postmodern skeptical view that "it is all a matter of interpretation." Philosophy does not end with interpretation, but begins here.

Every interpretation can be, and must be, tested for coherence and meaning. RP affirms that the self-evident truths of rationalism (Descartes' *cogito* or Jefferson's self-evident truths) are not logically basic, even though they are taken as properly basic. The alternatives of absolute idealism and naturalism require a response.

Rational Presuppositionalism is to be distinguished from fideistic presuppositionalism, in which one moves from Scripture (the Triune God of the Bible) to reason. RP is to be distinguished from axiomatic presuppositionalism, in which one begins with the Scripture as one's set of axioms.

---

3. Gangadean, *Philosophical Foundation*, 287-292.

4. Gangadean, *History of Philosophy*, 9-12.

5. Gangadean, *Philosophical Foundation*, 117-118.

RP is to be distinguished from reformed epistemology, in which one begins with what is taken as properly basic beliefs.[6] RP is to be distinguished from evidentialism, in which one seeks to argue from miracles to God. RP is to be distinguished from common sense realism, in which the objective existence of the external world is assumed.[7]

RP affirms that the clarity of general revelation is necessary for the inexcusability of unbelief and undertakes to show what is clear from general revelation by showing the alternatives of unbelief are contrary to reason.[8] It is to be distinguished from all attempts to answer historical criticism of the Scriptures without first establishing the clarity of general revelation.

RP begins with an affirmation of the nature of reason based on the reality of thought. Reason is to be defined in itself, in its use, and in us.[9]

Reason in itself is the laws of thought. Most basically, these are the law of identity: *a* is *a*; the law of non-contradiction: not both *a* and *non-a*, at the same time and in the same respect; and the law of excluded middle: either *a* or *non-a*. Other laws of thought are based on these laws. To doubt these laws is to lose all distinctions and to cease to think.

Reason in its use is formative, critical, interpretive, and constructive. Reason is used to form concepts, judgments, and arguments, which are the forms of all thought. Whenever there are thoughts, reason is being used formatively. Reason is used critically as a test for meaning. It is applied especially to basic beliefs as a test for meaning. If a belief, upon analysis, violates a law of thought, it lacks meaning and cannot be true. Reason is used to interpret experience in light of one's basic beliefs. No experience is meaningful without interpretation, and every interpretation can and must be tested for meaning. And lastly, reason is used to construct a coherent world and life view upon one's basic belief. Worldviews are manifest in cultures. They are held more or less consciously and more or less consistently and, therefore, continually face the internal and external challenges of reason.[10]

---

6. Gangadean, *History of Philosophy*, 175-179.

7. *Paper No. 3.*

8. *Paper No. 3;* Gangadean, *Philosophical Foundation*, 71-161.

9. Gangadean, *Philosophical Foundation*, 10-15.

10. *Paper No. 19.*

Reason is always being used formatively. It is often used constructively, without first being used critically. It is sometimes used interpretively without realizing it. Reason in itself is not fallible, but a person may fail to use reason critically and fully.

Reason does not succeed only if it persuades subjectively, but if it answers objections with an objectively sound argument. Many objections against reason and rationalism are really against what amounts to a failure to use reason.[11] Reason in itself must therefore be distinguished from reason in its use.

Reason in us is natural, ontological, transcendental, and fundamental. Reason is natural, not conventional. It is universal, the same in all persons. Reason as the laws of thought is the common ground among all thinkers. What distinguishes us is not reason, but the willingness to use reason. What distinguishes us is not our assumption, but the willingness to critically examine our assumption for meaning.

Reason is ontological. It applies to being as well as to thought. There are no square-circles, no uncaused events, no being from non-being. It applies to all being, including the highest being. God is not both eternal and not eternal, at the same time and in the same respect. Matter is not both extended and not extended, at the same time and in the same respect.[12] There is no noumenal realm or dimension in which reason does not apply, but to which faith gives access.[13] While the mysteries of faith do not originate in reason, they do not go against reason. Miracles are not against the laws of reason, but against a law of nature. Reason, as an aspect of God's being, is eternal. The laws of nature are created. Paradoxes are puzzling to reason insofar as assumptions present and at work are not yet critically examined and corrected. Finite beings cannot have exhaustive or comprehensive knowledge of anything, but the unknown is not against the laws of reason.

Reason is transcendental. It is authoritative and self-attesting. It is transcendental in that it stands above thought and makes thought possible. It cannot be questioned, but makes questioning possible. Statements about general and special revelation (Scripture) can and must

---

11. Gangadean, *History of Philosophy*, 131-137.

12. Gangadean, *History of Philosophy*, 38.

13. Gangadean, *History of Philosophy*, 151-153; Gangadean, *Philosophical Foundation*, 109-110.

be questioned, by reason, but reason itself as the laws of thought cannot be questioned. As transcendental, it cannot be argued for, even in a circular manner. In thought, what is of highest authority is self-attesting, and only reason is self-attesting.[14] Scripture assumes reason as that by which Scripture is to be understood. Scripture, if it is to be received, must be spoken in the name of God; that is, it must be consistent with the nature of God known from general revelation. There is not and cannot be any conflict between reason, general revelation, and Scripture. Scripture is set against all other forms of special revelation, not against reason and general revelation.

Reason is fundamental. It is fundamental to other aspects of human personality. Feelings are directed by belief about the good, and thought and feeling move the will to act. Feeling and will are not independent of or contrary to belief. Conflicts within the understanding are manifest in conflicts in feeling and will. Unnoticed, these misunderstandings, as conflicts within our thoughts, lead to apparent conflict between thought and feeling, etc. Our deepest need is for meaning. Our deepest misery is in the awareness of the lack of meaning. Meaninglessness is a fundamental aspect of spiritual death, and, sometimes, physical death is sought as an escape from spiritual death. Boredom comes from meaninglessness, in which the creation, apart from or in place of the Creator, cannot satisfy. Failure to be rational is experienced as guilt, from which escape is sought in the unending rationalizations of self-justification. Our greatest happiness is from the use of reason in understanding the creation, when this understanding leads to the knowledge of God.

The first application of RP is to the question *what is real?* It clarifies the subjective factors of integrity and commitment to reason as preconditions to knowledge. It prevents further discussion, which would be fruitless if these preconditions are not in place.

We begin with the question *what is real?* because existence is our most basic concept, and eternal existence (without beginning) is more basic than temporal existence (with beginning).

To show that *some is eternal* is true, we show that the contradiction *none is eternal* cannot be true. *None is eternal* implies that *all is*

---

14. Gangadean, *Philosophical Foundation*, 298-299.

temporal, all had a beginning, all came into being. If all came into being, it would have come into being from non-being, which is impossible.

Hence, *none is eternal* cannot be true, and its contradiction *some is eternal* must be true. *All came into being from non-being* is not the same as creation *ex nihilo*, in which God is eternal and acted to create.[15]

By *non-being* is meant the absence of all being whatsoever, not just the absence of all visible being. An unending series of finite and temporal beings having the power to create *ex nihilo*, is not an objection that has been (or, upon analysis, can be) made.

If it is agreed that it is clear to reason that there must be something eternal, we can go on to the next step in showing what is clear.[16]

---

15. Gangadean, *Philosophical Foundation*, 61-68.

16. *Paper No. 102*; Gangadean, *Philosophical Foundation*, 71-284.

Paper №· 102

THE CLARITY OF
GENERAL REVELATION

*God's Eternal Power and Divine Nature,
and the Moral Law*

GENERAL REVELATION IS WHAT MAY BE KNOWN of God by all men, everywhere, at all times. What is clear from general revelation is his eternal power and divine nature and the moral law.[1]

The clarity of general revelation is the basis of the inexcusability of unbelief and of the necessity of redemptive revelation in Scripture.[2] Because general revelation is clear, those in unbelief regarding the existence and nature of God and of the moral law have no reason for their unbelief.

To deny what is clear requires the denial of reason. The clarity of general revelation, under the condition of moral and natural evil, leads to recognition of the necessity, content, origin, and existence of Scripture. This further leads to the recognition of the transmission, completion, translation, clarity, sufficiency, and interpretation of Scripture.[3] The clarity of general revelation is necessary in order to avoid misinterpretation of Scripture.

---

1. *Romans 1:18-20; 2:14-15.*

2. *Paper No. 12.*

3. *Paper No. 11.*

If non-believers are responsible for seeing through the inexcusability of their unbelief, believers are all the more so. If we have come to understand what is clear, we should be able to show what is clear.[4] We should be able to take thoughts captive that are raised up against the knowledge of God.[5]

But believers still have sin and have to contend with the noetic effect of sin in themselves. Believers have to struggle to avoid being taken captive by prevailing unbelief in the culture in which they live. But by recognizing the need for the renewal of one's mind, by benefiting from the understanding already achieved in Historic Christianity, and by engaging with the remaining internal and external challenges to the Faith, believers can come to a mature understanding of the clarity of general revelation.

Rational Presuppositionalism is an epistemological method which seeks to settle disputes by thinking of the less basic in light of the more basic and critically analyzing assumptions for meaning. By Rational Presuppositionalism, we can understand the major steps in showing the clarity of general revelation.

1. Show the necessity for clarity in general against skepticism, and the necessity for clarity in particular for Christian theism, against fideism.

2. Show, by ontological argument, that there must be something eternal. This is a paradigm of what is clear to reason. Rational Presuppositionalism requires agreement here before going any further in metaphysics. If this cannot be known, nothing can be known and dialogue is not possible.

3. Show, by cosmological arguments, that only some (God) is eternal; that is, show theism vs. all forms of non-theism. This requires showing that matter exists and that matter is not eternal; that the soul/spirit exists and the soul is not eternal.

    To show the material world is not eternal, it must be shown that the material world is not self-maintaining (vs. material monism— all forms of scientific materialism and cosmological naturalism).

---

4. *Paper No. 110; Paper No. 39.*

5. *2 Corinthians 10:4-5.*

To show that the soul exists, it must be shown that the mind is not the brain. To show the individual soul exists, it must be shown that there is not one mind only and its ideas (vs. spiritual monism—absolute or Vedantic idealism).

To show that the material world exists (vs. ordinary idealism), it must be shown that the cause of what is seen is not my mind or another mind, but outside all minds.

To show that the soul is not eternal (vs. all forms of dualism—Greek, Indian, Persian, and Mormon, and reincarnation), it must be shown that the soul experiences unique events.

4. Show, by teleological argument, that the natural order is by design (that is, show special creation) vs. all forms of evolution—natural and theistic.

5. Show, by teleological argument, that, in divine providence, moral and natural evil serve the divine purpose (that is, show the Ironic Solution to the problem of evil) vs. naturalistic and Free Will solutions.

6. Show the moral law, structured into human nature by creation, is clear, comprehensive, and critical, the same in content as the law given by special revelation.

7. Show the necessity, content, origin, and existence of special revelation (vs. deism). Further, show the transmission, completion, translation, clarity, sufficiency, and interpretation of special revelation.

8. Show Christian theism (vs. all forms of non-Christian theism—that is, Judaic and Islamic theism), based on general and on special revelation.

9. Show the response to past challenges to Christian theism, based on general and on special revelation, and summed up in the ecumenical and historical creeds (Gnosticism, Trinity, Incarnation, predestination).

10. Show the response to continuing external and internal challenges to Christian theism (faith vs. reason, otherworldliness and secularism vs. knowledge of God, continuing divisions within theism vs. unity of the faith).

Paper № 103

———

THE NOETIC EFFECT OF SIN
The Effect of Moral Evil on the Mind of Man

IT IS THE NATURE OF SIN (MORAL EVIL) TO NOT SEEK the good, to misunderstand the good, in ignorance to call good evil and evil good, to oppose the good in light of one's misconception, and to avoid and resist correction by self-deception and self-justification. The effect of moral evil on the mind of man is called the noetic effect. It began with the fall of man and is removed gradually in the redemption of man.

Scripture (the biblical worldview of creation–fall–redemption) assumes the clarity of general revelation.[1] Sin begins in the failure to seek and understand what is clear about God. This sin is universal.[2] This sin is deep.[3] This sin is destructive.[4] The neglect of not seeking is set against the necessity for seeking: he that comes to God must believe that he is and that he is the rewarder of those that diligently seek him.[5] The reward of diligently seeking God is knowing him. Eternal life is knowing God.[6]

———

1. *Romans 1:20.*
2. *Romans 3:10-11.*
3. *Jeremiah 17:9.*
4. *Romans 6:23.*
5. *Hebrews 11:6.*
6. *John 17:3.*

The noetic effect of sin is first seen in the Garden of Eden. Man is called to know God through the work of dominion. Left to himself, man turns from the knowledge of God as the good. When tested (regarding his understanding of good and evil, and life and death) he failed. He believed the falsehood: "You shall not surely die . . . you shall be like God knowing good and evil."[7] The outward act of eating of the tree of the knowledge of good and evil revealed the inward state of not seeking and not knowing God. He lost sight of the radical difference between God as Creator and man as creature in knowing good and evil. He had put himself in the place of God to determine good and evil.

Good for a being is based on the nature of that being. God knows good and evil, not by discovery, but by determining the nature of beings by the act of creation. Adam was to know good and evil by discovering the nature of beings. Man cannot be like God in knowing good and evil because man is a creature, not the Creator. He cannot determine the nature of things. Adam, by not seeking the knowledge of God as the good, failed to understand what is clear about God—that God is the infinite and eternal Creator, and that man is a finite, temporal creature. This, the original sin, is the origin of all sin in all men. Sin is the failure to understand what is clear about God.

As the inward act of sin of not seeking and not understanding is exposed by the outward act of unrighteousness (eating), man experiences shame in his nakedness. Shame is the first natural and inward call back from sin. It is the call of conscience. Man avoids this call back through self-deception, by covering his nakedness. God calls man back a second time, outwardly, by a call to self-examination in asking: where are you? Man resists the second call by self-justification, blaming the woman and God himself for his own disobedience. God calls man back a third and final time by imposing on man the curse (toil and strife, and old age, sickness, and death) and by the giving of the promise (the seed of the woman will crush the head of the serpent).[8] Man responds to the third call by repentance and faith. He is justified by God in being covered with the coats of skin (forgiveness through the death of another), and is to be sanctified through suffering, by expulsion from the Garden to live under the curse.

---

7. *Genesis 3:5.*

8. *Genesis 3:15.*

Sin is permitted by God and is made to serve his purpose. It deepens the revelation of his justice and mercy. If it is removed abruptly, the revelation will not be deepened. If it is not removed, the revelation will not be seen. Sin, as unbelief, is permitted to work itself out in human history in every form and degree of combination with belief. In this age-long and agonizing conflict, good overcomes evil. The seed of the woman crushes the head of the serpent, according to the promise.[9]

Although forgiven in Christ, sin remains in believers, along with its noetic effect. Believers continue to fail to understand what is clear about God from general revelation. This failure to seek and to understand the clarity of general revelation is overlooked in self-deception and resisted in self-justification. Natural evil (the curse) continues to call men back from moral evil (sin). Suffering calls men to stop and think about basic things, about meaning and purpose, about God and man, about good and evil, about life and death. Suffering the curse and agonies of the spiritual war of belief vs. unbelief continues as long as the noetic effect of sin remains.

The clarity of general revelation cannot be denied without denying the inexcusability of unbelief. But clarity cannot be affirmed without being required to show the clarity of general revelation. As a result, the doctrine of clarity has been left in the dark. Believers continue to show a disregard for the clarity of general revelation and a disinclination to show the inexcusability of unbelief.[10] This, and other closely connected doctrines, has been held more or less consciously, and more or less consistently.

Self-deception about diligently seeking to know God continues; self-justification for not knowing what is clear about God continues; the suffering of toil and strife, and old age, sickness, and death continues as God's call back to stop and think. Insofar as we do not stop and think, our understanding remains in darkness. What we profess to believe becomes emptied of meaning or filled with misunderstanding. One's entire worldview is affected by one's understanding of good and evil.

The failure to understand what is clear from general revelation continues in the failure to understand what is clear from special revelation.

---

9. Gangadean, *Philosophical Foundation*, 156-161.

10. *Paper No. 61; Paper No. 62.*

The divisions in the Church in understanding Scripture reflect the divisions in understanding general revelation. Sin has affected the entire Christian worldview by distorting understanding of foundational teachings. The following briefly mention some of this misunderstanding, with further explanation below.

Moral evil is not seen as the failure to understand what is clear about God. It is seen as a willful act of disobedience of a command of God. Faith is not seen as based on understanding and evidence. It is seen as a choice to believe above, apart from, or against evidence. The wages of sin is not seen as spiritual death, present and inherent in sin. The wages of sin is seen as hell, which is future and imposed. Eternal life is not seen as the knowledge of God. It is seen as the absence of the curse in heaven.

1. The noetic effect affects our understanding of sin (moral evil).

Sin is the failure to seek and to understand what is clear about God (divine nature) and man, and good and evil (moral law). Sin is not fundamentally the willful outward act of disobedience of a command of God.[11] Adam believed what was false about God and about sin and death before he ate; and he ate because of his unbelief. Sin is coming short of seeing the glory of God. This is the sin which is universal, and of which all must repent. Yet, personally and corporately, the Church repents of fruit sin, but not root sin. We think of ourselves as concerned to know the truth even when we fail to know what is clear. We resist responsibility for knowing what is clear by denying clarity (no one knows), or making it impossible to know (reason is finite/fallen), or irrelevant to faith (deep down everyone knows). The noetic effect of sin is covered by hypocrisy through self-deception and self-justification. Integrity, by self-examination and by discipline, is necessary and sufficient to overcome hypocrisy, and to know what is clear about God.

What can be known of God is revealed by the Word of God. Man, in his fallen state, resists and rejects the Word of God in every form: in himself as reason;[12] in creation as general revelation;[13] in history as

---

11. *Paper No. 120.*

12. *John 1:4-5.*

13. *John 1:10.*

special/redemptive revelation;[14] in person as Jesus Christ, the Word incarnate.[15]

2. The noetic effect affects our understanding of spiritual death.

The wages of sin is death,[16] not hell as is commonly conceived. Death here is spiritual, not physical. Spiritual death is present and inherent in sin, whereas hell, as a literal lake of fire, is future and imposed. Hell, in biblical language, is a symbolic representation of spiritual death. It is called the second death.[17] Taken literally, hell, as a lake of fire, is without meaning. Spirits are not affected by physical fire. To appeal to a continual miracle in order to make the literal hell possible is to deny God's justice and to invite blasphemy.[18] The fear of hell (avoiding natural evil) is not the fear of God (avoiding moral evil). There is a necessary connection between sin (not seeking, and not understanding) and death (meaninglessness, boredom, and guilt). Understanding the connection between sin and death creates the fear of the Lord, which moves us to diligently seek him. Thus, the fear of the Lord is the beginning of wisdom.

3. The noetic effect affects our understanding of the curse (natural evil).

The curse of toil and strife, and old age, sickness, and death, is God's call back from sin, not punishment for sin. There are two kinds of death as well as two kinds of resurrections: physical and spiritual.[19] The wages of sin is spiritual death, not physical death. It is part of the noetic effect of sin to avoid and resist the curse as God's call to repentance of failing to see what is clear.

Physical death is not original in the creation. Physical death is not inherent in sin. Physical death is imposed because of sin. It is the third and last call back from sin. (The first call back of shame is avoided by

---

14. *John 1:11.*

15. *John 1:14.*

16. *Romans 6:23; Genesis 2:17; Ephesians 2:1.*

17. *Revelation 20:14; 21:8.*

18. *Romans 2:24.*

19. *John 5:24-29; John 11:25; Revelation 20:6.*

self-deception, and the second call back to self-examination is avoided by self-justification.) The noetic effect of self-deception and self-justification objectively require the curse and at the same time subjectively resist the curse. Although the curse is sometimes referred to as punishment and sometimes as chastening, it is not punishment in the strict or absolute sense of the term. Physical death cannot (in the strict sense) be considered punishment for sin, in this life or the next. If physical death were punishment for the believer, then Christ did not bear the full penalty of sin. If physical death were punishment for the non-believer, there would be no resurrection for the bodies of non-believers. If the curse were punishment for both believers and non-believers, there would be some proportionality in its manifestation. But the most righteous, for example Job, often suffer more than others, and the wicked often prosper more than the righteous.[20]

The curse serves several purposes in relation to sin. Its serves to restrain all from sin, to recall non-believers from sin, and to remove the sin remaining in believers. In all the suffering of the curse, there is a call to stop and think deeply about good and evil, about the meaning and purpose of life. It is a call to know God. The curse is intensified in history to become famine, war, and plague. At death, there is no further call back. A person continues in the condition in which they died. The curse is fully removed, not at death, but at the end of this age in the resurrection, when all things have been subdued to Christ.[21] The last enemy to be destroyed is death.

4. The noetic effect affects our understanding of eternal life.

Eternal life is to know God.[22] Eternal life is not heaven. Eternal life begins in this life, at regeneration. Heaven begins after this life. God makes himself known through his works of creation and providence (providence includes redemption in history). God is a Spirit, immortal and invisible, whom no man has seen nor can see.[23] God cannot be seen directly in heaven apart from his works. Creation is revelation,

---

20. *Psalm 75.*

21. *1 Corinthians 15:25-28.*

22. *John 17:3.*

23. *1 Timothy 6:16.*

necessarily, intentionally, and exclusively. In heaven, after death, and before the resurrection, in the intermediate state, the fullness of blessing is not received, but is awaited. Departed believers await the completion of the work given to man in history.[24] Through the work of dominion, the earth is to be filled with the knowledge of God as the waters cover the sea.[25]

Dominion (developing the powers latent in the creation—in one's self and in nature) is necessary for knowledge of the creation. And knowledge of the creation is necessary for the knowledge of God. The fullness of life is not absence of the curse, but the fullness of the knowledge of God. To expect life without knowledge of God is contrary to human nature. To expect fullness of life apart from the completion of dominion is false hope. To expect the work of dominion to be done by Christ at the Second Coming, supernaturally, apart from the Church, is to misunderstand the nature of knowledge through dominion.[26] To expect the knowledge of God through the work of dominion is true hope.

Due to sin and its noetic effect, the work of dominion is not set aside, it is deepened. The noetic effect is opposed by a spiritual war. With the curse in natural evil is given the promise in redemptive revelation: between good and evil (light and darkness, truth and falsehood, belief and unbelief), there is a spiritual war, which is age-long and agonizing, in which good eventually overcomes evil.[27] Every thought raised up against the knowledge of God will be made subject to Christ. Dominion now extends over sin.[28] The spiritual war is fought asymmetrically. Truth uses reason to persuade; falsehood uses threat and slander and the entire range of pseudo-arguments commonly called informal fallacies.[29] There is enmity, hostility, and hatred toward what exposes falsehood. Removal of this hostility requires a redemptive change of heart by regeneration. Truth prevails: "the light shines in the darkness

---

24. *Hebrews 11:13, 39-40.*

25. *Isaiah 11:9.*

26. Gangadean, *Philosophical Foundation*, 207-219.

27. *Genesis 3:15.*

28. *2 Corinthians 10:4.*

29. Gangadean, *Philosophical Foundation*, 45-48.

and the darkness cannot overcome it or withstand it."[30] The rational requirements of human nature cannot be eradicated. The need for meaning, found only in the knowledge of God (eternal life), remains.

5. The noetic effect affects all our basic beliefs.

The noetic effect affects our understanding of faith and reason and the inseparability of the two. It affects our interpretation of Scripture and of literature. It affects our understanding of good and evil, and why there is evil, and how evil serves the good. It affects our understanding of the moral law written on the hearts of all men and how the law serves the good. It affects our view of world history and Church history and human propensity toward apostasy. It affects our understanding of human conflicts and is the source of all conflicts and of every kind and degree of evil (in and between persons, in each household, in and between churches, in and between nations, and most comprehensively summed up between two ways, two kingdoms, two cities: the City of God and the City of Man). It affects our eschatology and our interpretation of all of life.

We can progress in overcoming the noetic effect:

1. by acknowledging the nature of sin at its root and its continued existence in us.

2. by acknowledging the curse (toil and strife, and old age, sickness, and death) as imposed by God as a continuing call to stop and think.

3. by acknowledging the good as the knowledge of God and the goal of filling the earth with the knowledge of God.

4. by acknowledge the work of the Holy Spirit leading us into all truth through the work of the pastor-teachers and summed up in the creeds of the Church.

5. by acknowledging the continuing internal and external challenges to the faith as God's call to take all thoughts captive which are raised up against the knowledge of God.

---

30. *John 1:5.*

ESCHATOLOGY

The Earth Shall Be Full of the Knowledge of God

ESCHATOLOGY HAS TO DO WITH THE END. It has to do with our hope. It has to do with what we can expect in the future. Eschatology has a broader and a narrower aspect. The broader aspect has to do with the goal, or end, of human existence.

The first question of the Shorter Catechism is: "What is the chief end of man?" It is the more basic aspect of eschatology. The narrower aspect has to do with how and when this chief end of man is realized. If we understand what is more basic, we will understand what is less basic.

If we agree on the chief end of man, we can overcome the divisions regarding premillennial, amillennial, and postmillennial eschatologies. If we keep in mind the method of Rational Presuppositionalism and the problems of the noetic effect of sin, we can come to the unity of the faith in relation to eschatology.

From general revelation, from Scripture, and from Historic Christianity (summed up in the Westminster Confession of Faith) we can know that eternal life—the good for man—is the knowledge of God,[1] and that the earth shall be full of the knowledge of God as the waters cover the sea.[2]

---

1. *John 17:3.*

2. *Isaiah 11:9.*

We know that creation reveals the glory of God[3] and that knowledge of God's glory comes through the work of dominion given to man in the beginning. The hope of life in knowing God is assumed and affirmed throughout Scripture from the beginning to the end.

1. Sabbath

The Sabbath is the single, greatest, continuing affirmation of hope for mankind. Man is made in the image of God. As God worked and completed his work of creation, so man will work and complete his work of dominion. As creation is revelation, dominion brings knowledge of this revelation. As a result of the corporate work of mankind through the ages in ruling over the creation, the earth will be filled with the knowledge of God as the waters cover the sea.

2. The seed of the woman

In sin, man turned away from knowing God as the good. He put himself in the place of God to determine good and evil. God permits evil to serve the good—to deepen the revelation of his glory, especially his justice and mercy. His mercy is seen in the promise of redemption, and in the curse which restrains, recalls from, and removes moral evil. God established a spiritual war between believer and non-believer which is age-long and agonizing, with the promise that good (the seed of the woman) will overcome evil (crush the head of the serpent).

3. Noah

In the first age of human history, God permits evil to come to maximum expression. Yet his purpose is not frustrated. Noah, in faith and hope, builds the ark in which he preserves the promise of redemption and the work of dominion attained thus far. In doing so, he comforts us (mankind) in the labor and painful toil of our hands caused by the ground the Lord has cursed. Hope is preserved through the greatest darkness, and continues, with further restraints on evil by increased toil and diminished lifespan.

---

3. *Isaiah 6:3.*

4. Abraham and the patriarchs

Apostasy has become worldwide again at Babel and further restrained by the division of mankind. While mankind is left to go on in apostasy, God chooses to fulfill the promise of redemption for all of mankind through Abraham. In Abraham's seed all the families of the earth will be blessed. The promise continues through Isaac and Jacob and his sons, who are seeking the City of God, a city with foundations, which is the kingdom of God on earth, in the Promised Land.

5. Moses

Moses sought this City too. He left the power and glory of Egypt for the promise in Christ. He led the people out of Egypt by God's power and gave them the law of God for the kingdom of God. The way of life through atonement, sanctification, and service is taught, culminating in the Feast of Ingathering (of all peoples) and the full removal of all debt (Jubilee).

6. Joshua

After the first generation leaving Egypt did not enter the Promised Land because of their unbelief, Joshua leads the next generation in the conquest of Canaan. Joshua's conquest is a pattern for the Church to overcome all worldviews of the nations raised up against the knowledge of God, rather than fear the giants of opposing systems of thought, and wander in the wilderness in unbelief.

7. David and the Psalms

David and others in the Psalms sing of the person and work of Christ, both in his suffering and his glory. Christ is raised from the dead and appointed to reign now.[4] All the ends of the earth will remember and turn to the Lord and all the families of the nations will bow down before Him. All of creation is brought to praise the Lord whose splendor is above the earth and the heavens.

---

4. *Psalms 2, 22, 67, 72, 110, 148,* and *150.*

8. The Prophets

All the prophets speak of God's judgment of famine, war, and plague on sin, and of God's restoration of His people. This restoration extends beyond the near future into the Gospel age, in which the nations are brought into the house of God. All nations stream to it[5] until the earth is filled with the knowledge of God.[6] The comfort of restoration extends to the new heavens and the new earth.[7] Ezekiel sees the restoration in the vision of the dry bones[8] extending as a river from the Temple to all mankind.[9] Daniel sees the kingdom of God grow from the Rock that struck the image of the worldly kingdoms and became a huge mountain that filled the whole earth.[10] Jonah's life prefigures the resurrection of Christ and the call of the nations to repentance. Joel anticipates the outpouring of the Spirit on multitudes in the Valley of Decision.

9. Jesus

Jesus is the seed of the woman who came to destroy the works of the devil. He is the seed of Abraham in whom all the families are to be blessed. He is the Lamb of God who takes away the sin of the world. He is the anointed prophet, priest, and king, whose kingdom is to rule over all the earth. He is the Word of God, the Son of God, incarnate. He taught the character of the kingdom and the law of the kingdom in his Sermon on the Mount. He taught that the goal of the will of God and the coming of the kingdom is that the name of God would be hallowed (that God would be glorified in all that by which he makes himself known). He taught that the kingdom will grow gradually to its fullness (as a mustard seed, and as leaven). Though few at first are saved, and though Jerusalem will be destroyed,[11] he commanded his followers to make disciples of all nations, and he sent the Holy Spirit to enable them to do this work.

---

5. *Isaiah 2.*

6. *Isaiah 11.*

7. *Isaiah 40; 66.*

8. *Ezekiel 37.*

9. *Ezekiel 47.*

10. *Daniel 2:34-35.*

11. *Matthew 23-24.*

10. Paul

The apostle Paul taught that where sin increased, grace increased all the more.[12] He taught that God placed all things under Christ who, through his body the Church, is to fill everything in every way,[13] that through the work of the Spirit in the ministry of pastor-teachers, the Church is to attain to the unity of the faith, to the whole measure of the fullness of Christ.[14] He taught that all Israel will be saved when the fullness of the gentiles has come in;[15] that Christ will reign until he has put all his enemies under his feet, the last enemy to be destroyed, at his second coming, is death.[16]

11. Peter

Peter exhorts his readers to be patient in suffering for the cause of Christ; that although false teachers are bold and arrogant, God rules, as in the days of Noah, when he brought that world to a sudden end. So too now the world of wickedness will be destroyed. Believers are to speed the coming of that day by their witness. The rule of spiritual forces of evil in the heavenly realms (the heavens) will be destroyed and the fundamental principles (the elements/*stoicheia*) of the world will be destroyed suddenly. In the place of the old, believers look for a new heaven and a new earth, in which the will of God is done.

12. John

John's Revelation brings the blessing of hope to all who read it and take it to heart. The time is near to readers in every age. After a seven-fold description of the state of the Church in John's age, the rule of God through the curse and the promise in an age-long spiritual war is unveiled in a seven-fold vision: the seven seals, the seven trumpets, the woman and the dragon, the seven bowls, the woman on the beast, the age-long spiritual war (Armageddon—fought with the sword coming

---

12. *Romans 5.*
13. *Ephesians 1.*
14. *Ephesians 4.*
15. *Romans 11.*
16. *1 Corinthians 15.*

out of the mouth), the thousand-year rule of believers (the millennium, in which all rule, who are raised from the dead spiritually—the first resurrection). Each vision covers the entire period of Christ's rule, from the first to the second coming. Each vision depicts the spiritual war between believers and non-believers under different aspects. Each vision shows the conquest of the kingdom of God over the kingdom of darkness. John's Revelation ends with the consummation of the kingdom of God. The work given to mankind in the Garden of Eden is completed by Christ through the Church. The City of God, perfected in beauty, comes down from heaven to earth. The river of life flows through the middle of the city, bringing blessing to all nations, life in its fullness. The hope of the Sabbath, of work and rest, is fully realized. The earth is filled with the knowledge of God as the waters cover the sea.

Paper N<u>o.</u> 105

———

THE REGULATIVE PRINCIPLE

OF WORSHIP

According to the Revealed Will of God

GENERAL REVELATION, SCRIPTURE, AND Historic Christianity (the Westminster Confession of Faith) call us to worship God as he is in truth, and not according to our own imagination. They call us to worship God with all the heart and not merely outwardly, in vain.

"The light of nature shows that there is a God, who has lordship and sovereignty over all, is good, and does good unto all, and is therefore to be feared, loved, praised, called up, trusted in, and served, with all the heart, and with all the soul, and with all the might. But the acceptable way of worshipping the true God is instituted by himself, and so limited by his own revealed will, that he may not be worshipped according to the imaginations and devices of men, or the suggestions of Satan, under any visible representation, or any other way not prescribed in the Holy Scripture."[1]

The principle which regulates worship limits worship to the revealed will of God. The second commandment requires the receiving, observing, and keeping pure and entire, all such religious worship and ordinances as God has appointed in his Word.[2] It forbids the worshiping

---

1. *WCF 21.1*; Gangadean, *The Westminster Confession*. See Questions 93-99; *Paper No. 104* and *134-135*.

2. *SCQ. 50*; Gangadean, *The Westminster Catechisms*. See SCQ. 52.

of God by images, or any other way not appointed in his Word.[3] The second commandment affirms the regulative principle of worship which limits worship to what God has revealed in his Word. The regulative principle includes what is commanded; it does not include what is not commanded as well as what is explicitly forbidden. Jesus taught that God is Spirit, and his worshipers must worship in spirit and in truth.[4]

The book of Psalms in the Scriptures is given for singing, which is an ordinary part of public worship. "The reading of the Scriptures with godly fear, the sound preaching and conscionable hearing of the Word, in obedience unto God, with understanding, faith, and reverence, singing of psalms with grace in the heart . . . are all parts of the ordinary religious worship of God."[5]

The Psalms alone, and not any songs of human composition, are to be used in singing in the corporate worship of God. Our own heart, which in this life remains affected by sin and comes short of the glory of God, is not sufficient to represent the truth of God, to be confessed immediately in singing by all. A broken and a contrite heart will not put its fallible thoughts of God in place of God's revelation of himself.[6]

Biblical piety is in contrast to zeal without knowledge. We are sanctified by knowing the truth of God.[7] Singing the Psalms with understanding develops true spirituality. The Psalms affirm the nature of God as both just and merciful. They affirm the biblical worldview of creation–fall–redemption in all aspects. They affirm the will and purpose of God in history in his law and kingdom. They affirm, with hope, the full force of spiritual warfare faced by believers in every age. They are intimately acquainted with the whole range of human emotions. They are always God-centered and not self-centered. They are Christ-centered in his person and his work, on earth and at God's right hand.

Through singing the Psalms, the Word of Christ comes to dwell in us richly,[8] and we are filled with the Spirit.[9] The Psalms are to be sung, not as a matter of prudence or preference merely, but as the expression of love for God as he is in truth, not as we might imagine him to be.

---

3. *SCQ. 51.*

4. *John 4:24.*

5. *WCF 21.5.*

6. *Job 42:5-6.*

7. *John 17:17.*

8. *Colossians 3:16.*

9. *Ephesians 5:18-19.*

Paper No. 106

———

THE GOOD AND HEAVEN
The Good Is Not the Beatific Vision

The good is the end in itself, man's chief end, the highest value, sought for its own sake, the *summum bonum*.

The beatific vision is said to be the immediate vision/experience of God, apart from creation, accessible to all in heaven.

As we understand the good and the beatific vision, we will understand the good is not the beatific vision or heaven as the immediate fulfillment of human happiness.

1. Characteristics of the good

The good is objectively clear, from general revelation (GR), special revelation (SR), and Historic Christianity (HC).

From General Revelation:

i. The good for a being is based on the nature of that being: all beings have a nature/essence, that distinguishes them from other *kinds* of beings.

ii. There is a unity of diversity in the nature of a being.

iii. The good for a human being is based on human nature. There is a human nature consisting of the set of qualities which *all* humans have, that they *always* have, that *only* humans have, that distinguishes humans from all non-humans: animals, angels, God, plants, non-living beings.

iv. There is a unity of diversity in human nature: the larger *formal* aspect, the narrower *content* aspect, the triune personality, the body/soul unity, the male/female unity, the temporal/historical/background factor, and the unique, singular, distinguishing factor.

v. Man is a *rational* animal; reason in man is natural, ontological, transcendental, and fundamental to all other aspects of his being.

vi. Good for man as a rational being is the use of his reason to the fullest. Reason is used to understand the nature of things. The nature of things created reveal the nature of God. Therefore, the good for man as a rational being is the knowledge of God.

vii. The knowledge of God is based first on GR, not gnostic (based first on SR); the knowledge of God is rational/cognitive, not mystical/non-cognitive/experiential.

From Special Revelation/Scripture:

i. From creation, man is the image of God, a person who can know all other persons (including God). He can think, reason, and understand revelation. Creation is revelation, necessarily, intentionally, and exclusively; it is full and clear. Man is given dominion over the creation, a task which is corporate, cumulative, and communal, by which mankind is to glorify God. The end of the work of dominion is the earth filled with the knowledge of God as the waters cover the sea.[1] The Sabbath affirms that man will complete the work of dominion.

ii. Eternal life is knowing God.[2] Eternal life begins in this life and continues into the next life; it does not merely begin in the future life in heaven.[3] The good *is* eternal life.

iii. The fall of man is permitted in order to *deepen* the revelation of God, especially God's justice and mercy in redemption.

---

1. *Isaiah 11:9.*

2. *John 17:3.*

3. *John 5:24.*

iv. Redemption is by the curse (as a call to repentance) and by promise (through a spiritual war, which is age-long and agonizing, good will overcome evil[4]). In this *spiritual* war, the believer is to take captive every thought raised up against the knowledge of God.[5]

From Historic Christianity:

i. Historic Christianity is the work of the Holy Spirit guiding the Church into all Truth.[6]

ii. Historic Christianity responds to challenges to the faith throughout the history of the Church. This insight is cumulative, to depart from which, without sufficient reason manifest in discussion, is to deny the unity of the faith. Traditional Christianity is not Historic Christianity.

iii. Historic Christianity began with the Council of Jerusalem (A.D. 51), and continues in the Apostles' Creed, Nicea, Carthage, Chalcedon, Orange, and, from the Reformation period, is summed up in the Westminster Confession of Faith (WCF, 1648).

iv. WCF is doxologically focused: man's chief end is to glorify God and to enjoy him forever, in all that by which he makes himself known, in all his works of creation and providence.[7] The outcome of glorifying God is the earth filled with the knowledge of the Lord as the waters cover the sea. There is no enjoying of God without glorifying God.

v. Challenges since the Reformation remain to be answered: fideism and divisions in the Church vs. skepticism and pluralism in the world; mere otherworldliness in the Church vs. mere this-worldliness in the current culture wars. These pairs of conflicting views are antinomies, both of which are mistaken, since both share the same set of assumptions regarding good (creation and revelation) and evil (clarity and inexcusability).

---

4. *Genesis 3:15.*

5. *2 Corinthians 10:4-5; 1 Corinthians 15:25; Revelation 19:11-21; 20:1-3.*

6. *John 16:13; Acts 15; Ephesians 4.*

7. *SCQ. 1, 101; WCF 4.1, 5.1.*

2. Reasons for conflicting views and response

i. Some claim that God is unknowable by reason from creation; God is infinite and man is finite (Barth).

Response:

God as Creator *ex nihilo* is not merely infinite, but infinite in all his attributes—being, wisdom, power, holiness, justice, goodness, and truth (vs. *Advaita*/non-dual Vedanta's attributeless Nirguna Brahman; and vs. God in Islam who is beyond all attributes). Man is the finite, temporal, changeable image of God. Creation is revelation, necessarily, intentionally, and exclusively. In knowing himself, man can have knowledge of God.

ii. Some claim reason is either finite or fallen or both. The finite cannot grasp the infinite, without paradox. God is incomprehensible, past finding out. Those stuck in the meshes of intellect are worse than dogs . . . incorrigible, hopeless, and destined to doom (Buddhism).

Response:

Reason is ontological, it applies to being, all being, God's being. God is not both eternal and not eternal, at the same time and in the same respect. There is unity of diversity but no paradox in *any* being; the problem lies in the non-theistic presupposition that all is eternal or all is one/becoming.

Man has true knowledge of anything only in part; he knows nothing comprehensively or exhaustively. Man can grow in knowledge without end, in depth and breadth, as the waters cover the sea. Reason is transcendental; as the laws of thought, it cannot be fallen.

iii. Some claim the noumenal (God) cannot be known by man in time, in or from the phenomenal realm (Kant).

Response:

The distinction between the two realms requires reason, or must not be made at all; and, causality applies objectively between the noumenal cause and the phenomenal effect or all the world is an uncaused event, and meaningful predication ceases.

iv. Some claim we can have only negative knowledge of God which does not satisfy the heart of man to know God (Aquinas).

Response:

Man can never know God as God knows himself; man can never be infinite, eternal, and unchangeable in himself or by infusion. Man knows God only by God's self-revelation in creation, which is very good in itself and as revelation. This is *positive* knowledge of God that fills the heart with great delight.

v. Some claim the need for a special work/grace to dispose the heart of man to desire what he knows, a *bonum superadditum* based on the doctrine of the primacy of the heart as feeling or emotion (J. Edwards, J. Gerstner, R.C. Sproul, J. Piper).

Response:

Man is sanctified (made holy) by knowing the Truth. Knowing the truth under sin is through suffering (by expulsion from the Garden to live under the curse). Job came to see what he had not seen before through a trial of faith.[8] Man is transformed by the renewing of his mind. There is a change in cognitive content, not merely a supernatural change in attitude apart from content. Holiness as purity of heart removes doublemindedness. Without holiness, no one can see God.[9]

3. Reasons for the beatific vision

i. Desire for ecstasy/bliss in unitive love (depicted in Bernini's sculpture of Teresa of Avila in the Vatican).

ii. Continuing desire for euphoria/bliss in ordinary life vs. depression.

iii. Continuing desire for the oceanic feeling of oneness as in mother/infant relation.

---

8. *Job 42:3-6.*

9. *Hebrews 12:10-14.*

iv. Reaction to arid intellectualism in theology (Aquinas) or in Romantic reaction to Enlightenment rationalism.

v. Desire for escape from life on earth as a vale of tears (widespread in history).

vi. Desire for escape by suicide by the sensitive and thoughtful from the slings and arrows of outrageous fortune (Hamlet).

vii. Life at its best under the sun is still vanity (Solomon).

viii. Life is as a tale that is told, spent in labor and sorrow (or full of sound and fury signifying nothing) (Moses, *Psalm 90*).

ix. The songs of pop culture constantly portray romantic love as the good. Love without the good fails to satisfy and often ends in heartbreak.

x. The vast majority of human beings seek virtue or happiness as the good. Without a sufficient good in this life, the default is the good in the life to come.

4. Response to appeal to experience

i. No experience is meaningful without interpretation; this mystical experience has been interpreted in many ways by naturalism, dualism, spiritual monism, Buddhism, and animism. A valid interpretation must be logically coherent. Only theism retains coherence, and consistent theism does not teach or allow for the good as heaven in the afterlife.

ii. Happiness is not the good, but the *effect* of possessing the good.

iii. Love is not the good, nor is a person the good; in true love, we seek the good for the other person.

iv. The curse of toil and strife, and old age, sickness, and death is God's call back from moral evil (sin and spiritual death), to exercise moral and natural dominion in the earth.

v. Without the good, the practical and psychological virtues of the many can become vices, which hinder achieving the good for all.

5. Scriptural passages used in support of the beatific vision and response

    i. We shall see him face to face;[10] Moses spoke to God face to face.[11]

Response:

God is a spirit and does not literally have a bodily face. No man has ever seen God.[12] The Son of God, who is the Word of God in its fullness, the *Logos*, makes God fully known. God is a Spirit, immortal, invisible, dwelling in the light which no man can approach unto, whom no man has seen, nor can see.[13] Face to face is seeing the nature of God plainly, beyond types and shadows.

    ii. The Mount of Transfiguration experience is seen as a foretaste of what is to come.

Response:

The disciples' seeing Jesus transfigured was not transformative. That came later as their understanding was opened to the Scriptures.

    iii. To be absent from the body is to be present with the Lord, which is better by far.[14]

Response:

If one's work is done, it is better to depart. But Paul knew he had to remain to build up the saints in the faith.

Abraham died in faith, still waiting for the promised City with foundations. Those who die before the resurrection are still waiting for the work on earth to be completed.[15]

    iv. Heaven is seen as a return to the Garden of Eden, prior to and without the curse, often as some type of hedonic surfeit.

---

10. *1 Corinthians 13:12.*

11. *Exodus 33:11.*

12. *John 1:18.*

13. *1 Timothy 6:16.*

14. *2 Corinthians 5:8; Philippians 1:21-26.*

15. *Hebrews 11:10, 39-40.*

Response:

The Garden was the beginning, not the end. Mankind was to move from the Garden to the City of God,[16] the completion of the work of dominion and its expression in culture. The fullness of blessing and inheritance is found only in the City of God, the kingdom of God presently coming on earth.

v. Since happiness evades most in this life, it is eagerly hoped for in the next life.

Response:

Happiness evades most because most do not glorify God and so cannot enjoy God. Happiness is the effect of possessing the good, which is the knowledge of God through dominion. The good apart from the work of dominion is false hope. Work without a lasting good is no hope.

6. The good is not the beatific vision in heaven

i. The good is rational, based on human nature; the beatific vision is not.

ii. The good is continuing from this life to the next; the beatific vision is not.

iii. The good is clear, grounded in human nature; the beatific vision is not.

iv. The good is the source of unity in all and for all; the beatific vision is not.

v. The good is consistent with GR, SR, and HC; the beatific vision is not.

vi. The good preserves the distinction between God and man; the beatific vision does not.

vii. The good preserves meaning in history; the beatific vision does not.

---

16. *Revelation 21.*

   viii. The good is necessary to restore the Church; the beatific vision cannot.

   ix. The good is necessary to overcome the first and root sin of mankind in becoming like God knowing good and evil; the beatific vision is an expression of that sin.

   x. Only the good is fulfilling, ultimate, and transformative; the beatific vision is not.

7. The good: past and at present

   i. In theodicy of the Fall, God permits evil in order to deepen the revelation of his glory in creation. In redemption, sin is allowed to work itself out in world history, while being *gradually* removed.

   ii. The noetic effect of sin blinds man to the nature of sin.[17] Root sin blinds man to all sin. Root sin is first historically (in Eden), ontologically (in the First Commandment), and existentially (in human self-awareness).

   iii. Misunderstanding good and evil is first existentially. What is first is foundational. What enters first historically is removed last historically.

   iv. There have been many cycles of apostasy in the Church. Many civilizations have perished in the world. After many cycles culminating in the Crucifixion, the second diaspora occurred. Judaic literalism and legalism were rejected in the Council of Jerusalem (A.D. 51).

   v. The Church expanded into a world taught by Athens. The Apostles' Creed rejected Greek dualism, and with it Greek gnosticism and mysticism. Yet, otherworldliness in monasticism and celibacy captured the best minds.

   vi. Augustine and Aquinas in "spoiling the Greeks" built upon Plato and Aristotle.[18] Lacking in the doctrine of sin grounded in clari-

---

17. *Paper No. 103.*

18. Gangadean, *History of Philosophy*, 111-114, 121-126.

ty and inexcusability, the Church gave Greek philosophy a pass and the Church has been spoiled.

vii. By rebuilding upon the Historic Christian Faith from prior councils and creeds, the Church in the Reformation got to the doxological focus of the Westminster Confession of Faith (1648). Subsequent generations failed to build upon the focus that man's chief end is to glorify God in all that by which he makes himself known.

viii. The challenges of Modernism (Enlightenment naturalism and secularism) and Postmodernism (skepticism and pluralism) remain. The Church's response of otherworldliness and fideism are inadequate antinomies, building on the same worldly assumptions.

ix. At present, we are nearing a crisis of a perfect storm. Four cycles of history are converging. Post-Babel, post-Western/Christian, post-Reformation, and post-pluralism/Critical Theory are upon us. Can the Church rebuild its foundation or do we face a world-wide collapse of Modernity?

x. There is hope in thinking foundationally, in restoring the cornerstone. The stone the builders rejected has become the chief cornerstone. The fear of the Lord is the beginning of wisdom. By wisdom, using the ordinary means ordained and blessed of God, the Church can rebuild, beginning with understanding good and evil.

Paper №· 107

———

A RESPONSE TO
CRITICS OF CLARITY

*Common Ground Applied to
Avoid Meaningless Disputes*

PART II

(Continued from Paper No. 23)

OBJECTIONS TO COMMON GROUND
AND RESPONSES

The following objections deny Common Ground. A response is made
to each objection.

14. *Objection:* If some things are clear, and knowledge is justified,
true belief (in the strong sense), you need to give a philosophical
proof that *a is a.*

Response:

    i. There are several levels of "clear": self-attesting, self-evident,
self-referentially absurd, and clear to reason.

        1) Reason, as the laws of thought, is self-attesting; it cannot be
questioned because, as the laws of thought, it makes questioning (one form of thought) possible. No attempt has ever

been made or can be made to prove the laws of thought by using (assuming) the laws of thought.

2) Only reason is self-attesting and is therefore most authoritative.

3) It is self-evident that we think (use the laws of thought) and it is self-evident that there are laws of thought—reason in itself *is* the laws of thought. What is self-evident needs no proof because it is immediately evident and known without inference.

4) It is clear that something exists (vs. nothing exists). To deny this is SRA (self-defeating vs. defeated by another).

5) It is clear that the self exists (vs. *Advaita*) since the denial involves a contradiction and it is SRA.

6) It is clear that there must be something eternal since the denial involves a contradiction (by *reductio* argument).

7) It is clear that the material world is not eternal (assuming common ground that the material world exists and the definition of the material world). This is based on what is more basic by RP—that there must be something eternal.

8) It is clear that natural evil (physical death) is not original. This is based on RP—that only some is eternal and analysis of infinite power and goodness (what God could, would, and must do, and therefore actually did).

ii. Proof applies to some things that are clear (#5-8); it does not apply to other things that are clear (#1-4).

15. *Objection:* A practical (pragmatic) proof is not a philosophical proof. An SRA is a practical proof.

Response:

i. An SRA, like an uncaused event, is both a practical and a logical objection. An uncaused event implies *being* from *non-being*, which renders the logical distinction between *being* and *non-being* (and all other distinctions) meaningless.

ii. We can neither cease to think (practical) nor think what is meaningless (logical).

iii. Denial of the light of reason (life) leaves us in the darkness of meaninglessness (death).

iv. Thinking is the most basic activity of rational life; one cannot think what is unthinkable/meaningless; one cannot live death. The need to think remains; the light shines in the darkness. An SRA is not only impossible in this world; it is impossible in all possible worlds.

16. *Objection:* I don't understand a word you are saying ("much learning doth make thee mad"—Festus to St. Paul[1]).

Response:

i. Either the person does not understand because the words are without meaning and no one can understand.

1) But many do understand. Are they all mad?

2) Specify the criteria to distinguish meaning from no meaning—is it other than the laws of thought as the test for meaning?

ii. Or, there is an irrational antipathy and this is an *ad hominem*— speaking against a person rather than what is being said. In which case, we wait for a response to what is said.

17. *Objection:* This is not the way philosophy is currently done.

Response:

i. Styles in philosophy change. What is current now may not endure ages away. Styles depend on substantive differences. The styles of Plato and Aristotle arose from epistemological differences.

ii. A descriptive claim is not a normative claim of what philosophy should be.

---

1. *Acts 26.*

    iii. *Philosophical Foundation*[2] offers an answer to the question "what is philosophy?" that is classical/essential and comprehensive.

    iv. CG is the set of conditions which make thought and discourse possible. Critics of clarity must address CG in order to speak meaningfully.

18. *Objection:* We should be epistemically humble; lack of clarity/certainty is epistemically humble.

    Response:

    i. Submission to the Word of God is epistemically humble. The Word of God and Historic Christianity affirm clarity and inexcusability (sin).[3]

    ii. Public criticism of persons without prior agreement on positions leads to *ad hominems* and is not epistemically humble.

19. *Objection:* Why should we be that concerned about clarity? Most are not. The concern is peculiar and exclusive.

    Response:

    i. Clarity concerns meaning at the most basic level of thought. No meaning here affects loss of meaning everywhere (nihilism).

    ii. If there is no clarity, then there is no inexcusability (sin), and no need for the gospel of Christ.

    iii. *Argumentum ad populum* (most don't have that concern) must reckon with (a) no one (left to oneself) seeks God, (b) all are being called to stop and think through the curse (toil and strife, and old age, sickness, and death).

20. *Objection:* I believe it is clear, but I can't give a proof.

    Response:

    i. Proof (for truth) is not relevant where there is a test for meaning. Meaning is more basic than truth. If there is no meaning, then there is no (possible) truth.

---

2. Gangadean, *Philosophical Foundation*, 6-10.

3. *Romans 1:20; WCF 1.1.*

ii. Self-attesting, self-evident, and self-referentially absurd are immediately clear by test for meaning (not by proof for truth).

21. *Objection:* If I don't see what is clear, how can I hold to the Principle of Clarity (PC)?

    Response: Holding to clarity in principle (as part of CG) is not the same as showing what is clear. PC is a necessary condition for one's thought.

22. *Objection:* Why is CG necessary? It seems a merely arbitrary imposition.

    Response:

    i. CG is the set of necessary conditions for thought and discourse; it (basic CG) begins with reason as the laws of thought and test for meaning, and ends with PC. CG extends to every level of dispute: more basic, then less basic.

    ii. If there is no meaning, then it is a meaningless dispute; we should avoid, by RP, meaningless disputes.

    iii. Meaninglessness is the condition of spiritual death—the wages (inherent consequence) of sin (not seeking, not understanding, not doing what is right).

    iv. CG is to be applied as universally as sin and spiritual death is universal.

    v. More so when dealing with matters that have been disputed.

    vi. Most so when dealing with a contentious person.

    vii. Everywhere and always, we should avoid meaningless disputes (chain and bind the adversary—the light shines in the darkness[4]).

23. *Objection:* There is always an unknown, therefore uncertainty, and therefore no clarity.

    Response:

    i. The unknown must be distinguished from the unknowable as well as from the known. An unknown at a less basic level does

---

4. *Revelation 20; John 1:5.*

not affect or set aside what is known at a more basic level. In this sense, we know in part. Human knowledge is finite—it may grow forever and still be finite.

ii. If any worldview is coherent in its essence (more basic), then non-essential (less basic) differences in that world may not now be known, and may remain an unknown, without unsettling what is known at the more basic level.

24. *Objection:* Clarity is neither possible nor necessary.

Response:

i. If clarity is not possible, then nothing is clear, and no distinction is clear, and no meaning is possible. If all is meaningless, then we should be silenced.

ii. If clarity is not possible, then inexcusability is not possible, and therefore morality is not possible, and the gospel is not necessary.

25. *Objection:* Clarity is presumptuous—who has or can claim it?

Response:

i. Scripture claims it: What may be known of God is clear so that they are without excuse.[5]

ii. The Historic Christian Faith claims it: The light of nature, and the works of creation and providence do so far manifest the goodness, wisdom, and power of God, as to leave men inexcusable.[6]

26. *Objection:* Clarity is mere philosophy (head knowledge); what is needed is more piety (godliness).

Response:

i. Zeal without knowledge is mere pietism; it is not true piety.

ii. Holiness is based on truth: Sanctify them through thy truth: thy Word (Logos) is Truth.[7]

---

5. *Romans 1:20.*

6. *WCF 1.1.*

7. *John 17:17.*

    iii. We are transformed by the renewing of our minds; knowing the truth sets us free.[8]

    iv. Knowing words is not understanding meaning; having the foundation (elementary truths) is necessary for spiritual maturity.[9]

27. *Objection:* Clarity has little to do with the psychological and practical necessities of life.

    Response: Natural evil consists of toil and strife, and old age, sickness, and death; it is intensified in war, famine, and plague. It is imposed by God to restrain, recall from, and remove moral evil; moral evil is to neglect, avoid, resist, and deny one's reason in the face of what is clear about God; natural evil is God's call to stop and think to see what is clear. The psychological and practical necessities arise from the (as a) call to see what is clear, therefore clarity has everything to do with the necessities of life.

28. *Objection:* If it is so clear, why don't I see it?

    Response:

    i. Left to oneself, no seeks and no one understands what is clear.

    ii. If we don't have a concern for consistency and accept the necessity for clarity to have meaning and morality, we will not seek.

    iii. Seeing clarity requires a commitment to reason as the test for meaning.

    iv. Seeing clarity requires critical thinking applied to unexamined assumptions.

    v. Seeing clarity is cumulative; it is a step-by-step process from more basic to less basic.

    vi. In short, without CG we won't see what is clear.

---

8. *Romans 12:2; John 8:32.*

9. *Hebrews 6:1.*

29. *Objection:* Proof of what is clear is not persuasion.

Response: Persuasion without proof is blind faith; it is based on pseudo-argument, not sound argument. Biblical faith has evidence for what is not seen.[10]

30. *Objection:* Clarity is not necessary for the good.

Response:

i. Clarity is necessary for the knowledge of God through the work of dominion.

ii. Clarity is necessary to take thoughts captive and to disciple the nations.

iii. Clarity is not necessary for the good, understood as a beatific vision of God in heaven or a return to a paradise.

iv. Clarity is necessary for meaningful thought; without clarity, Christ and the cross is emptied of meaning.

31. *Objection:* God is not like that—to hold people inexcusable.

Response:

i. God will not hold him guiltless who takes his name in vain.[11]

ii. Clarity and inexcusability are not imposed; inexcusability is inherent in clarity, and clarity is inherent in the order of creation.

iii. Sin and death are not imposed; sin is inherent in clarity and inexcusability, and death is inherent in sin.

iv. The wages of sin are inherent in sin; spiritual death (meaninglessness, boredom, and guilt) is inherent in sin (not seeking and not understanding).

v. The wages of sin is spiritual death, not physical death (present and imposed) or hell (future and imposed).[12]

---

10. *Hebrews 11:1.*

11. *Exodus 20:7.*

12. *Romans 6:23.*

32. *Objection:* To know what is clear requires work. Salvation is by grace, not work.

   Response:

   i. Reason is the most basic form of the Word of God that comes to man (the life of the *Logos* in man, as light, by which man sees/understands what is clear about God).

   ii. The Holy Spirit works by and with reason (the Word), not apart from reason. The Holy Spirit works to convince, persuade, enlighten, and illuminate the mind with sound argument, not apart from sound argument.

   iii. The use of reason to know what is clear is not opposed to or independent of grace, but is itself a work of grace. The use of and proper response to sound argument is not a purely natural occurrence, but is itself something of a miracle.

   iv. We die spiritually when we deny our reason. The Holy Spirit restores us to life by restoring the life of reason in us.

33. *Objection:* I don't define knowledge as absolute certainty.

   Response: No one does insofar as *absolute* is associated with the divine. But humans can have maximal certainty about basic things, like *a is a* and *some things are clear* (e.g., There is no *being* from *non-being* (*being* is not *non-being*)).

34. *Objection:* I don't know clarity by reason, but by intuition (or, I know reason by intuition).

   Response:

   i. Meaning is more basic than truth.

   ii. Reason is the test for meaning. What violates a law of thought (*a is non-a*) has no meaning (self-evident).

   iii. The opposite of what is known by intuitional awareness (immediate/non-inferential) can still be thought and may be true.

   iv. The opposite of what is known by reason cannot be thought and cannot be true.

35. *Objection: God exists* is not necessarily true.

   Response:

   i. Contradictory statements cannot both be true and cannot both be false.

   ii. If the contradiction of *God exists* cannot be true, then *God exists* must be true.

36. *Objection:* I don't have to prove (it is clear) God exists. God (the Holy Spirit) can show it (by a miraculous sign?).

   Response:

   i. If a person knows basic things are clear from general revelation, they can show what is clear.

   ii. If a person knows what is more basic, they can show what is less basic.

   iii. Miraculous signs accompany truths of special revelation, which must be consistent with clear general revelation.

   iv. All persons are called to know clear general revelation and to show clear general revelation.

37. *Objection:* What is maximal clarity?

   Response:

   i. Maximal clarity is necessary and sufficient for inexcusability.

   ii. Doubt or denial of maximal clarity of basic beliefs leads to loss of all meaningful distinctions. If *being* can come from *non-being*, there is no meaningful distinction between *being* and *non-being*.

   iii. Rational Presuppositional epistemology (vs. all non-RP) maintains thinking is presuppositional (the less basic in light of more basic) and some things are clear (vs. nothing is clear). Given RP, basic things are clear and are clear to reason (vs. various forms of experience).

   iv. Basic things are maximally clear (nothing clearer) (vs. absolutely clear), sufficient for inexcusability. Denial of what is maximally clear is a denial of one's rational nature (sin) and leads to spiritual death (meaninglessness, boredom, and guilt).

38. *Objection:* Objection to clarity based on pseudo-argument vs. real argument.

    Response:

    i. A pseudo-argument does not engage with a real argument.

    ii. Objections to a real argument will show it is either invalid or unsound.

    iii. Pseudo-arguments are informal fallacies that are irrelevant to a real argument.

    iv. A pseudo-argument is used to neglect, avoid, resist, and deny reason—a progressive hardening into anti-intellectualism (from walk to stand to sit in the seat of scorners[13]).

39. *Objection:* If I know what is clear, why do I have to show what is clear?

    Response:

    i. A person may fail to know what is clear even while claiming to know what is clear.

    ii. A person may think they know what is clear by using an epistemological method other than Rational Presuppositionalism (e.g., intuition or common sense), which does not amount to objective (vs. subjective) proof.

    iii. If one knows what is clear, one should be able to show what is clear, and be able to overcome commonly held objections to what is clear.

40. *Objection:* Only God (and not self or others) can bring us to see what is clear.

    Response:

    i. It is *not* in question that God, as Creator, ruler, and redeemer, convicts us of sin (of not seeking) and of the death of not

---

13. *Psalm 1.*

understanding what is clear. What *is* in question is how God does so.

ii. Inwardly: God restores the life (light) of reason in us to see the emptiness of life without God—this occurs when spiritual death in us (meaninglessness, boredom, and guilt) is seen as due to sin (not seeking and understanding).

iii. Outwardly: How then shall they call on Him in whom they have not believed? And how shall they believe in Him of whom they have not heard? And how shall they hear without a preacher? And how shall they preach unless they are sent? As it is written: "How beautiful are the feet of those who preach the gospel of peace, Who bring glad tidings of good things!" But they have not all obeyed the gospel. For Isaiah says, "Lord, who has believed our report?" So then faith *comes* by hearing, and hearing by the word of God.[14]

SUMMARY

1. Neither skepticism nor fideism can set aside reason.

2. Critics of clarity try to set aside reason to avoid discussion, which shows the inexcusability of unbelief.

3. The light of reason is irresistible: it cannot be overcome and it cannot be withstood.

4. Reason in man (made in the image of God) cannot be eradicated from human nature.

5. The light shines in the darkness and the darkness comprehended it not.[15] Reason is self-attesting.

This paper is posthumously published
based upon the original work of Dr. Surrendra Gangadean
and has been edited by The Logos Foundation Editorial Board.

---

14. *Romans 10:14-17.*

15. *John 1:5.*

Paper No. 108

_____

ANAPOLOGIA VS. *DIALOGIA*

ANAPOLOGIA—WITHOUT REASON

1. Human beings are thinking (rational) beings made in the image of God. We are called to use our reason to find meaning in seeing what is clear about God.

2. Left to oneself, no one seeks God, no one understands, no one does what is right.[1] We neglect, avoid, resist, or deny reason in the face of what is clear about God (NARD). To fail to see what is clear about God is to be without reason/*anapologia*/inexcusable.[2] "NARDing" is the anti-intellectual response to an intellectual challenge.

3. Slander (personal attack, abusive *ad hominem*, speaking against the person rather than what the person said) is the chief way to NARD. Charging others with being mindless is the chief way to slander.

4. In the spiritual war between truth and falsehood and good and evil, within each person, NARDing is spiritual suicide. It is to deny the rational dignity of oneself. Spiritual suicide brings spiritual death: meaninglessness, boredom, and guilt. In the spiritual war between persons, charging others with being mindless is spiritual murder; it is to deny the rational dignity of others. Spiritual suicide naturally leads to spiritual murder which, when developed, leads to all killing and war.

_____

1. *Romans 3:10-11.*

2. *Romans 1:20.*

DIALOGIA—REASONING WITH

1. Dialogue

In place of NARDing and slander, we are called as rational beings to dialogue where there are disputes. Dialogue requires Common Ground in that which is self-evident.

Dialogue (reasoning with) assumes:

i. Reason in itself is the laws of thought, which make thinking possible and which are self-evident. Reason, therefore, is the test for meaning.

ii. Integrity—a concern for consistency: what is logically self-contradictory is meaningless; what is existentially self-contradictory is absurd.

iii. Rational Presuppositionalism—thinking is presuppositional: we think of the less basic in light of the more basic; if there is agreement on what is more basic, there can be agreement on what is less basic. Reason as the laws of thought is most basic.

iv. The Principle of Clarity: some things are clear; the basic things are clear; the basic things (about God and man and good and evil) are clear to reason.

2. First Things

The basic (first) things concern the clarity of general revelation (GR) and the inexcusability of unbelief.[3] GR is what can be known by all men, everywhere, at all times. It focuses on the eternal power and divine nature of God and on the natural moral law grounded in human nature. First things concern epistemology, metaphysics, and ethics.

i. Epistemology is concerned with whether knowledge is possible, whether some things are clear to reason.

a. Unless some things are clear from GR, neither meaning nor morality is possible (nihilism). There can be no inexcusability

---

3. *Romans 1:20; 2:14-15.*

for unbelief (no sin) and therefore no need for redemption or Scripture (redemptive revelation).

b. Skepticism (which says knowledge is not possible) must show how skepticism, consistently held, does not lead to nihilism (the loss of all meaning), or, how talk without meaning is not self-referentially absurd (SRA).

c. Fideism (which says proof for the existence of God is not necessary, or possible, or relevant, for faith) must show how inexcusability for unbelief (moral evil or sin) is possible without the clarity of GR, or, if it is clear that God exists, must show how it is clear.

Neither the existence of God, intuitively held, (as in: "We hold these truths to be self-evident, that all men are created equal . . .") nor Scripture, is self-evident. But the *Logos*, as reason, is self-evident.

ii. Metaphysics is concerned with the nature of being. In this context, it is concerned with the existence and nature of God and the nature of man.

a. It is clear to reason that there must be something eternal and that only some (God the Creator) is eternal vs. all is eternal in some form or other.

b. It is clear to reason that God the Creator is a Spirit, infinite, eternal, and unchangeable, in his being, wisdom, power, holiness, justice, goodness, and truth, and that man is created in the image of God.

c. It is clear to reason that since God is all good and all powerful, creation in the beginning must have been very good, that natural evil is due to moral evil, that physical death was imposed as a call back from spiritual death.

iii. Ethics is concerned with the question whether there is rational justification for the answer to the question, "What is the good?"

a. It is clear to reason that the good is the end in itself, man's chief end, the highest value chosen for its own sake; that virtue is the means to the good; that (lasting) happiness is the effect of possessing what is the good.

b. It is clear to reason that the good for man is based on human nature; that the good for man as a rational being, made in the image of God, is the use of reason to understand the nature of creation, which reveals the nature of God.

c. It is clear to reason that the natural moral law is grounded in the fundamental features of human nature which are knowable to all.

3. General Revelation Requires Special Revelation

Given the universal reality of moral and natural evil, mankind stands in need of redemption.

Scripture as special/redemptive revelation reveals how God is both just and merciful to mankind in sin.

Christ, the *Logos*/Word of God incarnate, takes away the sin of the world by his death/crucifixion and rules through his resurrection to bring the world to know God.

Paper № 109

———

THE SPIRITUAL WAR

Its Many Dimensions

1. The promise of redemption is given to Adam in the Garden after the Fall. It is given in these words: I will put enmity between you (Satan, the tempter) and the woman, between your seed and her seed; he will crush your head and you will strike his heel.[1]

2. There will be a spiritual war; it will be age-long and agonizing; good will overcome evil. The seed of the woman (Christ—in the place of Adam) will undo what Adam did (take away our sin) and do what Adam failed to do (make God known).

3. It is a spiritual war (not physical), between belief and unbelief, between the truth of God (the Logos, the Word of God; truth in its fullness) and falsehood (the lie of the devil, human autonomy, you shall be as God knowing good and evil).

4. The war between belief and unbelief is first within each person and then between persons, within each family and between families, and collectively, between the kingdom of God and the kingdom of darkness.

---

1. *Genesis 3:15.*

5. It is between the light of reason (In him was life, and the life was the light of men[2]) and the darkness of non-rationalism (non-cognitive approaches to life) and anti-rationalism (resistance to rational approaches to life). The light shines in the darkness and the darkness cannot overcome it or withstand it.[3]

6. It is between the Church and the world. "Marvel not, my brethren, if the world hates you."[4] "Be of good cheer, I have overcome the world."[5] "The gates of hell shall not prevail against it."[6] "They overcame him by the blood of the Lamb, and by the word of their testimony."[7]

7. We wrestle not against flesh and blood, but against principalities and powers, against the rulers of the darkness of this world, against spiritual wickedness in high places.[8] We wrestle against the lies of Satan, embodied in worldviews which are entrenched in positions of authority.

8. Every believer, in every age, struggles against the enmity of the world, the flesh, and the devil. From the flesh (fallen human nature) arises the lust of the eyes (for beauty), the lust of the flesh (for pleasure), and the pride of life (the folly of human wisdom).

9. And take up the sword of the Spirit which is the Word of God.[9] The Word of God is sharper than any two-edged sword, piercing even to the dividing asunder of soul and spirit and of the joints and marrow, and is a discerner of the thoughts and intents of the heart.[10]

---

2. *John 1:4.*

3. *John 1:5.*

4. *1 John 3:13.*

5. *John 16.33.*

6. *Matthew 16:18.*

7. *Revelation 12:11.*

8. *Ephesians 6:12.*

9. *Ephesians 6:17.*

10. *Hebrews 4:12.*

10. The weapons we fight with are not the weapons of this world. We demolish arguments and every pretension that sets itself up against the knowledge of God. And take every thought captive to the obedience to Christ.[11]

11. It is against the kingdom of darkness: the False Prophet (education without the Word/Logos of God), the Harlot (the economy without the law of God), and the Beast (politics without the law of God—the mark of the Beast is the law of man in place of the law of God, on the forehead and on the hand).[12]

12. The spiritual war is depicted as a physical war and is sometimes called Armageddon.[13] It is a spiritual war, not physical, because it is fought with a sword that comes out of the mouth.[14] Through this war, Christ, the Word of God, and his followers, make disciples of all nations.

---

11. *2 Corinthians 10:4-5.*

12. *Revelation 12–20.*

13. *Revelation 19:11-21.*

14. *Revelation 19:15, 21.*

Paper № 110

―――

ON CLARITY

Concern for Consistency in Thought and Action

1. If nothing is clear, there can be no meaning. Consistently held, it leads to nihilism. Thinking is presuppositional. If the more basic is not clear, then nothing is clear. The basic things are about the infinite and the eternal, and therefore about God. One's view about God determines one's view of human nature, and good and evil.

2. Clarity about basic things is propositional knowledge (true vs. false); it is not non-cognitive awareness, which is neither true nor false.

3. Clarity is not immediate and non-inferential vs. common sense realism and the *sensus divinitatis*; it must be able to answer objections.

4. What is clear must first be objectively clear; it need not be subjectively clear.

5. Knowledge is the basis of holiness and righteousness; it is not opposed to these.

6. Finitude and incomprehensibility are not opposed to clarity.

7. The Fall and sin affect man's willingness to seek and understand; it does not affect reason in itself and objective clarity.

8. Clarity about the basic things (the foundation) is for all, not just for some.

9. Lack of knowledge of proof does not imply there is no proof; if thinking is presuppositional, proof would be a step-by-step process, not by a single argument.

10. Proof is not independent of historically cumulative insight; progress is built upon the internal and external challenges to prior claims of proof.

11. Clarity is consistent with and implicit in understanding root sin as not seeking, not understanding, and not doing what it right.

12. Understanding the inherent connection between sin and spiritual death moves one to seek and to understand what is clear about God.

13. It is clear that man's chief end is to glorify and enjoy God in all that by which he makes himself known, in all his works of creation and providence.

14. If general revelation is not clear and does not lead to the necessity for special revelation, then unbelief is excusable.

Paper № 111

———

COMMON CHRISTIAN
MISCONCEPTIONS ABOUT REASON
A Response

1. **Reason and Sin:**[1] Reason is fallen. The effects of the Fall or the no-etic effect of sin blinds man or distorts his reason.

   Response: Reason is not affected by the Fall any more than our sight is affected by the Fall. The Fall affected our willingness to use reason, not reason itself.

2. **Reason and Authority:** Reason is not autonomous. Reason is used to support vain philosophy. In the name of reason, men have turned away from God.

   Response: Reason is the Word of God in all men.[2] It cannot be opposed to the Scripture. One has to deny reason to avoid seeing God. Those who deny God in the name of reason have failed to use reason fully.

3. **Reason and Conversion:**[3] Reason is ineffectual. Reason does not persuade anyone to believe in God.

---

1. *Paper No. 103.*

2. *John 1:4.*

3. Gangadean, *Philosophical Foundation*, 36-37; Gangadean, *The Westminster Confession*. See Questions 49-52; Gangadean, *The Westminster Catechisms*. See LCQ. 67.

Response: The light of reason exposes inconsistencies in our understanding and thus compels change. It is life unto life to those who believe or death unto death to those who do not believe. It accomplishes God's intended purpose.

4. **Reason and Scripture:**[4] Scripture is the authority, not reason. Since Scripture is sufficient, reason is not necessary.

Response: Reason is the laws of thought. It is necessary in order to understand God's self-revelation in nature/creation and in Scripture. Reason is necessary to expose inconsistencies both in false prophets and in false interpretations of Scripture.

5. **Reason and Faith:**[5] Reason is opposed to faith. We walk by faith, not by reason. We are not supposed to question our faith or seek proof for faith.

Response: Faith is opposed to sight, not reason. By faith we understand or see what is invisible.[6] Faith grows as our understanding grows. Faith is tested as our understanding is tested. Understanding grows through the use of reason.

6. **Reason and Clarity:** Reason is not needed for clarity. All men deep down already know God, instinctually.

Response: Clarity of general revelation is necessary for inexcusability and reason is necessary to understand what is clear about God's divine nature. Objections to what is clear must be shown to be logically impossible.

7. **Reason and Feelings:**[7] Reason is cold and does not allow for feelings. The heart and the head may be opposed. What is needed is heartfelt religion.

---

4. Gangadean, *The Westminster Confession.* See Questions 4-12; Gangadean, *The Westminster Catechisms.* See LCQ. 4-6; *Paper No. 14, 26, 56, 112, 114,* and *141-150.*

5. Gangadean, *Philosophical Foundation,* 32-45, 121-127; Gangadean, *History of Philosophy,* 3-12, 163-167; *Paper No. 21, 28, 98,* and *128-129.*

6. *Hebrews 11:1-3.*

7. Gangadean, *Philosophical Foundation,* 43-45, 178-179.

Response: Feelings always arise out of beliefs. The conflict is not between the head and the heart, but between a consciously held belief and another belief which is held less consciously. Knowledge of the truth makes us holy.

8. **Reason and Will:**[8] We may know the truth and not do it. We may know the truth and rebel against what we know. The will is independent of the intellect.

   Response: We think we are justified when we do what we do. Those who kill believers think they do God's service.[9] Christ prayed: Father, forgive them; for they know not what they do. Knowing the truth sets us free from the power of sin.

9. **Reason and Common Ground:** There is no common ground with the non-believer. Neutrality is a myth. Nothing in God's universe is neutral.

   Response: All human beings are created with the same human nature. Our created nature as rational beings is common ground. Common ground does not mean neutral ground. A person must deny their rational nature to avoid seeing God.

10. **Reason and Repentance:** Sin is the outward act of disobedience. We repent of sin when we turn away from disobedience.

    Response: Root sin is not fruit sin. Root sin begins in failure to see what is clear. Radical repentance requires coming to see what is clear. If we cannot show what is clear, then we continue to avoid reason and the root of sin remains in us.

11. **Reason and God:** God is not bound by reason. The miracles and mysteries of God are above reason.

    Response: God's being is rational. God is not both eternal and not eternal, at the same time and in the same respect. The mysteries of God are not contrary to or above reason. Miracles go against the laws of nature, not the laws of reason.

---

8. *Paper No. 120.*

9. *John 16:2.*

12. **Reason and the Holy Spirit:** Regeneration from death to life is a work of the Holy Spirit, not the work of human reason. Salvation is by grace, not by reason.

   Response: The life of the Word of God is in all men as reason: In Him was life and that life was the light of men. We die spiritually when we deny our reason. The Holy Spirit restores us to life by restoring the life of reason in us.

Paper N⁰· 112

———

Why General Revelation
Is Basic in the
Christian Worldview

1. Historic Christianity is redemptive—it assumes the reality of sin and death from which we are redeemed. In the divine justice, sin and death require the clarity of general revelation and the inexcusability of unbelief. To fail to understand clarity is to fail to understand divine justice and mercy.[1]

2. Creation is revelation, necessarily, intentionally, and exclusively. God created and rules to make his glory known. The whole earth is full of his glory. Man is called to know God's self-revelation in his works of creation and providence. To make knowledge of this revelation unnecessary is to deny God's wisdom and purpose in creation and history.[2]

3. Natural evil is God's call back from moral evil, the failure to seek and to understand what is clear about God. Toil and strife, and old age, sickness, and death are a call back from sin and spiritual death. Natural evil is imposed by grace to restrain, to recall from,

---

1. Gangadean, *The Westminster Confession.* See Questions 4-12; Gangadean, *The Westminster Catechisms.* See LCQ. 4-6; *Paper No. 14, 26, 56, 112, 114,* and *141-150.*

2. Gangadean, *The Westminster Catechisms.* See Appendix 4.

and to remove moral evil. It calls us to stop and think deeply about what is clear.

4. The moral law is written on the hearts of all men.[3] It is the way of life for mankind, the means to the good in every dimension of life. It requires man to know and to acknowledge God (First Commandment), to not lightly and thoughtlessly regard that by which God makes himself known (Third Commandment).

5. Man's chief end is to glorify God and to enjoy him forever. Through the work of dominion, given to man from the beginning, man was to know God's glory and to make his glory known. Eternal life is to know God. Sin was permitted to serve God's purpose, by deepening God's self-revelation and enlarging the work of dominion.

6. Prayer is an offering of our desires in keeping with the will of God. The first and fundamental petition of all prayer (Hallowed be thy name) is that God would enable us to glorify him in all that by which he makes himself known. God makes himself known through his works of creation and providence.

7. In the Great Commission, the Church is called to make disciples of all nations. This requires believers to take every thought captive which is raised up against the knowledge of God. This work begins with internal challenges of misunderstanding which divide the Church, and extends to external challenges of unbelieving worldviews.

8. Having faith is necessary to please God. Faith is the substance (underlying support) of things hoped for, the evidence of things not seen. By faith, God's eternal power and divine nature are understood from the things which are made. Trust in God and the understanding of Scripture are based on understanding what is clear about God.[4]

---

3. Gangadean, *Philosophical Foundation*, 171-284; Gangadean, *History of Philosophy*, 61-69; Gangadean, *The Westminster Catechisms*. See LCQ. 91-148.

4. Gangadean, *Philosophical Foundation*, 32-45, 121-127; Gangadean, *History of Philosophy*, 3-12, 163-167; *Paper No. 21, 28, 98,* and *128-129.*

9. Historic Christianity as it is summed up in its creeds is doxological. The creeds reflect the work of the Holy Spirit leading the Church into deepening understanding. The Westminster Confession of Faith is not focused on salvation narrowly understood, but on the praise of the glory of God revealed in all his works of creation and providence.

10. Christianity is eschatological. History will come to an end. The Sabbath marks the completion of work, both for God and man. Christ returns when the work is completed. He is to rule to fill everything in every way through his body the Church, to make God known. The earth will be filled with the knowledge of God as the waters cover the sea.[5]

---

5. *Paper No. 104* and *118-119*.

Paper N<u>o.</u> 113

————

HISTORIC CHRISTIANITY
Contrasted to Popular Christianity

1. What is Historic Christianity?

    i. Historic Christianity is the result of the work of the Holy Spirit leading the Church into all truth.[1]

    ii. This work is done through the pastor-teachers who respond to foundational challenges to the faith in every age.[2]

    iii. After much discussion in Church councils, a common understanding is reached which is expressed in the creeds of the Church.

    iv. Current challenges focus on the antinomies of faith vs. reason and on the value of this life vs. the after-life.

    v. Through overcoming these challenges, the Church attains to greater unity of the faith and fullness in God.[3]

2. How is Historic Christianity to be contrasted to Popular Christianity?

    i. Human beings are finite and fallen and therefore hold their beliefs more or less consciously and consistently.

———————

1. *John 16.*

2. *Acts 15.*

3. *Ephesians 4.*

ii. Historic Christianity is more conscious and consistent than Popular Christianity because Historic Christianity is built on the historically cumulative insight of the creeds whereas Popular Christianity is largely indifferent to how beliefs shape our lives.

iii. Historic Christianity is concerned with the goal of the knowledge of God whereas Popular Christianity is concerned with the goal of heaven.

iv. Historic Christianity is concerned to take thoughts captive which are raised up against the knowledge of God whereas Popular Christianity is unconcerned to give a reason for one's belief.

v. A significant change in understanding foundational truths about good and evil is necessary in order to change from a popular to a historic level of Christianity.

3. What does Historic Christianity affirm?

i. Historic Christianity affirms the clarity of general revelation and consequently the inexcusability of unbelief in all forms of skepticism and fideism.

ii. Historic Christianity affirms the biblical worldview of creation–fall–redemption and the need to consistently interpret Scripture in the context of this worldview.

iii. Historic Christianity affirms the work of the Holy Spirit in Church history and the historically cumulative insight summed up in the creeds and confessions of faith: the first Council of Jerusalem,[4] the Apostles' Creed, the Creed of Nicea, the Council of Carthage, the Creed of Chalcedon, the Council of Orange, and last, the Westminster Confession of Faith.[5]

iv. Historic Christianity affirms that man's chief end is to glorify and enjoy God in all that by which he makes himself known—in all his works of creation and providence.

---

4. *Acts 15.*

5. *Paper No. 16*; Gangadean, *The Westminster Confession*; Gangadean, *The Westminster Shorter and Larger Catechisms.*

v. Historic Christianity affirms that the gospel is for everyone and that the goal of life is that the earth will be filled with the knowledge of God as the waters cover the sea.[6]

---

6. *Isaiah 11:9.*

Paper N<u>o.</u> 114

———

THE GOSPEL

For Everyone

**The Gospel is the good news of God's salvation.
It is for everyone.**

1. All have sinned.

i. *There is no one righteous, not even one; there is no one who understands, no one who seeks God.*[1]

Unrighteousness (fruit sin) arises from not seeking and not understanding (root sin). While fruit sin may differ, root sin is the same and present in all.

ii. The inexcusability of unbelief arises from the clarity of general revelation:

Since the creation of the world God's invisible qualities—his eternal power and divine nature—have been clearly seen, being understood from what has been made, so that men are without excuse.[2]

The law of God (summed up in the Ten Commandments) is written on the hearts of all men.[3]

---

1. *Romans 3:10-11.* Basic truths of Scripture are not limited to the verses cited in this paper, but are assumed and implied throughout Scripture.

2. *Romans 1:20.*

3. *Romans 2:14-15.*

The moral law is clear because it is grounded in human nature. It is the rule of life for all men, everywhere, at all times.

iii. What is clear is not understood because, left to oneself, no one seeks God. One has to neglect, avoid, resist, or deny reason to avoid what is clear.

Therefore, all have sinned.

2. All under sin are in spiritual death.

i. *The wages of sin is death.*[4]

There are two kinds of death as well as two kinds of resurrection: physical (of the body) and spiritual (of the soul).[5]

As for you, you were dead [spiritually] in your trespasses and sins.[6]

I am the resurrection and the life. He who believes in me will live, even though he dies [physically]. And whoever lives and believes in me will never die [spiritually].[7]

ii. The wages of sin is spiritual death, which is present and inherent in sin, not future and imposed, as hell is commonly conceived. (The lake of fire is the second (spiritual) death.)[8]

iii. Spiritual death is meaninglessness, boredom, and guilt which are inherent in not seeking and not understanding. Man is given up by God to follow the desires of his heart.[9] The emptiness of life without God leads each individual to all the excess of unrighteousness.

Corporately, idolatries which originate in misconceptions about God lead to divisions, apostasy, cultural decay, and finally, to cultural collapse.[10]

---

4. *Romans 6:23; Genesis 2:17.*

5. *Revelation 20:6.*

6. *Ephesians 2:1-6.*

7. *John 11:25.*

8. *Revelation 20:14; 21:8.*

9. *Romans 1:24, 26, 28.*

10. *Romans 1:21-31.*

The wages of sin is spiritual death, both individually and corporately.

3. All are called to repentance.

i. The root sin of not seeking and not understanding is manifest in doing what is forbidden (the outward act of eating).[11]

ii. God calls man back first through conscience (the sense of shame).

This call back has been avoided by self-deception.[12]

iii. God calls man back again through others, by question: "Where are you?"

This call back has been resisted by self-justification.[13]

iv. God calls man back finally through suffering (toil and strife, and old age, sickness, and death) to stop and think.[14]

Natural evil is imposed on mankind by God to restrain, to recall from, and to remove moral evil.

The call back through the curse is accompanied by the promise of redemption. The seed of the woman will crush the serpent.[15]

4. All who believe in Christ have everlasting life.

i. Only in the Scriptures is God's promise of redemption in Christ revealed.

Christ is the Son of Man, in the place of Adam, who will undo what Adam did and who will do what Adam failed to do.[16]

ii. Only in Jesus Christ is the promise of redemption fulfilled.[17]

---

11. *Genesis 3:1-6.*

12. *Genesis 3:7.*

13. *Genesis 3:8-13.*

14. *Genesis 3:16-19.*

15. *Genesis 3:15.*

16. *Genesis 3:15; Romans 5:17-18; 1 Corinthians 15:21-22.*

17. *John 3:16, 14:6.*

Jesus is the Christ, the Son of God, the Word of God incarnate, who forgives sin and who makes God known.[18]

iii. Only by Christ's vicarious atonement on the cross does the mercy of God satisfy the justice of God.[19]

Christ is the Lamb of God who takes away the sin of the world.[20]

iv. Only by repentance of sin and faith in Christ is redemption realized.[21]

Christ is Prophet, Priest, and King who by his Word and Spirit brings his people to the unity of the faith and to the fullness of God.[22]

5. The promise of redemption is for all mankind.

i. Eternal life is knowing God.[23] It does not begin in the afterlife in heaven as is commonly conceived; it begins and grows in this life—Christ rules to make God known.[24]

ii. Under Christ's rule, all nations are to be discipled and taught to observe all he has commanded.[25]

iii. Under Christ's rule, the work of dominion will be completed.[26]

iv. Under Christ's rule, the earth will be full of the knowledge of the Lord as the waters cover the sea.[27]

---

18. *John 1:1-18.*

19. *Romans 3:21-26.*

20. *John 1:29.*

21. *1 John 1:9; Hebrews 11:6; Ephesians 2:8-9.*

22. *Ephesians 3:19, 4:9-14; John 16:13.*

23. *John 17:3.*

24. *John 17:26.*

25. *Matthew 28:19-20.*

26. *Genesis 1:28; 1 Corinthians 15:25; 2 Corinthians 10:4-5.*

27. *Isaiah 11:9.*

Paper №· 115

———

DOXOLOGICAL CHRISTIANITY

1. *Doxological* Christianity means everything intentionally and ultimately is directed to the praise and glory of God—***Soli Deo Gloria***.

2. The Westminster Confession of the Faith supports *doxological* Christianity.

    i. WCF 1.1: The glory of God is clearly revealed to all men making them inexcusable for unbelief.

    ii. WCF 2.2: God has all glory in and of himself, and manifests his own glory in, by, unto, and upon his creatures.

    iii. WCF 3.3: God's eternal decree is for the manifestation of his glory.

    iv. WCF 4.1: God created to reveal his glory.

    v. WCF 5.1: God's rules to the praise of his glory.

    vi. WCF 6.1: God permitted the Fall for the praise of his glory.

3. To be *doxologically* focused is to be concerned with living our entire life as a living sacrifice to him, wholly consumed by the will of God.[1]

4. To be *doxologically* focused requires us to completely deny our self (self-life), and take up our cross daily and follow Christ.[2]

---

1. *Romans 12:1.*
2. *Matthew 16:24.*

5. To be *doxologically* focused is to be ultimately concerned with holiness, being conformed into the image of Christ,[3] perfecting that holiness in the fear of the Lord,[4] to renew our minds, to know what is pleasing to the Lord,[5] to mediate on the moral law,[6] dying to sin and living to righteousness.[7]

6. To be *doxologically* focused is to be ultimately concerned with the law of God, in all of life, written on the hearts of all men by creation, knowing that obedience leads to his glory, the hallowing of his name in all the earth.[8]

7. To be *doxologically* focused requires whole-hearted diligence in seeking after him. To love him with all our heart, mind, soul, and strength,[9] seeing him as he is, and that he is the rewarder of those who diligently seek him,[10] knowing he is our shield and exceedingly great reward,[11] trusting and acknowledging him in every area of our life,[12] looking to him for our daily bread.[13]

8. To be *doxologically* focused is to seek first and foremost the kingdom of God and his righteousness.[14]

---

3. *Romans 8:29.*

4. *2 Corinthians 7:1.*

5. *Romans 12:1.*

6. *Psalm 1:2.*

7. *1 Peter 2:24.*

8. *Isaiah 11:9; Matthew 6:9.*

9. *Deuteronomy 6:5.*

10. *Hebrews 11:6.*

11. *Genesis 15:1.*

12. *Proverbs 3:5.*

13. *Matthew 6:11.*

14. *Matthew 6:33.*

Paper №· 116

––––––

THE KNOWLEDGE OF GOD
VS. THE HOPE OF HEAVEN

**The hope of heaven is a pretension that has been
set up against the knowledge of God.**

1. Eternal life is not heaven. Eternal life is knowing God.[1]

2. Eternal life is not to be understood in light of heaven. Heaven is to
    be understood in light of eternal life.

3. Heaven is then, not now. Eternal life is now and then.

4. God cannot be seen in heaven. God is to be seen through his works
    of creation and history.

5. Heaven is not God's dwelling place. God dwells in those who love
    and obey Him.

6. Heaven is sought as the escape from natural evil, the curse. Eternal
    life is the removal of moral evil. Seeking heaven rather than eternal
    life reverses God's order.

7. Heaven is based on what is to be seen. Eternal life is based on what
    is to be understood.

––––––––––––

1. Gangadean, *The Westminster Catechisms.* See SCQ. 1 and Appendix 4; Gangadean, *The Westminster Confession.* See Question 25; Gangadean, *Philosophical Foundation*, 171-177, 208-
   211; Gangadean, *History of Philosophy*, 61-64; *Paper No. 6, 42, 106, 115* and *117.*

8. At death, one goes to the intermediate state, not the final state. In the intermediate state, the soul is without body. Those in the intermediate state have not received what has been promised. They, without those on earth seeking dominion, cannot be made complete.

9. It is not obvious that heaven is the place of Christ's resurrected body. Paul, when caught up to the third heaven, did not know if he was in his body or out of his body.

10. The final state is not away from earth nor a return to the Garden of Eden. It is the City of God which is coming down on earth. It is the completion of the cultural mandate through which the earth is filled with the knowledge of God as the waters cover the sea.

Paper №· 117

———

KNOWING AND
MAKING GOD KNOWN

1. We are called to know God and make God known.

2. Man's chief end is to glorify God and to enjoy him forever.[1]

3. We are to glorify God in all that by which he makes himself known.[2]

4. God makes himself known in all his works of creation and providence.[3]

5. We are to actually, intentionally, and increasingly seek to glorify God. Not to do so is the beginning of sin.

6. When they knew God, they glorified him not as God, neither were thankful.[4]

7. The most basic thing that can be said about God, to glorify God, is that God and only God is eternal.

    i. In the beginning God created the heavens and the earth.[5]

———

1. *SCQ. 1.*
2. *SCQ. 101.*
3. *WCF 4.1, 5.1.*
4. *Romans 1:21.*
5. *Genesis 1:1.*

God is without beginning (eternal); all else had a beginning (is temporal); only some (God) is eternal. And what is eternal brought into existence (created) what is not eternal.

ii. God speaks of himself as the one who is, was, and is to come.[6]

iii. God reveals his name as I AM, the self-existing or eternal one.[7]

iv. Since the creation of the world, God's invisible qualities—his eternal power and divine nature—have been clearly seen, being understood from what has been made, so that man is without excuse.[8]

v. The whole earth is full of his glory.[9] The heavens declare the glory of God;[10] they will perish, but you remain.[11]

8. The first and most basic truth to be known and made known in glorifying God is that God, and God alone, is eternal. In general revelation terms, only some is eternal. There are several reasons why we must know and show this:

i. Glorifying God requires us to know and to show (1) that there must be something eternal and (2) that only some is eternal: matter (the material universe—the heavens and the earth) exists and matter is not eternal; the soul (individual self, spirit, mind, consciousness) exists and the soul is not eternal. All things were created by God.

ii. Clarity and inexcusability and taking thoughts captive[12] requires us to know and to show what is clear from general revelation.

iii. Knowing God (eternal life[13]) requires us to know this. We see his infinite justice in understanding what is sin and what is spiritual death, and we see his infinite mercy in understanding how

---

6. *Revelation 1:4, 8; 4:8, 11:17.*

7. *Exodus 3:14.*

8. *Romans 1:20;* Historic Christianity in *WCF 1.1.*

9. *Isaiah 6:3.*

10. *Psalm 19:1.*

11. *Psalm 102:26.*

12. *2 Corinthians 10:4.*

13. *John 17:3.*

we were brought out of sin and death by the work of Christ as our Savior and Lord.

iv. Becoming mature[14] and attaining to the unity of the faith[15] requires us to have the basic truths of the foundation in place.

v. Making disciples of all nations[16] (glorifying God by bearing much fruit that lasts[17]) requires us to know and to show what is clear about God and his law written on the heart of man.

---

14. *Hebrews 6:1.*

15. *Ephesians 4:13.*

16. *Matthew 28:20.*

17. *John 15:8, 16.*

Paper NΩ. 118

_____

ESCHATOLOGY

Based Upon the Doxological Focus

Eschatology is the study of the end or the goal of life. It includes how and when that goal is reached. Understanding the end or the goal of life is basic to all we think and say and do. In general revelation, the goal is called the good; in Scripture, it is called eternal life; in Historic Christianity, it is called man's chief end. In general revelation, the good for man as a rational being is the knowledge of God. In Scripture, eternal life is knowing God.[1] In the Westminster Standards, man's chief end is to glorify God,[2] in all that by which he makes himself known,[3] in all his works of creation and providence.[4] The focus on the knowledge of God in eschatology is called the *doxological focus*.

The following is a brief outline summary of the doctrine of eschatology based upon the doxological focus.

1. Creation: The Sabbath

Man is the image of God. As God's work of creation is self-revelation, man's work of dominion is to attain the knowledge of God's self-revelation. As God completed his work of creation, mankind

_____

1. *John 17:3.*
2. *SCQ. 1.*
3. *SCQ. 101.*
4. *WCF 4.1, 5.1.*

will complete their work of dominion. Observing the Sabbath is a continual and perpetual reminder of man's purpose and hope: the earth shall be full of the knowledge of the Lord as the waters cover the sea.[5]

2. Fall and Redemption: The Curse and the Promise

God permitted the fall of man having purposed to order it to his own glory. The Fall and redemption deepen the revelation of God's glory. Evil as unbelief is allowed to work itself out in world history in every form and degree of admixture with belief. In an age-long and agonizing conflict between good and evil, good eventually prevails. The curse of toil and strife, and old age, sickness, and death is imposed on mankind to restrain, recall from, and remove moral evil. The promised Seed of the woman will crush the head of the Serpent.[6] Christ, in the covenant place of Adam, will undo what Adam did (by dying for our sins) and do, by his reign, what Adam failed to do (fill the earth with image-bearers of God through making disciples of all nations).

3. Abraham: The Father of the Faithful

God permitted sin to reach maximal level before the Flood. He preserved the work of dominion through Noah and deepened the restraint of the curse after the Flood. God further restrained sin at Babel by dividing the people who were united in apostasy. God called Abraham out of Ur of the Chaldees and promised him a city with foundations[7] and that in him all the families of the earth will be blessed. The city with foundations is the kingdom of God, the Church, which extends to all the families of the earth who become children of Abraham and heirs of the promise through faith in Jesus Christ.[8]

---

5. *Genesis 1:26-28, 2:2-3; Exodus 20:8-11; Isaiah 11:9.*

6. *Genesis 3:14-19.*

7. *Hebrews 11:10.*

8. *Galatians 3:29.*

4. The Prophets: From Moses to Malachi

Through the prophets, the promise of God's kingdom was preserved and deepened even as the restraint on apostasy by the curse
was deepened through war, famine, and plague. By types and shadows in the ceremonial worship, by promises and prophecies given
through the prophets, and by God's acts of judgment and restoration, the revelation of the person and work of Christ is deepened.
He is revealed as God's prophet, priest, and king who will accomplish the Lord's purpose on earth.

5. Christ: Fulfillment of the Promise

Christ, by his teaching and ministry of miracles and signs, by his
death and resurrection, by his ascension and session at the right
hand of God, has accomplished redemption and is fulfilling what
was promised. He taught the gradual growth of the kingdom to
its fullness (parable of the mustard seed and yeast);[9] he commanded his disciples to make disciples of all nations; he sent the Holy
Spirit to enable them to do this work; and he promised his presence until the end of the age when the work is completed and he
returns in person.[10]

6. Paul: More Than Conquerors

Paul taught that in and through the age-long and agonizing spiritual war, in the struggle against sin in believers[11] and in the world,
Christ is reigning so that all things work together for the good of
those who love God, so that we are more than conquerors through
him who loved us. In this spiritual war, we are to take captive
every thought raised up against the knowledge of God.[12] In this
war, Christ will reign until all his enemies are put under his feet,

---

9. *Matthew 13:31-34.*

10. *Matthew 28:18-20; 1 Corinthians 12:23-26.*

11. *Romans 7.*

12. *2 Corinthians 10:4-5.*

the last enemy, death, will be destroyed by the resurrection of the dead at his return.[13]

7. John: The Seven Visions of the Book of Revelation

In the Book of Revelation, John is given 7 visions, each of which covers the course of the conflict between Christ's kingdom and the kingdom of darkness, from Christ's ascension and rule at the right hand of God to the consummation of the age. Through the call back of the curse and the proclamation of the gospel, in a spiritual war which is age-long and agonizing, Christ through the Church overthrows Satan's kingdom and establishes the everlasting kingdom of God, the City with foundations, sought by the people of God in all ages.[14]

The focus on the earth being filled with the knowledge of God through the work of dominion (the doxological focus) is opposed to the view that there is a direct (beatific) vision of God in heaven, so that the revelation in creation and providence may be bypassed.

This is based upon:

1. There is no knowledge of God apart from revelation.

2. There is no revelation of God apart from his works of creation and providence. God is a Spirit, immortal and invisible, dwelling in unapproachable light, whom no man has seen or can see.[15]

3. There is no knowledge of creation apart from man's work of dominion by which the powers latent in man and the creation are developed.

The doxological focus is opposed to the view that believers upon death receive full and final blessedness in heaven.

---

13. *1 Corinthians 15:25-26.*

14. *Revelation 21.*

15. *1 Timothy 6:16.*

This is based upon:

1. Those who have died have not received what was promised; they without us are not made complete.[16]

2. Those who have died await the resurrection of their bodies upon the completion of Christ's rule.[17]

3. Those who have died desire and see the earth being filled with the knowledge of God through the rule of Christ.[18]

The doxological focus is opposed to the view that the kingdom of God comes either suddenly or does not come fully.

This is based upon:

1. God permits evil to come to full expression in history and to be removed gradually in order to deepen the revelation of his glory.

2. God's kingdom, expanding to the ends of the earth, began with Christ's rule at the right hand of God. It includes all who are regenerated by his Spirit.

3. God's kingdom grows to its fullness by displacing the kingdom of darkness.

---

16. *Hebrews 11:13, 39-40.*

17. *1 Corinthians 15:25-26.*

18. *Isaiah 11:9.*

Paper Nº· 119

———

PAULINE ESCHATOLOGY

Pauline theology (including his eschatology) is a natural expression of his biblical worldview of creation–fall–redemption.

1. Through conversion, he comes to understand Christ as fulfilling the promises of the Old Testament Scriptures. He is appointed apostle to the gentiles to fulfill the work of Christ.

2. He sees the fullness of God in Christ, who is to fill everything in every way. He sees Christ in the place of Adam who comes to undo what Adam did and to do what Adam failed to do.

3. He sees Christ ruling/seated at the right hand of God, and believers ruling with him, being seated with Christ in the heavenly realm, through which rule every knee shall bow to Christ.

4. He sees the spiritual war is against the world, the flesh, and the devil. He sees the need to take every thought captive raised up against the knowledge of God. He sees Christ will return to raise the dead when all his enemies are subdued to him. He himself has fought the good fight, at every level. In Christ, we are more than conquerors.

5. He sees the good as the knowledge of God in Christ, in whom dwells all the fullness of the Godhead bodily. He counts all previous privileges as worthless by comparison.

6. He sees the sovereignty of God in creation–fall–redemption is for the praise of his glory, including the falling away and the restoration of Israel.

7. He sees the need for the Church to attain the unity of the faith in order to attain to the fullness of Christ.

8. He seeks, with Abraham, and with the saints in every age, the City of God with foundations. He sees the need for foundation to attain maturity, fruitfulness, unity, and fullness. As a wise master-builder, he lays the foundation.

9. He sees our inheritance in the City of God that comes about by activity which is corporate, cumulative, and communal. Those who have gone before us have not yet received the things promised; they, without us, are not made complete.

10. He sees God's discipline connected with the Lord's Supper (the Passover) in Israel (A.D. 70) and in the Church. We are not to divide the body of Christ by false teaching, but proclaim the true meaning of his death in order to disciple all nations, until he comes.

Paper № 120

———

CONTRA VOLUNTARISM

The Will Is Not Independent of the Intellect

INTRODUCTION

1. In the Church, voluntarism is a prevailing epistemological assumption, among others (e.g., literalism, fideism, intuitionism).

2. Voluntarism affirms that the will acts independently of and can be in opposition to the intellect (what one knows/understands).

    i. That we may know the truth and not do it—due to weakness of the will (*akrasia*).[1]

    ii. That we may know the truth and rebel against what we know (knowing the truth and willfully suppressing it).[2]

    iii. That we may knowingly do evil.

    iv. That knowledge is not sufficient for morality.

3. The basis of inexcusability before God:

    i. Voluntarism assumes that if one does not have knowledge (particularly that God exists), one cannot be held responsible.

---

1. *Romans 7:15.* "For what I would, that I do not." Paul expresses here what is sometimes taken as a classic statement of the weakness of the will. This should not be taken so as to negate other passages which speak on the subject.

2. *Romans 1:18* is the classically used text to support suppressionism.

   a. All men know God deep down inside (subjectively).

   b. Inexcusability is a matter of knowledge knowingly suppressed or rejected.

ii. Voluntarism is set in contrast to the view of *culpable ignorance*— sin is fundamentally the failure to seek and understand (know) what is objectively clear about God (and man, and good and evil). Objective clarity is sufficient for responsibility.

   a. The objective revelation of God is never subjectively realized (it fails to "get through") apart from seeking.

   b. Inexcusability is a matter of clear and present truth unacknowledged.

Is the doctrine of voluntarism the truth or is it an error, an uncritically held epistemological assumption, which hinders the knowledge of God and divides the body of Christ?

PART I:
The nature of man is not consistent with voluntarism.

1. Scripture affirms that from the very nature of man as fallen, none understand.

   None is righteous, no, not one; no one understands; no one seeks for God. All have turned aside; together they have become worthless; no one does good, not even one.[3] This is the universal state of mankind ("not even one"). No one understands because no one seeks (culpable ignorance). Seeking leads to understanding, and understanding to doing what is right/good.

2. There is a natural unity and a natural order for unity in each person (in the human personality) between intellect, emotion, and will.

   What we think/believe about the good directs desires/feelings, and together they both move the will. We desire what we believe is the

---

3. *Psalm 14:1-3; Psalm 53:1-3; Romans 3:10-12.*

good and act to achieve what we desire (It is the belief that God rewards those who diligently seek him that leads to seeking him[4]).

3. From Scripture and Historic Christianity, man is created in the image of God, in knowledge, holiness, and righteousness.[5]

Holiness comes through knowledge of the truth—*Sanctify them by the truth: your word is truth.*[6] Knowledge and holiness lead to righteousness. *Then you will know the truth, and the truth will set you free.*[7] Voluntarism assumes that knowing the truth does not set a person free from moral bondage (the power of sin). The process of sanctification takes place throughout one's entire life, even to the point of death, due to unbelief (lack of knowledge), which is covered over by layers of self-deception and self-justification.[8]

4. Man is not divided within this order (intellect, emotion, will).

The apparent conflict/split between the aspects of human personality (intellect vs. will, etc.) is to be explained by inconsistencies and insufficiencies first in one's understanding, and subsequently a split in the desires, and the will (within each aspect)—a split between two whole conflicting orders. It is between knowledge, holiness, and righteousness on the one hand, and unbelief, unholiness, and unrighteousness (the flesh/old man) on the other hand.[9] Man is fallen in all aspects of his heart and likewise needs to be recreated in all aspects. Because we are often aware of the desires/will of the flesh, and not the unbelief of the flesh, we think the opposition is between the desires/will of the flesh and the belief of the regenerate man. The conflict is fundamentally in the intellect, between belief and unbelief. And we hold our beliefs more or less consciously and consistently.

---

4. *Hebrews 11:6*

5. *Ephesians 4:24; Colossians 3:10; SCQ. 10.*

6. *John 17:17.*

7. *John 8:32.*

8. See *Paper No. 14* for the paradigm account of this in *Genesis 3*.

9. *Ephesians 4:22-24; Colossians 3:9-10; 1 Peter 1:14-16; Galatians 5:17.*

PART II:
Christ does not teach voluntarism.

1. Christ prays on the cross: *Father, forgive them; for they know not what they do.*[10]

   The greatest rebellion against God is not attributed to the willful suppression of the truth, but to culpable ignorance. They need to be forgiven particularly for not knowing that which they should have known. Here, this is revelation that is as clear in its compounded sense (the Word of God in general revelation + special revelation + Incarnate) as one could possibly get—Jesus is in their very midst. He does not teach voluntarism regarding sin against himself, but rather culpable ignorance. If this is true of the clearer revelation, all the more it is true of other revelation. This is of critical and central importance because it reflects the mind/attitude of Christ.

2. Christ warns his disciples: *Indeed, the hour is coming when whoever kills you will think he is offering service to God. And they will do these things because they have not known the Father, nor me.*[11]

   We think we are justified when we do what we do. We can think we know when we don't know. We can call evil good, and good evil. They think they are doing God's service (and that this should be done), not that they are against God. When Paul testified before King Agrippa of his former persecution of the Church, he said, *I too was convinced that I ought to do all that was possible to oppose the name of Jesus of Nazareth.*[12] When Jesus was before the Sanhedrin, the high priest rent his garment thinking he was killing a blasphemer.[13] This is culpable ignorance, not willful suppression of what one knows.

3. Christ speaks of unbelievers: *You will be ever hearing but never understanding; you will be ever seeing but never perceiving. For this people's heart has become calloused; they hardly hear with their ears, and they have closed their eyes. Otherwise they might see with their eyes,*

---

10. *Luke 23:34.*
11. *John 16:2-3.*
12. *Acts 26:9.*
13. *Matthew 26:65.*

*hear with their ears, understand with their hearts and turn, and I
would heal them.*[14]

Jesus confronts the sinner as ignorant and unwilling (not seeking)
to know the truths of God. The emphasis of Christ's words reveals
a problem with the cognition of the truth and not a willful rejection of it. They have shut their eyes (of the mind), they have shut
off their reason (not seeking), and so they don't see (understand)
what is clear about God. This is culpable ignorance, not that they
believe and do not believe at the same time.

4. Christ challenges those in authority (leaders/teachers): Two examples: Christ asked 1) whether John's baptism was of God or of
man,[15] and 2) who David's Lord was in Psalm 110.[16]

Jesus' apologetic efforts were consistently aimed at showing where
the assumptions of others were clearly at fault and how they were
responsible for their obstinacy in not seeking and not knowing the
clear truths of God. He knew that the questions he raised would
serve to expose and demolish the uncritically held assumptions of
those in authority, those who were in positions of instruction in the
faith. Many of Christ's debates ended in silence, revealing that the
truth is clear and that sinful man must turn off his mind not to see it.

5. Christ teaches Israel's teacher: *Are you the teacher of Israel, and do
not know these things?*[17]

Nicodemus failed to understand man's need for regeneration. He
didn't know the basics—the foundation of the faith. Without the
foundation, he couldn't understand the teaching of the Word of
God in the Old Testament (he took the sign for the reality in the
case of circumcision) or the Word of God Incarnate (the epistemological assumption of literalism hindered him from understanding
the meaning of "born again"). Both spoke of the same reality—the
need for regeneration. Nicodemus should have known this, but

---

14. *Matthew 13:14-15.*

15. *Matthew 21:23-27.*

16. *Matthew 22:41-46.*

17. *John 3:10.*

overlooked it. This failure (culpable ignorance) is the effect of having not diligently sought out the clear truth of God and cannot be attributed to any type of suppressed knowledge.

6. Christ admonishes and teaches his disciples:

   i. *"How foolish you are, and how slow to believe all that the prophets have spoken! Did not the Messiah have to suffer these things and then enter his glory?" And beginning with Moses and all the Prophets, he explained to them what was said in all the Scriptures concerning himself. . . . They asked each other, "Were not our hearts burning within us while he talked with us on the road and opened the Scriptures to us?"*[18]

   ii. *They were startled and frightened, thinking they saw a ghost. He said to them, "Why are you troubled, and why do doubts rise in your minds? . . . "Everything must be fulfilled that is written about me in the Law of Moses, the Prophets and the Psalms." Then he opened their minds so they could understand the Scriptures.*[19]

The gospels reveal the same psychological effect of regeneration and sanctification time and time again—coming to see the truth of what had not before been understood because of a lack of seeking to know the truth of God. Even in everyday life it is common that when believers come to the Lord, they do so through a process of realizing that their past assumptions and basic beliefs no longer make any sense in the light of God's clear and compelling truth. Furthermore, time and time again we see Christ admonishing his followers for being of dull mind and slow in understanding, but never do we see Christ admonishing them for anything that can be categorized as willful suppression of the truth. Even the disciples who were with him for three years, who he had told a number of times explicitly that he was going to die, did not understand as they should have.

---

18. *Luke 24:27, 32.*

19. *Luke 24:37-38, 44-45.*

7. Christ continually focuses on culpable ignorance:

    i. *If you believed Moses, you would believe me, for he wrote about me. But since you do not believe what he wrote, how are you going to believe what I say?*[20]

    ii. *Then they said to Him, "Where is Your Father?" Jesus answered, "You know neither Me nor My Father. If you had known Me, you would have known My Father also."*[21]

    iii. *". . . for if you do not believe that I am He, you will die in your sins." Then they said to Him, "Who are You?" . . . They did not understand that He spoke to them of the Father.*[22]

    iv. *"If you abide in My word, you are My disciples indeed. And you shall know the truth, and the truth shall make you free." They answered Him, "We are Abraham's descendants, and have never been in bondage to anyone. How can You say, 'You will be made free'?" Jesus answered them, "Most assuredly, I say to you, whoever commits sin is a slave of sin.*[23]

    v. *"Abraham is our father," they answered. "If you were Abraham's children," said Jesus, "then you would do what Abraham did. . . . "The only Father we have is God himself." Jesus said to them, "If God were your Father, you would love me, for I have come here from God. . . . Why is my language not clear to you? Because you are unable to hear what I say. You belong to your father, the devil . . . not holding to the truth, for there is no truth in him. . . . for he is a liar and the father of lies. Yet because I tell the truth, you do not believe me!*[24]

    vi. *My Father, whom you claim as your God, is the one who glorifies me. Though you do not know him, I know him. If I said I did not, I would be a liar like you.*[25]

---

20. *John 5:46-47.*

21. *John 8:19.*

22. *John 8:24-25, 27.*

23. *John 8:32-34.*

24. *John 8:39, 41-45.*

25. *John 8:54-55.*

Time and time again, the gospels reveal a Christ who taught concerning what people *did not* already know or realize, yet *ought* to have. They think they know when they don't. Thinking is presuppositional—the less basic in light of the more basic. They think they know who their father is. If Abraham was their father, then they would understand (have faith) as Abraham did, and rejoice at seeing Christ. If God was their father (if they knew God), then they would know, love, and obey Christ. They would know that he was sent from God. If they understood and believed God's revelation through Moses, then they would understand and believe God's revelation through the person and work of Christ. Because they do not understand the true fundamental nature of sin (as the failure to seek and understand what is clear about God), and therefore how one is saved/set free from sin, they do not see their need for redemption in Christ. They are not able to understand (see/hear) what is clear (what else could our Lord have said to make himself any clearer?) because they are not seeking to know. Instead, they have believed the lie (and the father of lies) in place of the truth (thinking they know the truth). Never do we see Christ appealing to suppressed knowledge, but always to the blindness of unbelief and the unwillingness of sinful man to seek after the clear truth of God.

8. Christ prays in his High Priestly Prayer for all those who would believe:

   i. *Father, the hour has come. Glorify Your Son, that Your Son also may glorify You, as You have given Him authority over all flesh, that He should give eternal life to as many as You have given Him. And this is eternal life, that they may know You, the only true God, and Jesus Christ whom You have sent.*[26]

   ii. *Sanctify them by the truth: your word is truth.*[27]

   iii. *I do not pray for these alone, but also for those who will believe in Me through their word; that they all may be one, as You, Father, are in*

---

26. *John 17:1-3.*

27. *John 17:17.*

Me, and I in You; that they also may be one in Us, that the world may believe that You sent Me.[28]

iv. *O righteous Father! The world has not known You, but I have known You.*[29]

v. *I have made you known to them, and will continue to make you known.*[30]

Christ is praying to his Father just before his arrest and trial, anticipating that he is about to suffer and die. This prayer is a culmination of all his work, leading up to what he is about to accomplish. It is highly focused and its concern is for the glory of God. God is glorified as one knows and makes God known. Christ tells us that eternal life for man is *knowing God*. The world (unbelievers), in spiritual death, does not know the true God. This is the universal sin for which all men are without excuse, and stand in need of salvation. (If all men really know God deep down, do they have saving knowledge deep down?). Believers are sanctified (cleansed of sin) as they grow (mature) in the truth of the knowledge of God, and bear fruit in making God known to others. This requires the Church to respond to challenges (internal and external), demolishing arguments and *every* pretention raised up against the knowledge of God.[31] As the Church is led into *all* truth, through the work of the Holy Spirit,[32] it is brought to *perfect* unity in the faith, in the knowledge of God, to the fullness of Christ.[33] The outcome of glorifying God (unity in knowing and making God known) is that the world will believe—the *earth* shall be *full* of the knowledge of the glory of the Lord as the waters cover the sea.[34] Christ came full of grace (by which forgiveness comes) and truth (by which eternal life, the knowledge of God, comes in fullness).[35]

---

28. *John 17:20-21.*

29. *John 17:25.*

30. *John 17:26.*

31. *2 Corinthians 10:4-5.*

32. *John 16:13.*

33. *Ephesians 4:13.*

34. *Isaiah 11:9; Habakkuk 2:14.*

35. *John 1:14, 17.*

PART III:
Examples of Scripture do not teach voluntarism.

1. Adam and Eve—the original sin.

> The temptation was a time of testing of Adam and was directed at the heart of what Adam understood to be true regarding the nature of God, man, and good and evil. It was designed to reveal: Was he seeking the good, the clear truth of the knowledge of God, or was he seeking to determine the good for himself? The temptation came in the form of an argument (addressed to the intellect) directly contradicting God's command that both Adam and Eve would surely die upon eating. The serpent tactfully insinuated that God is either ignorant or a liar, both of which God *clearly* cannot be. Furthermore, a reason (premise), "for you shall be as God knowing good and evil," was given to support this contradiction (conclusion). Just as it is clear that God is infinite, eternal, and unchangeable in all his attributes (including wisdom and truth), and so cannot be ignorant or a liar, it is clear that man, who is finite, temporal, and changeable, can *never* be as God in knowing good and evil. God, as Creator, determines good and evil. Man, a creature, is to discover good and evil by understanding the nature of things as created by God. Adam and Eve were responsible to know this most basic and clear distinction. But man is changeable in knowledge, holiness, and righteousness. Eve was deceived—she believed the lie and justified her act on the basis of seeking wisdom apart from any reference to God. Adam had turned aside—he had ceased to seek, and therefore did not retain the knowledge of God as the good for himself and for his wife, and instead determined the good by what pleased him. There was unbelief (they had turned aside) before they ate. The outward act of eating of the fruit (unrighteousness) was the manifestation/result of the inward reality of determining good and evil for oneself (unholiness) due to failing to seek and understand what is clear about God (unbelief). Because of the clarity of general revelation, unbelief is inexcusable.

2. Job

Job was said to be the most righteous man in his time. He felt he had integrity, and in his affliction, he questioned God's justice. He had gone further than all others, but had failed to continue as he should have. He was blameless, but not sinless. When questioned by God, Job's sin was revealed—he found that he came short in his seeking and understanding God's revelation of himself in his works. There was a culpable lack of knowledge. *You asked, 'Who is this who hides counsel without knowledge?' Therefore I have uttered what I did not understand . . . I have heard of You by the hearing of the ear, But now my eye sees You.*[36] Job came to see what he had not seen before. He then felt self-abhorrent, and humbled himself, and repented in dust and ashes. Subjective sincerity is not objective integrity. God wanted Job to be holy, without which no one will see the Lord.[37]

3. David

Did David knowingly do evil when he committed adultery with Bathsheba? David's adultery arose in the context of not pursuing the good in his call as king to engage in war: *At the time when kings go off to war . . . David remained in Jerusalem. . . . and walked around on the roof of the palace.*[38] David, as the warrior king of the Lord's army, should have continued giving himself to diligently seeking the knowledge of God through leading the advancement of God's kingdom. To heighten this, Uriah, in contrast to David, would not go in to be with his own wife while the soldiers were in battle. He acted in faith with integrity, keeping his eyes on the good—a reproof to David (and from a Hittite). David had turned aside, lost sight of the goal/hope (the glory of God), and turned his eyes to covet Bathsheba (the enchanted life vs. the crucified life). Man is changeable. If he doesn't continue growing, even what he has can be lost. Perhaps because of his many successes (God had abundantly blessed him), David was taking it easy, became restless and discontent, and needed to fill the emptiness in his life (vs. finding his

---

36. *Job 42:1-6.*
37. *Hebrews 12:14.*
38. *2 Samuel 11:1-2.*

enjoyment in glorifying God). This is not to say that David didn't know, in some sense, that adultery was wrong (he tried to cover it up, ultimately having Uriah killed), and should have even on that basis not committed adultery. But his failure to withstand the temptation was *fundamentally* due to a lack in seeking the knowledge of God as the good. To know what is right and do what is wrong is not the same as to know what is good and do what is wrong. The right/duty (virtue) is a means to the good and is justified in relation to the good. David's justification for the right could not stand up under pressure. When David repented, he prayed, *Behold, You desire truth in the inward parts, And in the hidden part You will make me to know wisdom. . . . Wash me, and I shall be whiter than snow. . . . Then I will teach transgressors Your ways, And sinners shall be converted to You.*[39] God revealed to David the hidden power of sin that remained in him so that he might be sanctified. David recognized his need to be forgiven and cleansed[40] of this root sin (of failing to know God) by learning truth in his inmost being. (The best of men—a man after God's own heart—have root sin remaining.) And out of his inmost being would flow rivers of living water—glorifying God in making this truth known.

4. Peter

Peter had received revelation from God about the identity of the Messiah and confessed, *You are the Christ, the Son of the living God.* And Jesus pronounced a blessing on him. *Blessed are you, Simon Bar-Jonah, for flesh and blood has not revealed this to you, but My Father who is in heaven.*[41] Just after this confession, Jesus then tells his disciples that he is going up to Jerusalem to die, and Peter takes him aside, attempting to correct him. *"Far be it from You, Lord; this shall not happen to You!" But He turned and said to Peter, "Get behind Me, Satan! You are an offense to Me, for you are not mindful of the things of God, but the things of men."*[42] Though clearly regenerate, Peter insisted that Jesus as Messiah could not be made to

---

39. *Psalm 51:6-7, 13.*

40. *1 John 1:9.*

41. *Matthew 16:16-17.*

42. *Matthew 16:22-23.*

suffer. Peter's attempted suppression of the truth of Christ's mission stemmed from a false assumption that was born of *not seeking* what God had *clearly revealed* of his redemptive plan in Scripture. Shall we assume that Peter was rebelliously suppressing an innate understanding that the Messiah had to suffer, or shall we instead assume that Peter wrongly believed that the atonement for sin would come without the shedding of the Messiah's blood? Jesus openly rebuked a lack of understanding in Peter—the Messiah must die to undo what Adam did. Peter had a worldly view of the Messiah (expecting Christ to bring a physical kingdom) mixed in with the true revelation of who Christ was. Belief mixed with unbelief. This split occurring in the understanding is further manifested in the dramatic example of Peter's denial of Christ. When Jesus was arrested and taken into trial, Peter's world(view) fell apart due to this hidden contradiction in his understanding, which he soon realized, and he was later willing to die for the one he had earlier denied. It was not due to *akrasia*, a weakness of the will, nor was his denial due to any supposed conflict between thought and feeling.

5. Paul

Concerning his own life in sinful unbelief, we have the words of Paul himself: *though formerly I was a blasphemer, persecutor, and insolent opponent. But I received mercy because I had acted ignorantly in unbelief.*[43] Paul, someone no longer suppressing the truth, recognizes having acted out of lack of knowledge. Clearly, ignorance is a matter of not knowing what is true—not a matter of suppressing what is true. One who knowingly suppresses the truth cannot also be suppressing the truth ignorantly. Some might say that Paul knew general revelation, but not special revelation. Regardless, it is relevant in that what Paul did was due to a lack of understanding. And with respect to general revelation, Paul had a misconception (unbelief) in his mind regarding the infinite justice of God. He sought to establish his own righteousness by obedience to the law—even as he spoke about the Jews, who acted out of zeal *without knowledge* and were *ignorant* of God's righteousness.[44] So, Paul's example (I acted

---

43. *1 Timothy 1:13.*

44. *Romans 10:2-3.*

ignorantly in unbelief) can be used as a paradigm for all who persecuted the Church at that time. Additionally, when Paul was called
to repentance directly by Christ, Christ identifies Paul's persecution of the Church as sin against himself. *"Saul, Saul, why are you
persecuting Me?" And he said, "Who are You, Lord?" Then the Lord
said, "I am Jesus, whom you are persecuting."*[45] This further clarifies
that voluntarism is not taught regarding sin against Christ himself.

6. Moses

Moses and Aaron rebelled against God.[46] This need not be interpreted by saying that rebellion is deliberately acting against what
one knows. One's motivation for action may change according to
circumstances. There may be an exasperation or provoking or a fear
(a change), but not knowledge one deliberately rebels against. There
may be unbelief or a false belief taking prominence under strenu-
ous circumstances where one is pressed to their limits. One's un-
derstanding/belief is revealed through trials of faith. *Because you did
not believe Me, to hallow Me . . .*

7. Pharaoh

Pharaoh hardened his heart. God's increasing revelation came to
Pharaoh and he had to increasingly harden his heart in response—
resisting (stopping) the revelation from coming in. He is emblemat-
ic of the human heart in its fallen condition, showing the depth in
unbelief one may go to neglect, avoid, resist, and deny the knowledge of God (especially his mercy revealed in the curse—death of
firstborn, drowning in the sea). God appointed Pharaoh for the
very purpose of making his glory known, while Pharaoh remained
in darkness of unbelief—he did not know and acknowledge God
as he should.

8. Israel at Kadesh Barnea

At Kadesh Barnea, *the* classic case of rebellion of God's people occurs. The whole community is involved and as a result, God caused

---

45. *Acts 9:4-5.*

46. *Numbers 20:11-12, 24.*

that generation to wander and die in the wilderness. Was this a case of knowing and not doing? Ten spies came back with a bad/false report that Israel was far inferior to their enemy, which caused fear to spread among the people who falsely believed that they would die.[47] This is not a high-handed rebellion, but one that arose from unbelief and a lack of faith. This is culpable ignorance. Instead of remembering and taking to heart what God had done in delivering them out of the power of Egypt and seeing his works/provision day after day, they disregarded it and treated God with contempt, not believing in or trusting him.[48] They lightly and thoughtlessly regarded that by which God makes himself known. They saw what he did, but did not know who he was.[49] It wasn't that they knew they could go in and take the land, but that they failed to know God (in contrast is the faith of Joshua and Caleb). The continued willful rebellion of the people in the wilderness was a result of their unbelief.[50]

9. Korah's Rebellion

In Korah's rebellion, men of renown in the congregation of Israel rose up against Moses and Aaron, God's appointed authority over the people. This was warned against explicitly. And yet, they deliberately did it. Did they believe that Moses and Aaron were the only ones chosen by God to lead the people? This is precisely what they did not believe (their unbelief). *You take too much upon yourselves, for all the congregation is holy, every one of them, and the Lord is among them. Why then do you exalt yourselves above the assembly of the Lord?*[51] In light of the objective clarity of the cumulative revelation of God's glory, the people murmur and complain, object to God's order of authority, and take the name of God in vain, bringing God's judgment. They sought to arrogate to themselves God's authority in pride, presumption, arrogance, and contumacious behavior. They thought they knew better than the authority (God, and Moses and Aaron) when they did not know—culpable ignorance.

---

47. *Numbers 13:31-33; 14:1-9.*

48. *Numbers 14:11*

49. *Psalm 95:9-10.*

50. *Psalm 78:7-8, 11, 17-22, 32, 40-42; Hebrews 3:12-19; 4:2.*

51. *Numbers 16:3.*

They came judging instead of examining their uncritically held, self-refuting assumption. They judged the authority chosen by God to rule in God's house. And they despised chastening. To put an end to this, Aaron's rod, along with the others, was placed before the tabernacle to testify to the truth. As a permanent witness for the people of God, Aaron's rod that budded, blossomed, and brought forth fruit was placed in the Ark of the Testimony.[52] The disregard (not seeking and not understanding) of what is clear about God and his Word led to Korah's rebellion and death. In contrast, resurrection life (Aaron's rod) comes through (knowing) the Word of God.

10. Jonah

Jonah ran away from the Lord's call to preach to Nineveh. Was there any lack of knowledge in Jonah? It seems that God told him what to do and he simply did not do it—he knew and he rebelled against God. After finally heeding God's call and seeing God's mercy to Nineveh, Jonah said in anger, *Isn't this what I said, Lord, when I was still at home? That is what I tried to forestall by fleeing to Tarshish. I knew that you are a gracious and compassionate God . . .*[53] God questioned his anger. Jonah was then angry concerning the plant that came up overnight and then perished, which God provided for Jonah's comfort. God again questioned his anger. Why was Jonah angry and why did he want to die? He wanted the Lord to bring justice on (destroying) the Ninevites (vs. mercy) because, by implication, in sparing them they would eventually destroy Israel (as God's instrument). Jonah came up short (a lack) in understanding the greatness of God's graciousness and compassion. He was concerned for temporal blessing—Israel's well-being in not being physically destroyed. He was concerned about Israel's outward enemy (Assyria) being cut off over and against the inward enemy of sin being destroyed (the destruction of Israel outwardly = the preservation of Israel inwardly).[54] He was concerned about his own creature comfort (pictured with the plant)—looking into the future, he didn't want to face trouble/stressful conditions (like

---

52. *Numbers 17:10.*

53. *Jonah 4:2.*

54. *Amos 9:11-15; Hosea 2:14-23; 3:4-5.*

Elijah). Jonah didn't deserve mercy in deliverance from his disobedience. He also didn't deserve the plant, just as Nineveh didn't deserve mercy. But Jonah was concerned about the plant and not Nineveh, yet God created them both—which is greater? So, Jonah needed to be pushed to see God's graciousness and redemptive/resurrection power (the sign of Jonah) in a greater way.

11. The devil and the demons

The devil and the demons make professions of belief. Do they know and not do? They may not deny the existence of God per se, but they deny the nature of God. 1) When Satan challenged God in relation to Job, Satan failed to understand and believe in the sovereignty of God and the perseverance of the saints. He misunderstood the goodness of God and the love of man toward God—does man only love God for what God gives him? This is precisely the point that is settled in the book of Job once and for all, silencing Satan, and deepening the revelation of the glory of God for all to see. 2) When Satan worked to bring about the destruction of Christ, did he know and understand the Scripture, that this would be the fulfillment of prophecy (advancing the kingdom of God and destroying the works of the devil)? 3) When the devil (as the power behind the king of Babylon) said in his heart, *I will ascend into heaven, I will exalt my throne above the stars of God; I will also sit on the mount of the congregation . . . I will be like the Most High,*[55] he blurred the distinction between himself (a finite creature) and God. 4) Likewise, when the devil said in the Garden of Eden, *you shall be as God knowing good and evil*, did he fail to understand this radical and basic distinction between the infinite, eternal, and unchangeable and the finite, temporal, and changeable? 5) When the demons profess that Jesus is the Son of God, clearly they believe that he exists and that he is very powerful, but do they believe that he is omnipotent? Do they believe that God is infinite, eternal, and unchanging in all his attributes and that they are finite creatures? 6) In the book of James it says, *You believe that there is one God. Good! Even the demons believe that—and shudder.*[56]

---

55. *Isaiah 14:12-14.*

56. *James 2:19.*

First, the context in which this passage is given speaks about faith without works/deeds being dead. This dead faith is one claiming (merely professing) to believe, not that they actually believe. It is saying and not doing. It is not a split between the intellect and will. Our faith/understanding is shown by our deeds. True genuine faith will result in actual appropriate deeds—faith and deeds working together.[57] This is opposed to antinomianism (mere profession without deeds) and legalism (mere deeds without understanding). Second, for one to claim they believe God is one is not the whole system of theology—there is much more to the nature and purpose of God. The meaning of what is claimed is not clear—it is ambiguous whether there is genuine belief. Mere profession is not enough, even if it evokes a certain emotion (trembling). The devil and the demons may know much about the being of God, but do not understand him as he truly is.

12. King Agrippa

When Paul testified before King Agrippa concerning Christ he said, *I am saying nothing beyond what the prophets and Moses said would happen . . . do you believe the prophets? I know you do.*[58] What is Paul saying here—in what sense does Agrippa believe? Does he genuinely believe with understanding (know) so that the inference should follow—he should believe what Paul said? (As when Jesus said, *If you had believed Moses, you would have believed me.*) Was this spoken in a context of courtesy, the way Paul spoke to the Athenians, quoting some of their own poets and appealing to what they should know, or claim or profess to know (appealing to their better knowledge)? Agrippa did not believe what Paul said. *Do you think that in such a short time you can persuade me to be a Christian?* He was not persuaded. It is not that he knew and did not believe.

---

57. *James 2:22.*

58. *Acts 26:22-28.*

PART IV:
Other passages of Scripture do not teach voluntarism.

1. *And now, brothers, I know that you acted in ignorance, as did also your rulers. But what God foretold by the mouth of all the prophets, that his Christ would suffer, he thus fulfilled.*[59]

   In light of the people's amazement at the miracle of the lame beggar, Peter called them to repent and understand that this was done by faith in the name of Jesus, God's servant, whom they crucified. And Peter emphasized that this sin against Christ (the ultimate manifestation/fruit of sin) arose from a lack of knowledge (root sin)—culpable ignorance. They had killed the very Author and giver of life, in whom was life and that life was the light of men[60]—the Word of God in man as reason, making us the image of God. We would never crucify the Word of God incarnate without first crucifying the Word of God in us (shutting our eyes—not seeking or understanding). But God used this very sin of ignorance and resultant rejection and killing of Christ to fulfill what was foretold through all the prophets. Furthermore, Peter emphasized that the leaders of the people were guilty of this sin also. It is not only the Romans who were ignorant (as some have said concerning Christ's prayer, *Father, forgive them; for they know not what they do.*).

2. *For since, in the wisdom of God, the world through wisdom did not know God, it pleased God through the foolishness of the message preached to save those who believe.*[61]

   None of the rulers of this age knew; for had they known, they would not have crucified the Lord of glory.[62]

   But the natural man does not receive the things of the Spirit of God, for they are foolishness to him; nor can he know them, because they are spiritually discerned.[63]

---

59. *Acts 3:17.*
60. *John 1:4.*
61. *1 Corinthians 1:21.*
62. *1 Corinthians 2:8.*
63. *1 Corinthians 2:14.*

Paul, warning believers who are divided because of worldliness in their thinking, distinguished between the wisdom of the Word of God in contrast to the wisdom of the world. What is foolishness to those in unbelief is such because they have not understood it, and they have not understood it because they have not sought the clear truths of God. Unbelieving man in spiritual death is unwilling and therefore unable to know God. The word of the cross is folly to those who are perishing, but to us who are being saved it is the power of God. Those who do not see their sin of not seeking and understanding what is clear about God, and the spiritual death inherent in this, do not and cannot understand the meaning of the cross (Christ and him crucified). Therefore, it is foolishness to them and their lives are not transformed by the power of this understanding. There is an inseparable connection between knowing and doing. If the rulers of that age had understood the wisdom of God, they would not have sinned against Christ, crucifying the Lord of glory. By the working of the Spirit, the light of the Word of God in us is restored, regenerating and illumining our minds to see and understand the knowledge of God.

3. *And do not be conformed to this world, but be transformed by the renewing of your mind, that you may prove what is that good and acceptable and perfect will of God.*[64]

Man is transformed by the renewing of his mind. There is a change in cognitive content, not merely a supernatural change in attitude apart from content. It is in understanding God's mercy (explained in Romans 1–11) that men are to devote themselves to God and to do his will in all things.[65] Knowledge leads to holiness and righteousness.

4. *And even if our gospel is veiled, it is veiled to those who are perishing. The god of this age has blinded the minds of unbelievers, so they cannot see the light of the gospel of the glory of Christ, who is the image of God.*[66]

---

64. *Romans 12:2.*

65. *Romans 12:1-2.*

66. *2 Corinthians 4:3-4.*

Though believers can come to see the error of their uncritically held assumptions (such as Peter), unbelievers are forever unwilling to seek after and acknowledge the clear truth of God (the same sentiment as mentioned in 4.2 above and 4.5 below). We see an example of Paul's above emphasis nowhere better than with the teachers of the Law. These individuals were operating from age-old assumptions about the nature of the Messiah that ran in direct contrast with the life and teachings of Christ. Their problem was that *in light of* their own entrenched assumptions they would not and could not see the truth and consistency of Christ's claims. They hated Christ not because they knew he spoke the truth and could not stomach it, but because what he preached did not align with their beliefs (Messianic and otherwise) and also because he brilliantly exposed their illegitimate authority. We should expect the spiritually blind to be unwilling to seek after and understand spiritual truths—resorting instead to blind authoritarianism and militant self-justification.

5. *They know nothing, they understand nothing; their eyes are plastered over so they cannot see, and their minds closed so they cannot understand. No one stops to think, no one has the knowledge or understanding . . . he cannot save himself, or say, "Is not this thing in my right hand a lie?"*[67]

Clearly, this passage is best interpreted to mean that God's objective revelation is not subjectively realized by the one in unbelief. He instead unknowingly holds to a lie (an idol—a misconception of the knowledge of God).

6. *Assemble yourselves and come; draw near together, you survivors of the nations! They have no knowledge who carry about their wooden idols, and keep on praying to a god that cannot save.*[68]

Every man is stupid and without knowledge; every goldsmith is put to shame by his idols, for his images are false, and there is no breath in them.[69]

---

67. *Isaiah 44:18-20.*

68. *Isaiah 45:20.*

69. *Jeremiah 10:14.*

7. *Hear, O heavens, and give ear, O earth; for the Lord has spoken: "Children have I reared and brought up, but they have rebelled against me. The ox knows its owner, and the donkey its master's crib, but Israel does not know, my people do not understand." Ah, sinful nation, a people laden with iniquity, offspring of evildoers, children who deal corruptly! They have forsaken the Lord, they have despised the Holy One of Israel, they are utterly estranged.*[70]

God called witness to the spiritual condition, the sin of his people. His children, raised in the Lord's house, turned away in deliberate, willful, resistant rebellion (the enormity/extent of sin). This is due to their failure to understand/know God (the root/essence of sin).

8. Ezekiel states 70+ times: *And they shall know that I am the Lord*

As a prophet of the captivity, this repetition from Ezekiel assumes and emphasizes this lack of knowledge in the people during this period. God brought affliction on them for this reason. He rules to make himself known in judgment that his people might come to know him in blessing.

9. *My people are destroyed for lack of knowledge; because you have rejected knowledge, I reject you from being a priest to me. And since you have forgotten the law of your God, I also will forget your children. . . . they exchanged their glorious God for something disgraceful.*[71]

A formal charge of adultery was brought by God against his people. In the spirit of prostitution (worldliness/idolatry), the people sought satisfaction in the creation vs. the Creator, satisfaction in the gift vs. the giver, and protection and provision apart from their provider/husband (God). There was no faithfulness or steadfast love in the land, which manifested in various forms of corruption and violence, bringing destruction and judgment. It is pointedly identified that this was because there was no knowledge of God in the land. And there was no knowledge because the priests who were to teach and hold the people accountable had rejected and forgotten the Word of God. They had exchanged the truth about God for a

---

70. *Isaiah 1:2-4.*

71. *Hosea 4:1-7.*

lie.[72] The judgment declared: the spirit of prostitution was in their heart, rooted in not knowing God.[73]

10. *So you are ignorant of the very thing you worship—and this is what I am going to proclaim to you. The God who made the world and everything in it is the Lord of heaven and earth and does not live in temples built by human hands. And he is not served by human hands, as if he needed anything. . . . we should not think that the divine being is like gold or silver or stone—an image made by human design and skill. In the past God overlooked such ignorance, but now he commands all people everywhere to repent.*[74]

Paul, distressed by the glory given to idolatry in Athens, reasoned with the philosophers from general revelation addressing their uncritically held assumptions. He did not assume they already knew God deep down, but rather sought to make known the true God who was unknown to them—of whom they were culpably ignorant. They held to polytheism intermingled with dualism. They thought of God as finite, being served by human hands.

11. *For what I would, that I do not.*[75]

Paul expresses here what is sometimes taken as a classic statement of the weakness of the will (*akrasia*). The person wants to do what they believe is good and fails to do it. As initially addressed in 1.4 above, there is not a split between intellect, desires, and will in the nature of man, but rather a split between two whole conflicting orders. There is an irreconcilable war between good and evil, between the old sinful nature, which remains in us after becoming believers, and the new nature we have in Christ, which makes us desire to do the will of God.[76] This is a spiritual war, which goes on fundamentally in the mind of a believer, between belief and unbelief. We may know/believe a truth in the sense of having a mere minimal assent, but do not draw out implications about this

---

72. *Romans 1:23, 25, 28.*

73. *Hosea 5:4.*

74. *Acts 17:23-25, 29-30.*

75. *Romans 7:15.*

76. *Ephesians 4:22-24; Colossians 3:9-10; 1 Peter 1:14-16; Galatians 5:17.*

truth that we should. We may wrestle with a problem at the level of knowing we should or should not do something, but not get to the deeper, underlying, relevant cause connected to knowing who God is (or in the measure that we should know). It is this greater knowledge of God that is sanctifying, transforming, and sets us free. Repentance is needed at this deeper level of failing to know what we should. Thus, the *akrasia* view about the weakness of the will is really a weakness of understanding.

12. *Formerly, when you did not know God, you were enslaved to those that by nature are not gods. But now that you have come to know God, or rather to be known by God, how can you turn back again to the weak and worthless elementary principles of the world, whose slaves you want to be once more?*[77]

Paul affirms that the Galatians, formerly as unbelievers, did not know God. Instead, or in place of knowing the true God, they were subject/enslaved to false gods (unbelief). He speaks of this as being enslaved to the elementary principles of the world (*stoicheia*)[78] in the analogy of being like a child who is under rules and regulations (guardians and managers) before the appointed time of receiving their inheritance. These are the first principles of unbelief in the world (all false worldviews)—seeking life/salvation/justification under these principles. But these Galatians have come to know God and salvation in Christ, and are no longer a slave to these principles, but a son, and as a son, an heir of the inheritance of the kingdom of God. Yet now, they are turning from Christ by seeking to be justified by observing the Law. Is it while now knowing God, they are willfully turning away? Paul compares their turning to the observance of the Law (keeping special days) to be justified as if this were the same thing as going back to being enslaved to the false gods. It is the same in essence. They are turning back (backsliding) to meaningless (emptied of meaning)/worthless principles. Out of this unbelief comes their observances. If they understood the meaning of the Law/historical observances (vs. emptying them of meaning), then they would know that these

---

77. *Galatians 4:8-9.*

78. *Galatians 4:3.*

were a guardian, a tutor, bringing them to Christ—to be justified by faith (not by observing the Law).[79] They were types and shadows pointing ahead to the reality in Christ—when the fullness of time had come, they would receive the inheritance. In God's redemptive purpose, believers are called to come to full maturity in Christ—from being a child (immature) to the fullness (mature) of the inheritance in the knowledge of God (the City of God). The foundational, elementary, first principles of faith (in the City of God) must displace the first principles (*stoicheia*) of unbelief in the world (in the City of Man).[80] Foundation is necessary for maturity, fruitfulness, unity, and fullness.[81]

PART V:
Romans 1 does not teach voluntarism.

The classical passage used in support of voluntarism is Romans 1:18-21. The above analysis concerning the nature and condition of man, the words and teaching of Christ, and the various relevant examples and passages of Scripture—that men are without excuse for not understanding and believing in what God has clearly revealed of himself—should be kept in mind when coming to and uncovering the meaning of this passage.

1. Objective clarity does not imply subjective clarity.

   This passage is teaching that there is a revelation of God that is objectively clear (general revelation). Whether human beings know it clearly and suppress it is another matter. We need not uncritically assume that objective clarity implies subjective clarity. "Is plain to them" and "clearly seen" need not be interpreted as actually seen, but can rather be interpreted as being clearly revealed, objectively, or that it is easily knowable by all (it is intelligible). A robust Reformed apologetic must never be willing to grant too much to the unregenerate mind in terms of what it knows to be true of God.

---

79. *Galatians 3:24.*

80. *Colossians 2:8, 20; 2 Peter 3:10, 12; Galatians 4:3, 9; Hebrews 5:12; 6:1.*

81. *Hebrews 6:1-2; Ephesians 4:11-13.*

If it is the case that the unregenerate mind does not seek and does not understand God's revelation,[82] why ought we to insist that they know the truth of God? After all, the Holy Spirit not only regenerates our deadened minds so that we may confess belief in Christ, he also must first work in opening our minds to seek and understand what we before did not comprehend about the truths of the Spirit, as Paul speaks about in 1 Corinthians.

Likewise, subjective clarity does not imply objective clarity. We may feel so certain about and really believe something, yet it may not be true objectively. Many rely on intuition, which fails to see that this is not a morally ideal world, and assume that if something is subjectively clear, then it is objectively clear.

2. Suppressing the truth does not imply that one knows it as truth.

We need not assume here that unbelievers suppress the truth while at the same time knowing it, but instead, suppress and hinder the truth of God principally by the mountain of lies and falsehood they concoct out of their darkened and ignorant minds (culpable ignorance). Paul's emphasis is to set up the idea that the truth of God, *both* specially and generally revealed, has been systematically suppressed, hindered, and held down by false assumptions and lies. This can be seen from the many examples given above. Paul persecuted the Church and was suppressing the truth by his unrighteousness (his wicked deeds), but acknowledged that this was done ignorantly in unbelief.[83] This came out in a whole way of life—from unbelief to unholiness (zeal without knowledge)[84] to unrighteousness. The root of sin is the *inexcusability of unbelief*. Paul is teaching that all men are inexcusable for 1) failing to know/believe what is clearly revealed about God, and 2) in place of believing in God, they believe what is false, using this unbelief/falsehood to suppress the truth of God. They do so by seeking to justify their unbelief, by giving reasons against the truth and in support of their falsehood. But they are without excuse (*anapologia*—without a reason)—they can

---

82. *Romans 3:10-11.*

83. *1 Timothy 1:13.*

84. *Philippians 3:6; Galatians 1:13-14.*

and should see that their unbelief is clearly incoherent and false, collapsing under critical analysis. Ultimately, in order to hold on to their unbelief, they try to suppress the Word of God (in man, as light[85])—they neglect, avoid, resist, or deny reason in the face of what is clear (shut their eyes rather than give up their contradiction). Yet reason in man is ineradicable and irresistible.[86]

Likewise, believers, insofar as they have sin remaining in them, suppress the truth by their root ignorance and unbelief. Growing in knowledge/belief of the truth suppresses the remaining unbelief in the believer. In this psychological state, we may not understand our own experience—we may think we know our own hearts, when we don't.

3. This passage teaches that the *content* of what is clear in general revelation is a full (vs. bare) revelation of the knowledge God.

Paul teaches that since the beginning of history up until the present day, God's invisible qualities—namely, *his eternal power* and *divine nature*—have been manifested to all persons. Additionally, in the next chapter, he tells us that all are accountable for knowing *the law of God* as it is written on the hearts of all men (structured into their very being). The existence (eternal power), nature (God is a Spirit, infinite, eternal, and unchangeable, in his being, wisdom, power, holiness, justice, goodness, and truth[87]), and law of God is a full general revelation of the knowledge of God. The whole earth is full of his glory.[88] None can escape the revelation.[89] There is no speech or language where their voice is not heard. Nothing is hidden from the heat of the sun.

If everyone knows God deep down, then the content of everyone's belief should be the same as what is taught here—especially in those who claim to no longer be suppressing the truth. The account from

---

85. *John 1:4.*

86. *John 1:5.*

87. *SCQ. 4.*

88. *Isaiah 6:3.*

89. *Psalm 19.* Here, David highlights both creation and the moral law connected to the content of the knowledge of God.

those who hold to a voluntaristic view of *sensus divinitatis* is varied (they do not agree) and generally bare.[90] Anything less than what this passage details (the full revelation) is too bare a knowledge to satisfy inexcusability. Appealing to the worship of sticks and stones does not show they know God, but rather that they *do not* know God—they worship an idol (a false view of God). This is the same for those who worshipped the sun in the civilizations of the past (it is not eternal—it is finite in size, giving off heat, therefore will burn out) and those who worshipped a higher power, like Zeus (a higher power is not the highest power—the eternal power, nor is Zeus infinite and unchangeable). The formal aspect of human nature (a sense that something ought to be worshipped) is not the specific content (the true knowledge of God). This view of *sensus divinitatis* leaves these beliefs as excusable, and therefore provides no basis for sin, and therefore no need for redemption through Christ and him crucified. This is precisely what Paul is seeking to establish in this chapter—man's need for redemption, understood in light of his condition in sin and spiritual death (under the wrath of God).

An alternative view of *sensus divinitatis*, which is not in conflict with Romans 1, is that men have inscribed within their heart the concepts (of the qualities of infinite, eternal, and unchangeable) which apply to God—they are inescapably in all who think. We have and apply these concepts (along with finite, temporal, and changeable) to beings we think about (a being is either finite or infinite, temporal or eternal, etc.). So, by nature, we think the true God either exists or does not exist.

4. This passage teaches that the *means* (by which we understand) and the *source* of the knowledge of God is by inference/mediate knowledge from the creation (vs. intuition/immediate knowledge).

90. John Calvin, *The Institutes of the Christian Religion*, trans. and ed. Ford Lewis Battles (Grand Rapids, MI: W.B. Eerdmans, 1987), Book 1, Chapter 3; Charles Hodge, *Systematic Theology* (Peabody, MA: Hendrickson Publishers, 1999), Volume 1, 191-195; Cornelius Van Til, *The Defense of the Faith* (Phillipsburg, NJ: P&R Publishing, 1967); Alvin Plantinga, *Warranted Christian Belief* (Oxford: Oxford University Press, 2000); K. Scott Oliphant, *Reasons for Faith: Philosophy in the Service of Theology* (Phillipsburg, NJ: P&R Publishing, 2006), 134.

Those who hold to a voluntaristic view of *sensus divinitatis* say the knowledge of God is intuitively/immediately known (that it spontaneously "gets through"). Yet the Scripture here says, *being understood from what has been made.* This emphasizes that it is mediated through and understood from the creation (as the source). The knowledge of God is through knowledge of God's self-revelation (*God has made it plain*) in the creation (which unfolds in providence/history). The act of a being necessarily reveals the nature of that being. God's act of creation reveals the existence and nature of God the Creator. What is objectively revealed in the creation[91] can become subjectively known[92] if we engage our minds (seek) to understand the meaning of that revelation as structured in the nature of things created. The knowledge of the creation is through the work of dominion, given to man in the Garden.[93] Dominion requires naming (grasping the nature of) all beings in all their parts and relations, and developing this nature/essence, the excellence/glory in all beings, so as to make known the glory of God. Understanding is more than grasping a concept or holding a judgment/belief. Understanding requires an argument or inference (a reason for the hope/belief in you[94]—how do you know it's true?). One may believe something subjectively, but may not be justified in holding that belief. Understanding or knowledge in this sense is justified true belief—it requires objective proof (evidence), known by reason and inference/argument. It is the substance of things hoped for, the evidence (underlying support) of the invisible.[95] Faith is understanding (vs. fideism). It is understanding that the world was framed by the Word of God, so that the things which are seen (creation) were not made of things which are visible.[96] It is understanding that God exists and that he is the rewarder of those that diligently seek him.[97] Understanding is by seeking, through the use of reason (the Word of God

---

91. *Isaiah 6:3; Psalm 19.*

92. *Isaiah 11:9; Habakkuk 2:14.*

93. *Genesis 1:28.*

94. *1 Peter 3:15.*

95. *Hebrews 11:1.*

96. *Hebrews 11:3.*

97. *Hebrews 11:6.*

in man). Being made in the image of God as rational beings does not necessitate *actual* knowledge, but entails the *capacity to understand* God's revelation. Men are inexcusable for not seeking and therefore not understanding this revelation.[98] Objective clarity is *sufficient* for responsibility.

If the knowledge of God is by an intuitively/immediately held belief, when arguments (rational defeaters/claims) are raised against this belief, which should one follow? It is not self-evident that intuition must override reason. Moreover, the deliverances of intuition can and must be interpreted.

5. If one claims to have knowledge, one should show this knowledge.

First, if the truth (the knowledge of God) is clear and known by you (especially if you are no longer suppressing the truth), can you show it (give a reason for the hope that is in you)? One should use the *means*/demonstrate (by inference/argument) the *content* (the full revelation) of the knowledge of God from the *source* (creation). This is consistent with a faithful interpretation of Romans 1. One should be able to argue for the infinite, eternal, and unchangeable, being, wisdom, power, holiness, justice, goodness, and truth of God from general revelation (not special revelation). One should be able to show the moral law of God written on the hearts of all men—minimally deriving the content of the Ten Commandments/moral laws from human nature (not special revelation).

Second, all the more so, if the Christian is calling others to repentance and the need for redemption in Christ, not only should they be able to demonstrate the above, but they should be able show the inexcusability of unbelief. To merely affirm that "everyone deep down knows God and is suppressing it" does not show clarity by showing the inexcusability of unbelief. Not only is it clear that God exists, it is clear that *all* opposing beliefs are incoherent and false. The Christian must be able to demonstrate the substantial incoherence of all ideas raised up against the knowledge of God.[99] From what is clear generally, the Christian is called to silence, rout, and

---

98. *Romans 3:10-11.*

99. *2 Corinthians 10:4-5.*

completely demolish their strongholds (arguments and pretentions). The truth of God is clear; and the Church's apologetic must be reinvigorated in that truth. As Christ our Lord took all thoughts captive and did not appeal to a suppressed knowledge within the unbeliever (or the believer with unbelief remaining), so too must we fight. Witness is limited to what we know; what we know is limited to what we can show.

6. This passage requires a corporate sense of apostasy.

For although they knew God, they neither glorified him as God nor gave thanks to him, but their thinking became futile and their foolish hearts were darkened. Undoubtedly, Romans 1:21 is the *locus classicus* for those who assert that all persons in unbelief willingly suppress what they know to be true of God as their Creator. Upon first impression, this verse appears to say as much and nothing less. But upon examination of both the context of this verse as well as the history of mankind in biblical revelation, interpreting the verse in this way is not warranted. Rather the passage requires this to be understood as describing a *corporate* sense of apostasy—a corporate, historical progression into sin (not ahistorical—the history of each and every person). Not each and every one goes through the process and into the depths of depravity described here—making and worshipping idols and creeping things, engaging in unnatural relations, being filled with every kind of wickedness, progressively going down into being senseless, faithless, heartless, and ruthless. This is describing sin in its historically cumulative and communal sense.

While Paul uses Romans 1:20 to speak of that clear universal revelation of God that holds all men without excuse to this very day, verse 21 can be understood as documenting how God's clear *special revelation* has undergone an unmistakable pattern of generational decay in what people knew to be true of God and of his commands. In short, since none seek and none understand, what God has specially revealed of himself has been just as neglected from the beginning as has his general revelation. Starting from a truly biblical framework, the reader of Romans 1:21 would have to admit that all persons descended from Adam and that there was a slow, but progressive neglect, distortion, and dissolution of God's special revelation originally transmitted to our first father. While it is demonstrably true that God has not manifested himself specially to all persons, the entire human race does spring from an original historical point that was saturated with God's special revelation. For example, because of the effects of sin and spiritual death (not seeking, not understanding), what Cain learned from his father concerning God quickly became something less than glorifying to God. While Cain knew enough to bring sacrifice, he did not care enough to understand, in contrast to Abel, the tremendous significance of the bloody sacrifice. More or less, this generational pattern of revelation decay carried all the way to the Flood, where only Noah and his sons were left with God's original and undistorted special revelation.

As also occurred with the immediate descendants of Adam, from this post-Flood historical point the generations of men slowly moved further and further away from what Noah and his sons had preserved of God's special revelation. While it is true that an Aztec warrior could not be held personally accountable for what Ham and his descendants *once* knew of God, he is held accountable for failing to know of what God has clearly revealed of himself generally. What Paul says in Romans 1:21-32 concerning the debasing practices of mind and body committed by those of darkened intellect can be easily interpreted as a pre and post-Flood indictment of how sinful man slowly but surely dissolves the truth of God, turning it into a detestable and distorted lie. The history of Israel shows time and time again that although they knew of God as a nation and as individuals, they consistently failed to seek after the knowledge of God, wherein the truth dissolved into gross idolatry.

Whereas all persons are responsible to see what is clear of God from general revelation, there are those specifically who are under special indictment for their failure to seek after and understand God's special revelation as well. The generational decay in the book of Judges is a perfect example of how special revelation can be both known and disregarded because of a lack of seeking God earnestly. *After that whole generation had been gathered to their fathers, another generation grew up, who knew neither the Lord nor what he had done for Israel. Then the Israelites did evil in the eyes of the Lord and served the Baals. They forsook the Lord, the God of their fathers, who had brought them out of Egypt. They followed and worshiped various gods of the peoples around them.*[100] Furthermore, we saw this also in the passage from Hosea above (4.9).[101] And lastly, Jeremiah says, *Has a nation ever changed its gods? (Yet they are not gods at all.) But my people have exchanged their Glory for worthless idols.*[102] One may neglect or distort what they have been taught of God, not because they rebelliously loathe its content, but because in spiritual death they have not uncovered its true significance and, thus, cannot discern its meaningfulness for their lives. One can see a pattern emerge in the Scripture regarding complacency and pseudo-religiosity in the life of God's people that inevitably leads to a defective reinterpretation of God's revealed will. From the history of Israel alone, the reader of Romans 1:21 need not assume that Paul is speaking about first century Gentiles who willingly suppress an innate knowledge of God. Instead, one need only assume that Paul is alluding to God's historical special revelation, which, though clearly given to the race of man at times, has been systematically debased and forgotten by generation after generation.

Along with verse 21, verse 32 has been used to help substantiate the theory that men willingly suppress what they know to be true of God. Nowhere does verse 32 allude to the idea of man possessing a formal and specific knowledge of God; for it is quite easy to see how man can have the law of God in the very structure of their being (written on their hearts)[103] and have no understanding of God specifically as Creator. Though nearly all societies demonstrate a universal law code, and all men act against their consciences, it is not the same thing to suggest that all men willingly suppress a formal and immediate knowledge of God within them.

7. The explication of the wrath/justice of God detailed within this passage is consistent with sin understood as not seeking, not understanding, and not doing what is right (Paul's definition).[104]

---

100. *Judges 2:10-12.*

101. *Hosea 4:6-7.*

102. *Jeremiah 2:11.*

103. *Romans 2:14-15.*

104. *Romans 3:10-11.*

Paul teaches that *the wrath of God is being revealed* against the sin of man. This is being described as present (*is being revealed*) and inherent in sin (not future and imposed). The inherent consequence of not seeking and not understanding is meaninglessness (darkened mind), boredom (burning in desires without satisfaction), and guilt (the torment of conscience due to transgressing the law of God), all without end (the bottomless pit—downward progression). This is spiritual death (not physical death—imposed as a merciful call back from sin).[105] Infinite/divine justice (wrath) is ontological.

As seen in what was outlined in the prior point concerning the historical progression into apostasy, there is a change from knowing to not knowing. Although they at some point *knew* (to whatever degree) or were given the revelation, *they neither glorified him as God nor gave thanks to him . . . they became fools and exchanged the glory of the immortal God . . . They exchanged the truth of God for a lie . . . they did not think it worthwhile to retain the knowledge of God.*[106] Paul repeatedly emphasizes the mind and not the will as fundamental in this progression. It begins with the *omission* of not glorifying God as God and not being thankful to him. This is to fail to keep the first commandment, which requires us *to know and acknowledge God to be the only true God, and our God, and to worship and glorify him accordingly.*[107] It is to fail to hallow God's name—*to glorify him in all that by which he makes himself known* (including the clarity of general and special revelation).[108] To glorify God is to know God and make him known. In the most concise and focused summary of what sin is, Paul says that all have sinned by coming short of the glory of God.[109] It is a denial of eternal life as knowing God, man's chief end—*to glorify God and to enjoy him forever.*[110] There is an intrinsic and inescapable connection between glorifying and enjoying God, manifested in thankfulness to God for his countless blessings—ultimately which is the knowledge of God that comes

---

105. *Romans 6:23; Ephesians 2:1; Genesis 2:17.*

106. *Romans 1:21, 23, 25, 28.*

107. *SCQ. 46.*

108. *SCQ. 101.*

109. *Romans 3:23.*

110. *SCQ. 1.*

from diligently seeking him.[111] Not giving thanks to God is the beginning of the outward manifestation of apostasy (turning away, showing a lack of understanding). It is to become a fool, who *cannot understand* the blessings of God and how profound are his thoughts, and so cannot give thanks.[112] In this, the wrath of God is revealed— *but their thinking became futile and their foolish hearts were darkened. Although they claimed to be wise, they became fools . . . Therefore God gave them over in the sinful desires of their hearts . . . God gave them over to shameful lusts. . . . he gave them over to a depraved mind, to do what ought not to be done.*[113] In this condition of spiritual death (inherent consequence), entailing the destruction of the self or the soul of man, Paul again emphasizes the mind of man as ontologically fundamental. The mind becomes futile, not understanding the meaning of things (starting with misconceiving of God, blurring the distinction between Creator and creation). Given the nature of man as rational, the demand for meaning/understanding is inextinguishable.[114] When one does not find enjoyment in knowing God (leaving their first love), they are left unsatisfied (boredom) and they try to overcome/fill that emptiness by seeking enjoyment in the creation (apart from God), which leads to transgression and ultimately, excess and perversion, bringing shame and guilt. Apart from the redemption of God, this death continues in a downward cycle, unendingly. This is how the human psyche is ontologically structured by God.

IMPLICATIONS

The question of voluntarism vs. culpable ignorance is not just a theoretical question.

1. It has to do with our understanding of what sin is, and therefore redemption from sin.

---

111. *Hebrews 11:6.*

112. *Psalm 92.*

113. *Romans 1:21, 22, 24, 26, 28.*

114. *John 1:4-5.*

2. It has to do with apologetics—our witness to the non-believer. God calls all believers to give a reason for the hope we have within. Holding to the doctrine of voluntarism excuses one from having to show the clarity of general revelation and the inexcusability of unbelief/sin (by saying that persons already know). This does not give a basis for doing apologetics.

3. It has to do with our own sanctification. The Lord says that we are to be sanctified in knowing the truth.

4. It has to do with our understanding of the Word of God, authority, and reason.

5. It has to do with what is perhaps best characterized as an anti-intellectual attitude in the Church. This can be anywhere from a disregard for the life of the intellect, to a resistance, to perhaps hatred and despising of it.

6. All of these culminate in saying, it has to do with the very goal of the Christian life. If the goal is the earth being filled with the knowledge of God,[115] and this knowledge involves the mind being used fully,[116] then we can see how this question of knowing and not doing, and what is knowledge, is intimately connected to these very basic things.

The commonly held goal of salvation focused on heaven (rather than eternal life in knowing God), supported by literalism, fideism, intuitionism, and voluntarism, comes short of the glory of God and has been the *chief hindrance* to the goal of the knowledge of God through the work of dominion.

BENEFITS IN ASSUMING CULPABLE IGNORANCE (VS. VOLUNTARISM)

1. The Christian is not stuck with the ugly paradox of the unbelieving believer. Romans 1:18-21 need not be a difficult passage. The perspicuity of Scripture demands that such a crucial issue as this

---

115. *Isaiah 11:9; Habakkuk 2:14.*

116. *Mark 12:30-31.*

be relatively easy to comprehend, as opposed to being intrinsically enigmatic.

2. The position of culpable ignorance is consistent with the whole of Scripture, and is not primarily founded on one particular verse. Moreover, there is nothing heretical in this position that makes it immediately less appealing than the assumption that unbelievers knowingly reject the truth of God.

3. As opposed to the assumption that unbelievers resist the truth of what they know about God, the position of culpable ignorance carries with it no voluntaristic baggage—the will warring against the intellect. The issue is fundamentally an intellectual one, not an ethical/moral one (our actions).

4. The position of culpable ignorance upholds the cultural mandate, whereby we master the lies that suppress the truth and expose the incoherence of those thoughts raised up against the knowledge of God.

This paper is posthumously published
based upon the original work of Dr. Surrendra Gangadean
and has been developed by The Logos Foundation Editorial Board.

Paper No. 121

THE KNOWLEDGE OF GOD
VS. MYSTICISM

1. Mysticism denies the necessity of the intellect for the knowledge of God and the sufficiency of this knowledge for morality.

2. Mysticism denies the unity of the human heart in knowledge, holiness, and righteousness, and the primacy in order of the prophetic function over the priestly and kingly functions in each person and in our corporate functions.

3. Mysticism has many faces and appears in all major religions as well as in secular forms.

4. Mysticism is present in Christianity in the form of pietism and is a major force behind the otherworldly attitude and the presence of anti-intellectualism that have dominated the lives of Christians and the Church.

The following are some common forms of mysticism in Christianity today:

1. The heart is independent of the head. We can have knowledge in our heads without any feeling in our hearts. We can have feeling in our hearts without having knowledge in our heads.

2. The heart may be opposed to the head. There may be a conflict between what we are thinking and what we are feeling.

3. There is a primacy of the heart over the head. People are said to know that God exists and yet hate what they know so that they do not acknowledge God to be their God.

4. We may know by intuition what is in the heart of another person. And besides this, there are many things which are known by intuition.

5. There are certain religious experiences which we may have, which give certainty without any need for interpretation. These experiences are thought to be self-certifying.

6. It is possible to have direct knowledge of God, if not now, at least in heaven, when all shall behold the face of God. This is commonly known as the beatific vision of God.

7. The psychological-therapeutic approach to solving personal problems does not require theological-philosophical knowledge.

8. Holiness is not dependent in knowledge. It is possible to have zeal without knowledge. Knowledge is not necessary and sufficient for holiness.

9. There is certainty about the things of God that comes independently of reason and understanding and is the result of the direct working of the Holy Spirit.

10. Though Christians are to have a deep and disciplined respect for the life of the mind, no thoughtful Christian considers it the only or indeed the best way to glorify God. It is neither sufficient nor necessary for glorifying God.

Paper № 122

CONTRA CHARISMATIC DISTINCTIVE

Charismatic Theology maintains that one can be a believer in the New Testament period and not have *the baptism of the Holy Spirit*, that one has to have a distinct, if not separate, experience of baptism in the Spirit, which is ordinarily accompanied by speaking in tongues. In holding to this position, Charismatics maintain that the position of Historic Christianity is mistaken and does serious harm to the spiritual lives of believers, serious enough to divide the Church over it.

Is this position the truth or is it an error which hinders the knowledge of God and divides the body of Christ?

1. **Continuing supernatural revelation is against the nature of Scripture.**

   When scriptural revelation is complete, partial revelation (*the word of prophecy, the word of knowledge, tongues, and interpretation*) are done away with and put aside. Since Christ has come and accomplished the work of redemption, and the Apostles have interpreted his Word and works for us, there is no more scriptural revelation now.

2. The display of power as proof is against the clarity of general revelation.

Miracles are not clearer than general revelation in convincing unbelievers. Miracles do not prove anything apart from whether the person is speaking what is true about God.

3. Separate experience of Spirit baptism is against God's covenant in history.

The baptism of the Holy Spirit as a *separate experience from conversion* was the case for those of the transitional period *only*, from the Old to the New Testament. Those who were saved before Christ sent his Spirit had to have a separate experience. Only they had the tarry of the Spirit. No separate experience is recorded for anyone other than the Apostles, the Samaritans, Cornelius's household, and the believers from Ephesus.

4. Edification apart from the understanding is against the nature of man.

Understanding is *necessary for edification*. Paul said he would rather speak five words with his mind, than ten thousand words in a tongue.[1] We are sanctified through knowing the truth.[2] Knowledge produces holiness and righteousness. We are transformed by the renewing of our minds.[3] The Holy Spirit does not sanctify us mystically apart from our understanding. The knowledge that sanctifies is the knowledge of God which is eternal life,[4] not the charismatic gift of the word of knowledge.

5. A deliverance ministry is false and against God's compassion in natural evil.

The working of miracles served as signs of the apostolic ministry—that God had sent them and their word was to be received

---

1. *1 Corinthians 4:19.*
2. *John 17:17.*
3. *Romans 12:2.*
4. *John 17:3.*

as authoritative for the Church. To seek miracles as a way out of the *curse* of toil, strife, and sickness, is to deny God's call to repentance from self-deception and self-justification in not seeking him diligently.

6. Mystical feelings as self-induced are against knowledge through dominion.

Special feelings of the presence of the Spirit when sought for and used for guidance are often self-induced and become a substitute for the knowledge of God revealed through his works of creation and providence, known only through the exercise of dominion.

7. Experience is interpreted apart from and against the written Word.

The experience of what is interpreted as speaking in tongues is not self-evident. The cause of strange utterances can be psychological, and the cause of speaking a foreign tongue need not be of the Holy Spirit.

8. The trichotomy doctrine is either confused or false or both.

To separate man into body, soul (as carnal mind), and spirit (as a special faculty for communing with God), fails to see the different senses in which the term is used in Scripture and is a false understanding of what is our mind and our spirit.

Paper N⍛· 123

Non-Cognitivism
Introductory Remarks

1. Non-Cognitivism (NC) is a claim about knowledge by reason as not possible or necessary, or relevant. It is indistinguishable from skepticism and fideism, which share the assumption that nothing is clear.

2. NC utterances are neither true nor false nor both nor neither—they cannot be objected to (but neither can they object to anything).

3. NC assumes a view about man: reason is not natural/common ground; reason is not fundamental in human beings.

4. NC assumes a view about metaphysics: reason is not ontological—there are no essences or natures per se (nominalism vs. realism).

5. NC assumes a view about epistemology: reason is not transcendental and conceptual distinctions are distortions.

6. NC assumes a view about ethics: it is for freedom and autonomy vs. "fixed causality"; for creativity and openness (without limits); for inclusion and harmony vs. "exclusion."

7. NC is for the pragmatic/aesthetic/poetic/mythic narrative; for diversity and particularity vs. essentialism as reductionism.

8. NC does not affirm reason as a test for meaning.

9. NC is not concerned about a concern for consistency.

10. NC, if consistently applied, would eliminate all words and thought.

11. NC seeks to move beyond thought to being without thought.

12. NC must deny the eternality of the Logos/Word and therefore must end in silence, without a word (cf. the quatralemma: it isn't is; it isn't isn't; it isn't both; it isn't neither).

Some instances of NC:

1. Hindu/Buddhist enlightened states

2. Islamic thought through al-Ghazali on the nature of God and man and good and evil

3. Taoism, Confucian "relational virtuosity"

4. All forms of mysticism, including the "beatific vision" of God

5. Kant's *noumena*

6. Naturalist's view of human thinking seen in Marx, Nietzsche, Freud

Paper № 124

———

ON ISLAM[1]

1. Islam professes to build upon Judaism and Christianity, yet Islam rejects the central teaching of both regarding vicarious atonement seen in *Yom Kippur* and the crucifixion. It rejects the necessity for and the reality of the crucifixion of Christ.

2. In its cry *"Allahu Akbar!"* God is confessed to be great, in both justice and mercy. Yet when God is merciful, God's mercy does not satisfy his justice, but sets it aside.

3. Islam maintains that the Quran is given by God and also preserved by God. Yet the Scriptures of the Old and the New Testaments, which are also said by Islam to be given by God, are said not to be preserved by God.

4. Islam affirms the justice of God in those who perish in unbelief outside of Islam, but it does not show the inexcusability of unbelief based on the clarity of general revelation. Why is there any need for scripture in the first place and how can it be known that the Quran is that scripture in light of the claims of other writings to be scriptures?

5. Islam affirms the justice of God in hell, which is future and imposed, rather than in spiritual death, which is present and inherent in sin.

---

1. Gangadean, *Philosophical Foundation*, 191-192; Gangadean, *The Westminster Confession*. See Questions 7, 10, 19, 43, and 95; *Paper No. 91*.

6. Islam affirms heaven as a sensual paradise rather than eternal life as the knowledge of God. It fails to affirm creation is revelation and the knowledge of God through the work of dominion.

7. Islam fails to explain natural evil (toil and strife, and old age, sickness, and death) as imposed by God as a call back from moral evil (the failure to seek and to understand what is clear about God).

8. Islam rejects, as idolatry, the doctrine of the Trinity in which each person shares the same divine nature, yet believes in a being as God which lacks the divine nature of infinite and eternal justice and mercy.

9. Islam rejects Christianity based on a misrepresentation of Christ as the son of God by Mary, rather than Christ as the eternal Son of God who became incarnate through Mary.

10. Islam permits and encourages the use of force in *jihad* to propagate its teachings rather than the use of reason in proclamation and persuasion.

11. Islam upholds and seeks to impose *sharia* (positive law knowable only by revelation) on all men as the law of God, rather than the moral law of God which is written on the hearts of all men, and knowable by all men without special revelation.

12. Islam does not permit freedom of thought to its citizens. It does not permit freedom of speech to teach other views or freedom of choice to convert out of Islam.

13. Islam is willing to adopt victim status and to blame outsiders for its present state, rather than to accept responsibility for the practical and social implications of its worldview and policies.

Paper №· 125

———

SHAMANISM

1. Shamanism is not a primitive stage in religious development.

2. A form of "theism" is present before and during shamanism—in China, Africa, Indonesia, in Native American religion, and in all cultures of the world.

3. There are many forms of contact with powers and spirits.

    i. In magic, the contact is with an impersonal force—mana.

    ii. In animism, the contact is with local spirits in animals, places, and things.

    iii. There is widespread belief that the spirit of the deceased makes contact with the living, directly, or in circumstances, or through mediums.

    iv. In Gnosticism, there is believed to be contact with higher spirits which impart secret knowledge to human beings, into which a person may be initiated.

    v. Psychic phenomena are often described as special powers of the adept or the activity of spirits. Out of body experiences, knowledge of previous lives or of the thoughts of others, poltergeist phenomena, contact with familiar spirits, and possession by spirits are examples of psychic phenomena.

    vi. Divination (foretelling the future) by countless means is a widespread practice. Tarot cards, tea leaves, the I-Ching, phrenology, palmistry, astrology, and reading the entrails of animals are a few forms of divination.

4. God in shamanism is not believed to have much to do with the daily affairs of man. He does not actively rule the creation. So, God is not actively sought or appeased in shamanism.

5. The benefits sought after in shamanism are natural blessings—the avoidance of natural evil having to do with sickness, crops, child-birth, enemies, and loss of powers.

6. In shamanism, there is a widespread sense of fear of the activity of spirits along with a fatalistic resignation to omens of what is about to take place.

This paper was originally developed for a World Religions course.

Paper № 126

———

THE BAHÁ'Í FAITH

1. Bahá'í teaches the oneness of God, the oneness of religion, and the oneness of mankind.

2. Bahá'í teaches the harmony of science and religion.

3. Bahá'í teaches progressive revelation.

4. The prophets, in Bahá'í teaching, are Abraham, Krishna, Moses, Zoroaster, Buddha, Christ, Mohammed, the Báb, Bahá'u'lláh.

5. The prophets are the only way to know God. God's essence cannot be known by experience or reason.

6. The prophets are intermediaries between man and God; they are a third reality; they have a divine soul and a human body.

7. The prophets come to revive man's spiritual life and to establish a new civilization.

8. The physical universe is a creation of God, but it has always existed. Creation is a continuous process.

9. Man has always existed somewhere in the universe. He evolved from a lower form, but from the beginning he was potentially man. He is a distinct species.

10. In the individual man, soul and mind existed from the beginning. The soul does not really enter or leave the body.

QUESTIONS ON THE BAHÁ'Í FAITH

1. If it is impossible to know the essence of God because we are finite, then can the prophet make this known to us? And if we can know attributes of God, do we need the prophet to make this known?

2. On the nature of the prophet: can there be a human body without a human soul?

3. Are the prophets a third reality, or a combination of the divine and the human?

4. If Bahá'u'lláh is Christ returned, is there one prophet or many?

5. How can a prophet be recognized? Do they identify themselves to others? Abraham, Moses, and Mohammed did not claim to be more than human.

6. Was there a prophet to the Chinese? To the Aztecs? To the Greeks? Could Socrates or Confucius or Joseph Smith be prophets? If all need prophets, why do all not have prophets?

7. Why are some prophets such near contemporaries since they are said to come in different ages? Why the Báb and Bahá'u'lláh? Why Zoroaster and the Buddha?

8. Must civilizations end and new ones begin? Can civilizations continue? Is the kingdom of God the same as a civilization? Does the kingdom of God grow continuously in history?

9. If man has always existed somewhere in the universe and the universe has always existed, is man therefore eternal as a species? How long has man been evolving? Does only the body of man evolve? Is man still evolving? Will evolution ever stop?

10. Is the process of creation unique in any sense or is the process the same as an endless cycle that is ever recurring?

This paper was originally developed for a
World Religions course.

Paper № 127

___

GOD IS CREATOR AND RULER VS. DEISM[1]

1. **Deism is most commonly met in those who say they believe in God, but not the one in the Bible.**

   In the name of reason, they claim belief in the God of general revelation and see no rational grounds for believing in the God of Scripture.

2. **Deists cannot account for the reality of physical death and its implications, given their conception of God as Creator and not ruler.**

   There are three parts of this proof:

   i. Physical death was not a part of the original creation.

      If God is all powerful, then he *could* create a world without natural evil.

      If God is all good, then he *would* create a world without natural evil.

      If God could and would, then he *must* have created a world without natural evil.

      If God must have done so, then God *did*.

___

1. Gangadean, *Philosophical Foundation*, 190-191.

Therefore, original creation was without natural evil. ("it was very good."[2])

ii. Physical death was imposed on man as a call back from sin.

If natural evil was not original, then it was imposed by God because of man's change.

Natural evil was not imposed in justice as punishment of moral evil.

Justice is not imposed as arbitrary, but is necessary and inherent to moral evil.

Natural evil was imposed in mercy as a call back from moral evil.

Natural evil consists of toil and strife, and old age, sickness, and then physical death, which is the final call back.

It is a drastic call back.

As drastic, it presupposes deep resistance (self-deception and self-justification) to see what is clear about God.

iii. Natural evil, as a merciful call back, requires redemptive revelation.

God cannot deny the requirement of infinite justice; the penalty must be paid.

How God will be both just and merciful to man cannot be known from general revelation. (How can the penalty be both paid by man and not paid by man?)

It is necessary for man to know this if he is to come back to God as both just and merciful.

Therefore, natural evil, as a call back, requires redemptive revelation.

3. **Since God acts in history in imposing natural evil, and since natural evil requires redemptive revelation, deism is contrary to reason in denying that God acts in history and in denying the need for redemptive revelation.**

---

2. *Genesis 1:31.*

Paper N<u>o.</u> 128

———

ABRAHAM'S FAITH[1]

The Elements of Abraham's Faith in Offering up Isaac

1. He understood God's purpose in creation and history.

He grasped and applied the biblical worldview in his own life and lifetime.

He considered and understood the what, why, how, and who of the blessing of God in the manifold aspects of his call out of Ur of the Chaldees.

2. He understood the meaning of sacrifice.

The sacrifice was vicarious atonement: the innocent in the place of the guilty; not the animal itself which is but a sign of one to come in the place of Adam.

3. He understood the meaning of circumcision.

Circumcision is the sign of a new heart; regeneration; spiritual resurrection; needed by all, including Abraham and Isaac.

---

1. Gangadean, *Philosophical Foundation*, 32-45, 121-127; Gangadean, *History of Philosophy*, 3-12, 163-167; *Paper No. 21, 28, 98,* and *129.*

4. He understood the meaning of the name "Isaac."

God can and does bring life out of death (out of the deadness of Sarah's womb); by promise, not by works; he called the name "Isaac/ Laughter" innumerable times.

5. He understood the blessing is through Isaac.

The blessing is not through another: not through Lot or Eliezer, or Ishmael, or any yet to be born of him; he reasoned that God must and will raise Isaac from the dead in order to fulfill the promise;[2] he did not obey with resignation to the loss of Isaac.

6. He understood his relation to the one to be sacrificed.

Take now your son, your only son Isaac, whom you love, and go to the land of Moriah; and offer him there for a burnt offering upon one of the mountains which I will tell you of.[3]

7. He understood as a prophet does.

He sees what God himself will do: *God will provide himself a lamb for a burnt offering.*[4] He sees how God will do it by doing what God will do.[5]

---

2. *Hebrews 11:17-19.*

3. *Genesis 22:2.*

4. *Genesis 22:8.*

5. *John 8:56.*

Paper N<u>o.</u> 129

———

FAITH AND REASON IN THE
LIFE OF ABRAHAM[1]

1. It is common to think faith is distinct from reason and may even be opposed to reason. A classic example of this is Kierkegaard's analysis of the faith of Abraham in his work, *Fear and Trembling.* If the events of Abraham's life leading up to the sacrifice of Isaac are analyzed, we can see the movement is not going beyond reason, but the fulfillment of reason. In all of the earlier events, he shows some knowledge of the good and the means to it.

2. In the call to leave Ur of the Chaldees for an unknown Promised Land, he reveals his rejection of the kingdoms of this world for the kingdom of God, a city with foundations whose maker and builder is God. He does not conceive the good in earthly political terms. Earthly kingdoms not built on the faith in God are doomed to failure. Sin brings death.[2]

3. The promise that through him all nations will be blessed assumes a sense of universal history, the need of all men for blessing, the origin of sin and death in Adam, in what that blessing consists, and the promise of the coming of this blessing from the beginning. This

---

1. Gangadean, *Philosophical Foundation,* 32-45, 121-127; Gangadean, *History of Philosophy,* 3-12, 163-167; *Paper No. 21, 28, 98,* and *128.*

2. *Genesis 12:1; Hebrews 11:10.*

blessing involves the removal of sin and its effects, including physical death.[3]

4. In the many instances of sacrifice, he shows some understanding that sin is removed through the death of another so that the blessing of all nations likewise requires the removal of sin through sacrifice. He had some idea of the sacrifice to come.[4]

5. He lived as a stranger in the Promised Land. The good was not heaven apart from earth. He could not inherent the promise by death, but only by being raised from the dead. While the land is not itself the good, it is closely connected to the good so that all nations blessed is connected to all of the earth.

6. He knew more clearly after the battle with the kings that God himself, not something that can be given by God, is the good, his exceeding great reward. He must have had some sense that the good was knowing God and that evil was failure to know God.[5]

7. He knew that the promise will be fulfilled only by utter dependence on God. No human strategy could bring about the promised child. Only God could bring life out of the deadness of Sarah's womb. By seeing Isaac every day, he was reminded of this dependence on God to bring life out of death.[6]

8. He knew that God could raise the dead, would raise the dead, and must raise the dead, to fulfill the promise that he made. He had known the voice of God for many years, fulfilling what had been promised. He knew Isaac was the one through whom the promise would be fulfilled. He could and did reason that God would raise Isaac from the dead to fulfill the promise.[7]

---

3. *Genesis 12:2.*

4. *Genesis 12:7-8.*

5. *Genesis 15:1.*

6. *Genesis 18:19; 18:14; 21:3.*

7. *Hebrews 11:19.*

9. He knew that animal sacrifice was not enough to cover sin. He knew that the sacrifice of another like himself could not take away his sin. Yet he knew also that sacrifice was for the removal of sin and that what he was called to do was to sacrifice Isaac. He believed that God would provide the lamb for the burnt offering and saw in a figure how this would be done in the offering up of His own son whom He loved.[8]

---

8. *Genesis 22:8; Mark 12:6.*

Paper N<u>o.</u> 130

————

MAJOR SECULAR
ETHICAL THEORIES

**Secular ethical theories attempt to find
the basis of morality in some aspect of human nature.**

1. ETHICAL EGOISM seeks the moral absolute in individual desire. One ought to seek one's own interest (pleasure) without regard for anyone else. It is hedonistic (happiness or pleasure is the good). It was examined by Plato (Thrasymachus); it was taught by Hobbes (1660) and Ayn Rand (1950).

2. UTILITARIANISM[1] seeks the moral absolute in collective desire. One ought to do that which would produce the greatest amount of happiness for the greatest number of people. It was taught by John Stuart Mill (1870). It is implicit in Marxism.

3. DEONTOLOGY[2] seeks the good in a will that is governed by reason apart from desire. Moral duty should be done for duty's sake. One should act only on those rules of action which one can will to become universal laws. This was taught by Kant (1790).

4. EXISTENTIALISM[3] finds the good by an act of will which determines the good independent of there being any essential qualities in

---

1. Gangadean, *Philosophical Foundation*, 174.

2. Gangadean, *Philosophical Foundation*, 172-174; Gangadean, *History of Philosophy*, 154-158.

3. Gangadean, *History of Philosophy*, 163-170; Gangadean, *Philosophical Foundation*, 121-124.

things. Man is the sole determiner of meaning and by taking full responsibility for one's choice man achieves authentic existence. This was taught by Sartre (1950).

5. NATURALISM seeks the good in individual instinct. Human beings unfettered by artificial conventions are naturally good and should live according to the instinctive promptings of their nature. The uncivilized man is naturally noble. Civilization corrupts man. This was taught by Rousseau (1770) and by Lao Tzu in Taoism (500 B.C.).

6. TRADITION seeks the good on the wisdom of collective instinct expressed in a way of life that has been handed down from ages past to the present generation. There is no higher standard that the tradition itself. There is an element of tradition in all cultures in teaching the young, but it is especially present in the teachings of Confucius in China (500 B.C.) in the reverence shown toward ancestors.

7. HUMANISM seeks the good in the actualization of all of one's potential. No particular aspect is especially chosen over another. One ought to realize the fullness of one's humanity. How we know what our nature is like apart from knowing what is real becomes a critical issue. This was taught by Aristotle (330 B.C.) and Maslow (1980).

8. STOICISM seeks the good in denial of desires. Like all philosophies of asceticism, desires are seen as a hindrance to the good. Eastern asceticism radically denies desires by denying the reality of the self which has these desires. This was taught by Epictetus (300 B.C.) and Shankara (A.D. 800).

9. CONTEMPLATION seeks the good in the exercise of the intellect. In Plato, the object of knowledge is attained apart from the use of the senses. This knowledge is difficult to attain for Plato and it is reached only by a few, if any at all, in this life. Plato was a major philosopher influencing Western philosophy. He lived in Athens (427–347 B.C.).

This paper was originally developed for an
Introduction to Philosophy course.

Paper N⁰· 131

ASSUMPTIONS IN DISCUSSING CHRISTIANITY AND POLITICS

1. The office of civil magistrate is ordained by God for his glory and the public good.[1]

2. In addition to the State, God has ordained the Family and the Church. No institution is total (over all); each institution is equally under the moral law given by God.[2]

3. The moral law is written on the hearts of all men, as well as given in Scripture.

   It is objectively clear from general revelation.[3]

   All men are under moral obligation to obey the law written on their hearts.

   All men are under civil obligation to obey the civil aspects of the moral law.

4. Culture is determined by and embodies the dominant worldview.

   Culture includes law, politics, education, arts, and more.

   A worldview is based on answers to basic questions.

---

1. Gangadean, *The Westminster Confession*. See Questions 103-106.

2. Gangadean, *Philosophical Foundation*, 221-229.

3. *Romans 2:14-15*; Gangadean, *Philosophical Foundation*, 171-284; Gangadean, *History of Philosophy*, 61-69; Gangadean, *The Westminster Catechisms*. See LCQ. 91-148.

    i. How do we know?

    ii. What is real? How did things come to be?

    iii. What is the goal of life and how do we achieve it?

The dominant worldview holds public authority and public authority is based on what appears rational.

5. There is a spiritual war between good and evil, between belief and unbelief, which is age-long and agonizing.

    The outcome of this war is that good will overcome evil.[4]

    i. Believers are to be salt and light in the world. If they are not, they will be cast out and trampled under feet.[5]

    Believers are to be one that the world might believe.[6]

    ii. Believers are to take thoughts captive which are raised up against the knowledge of God.[7]

    iii. The will of God is to be done on earth as it is in heaven.[8]

    This is done as believers make disciples of all nations, teaching them to observe all that Christ has commanded.[9]

    iv. If believers obey God's law, they will be the head and not the tail of the culture.[10]

    v. God rules by his grace and by his power over men and nations to make himself known.[11]

---

4. *Genesis 3:15.*

5. *Matthew 6:13-15.*

6. *John 17:21.*

7. *2 Corinthians 10:5.*

8. *Matthew 6:10.*

9. *Matthew 28:19-20.*

10. *Deuteronomy 28:13, 44.*

11. *SCQ. 102; LCQ. 191; Acts 17:26-27; Ezekiel*—stated 70+ times.

Paper N<u>o.</u> 132

_____

REASON, RELIGION, AND PUBLIC EDUCATION

1. Reason, the Self-Evident, and Public Discourse: "We hold these truths to be self-evident . . ."

i. Is the self-evident necessary for public discourse? (clarity vs. skepticism, fideism, and nihilism)

ii. What is self-evident: testimony, intuition, common sense, science, reason?

iii. Man is a thinking being, a rational animal, (image of God?); reason as the laws of thought is self-evident: it makes thought possible; it cannot be questioned but makes questioning possible.

iv. Common Ground: Reason, Integrity, Rational Presuppositionalism, the Principle of Clarity.[1]

v. Reason and human nature: the good for man as a rational being: human well-being vs. harm to oneself (acting contrary to one's nature).

vi. Reason, participation in human society, and human rights/dignity.

vii. Reason, clarity of the moral law, and civic culture.

_____

1. *Paper No. 2.*

2. Religion: "Congress shall make no law respecting an establishment of religion . . ."

i. What is the wall of separation: interpretation of constitutional law.

ii. What is religion: defined by examples; are there limits regarding Church and State?

iii. What is religion: defined by essence: the (set of) beliefs used to give meaning to one's experience.

iv. Five implications: cognitive, universal, inseparability of faith and reason, classification, and conflict (internal and external conflict; exclusivism vs. inclusivism).[2]

v. Religion and rational discourse: any restrictions by skepticism or fideism?

3. Public Education: must public education be religiously neutral?

i. The paradox of public education: can education be religiously neutral?

ii. An antinomy: equal fideism or equal skepticism or neither?

iii. Critical thinking is not neutral with respect to truth: if reason shows that God exists, is reason "contrary to the Constitution"?

iv. Internal solution: pursue the critical use of reason within the limits of general revelation vs. default skepticism and fideism.

Is there a point at which the use of reason "becomes religious"?

Reason is common ground (necessary and universal), but it is not neutral ground.

Natural religion is based on general revelation (equally accessible to all by reason and experience).

Revealed religion is based on special revelation (testimony—not equally accessible to all).

v. External solution: restore education to the non-governmental private sphere and adjust tax policy accordingly (home school, private, charter, voucher, accreditation); pluralize/choice vs. monopolize.

---

2. *Paper No. 89.*

Paper № 133

———

WHEN DOES HUMAN LIFE BEGIN?
The Soul and Life Are One and the Same

Many have allowed for abortion on the basis of the claim that we don't (can't) know when human life begins because we don't (can't) know when the soul enters the body.

This response is directed to those theists who believe the soul is added by God to an already living being. It is not directed to those who deny (1) that God exists, or (2) that man has an immortal soul, or (3) that the soul is added by God to an already living being. There are other arguments against these, which are not presented here.

This argument has two parts:

1. To show that life begins at conception.
2. To show that the soul and life are one and the same (the minor premise of the first argument).

PART I

Major premise: If the soul and life are one and the same, then human life begins at conception.

Minor premise: The soul and life are one and the same.

Conclusion: Therefore, human life begins at conception.

Symbolically stated:
[abbreviations: S (the soul); L (life); LBC (life begins at conception)]

$(S \equiv L) \supset LBC$

$(S \equiv L)$

$\therefore LBC$

The reason for the major premise is that the fetus is alive in every ordinary sense of the term from the moment of conception. If the soul and life are one and the same, and the soul makes for human life, then human life is present from conception.

PART II

The reason for the minor premise in Part I is based on the immediately given awareness that in a person there are *not* two centers of awareness, but only one center of awareness, which is the self or the soul.

More specifically, the soul is said to be what is aware. But life without the soul also is aware (animals without souls also perceive). So, if the soul is not one and the same as life (in humans), the soul *plus* life (in humans) would be *two* centers of awareness in each person. Since it is clear that there are not two centers of awareness in each person, but only one, it follows that the soul and life are not two things, but one and the same in humans.

Symbolically and more succinctly stated:
[abbreviations: S (the soul); L (life); 2CA (two centers of awareness)]

$(S \neq L) \supset 2CA$	If the soul is not the same as life, then there are two centers of awareness.
$\sim 2CA$	It is not the case that there are two centers of awareness in a person.
$\therefore \sim (S \neq L)$	Therefore, it is not the case that the soul is not the same as life.
$\therefore (S \equiv L)$	Therefore, the soul *is* the same as life.

This supports the minor premise of the first argument in Part I.

Paper N⁰ 134

_____

WORSHIP, THE SABBATH, AND THE CHURCH

1. Worship

We are not free to worship God as we see fit.

We are to worship God as he has commanded.

The regulative principle of worship is declared in the Second Commandment.[1]

Worship is required by the light of nature and regulated by the Scriptures.

Ordinary religious worship includes keeping the Sabbath day holy, preaching, prayer, singing of psalms, and sacraments.[2]

2. The Sabbath

The Sabbath is a day of rest and worship, appointed by God from the beginning, to commemorate the completion of the work of creation. It also confirms to mankind the hope of completing the work of dominion.[3]

---

1. Gangadean, *The Westminster Catechisms*. See LCQ. 107-110; Gangadean, *The Westminster Confession*. See Questions 93-99.

2. *WCF 21.1-8.*

3. *Genesis 2:2-3*; Gangadean, *The Westminster Catechisms*. See LCQ. 115-121.

As creation and history reveal the glory of God, man's work of dominion brings knowledge of the glory of God.[4]

3. The Day of Worship

Since the completion of Christ's work of redemption, the Church has observed the first day of the week as the Lord's Day, the Christian Sabbath, on which the Church assembles for worship.[5]

Believers are not to forsake the assembling of themselves together for worship.[6]

4. Daily Worship

God is to be worshiped everywhere, in spirit and in truth, in private families daily, as well as each one by himself.[7]

Personal and family devotion consist in the reading of Scriptures, the singing of Psalms, and in prayer.

5. The Church: the pillar and foundation of the truth

The Church is the pillar and the foundation of the truth. It is ordained by God to bring his Word of truth to mankind.[8]

The Holy Spirit leads the Church into all truth by enabling its teachers to respond to challenges to the truth in every age.[9]

Pastor-teachers, after much discussion, come to agreement, which is expressed in statements of faith, for the benefit of all believers.[10]

---

4. *Isaiah 6:3; 11:9.*

5. *1 Corinthians 16:1-2; Acts 20:7; Revelation 1:10.*

6. *Hebrews 10:25*; Gangadean, *The Westminster Confession*. See Question 99.

7. Gangadean, *The Westminster Confession*. See Question 97.

8. *1 Timothy 3:15.*

9. *John 16:13.*

10. *Acts 15.*

6. The Church and Sacraments

A sacrament is a holy ordinance instituted by Christ, wherein, by sensible signs, Christ and the benefits of the new covenant are represented, sealed, and applied to believers.

The sacraments of Baptism and the Lord's Supper are given to the Church and are administered by those in oversight to believers who make a credible profession of faith.[11]

7. The Church and Good Works

We are God's workmanship, created in Christ to do good works.[12]

Good works are not anything we might do out of zeal without knowledge.

Pastor-teachers, in teaching the Scriptures, prepare God's people for works of service.[13]

8. The Church and Sanctification

God's people, who are forgiven in Christ, must be sanctified by knowing the truth.[14]

Believers are not to be conformed to this world, but are to be transformed by the renewing of their minds.[15]

Believers are not to remain infants, but are to grow to maturity by being taught the foundational truths of God's Word.[16]

Believers are to be members of that branch of the Church which most fully holds to the truth of God's word. They are to submit to those in oversight who watch for their souls.[17]

---

11. Gangadean, *The Westminster Confession*. See Questions 116-118; Gangadean, *The Westminster Catechisms*. See LCQ. 161-177.

12. *Ephesians 2:10.*

13. *Ephesians 4:11; 2 Timothy 3:16.*

14. *John 17:17.*

15. *Romans 12:1-2.*

16. *Ephesians 4:12-13; Hebrews 5:11–6:3.*

17. *Hebrews 13:17.*

9. The Church and Discipleship

The Church is called to make disciples of all nations.[18]

To disciple others, believers must first be discipled by being taught to obey all that Christ has commanded.[19]

Believers are not to be taken captive by the thoughts of this age, but are to take every thought captive which is raised up against the knowledge of God.[20]

10. The Church and Fellowship

The Church is the body of Christ, the fullness of him who fills everything in every way.[21]

The Church grows and builds itself up in love as each part does its work.[22]

Members of the Church are called to love each other as Christ loves us and to build each other up in the faith.[23]

18. *Matthew 28:20.*
19. *Matthew 28:20.*
20. *2 Corinthians 10:4-5.*
21. *Ephesians 1:21-22.*
22. *Ephesians 4:16.*
23. *John 13:34; Romans 15:2.*

Paper N⁰· 135

———

ON WORSHIP

1. Man is to worship God in spirit and in truth.[1]

2. To worship God in truth is to acknowledge the truth of the glory of God.

3. God, as Creator, upholder, and redeemer, is worthy of all praise, honor, and glory. Worship is due to him alone and not to any creature. "You shall have no other gods before me."[2]

4. God, who is infinite, eternal, and unchangeable in his being, wisdom, power, holiness, justice, goodness, and truth, is not to be likened to the finite, temporal, and changeable creature.[3]

5. All misconception of the nature of God in thought or by visible representation is idolatry. Divisions among those who profess belief in God are rooted in idolatry. "You shall not make for yourself an idol (in the likeness of any creature)."[4]

6. All have sinned and come short of the glory of God.[5] Some sin remains in all men during this life. Since all of our conceptions come short of God's glory, worship in the Church must be based on truth revealed by God in Scripture.

———

1. *John 4:24.*
2. *Exodus 20:3.*
3. *Romans 1:20-24; Genesis 3:5.*
4. *Exodus 20:4.*
5. *Romans 3:23.*

7. The acceptable way of worshiping the true God is instituted by himself, and so limited by his own revealed will, that he may not be worshiped according to the imaginations and devices of men.[6]

8. Since the fall of man, worship must be through the mediation of Jesus Christ who alone, as priest, atones for sin and intercedes for man.[7]

9. The Book of Psalms is given by God for singing in the worship of God in the Church. Only the Psalms embody true piety in keeping with the whole truth of God.

10. True worship of God is neither in outward form without understanding, nor in zeal without knowledge, but by the Spirit of God who makes God's truth known to men.[8] "You shall not take the name of the Lord your God in vain."[9] God must be worshiped in spirit and in truth.

---

6. Gangadean, *The Westminster Confession*. See Question 93.

7. Gangadean, *The Westminster Confession*. See Question 94.

8. *John 16:13.*

9. *Exodus 20:7; Matthew 15:18-19.*

Paper N<u>o.</u> 136

———

ON PRAYER[1]

1. *Our Father Which Art in Heaven*

The preface of the Lord's Prayer teaches us to draw near to God with all holy reverence and confidence, as children to a father, able and ready to help us; and that we should pray with and for others.[2]

i. Your Father knows what you need before you ask him.[3]

ii. How much more will your Father in heaven give good gifts to those who ask him.[4]

iii. As a father has compassion on his children, so the Lord has compassion on those who fear him.[5]

iv. How much more should we submit to the Father of our spirits and live.[6]

v. Jesus called out with a loud voice, "Father, into your hands I commit my spirit."[7]

1. Gangadean, *The Westminster Confession*. See Question 95; Gangadean, *The Westminster Catechisms*. See LCQ. 178-196.

2. Gangadean, *The Westminster Catechisms*. See SCQ. 100.

3. *Matthew 6:8.*

4. *Matthew 7:11.*

5. *Psalm 103:13.*

6. *Hebrews 12:9.*

7. *Luke 23:46.*

We are to avoid no prayer and vain prayer. We are to pray according to the Word of God.

2. *Hallowed Be Thy Name*

In the first petition, we pray that God would enable us, and others, to glorify him in all that whereby he maketh himself known; and that he would dispose all things to his own glory.[8]

  i. Now this is eternal life: that they may know you, the only true God, and Jesus Christ, whom you have sent.[9]

 ii. God saw all that he had made, and it was very good.[10]

The whole earth is full of his glory.[11]

iii. Since the creation of the world God's invisible qualities, his eternal power and divine nature, have been clearly seen, being understood from what has been made, so that men are without excuse.[12]

 iv. God blessed them and said to them, "Be fruitful and increase in number; fill the earth and subdue it."[13]

  v. For the earth will be full of the knowledge of the glory of the Lord as the waters cover the sea.[14]

We are to avoid worldliness and otherworldliness. God is known by creation and history.

3. *Thy Kingdom Come*

In the second petition, we pray that Satan's kingdom may be destroyed; and that the kingdom of grace may be advanced, ourselves

---

8. Gangadean, *The Westminster Catechisms*. See SCQ. 101.

9. *John 17:3.*

10. *Genesis 1:32.*

11. *Isaiah 6:3.*

12. *Romans 1:20.*

13. *Genesis 1:28.*

14. *Isaiah 11:9; Habakkuk 2:14.*

and others brought into it, and kept in it; and that the kingdom of glory may be hastened.[15]

i. Seek first the kingdom of God and his righteousness.[16]

ii. Go and make disciples of all nations.[17]

iii. We demolish arguments and every pretension that sets itself up against the knowledge of God.[18]

iv. The kingdom of heaven is like a mustard seed.[19]

The kingdom of heaven is like yeast.[20]

v. He must reign until he has put all his enemies under his feet.[21]

We are to avoid no hope and false hope. The kingdom of God grows gradually to its fullness.

4. *Thy Will Be Done on Earth as It Is in Heaven*

In the third petition, we pray that God, by his grace, would make us able and willing to know, obey, and submit to his will in all things, as the angels do in heaven.[22]

i. Do not turn from the law to the right or left; meditate on it day and night.[23]

ii. The law of the Lord is perfect, restoring the soul.[24]

iii. These laws are to be on your hearts. Impress them on your children.[25]

---

15. Gangadean, *The Westminster Catechisms.* See SCQ. 102.

16. *Matthew 6:33.*

17. *Matthew 28:19.*

18. *2 Corinthians 10:4.*

19. *Matthew 13:31.*

20. *Matthew 13:33.*

21. *1 Corinthians 15:25.*

22. Gangadean, *The Westminster Catechisms.* See SCQ. 103.

23. *Joshua 1:7.*

24. *Psalm 19:7.*

25. *Deuteronomy 6:5.*

   iv. The nations show the work of the law is written in their hearts.[26]

   v. Love the Lord your God with all your heart and with all your soul and with all your mind. And love your neighbor as yourself.[27]

We are to avoid no law and man's law. God's law is the rule for all of life.

5. *Give Us This Day Our Daily Bread*

In the fourth petition, we pray that of God's free gift, we may receive a competent portion of the good things of this life, and enjoy God's blessing with them.[28]

   i. Do not worry, saying, "what shall we eat or drink or wear."[29]

   ii. Having food and raiment, let us be content.[30]

   iii. Cast all your care upon him, because he cares for you.[31]

   iv. My God shall supply all your needs according to his riches in Christ.[32]

   v. I can do all things through Christ who strengthens me.[33]

We are to avoid no trust and mistrust. We are to trust in God in using ordinary means.

6. *And Forgive Us Our Debts as We Forgive Our Debtors*

In the fifth petition, we pray that God, for Christ's sake, would freely pardon all our sins; which we are the rather encouraged to ask, because by his grace we are enabled from the heart to forgive others.[34]

---

26. *Romans 2:15.*

27. *Matthew 22:37.*

28. Gangadean, *The Westminster Catechisms*. See SCQ. 104.

29. *Matthew 6:31.*

30. *1 Timothy 6:8.*

31. *1 Peter 1:5.*

32. *Philippians 4:19.*

33. *Philippians 4:13.*

34. Gangadean, *The Westminster Catechisms*. See SCQ. 105.

i. Then Jesus said, "Father, forgive them; for they know not what they do."[35]

ii. Bless those who persecute you; bless and do not curse.[36]

iii. For all have sinned and come short of the glory of God.[37]

iv. If we confess our sins, he is faithful and just and will forgive us our sins and cleanse us from all unrighteousness.[38]

v. If you forgive not men their sins, your Father will not forgive your sins.[39]

We are to avoid excusing or accusing one another. God forgives us in Jesus Christ.

7. *And Lead Us Not Into Temptation but Deliver Us From Evil*

In the sixth petition, we pray that God would either keep us from being tempted to sin, or support and deliver us when we are tempted.[40]

i. Do not despise the Lord's discipline; because the Lord disciplines those he loves.[41]

ii. The trial of your faith is more precious than gold which perishes.[42]

iii. Each one is tempted when he is carried away and enticed by his own lust.[43]

iv. Watch and pray so that you do not enter into temptation.[44]

---

35. *Luke 23:34.*
36. *Romans 12:14.*
37. *Romans 3:23.*
38. *1 John 1:9.*
39. *Matthew 6:15.*
40. Gangadean, *The Westminster Catechisms*. See SCQ. 106.
41. *Hebrews 12:5.*
42. *1 Peter 1:7.*
43. *James 1:14.*
44. *Matthew 26:41.*

v. Whoever wants to save his life will lose it, but whoever loses his life for me will find it.[45]

We are to avoid denial of sin and despair in sin. We are sanctified by knowing the truth.

8. *For Thine Is the Kingdom, and the Power, and the Glory, Forever, Amen*

The conclusion of the Lord's prayer teaches us to take our encouragement in prayer from God alone, and in our prayers to praise him, ascribing kingdom, power, and glory to him; and, in testimony of our desire, and assurance to be heard, we say, Amen.[46]

i. In him we live and move and have our being.[47]

ii. All things were created by him and for him; by him all things consist.[48]

iii. God works all things after the counsel of his own will to the praise of his glory.[49]

iv. And he shall reign for ever and ever.[50]

v. To him who sits on the throne and to the Lamb be praise and honor and glory and power, for ever and ever.[51]

We are to avoid self-centeredness and man-centeredness. All of life is centered in God.

---

45. *Matthew 16:25.*

46. Gangadean, *The Westminster Catechisms.* See SCQ. 107.

47. *Acts 17:28.*

48. *Colossians 1:16.*

49. *Ephesians 1:11.*

50. *Revelation 11:15.*

51. *Revelation 5:13.*

Paper № 137

———

ON EVANGELISM

1. It is clear that God exists.

Since the creation of the world, God's invisible qualities—his eternal power and divine nature—have been clearly seen, being understood from what has been made, so that men are without excuse.[1]

2. Our failure to see what is clear results in spiritual death.

i. The wages of sin is death.[2]

ii. Spiritual death is inherent in sin. The shutting of our eyes to avoid what is clear brings meaninglessness, boredom, and guilt.

3. God calls us back to conscience, through others, and through suffering.

i. We resist God's call to conscience by self-deception.[3]

ii. We resist God's call through others by self-justification.[4]

iii. Therefore, God imposes the suffering of toil and strife, and old age, sickness, and death as his continuing call to repentance.[5]

---

1. *Romans 1:20.*

2. *Romans 6:23; Ephesians 2:1; Genesis 2:17.*

3. *Genesis 3:7.*

4. *Genesis 3:9-13.*

5. *Genesis 3:14-19.*

4. Scripture tells us how God is both just and merciful to man in Jesus Christ.

   i. God cannot deny his justice while being merciful.

   ii. Only the Bible reveals how God is both just and merciful.

   iii. Christ, the Son of God incarnate, died in the place of those who put their trust in him.[6]

BASIC QUESTIONS

1. For what does God hold all men accountable?

What may be known about God is plain to them, because God has made it plain to them. For since the creation of the world God's invisible qualities—his eternal power and divine nature—have been clearly seen, being understood from what has been made, so that men are without excuse.[7]

2. What is man's natural response to God's general revelation?

All have sinned and come short of the glory of God.[8]

There is no one righteous, not even one; there is no one who understands, no one who seeks God.[9]

3. What is the consequence of sin?

The wages of sin is death.[10]

You must not eat from the tree of the knowledge of good and evil, for when you eat of it you will surely die.[11]

---

6. *John 3:16.*

7. *Romans 1:19-20.*

8. *Romans 3:23.*

9. *Romans 3:10-11.*

10. *Romans 6:23.*

11. *Genesis 2:17.*

4. Is there any hope for man's salvation?

For God so loved the world that he gave his one and only Son, that whoever believes in him shall not perish but have eternal life.[12]

5. Can any man by his own effort save himself?

It is by grace you have been saved, through faith—and this not from yourselves, it is the gift of God—not by works, so that no one can boast.[13]

6. What must one believe in coming to God?

Without faith it is impossible to please God, because anyone who comes to him must believe that he exists and that he rewards those who earnestly seek him.[14]

7. What is the eternal life promised to those who seek God?

Now this is eternal life: that they may know you, the only true God, and Jesus Christ, whom you have sent.[15]

8. How does one grow up in Christ?

Like newborn babies, crave pure spiritual milk, so that by it you may grow up in your salvation, now that you have tasted that the Lord is good.[16]

9. Is any trial of our faith too great?

No temptation has seized you except what is common to man. And God is faithful; he will not let you be tempted beyond what you can bear. But when you are tempted, he will also provide a way out so you can stand up under it.[17]

---

12. *John 3:16.*
13. *Ephesians 2:8-9.*
14. *Hebrews 11:6.*
15. *John 17:3.*
16. *1 Peter 2:2.*
17. *1 Corinthians 10:13.*

10. What are we to do when we sin?

If we confess our sins, he is faithful and just and will forgive our sins and purify us from all unrighteousness.[18]

11. How can we know the Holy Spirit is working in us?

The fruit of the Spirit is love, joy, peace, patience, kindness, goodness, faithfulness, gentleness, self-control.[19]

12. What is the goal of Christ's salvation?

The earth will be full of the knowledge of the Lord as the waters cover the sea.[20]

---

18. *1 John 1:9.*
19. *Galatians 5:22.*
20. *Isaiah 11:9.*

Paper N⁰· 138

CONCERNING MARRIAGE[1]

So God created man in his own image,
in the image of God he created him;
male and female he created them.[2]

1. Under God or Unto Self

i. This is the first and most basic point to consider in thinking about marriage. Every point to be considered later will be decided by this first point.

ii. Is marriage being considered in light of God's goal for human life or apart from God's goal?

iii. Is one's partner a helpmeet in the goal of the knowledge of God through dominion or is marriage for self (companionship or children) considered apart from God's purpose?

iv. Under God, marriage is the most important decision a person makes in life. The decision is to be made with prayerful thought and foresight and not be left merely to instinct, intuition, and tradition or circumstance.

---

1. Gangadean, *The Westminster Confession*. See Question 107; Gangadean, *Philosophical Foundation*, 245-254.

2. *Genesis 1:27.*

2. Blessing or Curse

    i. Some consider marriage as a blissful union in which the two live happily ever after.

    ii. The experience of many is that their marriage has been a personal disaster, or that if marriage lasts, it is more often a life of quiet desperation.

    iii. The biblical view is that marriage under God is a great blessing. Since, however, man has a struggle with sin in living under God, marriage is accompanied by trouble in the flesh. For those who seek God in the midst of their troubles, God causes these troubles to serve his purpose and further their good. Marriage under God is full of hope.

3. To Be or not to Be—Married

    i. Not everyone has the ability to live as a single person.[3]

    ii. Those who long to be with another and who have distracting thoughts about the opposite sex should consider that they do not have the ability to be single. They should consider getting married, under God.

    iii. The Scripture teaches that it is better to marry than to burn with desire.[4]

    iv. A person must be honest before God and others in recognizing his or her need. Where needs are not acknowledged, the person does not give careful thought to use of God-ordained means to satisfy those needs. They are then often satisfied in unlawful ways.

4. Preparation[5]

    i. Ordinarily, a person cannot consider finding one's life-partner without knowing what their calling in life before God is to be.

---

3. *Matthew 19:11-12.*

4. *1 Corinthians 7:8-9.*

5. Gangadean, *Philosophical Foundation*, 252-253.

   ii. Ordinarily, one is not prepared for marriage until the financial needs of a family can be provided for.

  iii. Marriage without due preparation is possible, but it increases hardships in some ways.

  iv. One should seek to prepare oneself for marriage before thinking about finding the other.

5. Finding One's Other

    i. The choice of marriage should be based on knowledge of the other and not on fantasy.

   ii. The outward signs are not to be taken as always accompanied by the inward reality.

  iii. What is sought in marriage is one's complement, that which will complete each other.

  iv. Finding one's complement is through courtship, which submits to parental oversight.

6. What Is Basic

    i. There must be a clear common understanding of God's purpose for human life.

   ii. There must be a proven commitment to the means to seeking this goal.

  iii. The man must be able to exercise godly oversight; the woman must be willing to submit to his godly oversight.

  iv. The basics should be in place from the start and not added later.

7. Providence

    i. Obedience to God in finding one's other requires recognizing God's providence on one's life and the use of ordinary means.

   ii. A person is to avoid running ahead of or lagging behind God's providence.

iii. There is a time and a season for everything. One is to consider building one's life together from the time of one's youth and not later in life when independent patterns become set.

8. Roles

i. Marriage assumes an original difference between male and female as created by God in his own image.

ii. Recognizing these differences is essential to observe God's ordained order for marriage.

iii. The responsibility of the husband is to love his wife as Christ loved the Church.[6]

iv. The responsibility of the wife is to submit to her husband in the Lord.

9. Plans

i. There are some practical decisions that have long-term effects on the wellbeing of marriage. It is wise to have a common understanding of what is to be expected.

ii. In deciding where to live, family, and church community should be given careful thought.

iii. There should be a common understanding about family planning.

iv. There should be agreement about who should work and who should care for the children.

v. There should be plans to avoid competing careers and for the continual growth of both.

10. One Flesh

i. Marriage is constituted by sexual union, even if the union is considered casual.[7]

---

6. *Ephesians 5:22-23.*

7. *1 Corinthians 6.*

ii. Marriage is consummated by the sexual union of those who are lawfully married.

iii. Marriage is broken by adultery, unless the offended person is pleased to be reconciled.

iv. In marriage, a primary concern of each is to learn to please the other.[8]

v. In marriage, one is not to deprive the other or abstain except by mutual consent.[9]

11. Vows[10]

i. In the covenant of marriage, vows are to be made to each other before God and man.

ii. Vows before God are to be according to his Word.

iii. Vows are to recognize the different responsibilities and needs of each in the marriage.

iv. Marriage vows are for life, for better or worse, until death do us part.

v. Vows, as the most thoughtful commitment, require knowledge of oneself and the other.

12. Unity

i. What God has joined together man must not put asunder.

ii. Husband and wife must forsake all others. All past competing relations are forever over.

iii. Husband and wife must leave father and mother and cleave to each other.

iv. Parents must let go and not interfere. The parental role ends when marriage begins.

---

8. *1 Corinthians 7:32-35.*

9. *1 Corinthians 7:5.*

10. Gangadean, *The Westminster Confession*. See Questions 100-102.

    v. Friends and community must support and not hinder the new relation.

   vi. All witnesses to the vow must encourage and hold both accountable for keeping their vow.

Paper № 139

———

THE BLESSING
OF CHILDREN

PRELIMINARY CONSIDERATIONS

1. If you were Abraham's children, you would do the things Abraham did.[1]

2. Nor because they are descendants are they all Abraham's children.[2]

3. If you belong to Christ, then you are Abraham's seed.[3]

4. Those who believe are children of Abraham.[4]

5. You belong to your father the devil.[5]

6. More are the children of the desolate woman than of her who has a husband.[6]

7. He cuts off every branch in me that bears no fruit.[7]

---

1. *John 8:39.*
2. *Romans 9:7.*
3. *Galatians 3:29.*
4. *Galatians 3:7.*
5. *John 8:44.*
6. *Isaiah 54:1; Galatians 4:27.*
7. *John 15:2.*

8. This is to my Father's glory, that you bear much fruit, showing yourselves to be my disciples.[8]

9. I chose you and appointed you to go and bear fruit—fruit that will last.[9]

10. Go and make disciples of all nations, teaching them to observe all things whatsoever I have commanded you.[10]

11. The man who hears the Word and understands it . . . produces a crop, yielding a hundred, sixty, and thirty times what was sown.[11]

12. Look at the fields! They are ripe for harvest . . . I sent you to reap what you have not worked for.[12]

SOME IMPLICATIONS

1. There are physical children and spiritual children.

2. The blessing of children to Abraham is the blessing of spiritual children.

3. We can be fruitful spiritually without being fruitful physically.

4. We can be fruitful physically without being fruitful spiritually.

5. God wants us to be fruitful spiritually even if we are not fruitful physically.

6. God wants us all to be fruitful.

7. We are fruitful when we make disciples of all nations.

8. God wants us to be fruitful spiritually more than we are fruitful physically.

9. Bearing much fruit that lasts shows that we are his disciples.

---

8. *John 15:8.*

9. *John 15:16.*

10. *Matthew 28:20.*

11. *Matthew 13:23.*

12. *John 4:35-38.*

Paper № 140

———

ARGUMENT FOR
PAEDOBAPTISM

1. All who are saved are saved by the covenant of grace.

Abraham was saved.

Therefore, Abraham was saved by the covenant of grace.

   i. There is a covenant of grace. We are saved by grace through Christ as our representative head.

   ii. The covenant of grace is made with Christ who fulfills the covenant of works made with Adam, in whom all die.

  iii. All persons throughout history are under the covenant headship of one or the other, but not both.

  iv. The covenant of grace did not begin with the New Testament.

   v. The covenant of grace is not identical with the New Testament.

  vi. The New Testament is a new administration of the one covenant of grace; it is not another covenant of grace.

2. Circumcision was God's sign to men of regeneration and all it implied.

Regeneration is in, by, and for the covenant of grace.

Therefore, circumcision was God's sign to men of the covenant of grace.

   i. The sign of the covenant is not the reality it signifies.

  ii. The sign of the covenant does not confer the reality it signifies.

 iii. The sign of the covenant is not always accompanied by the reality it signifies.

 iv. The sign is ordinarily connected with the reality before or after the sign is given, when the sign is administered with godly oversight.

3. **The sign of the covenant of grace (circumcision) was to be applied to infants.**

   Baptism signifies the same thing that circumcision signifies (regeneration) and replaces circumcision in the New Testament.

   Therefore, baptism as the sign of the covenant of grace in the New Testament is to be applied to infants.

   i. Infant children were included in the visible community of the covenant of grace by having the sign applied to them by those in oversight in the community.

  ii. Persons having the sign of the covenant who do not walk according to the covenant, and who do not seek forgiveness of their sins according to that covenant, are covenant-breakers and are therefore to be excluded from the visible community until they repent.

 iii. The exercise of godly discipline preserves the purity of the visible covenant community.

 iv. The sign of the covenant may be changed, but the substance cannot be changed without changing the covenant itself.

Paper № 141

———

THE BIBLICAL WORLDVIEW

PART I

Hermeneutics for a Biblical Worldview

Hermeneutics is concerned with how to interpret or understand the meaning of general and special revelation. We become more conscious and consistent in understanding meaning in response to challenges to interpretation. By discussing hermeneutics first, misinterpretations and strife can be avoided. Hermeneutics applies to the formation of a biblical worldview, which is a comprehensive understanding of general and special revelation.

Five factors determining hermeneutics will be introduced here. These hermeneutical factors will guide response to questions raised in relation to these.

1. Common Ground

Common Ground (CG) is the necessary condition for thought and discourse: all discourse or dialogue is based on CG and without CG discourse naturally ends. The four elements of CG are: Reason, Integrity, Rational Presuppositionalism, and the Principle of Clarity, in which the latter flows from the former.

i. Reason[1]

It is self-evident that we are thinking beings and that there are laws of thought—reason in itself is the laws of thought (the law of identity, non-contradiction, and excluded middle).

Reason, as the laws of thought, is the test for meaning and is itself self-attesting—it cannot be questioned because it makes questioning possible.

ii. Integrity[2]

Integrity is a concern for consistency, both logical (in the relation between ideas) and existential (put into practice). We are more or less conscious and consistent. We should be more conscious and consistent.

iii. Rational Presuppositionalism[3]

Thinking by nature is presuppositional: we think of the less basic in light of the more basic; if we agree on the more basic, we can agree on the less basic.

iv. The Principle of Clarity[4]

Some things are clear (vs. skepticism/fideism/nihilism); the basic things are clear (based upon Rational Presuppositionalism); the basic things (about God and man and good and evil) are clear to reason.

2. The relation of general revelation (GR) and special revelation (SR)

i. The Principle of Clarity (PC) affirms the clarity of GR (cGR). If there is no cGR, then *nothing* is clear (hence skepticism/relativism/subjectivism/nihilism).

---

1. Gangadean, *Philosophical Foundation*, 10-15; Gangadean, *History of Philosophy*, 25-35; *Paper No. 2, 5, 44, 48, 50, 57, 92,* and *111.*

2. Gangadean, *Philosophical Foundation*, 199-205; Gangadean, *History of Philosophy*, 3-12; Gangadean, *The Westminster Catechisms.* See LCQ. 111-114; *Paper No. 2, 51,* and *64.*

3. Gangadean, *History of Philosophy*, 19-23; *Paper No. 2, 52, 95-96,* and *101.*

4. Gangadean, *Philosophical Foundation*, 3-5, 287-292; Gangadean, *The Westminster Confession.* See Question 4; *Paper No. 2, 35, 39, 41, 43, 53,* and *102.*

ii. If there are no meaningful distinctions/nihilism (no cGR), then morality is not possible and there is no meaningful possibility of moral evil (i.e., sin or redemption from sin).

iii. cGR applied to the problem of evil shows natural evil (NE) is imposed by God to restrain, recall from, and remove moral evil (ME). NE requires special (redemptive) revelation to show how God can be both just and merciful to man in sin.

iv. SR, as redemptive revelation, assumes cGR. If there is no cGR, there can be no sin and redemption.

v. SR explicitly asserts cGR as the basis of the inexcusability of unbelief.[5]

vi. Historic Christianity, summed up in the Westminster Confession of Faith (1648), explicitly asserts cGR as the basis of the inexcusability of unbelief.[6]

vii. In light of longstanding objections to appeals to any SR, it is necessary to show the steps from GR to SR: the necessity for SR, its content, origin, existence, transmission, completion, translation, clarity, sufficiency, and interpretation.[7]

3. The Word of God

The Word of God makes God known. It is the highest and final authority in all disputes. The doctrine of the Word of God is summed up in the Prologue of the Gospel of John and in subsequent passages.

i. The Logos is the eternal Word of God, the Son of God, who makes God known.[8] This is the first and most basic sense of the Word of God.

---

5. *Romans 1:20.*

6. Gangadean, *The Westminster Confession.* See Question 4. It should be noted that this is the very first chapter, section, and line of the Confession.

7. *Paper No. 11.*

8. *John 1:1.*

ii. The life of the Logos is in all men as light, by which men see/understand; that light is reason in all men.[9] It is opposed by the darkness of unbelief, which cannot overcome or withstand the light.

iii. The Logos, as Creator, is revealed in the world created (general revelation), but men failed to understand the revelation of the Logos.[10]

iv. The Logos came to the covenant people in history (through the prophets) as special revelation/Scripture, but was not received.[11]

v. The Logos, resisted and rejected as reason, general revelation, and special revelation, comes again to man, incarnate in Jesus Christ, and was crucified, and so brought the fullness of grace and truth (bringing a deeper revelation of God by grace— through which sin is forgiven and by which man is brought to the truth).

vi. Christ sent the Holy Spirit to lead the Church into all truth. The historically cumulative insight gained in response to challenges is summed up in the creeds and confessions of Historic Christianity.[12]

vii. The Holy Spirit brings persons into the truth of the Logos/the Word of God by the work of regeneration and sanctification.[13]

4. Man, the image of God[14]

The knowledge of God and the knowledge of self are reciprocally related. There are several aspects of man as the image of God.[15]

i. The larger aspect (the essence of man) consists of formal qualities that all men always have and that distinguish man from all other creatures: man is finite, temporal, and changeable in his being,

---

9. *John 1:4.*

10. *John 1:10.*

11. *John 1:11.*

12. *John 16:13.*

13. *John 3:3; 8:32; 17:17.*

14. Gangadean, *The Westminster Confession.* See Question 25; Gangadean, *The Westminster Catechisms.* See LCQ. 17.

15. These are further developed in *Paper No. 144.*

wisdom, power, holiness, justice, goodness, and truth. God has these qualities in an infinite, eternal, and unchangeable way that sets him apart from all creatures.

ii. The narrower aspect gives content to what is regarded as truth (connected with knowledge), beauty (connected with holiness), and goodness (connected with what we ought to do), and reflects man's changeability between belief and unbelief.

iii. Man is a triune personality, in the image of the Triune God. There is an order and unity in man's heart between knowledge, holiness, and righteousness, variously reflected and understood through human history.

iv. Man is a body/soul unity, requiring discernment in understanding the relation of both aspects.

v. Man is male/female unity, requiring the understanding of both aspects in God.

vi. Man's development, in his nature, is shaped by background factors in his particular history.

vii. Each person uniquely reflects the image of God; the various aspects of human nature are to be understood in an ordered way from the larger aspect to the unique aspect.

5. Rational Presuppositionalism

Thinking by nature is presuppositional; we are to understand the less basic in light of the more basic. Reason, as the laws of thought, is most basic and is the test for meaning, hence the name Rational Presuppositionalism (RP).

i. We are to think of meaning in light of reason (meaning/reason), truth/meaning, experience/basic belief, finite and temporal/infinite and eternal, conclusion/premises.

ii. In general revelation or philosophy, we are to think of ethics (good and evil) in light of metaphysics (the nature of the eternal and of man), which must be thought of in light of epistemology (what is clear to reason).

iii. In special revelation or Scripture, we are to think of redemption in light of the Fall, and the Fall in light of creation.

iv. RP is opposed to all forms of empiricism, which fails to notice that all experience (tradition/testimony, common sense, intuition, science) must be interpreted in light of basic beliefs. RP is opposed to literalism as the outcome of empiricism.

v. RP is opposed to all forms of rationalism, which use reason as a source of truth, or use it constructively rather than its first use as a test of meaning. RP is therefore opposed to allegoricalism, which is the outcome of the use of "rational" non-theistic assumptions to interpret theism.

vi. RP affirms the hermeneutics of contextualism: the several layers of context must be observed in interpretation from more basic to less basic: from cGR, to SR (the foundation of creation–fall–redemption in Genesis 1–3), to Historic Christianity (summed up in the creeds and confessions), to book, to chapter, to verse, and to word, in that order.

vii. RP holds out the hope that, beginning with Common Ground and the clarity of GR, longstanding disputes in GR and SR can be settled, that unity of the faith and the knowledge of God can be attained.

This paper is posthumously published
based upon the original work of Dr. Surrendra Gangadean
and has been edited by The Logos Foundation Editorial Board.

Paper №· 142

———

THE BIBLICAL WORLDVIEW

PART II

Biblical Cosmology: Creation Ex Nihilo

1. The relation between special/redemptive revelation and cosmology

Does Scripture speak to the question of cosmology/science?

i. Context of special/redemptive revelation:

    a. It shows how God can be both just and merciful to man in a state of sin and death. It assumes the need for redemption from sin.

    b. Sin is not seeking, not understanding, and not doing what is right.[1] Because there is a clear general revelation (assumed by Scripture), failure to see what is clear (unbelief) is without excuse.[2] The inherent consequence of sin is spiritual death[3]—meaninglessness, boredom, and guilt. Christ came as the Lamb of God to take away the sin of the world. He came to undo what Adam did (by his death on the cross he atones for sin)

---

1. *Romans 3:10-11.*

2. *Romans 1:20.*

3. *Romans 6:23; Ephesians 2:1.*

and to do what Adam failed to do (rule/exercise dominion to make God known).

ii. Special revelation is given by God to all men for the purpose of knowing God. This is in contrast to the view that it was written by a limited man (Moses) to a limited audience (the Hebrews, at that time, with their worldview) for a limited purpose (e.g., to wean them away from idolatry). They could and should have known that idolatry is wrong from what is clear about God in general revelation and that God who gives this special revelation is holding mankind responsible for the failure to seek and understand what is clear about him.

iii. Since cosmology is a fundamental/foundational aspect of knowing God, special revelation must be consistent with clear general revelation and understood in the context of the goal of knowing God. Sin is coming short of the glory of God.[4] Redemption brings man to know and make known the glory of God. So, we should expect (it is reasonable to read) the Scripture as having a revelation concerning cosmology—the origin of the cosmos; God as the creator of the cosmos.

2. Definition of "God" from clear general revelation (from a minimal to a maximal definition)

i. God is a higher power.

ii. God is the highest power (none higher—he is not brought into existence by another and therefore not dependent on another for his being).

iii. God is eternal (from ii.).

iv. Only God is eternal (from i.+ii.) (all else is temporal—brought into being by what is eternal).

v. God is Creator *ex nihilo* (all else is brought into being by God from nothing—no pre-existent material).

vi. God, as Creator *ex nihilo*, is a Spirit (he is other than the created material world), infinite (having power to create *ex nihilo*), eternal,

---

4. *Romans 3:23.*

and unchangeable in being, wisdom, and power (as Spirit and Creator, he has knowledge and will, which reflect understanding of the things created and the power to bring this about).

vii. Man is created by God and is a body/soul unity—a thinking and sentient being. He is created in the image of God: finite, temporal, and changeable in being, wisdom, power, holiness, justice, goodness, and truth (the last four being moral attributes). From this self-knowledge, one can know that these moral attributes are also in God, as creator of man, in an infinite, eternal, and unchangeable way.

3. Objections and/or alternatives to the idea of creation *ex nihilo* (God the Creator)

i. Being from non-being—the world came out of absolute non-being:

a. This is the affirmation of an uncaused event.

b. Steady-State theory—hydrogen atoms come into being from nowhere.[5]

c. Vacuum fluctuation in space—moving from a true vacuum (no matter, no energy) to a false vacuum (energy, but no matter) to the Big Bang.[6]

Response: Being from non-being is logically incoherent/impossible.[7] Physical being comes from non-physical being (spirit). This spirit is God creating *ex nihilo*.

ii. It is logically impossible:

a. It is like magic (i.e., God simply waves his hand to bring about the world)—no one really believes in magic.

b. Example from longstanding tradition: Nagarjuna (Buddhist dialectician)—boldly declared the doctrine of No-origination:

---

5. Gangadean, *Philosophical Foundation*, 78.

6. Gangadean, *Philosophical Foundation*, 76-77.

7. Gangadean, *Philosophical Foundation*, 61-63.

"Never and nowhere can anything be produced."[8] There is only a transformation of what is already existing.

Response: There are analogies to creation *ex nihilo* in human experience that show it is not logically impossible. A neural impulse is not a mental image (the mind is not the brain) and there is a transition from the impulse to the image.[9] As matter affects mind, so mind affects matter. A mental event (the intention to move my arm) can cause a physical event (the movement of my arm).[10]

iii. Pantheism—all is one:

    a. Emanations or transformation of the one/God (each being is a part of God).

    b. Ramanuja—qualified non-dualism.[11]

    c. Thales—all is water; this ultimate reality/substance is alive/ has soul in some sense, and this is used to account for the source of motion.

    d. Animism (in the teachings of tribal religions)—life-force in all things; nature is alive, suffused with spirits.

    e. Gaia/eco-mysticism.

Response: Spirit and matter can and must be distinguished. The human spirit/soul[12] and the material world are not eternal.[13] Logical objections against saying there is one spiritual reality composed of parts: 1) All the parts cannot be finite and eternal; 2) All the parts cannot be infinite and eternal.[14]

---

8. Gangadean, *Philosophical Foundation*, 115-117.

9. Gangadean, *Philosophical Foundation*, 82-86.

10. Gangadean, *Philosophical Foundation*, 142.

11. Gangadean, *Philosophical Foundation*, 112-115; Gangadean, *History of Philosophy*, 115-119.

12. Gangadean, *Philosophical Foundation*, 132.

13. Gangadean, *Philosophical Foundation*, 73-80.

14. Gangadean, *Philosophical Foundation*, 114.

iv. The world is an illusion:

    a. What is not rational is not real (e.g., a square-circle—it cannot exist).

    b. Parmenides; Zeno's Paradoxes—motion; since it cannot be rationally grasped, it cannot exist; it only appears to exist.

    c. Shankara—the world is neither real nor unreal; it is *maya* (illusion).[15]

Response: The physical/material world exists—the cause of what I see/perceive is not my mind or another mind, but outside all minds.[16] The individual soul exists. The mind is not the brain—neither in perception (a mental image is not a neural impulse and the self/perceiver is not a mental image),[17] nor in conception (a judgment is not reducible to motion of atoms in the brain).[18] And the individual mind/self is not an illusion.[19]

v. Dualism—matter and spirit are eternal:

    a. God is not the creator of matter; the demiurge is at best finite and co-eternal.

    b. Many finite gods (as in Greek polytheism) vs. one.

    c. Plato—ordinary dualism;[20] Aristotle—dependent dualism.[21]

Response: Neither matter nor individual souls are eternal.

vi. Material monism—all is matter and matter is eternal:

    a. There is no thinking being involved in the process.

    b. Goes from an undifferentiated chaos to the ordered cosmos. This goes through an eternal cycle.

---

15. Gangadean, *Philosophical Foundation*, 110-112.

16. Gangadean, *Philosophical Foundation*, 107-108.

17. Gangadean, *Philosophical Foundation*, 82-86.

18. Gangadean, *Philosophical Foundation*, 80-82.

19. Gangadean, *Philosophical Foundation*, 111-112.

20. Gangadean, *Philosophical Foundation*, 131-132; Gangadean, *History of Philosophy*, 87-91.

21. Gangadean, *Philosophical Foundation*, 132-134; Gangadean, *History of Philosophy*, 93-105.

    c. Self-organizing—organizes itself by time and chance over long periods of time.

    d. Self-generating forces in the universe; *Om mani padme hum* (chanted in Buddhist circles)—the universe is self-existing, self-explaining, self-maintaining, and self-generating; the view on the Tao may be likened to this.

Response: The material world is not eternal. Spirit exists.

4. Introductory textual analysis (Genesis 1:1-2)

   i. *In the beginning*

    a. This is speaking about a beginning, in the ordinary sense of the word. Time began. Time could not be said to begin if there was anything else eternal besides God. If time involves change—matter changes and finite minds change (one thought after another), then time began with creation.

    b. This is in contrast to an eternal cycle.

   ii. *God*

    a. Elohim: The Almighty.

    b. Coupled later with the eternal, Yahweh (Jehovah) Elohim—the self-existing one; the LORD God.

    c. Uniplurality—there is both a unity and plurality present in Elohim (God is plural and yet one); understood and expressed in the doctrine of the Trinity.

   iii. *created*

    a. Two views of creation: *ex nihilo* (infinite deliberate wisdom—knowledge and power) vs. forming something that is pre-existent (dualism—limitations of the demiurge).

    b. In light of clear general revelation, matter is not eternal (no pre-existing material).

    c. Scripture/special revelation must be consistent with clear general revelation.

   iv. *the heavens and earth*

a. This is the substance of the universe. This is in contrast to a multiverse (which is incoherent when the idea of a universe is understood).

b. This substance is in the form of water. "Deep" suggests water (4.6 below); this is made more explicit in the next phrase (4.7).

c. Water has an understandable essence and the vastness of this entire substance/body has implications (e.g., there are forces already operating in this reality of water).[22]

v. *and the earth was without form, and void*

a. Two interpretations: it was not yet formed vs. it was formed and then became unformed (lost its form) or it was created with form but subsequently is without form, immediately connected with the original creation (heavens and earth).

b. In light of several accompanying passages, the interpretation that it was not yet formed should be taken.[23]

c. Original creation (the substance of the universe) without form implies formation in subsequent creation. Subsequent creation is by forming and filling what is without form and void.

vi. *and darkness was upon the surface of the deep*

Was there no light anywhere? On the earth? In the heavens?

vii. *And the Spirit of God moved upon the face of the waters*

The Spirit is present, hovering, brooding—this is a way of speaking about providence. Upon God's creating, providence begins immediately, in which the Spirit is upholding, directing, disposing, and governing all the creation, from the greatest to the least, to the praise of his glory.[24]

*This paper is posthumously published
based upon the original work of Dr. Surrendra Gangadean
and has been edited by The Logos Foundation Editorial Board.*

---

22. See *Paper No. 143.*

23. See *Paper No. 143.*

24. Gangadean, *The Westminster Confession.* See Questions 24-25.

Paper N⁄o. 143

———

THE BIBLICAL WORLDVIEW

PART III

Biblical Cosmology:
Subsequent Creation by Forming and Filling

1. **Is there a conflict between science and religion (especially with respect to the age of the earth)?**

   This is a complex question as it involves what is meant by science and what is meant by religion. Religion may be natural religion (general revelation) or revealed religion (special revelation) and involves the question of interpretation/understanding their meaning and relation.[1] Science involves experience/observation which requires interpretation—science will vary depending on what interpretive assumption is used.

   i. There is a conflict which is more deeply rooted, going back to the question of Common Ground.

   ii. We are more or less conscious and consistent with respect to the use of reason, Rational Presuppositionalism, and the Principle of Clarity.

---

1. *Paper No. 141.*

iii. The conflict is in each person, not just between believers and non-believers. It is a conflict between belief and unbelief in each person, with one being more basic than the other.

iv. Believers and non-believers both have uncritically examined assumptions. Both compromise the Principle of Clarity by fideism or skepticism.

v. The compromise of the Principle of Clarity is revealed in the textual analysis of Genesis 1.

2. In original creation (OC), God is Creator *ex nihilo*. What happens after OC depends on what happens in OC.

What was created in the beginning: the substance of the universe without form, or the substance of the universe in the form of the heavens and the earth (formed separately)?

i. If OC is with form, then the sun is already in existence as part of the heavens, which is already separated from the earth, and there is light.

ii. If OC is with form, then there are solar days (and nights) after Genesis 1:1a. This affects the interpretation of time and age.

iii. OC with form is not consistent with darkness over the face of the deep (except for at most 12-hour periods, since solar days are already present).

iv. OC with form is not consistent with the subsequent creation of light, since light already exists.

v. OC with form is not consistent with the subsequent formation of the firmament and the formation of the earth.

vi. OC with form is not consistent with the formation of the sun and stars as lights (light bearers) on the fourth day.

vii. OC with form implies the earth became formless (and vice versa—to say the earth became formless implies it was originally created with form) vs. the earth was not yet formed.

viii. Earth becoming formless (after OC with form) allows for a gap of time (measured in 24-hour days, since the sun is already present) between OC with form and the earth becoming form-less (between verses 1 and 2).

The gap is said to be long enough to explain fossil remains. One of the reasons this is introduced is to lessen any perceived conflict between science and religion, between the old earth and young earth views.

ix. Fossils are found in distinct sedimentary strata formed either by many distinct floods (laid down by water) over a long period of time or by one flood over a short period of time.

x. Old earth (OE) vs. young earth (YE): both assume original creation with form.

OE assumes: a) OC with form, b) solar days after Genesis 1:1, c) animal life and many floods before the creation of light in Genesis 1:3.

YE assumes: a) OC with form, b) solar days after Genesis 1:1, c) one flood (Genesis 7-8).

xi. OC without form better explains darkness, light, and the firmament, which are not explained by OC with form.

In OC without form, there is no time gap, no animal life before Genesis 1:3, no fossils, and no floods.

xii. OC without form implies formation in subsequent creation (SC).

It implies an alternative cosmology in the formation of time and space and matter.

SC is building upon the conditions brought into existence by OC.

Subsequent creation is by forming and filling what is without form and void:

3. Creation of light (Day 1)

i. The substance of the universe is water (the deep). There is darkness over the surface of the deep—there is no light.

Dimension: The mass of this body of water, given the current understanding of the size of the cosmos, is about 1 light-year across. This is vast to the point of being stupendous, beyond our imagination. This constitutes the substance of the universe.

Condition: It is in the form of water. Hydrogen and oxygen atoms are present in a combination, as well as subatomic particles. In considering the vastness of this body, it is subject to various forces operating, including gravity and the effect this has on the atoms deep within this body.

ii. Light, as we know it, is formed by thermonuclear reaction. This process strips down atoms, allowing for a recombination, and out of this the other elements of the universe are formed. This process does not simply come about naturally. It comes about by a supernatural process supervening on natural processes. *The Spirit of God moved upon the face of the waters.* It is providential, which involves upholding, directing, disposing, and governing the creation. It is at the Word of God ("Let there be . . ."—fiat creation) that this process brings into existence light. The creation/physical universe, created by the Word of God, can be understood by man because that Word of God is in man.[2]

iii. *And God saw the light, that it was good.* It is just what God intended it to be, by infinite power and wisdom (no limit). Ultimately, creation is intended to reveal who he is. It is also necessarily a revelation—the nature of God is necessarily revealed in the acts of God. Furthermore, creation is revelation exclusively (i.e., revelation of God's wisdom and power, as it is revealed in the creation, is not possible apart from creation). So, creation is revelation: necessarily, intentionally, and exclusively. This has significant implications for how we understand the rest of biblical cosmology and the doctrines of creation–fall–redemption.

4. Creation of the heavens/the firmament/space (Day 2)

i. God said, again by fiat, *Let there be a firmament in the midst of the waters.*

---

2. *John 1:4.*

ii. The waters that were created in this vast body are separated—the waters that were above from the waters below. This subsequent creation then, which is by formation, is by separation.

iii. By implication, everything was in one place and expanded from one place—stretched out. This is like, in some respects, the Big Bang view (one version—with a center). It is sometimes referred to as a white hole cosmology (expanding from a center vs. contracting). So, the water below the firmament is at or near the center of everything.

iv. The amount of energy from within this vast body of water (comprising the entire substance of the universe) is much greater than one sun releasing light. This energy is released, causing the entire universe to expand.

5. The dry land appears (Day 3)

i. At the Word of God, the waters that were under the firmament (which are at or near the center of everything) are gathered together in one place and the dry land appears.

ii. Therefore, the Earth and sea are formed by separation.

iii. The Earth is filled with vegetation by the Word of God: grass, herbs, trees.

iv. It is emphasized that each of these is *after its kind*. Subsequent creation is the forming of kinds (and larger categories inclusive of several kinds—there are several kinds of trees etc.).

v. *And God saw that it was good.* As this is repeated, we should be reminded, as it was with the light, that creation is revelation. The visible reveals the invisible—it can reveal it symbolically and it can reveal it naturally in terms of understanding causes by inference (e.g., God is light (spiritual light) and the physical light symbolically speaks of that spiritual light).

6. Creation of the sun, moon, and stars (Day 4)

i. These are lights. They are intended to give light on the earth—light bearers; different from the creation of light itself.

    ii. They are used to divide the day from the night, the light from the darkness, and to measure days and years.

    iii. They are also for signs and seasons.

    iv. At this point, the fourth day, one can say that solar days begin. Before the sun is formed, one cannot speak about solar days. This is understood in the context of OC without form.

7. Creation of the living creatures in the waters and the birds of the air (Day 5)

    i. *God said, Let the waters bring forth abundantly* . . . We should understand that "abundantly" applies to the kinds of living creatures more than the numbers; there is a vastness of kinds that are being formed and, as we will see below, the numbers are going to increase.

    ii. Again, it is emphasized that God formed, by fiat creation, each kind, great and small, separately and distinctly. Attention can be given to what constitutes a kind and what constitutes a change within a kind.

    iii. *And God blessed them, saying, be fruitful, and multiply, and fill the waters . . . let birds multiply on the earth.* Subsequent creation is by forming and filling. Each kind is to increase in number and fill the waters/earth, which comes about by the blessing of God (the first place this is mentioned). This implies starting with few in number.

8. Creation of the living creatures of the earth (Day 6)

    i. These are characterized as beasts, cattle, and creeping things.

    ii. There are many kinds in each of these broad categories, and each is separately and specially created.

    iii. Man, the image of God (examined in *Paper No. 144*).

*This paper is posthumously published
based upon the original work of Dr. Surrendra Gangadean
and has been edited by The Logos Foundation Editorial Board.*

Paper No. 144

THE BIBLICAL WORLDVIEW

PART IV

Biblical Cosmology:
Man, the Image of God

1. The nature of man and the good for man

i. *And God said, Let us make man in our image, after our likeness.* The sixth day is completed with the subsequent creation of man.

ii. Man is distinct in kind from *all* animals. The reference to kinds has been repeated—plants, sea life, birds, and animals. In contrast, man is distinct in kind, not just as one among many animals, but from all animals.

iii. It is self-evident that man is a thinking being. There are three acts of thought/reason. We form: 1) concepts—grasping the essence of a thing, 2) judgments—joining two concepts, 3) arguments—joining two judgments to infer a conclusion.[1]

iv. Man is a sentient being—he has five bodily senses: see, touch, taste, smell, and hear. In this respect, he is like other animals.

v. Man is a rational animal. It is self-evident that there are laws of thought—reason in itself is the laws of thought. Therefore, man is not merely an animal, he is a rational animal—a body/soul unity.

---

1. *Paper No. 75*; Gangadean, *Philosophical Foundation*, 49-59.

   vi. To deny rationality (or to neglect, avoid, or resist rationality) in oneself or in others is to deny one's dignity as a human being. Rationality in man, as a rational animal, constitutes the essence of man.

       This is set in contrast to man as animal only, without reason, or man as some kind of divine being that stands beyond, above, or apart from reason.

   vii. Knowledge, understanding, and wisdom, which man has based on his rationality, enable man to rule over the creation. From this, inferences concerning the good for man can be drawn.

  viii. From general revelation: the good for man, as a rational being, is the use of reason to its fullest, to understand the nature of things created, which reveals the nature of God. So, creation is revelation (necessarily, intentionally, and exclusively) and the good for man is the knowledge of God. And this revelation is full and clear in the creation, in all its vast array (by forming and filling). It is full (not infinite) in the sense that it cannot be exhausted by man as a finite being.

   ix. From special revelation/Scripture: eternal life (the good) is knowing God.[2]

    x. From Historic Christianity (summed up in the Westminster Confession): Man's chief end is to glorify God,[3] in all that by which he makes himself known,[4] in all his works of creation and providence.[5]

   xi. The Logos, by whom all things were made,[6] is in all men as the light of reason.[7] This is the light by which man sees/understands intellectually.

---

2. *John 17:3.*

3. *SCQ. 1.*

4. *SCQ. 101.*

5. *WCF 4.1, 5.1.*

6. *John 1:3.*

7. *John 1:4.*

The Logos in man, as reason, enables man to understand the Logos revealed in the creation.

xii. The process of understanding the fullness of God's self-revelation in the Logos (in general and special revelation) is corporate (requires the activity of all men), cumulative (throughout history), and communal (the more this knowledge is shared, the more it increases).

2. Man is to exercise dominion over the creation: *Let them have dominion . . .*

i. In dominion, man is to *name* the creation and *rule* over the creation (developing the powers latent in himself and in the creation). To name is to grasp the nature/essence of a thing. *Whatever the man called each living creature, that was its name.* He is to name/grasp the nature of things in relation to himself.

ii. Dominion, naming and ruling, is corporate, cumulative, and communal: *God blessed them, and God said to them, "Be fruitful and multiply; fill the earth and subdue it; have dominion over [it]."* To complete the work of dominion, to name and rule over the creation, in all its vast array, will take all of mankind throughout all of history. Through this, man comes to know the nature of things more fully, through which he comes to understand the nature of God—to grasp the Logos that is revealed in the creation (biologos, anthropologos, psychologos, etc.).

iii. Dominion is for God's purpose—to reveal his glory (necessarily, intentionally, and exclusively) in, by, unto, and upon his creatures. He does not derive any glory from them, but manifests his glory naturally in all of his works.[8]

iv. Dominion is for man's chief and—to glorify God—to know and make known God's glory. Both God's purpose and man's purpose coincide in the call to exercise dominion.

v. The outcome of the completion of dominion is that the earth will be filled with the knowledge of God as the waters cover the

---

8. Gangadean, *The Westminster Confession.* See Question 14.

sea.[9] The revelation is full and clear, and the knowledge of this revelation will be full (not an inch deep and a mile wide, but as the waters cover the sea). The vastness/fullness of this knowledge speaks to its inexhaustibility—the good for man is inexhaustible.

The Sabbath affirms the hope of man's completion of his work of dominion, as God completed his work of creation. Dominion without knowledge is no hope; knowledge without dominion is false hope (the beatific vision).

3. The image of God is complex: a unity of diversity

i. The larger aspect: man is finite, temporal, and changeable in being, wisdom, power, holiness, justice, goodness, and truth.

   a. All human beings have these qualities, always; fallen man is fully human—in the larger aspect. Fallen man is still man.

   b. It is self-evident that man has the communicable attributes of God (being, wisdom, power, holiness, justice, goodness, and truth) in a finite, temporal, and changeable way. Only God is infinite, eternal, and unchangeable (incommunicable attributes—they cannot be given to any creature).

   c. Idolatry begins in confusing the finite and the infinite (this occurred in the Fall—*you will be like God, knowing good and evil*). We are to understand the nature of man and the nature of God, and the distinction and relation between the two.

   d. In the simplicity of God, there is no tension among any of his attributes—particularly, the attributes of mercy and justice; mercy does not set aside justice; rather, the highest expression of justice is also the highest expression of mercy—both of these coincide in the death of Christ (the doctrine of the atonement). This is at the heart of special/redemptive revelation—how God can be both just and merciful to man in his condition of sin and death.

   e. The infinite includes the finite; the finite does not include and can never include/become the infinite. Man is forever

---

9. *Isaiah 11:9.*

the image of God; the image (in the larger aspect) can never be eradicated—man can never overcome his rationality in his need for meaning. *The light shines in the darkness, and the darkness has not overcome it.*[10] Without meaning, it is the source of man's greatest pain. With meaning, it is the source of man's greatest joy.

ii. The narrower aspect: man can change; he can change in knowledge, holiness, and righteousness:

   a. in knowledge: from belief to unbelief, from understanding to misunderstanding (and vice versa).

   b. in holiness: from seeking the good (the knowledge of God) to seeking his own glory.

   c. in righteousness: from obeying God's law (to love God) to obeying man's/his own law.

When man changes, he does so in all three aspects together (not just one or two)—they are not in conflict with one another; there is a split down the middle of his whole inner being—the Fall affects every aspect of the heart of man (total depravity).[11]

iii. Man is a triune personality, in the image of the Triune God.

   a. The most common way this is spoken of is intellect, emotion, and will.

   b. In Scripture, this is spoken of as knowledge, holiness, and righteousness.

   c. In the Old Testament, those distinctions are spoken of in terms of the offices of prophet, priest, and king.

   d. Man is to love God with the whole heart: mind, soul, and strength.

   e. If he does not love God with his whole heart, seeking him diligently to understand what is clear, his entire being will be

---

10. *John 1:5.*

11. *Paper No. 120* and *18.*

affected. There will be a disunity within man's being and a
disorder in his life (corporately, in the life of culture).

The manifestation of this can be seen in the conflict of those
saying, "I am of Paul" (more prophetic), or "I am of Apollos" (more priestly), or "I am of Cephas" (more kingly).[12]
These divisions continue with us still and account for divisions within Christendom.

iv. Man is a body/soul unity.

   a. The visible body reveals the invisible soul.

   b. Physical death reveals something about spiritual death. The
   two should be distinguished properly (e.g., the wages of sin is
   spiritual death, not physical death).[13] Physical death becomes
   a sign that is imposed upon man, through the curse, of the
   condition of spiritual death—calling man to repentance. Just
   as there are two kinds of death, there are two kinds of resurrection, one of the soul and one of the body.[14]

   c. Miracles of healing in the New Testament (e.g., from blindness, leprosy, being lame, or physical death) are signs of a
   spiritual reality.

   d. They are a unity (vs. one independent of the other, in a kind
   of dualism) and, therefore, one affects the other—the mind
   affects the body and the body affects the mind.

   e. There is an order between the two—the soul leads and rules
   the body. Man is not genetically determined, but rather the
   soul leads the body in matters of knowledge, holiness, and
   righteousness.

v. Man is a male/female unity.

   a. Male and female in the image of God reveal God as Creator
   and upholder (providence) of all things. Both aspects (the

---

12. *1 Corinthians 1:12-13.*

13. This is further developed in *Paper No. 147.*

14. *Ephesians 2:1; Colossians 2:13; John 11:25-26; John 5:25; John 5:28-29; Revelation 20:6,
14; 21:8.*

masculine and feminine) are fundamentally spiritual qualities. Man is a male/female unity reflecting the unity and order of those qualities in God.

Failing to understand the nature of male/female differences leads to distortion and division in gender wars.

    b. Just as both aspects are in God, both were in one person (in man).

    c. The visible differences of male and female reveal (become a sign of) the invisible (spiritual) differences of the masculine and feminine.

    d. What was one nature (in one person) became two persons (male and female), which were to become one flesh.

    e. The covenant of marriage (the relationship between man and woman) reveals the covenant of creation (in which God established a permanent relationship between himself and mankind). This covenant of creation is completed in Christ and the Church.

  vi. Man is finite, temporal, and changeable in time and place.

    a. Man is historically situated.

    b. Man is historically influenced.

    c. Man is historically developed.

    d. Yet man is not historically or geographically determined.

    e. Rather, man is covenantally determined—whether he is in Adam (the covenant made with Adam) or in Christ (the covenant made with Christ).[15]

  vii. Man is a unique personality.

    a. Man's uniqueness is irreducible to other aspects and factors of his being.

    b. It is revelational of God in a unique way.

    c. It is continuing forever.

---

15. This is further developed in *Paper No. 145*.

4. Creation is very good

  i. *And God saw everything that he had made, and, behold, it was very good.* It was very good because *all* of creation reveals God and reveals him clearly.

  ii. It was very good, together, because the completion of the work of creation in all its vast array is a full revelation. It speaks of plenitude, but not infinitude.

It is estimated, currently, that there are 100 billion stars in each galaxy, and there are 100-200 billion galaxies. Although we are now discovering how vast the physical universe is, in doing a critical analysis of biblical cosmology, we should have understood and anticipated this from what is said in many other places in Scripture from the beginning (e.g., *as the stars of the heaven and as the sand which is on the seashore . . . which cannot be numbered for multitude;*[16] God stretched out the heavens[17]—the expansion of the firmament, from one source). The biblical revelation of cosmology gives a view from the beginning of what human beings have gathered slowly over time (or in leaps and bounds from time to time) in history, operating with a limited understanding based on observation.

  iii. The animals were given green vegetation for food in the beginning.

  iv. There was no physical death for man, as he was created.

  v. Altogether, creation was very good—there was no natural evil (the curse) before and apart from moral evil in the Fall.

*This paper is posthumously published
based upon the original work of Dr. Surrendra Gangadean
and has been edited by The Logos Foundation Editorial Board.*

---

16. *Genesis 22:17; 32:12; Deuteronomy 1:10; 10:22.*

17. *Isaiah 40:22; 42:5; 44:24; 45:12; 48:13; 51:13; Jeremiah 10:12; 51:15; Zechariah 12:1; Job 9:8; Psalm 104:2.*

THE BIBLICAL WORLDVIEW

PART V

The Fall:
The Covenant of Creation and the Temptation

INTRODUCTION

1. All non-theists, all non-Christian theists, and strict literalists deny the idea of a covenant of creation (the Fall). Understanding the Fall is essential/necessary to understand the Christian Faith.

2. *Objection 1:* There is no literal mention of the word "covenant."

   Response 1: From special revelation: *representation* is the essence of covenant. One person acts for another.

   i. *For as in Adam all die . . .*[1] All descendants of Adam have been affected by his act.

   ii. By one man sin and death entered the world.[2] Again, by one man an effect came on everyone else.

   iii. A covenant is necessary to understand the person and work of Christ. He comes to undo what Adam did and to do what Adam

---

1. *1 Corinthians 15:22.*
2. *Romans 5:12-21.*

failed to do—he is the covenant head in the place of Adam, after the Fall.

Christ must suffer (paying the penalty of sin—to undo) and then enter his glory as covenant head (to rule in the place of Adam to make God known).

As Savior: he is the Lamb of God who takes away the sin of the world (*vicarious* atonement—another in your place).

As Lord: he is ruling, through his people, to make God known.

Response 2: From general revelation: the idea of a covenant can be derived.

   i. From the Problem of Evil: any evil (moral or natural) is not original in the creation.

     Argument:

     If God is all powerful, then he *could* create a world without evil.

     If he is all good, then he *would*.

     If he could and would, then he *must* have.

     If he must have, then he *did*.

  ii. Yet we are born into a world with natural evil (in nature and in man). It is not inherent in moral evil/sin (as punishment); it was imposed by God, not arbitrarily, but as a call back from moral evil.

 iii. Therefore, natural evil is due to moral evil; from the act (the moral evil) of one man (the first man), all have been affected.

 iv. As a result of the one man's sin and its effect on us,[3] it can be explained that all (universal) have sinned; no one seeks God, no one understands. So, both moral and natural evil go back to this act of the first man—the covenant head.

3. *Objection 2:* Covenant headship is not fair; it is not just to be punished for the sin of another.

---

3. *Paper No. 103.*

Response 1: Imputed sin and guilt is not actual sin and guilt. In the Fall, the sin and guilt of Adam is imputed to all.

Response 2: Spiritual death (meaninglessness, boredom, and guilt) is inherent in actual sin.

Response 3: Natural evil is not punishment; it serves to restrain, recall from, and remove moral evil in man; as a call back (to stop and think), it is mercy.

Response 4: Man, as a rational being, is always free to use his reason to see what is clear (to avoid/overcome moral evil). He does not find himself as a victim without freedom.

Response 5: Christ's vicarious atonement (death on the cross) is both just (to pay the penalty) and merciful (his righteousness is imputed to us, and we are accepted on this basis—triple imputation: Adam's sin to us, our sin to Christ, Christ's righteousness to us). There is no conflict between God's justice and mercy.

THE COVENANT OF CREATION

1. Purpose: to establish man in everlasting/permanent relationship with God.

    i. Man in himself is changeable (finite, temporal, changeable).

    ii. Through the act of one man, a covenant head, in the first man Adam, all his descendants will be represented.

    iii. All of life and history flows from one source by covenant representation.

2. Probation

    i. Man's obedience to the will of God is to be tested for a time.

    ii. Should he obey, he and all in him will be established in life by the covenant.

    iii. Should he disobey, he and all in him will surely die (spiritual death).

3. Manifestation

    i. The whole account of Genesis 2:4-25 makes the idea of covenant manifest (i.e., through one, all are affected). Here, an account of the creation is being given in the context of the covenant (connected with the created order).

    Genesis 1 speaks about God as the Almighty Creator (Elohim). In addition to this, in Genesis 2 it begins by speaking of *The LORD God* (Yahweh/Jehovah Elohim)—the "Covenant-Keeping God." This gives a definite indication of a new type of relationship between God and man coming into focus.

    ii. The centrality of the Garden of Eden (and the rivers flowing out) in space (geographically) represents the centrality of the covenant of creation to history (flowing out in time from the Garden). The visible spatial representation shows that all of life (biologically, geographically, and historically—all the unfolding events of history) flows out from this one place and from this one man, this covenant representation.

    iii. In the center of the Garden are the tree of life and the tree of the knowledge of good and evil. The visible trees make manifest the invisible choice between two ways—between good and evil, between life and death. This is representative of the choice all men have continually between good and evil.

    iv. The covenant of marriage of man and woman. The latter part of Genesis 2 focuses on this relation and their being united/one flesh for the purpose for which God created them.

        a. Man is a body/soul unity, in the image of God, distinct from the animals (he is called to name them).

        b. Man is to name the creation; naming requires grasping the nature/essence of things in all their parts and relations (e.g., within a being; within the brain; within the DNA; the relation of man to all other creatures and the environment).

        Naming the creation is necessary for ruling (developing/making manifest all the powers latent in) the creation.

        Naming the creation is as vast and complex as all of creation.

   c. Only man, made in the image of God, can name and rule the creation. No animal is suitable to help man.

   The vastness of the task of dominion requires a vast number of human beings.

   d. Man is a male/female unity in the image of God—one person with a diversity of aspects. What was united in one person was separated (the masculine and feminine aspects became incarnate) into two persons, in man and woman.

   e. Man and woman are to be united in a covenant of marriage, to be fruitful and multiply, to fill the earth and to rule over it.

   f. Dominion by all of mankind through all of history is to fill the earth with the knowledge of God as the waters cover the sea. Dominion is at the core of the very being of man.

   g. The visible covenant of marriage between man and woman reveals the invisible covenant of creation between God and man. This finds its consummate expression in Christ and the Church (the Bride of Christ).[4]

THE TEMPTATION

1. A temptation is a test, an examination, during one's period of probation.

2. Neither the temptation, nor the tempter, is the cause of sin, but reveals (makes manifest) if a person is in sin.

   i. Some object to the idea of Satan in the form of a talking snake—this appears ridiculous and is therefore dismissed. Behind the dismissal is the idea that there is no supernatural, because if this is allowed, the door will be opened for all kinds of absurdity/silliness. This presents a false dichotomy of all or nothing. Rather, at best, the tempter (and temptation) is the occasion (not the cause) of sin, making manifest what is already present.

---

4. *Revelation 21.*

ii. It is necessary for this to become manifest (clear) so one cannot argue and get around it.

God is neither the tempter, nor the author of sin. A man is tempted when he is drawn away by his own desires.[5] Man is always free to do as he pleases (to use his reason to see what is clear, if he desires).

3. The temptation is addressed to man as a rational being; it examines his knowledge of God, whether or not he has been pursuing the knowledge of God as the good.

4. The temptation comes in the form of an argument: the conclusion, "you shall not surely die," is a flat contradiction of what God said: "you shall surely die." The reason given (the premise) is: "For God knows that . . . you will be like God, knowing good and evil." The premise is more basic than the conclusion. If one is brought to believe the premise, they will be persuaded to believe the conclusion.

5. Good and evil for man.

   i. It is clear to reason that good for a being is according the nature of that being (the good for man as a rational being is the use of his reason to the fullest to understand the nature of things, and therefore the nature of God).

   ii. It is clear to reason that God, as Creator, determines the nature of the creation and thus determines good and evil for that creature.

   iii. It is clear to reason that man is finite, temporal, and changeable, and cannot determine (create) the nature of the creature. Thus, man cannot be as God in knowing good and evil. God knows by determining; man knows by discovering.

   iv. Had man been seeking the knowledge of God as the good, he would have known these things. Instead, he believed what was false about God and man and good and evil (which are clear to

---

5. *James 1:13-14.*

reason—the Principle of Clarity).[6] This failure to seek and understand is inexcusable to man as a rational being.[7]

v. The temptation revealed that he had left off seeking the knowledge of God as the good.

vi. Man had put himself in the place of God, contrary to reason and the nature of things, to determine good and evil.

vii. The outward visible act of eating of the tree of the knowledge of good and evil revealed the inward invisible act of putting himself in the place of God to determine good and evil.

viii. The temptation and sin of the first man in the Garden is the archetype of all temptation and sin.

ix. The sin of not seeking and not understanding preceded the sin of the outward act of disobedience.

This paper is posthumously published
based upon the original work of Dr. Surrendra Gangadean
and has been edited by The Logos Foundation Editorial Board.

---

6. *Paper No. 2* and *53.*

7. *Romans 1:20; 3:10-11.*

Paper N⍛ 146

___

THE BIBLICAL WORLDVIEW

PART VI

The Fall:
Sin

1. From general revelation: sin is an act contrary to one's nature. It is to neglect, avoid, resist, or deny reason in the face of what is clear about God. It is every degree of acting contrary to our rational nature.

   i. An act contrary to one's nature is harmful or destructive to one's self (the nature expresses the essential qualities of the self).

   ii. Man's nature or essence is the deepest level of the self and is spiritual (rational/thinking).

   iii. To neglect, avoid, resist, or deny one's reason is an act of spiritual suicide.

   iv. The inherent consequence of spiritual suicide is spiritual death.

   v. Only the self can harm the self. (*A good man cannot be harmed either in life or in death*—Socrates; *Do not fear those who kill the body but cannot kill the soul;*[1] *What will it profit a man if he gains the whole world, and loses his own soul?*[2]—only a man can cause the loss of his own soul).

___

1. *Matthew 10:28.*

2. *Matthew 16:26.*

vi. To deny rather than affirm human nature in oneself is to act against human nature in others. This may be explicit or implicit.

To dehumanize the self (nature/essence, in one's own mind) is to dehumanize others (in one's mind, since the essence is the same in all men). This continues to dehumanizing in conversation (not addressing others as rational beings) and then using force rather than reason to bring about change in others.

vii. To put any secondary aspect of self above a more primary aspect is to deny human nature (i.e., the larger aspect, narrower aspect, triune personality, body/soul unity, male/female unity, background, uniqueness—in that order) (e.g., we are first human, and then we are male or female; we are first human, and then we are Greek or Jew etc.).

viii. To reverse the order within any aspect of human nature, denies human nature (e.g., in our triune personality, to put the practical or psychological (based on one's present level of self-consciousness) before the intellectual, is to deny human nature in oneself—this is a failure to see how our beliefs/thinking affect our feelings/desires and actions).

2. The clarity of general revelation regarding the existence and nature of God makes unbelief inexcusable.[3]

i. It is clear that man is a thinking being and that reason in itself is the laws of thought, the test of meaning, and is self-attesting.

ii. It is clear that reason is ontological: it applies to being as well as thought; that there is no being from non-being; that there must be something eternal.

iii. It is clear that matter exists (the cause of what I see is not my mind or other minds, but is outside all minds, and is therefore material), and that matter is not eternal (the material universe is not self-maintaining—in general, in its parts, and as a whole).

iv. It is clear that the soul exists (the mind is not the brain), and that the soul is not eternal (man's knowledge is always finite/growing).

---

3. *Romans 1:20.*

v. It is clear, therefore, that only some (God, the Creator) is eternal, and that God is infinite, eternal, and unchangeable in being, wisdom, power, holiness, justice, goodness, and truth.

vi. It is clear, therefore, that original creation was good, that natural evil is due to moral evil (sin).

vii. It is clear that how things operate currently (providence) does not explain how things originate in creation.

viii. It is clear that natural evil is imposed as a merciful call back to stop and think and that natural evil as mercy requires special revelation as redemptive revelation, to show how God is infinite, eternal, and unchangeable in both justice and goodness (mercy).

ix. It is clear that only Genesis 1–3 (and what builds on this) is consistent with clear general revelation and qualifies as redemptive revelation (because it answers the question of how God can be both just and merciful to man in the condition of sin and death).

x. It is clear that failure to know and acknowledge what is clear to reason, from the more basic to the less basic, is contrary to reason and is sin/moral evil, and is destructive to oneself as a thinking/rational being.

3. If there is no clear general revelation, then there is no rational possibility of sin, and therefore no necessity for redemption through Christ crucified.

4. From special revelation: sin is not seeking, not understanding, and not doing what is right.[4]

5. From special revelation: sin is not glorifying God as God;[5] it is coming short of the glory of God.[6]

6. Sin is rooted in unbelief; it is not an act of will contrary to knowledge.[7] Ignorance of what is clear is culpable.

---

4. *Psalm 14:1-3; Psalm 53:1-3; Romans 3:10-12.*

5. *Romans 1:21.*

6. *Romans 3:23.*

7. *Paper No. 120.*

Root sin must be removed to overcome (master) fruit sin.

7. Sin is autonomy (*auto-nomos*).

    i. It is being a law unto oneself, being lawless with respect to God's law; it is determining good and evil from what pleases self, being self-centered vs. God-centered.

    ii. From Historic Christianity: sin is any want of conformity unto, or transgression of, the law of God.[8]

    iii. The duty which God requires of man is obedience to his revealed will, the moral law, and is summed up in the Decalogue/Ten Commandments.[9]

    iv. The Decalogue is written on the heart of man[10]—it is grounded in the basic features of human nature; it is easily knowable by all.[11] It is not from God by divine command theory, nor from man by arbitrary/positive law, nor from mere custom/tradition.

    v. Being grounded in human nature, the moral law is for all men (universal), everywhere, at all times (perpetual/lasting); it is not culturally relative.

    vi. The moral law is comprehensive; it applies to all aspects of human nature, all areas of human life (public and private), and all levels of human life (inward and outward).

    vii. The sum of the moral law/Decalogue/Ten Commandments is to love the Lord our God with all our heart, with all our soul, with all our strength, and with all our mind; and our neighbor as ourselves.[12] The moral law and the law of love are one and the same.

    viii. The moral law is teleological (aimed at the good/eternal life/ knowledge of God); it is not aimed merely at duty/virtue/deontology, nor is it consequential/hedonic/focused on happiness.

---

8. Gangadean, *The Westminster Catechisms.* See SCQ. 14; Gangadean, *The Westminster Confession.* See Question 30.

9. Gangadean, *The Westminster Catechisms.* See SCQ. 39-41.

10. *Romans 2:14-15.*

11. *Deuteronomy 30:11-14.*

12. Gangadean, *The Westminster Catechisms.* See SCQ. 42.

ix. The good is the source of unity in each person and among all
persons, in each institution and among all institutions, in each
nation and among all nations.

x. The consequence of good vs. evil, of obeying vs. disregarding
the moral law, is spiritual life vs. spiritual death, which increases forever, unendingly.

*This paper is posthumously published
based upon the original work of Dr. Surrendra Gangadean
and has been edited by The Logos Foundation Editorial Board.*

Paper № 147

THE BIBLICAL WORLDVIEW

PART VII

The Fall:
Death and Theodicy

DEATH

1. All have sinned and come short of the glory of God.[1] The wages of sin is death.[2]

   There are two kinds of death, physical and spiritual (pertaining to body and soul). Failure to distinguish these brings confusion in understanding the wages of sin.

   There are accordingly two deaths and two resurrections, one of the soul and one of the body.

   i. *You that were* [past tense] *dead in trespasses and sins . . .*[3]—clearly, this is referring to spiritual death—present in this life—which is the result of trespasses and sins.

   ii. *I am the resurrection and the life. He who believes in me, though he may die [physically], he shall live. And whoever lives and believes in*

---

1. *Romans 3:23.*

2. *Romans 6:23.*

3. *Ephesians 2:1.* See also *Colossians 2:13.*

me shall never die [spiritually].[4] In this one passage, Christ speaks about both physical and spiritual death.

iii. *The hour is coming, and now is, when the dead [spiritually] will hear the voice of the Son of God; and those who hear will live [spiritually].*[5] *For the hour is coming in which all who are in the graves [physically] will hear his voice and come forth [physically] . . . to the resurrection of life . . . [or] condemnation.*[6] Again, Christ is speaking about two kinds of death and two kinds of life (resurrection).

iv. *Blessed and holy is he who has part in the first resurrection. Over such the second death has no power.*[7] The first resurrection (implying the second resurrection) is a spiritual resurrection, and the second death (implying the first death) is spiritual death. Spiritual death has no power over those who take part in the spiritual resurrection. Later, the lake of fire is spoken of as the second death.[8] So, there are two kinds of death and two kinds of resurrection.

2. The wages of sin is spiritual death, not physical death, nor a physical place (as in the common perception of hell).

3. Spiritual death, as the wages of sin, reveals the justice of God. Divine justice, which is infinite, eternal, and unchangeable, is not and cannot be arbitrary. The consequence of moral evil is inherent in sin and therefore present, not future and imposed (as in the popular notion of hell).

4. Spiritual death is meaninglessness, boredom, and guilt.

i. Loss of meaning is present and inherent in not seeking and not understanding what is clear about God.

ii. In meaninglessness, *all* words and thoughts are increasingly emptied of cognitive meaning and consequently of psychological and practical meaning also.

---

4. *John 11:25-26.*

5. *John 5:25.*

6. *John 5:28-29.*

7. *Revelation 20:6*

8. *Revelation 20:14; 21:8.*

iii. Words as (conventional) signs lose their significance (power of signification).

5. Meaninglessness leads to boredom (diminishing satisfaction) in all activities and, hence, to increasing excess, to the point of abuse, wantonness, and perversion.

There is a progression within the seven deadly sins (pride, envy, anger, greed, lust, gluttony, sloth). It starts with pride (thinking we know when we don't) to envy (with our view of self) and anger (when that is not satisfied) and then all the appetites of greed, lust, and gluttony—all under the condition of sloth (not just physical, but spiritual sloth in not seeking).

6. Excess leads to transgression/trespassing (crossing boundaries) and misery (in our feelings/desires) and guilt.

The self is the author of its own misery (you did it to yourself).

The torment of guilt and shame (that the self is blameworthy) cannot be escaped by all the subtleties of self-justification. Guilt is objective; shame is subjective.

7. The wages of sin is spiritual death, not physical death (from #2 above).

   i. Natural evil (the curse/physical death[9]) is imposed to restrain, recall from, and remove moral evil.

   ii. Natural evil is a call to stop and think. It is mercy, not justice. When we stop and think about basic things, moral evil begins to be removed.

   iii. Natural evil is not evenly distributed as justice requires.

   iv. Natural evil/physical death ends with the resurrection of the body; spiritual death as justice (punishment) goes on unendingly.

8. Infinite justice is not the intensification of natural evil, as imposed, to the greatest degree (such as a literal lake of fire/the fires of hell).

---

9. *Genesis 3:19.*

9. In several biblical phrases, figurative language/expression is used in speaking about spiritual death—the visible is used to speak of the invisible spiritual state. Figurative language should not be mistaken for something literal.

  i. The lake of fire (hell) is symbolic of destruction, which *for man* is spiritual and is sometimes called the second death.[10]

  Death and Hades, the beast and the false prophet, Satan, and anyone whose name is not found in the book of life (those who remain in spiritual death) are cast into the lake of fire.[11] Each are destroyed appropriately according to the nature of the function or the being.

  ii. *Outer darkness* is figurative for the darkness of mind (meaninglessness).

  iii. *Where the fire is not quenched* is figurative for desires burning without satisfaction (boredom).

  iv. *Where their worm does not die* is figurative for torment of conscience (guilt and shame gnawing as a worm).

  v. *The bottomless pit* is figurative for ever increasing miseries of spiritual death—it is unending (*No worst, there is none*[12]).

10. The literal doctrine of hell has five problems:

  i. It is inconsistent with reason—in terms of infinite, non-arbitrary justice; the body being consumed and having to be recreated every moment to continue in pain; spiritual beings (Satan) being cast into a literal/physical lake of fire; Death (not a being) being cast into a physical lake of fire.

  ii. It is inconsistent with Scripture, which speaks of the lake of fire as the second death. The Scripture is emphatic—the figurative is being explained literally as spiritual death.

  iii. It has caused many to stumble.

---

10. *Revelation 20:14; 21:8.*

11. *Revelation 20:10, 13-15.*

12. Gerard Manley Hopkins, *No Worst, There Is None.*

iv. It has caused God's name (his justice) to be blasphemed.

v. It has removed the true fear of God from man—the fear of spiritual death, present and inherent, not future and imposed. From the beginning: *In the day that you eat of it, you shall surely die.*

11. Only in seeing the connection of sin (not seeking, not understanding, and not doing what is right) and death (meaninglessness, boredom, and guilt) can the infinite justice of God be seen. We are called to see the glory/excellence of the divine justice.

12. The noetic effect of sin[13] is the darkness of mind in spiritual death, remaining as long as sin remains.

Sin remains in all persons to varying degrees throughout one's lifetime. All die; all are being called back; all have some sin remaining. Job (the most righteous man in his time) came to repent and see something of the glory of God that he had not seen before.

For believers, the noetic effect no longer operates when physical death is no longer a call back.

The self-centeredness in the noetic effect of sin hinders us from using reason to see what is clear about God. Self-centeredness avoids the critical use of reason in self-examination (because it takes the self as it is, and one's own thinking process, as what is should be, and therefore we don't want anything to challenge our position of being at the center).

The noetic effect involves several aspects of knowledge:

i. There is a failure to know (ignorance) arising from a failure to diligently seek God and to understand what is clear about God and man and good and evil.

There is a failure to glorify God as God arising from a failure to recognize God as the author of all good (no thankfulness).[14]

There is, in addition, self-deception about one's seeking to know. We like to think we are seeking, but this is not true if

---

13. *Paper No. 103.*

14. *Romans 1:21.*

we don't see that which is objectively clear about God and man and good and evil.

ii. There is (positive) misunderstanding (error) concerning basic things due to lack of self-examination.

Thinking becomes vain (self-contradictory) without recognizing it (the mind is darkened).[15] We prefer to remain less conscious and consistent.

There is self-justification about one's ignorance and error. The inexcusable is being excused. Ignorance and errors are either denied or explained away. Blame is shifted to others (Adam blamed his wife Eve, as well as God).

iii. We think we know when we do not (pride).

Professing themselves to be wise, they became fools.[16]

iv. We think others don't know.

The fool sits in the seat of the scornful.[17] He progresses to that position.

Scorn (ridicule and slander) is used in the place of reason and argument.

v. The noetic effect changes the infinite, eternal, and unchangeable nature of God to finite, temporal, changeable creatures, descending downward (from man to birds, beasts, and reptiles/creeping things).[18]

Nature, not God, is thought to be the Creator, to create and uphold all things (evolutionary view).

vi. The noetic effect of sin on the mind of man affects the whole heart, which includes man's desires and will.

---

15. *Romans 1:21.*
16. *Romans 1:22.*
17. *Psalm 1.*
18. *Romans 1:23.*

vii. As unholiness and desires, and unrighteousness and will/actions increase, a downward spiral of sin and self-deception and self-justification sets in, continues, and builds on itself.

viii. Only the increasing suffering of natural evil (the curse) can restrain, recall from, and remove the compounding moral evil of not seeking, not understanding, and not doing what is right, as well as the additional complication of self-deception and self-justification.

THEODICY

1. Theodicy seeks to show the divine justice and goodness in response to the problem of evil (POE): if God is all good and all powerful, why is there evil (moral and natural evil (ME and NE))?

2. The POE is not a contradiction and the solution does not have to remain a mystery/unknown.

3. Evil (ME and NE) can only be justified in relation to the good, not by free will or by virtue (i.e., suffering of one kind produces commensurate virtue; virtue is the means to the good), but only by the good, which is the knowledge of God.

4. ME (not seeking, not understanding, and not doing what is right) serves both to obscure the knowledge of God and to deepen the revelation of the glory of God.

The revelation of divine justice and mercy is deepened through ME and NE.

Consider the analysis of the parable of the prodigal son.[19] Briefly: his failure to see/understand leads him down a path in which NE increases until he comes to stop and think (comes to his senses) and returns home. During that process, the consequence (justice) of his unbelief (working itself out) is seen, as well as the mercy (forgiveness, grace, and love) of the father is seen when he returns and is received back.

---

19. For further development, see Gangadean, *Philosophical Foundation*, 156-161.

5. NE (as toil and strife, and old age, sickness, and death, increasing to war, famine, and plague) serves throughout one's life and throughout history to restrain, recall from, and remove ME; it calls man to stop and think (vs. ME).

6. ME is removed gradually; if it is removed abruptly, the revelation is not deepened; if it is not removed, the revelation is not seen. There is a spiritual war between belief and unbelief (in human lives and throughout history) that is age-long and agonizing, in which good overcomes evil vs. alternatives (sudden removal of evil/premillennialism—in the return of Christ, or no removal of evil/amillennialism—good and evil will struggle until the end of history).

7. The Ironic Solution to the POE: because of all the moral evil in the world/me, I cannot see what is clear about God (how it can be said that God is all good and all powerful).[20] At this point, the problem of evil ironically dissolves. The solution is simply: open your eyes; use your reason to see what is clear.

This solution is ironic because we should have seen/understood this problem given the nature of evil.

8. The Ironic Solution assumes:

   i. The clarity of general revelation and the inexcusability of unbelief (if this can be shown, then the solution can begin to work).

   ii. There is no other way to deepen the revelation (e.g., there is no beatific vision—a direct seeing of God—apart from the revelation in his works of creation and providence; there is not some other version of history (book, movie, virtual reality) that can supply/represent the experience of providence in the fall and redemption of mankind).

   iii. The good justifies the evil (this is true only for those who go through suffering and come to see the good).[21]

---

20. Gangadean, *Philosophical Foundation*, 161.

21. *Romans 8:18.*

9. Is there gratuitous evil in this life, from the trivial to the tragic (Job)?

Is this the best of all possible worlds (Leibniz)? Can we really have this kind of optimism or is this merely a faux-optimism (resulting in individual passivity)? Set in contrast to this, is seeing what we are called to do in an agonizing struggle against unbelief in ourselves and in others—a work that is being done corporately, cumulatively, and communally through history (the work of dominion), and that the sufferings we go through in this life serve that purpose— the purpose of which is the knowledge of God (the whole creation groans, waiting in earnest expectation for the appearing of the sons of God;[22] *We know that all things work together for good*[23]). This includes animal suffering of all kinds and even that which symbolically represents death to us (*Margaret, are you grieving / Over Golden-grove unleaving? / Leaves, like the things of man, you / With your fresh thoughts care for, can you?*[24]).

10. Is there gratuitous evil in the next life (in the duration of hell)?

i. Can one "walk out of hell" at any time one wishes?

There is no essential difference between spiritual death in this life and in the next life. In rational freedom, there is never a conflict between *want* and *can*.[25] Freedom to use one's reason to see what is clear about God is inalienable (it can never be taken away; it is part of one's essence). If one uses their reason to see what is clear, then the whole process of meaninglessness (spiritual death) will be reversed. In that sense, one *can* walk out of hell at any time one *wishes*. But empirically, the duration shows, that left to ourselves, we will never turn around (desire) to seek God (use our reason) to see what is clear. It is only by the sovereign grace of God that any do.

---

22. *Romans 8:18-22.*

23. *Romans 8:28.*

24. Gerard Manley Hopkins, *Spring and Fall.*

25. Gangadean, *History of Philosophy*, 153-154; Gangadean, *Philosophical Foundation*, 66, 167-168.

ii. Does duration deepen the revelation of divine justice?

Unending spiritual death (the bottomless pit) deepens the revelation of God's justice and mercy, forever.

iii. Are persons being used as means only (to reveal the divine glory) and not ends (some have tried to object with this on Kantian terms)?

It should be understood that the divine glory is manifest in, by, *unto*, and upon human beings.[26] It is not merely *in* them, it is *unto* them. So, the distinction between means and ends does not apply here.

iv. Does divine justice (in the duration of hell) violate mercy?

Does justice somehow set aside that God could be merciful—that he could stop this process after a thousand, or ten thousand, or ten billion years? In the simplicity of God, there is no tension among any of his attributes—particularly, the attributes of justice and mercy; justice does not violate (or set aside) mercy, and mercy does not set aside justice. Both reveal God's glory/excellence and are equally worthy of praise. In justice, God leaves unrepentant sinners in their sin and the consequence of spiritual death (ontological justice—the wages of sin). In mercy, God extends or withholds mercy as he pleases, according to the unsearchable counsel of his own will.[27]

Would annihilation be better? Some who misunderstand the divine justice see annihilation as better for God and for man. For God, it seemingly spares him from the charge of cruelty (gratuitous evil) by everlasting punishment. For man, it allows for cessation of being to an otherwise everlasting meaningless existence. Annihilationism fails to understand the ontological nature of infinite/divine justice, the purpose of God's eternal decree, and the deepening of the revelation of both his justice and mercy—past, present, and future.

---

26. *WCF 2.2.*
27. *WCF 3.7.*

Is voluntary soul-sleep (or a state of pure consciousness), which removes awareness of self and suffering, possible? This is an attempt at turning off the mind (the cessation of all thoughts, supposedly when and how long one wants) if one wants a rest from the spiritual death (meaninglessness) connected with the life of the mind. This is impossible because one's essence, as a rational being, determined by God, asserts itself. The light of reason cannot be extinguished in oneself; the demand of human nature for meaning is inextinguishable.[28] If one wants to object, in an attempt at self-justification, and say, "Why have you made me so?" then this is not intelligible—one would be using their reason to question their reason—"I want a reason why I don't want to use reason." This is self-referentially absurd.

The biblical concept of sin and spiritual death (justice) transforms the problem of a final theodicy.

This paper is posthumously published
based upon the original work of Dr. Surrendra Gangadean
and has been edited by The Logos Foundation Editorial Board.

---

28. *John 1:4-5.*

Paper № 148

THE BIBLICAL WORLDVIEW

PART VIII

Redemption:
The First and Second Calls to Repentance

1. **Man is fallen: redemption presupposes the Fall, and the Fall presupposes creation.**

   In redemption, we are being restored from our condition of the Fall, which was a fall away from creation—we are being restored back to our original purpose in creation, but in a deeper way, given the reality of sin.

   i. Under the covenant of creation, Adam disobeyed. Therefore, all are fallen in Adam. Without the covenant of creation, we cannot speak about the Fall (of mankind; it is not simply an event in one person's life).

   ii. His outward (visible) sin of disobedience in the act of eating of the tree of the knowledge of good and evil reveals his inward (invisible) sin of autonomy, of determining good and evil apart from and against God. The good, for Adam, was no longer the knowledge of God, but what pleased Adam.

   iii. Adam listened to his wife in opposition to the Word of God.[1] His desire for his wife came before his desire for God.

---

1. *Genesis 3:17.*

While the tempter spoke to the woman, Adam was with her and said nothing. She saw that the tree was good for food, pleasing to the eye, and desirable to make one wise (singling out this tree from others)—a special kind of knowledge apart from any reference to God. She ate and then turned and gave to Adam, and he ate.

iv. Both man and woman failed to recognize their thinking had become vain/empty of meaning/futile/contradictory without their knowing it.

When we look at the temptation (the argument, assumptions, words, and the meaning of the words being used), understanding/meaning was clearly lost with respect to the distinctions of God and man, infinite and finite, Creator and creature, and good and evil.

v. In the outward act of eating, their eyes were opened; they realized they no longer were righteous before God/they had disobeyed God (this was not right, in terms of God's command).

vi. Previously they were naked and felt no shame. Their physical/visible nakedness now became a sign (connected with the new reality) of their spiritual/invisible nakedness (that is, their lack of righteousness).

vii. In the intimate connection between the visible and the invisible, they now felt shame in connection with their physical nakedness.

2. The first call (back) to repentance: shame.

i. The feeling of shame is an inward recognition by one's conscience that one has sinned, is blameworthy, and that one deserves to be cut off (punished) for one's sin.

The prodigal son: "I am no longer worthy to be called your son." And he was willing to accept the consequence of loss of sonship, with its the rights and privileges. Dealing with this is necessary for repentance.

ii. Conscience is an inward moral sense in man, created by God, that judges the moral action of man, according to the moral law written on the heart of man. This includes the notion of being blameworthy and deserving to be punished.

iii. Conscience is neither originated by man (himself or human society) nor, therefore, can it be eradicated by man (he will go on forever with his conscience, which will bring up this shame and guilt forever and the unending torment connected with this).

But conscience can be conditioned for a time by false beliefs—there can be a conflict between one's intuitive belief (e.g., that God exists—which may be part of an original, Edenic, pre-fallen condition) and one's present belief system that appears to oneself as rational (e.g., that there is no God—based on what appears to be rational to them (all is matter; all is natural; all can be explained in those terms)). This conflict exacerbates the problem (next point).

iv. There may be ignorance of the moral law (even though it is written on our hearts), but this is without excuse (culpable ignorance) and is the first source (root) of shame (for the failure to know/to be rational).

Shame is directed against oneself—"You should be ashamed of yourself"—what the self has become, or how the self has acted. In self-justification, the perpetual attempt to give a reason for what we've done is our conscience striking out against us, saying, "You are made as a rational being; you should be rational; you have no excuse for your failure to be rational." This, ultimately, is what the shame of conscience is rooted in.

v. Shame, arising as a conviction of sin by one's own conscience, is God's first call to man to repent.

vi. Repentance (from the word *metanoia*) is a change of mind (regarding one's unbelief). It involves confessing one's sin (root and fruit) and in paying (or seeking forgiveness of) one's debt.

vii. Failure to repent and to satisfy divine justice leaves one with guilt (objectively) and shame (subjectively) remaining. One cannot live with shame (it is a very powerful feeling—a sense of unworthiness); we have to deal with it one way or another. Man avoids the first call to repentance by seeking to avoid shame.

viii. Adam and Eve sought to avoid shame by covering their physical nakedness. They sowed leaves together to cover their physical nakedness, which is now a reminder of the spiritual nakedness. This involved a deliberate effort showing intention (not casual).

ix. One's nakedness can be covered, but the covering cannot be covered (however many layers of covering). Their earlier state of nakedness without shame cannot readily be forgotten.

x. Only by an ongoing effort of precarious self-deception can the first call back through shame be, at best, tentatively avoided. It will come back again and again, leading to the second call back.

He that comes to God must believe that he is, and that he rewards those who diligently seek him.[2]

Yet in one's fallen condition, no one seeks God, no one understands, no one does what is right.

To the root sin of not seeking is now added the sin of self-deception regarding one's seeking to know the truth.

3. The second call to repentance: self-examination.

i. Any manifest presence (or reminder) of God (and the standard of his Word) is avoided by man in the state of sin and self-deception.

ii. Adam, in sin, heard God and feared (immediate feeling) and hid from his presence (revealing the noetic effect of a darkened mind—hiding from God, who is infinite in knowledge, is self-contradictory to the point of being absurd—this shows the precarious nature of self-deception).

iii. God calls to Adam: "Where are you?" This is the second call back.

a. God, who is infinite in knowledge, knows where Adam is, both physically and spiritually.

b. This is therefore a call to Adam for self-examination, to recognize his state of alienation from God (which has led him to hide from God).

c. This second call is external (going beyond the internal call of conscience); it is through another person (in this case God

---

2. *Hebrews 11:6.*

himself); the call is in the form of a question (vs. declarative) calling to spiritual self-examination.

iv. Existential honesty, confessing the effect of sin ("I was afraid . . . and I hid"), is not confession of sin (repentance requires the acknowledgement of sin as such).

v. When confronted with sin ("Have you eaten . . ."), in his state of sin and self-deception (with his autonomy and self-centered-ness—wanting to protect himself at any cost), man justifies himself by blaming others: "The woman you put here with me—she gave me some fruit from the tree, and I ate it."

This is not only ungentlemanly of Adam (to blame his wife), but it is much more—he excuses himself by blaming God (as if he were an innocent bystander; or, if God hadn't put the woman there, he would be alright).

vi. The woman, when confronted, blames the tempter: "The serpent deceived me, and I ate." While it may in fact be true that she was deceived (Satan being the occasion, not the cause of it), it is not an adequate justification (how can she be deceived regarding what is clear?).

vii. Human self-justification attempts to excuse what is inexcusable. Only God's justification can provide the righteousness that God requires of man by the covenant of creation.

Added to the root sin of not seeking is the sin of self-deception and, now, the sin of self-justification. These three realities and their extent, going to the point of blaming God, are necessary to understand the third call to repentance—the curse and the promise.

This paper is posthumously published
based upon the original work of Dr. Surrendra Gangadean
and has been edited by The Logos Foundation Editorial Board.

Paper N⍛ 149

———

THE BIBLICAL WORLDVIEW

PART IX

Redemption:
The Third Call to Repentance

THE CURSE AND THE PROMISE

1. God does not leave man in the state of sin, self-deception, and self-justification. God calls man back a third time.

   The third call back presupposes the rejection of the first two call backs. The purpose of the first two call backs was not frustrated by man's response.

2. The third call back is lasting and final; it is for all human beings everywhere, at all times. All men live and die under it. No nation, no tribe, no tongue, no class—rich or poor, high or low, Jew or Gentile, believer or non-believer, past or present—no one person is exempt.

   There is no further call back after death (the culmination of the curse).

3. The third call back consists of both the curse and the promise.

   The curse and the promise are given *together* (interwoven) and are not to be separated in thought or in proclamation.

4. The curse comes upon all of the creation and all mankind, and affects the entire realm of man's dominion. It is not on nature (the ground, plants, animals, etc.) apart from its relation to man (the whole creation groans, waiting in earnest expectation for the appearing of the sons of God[1]—man turning back to God and the original purpose for which God created him). So, both the Fall and redemption affect the creation.

5. The curse comes upon all animals.

    i. It comes upon some animals more than others, changing their form (to the serpent: "on your belly you shall go") and their food ("dust you shall eat").

    ii. It comes most upon the serpent, the instrument used by the tempter (that is, Satan—who is called the Old Serpent, the great dragon, Lucifer, and the Devil), and anticipates the humiliation and defeat of Satan in the figure of the serpent.

    iii. Originally, all animals had only green vegetation for food (the creation was *very good*). After the curse, some animals became carnivores (that is, devoured other animals for food)—their form was changed with the food.

    iv. The distinction between clean and unclean animals (those more affected by the curse) is a reminder to man of the curse and of man's fallen condition, and is a call to stop and think.

    Later, in connection with this distinction, are the kosher laws, Levitical cleansing, and contact with death making one unclean—in all of these, God is teaching and reminding mankind of the reality of the Fall and the curse (as a call back).

6. The promise

    i. God will reverse man's alliance with Satan in his believing Satan's lie. "I will put enmity between you [Satan] and the woman." Satan had seduced the woman through a lie, promising enlightenment/fulfillment apart from God.

    God puts enmity by sovereignly restoring man to the truth.

---

1. *Romans 8:18-22.*

ii. The enmity arises from the conflict of truth and falsehood and results, therefore, in a spiritual war between belief and unbelief, between good and evil, between truth and falsehood.

iii. The spiritual war cannot be fought with the weapons of physical war.

The weapons we fight with are not the weapons of the world. On the contrary, they have divine power to demolish strongholds. We demolish arguments and every pretension that sets itself up against the knowledge of God.[2]

iv. The conflict is being fought out in every person[3] (where the war begins), in every sphere of life, and at every level (spiritual war is, in this sense, a total war).

v. The spiritual war is age-long, between the seed of the woman (all those descendants who believe the truth) and the seed of the serpent (all those descendants who believe Satan's falsehood).

vi. The spiritual war is agonizing. Truth vs. falsehood is asymmetric warfare.

Truth can use only the light of reason; falsehood cannot use reason, but resorts to non-rational means (much repeated lies/propaganda and force).

vii. The cumulative failure to use reason to take false thoughts captive results in physical war.

Ideologies (pretentions, sleight of hand, and the cunning and craftiness of men in their deceitful scheming) that support physical war should be exposed and demolished, especially in light of the principle of the clarity of general revelation and Rational Presuppositionalism.

Only knowing and speaking the (relevant) truth (at the basic level—foundational truths about God and man, and good and evil) can overcome falsehood on which all injustice is based (including false teachings/misconceptions in the name of God—idolatry).

---

2. *2 Corinthians 10:4-5.*

3. *Romans 7.*

viii. The outcome of this spiritual war, which is age-long and agonizing, is that good will overcome evil.[4]

One who is to come (the seed of the woman—Christ) will spiritually crush the head of the serpent (destroy Satan and his lies).

Satan will strike his heel (inflict physical harm).

This now applies to those who believe the truth and those who do not. This can be seen all through Scripture and coming out in Revelation 19—Christ and his army wage war against Satan and his kingdom (including the false prophet, the harlot, and the beast). Ultimately, good will overcome evil because God, who is infinitely good, guarantees this (he will cause evil/unbelief to serve his purpose—to deepen the revelation of his justice and mercy). While there may be questions about what the outcome of a particular battle/stage of the war may be (often fought with much destruction/shedding of blood), there is no doubt about the outcome of the war.

ix. The one who is to come is in the place of Adam (according to the covenant of creation); he will do what Adam failed to do: he will hold to the truth and rule to make God known.

7. The curse brings sorrow in childbearing.

i. Children are born under the Fall in the covenant of creation.

They must face in themselves the conflict of good and evil.

Their hearts must be turned to the truth by God.

ii. The conflict of good and evil is manifest between parents and children, and between children, in the conflict between belief and unbelief.

The sorrow in childbearing is not referring primarily to physical pain at the time of childbirth, but the whole process of bringing children into the world in this conflict.

iii. The paradigm of sorrow in childbearing is manifest in the first children born on earth.

---

4. *Genesis 3:15.*

Cain did not receive the instruction from Adam (how sin is dealt with—the need for sacrifice symbolized in the coats of skin), nor from Abel's example, nor from God (who directly called him back to do what is right, to be accepted).

In unbelief, he was angry, envious that Abel was accepted and he was not, thought he was wronged, and slew his brother. We can be certain this brought sorrow to the heart of his parents.

iv. The conflict between belief and unbelief is the source of all strife on earth. It was and is the source of all violence, murder, and war.

It begins in each person and each household:

Do not think that I have come to bring peace to the earth. I have not come to bring peace, but a sword . . . a man's enemies will be those of his own household.[5] This should be understood in light of "I will put enmity between you and the woman."

Consider him who endured from sinners such hostility against himself, so that you may not grow weary or fainthearted. In your struggle against sin, you have not yet resisted to the point of shedding your blood.[6]

v. The promise of redemption (not just the curse bringing sorrow) is also extended to one's own household (children) in the signs of the covenant—circumcision (Old Testament) and baptism (New Testament).

vi. The promise of redemption restores the relationship between husband and wife.

Having sinned and turned from the good, Adam became a delinquent husband in not leading his wife by the Word of God—one of his first responsibilities as spiritual head.

His desire was for his wife without God, and as a result, she ruled over him (he listened to her voice instead of the Word of God).[7]

---

5. *Matthew 10:34-36.*

6. *Hebrews 12:3-4.*

7. *Genesis 3:17.*

In redemption, her desire will be for her husband, and he will rule over her by the Word of God.[8]

8. The curse comes on the ground and on man.

   i. Thorns and thistles reduce the fertility of the earth.

   ii. By toil and sorrow, in the sweat of his face, man eats bread. There is stress connected with work in every way.

   iii. The ground is cursed for man's sake, as a call to repentance.

   iv. Man is to return to the ground by death: *Dust you are, and to dust you shall return.*[9]

   v. The fullest dimension of the curse is in connection with physical death. Man returns to the ground, if not by some other way, certainly by old age, sickness, and death.

9. As sin increases, the curse increases: toil and strife, and old age, sickness, and death increases to war, famine, and plague, repeated through all of human history.

   For example: the curse was increased upon Cain; the life span was greatly reduced after the Flood (900+ to 70); strife was increased after Babel. It is corporate for all men, and comes individually on some men, groups, and nations.

10. The curse is not punishment; it is God's third and final call back to repentance. The curse ends with physical death; physical death is a reminder of spiritual death.

    The curse, as natural evil, serves to restrain, recall from, and remove moral evil.

    The curse is God's call to stop and think.

*This paper is posthumously published
based upon the original work of Dr. Surrendra Gangadean
and has been edited by The Logos Foundation Editorial Board.*

---

8. *Genesis 3:16.*

9. *Genesis 3:19.*

Paper N⁰· 150

THE BIBLICAL WORLDVIEW

PART X

Redemption:
Justification and Sanctification

GOD JUSTIFIES MAN THROUGH
REPENTANCE AND FAITH

1. **Man's response to the curse can be and has been varied.**

    i. He can harden himself (Cain, Pharaoh) and cause the curse to
    increase.

    This is a form of stoicism, of which there are many varieties and
    expressions.

    > *My head is bloody, but unbowed . . . I am the master of my fate,*
    > */ I am the captain of my soul.*[1]

    The contrast between: *Rage, rage against the dying of the light*[2]
    vs. ending one's life *Not with a bang but a whimper.*[3]

    The existentialist stance against suffering and death (and the ab-
    surdity of it all) by attempting to become a hero of the Absurd.

---

1. William Ernest Henley, *Invictus.*

2. Dylan Thomas, *Do Not Go Gentle Into That Good Night.*

3. T.S. Eliot, *The Hollow Men.*

He can curse the curse, in one form or another, showing some recognition of it. Bitterness and hardness may set in, which can lead to suicide or, under some conditions, euthanasia.

ii. He can be indifferent.

He may look at the curse (death) as natural, not natural evil; as something inevitable, not imposed as the curse.

An eco-mystic might see this as a cycle of life (death gives way to life, life gives way to death).

He may hold some other form of resignation/fatalism (this is the way it is and we should simply submit to it).

iii. He can be indulgent.

He can say: "Let's eat, drink, and be merry" (form of hedonism).

He may hold some form of Epicureanism—celebrating his love for the moment, seeking to escape/drown the pain of life (*Come, fill the Cup, and in the fire of Spring / Your Winter-garment of Repentance fling . . . A Jug of Wine, a Loaf of Bread—and Thou / Beside me singing in the Wilderness*[4]).

iv. He can murmur and complain.

He can say, "Why me?" "Why now?" "Why this way?" "It's too hard." "What about others?" "Why can't I be like others?" We often pine away in some form of envy.

v. He can simply endure it, under God (recognizing it is from God).

This comes out in the view of life as a veil of tears. The hope for relief or anything better is in the afterlife (heaven) when we have completely passed through this veil of tears.

vi. He can seek relief by divine intervention.

This may be by the prosperity gospel (if you believe in God, and name and claim this blessing, then it's yours), or by way of rapture (where Christ will return and take us out of this world, or

---

4. Omar Khayyam, *The Rubaiyat.*

change it radically, which is imminent), or by deliverance ministries/miracles to get one out of present suffering/affliction.

Or, this may be by natural means/some measure of dominion/struggle to overcome sickness or hardships (e.g., building dams to overcome drought).

vii. He can see suffering as a waste and seek to avoid it for himself by not having children, seeking abortion, or pursuing a higher quality of life.

viii. He can fear it and flee it.

He may think an apocalypse is coming upon us at any moment (the sky is falling—the end of the world as we know it).

ix. He can negotiate, bargain, compromise (between ourselves and God, or ourselves and others) to minimize and get around it.

Some persons have denied the faith to alleviate their suffering here.

x. He can do any combination of the above to any degree.

Human beings are very inventive in finding ways to minimize evil and suffering.

xi. Alternatively: He can receive the curse as the curse, as a call back from God to stop and think, as a trial of faith from God (praying, *Lead us not into temptation, but deliver us from evil*), to grow in the knowledge of God for personal sanctification.

xii. And, he can view the curse as an enlargement of the work of dominion (over sin and the curse), which is corporate, cumulative, and communal.

xiii. Man is called to both the personal and the communal aspects of human life as inseparable and mutually reinforcing aspects (from xi + xii).

2. Adam expresses his response to the third call back (the curse and promise): he repents.

i. Adam shows his repentance to the third call back by naming his wife Eve, because she was the mother of all the living.

There would be no redemptive history if there were not a third call back, or if Adam had not repented.

ii. His naming her Eve shows he decided to obey God (to have children in the context of dominion) under the curse (of toil and strife, and old age, sickness, and death upon him and his descendants) with hope in the promise (that the seed of the woman will crush the head of the serpent). If he had no hope in the promise, his children could rise up and curse him for what he brought into the world.

iii. God put enmity between Adam and Eve and the serpent by turning their hearts from unbelief, and self-deception, and self-justification (sin compounded to the third degree), to belief and faith in God's promise.

iv. The first step in the order of salvation (the *ordo salutis*), commencing with Adam's repentance, is God's sovereignly changing the human heart (by a rebirth, a regeneration, a spiritual resurrection—signified later in redemptive history by circumcision (in which one is to circumcise the heart and not the flesh merely) and baptism (which speaks about a new birth/being raised to newness of life in Christ)).

v. Man is restored from spiritual death to life.

This life is the life of the Logos, which is in all men as light (reason).[5]

In sin, man had neglected, avoided, resisted, or denied his reason in the face of what is clear about God.

The denial of his nature brought spiritual death.

It is by the restoration of the life/light of reason that man comes to see what is clear about God.

vi. The restoration to life brought awareness/conviction of death (meaninglessness) due to sin (of not seeking, not understanding, resulting in not doing what is right).

---

5. *John 1:4.*

vii. Conviction of sin and death (not just from, originally, the conscience, but) in this effectual calling (regeneration) brought *repentance* (a change in thinking, acknowledging/confessing sin as sin and death as the just consequence of sin) *and faith* in God's promise of redemption through the seed of the woman—the one who is to come in Adam's place.

3. God justifies man.

i. It is through repentance and faith that God justifies man.

The Scripture does not mention justification explicitly, but it does mention an act of God. *Unto Adam also and to his wife did the Lord God make coats of skin, and clothed them.*[6] In this act, God is clothing them with the righteousness of another who has died representing them in their place (atonement of sin).

ii. In the place of the covering of leaves (to cover guilt and shame, signified by nakedness), God provides coats of skin.

iii. The coat of skin signifies that their sin/unrighteousness/guilt is covered by the death of another.

iv. Wearing the coats of skin daily was a perpetual reminder of (the truth/meaning of) being covered through the death of another.

v. Vicarious atonement (payment for sin by another in one's place) is possible and required by the covenant of creation (fulfilled by the covenant of grace).

vi. By vicarious atonement, another in the place of Adam must undo what Adam did.

There is only one covenant head in the place of Adam.

The one who undoes what Adam did is the same as the one who does what Adam failed to do.

The one who dies to atone is the one who lives to rule.

Only by vicarious atonement, under the covenant of creation, does mercy satisfy the requirement of divine justice. God is both

---

6. *Genesis 3:21.*

infinitely, eternally, and unchangeably just and good/merciful. God cannot deny his justice; mercy cannot set aside justice.

The covenant of grace in Christ satisfies the demands of the covenant of works in Adam.

vii. By representation, in the covenant of creation, there is a three-fold imputation.

   a. The guilt of Adam's sin is imputed to all whom he represents (as would his righteousness have been, had he obeyed—both are present in the original covenant arrangement).

   b. The sin of all who are in Christ is imputed to Christ as covenant head in the place of Adam.

   Christ is the Lamb of God, who takes away the sin of the world.[7]

   c. The righteousness of Christ, in the place of Adam, is imputed to all who are united to him by faith. This act of imputation must be understood in the context of, not apart from, the first two.

viii. Salvation is by grace alone, through faith alone, in Christ alone, as revealed in the Scriptures alone, and all for the glory of God alone.[8]

GOD SANCTIFIES MAN BY KNOWLEDGE
ACQUIRED THROUGH SUFFERING

1. Those whom God justifies, he also sanctifies.

   i. The goal of sanctification is holiness, which is a devotion to the good as the glory of God.

   The connection between the holiness and the glory of God is seen in the angelic beings who cry, *Holy, holy, holy, is the Lord of hosts: the whole earth is full of his glory.*[9]

   ii. Holiness is manifest in beauty that lasts.

---

7. *John 1:29.*

8. *Paper No. 17.*

9. *Isaiah 6:3.*

Worship the Lord in the beauty of holiness.[10]

As lasting beauty, holiness is true beauty, compared with all else that only appears to be or is a sign of the reality.

iii. Sanctification is a process of cleansing, which begins upon the forgiveness of sin (not before, and not apart from).

iv. *If we confess our sins, he is faithful and just to forgive us our sins, and to cleanse us from all unrighteousness.*[11]

v. Justification is distinct from sanctification, but is inseparable from sanctification.

Many have shipwrecked their faith and brought harm to others by trying to work out theologies which separate the two or cause one to be collapsed into the other.

vi. Justification is by the imputation of Christ's righteousness in the context of the covenant of creation (which established representation, and therefore imputation).

It is not a (non-cognitive) infusion of righteousness (making one righteous). In justification, one is not yet cleansed of sin; one is accounted as righteous (on the basis of the righteousness of Christ, which covers one's sin).

2. Sanctification is a transformation of the believer through coming to know the truth.

i. *Be transformed by the renewing of your mind.*[12]

It is a cognitive process (involving the understanding) in coming to know the truth, which has the effect of transformation (which is not all at once, but is progressive over time and through history).

ii. *You shall know the truth, and the truth shall make you free.*[13]

---

10. *Psalm 96:9.*
11. *1 John 1:9.*
12. *Romans 12:2.*
13. *John 8:32.*

iii. Most explicitly, Jesus prays in his High Priestly Prayer: *Sanctify them by your truth. Your word [Logos] is truth.*[14]

iv. The Logos is the truth of the Word of God in its fullness, from foundation to its full expression in the Kingdom/City of God.

3. The expulsion: sanctification through suffering.

This is the major event in the history of redemption showing the distinction between justification and sanctification, how they are inseparable from one another, and the process of sanctification in which all men (who are justified) share and cannot avoid.

i. Having been justified, symbolized by God's provision of the coats of skin (one's nakedness is covered through the death/sacrifice of another), man is to be sanctified through suffering.

ii. Man is expelled from the Garden to live under the curse, leading to death.

   a. He is kept from access to the tree of life lest he "eat, and live forever."

   b. He is driven from the Garden; there is a reluctance/resistance to suffering (living under the curse) even though he accepted this.

   c. There is a guard set against any return: cherubim and a flaming sword are placed "to keep the way of the tree of life."

iii. Suffering of the curse (toil and strife, and old age, sickness, and death) is unavoidable in this life; all must die.

iv. Suffering through trials is for maturity and faith, to overcome ignorance and error in foundational beliefs/presuppositions, arising from personality and background (part of which is being fallen in Adam), and manifested in changes in mood (seeking or not seeking; belief mixed with unbelief—e.g., Peter is one moment walking on water and the next he is sinking; one moment he affirms who Christ is and the next, things that deny him).

---

14. *John 17:17.*

v. Foundation, being brought about by sanctification, is necessary for maturity in faith.[15]

It brings believers into fruitfulness, unity of the faith, and the fullness of Christ.[16]

As a result of sanctification, not only is there growth at an individual/personal level, but there will be unity in the Church at a corporate level—all divisions in understanding (of foundational beliefs, of who God is, and of the truth of Scripture) will be identified, addressed, and removed/overcome.

vi. Foundation is necessary to accomplish the work of dominion (*Be fruitful and multiply; fill the earth and subdue it*), which now includes making disciples of all nations.

Man is to, through the process of dominion, attain to an understanding of the fullness of the revelation that God has given of himself in creation and history.

vii. The work of dominion ends with rest (the Sabbath) when the earth is filled with the knowledge of God as the waters cover the sea.[17]

viii. Sanctification continues throughout one's lifetime and through history.

It does not continue after death (in some kind of purgatory) or after the end of history (after the Last Judgment).

Sanctification ends individually and corporately in the state of glory, bringing to completion the process of salvation.

This paper is posthumously published
based upon the original work of Dr. Surrendra Gangadean
and has been edited by The Logos Foundation Editorial Board.

---

15. *Hebrews 6:1.*

16. *Ephesians 4.*

17. *Isaiah 11:9.*

GLOSSARY OF TERMS

ambiguity a term is ambiguous if it has more than one meaning: equivocal—if it has two unrelated meanings (ring on a finger, ring of a bell); analogous—if it has two related meanings (blanket of snow or bed cover); all non-basic terms are also philosophically ambiguous, relative to basic belief; a term is univocal if it has only one meaning.

analogous like in some respects and unlike in other respects.

antinomy contrary positions both of which can be false at the same time because both share a common assumption—capitalism and communism; this-worldly and other-worldly; all is eternal and none is eternal; skepticism and fideism; virtue is the good and happiness is the good—a source of recurrent conflict within and between cultures.

argument the third act of reason (see concept and judgment) in which premises are used to logically support a conclusion (see validity and soundness).

basic belief a belief is basic in relation to another if it is assumed by that belief; material monism (all is matter) assumes that all is eternal; macro-evolution assumes all is matter; superior race assumes macro-evolution; naturalistic science assumes methodological naturalism, which assumes metaphysical naturalism (all is matter).

clarity applied to basic beliefs; a belief is clear to reason if the contradiction is not logically or existentially possible; e.g., there must be something eternal; clarity is necessary for meaning, morality, and inexcusability; one knows what is clear if one can show what is clear; what is clear can be known by anyone who seeks to know.

Common Ground	the set of epistemologically necessary conditions for thought and discourse: 1) reason—as the laws of thought; 2) integrity—as a concern for consistency; 3) Rational Presuppositionalism—as critical thinking applied consistently; 4) the Principle of Clarity—as necessary for meaning and morality; to engage in discourse without Common Ground is to engage in meaningless disputes.
common sense	takes appearance for reality: the sun rises in the east; the earth is flat; the color of the ocean is blue; there is an external world; based on what is common to sense perception, rather than common sense as practical wisdom; it takes the condition/position of the perceiver for granted.
concept	the first act of reason (see judgment and argument); in a concept the mind grasps the essence of a thing or class of things; set in contrast to an image, an act of the senses; concepts are either well-formed or not.
contradiction	contradictory statements differ in quantity (all or some) and quality (is or is not); they cannot both be true and they cannot both be false, at the same time and in the same respect; *all s is p* is contradicted by *some s is not p*; *no s is p* is contradicted by *some s is p* (see judgment).
creation *ex nihilo*	affirmed by historic theism, it is the belief that God created the world out of no pre-existing substance; in contrast to dualism where creation is by forming pre-existing matter, and to pantheism—in which the world is a part of God; it is the basis of affirming the infinite power and wisdom of God.
deconstruction	recognizes the constructive use of reason by providing an internal conceptual critique of a position; does not apply critical analysis to test the meaning of basic beliefs upon which construction occurs; calls into question reason in itself based upon the mere subjective use of reason.

deduction reasoning from what is more general or universal to what is less general or particular; from all men are mortal to Socrates is mortal; from saying it is true of all to saying it is true of each.

deism belief that the world was created by God, but not actively ruled by God; God did not act after creation to bring about natural evil in the world, or to give any redemptive revelation to mankind (Voltaire and Thomas Jefferson).

deontology a theory of ethics focused upon duty and virtue as the end of moral action, independent of and in contrast to consequences; affirmed by Kant; set in contrast to teleological ethics which sees virtue as means to the good.

determinism the belief that every event has a cause and that given the cause the effect necessarily follows; in contrast to libertarianism; hard determinists affirm causality and deny libertarian freedom; soft determinists affirm causality and freedom as doing what one desires.

dilemma in logic, a form of argumentation in which either of two alternatives available is unacceptable; used rhetorically to show how entirely unacceptable a position is.

dominion the exercise of rule or authority given to mankind to develop the powers latent in oneself and in the creation; based on the principle that creation is revelation, it is directed toward the good as knowledge of God; set in contrast to domination as rule for self-interest.

dualism the ontological position that reality consists of two distinct kinds of being—matter and spirit—both of which are eternal; affirmed in different forms of Greek thought by Plato and Aristotle; distinct from theism, although dualistic attitudes persist in popular forms of theism.

empiricism the epistemological position that all knowledge arises from sense experience; affirmed by John Locke; Hume drew out its skeptical implications; assumed uncritically in some claims made in the name of science; radical empiricism includes inner as well as sense experience.

epistemology theory of knowledge; a major branch of philosophy that deals with the questions "Is knowledge possible?" and "How do I know?"

essence the set of qualities that all members and only members of a class always have; human essence is said to be both rational and animal.

ethics ethics is concerned with giving a rational justification for an answer to the question "What is the good?" Ethics assumes choice, which assumes values and therefore the highest value, which is the good; what is sought in ethics is rational justification for one's view of the good.

evolution, naturalistic a purely natural explanation of the development from non-life to life, to more complex life, to hominid, to human; macro (not micro) evolution; internal disputes exist over gradual vs. non-gradual process; external challenges exist over the scientific vs. philosophical status of evolution.

evolution, theistic a synthesis of naturalistic evolution and belief in God; subject to criticism from both naturalists and theists as compromising essential features of each, and is therefore inadequate as a compromise position; it has been subject to revision in the direction of theism or naturalism.

ex nihilo from no previously existing matter.

existentialism focus upon the individual in an actual condition of crisis with respect to the absence of any rational way to choose; without God (Nietzsche, Sartre) or without reason (Kierkegaard), man is forced to authentic freedom; his existence precedes what he becomes by choice (essence).

faith faith is applied to belief in general, which cannot be verified through sense experience; faith is not opposed to reason; as truth cannot be separated from meaning, faith cannot be separated from reason; faith grows as understanding grows; it is tested as understanding is tested.

fideism   holding a belief without proof; proof is seen either as not relevant or not possible or may not actually be present; belief may be either theistic or non-theistic; fideism assumes basic things are not clear; belief without proof based on understanding loses all meaning.

freedom   doing what I want or please or choose, all things considered; applied to the most basic level of thought, I can use my reason if I want to; set in contrast to libertarian freedom: if *ought* implies *can*, then *can* assumes *want*; the want of a rational agent is always free.

friendship   friendship is reciprocal, lasting and shares the deepest concerns; it is therefore the effect of mutual commitment to the good; in contrast to other relations which are not reciprocal, lasting, or cannot share the deepest concerns because they are not based on mutual commitment to the good.

general revelation   what can be known of God by all persons, everywhere, at all times, through the ordinary means of knowing; in contrast to special revelation; the subject matter of natural vs. revealed religion.

good and necessary consequence   an inference of reason; what must be said, if other things are accepted as true; applied to analyzing concepts, judgments, and arguments; used in critical, interpretive, and constructive reasoning.

happiness   the effect of possessing what one believes to be the good; not sought for its own sake as the good, but naturally accompanying the possessing what is believed to be of highest value; lasting happiness is the effect of possessing what truly is the good.

hedonism   the ethical view that pleasure/happiness of one kind or another is the good (Epicurus, Mill).

hermeneutics   the process by which the meaning of a text or an event is understood; no experience is meaningful without interpretation; in general, we interpret what is less basic in light of what is more basic; we interpret our experience in light of our basic belief or worldview assumptions.

induction   reasoning from observation of instances of things to a general statement about that class of things; from observing that some crows are black to the general statement that all crows are black.

informal fallacy   an attempt to persuade by pseudo-argument (through appeal to what is not rationally relevant) rather than to prove by sound argument: appeal to fear and pity apart from the good; appeal to authority or popularity rather than reason; speaking against the person vs. what was said, etc.

integrity   integrity is grounded in a concern to be whole or unified in one's being; specifically, it is a concern for consistency over and against inconsistency, which is manifest in contradiction in thought; double-mindedness in desire and hypocrisy in what we profess and what we do.

intuition   an immediate awareness one has, apart from reason and the senses, of the connection between a (natural) sign and what it signifies; e.g., smile and friendliness, beauty and goodness; misleading if one thinks the sign is the reality, or that the sign is always accompanied by the reality.

judgment   the second act of reason in which two concepts are joined by affirmation or separated by negation: *all s is p, no s is p, some s is p, some s is not p;* judgments are either true or false and may be simple or complex; a statement is used to express a judgment (or proposition).

knowledge   justified true belief.

libertarianism   a view of freedom where *ought* implies *can*; one is free if one could have done otherwise; related to causality, if my act was caused, it could not have been otherwise; libertarianism denies determinism (every event is caused) in order to affirm freedom (Kant, William James).

literalism	the belief that understanding a text is free of interpretive assumptions; that preceding layers of context are not necessarily relevant; that meaning is explicit only and not also by inference; that understanding language figuratively is to be avoided whenever possible.
love	love seeks the good for the other; love is a moral virtue, not the good sought for its own sake; set in contrast to romantic love in which the other is considered the good; in theism, to seek the good as the knowledge of God is to love God and to love oneself.
matter	that which has size and is not conscious; can be measured.
metaphysics	a branch of philosophy which deals with the question, "What is real or eternal?"; it deals with *ontology*—the nature of being, whether being is matter or spirit; it deals with *cosmology*—how the cosmos came to be.
moral evil	an act contrary to the nature of one's being; for man as a rational being it is to neglect, avoid, resist, or deny reason in the face of what is clear; it is the failure to seek and to understand and to do what is right.
natural evil	in the context of an all powerful and all good Creator, natural evil is not original in the creation, nor inherent in moral evil; it is imposed by God to restrain, recall from, and to remove moral evil; it consists in toil and strife, and old age, sickness, and death, and all amplifications of these in famine, war, and plague.
naturalism	the worldview of material monism: only natural forces explain all phenomena of nature; applied to human culture, it is called secular humanism: only human effort explains all social phenomena; in the sciences, methodological naturalism in explanation (all knowledge is through sense experience) is used to support metaphysical naturalism—there is no God, no spirit or soul, and no afterlife.

nihilism   the loss of all meaningful distinctions in epistemology, metaphysics, and ethics; the inherent consequence of skepticism—the denial of all clarity; a position which cannot be maintained with integrity.

ontology   the study of being.

philosophy   philosophy can be defined in terms of its several features: *area*—foundation and goal; *attitude*—love of wisdom; *method*—critical use of reason; *application*—self-examination; *system*—a worldview.

postmodern   a cluster of skeptical responses to claims to objective truth in modern thought; it is anti-foundationalism, anti-realism, and anti-essentialism; it assumes reason is not ontological or transcendental, nor is thinking presuppositional; it privileges the subjective aspects of interpretation.

pragmatism   a theory of truth: a belief is true if it yields satisfactory consequences (if it works); also, a theory of meaning: the meaning of a belief is the conduct it is fitted to produce (William James); claims to settle metaphysical disputes; assumes skepticism and that what works is common ground.

presupposi-   what is assumed or presupposed in any given statement
tion   or belief; applied particularly to what is assumed in a person's *system* of beliefs or worldview; one's most basic belief about what is eternal.

prima facie   literally "on the face of it"; applied to epistemic justification, rights, duties, evidence, etc.; it leaves open the question of who bears the burden of proof and what is one's epistemic duty: is one obligated to search out objections before believing what is *prima facie* justified?

problem   if God is all good and all powerful, why is there evil?; if
of evil   God is all powerful, he could create a world without evil; if he is all good, he would create a world without evil; the problem is intellectual, to make sense of an apparent contradiction, and not empty basic terms of meaning.

Rational Presuppositionalism	thinking is presuppositional; we think of the less basic in light of the more basic: less basic/more basic, truth/meaning, experience/basic belief, conclusion/premises, finite/infinite, etc.; reason is the test for meaning; if we agree on what is more basic, we can agree on what is less basic.
rationalism	a reliance on reason as the source of knowing the truth; to be contrasted with reliance on sense experience or intuition or testimony; also, to be contrasted with reliance on reason as a test for meaning (Rational Presuppositionalism).
reason in its use	reason in its use is *formative*—used to form concepts, judgments, and arguments, which are the forms of all thought; *critical*—used as a test of meaning; *interpretive*—used to interpret experience in light of basic belief; and *constructive*—used to construct a coherent worldview.
reason in itself	reason in itself is the laws of thought: the law of identity—*a* is *a*; the law of non-contradiction—not both *a* and *non-a*; the law of excluded middle—either *a* or *non-a*; these laws make thinking possible; the common ground for all who think.
reason in us	reason in us is *natural*—the same in all thinkers; *ontological*—applies to being as well as to thought; *transcendental*—authoritative, self-attesting, cannot be questioned but makes questioning possible; and *fundamental*—to all other aspects of human personality.
redemptive revelation	scripture as redemptive revelation reveals how man is brought out of sin and death; scripture assumes all have sinned—no one seeks, no one understands, no one is righteous; all are in the state of spiritual death—meaninglessness, boredom, and guilt; redemption by vicarious atonement shows both divine justice and mercy.

reductio ad absurdum a form of reasoning which proves the truth of a position by showing the opposite cannot be true because it is reduced to logical absurdity; used to show there must be something eternal; used to show the strong sense of clarity necessary to establish inexcusability.

religion the belief or set of beliefs used to give meaning to experience.

science the attempt to increase knowledge of reality based on theory confirmed by observation in experiment; science is overextended and becomes a source of skepticism when it assumes empiricism, that all knowledge is from sense experience, or makes claims which go beyond experience.

sensus divinitatis the immediate awareness of divinity present in human consciousness; variously understood, ranging from a sense of dependence on a higher power to awareness of God as Creator and ruler, or as one having an innate sense of the qualities of infinite, eternal, and unchanging, which can only, upon analysis, be applied to God.

skepticism the epistemological view that knowledge is not possible, that nothing is clear; consistently held, skepticism leads to nihilism, the loss of all meaning.

Sola Scriptura a principle of authority which maintains that scripture is the only rule of faith and life; set in contrast to new revelations of the Spirit or traditions of men; not set in contrast to reason making inferences from scripture, nor to reason making judgments concerning circumstances common to human societies.

soundness an argument is sound if it is valid and its premises are true (see argument and validity); a rational person will believe the conclusion of a sound argument.

special revelation what is known of God through testimony and its transmission; usually contained in form of scripture; the subject matter of revealed theology in contrast to natural theology or religion.

spirit	that which has no size and is conscious (also known as mind, soul, or consciousness).
spiritual monism	the ontological position that all of reality is eternal and is spirit; set in contrast to material monism, dualism, and theism; matter only *appears* to exist; this reality may be absolute non-dual, beyond all qualities (Shankara) or qualified non-dual, where all is part of God (Ramanuja).
spiritual death	set in contrast to and analogous to physical death; the inward condition of meaninglessness, boredom, and guilt; inherent in moral evil as the failure to seek and to understand basic things that are clear to reason.
talent	an ability to achieve some aspect of the good; originating in one's being and unique in each; developed fully only in the vision of the good; it is given to each for all; the good, achieved by talent, is the source of lasting value and of the richness of life for all.
term	a word or group of words used to express a concept (see concept, essence, and ambiguity).
the good	the good is the end in itself, chosen for its own sake and not for the sake of anything else; it is the highest good (*the summum bonum*); it is the source of unity (in a person, between two persons, and between groups of persons); set in contrast to virtue as means to the good and happiness as the effect of possessing the good.
the Principle of Clarity	some things are clear, the basic things are clear, the basic things about God and man and good and evil are clear to reason; necessary for meaning and morality.
theism	belief in God the Creator who brought the universe and all things in it into being; God is a Spirit, infinite, eternal, and unchangeable, in his being, wisdom, power, holiness, justice, goodness, and truth; in contrast to deism, God in theism is both Creator and ruler of mankind in history.

tradition   a way of life handed down by and received on the basis of testimony, in contrast to reason, intuition, or sense experience; without critical analysis, traditions are affirmed to be equal, requiring radical pluralism, diversity, multiculturalism, cultural relativism, and tolerance.

transcendental   that which is higher; stands above; authoritative.

uniformitarianism a principle which holds that the forces now operating in nature have always operated, and in essentially the same magnitude; a naturalistic assumption first used in geology by Charles Lyell, and in biology by Charles Darwin.

utilitarianism   holds that pleasure is the good and that we are to act so as to maximize the greatest amount of pleasure for the greatest number of people; proposed by Jeremy Bentham and John Stuart Mill; set in contrast to ethical egoism—one should seek pleasure for oneself first, and to deontology—duty for duty's sake.

validity   an argument is valid if its premises logically support the conclusion (see argument and soundness).

virtue   virtue is not the good, but the means to the good; there are different kinds of virtues: instrumental (money, house, car), natural (health, beauty, talent), and moral (wisdom, courage, love).

wisdom   knowing the good and the appropriate means to achieving the good.

worldview   how a person understands the world based on answers to the basic questions; each culture is shaped by a worldview held more or less consciously and consistently; a culture grows or declines as its worldview increases or decreases in its capacity to provide meaning.

INDEX

203, 208, 214, 218, 229,
239-240, 244-246, 278, 289,
310, 318, 438, 447, 458, 482,
494, 505, 532-535, 538, 552,
560, 563, 583, 593, 604, 658,
664, 691, 754, 770, 774, 778,
787
total depravity, 113, 120, 729
totalitarian(ism), 58, 160, 172, 299,
321, 481
totalitarianism, 58, 160, 299
tradition, 12, 345-346, 355, 672
    and custom, 367
traditional, 199, 549
transcendental, 10, 17, 28, 196,
225, 256, 267-268, 276, 287,
294, 315, 371, 419-420,
524-525, 548-550, 655,
788-789, 792
transcendental argument, the, 17
translation(s), 72, 75, 118, 508,
527-529, 707
    of Scripture, 527
transubstantiation, 343
trial(s) of faith, 92, 200, 205, 209,
214, 247, 269, 307, 313, 491,
551, 624, 773
tribulation, the, 274
Trinity, the, 108-109, 140, 183,
250, 291, 336, 451, 479-480,
518, 529, 658, 716
triune, 6, 42, 98, 109, 205, 245,
248, 282, 328, 456, 522, 548,
709, 729, 742
    God of the Bible, 522
    nature of man, 42
    order, 282
    personality, 6, 282, 548, 709,
    729, 742
Triune God, 98, 109, 205, 245,
248, 522, 709, 729

    of the Bible, 522
Trivium, 261
truth, 46, 65, 104-105, 180, 183,
189, 200-201, 205, 209-211,
214, 221-222, 239, 252-253,
258, 265, 279, 301, 313, 321,
325, 332, 340, 368-370,
484-486, 491, 506, 512, 517,
537, 546, 560-562, 581,
611-613, 616-619, 622-623,
631, 636-637, 640, 647, 680,
683-684, 708-709, 767-768,
777-778
    and justice, 46, 64-65
TULIP, 116, 120

unbelief, 4, 35-36, 39-42, 85-86,
92-93, 113, 125, 175, 192-193,
240-241, 252, 263, 299, 308,
317-319, 326, 332-336, 348,
437-438, 448, 491, 500, 516,
523, 527-528, 533, 541,
571-573, 613, 620, 623-625,
634-637, 640-641, 657, 707,
754, 768-769
    is without excuse, 4, 7, 41, 163,
    175, 234, 241, 245, 308,
    326, 475, 493, 504
    of mankind, 82
unbeliever, the, 41, 92, 641
unconditional election, 113,
120-121
unconstitutional, 127-128
understanding, 22, 85, 97, 120,
131, 176, 204, 209, 217, 294,
310-311, 332, 335, 352,
373-375, 444, 460, 468, 488,
496, 511, 525, 534-535, 538,
578-580, 623, 628-630, 639,
645, 652
    saving, 204

ABOUT THE AUTHOR

DR. SURRENDRA GANGADEAN (1943–2022) was a professor of Philosophy at Phoenix College and at Paradise Valley Community College for forty-five years. Additionally, he taught from the pulpit at Westminster Fellowship for almost 30 years and taught courses at Logos Theological Seminary for over 25 years. Courses he taught include Introduction to Philosophy, Logic, Ethics, Philosophy of Religion, Eastern Religions, World Religions, Introduction to Christianity, Introduction to Humanities, Philosophy of Art, The Great Books, Philosophical Theology, Biblical Worldview, Biblical History, Church History, Systematic Theology, Biblical Hermeneutics, and Existential Hermeneutics. He received an M.A. degree in Literature from the University of Arizona, an M.A. degree in Philosophy from the University of Arizona, and a Ph.D. in Natural Theology from Reformed International Theological Seminary. He presented academic papers and public lectures on Natural Theology and the Moral Law. Dr. Gangadean was the organizing President of The Logos Foundation, which serves academic education in Liberal Arts and Theology.

www.ingramcontent.com/pod-product-compliance
Lightning Source LLC
Chambersburg PA
CBHW060847120626
46553CB00001B/2